Europe's Income, Wealth, Consumption, and Inequality

International Policy Exchange Series

Published in collaboration with the
Center for International Policy Exchanges
University of Maryland

Series Editors
Douglas J. Besharov
Neil Gilbert

SCHOOL of
PUBLIC POLICY

EUROPE'S INCOME, WEALTH, CONSUMPTION, AND INEQUALITY

Edited by

GEORG FISCHER

ROBERT STRAUSS

OXFORD
UNIVERSITY PRESS

OXFORD
UNIVERSITY PRESS

Oxford University Press is a department of the University of Oxford. It furthers the University's objective of excellence in research, scholarship, and education by publishing worldwide. Oxford is a registered trade mark of Oxford University Press in the UK and certain other countries.

Published in the United States of America by Oxford University Press
198 Madison Avenue, New York, NY 10016, United States of America.

Library of Congress Cataloging-in-Publication Data
Names: Fischer, Georg, 1952– editor. | Strauss, Robert, 1958– editor.
Title: Europe's income, wealth, consumption, and inequality /
edited by Georg Fischer and Robert Strauss.
Description: New York, NY : Oxford University Press, [2021] |
Series: International policy exchange series |
Includes bibliographical references and index.
Identifiers: LCCN 2020034429 (print) | LCCN 2020034430 (ebook) |
ISBN 9780197545706 (hardback) | ISBN 9780197545720 (epub) |
ISBN 9780197545737
Subjects: LCSH: Income distribution—European Union countries. |
Wealth—European Union countries. | Equality—European Union countries. |
European Union countries—Economic conditions—21st century.
Classification: LCC HC240.9.I5 E97 2021 (print) | LCC HC240.9.I5 (ebook) |
DDC 339.2/2094—dc23
LC record available at https://lccn.loc.gov/2020034429
LC ebook record available at https://lccn.loc.gov/2020034430

DOI: 10.1093/oso/9780197545706.001.0001

9 8 7 6 5 4 3 2 1

Printed by Integrated Books International, United States of America

CONTENTS

FOREWORD

This is a very timely book, coming at a moment when Europe strives to recover economically and socially from the COVID-19 pandemic. The pandemic has shaken our health, our jobs and economy, and our livelihoods. It struck the European Union (EU) Member States to different degrees, and some countries were severely hit. But all, without exception, are suffering profound economic dislocation, social hardship, and employment losses. The pandemic calls for a strong response of solidarity between countries, between regions, between citizens. Importantly, it calls for more EU solidarity.

The EU experience during the Great Recession and the Euro Crisis showed strongly that developments in one country or a group of countries can benefit or harm not only well-being in a single country but in the EU more broadly. Some chapters of this book show that certain measures adopted back then might have even exacerbated divergence rather than promoted convergence. New ways to approach European development and integration are therefore vital.

The authors take the long-term process of European integration as a starting point and look at the EU not as a conglomerate of individual countries but as an economic and political entity whose parts are closely interlinked politically and economically. This is an important change in perspective that underlines the responsibility of the whole EU for the well-being of all Europeans, independently of the Member State that they live in.

Though written before the pandemic, the issues raised with respect to income and inequality are central to policies for recovery. This book, which often takes a novel approach in the analysis of social trends and policies, can provide stimulus to EU and national policymakers. It argues that inequality in Europe is undermining its social cohesion and might have become an obstacle to sustainable economic performance. It recalls that doing more to offset growing inequality of income within most countries in Europe means addressing the sources of more divergent wages, salaries, and earnings (market incomes) and making tax systems for people and companies more progressive. It calls for rebalancing economic and social objectives in European economic policy coordination and underlines the potential for EU-wide social and economic policies, including initiatives on stronger collective bargaining and taxation of income, wealth, and digital activity. It is essential reading for all those needing to know about repairing and preparing for the next generation of Europeans.

—Nicolas Schmit
European Commissioner for Jobs and Social Rights

CONTRIBUTORS

VINCENT BAKKER
Doctoral Researcher
Department of Economics
Leiden University
Leiden, The Netherlands

ERLING BARTH
Research Professor, Institute for Social
Research
Oslo, Norway

GERHARD BOSCH
Professor Emeritus
Institut Arbeit und Qualifikation
University Duisburg-Essen
Duisburg, Germany

ANDREA BRANDOLINI
Economist
DG Economics, Statistics and Research
Banca d'Italia
Rome, Italy

AGNIESZKA CHŁOŃ-DOMIŃCZAK
Associate Professor
Institute of Statistics and Demography
SGH Warsaw School of Economics
Warsaw, Poland

LARS VAN DOORN
Research Staff, Department of Economics
Leiden University
Leiden, The Netherlands

ALPER DUMAN
Associate Professor
Economics
Izmir University of Economics
Izmir, Turkey

ANIL DUMAN
Associate Professor
Political Science
Central European University
Vienna, Austria

GEORG FISCHER
Senior Research Associate
Vienna Institute for International
Economic Studies
WIFO Associate
Wien, Austria

LUCIA GRANELLI
Economic Analyst
Policy Officer
DG ECFIN
European Commission
Brussels, Belgium

MARTIN GUZI
Assistant Professor
Department of Public Economics
Masaryk University
Brno, Czechia

MARTIN KAHANEC
Professor
School of Public Policy
Central European University, CELSI, FNE
UEBA, GLO
Bratislava, Slovakia

ZSÓKA KÓCZÁN
Associate Director, Senior Economist
Office of the Chief Economist
European Bank for Reconstruction and
Development (EBRD)
London, UK

MANOS MATSAGANIS
Professor
Department of Architecture and Urban
Studies
Polytechnic University of Milan
Milan, Italy

MÁRTON MEDGYESI
Senior Researcher
TARKI Social Research Institute
Budapest, Hungary

KALLE MOENE
ESOP
Department of Economics
University of Oslo
Oslo, Norway

BALÁZS PÁLVÖLGYI
Economist
Directorate General for Economic and
Financial Affairs
European Commission
Brussels, Belgium

AXEL WEST PEDERSEN
Professor
Norwegian Social Research - NOVA
Oslo Metropolitan University
Oslo, Norway

ALFONSO ROSOLIA
Economist
DG Economics, Statistics, and Research
Banca d'Italia
Rome, Italy

WIEMER SALVERDA
Professor Emeritus
AIAS-HSI
University of Amsterdam
Amsterdam, The Netherlands

SARA SAVASTANO
Director
Research and Impact Assessment
Division
IFAD
Rome, Italy

SLAVINA SPASOVA
Researcher at the European Social
Observatory, European Social
Observatory
Research Associate
Université Libre de Bruxelles, CEVIPOL
Brussels, Belgium

ROBERT STRAUSS
Formerly European Commission
Brussels, Belgium

ISTVÁN GYÖRGY TÓTH
Director
Tarki Social Research Institute
Budapest, Hungary

MAGDALENA M. ULCELUSE
Postdoctoral Researcher
Cultural Geography
University of Groningen
Groningen, the Netherlands

ANNELEEN VANDEPLAS
Economist
DG ECFIN, European Commission
Brussels, Belgium
Research Fellow
LICOS, KU Leuven
Leuven, Belgium

BART VANHERCKE
Director
European Social Observatory
Brussels, Belgium

OLAF VAN VLIET
Professor
Department of Economics
Leiden University
Leiden, The Netherlands

JOHANNES ZIEMENDORFF
Policy Analyst/Economist
DG ECFIN
European Commission
Brussels, Belgium

1

INTRODUCTION

AN OVERVIEW OF ISSUES AND TRENDS

Georg Fischer and Robert Strauss

This volume is the Europe volume in an international series on income, wealth, consumption, well-being, and inequality.[1] It focuses on the European Union (EU) and covers all EU Member States and other European countries that are in close association with the EU. It makes a specific point to look at the Union not as conglomerate of individual countries but as an economic and political entity whose parts are closely interlinked politically and economically and dependent on each other. Geographical chapters are complemented by chapters that analyse policy areas that are of specific relevance for the evolution of the income and well-being of the population and how gains and losses are shared.

Economic growth, improving economic performance, and rising incomes have been important objectives of European integration and the EU. It is important to note that the European Integration process, starting in the 1950s, had and still has broader objectives than improving incomes and economic growth. This has also something to do with the historical roots of integration (the topic of the following section of this Introduction).

Like almost everywhere in the world, Europeans, and in particular the media and political leaders, use income trends as a measure of progress. For a long time two issues have dominated the debate in this respect: catching up with the

---

1 The analysis in this and the other chapters was completed in the sutumn of 2019. The volume essentially does not cover events after that date such as the COVID-19 pandemic and related policy initiatives.

Georg Fischer and Robert Strauss, *Introduction* In: *Europe's Income, Wealth, Consumption, and Inequality.*
Edited by: Georg Fischer and Robert Strauss, Oxford University Press (2021).
© Oxford University Press. DOI: 10.1093/oso/9780197545706.003.0001

United States and the convergence of the performance of the less-developed (the Southern European) countries with the richer countries, in particular when Spain, Portugal, and Greece joined the European Community in the 1980s. While there was substantial progress in convergence in the two decades leading up to the Great Recession, since then the process of convergence between Southern European and Western European countries has not only stopped but massive divergence also emerged, putting convergence between the European countries back on the agenda. On catching up with the United States, there has been disappointment since the 1980s. This is reflected in the subsequent European economic policy integration strategies demanding structural reforms to increase growth potential and improve competitiveness, with less attention paid to social tensions and income distribution.

In 2010, the Europe 2020 Strategy stated that the average growth rate of 'Europe' has been structurally lower than that of its main economic partners. It listed many explanatory factors, including lower employment rates and that 'Europeans work 10% fewer hours than their US or Japanese counterparts' (discussed more in the following chapter). However, the Strategy can also be seen as opening discussion in a different direction because it recognized that not everybody benefits from economic growth, stating that both groups of individuals and territories were being left out. Consequently, the Europe 2020 Strategy adopted an ambitious target of reducing poverty and social exclusion (reviewed in Chapter 15).

Since 2010, concerns about income inequality have multiplied as a response to the social impacts of the Great Recession and the following Euro Crisis. This concern has also reached EU leaders. In 2017, they adopted the 'European Pillar of Social Rights', a document that set out which social and employment rights Europeans should have, an initiative motivated by growing social divergence and inequality in the EU. In 2019, the leaders considered that 'Inequalities . . . pose a major political, social and economic risk' and that addressing them is 'a societal imperative and economic asset' (European Council: A New Strategic Agenda). In essence, Europe faces two major challenges in relation to economic inequality: income inequality within countries and growing divergence in income levels between the richer Northern European and poorer Southern European countries (the catch-up of Central and Eastern European [CEE] countries is, however, continuing).

Research and public interest in economic inequality and poverty have been around for much longer, responding to the drastically increasing inequality in the United States and the more moderate increases in Europe since the 1980s. An important milestone was the comprehensive research effort 'The Gini Project' (funded by the European Commission Research Programme), an analysis of economic inequality in rich countries, covering 25 EU Member States and published in two volumes.[2]

---

2 The GINI Project (2014).

There is a growing literature on trends and drivers by country, in particular on the biggest European economies of France, Germany, and the United Kingdom, and often with an in-depth analysis of the drivers of economic inequality. In terms of updating knowledge on trends in European countries, the World Inequality Lab has studied the evolution of income distribution in 38 European countries from 1980 to 2017 and is an important and valuable source of information.[3]

International organizations have also researched economic inequality globally and issued specific reports on Europe. These organizations are not only good sources for country-specific information but they also point to the policy issues relating to this volume on well-being, income, and inequality. The Organisation of Economic Cooperation and Development (OECD) was a real forerunner with its 'Growing Unequal: Income Distribution and Poverty in OECD Countries' (2008), and it has since published a sequence of major reports: 'Divided We Stand: Why Inequality Keeps Rising' (2011), 'In It Together: Why Less Inequality Benefits All' (2015), 'A Broken Social Elevator '(2018), and 'Under Pressure: The Squeezed Middle Class' (2019), all dealing with OECD members including EU countries. In addition, the OECD published 'Rising Income Inequality in European Union' (2012) analysing income inequality in the EU economy as a whole and 'Understanding the Socio-Economic Divide in Europe' (2017). The latter set income and wealth inequality within a broader picture of changes in the labour market and of other social divides, including participation in and the quality of education. The report warns about impacts on social stability, finds that Europeans are increasingly more pessimistic about the future of their children, and notes that, without policy action, the socioeconomic divide is set to continue to grow.

The European Bank for Reconstruction and Development (EBRD) devoted the 2016–2017 Transition Report 'Convergence and Inequality' to 'equal opportunities in an unequal world'. The report analyses developments in 34 countries, including the post-communist Central and Eastern EU member countries, the Western Balkans, and Turkey. To pick out one result from this data-rich report, just 44% of the population of the post-communist countries saw long-term income convergence, with most but not all 'new' EU member countries doing relatively better and the Western Balkan countries substantially worse (European Bank for Reconstruction and Development [EBRD], 2017).

The World Bank published 'Toward a New Social Contract: Taking on Distributional Tensions in Europe and Central Asia' in 2018 (Bussolo et al., 2018a). It concludes that 'rising inequality [is] among the most serious problems of our times' and provides an abundant data and information on labour market, income, and wealth trends in all the countries of the region, including the EU

---

3   Alvaredo, Chancel, Piketty, Saez, and Zucman (2018).

Member States, the Western Balkans, Russia, and Central Asia. The report focuses on the link between growing social tensions, income inequality, and transformations in the labour markets and advocates a renewal of the (existing) social welfare institutions and protection in the labour market, as well as more progressive taxation (Bussolo et al., 2018).

Within the European Commission (EC), as the executive arm of the EU, the Employment and Social Policy department has analysed the issue for a long time.[4] More recently, the Economics and Finance department has begun to review the evidence and policies as well. The EC states that EU and Euro Area (EA) income inequality is relatively low when seen through 'a global lens' but that income concentration at the very top has been increasing in Europe as well over the 1980–2017 period.[5] The EC notes slow growth of bottom incomes as the main (statistical) reason for the increase in inequality since the crisis. This slow growth is of particular concern because increased poverty at the bottom of the income distribution can threaten growth through several mechanisms on both the supply and demand sides.

On policy, the Commission argues: 'Preventing and reducing inequality largely depends on Member State action and reforms. The EU's role is to support and complement the Member States' policies in the fields of social inclusion and social protection, through policy guidance and financial support for reforms'.[6] Hence, the Commission provides country-specific policy advice on addressing income inequality. Broadly, its view is that 'the tax and benefit system is the key policy lever for addressing income inequality' (which points to, for example, the negative effects of flat taxes) and that 'up-skilling of low-skilled workers has the most potential to counteract wage dispersion'. More specifically, it suggests a considerable tax shift from labour to income, wealth, and capital, including property and inheritance and suggests concern about the weaker capacity of Member States to redistribute wealth through the tax transfer system. Education, training, and the provision of quality social services is called for while ensuring access for all.[7] There is a recognition that policy coordination in areas such as taxes is important (and the Commission has proposed related action), but there is little reflection on the role of European integration in the development of income inequality. This is in contrast with globalization and trade (largely an exclusive competence of the EU), where the Commission argues: 'Crucially, how

---

4   See, for example, a detailed analysis in European Commission (2015), European Commission(2016) and European Commission (2018) as well as Maquet, Meyermans, and Duiella (2015). The Joint Research Centre of the EC is publishing a series of papers on inequality and fairness.

5   See https://ec.europa.eu/jrc/en/page/fairness-policy-briefs-series-182382 and European Commission (2019).

6   European Commission (2017).

7   European Commission (2019a: 10–11).

labour market institutions and policymakers respond can determine whether trade creates more or less inequality'.

The policy message from all these studies and major reports is that a fair distribution of income and economic opportunity should be a top priority. 'Inclusive growth' and 'sustainable growth' are related terms widely used by international organizations; we understand this as saying that economic inequality has become an essential challenge in terms of social cohesion and political legitimacy but also a threat to progress in economic development itself. The International Monetary Fund (IMF) has researched income inequality and growth[8]. It concludes that

> We find that longer growth spells—periods of strong, healthy, per capita growth are robustly associated with more equality in the income distribution. . . . A key implication is that it would be a gamble to think that distribution will take care of itself provided policy makers steadfastly pursue growth. Over longer horizons, avoiding excessive inequality and sustaining economic growth may be two sides of the same coin.[9]

Thus, in addition to the concern about political stability and social cohesion, there is also a strong economic case for the analysis of income development, convergence, and inequality.

1.1 THE PURPOSE AND STRUCTURE OF THIS VOLUME

The previous section highlighted the relevance of the research presented in this volume. In addition, this volume serves two other purposes. First, its purpose is to provide a synopsis for an international readership that naturally does not and cannot follow the European literature in detail. The volume provides an overview of broad trends in the countries of the EU and its close neighbours as well as the EU as a whole. Second, it takes the long-term process of European integration as a starting point. The volume looks at income and the well-being of the EU population as an entity that shares broad social and economic objectives, one of which is convergence of its parts. And it considers the commonalities and differences in institutions and policies as they might impact the situation, not just in one country but in the Union as a whole. Migration is a clear example for this interdependence. The EU experience during the Great Recession and the Euro Crisis shows strongly that developments in one country or a group of countries can harm not only well-being in an individual country but in the Union more broadly.

---

8   IMF (2011).
9   Berg and Ostry (2011), p. 3.

In terms of sharing the benefits of growth and well-being, this European inte-gration perspective translates into considering three levels of analysis: First, the distribution of welfare gains within a country; second, the relative position of the European countries and, in particular, whether there is convergence or diver-gence between countries with lower and higher levels of income and well-being; and, third, what happens to income distribution when looking at the popula-tion of the EU as a whole. At the EU level, are richer households gaining more than those in the middle or at the bottom, or are the lower income households catching up? These levels of analysis are interlinked. For example, convergence between countries can be combined with rising inequality and exclusion within the individual countries or even within the groupings of countries, so it is im-portant to look not just at convergence but also at who are and where are the beneficiaries of convergence between countries.

With the international reader in mind, we thought it useful to start with a short summary of European integration and the main social-economic characteristics of how opportunity and income are shared and the welfare of the population is protected (the European Social Model). This is followed by brief conclusions from the wealth of analysis provided in this volume. Against the variety of ex-isting literature, a volume targeted at an international readership should provide a broad overview of income and well-being developments in Europe, but we do not see the need, nor the capacity, for country-by-country reporting.

Chapters 2–7 cover the EU and those countries in close association geo-graphically. Chapter 2 provides an overview of developments in the EU and the EA as single entities, as well as individual member countries (e.g., some analyt-ical groupings). Chapters 3–6 cover groups of countries that are of particular rel-evance: France and Germany, the motor of European integration; the Southern European countries (most of which participated in European integration later and only after overcoming authoritarian regimes); and the CEE countries and the Northern European countries that were also not a party to European integration from the beginning. Chapters 7 and 8 look at countries that are not members but are closely associated with the EU: the Western Balkans and Turkey. One central question for the geographical chapters (except the Northern group) is, indeed, whether European integration allowed for convergence with the lesser devel-oped parts. Developments in the Northern European countries are of interest for another reason: these countries' institutions and societies best represent the core of the European Social Model. Given the tensions and pressures that Europe experiences, the question arises whether the Nordic countries were able to cope with these pressures and maintain a degree of social fairness and equity in the sharing of incomes and well-being.

By contrast, Chapters 9–15 consider policy areas of relevance to the theme of the volume. Of course, there are many potential such issues, and we have had to be selective, so the focus is on those central social institutions (comprising the European Social Model) that influence how income and welfare are shared in our economies. In line with the literature on the Social Model, we consider labour rights and the relations of organized labour and employers, universal social protection, services, and the policies used to promote equality of opportunity and, in particular, a general universal education system. Chapter 13, on the evolution of industrial relations, discusses the central mechanism for sharing market incomes between labour and capital. Chapter 10, on social protection, focuses on a system central to post-market income distribution by providing cash transfers or social services; and Chapter 9, on education, looks at how these systems shape the earnings capacity of individuals of different socioeconomic backgrounds. Chapter 11 is devoted to pensions, which are by far the biggest part of social protection, and Chapter 12 focuses on long-term care (LTC), the most recent addition to social protection. Social protection for people of working age is a focus not only in Chapter 10 but also in the final chapter of the volume. These chapters compare trends in countries and ask whether different policies or institutions lead to different, more or less equitable outcomes, and they also look at the impact of these policies and institutions at the EU level. Chapter 14 reviews the migration experience in Europe, which comprises migration from outside of the EU and, to another substantial degree, migration between European countries governed by specific rules ('free movement of workers'). The authors of that chapter describe those parts of the EU that benefited from migration and explore possible differences between different types of migration.

The last chapter, Chapter 15, summarizes, complements, and deepens the geographical analysis and asks whether the EU and not just individual countries can ensure an equitable sharing of gains in income and well-being at both Union and national levels. It reviews the relevant policies and institutions and explores the impact that EU integration has had and what contribution EU-level policies have made. In this context, it discusses the issue of the social dimension of EU policies, including the debate on the Social Union. Chapter 15 can be seen as an epilogue to the two parts of the volume, bringing together developments and policies in a forward-looking manner.

The international reader might well ask: Why is there so much emphasis on inequality and redistribution, because European levels of income inequality and poverty are less marked than in other parts of world, and the observed increases are often considered to be less dramatic? This deserves an empirical answer, which Chapters 2 and 15 provide mostly in relation to the United States. The second answer to this question is that progress in Europe was achieved by maintaining a balance between economic and social progress, both within the member countries and across them. So the question for this volume is not to determine why there such a concern but to evaluate if recent trends are consistent with this balancing of economic and social progress. To this end, this volume analyses both progress in achieving equitable well-being across Europe and excessive inequality and social hardships and their drivers.

1.2 WHAT IS EUROPE?

'Europe' is a geographical description. It usually covers the territory from Portugal in the west to that part of Russia up to the Urals in the east, and from Norway in the north to those countries lying along or within the upper part of the Mediterranean, including a part of Turkey around western Istanbul, to the south. Europe has a population of 740 million. Many European countries are in the EU, comprising 28 Member States between 2011 and 2019. The east of geographical Europe, covering Russia, the Ukraine, and other ex-USSR countries, is not represented in the EU. Nor are Iceland, Norway, Liechtenstein, and Switzerland, although they are members of the European Free Trade Association (EFTA), which has a free trade agreement with the EU. Iceland, Norway, and Liechtenstein also join the EU in the European Economic Area (EEA) forming a Single Market for the free movement of goods, services, capital, and labour. Turkey, in a customs union with the EU, and several Balkan countries have close ties and are often applicants to become full members of the EU though this will probably only happen after lengthy negotiation and review. The micro-states of San Marino, the Vatican, Monaco, and Andorra are currently negotiating a status similar to being part of the Single Market, with EEA-type rights and obligations. Meanwhile, Ukraine is developing its economic and political relations with the EU, as are some of the other ex-USSR countries.

It is not only geographical proximity that defines Europe; its countries also have a long-standing, shared history with cultural, including religious, connections. In addition, both World Wars were in large part wars between European countries (sometimes also comprising civil wars). Turkey, though geographically mostly in Asia, has been very European for much of the 20th century, and the Istanbul Region is one of the largest agglomerations in Europe.

This Europe, and indeed all of geographical Europe, has been shaped by the economic and political developments since World War II. Between 1945 and 1990, the Iron Curtain separated Eastern and Western Europe, with the former being largely state-planned economies. No countries in Europe currently have such central planning and Communist governments, but their legacy still shapes, if to a declining degree, those countries with a history of them. The EU has emerged out of the political initiatives taken in the 1950s, principally to prevent France and Germany fighting another war. The European Coal and Steel Community led to the European Economic Community involving France, Germany, and Italy and the three Benelux countries—Belgium, the Netherlands, and Luxemburg. The United Kingdom had decided not to join the original six and had initiated the European Free Trade Association (EFTA) in 1960 with six other non-members: Austria, Switzerland, Norway, Sweden, Denmark, and Portugal. For a decade or so before the United Kingdom and Denmark left to join the EEC, it was seen as a potential rival trade block although it had quickly negotiated a free trade agreement with the EEC.

The original six were joined by the United Kingdom, Ireland, and Denmark in 1973. Greece, Spain, and Portugal became members in the 1980s as their dictatorships were replaced by democratic governments; and Sweden, Finland, and Austria joined the by now renamed EU in 1995. These 15 Member States were joined by 10 more in the single largest enlargement in 2004, with the arrival of eight former Comecon economies together with Cyprus and Malta. In 2007 Romania and Bulgaria acceded and, most recently, in 2013, Croatia, the EU reaching 28 members . Turkey has been an applicant for EU membership since 1963; Serbia, Montenegro, Bosnia, the former republic of Macedonia (FYROM), and Albania are also candidates for membership. However, the EU fell to 27 Member States when the United Kingdom withdrew—'Brexit'—in January 2020.

The economic development of the Union can be summarized as follows. Until the first oil crisis in 1973, rapid economic growth was experienced, resulting from postwar rebuilding, a catching up with US productivity levels, accompanied by the finalization of a move of all but few workers out of agriculture as mechanization became widespread in the EU6 but also in what would become the EU15. Technological advances and the postwar baby boom helped to push up national output. Inflation was something of a threat in the 1960s, but became the major policy challenge in the mid-1970s. 'Stagflation' then became the key preoccupation as the quadrupling of oil prices fed a wage-and-price spiral to varying degrees in different countries while growth stagnated in the face of the increasing cost of imported energy. More subdued gross domestic product (GDP) growth compared with the 1950s and 1960s was seen from 1975 until the mid-1990s. Efforts to tame inflation and monetary instability combined with fewer opportunities for catching up with the United States and moving workers from agriculture to industry. The manufacturing sector also peaked as a share of national output,[10] and the service sector came to dominate employment and output although intra-EC and international trade was still concentrated on manufactured products. In the late 1990s, the growth of things digital began to shape the economy and societies.

Monetary instability, including several devaluations in the early 1970s, saw the first attempts at European monetary coordination, including setting up the European Exchange Rate Mechanism (the ERM or 'snake in the tunnel'). Its collapse led to establishing the European Monetary System (EMS) in 1979. The success of the latter prompted preparations for more far-reaching monetary coordination culminating with the launch of a single currency—the euro—in 1999. The Economic and Monetary Union (EMU), dating from 1990, is an umbrella term for the group of policies aimed at converging the economies of EU Member

---

10 This happened in the 1960s in the United Kingdom and early 1970s in France and Germany; see Nickell, Redding, and Swaffield (2002).

States in three stages. The policies cover the 19 Eurozone states, as well as non-euro EU members.

Each stage of the EMU consists of progressively closer economic integration. Only once a state participates in the third stage is it permitted to adopt the euro as its official currency. As such, the third stage is largely synonymous with the Eurozone. The euro convergence criteria are the set of requirements that need to be fulfilled in order for a country to join the Eurozone. An important element of this is participation for a minimum of 2 years in the European Exchange Rate Mechanism (ERM II), in which candidate currencies demonstrate economic convergence by maintaining limited deviation from their target rate against the euro. Nineteen EU member states, including most recently Lithuania, have entered the third stage and have adopted the euro as their currency.

Deepening the economic union of the Member States was always seen not just as an economic opportunity but as establishing deeper links between the populations of the member countries. This was particularly the case when the EU decided to move from a single market that included free movement of workers to a single currency. In economic terms, expectations centred around the efficiency gains to be expected from a single monetary and exchange rate policy and the greater weight the entity would have internationally, hence being better able to adjust to external shocks. Political expectations were also high: a Union of states that share a currency would be on an almost automatic route to deepening political unity because so many issues would need to be solved together. The reverse side of this belief, however, was that some fundamental policy issues were not solved when the currency union was established, such as the degree of fiscal federalism needed and the development of a real banking union.

From 2001, Europe saw sustained growth, falling unemployment, and convergence of income per head as the economies of poorer countries in the periphery grew more quickly, in part because the euro and European Central Bank monetary policy gave them negative real interest rates. Competitiveness was a concern, but optimism was high about the European integration project, which also brought about quite strong investment. The financial and economic crisis brought these seemingly happy times to an abrupt end. All Member States except Poland saw output drop and unemployment rise for at least a couple of years. Initially, the Great Recession was met by coordinated government expansionary policies, but as public debt increased, in large part due to bank bail-outs, markets became worried about the ability of some of the euro member countries to finance their debt. The very survival of the euro was questioned. The Euro Crisis was managed, but the depth of the crisis and, as many would argue, also certain aspects of how it was managed contributed to the worst hit countries (Greece, Spain, Portugal) seeing output in 2017 still lower than that in 2008 and unemployment and social deprivation much higher. Other countries, principally Germany, Poland, and Sweden, saw only short-lived recessions.

While crisis management preoccupied European policymakers much of the time during the past decade, there was also a more long-term change. Pure or narrow GDP growth no longer became the only goal. Ecological sustainability, spurred by increasing evidence of man-made climate change, and inclusive growth in the face of growing inequality became of equal importance. Since 2010, the EU has been formally pursuing smart, sustainable, and inclusive growth.

1.3 THE EUROPEAN SOCIAL MODEL

Europe is often seen as high taxing and high spending, with substantial parts of GDP going to the government and being transferred to citizens needing support, both as an investment (education, health) and as a more immediate income type (pensions, unemployment, social assistance, and sickness benefits). Many of the benefits financed by the state are available to all, irrespective of income: this is the case for education, at least up to the end of secondary and much of tertiary schooling; for most aspects of healthcare; and for income in old age through very high coverage of pension insurance as part of universal social security schemes. (It should be noted that the basic pension in many EU countries is means—or at least household-income tested). OECD figures (for 2015)[11] show that only EU and EFTA countries have shares of general government expenditure higher than 40%, with France and Finland around 55%. Japan has expenditures of 39%, and the United States has 37%. Not all such government expenditure is on welfare items, but approximately 70% is for welfare expenditures.

As shown in Figure 1.1 most European countries spend comparatively large shares of their national incomes on social protection and related public services such as social and care services and health. The widely quoted 'Golden Growth Report' of the World Bank[12] noted that Europe was the world champion in social expenditure, claiming that the countries of Europe had expenditures that were much higher than not only emergent economies, but also of other industrial economies. Attention is needed, however, when comparing the size of total social expenditure with other regions. The OECD shows that, taking account of private in addition to public social expenditures and related tax treatment, US social expenditure amounts to almost 30% of GDP, just below the estimated number for France and well above several Western and Northern European countries[13] (e.g., Austria and Spain spend 25% and Ireland and Norway around 20%).

It seems Europeans prefer to have social protection and services organized to a large extent in the public domain, with its related implications, of course, on the side of taxation and social security contributions. There are measurable results in

---

11   https://data.oecd.org/gga/general-government-spending.htm.
12   Gill and Raiser (2012).
13   See OECD (2016).

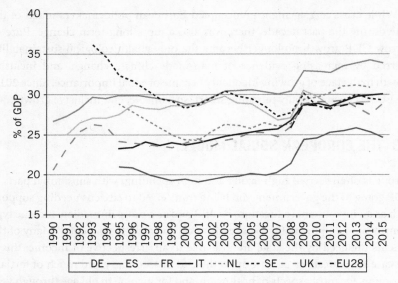

Figure 1.1 Social expenditure as per cent of gross domestic product (GDP).
Source: Eurostat, ESSPROSS.

terms of inequality and redistribution. The EU countries show a high degree of diversity in terms of level of income, economic structure, and culture. Hence it is no wonder that when looking at the EU as an economic entity market income inequality is equal to if not higher than in the United States economy. However, again looking at the EU as a single entity, inequality of disposable household income is substantially lower.[14] It is important to note that this reduction in inequality is largely through national tax and welfare systems and, given the small EU budget, only marginally through EU-level programmes.[15]

Indeed, social protection is one vital element of the European Social Model; however, there is more to it than this. Typically, the European Social Model is defined as a combination of social security and broader welfare policies providing universal coverage, labour rights, and organized industrial relations between workers and employers (thus ensuring freedom of association and autonomy) complemented by dialogue between social partners and government. Many would also include full access to general education as part and parcel of a universal system of social policies.

There is no uniform model of how either welfare or industrial relations are organized, and there is an extensive literature categorizing the different social models across Europe, starting with the analysis by Esping-Andersen.[16]

---

14 See Chapter 2 and Filauro (2017: 11–12).
15 See Pasimeni and Riso (2016).
16 Esping-Andersen (1990).

In the context of this introduction, the most important question is why so many European countries, including all in Western Europe, developed such combinations of guaranteed labour rights, industrial relations, and fairly large welfare systems, even as they differ greatly in detail and in their degree of inclusiveness. Two of the most eminent social philosophers, Jacques Derrida and Jürgen Habermas, provide a historical answer by referring back to why civil society welcomed individual liberty as an answer to the absolutist regimes that dominated Europe. They felt that the 'triumph of capitalism' needed to be accompanied by 'social justice':

> In Europe, those who have been affected by class distinctions and their enduring consequences understood these burdens as a fate that could be averted only through collective action. In the context of the workers' movement and the Christian socialist traditions an ethics of solidarity, the struggle for 'more social justice', with the goal of equal provision for all, asserted itself against the individualistic ethos of market justice that accepts glaring social inequalities as part of the bargain. Habermas and Derrida (2003)

In practice, the post-World War II period was decisive. Social protection was extended to guarantee universal coverage, labour rights were re-established and broadened where they had been the victim of fascist (and in the East after 1990, communist) regimes, and in many Western European countries different forms of corporatism developed. There is broad consensus among researchers and policymakers that this helped economic and social development in the decades of postwar reconstruction and especially during the long period of catching up with US productivity levels.

All the elements of the social model are in continuous evolution. Starting in the 1990s, activation of the unemployed and others of working age capable of working gained importance and led to considerable changes in the structure of welfare policies. In the 2000s, *social investment* became a catchword, meaning that reformed and well-designed social programmes should not be considered simply as transfers but as investments in the productive capacity of an economy. In the past few years, it has been argued that they are substantially threatened by recent developments such as globalization, digitalization, and neo-liberal post-financial crisis austerity policies.

While this fundamental discussion goes well beyond the scope of this volume, an important question to be reviewed is whether European countries where industrial relations and welfare systems are well developed cope better with moments of massive crisis in terms of loss of social welfare and employment.[17]

---

17 For the policies enacted during and after the Great Recession, see European Commission (2014), chapter 1, pp. 43–104.

Although there are substantial differences in practice, the EU Member States share common principles around which the 'models' are constructed. They have included these principles in a number of fundamental legal acts starting with the Treaty of Rome, the Charter of Fundamental Rights, and, most recently, the Proclamation of the Pillar of Social Rights. One of the questions discussed in the final chapter of this volume is whether there is a need for more European-level action to guarantee implementation and whether the fact that so many EU states share a single currency requires further coordination or harmonization. The following numbers show that welfare systems are in place in EU Member States, and some of the chapters in this volume review to what extent these systems contribute to what is now called *inclusive growth*.

The data on social security expenditure show interesting developments. Sweden was the highest spender by a long way in 1990, but has reduced its share in GDP significantly and is very much in the middle in 2015. France has seen a steadily growing share, and, at around 34% in 2015, sees the highest number. The United Kingdom was among the lowest in 1990 at 20%, but it has had much the same share as Sweden since 2010.

Did the biggest social spenders grow more slowly? France, Sweden, and the Netherlands all saw very or moderately respectable growth rates, while Italy did not. The lowest spender, Spain, saw fast GDP per capita growth until 2008, but then has seen prolonged recession. Considering the share of tax in GDP, high taxing France, Italy, and Sweden have seen rather different outcomes in terms of growth. Any causation, however, is even more complicated to establish as slow growth with fixed expenditures (including debt) needs ever-growing tax revenue to finance it. The sharp rise in Italy's share is surely in large part caused by slow growth. High social spending countries such as Sweden and the Netherlands clearly can also see high growth of GDP per capita and household disposable income. France, however, might find its social spending a greater challenge to finance with lower long-term growth.[18]

One of the main functions of government spending is redistribution and poverty relief, more often seen as making society more inclusive. Redistribution is not the only way determining how the benefits of growth are shared, however. In fact, wage and primary income dispersions and their changes are of great significance to achieve more or less equal net income distribution. In respect to inequality, what sort of challenges has the EU faced? In very broad terms, the data for the shares of the top 10% and the top 1% income earners/recipients show that countries tended to see a reduction in pre-tax inequality between 1970 and 1990, while it increased—quite sharply in some countries—between 1990 and the Great Recession. It then flattened out or even declined (see Figure 1.2).

---

18 There is an abundant literature on whether the European high tax and spending model is detrimental to growth, see, e.g., Sapir (2006) and Barr (2004).

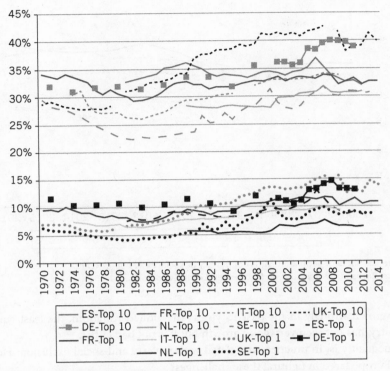

Figure 1.2 Distribution: shares in pre-tax national income of top 10% and top 1%.
Source: Wid.world database (http://wid.world/).

These broad trends encompass quite different national situations. The top 10% received between 23% and 43% of national income, while the top 1% received between 4% and 15%. Sweden has been continuously the most equal country measured by the share of the top 10%, with Denmark very similar, while the Netherlands has this distinction for the top 1%. The United Kingdom started the 1970s very much in the middle in terms of equality but, by 1990, with a steady, continuing increase, it had become the least equal country of those reviewed. Germany in recent years shows almost the same outcomes. Sweden, though relatively more equal, also saw quite a sharp rise, especially for the top 10%, from 1990—a period which coincided with the liberalization of financial sectors as well as the beginnings of the Digital Revolution throughout Europe.

Is more inequality associated with lower growth, a hypothesis increasingly being examined by international organizations such as the IMF and the World Bank? The facts just cited do not contradict this. Sweden and the Netherlands, the least unequal countries, were growing quite strongly throughout the period. Germany, though with less equality at least in the high share of the top 1%, has

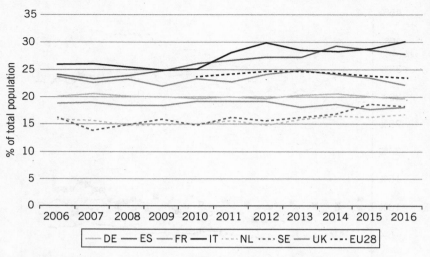

Figure 1.3 Share of population at risk of poverty or social exclusion (AROPE)
Source: Eurostat EU Statistics on Income and Living Conditions.

also grown strongly in the past 15 years. The United Kingdom, the least equal country, has not seen very good growth but it is not bad either.

Inequality is, in practice, associated with poverty and social exclusion: How has Europe fared in fighting these challenges?

The United Kingdom, together with Spain, has significantly higher poverty levels than the more egalitarian countries of the Netherlands and Sweden (see Figure 1.3).[19] Around 30% of the British population is poor (or, as the EU names it, 'at risk of poverty'), while at the other extreme the Netherlands sees a figure of only 17%. These numbers change relatively little year to year, but clearly there has been a significant increase since the financial crisis in both the best and worst performers. Interestingly, middle-ranking France and Germany have seen little change over the whole period 2006–2016; France even saw a decline since 2010. Using a different measure of poverty (income poverty at 50% of the median

---

19 The EU definition used is those at risk of poverty or severely materially deprived or living in households with very low work intensity. Persons are only counted once even if they are present in several sub-indicators. Those at risk-of-poverty are persons with an equivalized disposable income below the risk-of-poverty threshold, which is set at 60 % of the national median equivalized disposable income (after social transfers). Material deprivation covers indicators relating to economic strain and durables. Severely materially deprived persons have living conditions severely constrained by a lack of resources. Persons in households with very low work intensity are those aged 0--59 living in households where the adults (aged 18–59) worked 20% or less of their total work potential during the past year. See the extensive discussion in Chapters 2 and 15 on definitional and statistical issues.

household income), the OECD[20] shows that, for 2017, average EU performer Germany was at 10%, compared with the United States at 18%; Spain, the worst EU performer on this measure, was at 15%.

The chapters of this volume analyse these broad trends in far more depth, both empirical and conceptual, questioning also some commonly perceived views.

1.4 RESULTS AND BROAD CONCLUSIONS

Chapter 2, the first 'country' chapter, presents and analyses income, well-being, and inequality in the EU as a social and economic entity, reviewing the extraordinary importance of the process conducive to the Single Market and the Single Currency. The establishment of the Single Market, the gradual process of harmonizing the many rules governing markets as well as social rights, and the free mobility of people within the Union have clearly had consequences on the generation of income and the well-being of Europeans. These have become even more evident with the Single Currency: the common monetary policy as well as the need to keep public finances in check limit room for manoeuvring in national economic policymaking; financial markets understand these links and expect difficulties in one economy to extend potentially to the area as a whole. In EU language, the term is 'spillover', and a higher degree of economic policy coordination is therefore seen as necessary. In policy terms, the chapter argues for considering this economic entity as a social entity, too. This has implications on the assessment of Europeans' well-being because the reference becomes the whole EU and not individual national contexts. Accordingly, the chapter focuses on personal income as a proxy of well-being and argues that it is vital to measure inequality at the European level rather than just averaging national levels for foundational, analytical, and policymaking reasons.

Chapter 2 goes on to review the interaction between the performance of the EU as an entity and of its different parts. Based on national accounts, average living standards have improved considerably as the European integration process unfolded in terms of both increased real incomes and less time spent at work. This process went along with an individual convergence across the EU15 countries, and then the EU28 countries after the Eastern enlargements. At the same time, personal income distribution changed within each country: although patterns present important national specificities, there is a rough tendency of

---

20 The ratio of the number of people whose income falls below the poverty line, fixed at half the median household income of the total population. See https://data.oecd.org/inequality/poverty-rate.htm.

Note that there are differences between official European and US poverty statistics concerning the basis for calculating the income below which a household is considered to be in poverty. The OECD publishes comparable data. Related issues are again discussed in more detail in Chapters 2 and 15.

inequality to fall until the 1980s and to increase afterwards. The EU-wide inequality pattern reflects a combination of the trends observed for both between-country inequality (convergence in real GDP per capita) and within-country inequality (national patterns). As a result, EU28 income inequality has steadily declined, mostly as a result of the macroeconomic convergence of new accession countries. EU15 income inequality steadily fell until the mid-1980s, but picked up again with the economic turmoil following the Great Recession, largely reflecting the divergence between periphery and core countries in the EA. The United States provides a natural benchmark for the EU as a whole. The recent rise in EU15-wide inequality does not differ much from the increase observed in the United States, where, in line with other studies, the chapter finds that incomes are distributed more unequally than in the EU and, especially, the EA, due to the greater income redistribution achieved by European tax-and-benefit systems.

Using a common EU standard shows more progress in terms of poverty reduction. It also shows that the patterns of income convergence across Member States differ across categories of residents, thus calling for a more careful consideration of the personal and national dimensions of EU policies. This new analysis of household income distribution across the EU as an entity is making a major contribution to our understanding of well-being trends in Europe thus helping policymakers to develop a comprehensive welfare strategy to improve well-being across the EU.

France and Germany are often seen as the political and economic core of the EU. Chapter 3 focuses on these, the two largest economies of the EU comprising 36% of the EU28's GDP and (49% of the EA's GDP). It finds that the two economies rely on different growth models, with important social implications, and focuses on labour market features to explain this. Germany's postwar economic growth model is strongly based on exports, particularly of manufactured goods. This is underpinned by a more flexible collective bargaining system in Germany, marked by more involvement of workers in management through co-determination (*Mitbestimmung*) and more flexibility at the company level. In contrast, growth in France has traditionally focused on domestic demand, driven by its sizeable public sector and a lower household saving rate, with more antagonism between employers and workers and with a centralized collective bargaining system. With globalization and increasing internationalization of companies, manufacturing workers in Germany faced stronger external competition and were ready to accept muted wage growth to keep employment high. At the same time, collective bargaining coverage declined, and the Hartz reforms reduced the generosity of unemployment benefits, again leading to wage restraint by decreasing opportunity wages. While flexibility enabled adjustment and employment increased, disposable incomes in Germany became more unequal, income poverty increased, and a sizeable low-wage sector emerged.

Recently, the gap between the two growth models and the resulting differences in social outcomes appear to be narrowing. The 2010s saw a series of social measures in Germany that also made the labour market more inclusive. While in the 2000s there may have been a tradeoff between employment growth and employment quality, in the 2010s, both employment levels and employment quality improved. The introduction of the statutory general minimum wage in 2015 is a case in point. Wage increases exceeded inflation and productivity growth, while economic growth has increasingly relied on domestic demand. The earlier observed increases in disposable income inequality, income poverty, and in-work poverty appear to have largely halted or at least slowed, while unemployment remains low. This result is mirrored by a lower regional income inequality accompanied by a faster catching-up in the poorest regions. At the same time, in France, unemployment declined and a series of reforms have increased the flexibility of its labour market and reduced benefit generosity.

Southern Europe, emerging out of very different political and social structures, has displayed a long period of strong convergence followed by a rapid divergence since the Great Recession—this situation is reviewed in Chapter 4. The chapter suggests that living standards in Southern Europe largely converged to the EU average until the eve of the Eurozone crisis (except in Italy, where they peaked in the mid-1990s). These countries then lost ground relative to other Member States. The chapter shows the massive increase in employment in the region, reflecting fundamental changes in the underlying culture in the respective societies: in particular, a rise in women's workforce participation and tertiary education were a particular success story for young women. Thereafter, their destinies diverged: in Greece, the fall was greatest and the recovery most timid; in Italy, the decline was slow but steady; in Portugal and Spain, the economy turned the corner in 2012 and 2013, respectively, and started to bounce back, gradually closing the gap with the rest of the EU, although with the remaining gaps still very substantial. The chapter exposes a number of long-term impacts of the deep and long recession: the decline in employment for people with tertiary education was far more marked in the South than anywhere else and probably contributed to outward migration. Despite more favourable indicators and great progress in establishing universal healthcare since the 1960s, access to healthcare for lower income groups deteriorated in Greece and Italy. Similarly, poverty increased during the crisis in those countries where the pro-cyclicality in social policy expenditure was strong, an issue reviewed in several of the chapters. Inequality has increased during this period, after starting from higher levels than in other EU Member States, and it is likely to make a return to catching up more difficult. It is noted that Southern Europe is suffering from severe underinvestment, which, if not reversed, threatens its future growth prospects. Can convergence continue in Spain and Portugal and resume in Italy and Greece? The answer hinges on a variety of factors, internal and external, closely related to each other. External factors include the ability of policymakers at the European level to rebalance macroeconomic governance so that both core and periphery member states can prosper. Internal factors mainly concern political instability.

The CEE countries had a unique experience of initial fundamental transition followed by convergence towards Western Europe. Income, consumption, well-being, and inequality trends are analysed in Chapter 5, which presents this convergence but also an increasing diversity. A key common feature of the pre-crisis growth model in countries of the region was deep economic and institutional integration with the EU: they enjoyed significant capital inflows, and capital stock was upgraded with more productive assets that also allowed for technology transfers. The EU provided an important anchor for the region's institutional development and was not only a major source of private capital but also of public investment via the cohesion funds. During this development process, however, inequality increased in all CEE countries during the early years of transition, and while certain regions (e.g., capital cities), sectors (e.g., those dominated by multinationals), and social groups (the young, more educated) were able to reap the benefits of the development process, others remained left behind. The analysis of income inequality weighted economic performance (Table 5.4) makes this gap nicely visible. Convergence of the CEE countries is no guarantee against increasing differences within them. This has become a major political challenge and is certainly one of the sources of the success of avowedly 'illiberal' parties.

The crisis exacerbated these tensions as unemployment increased and government transfers were cut by austerity programmes. There were important differences between the experiences of CEE countries. Some of the more successful countries in terms of income convergence, the Baltic States, were also those with the biggest increases in income inequality. Slovakia and Poland, on the other hand, were able to achieve high levels of GDP growth without an excessive increase in income inequality. The Czech Republic and Slovenia, which were relatively more developed at the start of the transition process, recorded slower convergence to EU15 levels of income but recorded only moderate increase in inequality during the period studied. Figure 5.3 provides a fascinating picture of the relationship between income levels in CEE countries and the earlier EU members. An important issue that the chapter raises is the gap between the actual speed of convergence and the expectations of the populations: for example, the chapter demonstrates that although the share of household incomes below 40% of the EU15 average has declined dramatically, the income gaps remain very substantial.

It has been argued that the Nordic countries have developed the most adaptable version of the European Social Model. Chapter 6 reviews their social and economic performance, which seems to be indeed favourable but not unambiguously so. It notes that while the Nordic countries remain relatively affluent and egalitarian, inequality of disposable household income has been on the rise over the past 30 years. The inequality rise came at different times, with different intensities and with different mixtures of rising earnings inequality and declining social transfers. For a long time the Nordic countries were characterized by positive feedback between earnings compression and strong welfare states combined with high levels of employment. The chapter asks whether what we have seen in the recent past is a reversal: rising earnings inequality and reduction in welfare generosity going together—they call this the 'inequality multiplier'. This posits that, in addition to budgetary and economic pressures, there is also an element of declining readiness in a more differentiated society to share the benefits of growth and to adequately fund welfare programmes. The question really is to determine how far this process has advanced. And there the authors seem to have some hope: Nordic societies still enjoy high levels of trust so the potential is there for preserving and reinforcing what are, after all, still among the most equal and cohesive societies globally.

The non-EU countries in the Western Balkans and Turkey do interact strongly with the EU: two specific chapters, Chapters 7 and 8, look at income, consumption, and inequality trends in these countries that are closely influenced by European developments. The historical context, economic dynamics, demography, migration patterns, and, not least, the evolution of their political systems are important factors in the analysis. The Western Balkans (Chapter 6) is a region still coping with incomplete transition and the legacies of a boom-bust cycle, as most clearly reflected in still high unemployment rates. The chapter thus presents trends in inequality within the broader context of persisting high unemployment and perceptions of high and rising inequality. It is fundamentally a story of transition—the process, still unfinished, of transition from a system with an 'employer of last resort' and resulting job security to one with income gains for some parts of the population but widening inequality and increasing uncertainty that translate into reform fatigue and general feelings of discontent with the process of transition. The chapter can be seen as a counterfactual account to the preceding one on progress in CEE. Performance in the Western Balkans is in several respects still below the levels before transition in the former while well above its own the pre transition levels, and there are unprecedented high levels of dissatisfaction in the region. Recent announcements by Western European leaders point to some understanding of the dangers these situations entail for both individual European countries and the EU. The solution can only be found in a common effort to overcome the trap that exists between unfinished transition and the engagement of more developed European countries in investment in the private sector and policy support.

The chapter on developments in Turkey (Chapter 8) finds that, in the past 35 years, it has successfully transformed its inward looking and largely agricultural economy into an export-oriented and urban-based economy. The transformation has been achieved mostly in periods of dramatic reform embedded in business and political cycles. Nevertheless, there has only been partial success in terms of income convergence to EU standards. The biggest contributor to this success has been a structural change in the economy, shifting resources from agriculture into industry and services. The concomitant process of urbanization also enabled the government to deliver better public services. The Customs

Union agreement in 1995 and the EU candidate application in 1999 increased Turkey's international integration, thus enhancing the growth performance of the Turkish economy. The macroeconomic stability and institutional improvement after the 2001 economic crisis led to an acceleration in the convergence process. Nevertheless, in the most recent era, there have been significant setbacks for certain groups in terms of the regulatory environment, equality of opportunity, and access to markets and resources. One central issue illustrated in the chapter is gender equality, not only in broader societal terms but also in education and employment. Even in Istanbul, the economic powerhouse of Turkey, fewer than 36% of women of working age are counted as economically active (Table 8.8). This is, of course, partially the result of past developments. However, the future does not look much better because the share of young women not in employment, education, or training is, despite declining, still extraordinarily high (Figure 8.14). All this makes the outlook less favourable than one would expect when looking only at long-term trends but also points to areas where progress could be made perhaps comparatively quickly.

As discussed earlier, improving human capital was essential to the successful economic performance of Europe, and this importance is likely to grow. Chapter 9 looks at progress in investing in education and on educational access outcomes. It finds that populations across Europe are upgrading their educational attainment and that educational attainment is less strongly linked to parental background than it was for previous generations. However, important gaps remain in educational attainment. Moreover, educational attainment does not necessarily reflect skills attainment: the trend in foundation skills attainment over time is less clear. Furthermore, while lifelong learning is becoming increasingly important in today's fast-changing economy, the individuals who need it most may not always have access to adequate opportunities to upskill or reskill. Firms spend a lot more on training higher paid workers than lower paid, and those in and out of work frequently see little or no training. Finally, the chapter highlights that education and labour market outcomes vary substantially across countries. The United Kingdom, the Nordic countries, and Spain have reasonably good relative labour market outcomes for the low skilled. The countries still undergoing transition see low -skilled workers as having significantly worse employment, wages, and poverty levels than those with higher skills or qualifications. Furthermore, some of these countries in transition, which in many ways have built up successful economies, are those with the largest gaps in socioeconomic outcomes. Children of parents with low educational attainment or low -paying occupations have the weakest opportunities to do well. This is the case in Bulgaria, Poland, and Hungary. The structure of national education systems is deeply engrained in the institutional setup of an economy, intertwined with societal values and norms, and complementary to other institutions—not only within the world of education, but also those institutions governing labour markets, business investment, and social protection policies.

Chapter 10 looks at these social protection policies starting from the view that globalization, technological change, and migration form three major challenges for European labour markets and welfare states in the 21st century. These challenges are regarded as important sources of inequality between different groups within the labour market. It argues that globalization and technological change, via job polarization, affect the type of contract workers have with employers. It presents data which show that both the share of middle-skilled workers in low-paying jobs and the share of nonstandard employment have increased in many European countries. It hypothesises that the increased competition for low-paying jobs is associated with the rise of nonstandard employment and labour market flexibilization. An important and related question is how to ensure adequate social protection for workers under these non-standard forms of employment. This issue is explored in more detail in several country chapters and the EU has adopted related policy and legislative actions. The desired extension of social protection has resource implications. Chapter 10 analyses the role of the free movement of labour. New data illustrate that intra-EU labour migration from CEE countries to Western European countries has grown slowly but substantially since CEE countries have joined the EU. Free movement of labour is an important pillar of the Union. At the same time, it has been considered a challenge for welfare states because it can contribute to feelings of economic insecurity and may erode solidarity, which forms the basis for the provision of social policy.

The second part of Chapter 10 analyses how European welfare states and social policy have evolved over the past few decades. First, it shows that, in spite of budgetary pressure stemming from globalization and migration, most countries have increased the share of GDP spent on social policy. Until the financial crisis, social expenditure levels have converged across Europe, while the data show a pattern of divergence afterwards. Subsequently, it investigates to what extent the focus has shifted from classical social protection to social investment policies in order to enable workers to adapt themselves to new labour market transformations in all EU Member States. Furthermore, it demonstrates a novel way of correcting social expenditure data for the number of recipients. Analysing several policy programmes, it concludes that, in many countries, the shift from old to new social policies has been rather limited at best.

In terms of expenditure size, public support for well-being in old age is by far the biggest component of the European Social Model. It is also seen as the biggest success of the European welfare states—ensuring that people in old age do not suffer income poverty and do receive the healthcare they need. Chapter 11 discusses related trends in view of population ageing, the changing gender composition of the workforce, economic pressure, and changing societal needs including the evolution of household size and structure. Changes in the age structure of European populations mean that the current consumption and labour income age patterns are not sustainable. In the past decade, virtually all European countries changed their pension systems to meet the goal of their financial sustainability. The pressure of an increase in pension expenditure caused by demographic changes is offset by reducing pension transfers through changing benefit formulae or benefit indexing, as well as by increases in the effective pensionable age. The estimate of the impact of these two effects on the projected pension expenditure indicates that policy changes that lead to a reduction of benefit ratios are preferred over policies that lead to raising the official or formal retirement age. Thus, in the future, the amount paid per month to pensioner compared with the wages being earned will be reduced. These reforms of pension systems that tighten the link between lifetime earnings and pensions will translate in many countries into income inequalities within future generations of older people.

Increases in the official retirement age that are accompanied by a longer working life and therefore rising effective retirement ages would soften the tradeoffs discussed in that chapter. Hence it is no wonder that the chapter concludes that continuous efforts are needed to increase lifetime labour income. To this end it advocates mobilizing the potential of inactive people of working age. This includes, most importantly, tapping the potential of women in the labour market. While relevant in all European countries, this is most important in Southern European and CEE countries. The chapter also advocates investments in education, training, and adult learning that would improve the skills and competences of future workers, thus increasing labour productivity and earnings. This would increase the scope for vertical and horizontal redistribution, but, without specific policy action, it would not automatically reduce inequality within future older generations.

Europe devotes considerable resources to social services facilitating societal inclusion of individuals and families and enabling labour market participation and progress. In Europe, the public role concerning these services is particularly marked. Chapter 12 reviews trends in the provision of and access to long-term care, a growing component of social protection as society ages. It examines the main issues related to inequalities in access and affordability of LTC provision in the EU. Although, from a comparative perspective, Europe and in particular the EU as a region lead the field in providing LTC services to its citizens, significant inequalities in expenditure on LTC services and the benefits provided and in the situation of informal carers exist between Member States and even within individual countries.

The clear trend towards prioritizing home care in national policymaking and EU discourse has not always been matched by sufficient and affordable service supply, especially in Southern and Eastern European countries where home care remains underdeveloped. In some Member States, to some extent due to shortages in supply, there is an increasingly important trend towards the privatization and marketization of LTC and rapid growth of a commercial sector. The main consequences of these developments are growing out-of-pocket payments for beneficiaries resulting in greater inequalities and, in some cases, problematic monitoring of LTC quality. The high incidence of informal care in most EU Member States is also tackled. The above-mentioned issues of access and affordability, coupled with the lack or underdevelopment of special provisions for carers in many countries, are closely linked to this situation. This negatively impacts female labour market participation and the quality of work–life balance.

Migration has been a key aspect of economic and social development in Europe for decades. Chapter 14 looks at migration trends within and from outside Europe from the late 1950s until today. Free movement within the EU is one of its founding principles, but often more migration has occurred from outside rather than from within. The chapter looks at how in the 1950 and 1960s, it was Spain, Portugal, and Greece that exported many workers to the EU6, as did Turkey (and North Africa). This slowly halted in the 1970s, and then Spain, Portugal, and Greece joined the EU in the 1980s. With the collapse of the Iron Curtain, Eastern European countries picked up as the main sources for labour mobility in the 1990s and early 2000s. In 2004 and 2007, Eastern European countries joined the EU but have continued to be the major labour sending countries, together with the Balkans. The chapter shows that most of this immigration was of workers who did jobs largely not done by locals. The positive encouragement by host countries until the 1970s for migration was precisely because of labour shortages in sectors such as mining in Belgium or textiles in the United Kingdom. Though not actively covered by government programmes, the more recent migration trend is also mostly complementary to and not in substitution of existing jobs. The chapter provides the historical context for the past half-century in Europe, focusing specifically on the link between migration and economic development and inequality. It undertakes an empirical analysis and finds that immigration has contributed to reducing inequality within the 25 EU countries over the 2003–2017 period.

Typically, the European Social Model is defined as a combination of social security and broader welfare policies providing universal coverage, labour rights, and organized industrial relations between workers and employers, complemented by dialogue between social partners and government.

Chapter 13 covers industrial relations and inequality developments since the late 1990s, concluding that industrial relations are the most seriously damaged element in the European Social Model. It provides broad evidence on the decline in the organization of workers and employers and in the importance of collective bargaining and agreements, although there is a high degree of variation across countries. As the distribution of earnings determines to a large extent primary income distribution, what happens to industrial relations has a big impact on the equality of earnings and income. The decline in collective bargaining has contributed to a thinning out of middle-class earnings and to the concentration of wages at or somewhat above the minimum wage level. The chapter offers an in-depth analysis of the relationship between minimum wages, collective bargaining, and the share of low-income jobs and suggests a country group ty-pology for their interaction, showing the implications for earnings distribution in these economies. A wide coverage of collective bargaining is essential for maintaining or restoring middle-income earnings.

The chapter goes on to review the many reasons for this state of affairs, fo-cusing on the role of public policies and direct interventions into industrial re-lations practices. In the past two decades, policies have failed to strengthen or have weakened collective bargaining, and direct interventions have opposed or undermined collective bargaining. In Greece, these interventions contributed to a far stronger than expected fall in real wages.[21] The Greek case is of particular concern as these dramatic interventions in the industrial relation system was the result of the action of the IMF and the EU (EA states, the ECB, European Commission, and ESM). This involvement in policies that were in conflict with EU main objectives is one of the drivers of new labour policies initiated by Commission President Juncker (Fischer, 2018: 36) and led to a number of specific legal instruments to improve workers' rights and strengthen social dia-logue.[22] The chapter makes a strong case for a policy change at national and EU levels to restore or preserve one of the strong features of the European Social Model that has the potential to make economic development inclusive and sus-tainable. Strong collective bargaining by partners that captures the major struc-tural changes and supports public policy go together.

The final chapter (Chapter 15) looks at recent inequality and poverty trends from shortly before the 2008 Great Recession. It takes as a starting point what the 'country' chapters conclude on inequality and poverty. It finds that in this period

---

21 Yannis Stournaras, Governor of the Bank of Greece, in his analysis of the Greek lessons, agrees with the author on the gross underestimation of the contractive impact of the wages cuts but sees the reason for it lying in a wrong sequencing of the reforms mostly between labour and product markets: 'the idiosyncratic sequencing of struc-tural reforms led to real wages declining more than initially planned . . . . . households experienced a massive drop in purchasing power, and deepened the recession' See Stournaras (2018). Was it really an issue of sequencing? The chapter notes that product market regulation can also lead to a weakening of workers' positions in those sectors, thus reducing earnings and incomes.

22 Principle 8 of the Pillar of Social Rights reads,: '1. The social partners shall be consulted on the design and implementation of economic, employment and social policies according to national practices. They shall be encouraged to negotiate and conclude collective agreements in matters relevant to them, while respecting their au-tonomy and the right to collective action. Where appropriate, agreements concluded between the social partners shall be implemented at the level of the Union and its Member States. . . . . . . 3. Support for increased capacity of social partners to pro-mote social dialogue shall be encouraged'. Indeed, the EU foresees support for na-tional social partner capacity building through the European Social Fund and for the European organizations through the EU budget. For progress on the specific labour law initiatives, see the regular reports under https://ec.europa.eu/social/main.jsp?lan gId=en&catId=1310&furtherNews=yes.

the individual EU countries, and the EU itself, have been unable to make noticeable progress on poverty reduction and diminution of inequality. From these trends, it examines the main transmission mechanism from market incomes earnings to (post tax and benefits) household incomes, finding that inequality in wages is an essential determinant. It assesses the social transformation of household involvement in employment and its significant impact on income inequality and poverty. It also draws attention to the far less pronounced impact of redistribution on low-income working households.

It then reviews EU policy experiences and options for future improvement of Europe's social policymaking. Although Europe does not improve on the United States in market incomes, it does provide stronger redistribution in virtually all Member States, and this leads to a lower inequality of disposable household incomes (see also Chapter 2). The chapter also shows that national social policy expenditure has a strong impact on both poverty and inequality, finding that pension expenditures (because of their far bigger size) reduce poverty more than spending on social transfers for the adult population. On the latter, it picks up a point made in almost all chapters about the s negative impacts of pro-cyclical reductions in the period 2010–2014.

The chapter raises the question of poverty measurement and related targets. It discusses the merits of relative (monetary) poverty and of 'anchoring at a moment in the past'. Doing so would have shown clearly how much the income situation for lower income households deteriorated in Southern European countries during the recession. By the same token, anchoring at a past level means that, in growing economies, poverty falls almost automatically, a result the chapter's author finds questionable for material deprivation. No poverty measure will capture all aspects of social hardship, and choices have to be made. The adoption of the Europe 2020 target by EU leaders made such a choice: they wished to complement traditionally used relative income poverty with a measure of deprivation and exclusion from the labour market. The chapter also raises the question of how other widely recognized EU targets interact with inequality, such as higher employment rates and levels of tertiary education. None of them alone will lead to the desired effect. The (un)equal distribution of employment across households may affect income inequality. Reaching higher levels of employment facilitates social policy while low levels of employment do the opposite. On education, it is important to realize how the richest households often have two highly educated, high-earning members and, thus, reaching out to low-income populations is essential.

On the policy side, the European Pillar of Social Rights offers some perspective of improvement through its breadth and the diverse and effective instruments it brings in as a result. The chapter insists that the first priority remains the reduction of poverty, for which improvements in minimum income protection, child benefits, and minimum wages can all be pursued on the basis of the Pillar. It recalls that progress towards the social policy principles of the Pillar hinges on

Member State actions and on the capacity of the EU to encourage them to be undertaken.

The chapter emphasizes that the EU should be strong where joint action could make a real difference, with taxation being an important example of where the EU presently has little competence. Following from the analysis of the drivers of inequality and poverty at the household level, the chapter concludes by examining three areas where meaningful social policy action at the EU level could make a real difference: minimum wages, child benefits, and a tax credit for low-income working households.

1.5 KEY ISSUES

This volume shows that EU integration has broadly benefitted the social welfare of many people in Europe, but the chapters also show that this is not unambiguously the case. The benefits from integration were expected to be shared widely, almost automatically, but in reality they have not reached all population groups, regions, and sometimes countries, and integration can have adverse effects.

The chapters also confirm the concern of European leaders that the economic performance of the EU might still be less than satisfactory and that they are right to be worried about inequality: it undermines the social cohesion of the EU and its Member States, and it has become an obstacle for sustainable economic performance.

High or fast growing inequality or poverty is the opposite of inclusive welfare. Inequality is certainly an outcome variable. Market incomes have become more unequal since the 1970's in nearly if not all countries in Europe and, indeed, globally. Technological advances, especially digitalization, and globalization seem to have played some part in this. The decline of unionization, frequent but not universal in Europe, has also played a role. Government policy may have also been a partial cause, even if the intention was to increase opportunities for all (e.g., through educational reforms). Post tax (income) inequality has grown less, but governments' desires and perhaps abilities to tax and spend to bring this about appear weaker than before. This became particularly visible in the Great Recession: after 2 years of counter-cyclical policy, a switch to pro-cyclical austerity reduced social policy programmes just when they were urgently needed. Longer term investment in education and health was also scaled back.

Inequality is not only about poverty and increasing numbers of people with low incomes; it is also about those individuals with top incomes and corporations appropriating an increasing share of national income: hence taxation is central to this debate (but largely outside the scope of this volume). Furthermore, inequality is also about polarization and shrinking middle-income groups. This has a lot do with earning trends and with the way wages are set across Europe. While public policy cannot solve all the issues in this respect, a change towards strengthening collective bargaining and workers' and employers' organizations could certainly help.

Inequality can also be an input variable. More inequality can see a reduced propensity to consume and heightened resistance to change and adaptation or give rise to populism and political instability. The future of Europe is bound up with how rising inequality is treated by governments and others in positions of power. Europe's high levels of income, wealth, consumption, and well-being, amassed through decades of strong economic growth, depend on how inequality is addressed and develops in the years to come.

This volume looks at both inequality and poverty in depth—and it also goes beyond conventional analysis when considering trends in the distribution of incomes at the level of the EU as an entity as well as at the level of the EA. Within-country inequality trends differ between Member States, but, in general, the analysis confirms the long-term observation of a U-shaped curve, with the mid-1980s being the turning point followed by a levelling out at higher inequality in the early 2000s.

The current concern with inequality raises two issues. First, it and the linked concern about excessively high incomes and wealth comes with quite some delay. Why is there this late response by governments? Is it simply because the financial crisis followed by the European debt crisis required all the attention of politicians? Did it take time for both people and policymakers to realize that something had changed structurally? Was it that the Great Recession had very unequal impacts, with the general perception being that ordinary workers saw big job losses and salary cuts to pay for the mistakes of the largely untouched bankers? Or does the concern have something to do with expectations about what is to come—more digitalization and coping with climate change, which will almost certainly lead to massive shifts in employment structures that potentially sharpen redistributional tensions and might endanger social stability? Managing inequality today becomes a matter of urgency for those who want to promote technological change and address global warming with ambitious targets. In this sense the volume provides important and timely information for policymakers.

The second issue (as Chapter 2 points out) is that the years of the shift towards higher inequality are also those when EU economic integration made strong progress, with the implementation of a single market and preparation for the introduction of a single currency being key events. The implicit or explicit assumption that the EU economies would benefit from further integration was certainly correct, but the idea that it would be easy to compensate losers—and that this could be left to member countries with limited support from the EU—was much more questionable. Looking at the outcomes, the two key questions are whether losers have actually been compensated, and is this compensation what the people who work in sectors or regions that do not benefit from economic integration actually want? This presents a policy challenge that goes beyond the idea of 'compensating losers' largely at a national level. The EU already does something to address this issue (the Structural Funds and European Global Adjustment Fund), but these amount to around 0.5% of EU GDP and thus can only have a very limited impact. There is also a research challenge to assess how different populations across the Union have benefitted or lost from the deepening of the single market and from having a single currency, and whether policy has focused sufficiently on those affected negatively.

What about convergence and divergence? South–North convergence following the accession of Spain, Portugal, and Greece was one of the major achievements of integration (as explained in Chapter 4 on Southern Europe). Similarly, the CEE countries saw convergence in economic and social developments (again, as detailed in Chapter 5). The World Bank, as recently as 2018, called the EU a 'convergence machine'. While East–West convergence has continued up until now, South–North convergence ended with the financial crisis. Spain and Portugal lost many of the gains achieved in the preceding decade, have only recently returned to their 2008 levels of income, and unemployment levels remains high, considerably so for Spain. The most dramatic change concerns Italy. It has traditionally belonged to the group of rich Member States; in 1990, it had a GDP per capita level comparable to Germany's, but Italy's GDP per capita has steadily fallen below the EU average and is now some 30% lower than Germany's. In addition, household income, unemployment, and poverty have worsened in Italy, and this has had a deep impact on the credibility of the Union, given that convergence and cohesion are fundamental objectives of the EU project.

Chapter 5 on CEE countries discusses how European integration has contributed to their catching up. Are the lesser trends in the Western Balkans (Chapter 7) a true counterfactual, showing how important European integration has been, or is the causality actually in reverse? Did unfavourable political developments in the region and a lack of economic reforms and institution-building prevent similar positive developments? Or were the main European players, including the private sector, simply less ready to invest in and support growth because of their lack of economic interest and understanding of the importance of the region? Turkey is yet another country with a strong will to benefit from economic integration with the EU in the early years of the 21st century and a very different trend in the more recent period. In this respect, the volume raises more questions than answers and invites further research and thinking. One point, however, seems to confirm the need to look more deeply into how European integration is pursued. Progress in convergence between economies can leave certain population groups marginalized, and, if not addressed, this can endanger the whole integration process.

This volume makes a strong point for looking at Europe as an entity not only in the EU-wide income analysis but, as explained earlier, also by looking at the impact of economic integration and progress or regress in convergence between its parts. What are the conclusions when considering all household incomes across the EU as if they were accrued in one economic entity and the income distribution analysed for this entity, as is done for a single member country or for the United States? The traditionally used EU-level statistics on income distribution or monetary poverty are calculated as the weighted average of the national distributions. In policy terms, they tell us how the EU performs as the result of national policy efforts.

When comparing the two concepts of inequality, four interesting results emerge. First, market income inequality at the EU level is higher if calculated on the basis of the EU-level distribution. When decomposing within-country versus across-country components of inequality, the two chapters (Chapters 2 and 15), as do other studies, suggest a 20–25% contribution from across-country factors. Second, EU-wide inequality has declined more or less for the whole period for which we have data for the EU as an entity, including in recent years. Third, this has implications for comparisons with the United States. Usually, EU–USA comparisons are made using the weighted average of Member States for Europe (normally in purchasing power parity [PPP]), and this shows higher market income inequality in the United States. If one moves to the measurement of the EU as an entity, market income inequality is pretty much the same or on some estimates even higher for the EU, in particular when using nominal values or PPP adjustment also for the US states.

For the EU–USA comparison, differences in redistribution make all the difference. As expected, the much stronger redistribution (taxes, social protection, and social benefits) in the EU reduces inequality to a level below that of the United States but not as low as if using the weighted average used by Eurostat. A particularly interesting feature is what happened in the years 2008–2012, when the difference in inequality in disposable household income distribution was substantially smaller in 2010–2011, as shown in Chapter 15 (see Figure 15.7). This was due to a massive effort by the US federal government to fund a number of social programmes in a clearly anti-cyclical manner—something the US states could have not done. For the EU, such an extra effort can only be seen for the first 2 years of the crisis, as long as Member States were in position and ready to fund it. Later, those EU countries most in need of support for their populations could not continue such programme expansion and indeed saw quite the opposite: pro-cyclical cuts. The EU budget is simply too small and inflexible to offer such extra support. Is there a lesson to be learned for EU policymakers? For the moment, the debate about stabilization funding focuses on creating an EU budget or reinsurance schemes for national programmes[23], but could EU level programmes that directly support individuals in need, as some US programmes do, be an option to be included in the EU discussion?

---

23 As a last minute addendum, note that the EU response to the sharp decline in economic activity resulting from the Covid-19 pandemic, in particular the SURE programme, can be interpreted as a step towards a better system of fiscal policy coordination and an EU level stabilization effort. See European Commission (2020).

Finally, looking at the EU-level distribution itself allows different insights. One of the quantified objectives of the Europe 2020 Strategy is a reduction of the number in poverty and social exclusion by 20 million people, with monetary poverty being one component of the three used to measure this (see Chapter 15 for more details). Poverty, as calculated on the basis of the EU-wide income distribution, is substantially higher but continuously declining for the period for which we have data (see Chapters 2 and 13). The aggregated number of income-poor people (only this component of the EU target is here relevant here) was around 17% of those Europeans who lived in households with an income below 60% of the respective national median. Calculating the value for the EU as an entity saw this figure be substantially bigger—about 25% or, in absolute numbers, more than 120 million Europeans compared to 80 million. By 2015, despite the deep recession and austerity measures, the number calculated for the EU as an entity declined to 112 million or 23%, while the number based on national data increased to 86 million, with little change in the percentage, as pointed out in Chapter 2. Developments in the CEE counties are largely responsible for the overall decline in poverty and inequality measured at the EU level.

Some would argue that using the EU-wide measure would lead to an underestimation of poverty in the richer parts of Europe. We do not suggest that EU countries should abandon national poverty statistics or forget about setting themselves national objectives. But, interestingly, even the EU-wide measurement still leaves 10% of the population in the rich EA countries below the 60% poverty mark. And poverty gaps are far more similar for the two data definitions, suggesting that there are measurable deep pockets of poverty in all EU countries. Following from there, the last chapter would favour if EU poverty policies would aim at reducing the poverty gap. The key argument for complementing our statistical instruments rests in the fact that EU Member States are deeply linked through economic integration in the Single Market and through the Single Currency; thus, one also should ask what the corresponding social outcomes will be. But it should not be forgotten that inequality is a relative concept; people feel poor if those around them seem richer even if their own income is higher than in some faraway place. The poor German woman will feel poorer that the middle-income Estonian man even if she has a higher income. And the policies to redistribute market incomes are mostly national and thus voted on in national elections. Caution is needed when looking at EU-wide measurement.

The national and EU-level analyses identify groups that did not benefit (or benefitted less) from economic development in the longer run and in particular in the past decade: the poorly educated everywhere, single parents, and single earners supporting a multiperson household (most relevant in the South). The highly educated benefitted, with the notable exception of the South. The strongest income growth was recorded in double-income households with highly educated people. Chapter 9 contains a healthy warning on the differences in access and opportunity to participate in higher education and even more so in adult education between income groups but also between EU countries—suggesting that further polarization might result from these double differences.

Almost all chapters emphasize that social protection is an important ingredient for addressing poverty and inequality but also for rebuilding trust in public policies to make economic growth more sustainable and inclusive. Chapter 10 on social protection and Chapter 15 look at these systems in somewhat different ways: the former reviews whether the proclaimed shift from social transfers to a more active use has actually taken place, and the last chapter analyses the impact of social transfers on poverty and inequality, showing mixed results particularly for children and people of working age. Both chapters refer to the ongoing debate on who would benefit from a more active use of social expenditure (employment promotion, child and other care, training, and so on), the middle class or the poor? The empirical evidence seems to be mixed but suggests that one should pay attention to the risk that policy shifts could harm those most in need. A similar question might arise with an emphasis on promoting employment, a step often facilitated by programmes like childcare or care allowances, training, and adult education.

Could it be the case that, at a given moment in time, the observation might be correct that increases in employment might benefit households where one person already works and that care services might help double-income households, and thus not help necessarily the most vulnerable? But assuming that such programmes were absent, might there be even more single-earner households, leading to further increases in open poverty or households with incomes close to poverty? In our view the changes in our economies, societies, and labour markets require both prevention and cure. Thus the policy challenge is not to choose between reducing open poverty, in particular among the unemployed, and promoting decent employment opportunities including providing important social services, but to recognize that modern social policy and welfare will have to do both. While policymakers cannot ignore resource constraints, they might need to look at methods to overcome them not only by restructuring expenditures but also by reviewing how social policies are funded—which might give additional meaning to the discussion around taxation.

While retired people overall did relatively well, Chapter 11 also contains some warnings on both the sustainability of these gains and on their distribution. Important differences can be seen for the younger generation, who gained most in the CEE and did relatively well in the core EA countries, but who saw rising inequality within the group and lost out altogether in the South and also in the United Kingdom.

This volume concentrates on well-being measured in income. One interesting observation concerns income growth and the decline in working hours. As discussed in Chapter 2, working hours in Europe have, since the 1970s, declined much more markedly than in the United States, and some policymakers are worried. But perhaps Europeans prefer to transform some share of improved economic performance into shorter working time. Of course a lot depends on whether shorter working hours are voluntary and reasonably equally distributed or the results of, for example, precarious involuntary part-time employment. European countries have generally applicable schemes on sickness, maternity, paternity, and care leave (often paid), as well as on paid holiday and sometimes training leave, while in the United States similar leaves exist but are mostly for higher income workers. This observation raises the wider issue of whether well-being should be measured in income trends only, and, indeed, several chapters review evidence on other important dimensions of well-being, including material deprivation, labour market integration, health status, and life satisfaction. There is a wide literature on the broader concepts of well-being, and a similar compilation of trends across Europe would be a valuable contribution.

An EU-level perspective points to developments that require policy attention and again the question arises whether some of those trends—while not caused by EU integration—are shaped in the specific way they appear? Measures to raise efficiency in the single market could be accompanied by ensuring that workers in targeted sectors do not face a worsening of their working conditions. Making collective agreements in these sectors generally applicable is proposed as one way to achieve this. The recent EU directives on the labour contract, on paid care leave, and on the posting of workers, in the context of the European Pillar of Social Rights,[24] are steps in the same direction. One key message of this volume is that considering social well-being for the EU as an entity would give some guidance for reflecting about the role the EU could have in this respect.

This volume also seeks to assess the capacity of Europe to progress in sustaining high incomes and inclusive welfare: it identifies the essential policy challenges and reviews options on how to address them. It notes that there were episodes of divergence especially after the Great Recession, with South–North divergence questioning the very purpose of the EU in improving people's welfare. The depth of the crisis was in part due to divergent macroeconomic situations hidden, to a greater or lesser extent, by countries having a single currency. If divergence is not reversed, the political appeal of the EU will be quickly undermined in losing countries— hence the urgency of reforming the EMU architecture while addressing rising inequality and high levels of poverty .

---

24 The Proclamation of the Pillar of Social Rights by the European institutions recognizes the importance of addressing inequality, and the 20 principles could shape national policy and EU integration in this direction. To achieve this, the economic and social strands will need to be brought together into one stream of policy-making. A number of the principles have been translated into legal acts, mostly covering labour rights. In the area of social policies, the EU uses more policy coordination, 'herding' countries, as the final chapter calls it, to provide better protection. However, the question arises whether the EU should go further in the direction of binding acts, for example, on minimum income or EU-wide social schemes as Jürgen Habermas and Claus Offe advocate—see Fischer (2018).

Now, when the EU needs to consolidate the EMU with better policy coordination and stabilization tools based on stronger solidarity among EA countries, is the time to remember this lesson. In this context, it is interesting that proposals for a EU-level unemployment reinsurance scheme are now included in the programme of the Von der Leyen Commission, a tool that combines an EA stabilization function with social solidarity for the unemployed.[25]

In the broadest terms, the issues raised in this volume centre on rebalancing economic and social objectives in economic policy coordination, EU-wide social programmes, the taxation of income, wealth, and digital activity. These should be pursued further in both research and the policy debate.

Some readers might ask what are the main points where there is a need for more action by policymakers in Europe; seven priorities emerge from this volume.

First, used with prudence, *EU-wide rather than only aggregated national measurements of inequality and poverty* will help get a better feel for how European well-being is being perceived, and, as shown in this volume, results are markedly different. Beyond the research and analysis agenda, the policy case for doing so is because European integration and many EU-level policies do impact income generation and distribution.

Second, a more systematic use of indicators of wellbeing other than income, such as working time, health status, and life satisfaction.

Third, a core priority for action is tackling the causes of inequality in Europe which is undermining the social cohesion of the EU and the Member States. and has become an obstacle for sustainable economic performance. More must be done to *offset growing inequality of income within most countries in Europe.* This means addressing the sources of more divergent wages, salaries, and earnings (market incomes) and making tax systems for people and companies more progressive. Taxation of top incomes and wealth is identified as not only of being of particular importance but also a policy challenge requiring action at EU level.

A fourth priority is *reestablishing the importance given to investment in education and training,* particularly for those people in the lower 50% of household income. Adult education is an areas where inequality by education and income is particularly marked. This would be one key action to offset the negative effects of globalization and digitalization. *Spending more is necessary and spending better is essential* to improve education outcomes and thus the employability, productivity and incomes of the less advantaged.

---

25 See Fischer (2017), Beblavy et al (2017).

A fifth priority is *actively encouraging both employers' and workers' organizations and the use of collective bargaining* to stem or even reverse declining unionization; inequality would be stemmed or even reversed. The decline in union membership is both cause and effect of less collective bargaining in most countries in Europe.

A sixth priority is addressing the reasons for and *counteracting the divergences that have emerged between countries within the EU.* The financial crisis revealed hitherto little-known forces promoting divergence between Member States in terms of income but also productivity. Some of these were clearly linked with being part of a single currency—the euro. East–West convergence, somewhat counterintuitively, also remains an important issue because of inequalities that emerged within the newer member countries of the EU and because of migration within the EU.

The seventh and final priority is *completing or at least reinforcing the architecture of the EMU.* Most informed observers cite this also as an essential action to avoid divergence. Some form of *central fiscal capacity* to provide stabilization tools is essential in this respect. Given the challenges ahead, the size of this central fiscal capacity will have to be more than marginal.

ACKNOWLEDGEMENTS

The authors would like to thank Wiemer Salverda, Douglas Besharov, Neil Gilbert, David Arranz, Lieselotte Fuerst, Agnès Fondaire, and OUP's anonymous reviewers for the important contributions they made to the final draft of this chapter.

REFERENCES

Alvaredo, F., Chancel, L., Piketty, T., Saez, E., and Zucman, G. (2018). *World inequality report*. Paris: World Inequality Lab.

Barr, N. (2004). *Economics of the welfare state*. New York: Oxford University Press.

Beblavý, M., Marconi, G., and Maselli, I. (2017). *A European unemployment benefit scheme*. Brussels: Centre for European Policy Studies.

Berg G. A., and Ostry D. J.,(2011). *Inequality and Unsustainable Growth: Two Sides of the Same Coin?* IMF Staff Discussion Note, April 8 2011, SDN 11/08.

Bussolo, M., Davalos, M., et al. (2018). *Toward a new social contract: Taking on distributional tensions in Europe and Central Asia*. Washington, DC: World Bank.

Esping-Andersen, G. (1990). *The Three Worlds of Welfare Capitalism*. Princeton University Press, Princeton, NJ.

European Bank for Reconstruction and Development (EBRD). (2017). *Sustaining growth: 2016–17 transition report*. European Bank for Reconstruction and Development.

European Commission. (2014). Employment and social developments in Europe review. Brussels: European Commission.

European Commission. (2015). Employment and social developments in Europe review. Brussels: European Commission.

European Commission. (2016). Employment and social developments in Europe review. Brussels: European Commission.

European Commission. (2017). Addressing inequalities: European semester thematic factsheet. https://ec.europa.eu/info/sites/info/files/file_import/european-semester_thematic-factsheet_addressing-inequalities_en_0.pdf

European Commission. (2018). Employment and social developments in Europe review. Chapter 4, inequality of outcomes. https://ec.europa.eu/social/BlobServlet?docId=19888&langId=en

European Commission. (2019). Delivering inclusive growth. Technical note to the Eurogroup. Thematic discussions on growth and jobs. Brussels, 28 May 2019. https://www.consilium.europa.eu/media/39763/commission-note-on-inequality.pdf

European Commission. (2019a). Annual growth survey 2019: For a stronger Europe in the face of global uncertainty. https://eurlex.europa.eu/legalcontent/EN/TXT/PDF/?uri=CELEX:52018DC0770&from=EN

European Commission. (2020). ec.europa.eu/info/sites/info/files/about_the_european_commission/eu_budget/eu_sure_social_bond_framework.pdf.

Filauro, S. (2017). *European incomes, national advantages: EU-wide inequality and its decomposition by country and region*. EERI Research Paper Series (EERI RP 2017/05). Brussels: Economics and Econometrics Research Institute.

Fischer, G. (2017 May). *The US unemployment insurance, a federal-state partnership: Relevance for reflections at the European level*. IZA paper no. 129. Bonn: Institute of Labor Economics (IZA).

Fischer, G. (2018). Social Europe: The Pillar of Social Rights. In Nowotny, E., Ritzberger-Grünwald, D., and Schuberth, H. (eds.), *Structural reforms for growth and cohesion: Lessons and challenges for CESEE countries and a modern Europe* (pp. 41–42). Cheltenham, UK: Edward Elgar, pp. 41–42.

Gill, I., and Raiser, M. (2012). *Golden growth: Restoring the lustre of the European economic model: Overview (English)*. Europe and Central Asia Studies. Washington, DC: World Bank.

The GINI Project. (2014). Editors Salverda, W., Nolan, B., Checchi, D., Marx, I., McKnight, A., Tóth, I., and van de Werfhorst, H. *Changing inequalities in rich countries*. Oxford: Oxford University Press.

Habermas, J., and Derrida, J. (2003). February 15, or what binds Europe together: A plea for a common foreign policy, beginning in the core of Europe. *Constellations, 10*(3), 296.

Maquet, I., Meyermans, E., and Duiella, M. (2015). High and rising inequalities: What can be done about it (at EU level)? Analytical Web Note 6/ 2015, European Commission, DG Employment, Social Affairs and Inclusion. [https://ec.europa.eu/social/BlobServlet?docId=14556&langId=en

Nickell, S., Redding, S., and Swaffield, J. (2002). Patterns of growth. Centrepiece. academia.edu.

OECD. (2008) 'Growing Unequal: Income Distribution and Poverty in OECD Countries'. Paris: Organisation for Economic Cooperation and Development'.

OECD. (2011) 'Divided We Stand: Why Inequality Keeps Rising'. Paris: Organisation for Economic Cooperation and Development'.

OECD.(2012). 'Rising Income Inequality in European Union'. Paris: Organisation for Economic Cooperation and Development'.

OECD. (2015).'In It Together: Why Less Inequality Benefits All'. Organisation for Economic Cooperation and Development'. Paris: Organisation for Economic Cooperation and Development'.

OECD. (2016). From gross public to total net social spending, as a percent of GDP at market prices, 2013. Figure 4. http://www.oecd.org/els/soc/OECD2016-Social-Expenditure-Update.pdf

OECD. (2017). 'Understanding the Socio-Economic Divide in Europe'. Paris: Organisation for Economic Cooperation and Development'.

OECD. (2018).'A Broken Social Elevator'. Paris: Organisation for Economic Cooperation and Development'.

OECD. (2019). 'Under Pressure: The Squeezed Middle Class'. Paris: Organisation for Economic Cooperation and Development'.

Pasimeni, P., and Riso, S. (2016). The redistributive function of the EU budget. IMK at the Hans Boeckler Foundation, Macroeconomic Policy Institute. No. 174. https://ideas.repec.org/p/imk/wpaper/174-2016.html. Also available at SSRN, https://ssrn.com/abstract=3216375

Sapir, A. (2006). Globalization and the reform of European social models. *JCMS*, 44, 369–390.

Stournaras, Y. (2018). What lies in store for the eurozone? An assessment of the Greek bailout programmes: Has EU become wiser? Speech at The Economist: Southeast Europe-Germany Business and Investment Summit, 'Reassessing Europe's priorities.' Berlin, December 2018, BIS. https://www.bis.org/review/r181211b.htm.

2

THE DISTRIBUTION OF WELL-BEING AMONG EUROPEANS

Andrea Brandolini and Alfonso Rosolia

2.1. INTRODUCTION

European countries are engaged in a process of economic and political integration which has no parallel at the global level. It has taken place by steps over the past 60 years, moving from the original six countries that signed the Treaty of Rome on 25 March 1957 and formed the European Economic Community in 1958 to the 28 countries comprising the European Union (EU) in 2018, before the withdrawal of the United Kingdom. The common currency, the euro, was introduced in 1999 and is currently used by 19 countries. Integration has undeniably gone hand in hand with the continent's economic development, though establishing causal links is arduous. But how has the well-being of European citizens changed during such a long process?

In this chapter, we address this question by taking personal income as a proxy of well-being. Well-being is multifaceted and can be hardly reduced to income alone, but there is little doubt that it fundamentally depends on people's income: 'a crucial means to a number of important ends' (Anand and Sen, 2000: 100). Thus, investigating the evolution of the distribution of income among Europeans would go some way toward assessing the social progress of the European Union. This approach is rarely taken, however. Aside from data limitations, one important reason lies in the design of the integration process.

Creating a fairer and inclusive society is the declared aim of integration, but the political priority at the European level has always been the establishment of a common market. This has constantly been seen as the primary route to enhance

Andrea Brandolini and Alfonso Rosolia, *The Distribution of Well-Being among Europeans* In: *Europe's Income, Wealth, Consumption, and Inequality.* Edited by: Georg Fischer and Robert Strauss, Oxford University Press (2021).
© Oxford University Press. DOI: 10.1093/oso/9780197545706.003.0002

economic growth, and hence people's well-being, while devolving the attainment of social objectives to redistributive policies and welfare measures decided at the national level albeit subject to limitations due to EU membership. This approach has led to decoupling the assessment of macroeconomic convergence and territorial cohesion, thus focusing on countries or regions, from the evaluation of social exclusion and inequality, concerned with people living in nations taken in isolation.

Accordingly, Eurostat calculates the EU-wide statistics for poverty and inequality as 'the population-weighted arithmetic average of individual national figures' (Eurostat, 2017). This practice amounts to overlooking differences in income levels among countries, either in the setting of poverty thresholds or in the calculation of overall inequality. As Atkinson warned as early as 1989, whenever the at-risk-of-poverty threshold is set as a proportion of the national median, 'the impact of growth on poverty in the Community [depends] solely on what happens within each country', whereas it would be affected 'by the relative growth rates of different member countries' (1995: 71) if the threshold was proportionate to the overall EU-wide median.[1] Likewise, taking an inequality index that is exactly decomposable by population subgroups, Eurostat practice simply means ignoring the between-country component of European inequality. This exact decomposition does not hold for the two inequality measures standardly released by Eurostat, the income quintile ratio and the Gini index,[2] but even with these indices the level of EU inequality measured as an average of national levels clearly does not depend on how much, say, the average Dutch is richer than the average Slovakian: only within-country income gaps matter.

In this chapter we adopt a different perspective: we study the distribution of living standards among European citizens by measuring income distribution in the European Union as if it was a single country rather than taking it to be the average of national values. One straightforward implication is that measured

---

1   Differently from statistics based on household incomes, two European indicators use common standards across the EU: the *severe material deprivation* indicator counts persons who experience at least 4 out of 9 deprivation items due to lack of resources; the *low work intensity* indicator counts children and adults living in households where adults work a small proportion of their annual work potential. Together with the *at risk-of-poverty rate*, both indicators concur to define the headline indicator of the Europe 2020 strategy 'People at risk of poverty or social exclusion'. The notion of material deprivation was introduced to mitigate the shortcomings from using purely national standards in poverty measurement (e.g., Guio, 2005; Goedemé and Rottiers, 2011).

2   The income quintile ratio is the ratio of total income received by the richest 20% to that received by the poorest 20% of a country's population; the Gini index is the mean absolute difference of all pairs of incomes divided by the overall mean; it varies, for non-negative values, between 0 (perfect equality) and 1 (maximum inequality). Two common additively decomposable inequality measures are the mean logarithmic deviation and the Theil index; both belong to the broader class of the generalized entropy indices.

inequality does not depend on where a person lives within the European Union, whereas it does when using an average of individual national figures (Brandolini and Carta, 2016). At a more conceptual level, it means that the well-being of European citizens is assessed by reference to the whole of European citizens rather than to the people living in the same country, consistently with the fact that they share a single market and can move freely within the Union.[3] This different approach to inequality measurement may appear purely technical but it has, in fact, a deep political meaning which is discussed in the concluding section of this chapter.

The remaining of the chapter is organized as follows. We start Section 2.2 by summarizing the main dates of European integration. So far, we have loosely used the term 'European Union', but in the empirical analysis we need to be precise about the supranational aggregate to which we refer to. Throughout, we indicate by 'EU' the European Union (Community before 1993) in general, according to its varying historical composition, by EU15 the group of 15 countries that formed the European Union in 1995–2003, and by EU28 the group of 28 countries that form the European Union since July 2013 (but before the withdrawal of the United Kingdom). Similarly, EA stands for the Euro Area in its historical composition, EA12 for the group of 12 member states participating in the monetary union in the early 2000s, and EA19 for the group of 19 countries which currently share the common currency. We then use national accounts to describe the European economic development since World War II, taking the United States as a reference. These data show the considerable improvement of the average living standards in the European Union, both in terms of goods and services produced and in lower time spent at work. On average, differences among people living in different countries also diminished. This long-run process slowed with the sovereign debt crisis and the associated divergence between the 'core' and the 'periphery' of the EA.

---

3   This is an explicitly normative choice which does not require that Europeans actually take the whole EU as a reference to assess their living standards. Some authors have seen the 'Europeanization of reference groups' as a justification for adopting the EU-wide approach to the measurement of poverty and inequality based on the finding that, in the upper middle classes of new accession countries, people were and felt poorer than those belonging to the lower middle classes in most advanced European countries (Fahey et al., 2005; Delhey and Kohler, 2006; Fahey, 2007). As Fahey (2007: 45) writes, 'in the EU as a whole those who *are* disadvantaged on uniform EU-wide measures also tend to *feel* disadvantaged in proportion'. The issue is controversial (Heidenreich and Wunder, 2008; Whelan and Maître, 2009a, 2009b; Nolan and Whelan, 2011). Following a distinction suggested by Goedemé and Rottiers (2011), our choice is closer to the notion of 'publicly oriented' reference groups than to the concept of 'privately oriented' reference groups, which is used in the psychological literature on the assessment of personal outcomes.

While national accounts provide valuable evidence on the evolution of average living standards as the integration process has deepened, they are silent on how unequal the distribution of living standards has been among Europeans. We move to this question in Section 2.3. We first compare the distributions of real incomes in EU countries (except Croatia) in 2005 and 2015, using microdata from the EU Statistics on Income and Living Conditions (EU-SILC) and show that income disparities are considerable. We then turn to long-run changes and find evidence of some U-shaped pattern in most of the 12 countries considered, though the shape of the U greatly varies. Our brief review of the literature suggests that the reversal of postwar downward trends has been driven by a combination of general economic forces, such as globalization and technical change, and national policy choices. Despite their national specificities, these choices shared common objectives, such as making labour markets more flexible and reducing the redistributive role of government. Irrespective of the drivers, the substantial dispersion of personal incomes and its change over time must be taken into account in investigating the well-being of Europeans.

We examine the EU-wide income distribution and its evolution in Section 2.4. The evidence for old decades is fragile, but it seems to confirm some narrowing of income distribution until the mid-1980s, consistently with the macroeconomic evidence and with national patterns. With the more reliable data available for recent years, between 2005 and 2015 inequality shows a descending trend in the EU28 but a rising one in the EU15 and the EA. Expressing incomes at nominal market exchange rates raises estimates of inequality relative to adjusting incomes for international differences in price levels but has little effects on trends. Around 2015, incomes appear to be more unevenly distributed in the United States than in the European Union, and especially so in the EA. This outcome stems from the greater income redistribution achieved by European welfare states. We delve into inequality developments in the European Union during the past decade in Section 2.5, where we analyse the consequences of the Great Recession in 2008–2009 and the sovereign debt crisis in 2011–2012 for the geographic clustering of income inequality in the European Union and for specific sociodemographic categories.

In Section 2.6, we draw the main analytical conclusions and place our EU-wide analysis of inequality into the broader context of the social dimension of European integration. We discuss technical measurement aspects in Appendix 2.1 and review estimates of the EU-wide distribution in Appendix 2.2.

2.2 AN AGGREGATE VIEW OF POSTWAR DEVELOPMENTS

The process of European integration started in 1957, when Belgium, France, Italy, Luxembourg, the Netherlands, and West Germany signed the Treaty of Rome. The Treaty created the European Economic Community that came into force on 1 January 1958. Denmark, Ireland, and the United Kingdom joined in 1973; Greece followed in 1981; and Portugal and Spain in 1986. The Eastern German Länder became part of the European Community as a consequence of the country's reunification in October 1990.[4] In 1993, the Maastricht Treaty established the European Union, which was joined by Austria, Finland, and Sweden in 1995. The enlargement in 2004 brought 10 new member states into the Union: Cyprus, the Czech Republic, Estonia, Hungary, Latvia, Lithuania, Malta, Poland, Slovakia, and Slovenia. Bulgaria and Romania joined in 2007, and Croatia in 2013. On 1 January 1999, 11 countries irrevocably fixed the exchange rates of their currencies and adopted the euro: Austria, Belgium, Finland, France, Germany, Ireland, Italy, Luxembourg, the Netherlands, Portugal, and Spain. Eight countries joined in the following years: Greece (2001), Slovenia (2007), Cyprus (2008), Malta (2008), Slovakia (2009), Estonia (2011), Latvia (2014), and Lithuania (2015).

The different stages of the integration process are evident in the stepwise increase in EU population and employment (Figure 2.1; the vertical lines indicate the changes in EU membership). By virtue of this gradual accession of new countries, between 1958 and 2015, the population sharing EU membership tripled from 170 million to 514 million persons, although the population living in the whole of the 28 countries currently comprising the EU (EU28) only rose by around 30%. The number of people in employment follows broadly similar long-run tendencies. The impact of the Great Recession is evident in the sharp drop in employment in 2009, followed by a return to pre-crisis levels only in 2013 in the United States and 2 years later in Europe. European employment fell considerably also during the early 1990s, a period characterized by extensive restructuring in transition economies, by the German reunification, and by the currency crisis that forced Italy and the United Kingdom to leave the European Exchange Rate Mechanism in September 1992. The employment-to-population ratios show wide fluctuations, though not as large as in the United States. In Europe, the trend was downward until the mid-1980s. The higher ratios characterizing planned economies decreased during the transition to a market economy and aligned with those observed in the EU15 by the mid-1990s. In subsequent years, employment ratios went up until the Great Recession. In 2015, 45% of all persons were employed in the European Union vis-à-vis 47% in the United States. Note that these ratios refer to the whole population rather than only working-age persons, hence they reflect also changes in the demographic structure (e.g., ageing). While employment ratios are not too different from their values in the 1950s, despite wide fluctuations, the average annual hours of work per employed steadily fell. Since the 1950s, work hours have declined by more than a fourth in

---

4   In the remaining, West Germany and East Germany refer to the Federal Republic of Germany and the Democratic Republic of Germany before reunification, and the Western and Eastern Länder afterwards.

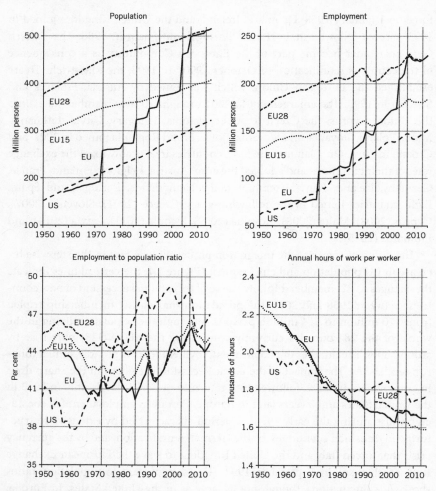

Figure 2.1 Population and employment in EU, EU28, EU15, and United States (1950–2015).
Source: Authors' elaboration on data from the Conference Board Total Economy Database™.
All figures are from the database (Original version) of November 2018 except for the figures for
West Germany in 1958–1990, which are from the database of May 2016. EU: totals for actual
EU member countries; EU15: totals for the 15 countries that formed the EU in 1995–2003;
EU28: totals for the 28 countries that form the EU since July 2013. The vertical lines indicate the
changes in EU membership.

the EU15, against around a tenth in the United States, as a result of both a shortening of working times and a spreading of part-time occupations. The considerable fall in the proportion of lifetime spent at work since World War II indicates a
rise in leisure time and an improvement in the well-being of a typical European.

Mean gross domestic product (GDP) per capita grew until the Great Recession
and then flattened out, both in the EU15 and the EU28 (Figure 2.2, top panels).
(Throughout, all statistics from national accounts are population-weighted

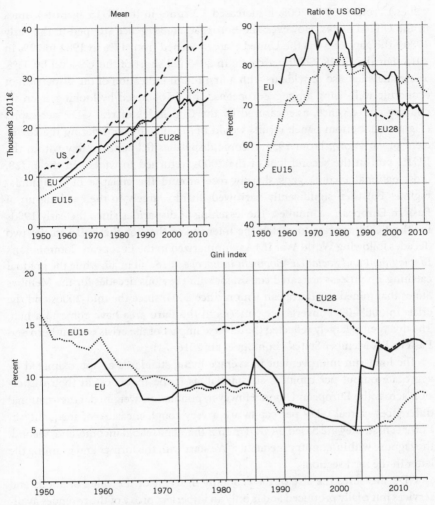

Figure 2.2 Real gross domestic product (GDP) per capita in EU, EU28, EU15, and United States (1950–2015).

Source: Authors' elaboration on data from the Conference Board Total Economy Database™ (Original version), November 2018. The figures for West Germany in 1958–1990 are obtained by rescaling the total for Germany based on separate figures for West and East Germany from the Conference Board Total Economy Database, May 2016. Real GDP is obtained by applying the EKS method; original values in millions of 2011 US$ at chained purchasing power parities are converted into 2011 euros by multiplying for the exchange rate in 2011 (0.719€/$). EU: totals for actual EU member countries; EU15: totals for the 15 countries that formed the EU in 1995–2003; EU28: totals for the 28 countries that form the EU since July 2013. The vertical lines indicate the changes in EU membership. All estimates are population-weighted values.

values.) From 1958 to 2008, it increased 3.5 times in the EU15 against 3 times in the United States. However, the European convergence stopped in the early 1980s: the gap vis-à-vis the United States widened from 17% in 1982 to 27% in 2015. For the EU28, GDP per capita in 2015 fell short of the US level by 33%. These statistics also provide us with a first rough indication of the dispersion of economic well-being among Europeans. This is obtained by looking at cross-country convergence, as measured by the Gini index of real GDP per capita (Figure 2.2, bottom panel; results would not change by considering the coefficient of variation). From 1958, income disparities fell considerably within the EU15, but, in the second half of the 2000s, returned to widen. In the EU28, cross-national income gaps sharply rose around the collapse of communist regimes but then significantly narrowed, thanks largely to the catching-up of Eastern European economies. The lessening of disparities since the early 1990s for the EU28 appears to match the intensity of that for the EU15 in the two decades following World War II.[5] As summarized in the European Commission's *Employment and Social Development in Europe 2016*, 'all in all, while the gradual catching-up process appeared consistent with previous decades for the Member States that joined the European Union since 2004, since the mid-2000s and the crisis in 2008–09, convergence patterns in the Euro area have come to a halt. The divergence largely reflected the adverse impact of the crisis on Southern and Eastern EA Member States' (Bontout et al., 2016: 74).

The long-run improvement in average living standards as approximated by aggregate output per capita is substantial, as is the reduction in their dispersion across the European Union. However, population-weighted, cross-national differences in real GDP per capita are a very rough measure of inequality in Europe: first, they are based on GDP rather than household income, and, second, they ignore within-country inequality. We start with the former and examine the latter in the next section.

GDP measures the size of the economy in terms of the value of goods and services internally produced and is only an imperfect proxy of the revenues available to (resident) households to sustain their living standard. It does not account

---

5   These national accounts data are estimated by the Conference Board, which regularly updates calculations originally made by Maddison (2001). While there is virtually no difference for the United States, the story partly changes for the EU according to the Penn World Table (Figure 2.A1 in Appendix 1). The EU15 mean GDP per capita grew much more substantially, by 4.5 times between 1958 and 2008; there is no income stagnation in the aftermath of the Great Recession. The gap relative to the United States was initially much larger, almost 60% in the early 1950s, but has kept narrowing, down to 23% in 2014; the corresponding value for the EU28 is 29%. As to income disparities, their decline in the EU15 during the 1950s and 1960s is more pronounced, while the rise after mid-2000s is slightly less intense. The different methodology used to adjust for variations in price levels, across countries and over time, is an important factor behind discrepancies between the two sources.

for the net flow of incomes earned and paid abroad, and it includes the resources used by governments to supply in-kind services and collective goods, as well as the profits (gross of capital depreciation) retained by businesses to sustain their investment plans. Resident households as a whole dispose of a spendable income which is, on average, less than two-thirds of GDP in the European Union (including small sole proprietorship enterprises and nonprofit institutions serving households [NPISH]); in small open economies such as Luxembourg and Ireland, this proportion falls well below 40%. The difference is not only in levels but also in dynamics, as shown for instance by the more limited fall of household gross disposable income (HGDI) during the Great Recession due to the effects of automatic stabilisers and stimulus packages (Jenkins et al., 2013; Atkinson, 2013). In national accounts, HGDI offers a better indicator of living standards than does GDP.[6]

Comparable time series for HGDI are released by Eurostat for all EU countries from 1995 onwards, with few exceptions. Real HGDI per capita, which is adjusted for cost-of-living differences both across countries and over time, as described in Appendix 2.1, is higher in the EU15 than the EU28, but the gap has been narrowing as a consequence of the faster growth of Eastern European economies (Figure 2.3). After a decade of relatively steady growth, the Great Recession severely hit the EU15, with real HGDI per capita falling by almost 5% between 2008 and 2013. In the remaining EU countries as a whole, income slowed but kept rising. This was not sufficient to maintain the Gini index for the EU28 on a steady descending trend because cross-national household income disparities within the EU15 abruptly increased during the sovereign debt crisis of 2012–2013. Figure 2.3 also reports data for the EA and the EA19 since the introduction of the euro in 1999. The time patterns for the EA19 resemble those for the EU15 but exhibit a larger fall in mean income and a steeper rise in the Gini index from 2007 to 2013.

The overall income growth since 1995 is lower for real HGDI per capita than for real GDP per capita in both the EU15 and the EU28. The narrowing of the distribution prior to the Great Recession appears more pronounced for HGDI than GDP, while the intensity of the subsequent rise looks about the same. In 2015, income dispersion in the EU15 is a fifth higher than in 1995 based on real

---

6   By including the value of social transfers in kind, 'adjusted' HGDI would be an even better indicator of living standards. As these transfers are generally not covered in household surveys, we focus here on HGDI to maintain consistency with the subsequent distributive analysis. An extensive literature shows that extending the income concept to include transfers in kind for education, healthcare, and housing (valued at market prices or actual cost) narrows the measured income distribution. For instance, Aaberge, Langørgen, and Lindgren estimate that in European countries 'inclusion of non-cash income reduces inequality by 15–25 per cent' and 'poverty rates . . . by 30–50 per cent' (2010: 339).

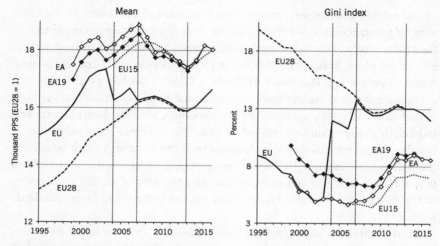

Figure 2.3 Real household gross disposable income (HGDI) per capita in EU, EU28, EU15, EA, and EA19 (1995–2016).
Source: Authors' elaboration on data from Eurostat, National Accounts (January 2019). Real HGDI is obtained by dividing the national series for HGDI by the purchasing power parities indices for HFCE (EU28 = 1) and by deflating the EU aggregates by the implicit deflator of household and nonprofit institutions serving households (NPISH) final consumption expenditure (index: 2010 = 100); the implicit deflator for EU is that for EU15 until 2003 and that for EU28 from 2004. Figures for the household gross disposable income for Spain (1995–1998), Croatia (1995–2001, 2013–2016) and the whole series for Malta are estimated on the basis of figures for nominal GDP. EU: totals for actual EU member countries; EU15: totals for the 15 countries that formed the EU in 1995–2003; EU28: totals for the 28 countries that form the EU since July 2013. The vertical lines indicate the changes in EU membership. All estimates are population-weighted values.

GDP per capita, but a fifth lower if measured with real HGDI per capita; income convergence within the EU28 is sizeable for both measures but greater for HGDI than GDP. Thus, the fall in inequality across EU nations during the past two decades is stronger for household incomes than domestic output.

To sum up, average GDP per capita in the EU15 almost quadrupled from the beginning of the integration process, closing some of the gap vis-à-vis the United States (though it still exceeded a quarter in the EU15 and was a third in the EU28 in 2015). Coupled with the large decline in time spent at work, these figures suggest a sizeable improvement in the well-being of the average European. Until the Great Recession, these income gains were larger in relatively poorer countries of the EU15 and the EA19, considerably reducing cross-country inequality. Significantly, this long-term process reversed during the sovereign debt crisis, following the divergent performances of the 'core' and the 'periphery' of the EA. As a consequence, convergence within the EU28 temporarily stopped, before resuming, driven by the catching-up of new accession countries.

2.3 INEQUALITY IN NATIONAL INCOME DISTRIBUTIONS

National accounts provide crucial insights on the long-run evolution of Europeans' incomes, hence indirectly of their well-being. This is especially the case if aggregate values refer to the part of national disposable income received by households, HGDI. The cross-national variation of HGDI per capita is a first proxy of European income inequality but a very imperfect one. It measures average income gaps *between countries*, but it ignores how unequally incomes are distributed among a country's inhabitants. Accounting for income distributions *within countries* is essential to estimate the EU-wide distribution at a point in time and ascertain its temporal pattern.

Figure 2.4 offers a snapshot of the national income distributions in all EU countries excluding Croatia in 2005 and 2015. To ensure the comparability of living standards, household incomes are adjusted for differences in household composition, by means of a standard equivalence scale, and for differences in cost of living across countries, by using proper price indices, as explained in Appendix 2.1. The box plots in Figure 2.4 show, for each country, the median value (the horizontal mark), the distance between the 25th and the 75th percentiles (the thick vertical bar) and the 5th and 95th percentiles (the two extremes of the thin vertical bar) of the distribution of real equivalized incomes among persons. Countries are arranged in ascending order of median real equivalized income. This ranking follows a known pattern, with Eastern European countries preceding Southern European countries, and then the remaining EU countries rather close to each other except for Luxembourg, which is clearly leading. This pattern is broadly similar in 2005 and 2015, but there are some notable changes, which are the legacy of the Great Recession and the following sovereign debt crisis: Greece moves down several positions, just above Romania, Bulgaria, and Hungary, whereas Germany goes up towards the top.

Income differences are sizeable not only between countries, as we know from national accounts data, but also within countries. In 2015, the Romanian median is only 17% of the Luxembourger median, and this figure falls to 9% if the comparison is made at the 5th percentile. For three-quarters of Eastern Europeans, household incomes are below or at most comparable to the incomes of the poorest quarter of those living in Central and Nordic countries. As this exercise assesses living standards within the European Union as a whole, the comparison in Figure 2.4 necessarily refers to absolute differences. In international comparisons of inequality, the real income gaps among countries are typically removed by expressing income levels as percentages of national medians. In such a case, income differences within Eastern European countries would not look so small compared to those within the other EU countries. In 2015, the 5th percentiles in Bulgaria and Romania are 21–22% of the national medians and just 8–9% of the 95th percentiles. These two countries exhibit the largest values

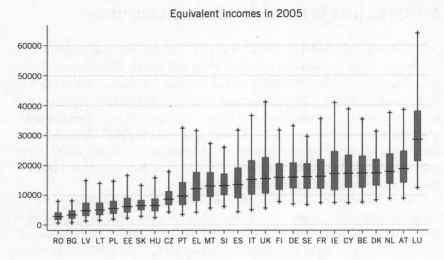

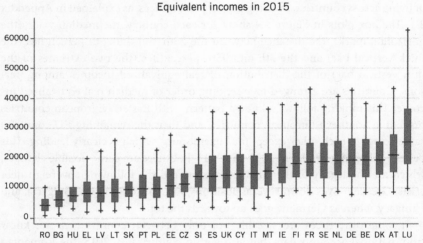

Figure 2.4 Real income distributions within EU countries (2005 and 2015).
Source: Authors' elaboration on data from EU Statistics on Income and Living Conditions
(EU-SILC) CROSS UDB 2005–2017 (version of October 2017). Equivalized disposable
household incomes; modified Organisation for Economic Cooperation and Development
(OECD) equivalence scale; nominal incomes in euro divided by the Price Level Index (PLI) for
household final consumption expenditure (HFCE), (EU28 = 1) and by the HFCE implicit deflator
(covering also nonprofit institutions serving households [NPISH]) for EU28 (index: 2010 = 100);
distribution among individuals.

of relative inequality, ahead of the Southern and Baltic States, taking the ratio
between the 95th and the 5th percentiles, but a similar ranking would emerge
looking at the Gini index.

The EU-wide measures of inequality that we discuss in the following sections
account for disparities both within and between countries. How much of the

overall inequality is explained by each component? Using exactly decomposable indices, they can be neatly set apart as they add up to the total. The within-country component is the weighted sum of the inequalities within each country, while the between-country component is the inequality that would result if each person had an income equal to his or her country's mean income, with weights depending on the index. Estimates based on two such decomposable indices, the *mean logarithmic deviation* and the *Theil index*, show that the within-country inequalities account for a proportion of total inequality, which is around 90% in the EA and the EU15 and around 75% in the more heterogeneous EU after eastern enlargements (Beblo and Knaus, 2001; Brandolini, 2008; Hoffmeister, 2009; Bönke and Schröder, 2014; Papatheodorou and Pavlopoulos, 2014; Filauro, 2018; Filauro and Parolin, 2019).

Clearly, the assessment of the evolution of well-being among Europeans cannot ignore how national income distributions have varied over time. In Figure 2.5 we illustrate the long-run inequality patterns in 12 EU countries as measured by the Gini index for disposable income and the share in taxable income of the top 1% of adult individuals.[7] The patterns tracked by the two types of series are far from being perfectly coincident, which is not surprising given that they measure inequality differently and refer to dissimilar income concept. Overall, however, the evidence gathered in Figure 2.5 consistently suggests that income distribution narrowed until around the 1980s. This is the case for all EU15 countries shown in Figure 2.5. Several factors contributed to reduce income inequality during the postwar Golden Age: on the one hand, strong and prolonged economic growth was accompanied by high levels of employment, rapidly rising wages and decreasing earnings dispersion, and, in general, a shift from capital to labour; on the other hand, expanding welfare states and progressive taxation boosted the redistributive role of governments. The increase in government transfers, in particular the development of old-age pension systems, was effective in narrowing the distribution of disposable income (e.g., Gustafsson and Palmer, 1997; Muffels and Nelissen, 1997; Uusitalo, 1989, for Sweden, the Netherlands, and Finland, respectively). While all eight EU15 countries share these developments to some extent, the relative importance of each factor differs across countries and subperiods. As regards the earnings

---

7 In Figure 2.5, the Gini indices from national studies are generally not comparable across countries but are internally consistent, except for a few statistical breaks (either ignored or adjusted for the absolute difference between old and new series in overlapping years). These figures are shown alongside the Gini indices from the Income Distribution Database (IDD) of the OECD, which are in principle cross-nationally comparable. The data for the top 1% income share are drawn from the World Inequality Database (WID). They are not comparable across countries (e.g., due to different definitions of taxable income and tax unit) and suffer from discontinuities (not shown), for example, due to changes in national tax laws. See notes to Figure 2.5 for details on sources and data characteristics.

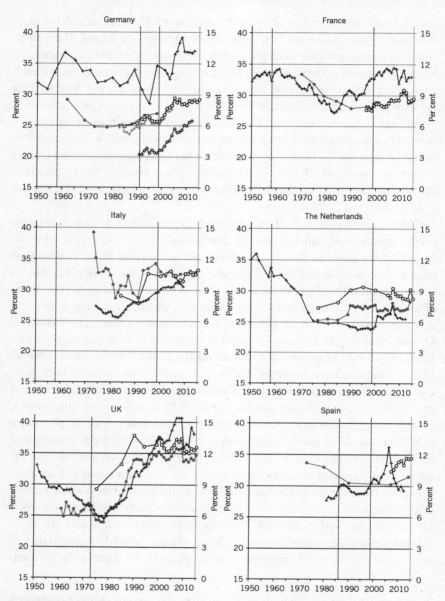

Figure 2.5 Continued

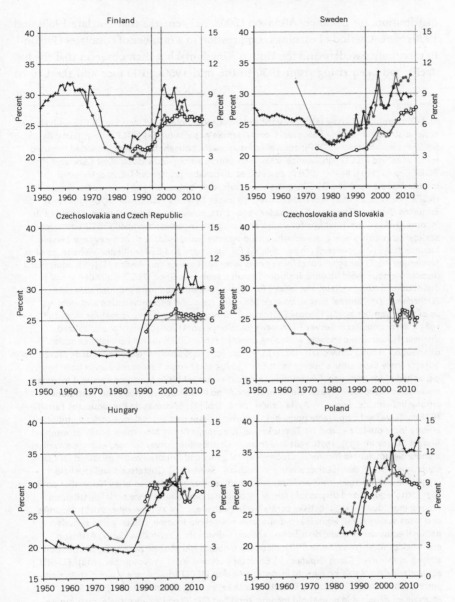

Figure 2.5 Gini index of disposable income and top 1% share of taxable income in selected EU countries (1950–2015).

Source: Vertical lines indicate first year of participation in EU and in EA, if applicable; additional lines indicate year of reunification for Germany and year of dissolution of Czechoslovakia for Czech Republic and Slovakia. In some cases, statistical breaks have been ignored or adjusted by linking series in overlapping years. *All countries:* (○) OECD (website, as of 25 November 2018), IDD: equivalized disposable household cash income, excluding imputed rents; square root equivalence scale; distribution among individuals; (+, right-hand scale) WID (website, as of 14 January 2019): pre-tax national income; distribution among adult individuals. *West Germany:* (•) Becker (1997, table 1) for 1962–1988 and Becker et al. (2003, table 3.3) for 1983–1998; Income

distribution, for instance, Atkinson (2008: 51) remarks that 'the late 1960s and 1970s were a period of earnings compression in a number of countries (Finland, France, Italy, Sweden, and the United Kingdom)', but then observes that the top decile had been rising from 1950 to the mid-1960s in France and the United

---

and Consumption Survey (EVS); equivalized disposable household income; OECD equivalence scale; distribution among individuals, only German population. (♦) SOEP Group (2015: 83–85); Socio-Economic Panel (SOEP); equivalized disposable household income, included imputed rents; modified OECD equivalence scale; distribution among individuals. *East Germany*: (◊) SOEP Group (2015: 83–85), SOEP; equivalized disposable household income, included imputed rents; modified OECD equivalence scale; distribution among individuals. *France*: (•) INSEE (website, as of 25 November 2018); Enquêtes Revenus Fiscaux for 1970–1990 and Enquêtes Revenus Fiscaux et Sociaux for 1996–2015; equivalized disposable household cash income, included imputations for undeclared property incomes; modified OECD equivalence scale; distribution among individuals, including only households with non-negative taxable income. *Italy*: (•) Brandolini (1999, table 13) for 1973–1975 and Banca d'Italia (website, as of 25 November 2018) for 1977–2014; Survey of Household Income and Wealth (SHIW); equivalized disposable household income, included imputed rents; modified OECD equivalence scale; distribution among individuals; figures for 1973–1975 estimated from grouped data. *The Netherlands*: (•) Centraal Bureau voor de Statistiek (personal communication and website, as of 25 November 2018), Income Distribution Survey (Inkomensonderzoek) for 1977, 1981, 1985 and Income Panel Survey (Inkomens Panelonderzoek) for 1989–2014; equivalized disposable household income, including imputed rents; CBS national equivalence scale; distribution among individuals. *UK*: (•) Institute for Fiscal Studies (website, as of 25 November 2018): Family Expenditure Survey for 1961–1992/93 and Family Resources Survey from 1993/94, adjusted for 'very rich' households using data from HMRC's Survey of Personal Incomes; equivalized disposable household income; modified OECD equivalence scale; distribution among individuals. *Spain*: (•) Ayala Cañón (2016: table 1): Encuesta de Presupuestos Familiares (EPF); equivalized disposable household income; square root equivalence scale; distribution among individuals. *Finland*: (•) Tilastokeskus (website, as of 25 November 2018): Household Budget Survey for 1971, 1976, 1981 and Income Distribution Survey for 1987–2015; equivalized disposable household income, including capital gains and imputed rents; modified OECD equivalence scale; distribution among individuals. *Sweden*: (•) Gustafsson and Uusitalo (1990: table 2) for 1967–1985 and Statistiska centralbyrån (website, as of 25 November 2018) for 1975–2013: equivalized disposable family income; national equivalence scale; distribution among individuals; (♦) Statistiska centralbyrån (website, as of 25 November 2018): Incomes and taxes survey (IoS); equivalized disposable household income, capital gains excluded; national equivalence scale; distribution among individuals. *Czechoslovakia*: (•) Atkinson and Micklewright (1992, table CSI1): disposable household income per capita; distribution among individuals. *Czech Republic*: (•) Eurostat (website, as of 25 November 2018): EU-SILC; equivalized disposable household income; modified OECD equivalence scale; distribution among individuals. *Slovakia*: (•) Eurostat (website, as of 25 November 2018): EU-SILC; equivalized disposable household income; modified OECD equivalence scale; distribution among individuals. *Hungary*: (•) Atkinson and Micklewright (1992, table HI1) for 1962–1987 and Gini Project (website, as of 25 November 2018) for 1982–2009: Hungarian Central Statistical Office Income Survey for 1962–1987, Hungarian Household Panel for 1992, 1995, 1996, TÁRKI Household Monitor for 1999–2009; disposable household income per capita; distribution among individuals. *Poland*: (•) Atkinson and Micklewright (1992, table PI1): Household Budget Survey (HBS); disposable household income per capita; distribution among individuals; (◊) Szulc (2006: table 2): Household Budget Survey (HBS), breaks in 1993 and 1997; equivalized disposable household income; national equivalence scale; distribution among households; (♦) Gini Project (website, as of 25 November 2018): Household Budget Survey (HBS); equivalized disposable household income; OECD equivalence scale; distribution among persons.

Kingdom, although not in West Germany. According to Piketty (2003: 1016), in France 'wage dispersion significantly widened between 1950 and 1967–68, and the sharp increases in the minimum wage implemented in the summer of 1968 and during the 1970s led to a significant decline in wage inequality until 1982–83, when the newly elected socialist government decided to freeze the minimum wage (wage dispersion has increased somewhat since then)'.

The downward movement of income inequality after World War II came to a halt during the 1980s. The turning point showed up first in the United Kingdom, roughly at the same time as in the United States, in coincidence with the electoral victories of Margaret Thatcher and Ronald Reagan, respectively. Earning disparities widened considerably and went along with a shift away from employment towards both unemployment and self-employment (Jenkins, 1995, 1996); the impact on the distribution of household disposable incomes was amplified by government policies aimed at reducing social spending and taxes on top incomes (Johnson and Webb, 1993; Atkinson, 2003). Inequality rose sharply in the United Kingdom until the 1990s and then flattened out; the reforms of income support and tax credits implemented by the Labour government played an important role in offsetting an otherwise ascending trend between the late 1990s and the mid-2000s (Bargain, 2012; Belfield et al., 2017).

In West Germany, disposable income inequality during the 1980s and 1990s either rose moderately or remained substantially stable depending on the source of data; government redistribution played an important role in mitigating market income inequality (Biewen, 2000; Bach et al., 2009; Fuchs-Schündeln et al., 2010; Corneo et al., 2014). Income distribution widened considerably during the first half of the 2000s, driven by developments in the labour market and changes in the tax system (Biewen and Juhasz, 2012; Bach et al., 2013). Since 2005, inequality has remained stable, even during the Great Recession, largely as a result of the expansion of employment opportunities (Grabka et al., 2012; Biewen et al., 2017). In France, income inequality began to rise at the end of the 1990s: Frémeaux and Piketty (2014) suggest that it was partly due to the lack of progressivity of the overall tax system, a feature that was reinforced during the 2000s. In the Netherlands, the Gini index recorded a leap in the late 1980s, but otherwise did not show any persistent upward tendency. The evidence from the top income series does not modify this conclusion once we take into account that the upsurge in 2001 reflects a break in the series and the blip in 2007 is due to a temporary tax relief on dividends (Salverda, 2017). Salverda et al. (2014) notices that tax-and-benefit reforms aimed at activating citizens to work (by restricting eligibility and shortening duration of benefits, lowering top tax rates, and introducing working tax credits) reduced the redistributive effects of social policy but might have sustained work participation and hence labour incomes.

In Italy, income inequality, as measured by the Gini index, rose sharply during the currency crisis of the early 1990s but much less during the double-dip recession from 2008 to 2013, despite a similar growth in (absolute) poverty ratios

(Brandolini et al., 2018). The widening of income distribution in the latter crisis offset the narrowing in the previous decade and was fairly contained in the face of the severity of the recession. The figures for the top income share also indicate a rise of inequality since the mid-1980s, but there are perceptible differences from the series for the Gini index in some subperiods (e.g., second half of the 1980s). In Spain, the Gini index decreased after the return to democracy and then hardly changed during the long economic expansion prior to the Great Recession save for temporary rises in economic downturns. This Spanish diversity, relative to the patterns observed in other advanced countries, disappeared with the Great Recession and the sovereign debt crisis, when the Gini index sharply increased (Pijoan-Mas and Sánchez-Marcos, 2010; Ferrer-i-Carbonell et al., 2014; Ayala Cañon, 2016). The top 1% income share has moved differently from the Gini index, largely because of the inclusion of capital gains that primarily account both for its dynamics and the 1987, 2000, and 2005 spikes (Alvaredo and Saez, 2009).

After the United Kingdom, Finland and Sweden are the two EU15 countries in Figure 2.5 that exhibit the steeper increases in inequality since the 1980s, although starting from very low levels. In both countries important drivers of inequality were the introduction of a dual income tax system in the early 1990s, which created strong incentives to shift earnings towards capital income and contributed to the rise of the top income shares, and the downsizing of social protection, which hit especially people at the bottom of the distribution (Blomgren et al., 2014; Jäntti et al., 2010, for Finland; Eriksson and Pettersson, 2000; Roine and Waldenström, 2008; Fritzell et al., 2014, for Sweden). In some years tax reforms also pushed investors to realise capital gains on equities, causing the spikes shown in the series.

As for Eastern Europe, a narrowing of income distribution in the 1960s and 1970s characterizes Czechoslovakia and Hungary (Atkinson and Micklewright, 1992),[8] while a sharp rise of inequality following the end of communist regimes is clearly visible in both countries and Poland. The available data show a flat trend during the 2000s in the Czech Republic and Slovakia, where taxation and transfers significantly mitigated market income inequalities (Kahanec et al., 2014), a stability followed by a fall after 2004 in Hungary (Fábián et al., 2014), and a modest growth in Poland since early 1990s (Letki et al., 2014). In East Germany, the Gini index also increased after the reunification (Biewen, 2000) but

---

8 As regards data availability and quality during the communist regime, Atkinson and Micklewright (1992: 74) note that 'in the case of the earnings distribution, not only is information available for Czechoslovakia, Hungary and Poland, but the similarities in the sources we use with the corresponding survey in Britain . . . are more striking than differences'. More generally, they observe that income data in these three countries have significant deficiencies, but all in all do not compare too unfavourably with corresponding British data.

by less than in the other three Eastern European countries; its movements match fairly closely those in West Germany.

We draw three conclusions from this overview of national trends in a selected group of EU countries. First, some U-shaped pattern is perceptible in virtually all countries, but timing, magnitude, and persistence of inequality movements differ. As Atkinson observed, 'it is misleading to talk of 'trends' when describing the postwar evolution of the income distribution. . . . It may be better for a number of countries to think in terms of 'episodes' when inequality fell or increased' (1997: 303). While common forces may have affected all European economies, countries' circumstances and policy choices led to distinct national patterns. Second, the causes of the reversal of postwar inequality downward trends seem to lie in labour markets becoming more 'flexible', in taxation reforms favouring high taxpayers, in the rolling back of welfare states. These tendencies are typically seen as the inescapable response to exogenous forces such as globalization and technological progress, but they also reflect radical changes in economic theory, policymaking, and social norms, which predate the establishment of the European Union in 1993 and the adoption of a common currency in 1999. The findings of Beckfield (2006, 2009) and Bertola (2010) that the deepening of European integration has been associated with a rise of within-country income inequality must be seen against this background. European integration may have facilitated the adoption of increasingly homogeneous policies, but it is reasonable to expect that countries would have gone roughly in the same directions irrespective of integration. The similarity between the patterns observed in Figure 2.5 for Sweden and Finland, two Nordic countries that differ in their participation in the monetary union, seems to back up this conjecture. Third, independently from the explanation of national experiences, Figure 2.5 confirms that income inequality has changed considerably within countries during the past half-century. This needs to be taken into account in the estimation of the EU-wide distribution over time.

2.4 ESTIMATES OF THE EU-WIDE INCOME DISTRIBUTION

Estimating the EU-wide distribution is a demanding exercise. Apart from important methodological choices (e.g., the adjustment for differences in cost of living across countries, the alignment of survey data to national accounts), it crucially depends on the availability of information on national income distributions. Ideally, one needs a database with cross-nationally comparable person- or household-level income data for all EU countries, such as EU-SILC in recent years. This permits consistent application of the same measurement assumptions to all income observations. Lacking microdata, the main alternative is to use summary statistics on national distributions. Borrowing approaches typically employed to estimate global inequality, a 'synthetic' EU-wide income distribution can be constructed by stacking the income means of all population quantile groups, ranked by income, comprising each national distribution, or by estimating national parametric distributions from available summary statistics. The gains from going back in time using existing tabulated data are counterbalanced by the impossibility of amending inconsistencies in underlying national distributions (e.g., due to differences in equivalence scales) and the understatement of measured inequality if income differences within quantile groups are ignored.[9] Due to data availability, direct estimates based on comparable microdata can only cover a relatively recent period spanning the years since the 1990s for the EU15 and the next decade for the EU28; synthetic estimates may extend over a longer period but are less accurate. In Figure 2.6, we report a selection of estimates of the Gini index for the EU15 (top panel) and the EU28 (bottom panel) as a whole, and for the United States as reference. In Appendix 2.2, we survey available estimates, their sources, and the underlying methodological assumptions.

For the EU15, the synthetic estimates by Morrisson and Murtin (2004), Darvas (2016), and Vercelli (2018) align distributive information to national accounts but differ in method and source of real GDP series; those by Bonesmo Fredriksen (2012) do not make any adjustment to national accounts and cover only 10 countries. The calculations by Vercelli suggest a steady decline of the Gini index between the late 1950s and the 1980s; the series shows ups and downs thereafter, but in 2014 it is back to the values of the mid-1980s. Vercelli (2018: 7) observes that 'there is statistical evidence of structural break . . . in 1984' and concludes that the reduction in the Gini index occurred 'almost entirely' between 1958 and 1984. Also Morrisson and Murtin estimate a fall between 1970 and 1980, though on much lower levels. For the period 1980–1995, they observe a stasis rather than Vercelli's small decline. Also Darvas calculates a substantial stability from 1988 to the mid-2000s, followed by an increase until 2015. For a subgroup of 10 EU15 countries, Bonesmo Fredriksen finds a rise of the Gini index between 1985 and 1995 and a further increase afterwards. Moving to direct estimates on microdata, Beckfield (2009) calculates a fall between 1980 and 2000 (gathering national data from different years around these two indicated years) and Troitiño Cobas (2007) finds a steady decline during the 1990s (considering only 11 countries for 1993–1996), similarly to Vercelli. For the second half of the 1990s, however, Benczúr, Cseres-Gergely, and Harasztosi (2017) observe little change despite using the same microdata as Troitiño Cobas. From 2005 onwards, the estimates by Benczúr, Cseres-Gergely, and Harasztosi (2017) and our own indicate a coherent pattern, leaving aside marginal differences in levels: inequality unequivocally increases.

---

9 On methodological problems arising in studies of income distribution in supranational entities, see Brandolini (2007) for the EU and Milanovic (2005), Anand and Segal (2008, 2015) and Atkinson (2017) for the world.

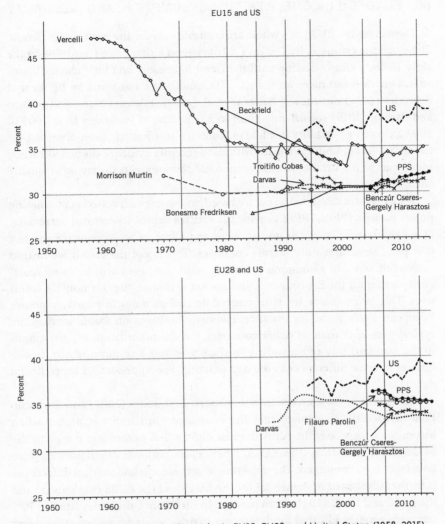

Figure 2.6 Long-run changes in the Gini index in EU15, EU28, and United States (1958–2015). *Source: Vercelli*: Vercelli (2018): synthetic estimates on World Income Inequality Database (WIID) data; adjusted to national accounts. *Morrisson Murtin*: Morrisson and Murtin (2004), synthetic estimates on World Bank data, break due to inclusion of East Germany since 1991; adjusted to national accounts. *Bonesmo Fredriksen*: Bonesmo Fredriksen (2012), synthetic estimates on OECD Income Distribution Database (IDD) data, excluding Austria, Belgium, Spain, Ireland, Portugal. *Darvas*: Darvas (2016), synthetic estimates on Standardized IDD (SWIID) data. *Troitiño Cobas*: Troitiño Cobas (2007), direct estimates on European Community Household Panel (ECHP) data, excluding Austria, Finland, Luxembourg, Sweden in 1993–1996. *Beckfield*: Beckfield (2009), direct estimates on LIS data, excluding Greece and Portugal, for various years around indicated year. *Benczúr Cseres-Gergely Harasztosi*: Benczúr, Cseres-Gergely and Harasztosi (2017), direct estimates on ECHP and EU Statistics on Income and Living Conditions (EU-SILC) data, excluding Croatia. *Filauro Parolin*: Filauro and Parolin (2019), direct estimates on EU-SILC data, excluding Malta (2006) and Croatia (2006–2008). *PPS*: Authors' elaboration on data from EU-SILC CROSS UDB 2005–2017 (version of October 2017), excluding Croatia. *US*: Andrews, Palesch, and Thomas (2015 and personal communication), direct estimates on Current Population Survey-Annual Social and Economic Supplement (CPS-ASEC) data; equivalized disposable household income; modified OECD equivalence scale; distribution among individuals. See Tables 2.A1 and 2.A2 in Appendix 2 for details.

Figures for the EU28 as a whole are available only for the most recent period. The synthetic estimates by Darvas (2016) suggest a sharp rise from 1988 to the early 1990s, a steady decline until the Great Recession, and little change thereafter. Our own estimates on the EU-SILC microdata and those by Bönke and Schröder (2014) not shown, Benczúr et al. (2017), Filauro (2018), and Filauro and Parolin (2019) consistently point to a reduction of inequality from 2005 to 2009 followed by stability until 2015, contrary to what has been observed for the EU15. These findings square with the aggregate evidence discussed earlier, hinting at the importance of macroeconomic developments in driving inequality changes.

The estimates discussed so far are based on incomes expressed at purchasing power parities (PPPs). PPPs provide the relative values, in national currencies, of a fixed bundle of goods and services and allow us to account for the fact that price structures differ across countries. This is not the case if we instead convert incomes to a common unit of account (e.g., the euro) by using fixed-euro parities for the EA countries and market exchange rates for non-EA countries. This latter choice tends to understate real incomes in relatively poorer European states since, for instance, labour-intensive nontradable services are typically cheaper than in richer countries. On the other hand, it corresponds to the standard way of measuring inequality within a country, which usually ignores internal differences in the cost of living. See Appendix 2.1 for technical details.

The choice of the conversion rate matters. Brandolini (2007) and Bonesmo Fredriksen (2012) calculate that the estimated Gini index is higher when incomes are expressed in euros than in PPS by 3–5 percentage points in the EU28 but by less than 2 in EU15, where cross-national differences in price levels are more contained. The importance of these methodological differences is further illustrated in Figure 2.7 for the EU15 and the EU28 (top panels) and the EA12 and the EA19 (bottom panels). In each panel, the series labelled PPS refers to incomes adjusted for differences in price levels across countries using the PPP indices for household final consumption expenditure (HFCE), while the series labelled Euro refers to incomes in euros converted by using the fixed-euro parities for EA countries and the average annual market exchange rates for non-EA countries. The series labelled PWM is the population-weighted mean of national values, which corresponds to the EU/EA figures regularly released by Eurostat. The last series is the Gini index in the United States, as estimated by Andrews, Palesch, and Thomas (2015) replicating as closely as possible Eurostat methodology on data from the Annual Social and Economic Supplement of the Current Population Survey (CPS-ASEC) of the US Census Bureau. This series refers to incomes unadjusted for price level differences across US states.

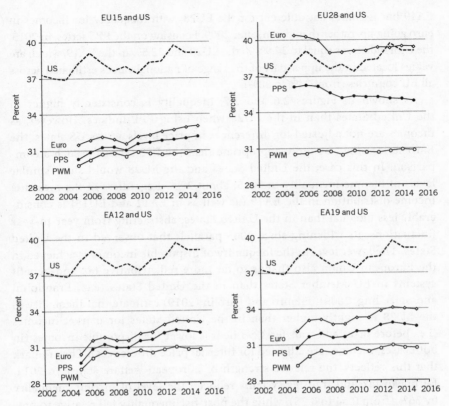

Figure 2.7 Gini index in EU15, EU28, EA12, EA19, and United States (2002–2015) by different definitions.
Source: Authors' elaboration on data from EU Statistics on Income and Living Conditions (EU-SILC) CROSS UDB 2005–2017 (version of October 2017) for EU15, EU28, EA12, and EA19 and from Andrews, Palesch, and Thomas (2015 and personal communication) for US; equivalized disposable household income; modified OECD equivalence scale; distribution among individuals. *Euro:* incomes converted to euros by market exchange rates; *PPS:* incomes in purchasing power standards; *PWM:* population-weighted means of national indices.

There is little change in inequality between 2005 and 2015 according to population-weighted averages, but this result is biased by the neglect of between-country inequality. Once the latter is considered, inequality is increasing in the EA19, as well as in the EA12 and the EU15, and decreasing in the EU28. The more pronounced widening of the income distribution is measured for the EA12, where the Gini index rose by about 2.5 percentage points between 2005 and 2015. As found in earlier studies, the Gini index is higher when incomes are converted to euro at nominal exchange rates—by more than 1 percentage point in the EA19 and about 4 points in the EU28. The trend looks the same for the

EA19 but is somewhat different for the EU28, with inequality for incomes in euro going up, rather than down, after 2009. Focusing on the PPS series, in 2015, the Gini index was equal to 34.9% in the EU28 and 32.5% in the EA19, which are values located in the upper part of the range of national values estimated across all EU countries (from 24% to 38%).

As shown in Figures 2.6 and 2.7, inequality is consistently higher in the United States than in the EU28 when using PPP indices. However, as incomes are not adjusted for differences in price levels across US states, the Euro series might be more appropriate than the PPS series for such a comparison. In this case, the United States and the EU28 would show similar levels of income inequality in 2015, about 39%. Regardless of the measure, income distribution in the EA19 (as well as in EA12 and EU15) is considerably less unequal than in the United States; abstracting from year-to-year fluctuations, its widening since 2005 parallels that observed in the United States. The lower level in the inequality of disposable incomes is achieved in the European Union also thanks to far more redistributive tax-and-benefit systems in EU Member States than in the United States (e.g., Brandolini and Smeeding, 2009). Filauro and Parolin (2019) estimate that inequality in the EU28 is slightly higher than in the United States for market incomes (i.e., before taxes and transfers), while it is lower for disposable incomes (in both cases, incomes are adjusted for internal price differences). They remark that this reflects 'the relative strength of European welfare states: in 2014, European tax and transfer systems reduced the level of income inequality by 36% (from 0.54 to 0.35), while the post-fisc inequality fell relative to pre-fisc inequality by 29% (from 0.53 to 0.38) in the United States' (Filauro and Parolin, 2019: 552). While European welfare states tend to be more redistributive than seen in the United States, they are however different from each other, inducing Caselli et al. (2016: 187) to observe that 'Country-level redistribution means that the geographic clustering of disposable incomes is even greater than the geographic clustering of market incomes. In other words, country-level redistributive policies reduce inequality, but give rise to a more heterogeneous Union'.

To sum up, the evidence for old decades is fragile, but it seems to confirm some narrowing of the EU15 income distribution until the mid-1980s. This is coherent with the downward trends observed for both between-country inequality (convergence in real GDP per capita) and within-country inequality (descending national patterns), although such a neat decomposition is not appropriate for the Gini index. With the more reliable data available for recent years, between 2005 and 2015, inequality exhibits an overall descending trend in the EU28 but a rising one in the EU15 and the EA. These recent tendencies are little affected by expressing incomes at nominal market rates rather than at PPPs. The inequality of disposable incomes in the European Union and, especially, the EA falls below the levels observed in the United States thanks to the operation of the European tax-and-benefit systems.

2.5 A LOOK INSIDE EU INEQUALITY DEVELOPMENTS IN THE PAST DECADE

As seen, between 2005 and 2015, the distribution of equivalized incomes became less unequal in the EU28 but more unequal in the EU15. By considering changes in the bottom and top deciles, Benczúr, Cseres-Gergely, and Harasztosi (2017: 5–6) observe that this EU15 development 'comes from the lower and only to little or no extent from the upper part of the distribution. Again, this process was driven mostly by changes for the Mediterranean, so powerful that it could induce a decrease and subsequently an increase in the overall EU15 inequality, despite the relatively small share of this country group'. This confirms the importance of what Caselli et al. (2016: 172) call 'geographic clustering' of income levels, or 'the fact that the relatively rich households and the relatively poor ones are geographically segregated'. Accordingly, we investigate the dynamics of income distribution in the European Union by taking a rather accepted, if arbitrary, clustering of countries: we split the 12 oldest EA members into CORE (Austria, Belgium, Finland, France, Germany, Luxembourg, the Netherlands) and PERIphery (Greece, Ireland, Italy, Portugal, Spain); we include in EUNEA the three EU15 non-EA countries (Denmark, Sweden, the UK) and in NEU15 the remaining 12 new accession countries (Bulgaria, Cyprus, Czech Republic, Estonia, Hungary, Latvia, Lithuania, Malta, Poland, Romania, Slovakia, Slovenia), which comprise seven EA members and five non-EA countries (Croatia is not included).

Figure 2.8 displays the *growth incidence curves* (GICs) for each country cluster. The GICs show the percentage cumulated growth rates between 2005 and 2015 for every percentile of the distribution of real equivalized disposable household incomes. Note that incomes are 'real' in a double sense: they have the same purchasing power in all EU countries because they are converted by means of PPP indices, and in both years because they are adjusted for the average inflation in the EU28 (see Appendix 2.1 for details). The observed reduction in the EU28 inequality reflected the much stronger growth of the bottom fourth of the distribution with respect to the other three-fourths. In turn, this stemmed mostly from the major improvements recorded in new accession countries (NEU15), where income growth was much stronger than in other EU countries along the whole distribution. In the other groups, developments in equivalized disposable incomes were more contained and homogeneous along the distribution, though qualitatively different: in the PERI countries, income fell throughout the distribution but very strongly at the bottom; income also declined in the EUNEA countries except for some rise at the bottom[10]; on the contrary, in the CORE

---

10 This negative pattern is dominated by results for the United Kingdom, whereas the profiles for Denmark and Sweden are very positive. See Figure 2.A2 in Appendix 1. This evidence for the UK may be affected by a statistical break in the EU-SILC series; other sources, such as national accounts and the estimates by the Institute for Fiscal Studies used in Figure 2.5, do not indicate any decrease in British household incomes.

countries, growth was positive at all income levels and increased by moving toward the top. Figure 2.8 provides a clear representation of how the recent divergence between core and periphery EU15 economies affected their income distributions: the income gap enlarged particularly at the bottom of the respective distributions but widened also at the top. The resulting changes in the overall EU distribution are shown in Figure 2.9, where we exploit the fact that the EU-wide density of equivalized income can be expressed as the weighted sum of country-group specific densities, with weights equal to population shares. The massive shift of the NEU15 population towards the middle of the EU-wide distribution and the raising share of the PERI population in its lower tail are evident by comparing 2005 and 2015.

To examine these changes in greater detail, we adopt an income-based definition of social class and divide the EU population into a low-income class (individuals with equivalized disposable income below 60% of the EU median value), a lower middle class (60–120%), an upper middle class (120–300%), and a high income class (above 3 times the EU median value). In line with our EU-wide perspective, we implement this classification using for all countries the

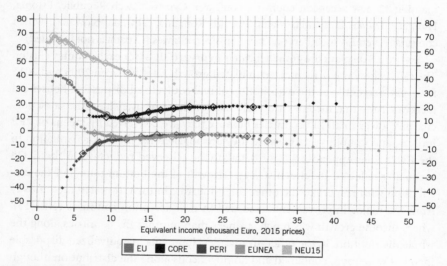

Figure 2.8 Growth incidence curves for EU28 and selected country groups (2005–2015).
Source: Authors' elaboration on data from EU Statistics on Income and Living Conditions (EU-SILC) CROSS UDB 2005–2017 (version of October 2017), excluding Croatia. The figure displays, for each country group, the percentage cumulated growth rates between 2005 and 2015 (y-axis) for every percentile of the distribution of equivalized disposable household income among individuals against their value (in purchasing power standards [PPSs] in 2005 (x-axis); only percentiles 3 to 97 are reported; hollow markers single out deciles of the corresponding distribution in 2005. CORE: Austria, Belgium, Finland, France, Germany, Luxembourg, the Netherlands; PERI: Greece, Ireland, Italy, Portugal, Spain; EUNEA: Denmark, Sweden, the UK; NEU15: Bulgaria, Cyprus, Czech Republic, Estonia, Hungary, Latvia, Lithuania, Malta, Poland, Romania, Slovakia, Slovenia.

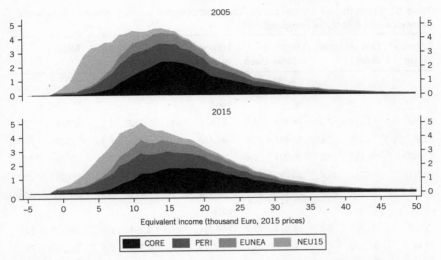

Figure 2.9 The composition of the EU28 equivalized income distribution (2005 and 2015). *Source:* Authors' elaboration on data from EU Statistics on Income and Living Conditions (EU-SILC) CROSS UDB 2005–2017 (version of October 2017), excluding Croatia; equivalized disposable household income; modified OECD equivalence scale; distribution among individuals; incomes in purchasing power standards (PPSs). *CORE*: Austria, Belgium, Finland, France, Germany, Luxembourg, the Netherlands; *PERI*: Greece, Ireland, Italy, Portugal, Spain; *EUNEA*: Denmark, Sweden, the UK; *NEU15*: Bulgaria, Cyprus, Czech Republic, Estonia, Hungary, Latvia, Lithuania, Malta, Poland, Romania, Slovakia, Slovenia.

same income thresholds as calculated on the EU28 distribution of equivalized disposable income (Table 2.1, panel A). In 2005, 122 million persons, or 25% of EU population, were at risk of poverty; that is, they had an equivalized disposable income below 60% of the EU-wide median value. About 63% of them were from new accession countries, where they accounted for three-quarters of that country-group population; another 20% was from periphery countries; and only 10% from core countries. In 2015, the number of persons at risk of poverty fell to 112 million individuals, or 23% of the EU population: only 48% were from new accession countries, while 31% were from periphery countries. Over the period, the incidence of low income in NEU15 countries fell from 75% to 54%, while that in periphery countries increased from 19% to 26%. At the upper end of the income ladder, the high-income class accounts for less than 3% of the EU population. The share in this class of people resident in core countries went up from 41% to 62%, whereas that of persons living in periphery countries decreased from 29% to 21%. Finally, the different income dynamics between new accession countries and periphery countries emerges in the composition of the (lower and upper) middle classes: while the share in these classes of NEU15 residents increased from 14% to 24%, that of PERI residents decreased from 57% to 51%.

The picture would be dramatically different using national thresholds, thus neglecting mean income differences between countries (Table 2.1, panel B). The

Table 2.1 Economic social classes in EU28 and selected country groups (thousands persons and percentage composition)

Country group	Low-income class		Lower middle class		Upper middle class		High-income class		Total	
A. Thresholds based on EU-wide median										
2005										
CORE	12,273	2.5	76,123	15.7	87,826	18.1	5,238	1.1	181,460	37.4
PERI	24,316	5.0	53,487	11.0	46,420	9.6	3,791	0.8	128,014	26.4
EUNEA	8,885	1.8	29,221	6.0	31,843	6.6	3,245	0.7	73,194	15.1
NEU15	76,732	15.8	20,797	4.3	4,069	0.8	621	0.1	102,219	21.1
EU28	122,206	25.2	179,628	37.0	170,158	35.1	12,895	2.7	484,887	100.0
2015										
CORE	11,797	2.4	68,017	13.7	98,114	19.7	8,191	1.6	186,119	37.5
PERI	34,390	6.9	54,928	11.1	40,095	8.1	2,718	0.5	132,131	26.6
EUNEA	12,657	2.5	35,212	7.1	29,678	6.0	1,854	0.4	79,401	16.0
NEU15	53,409	10.8	36,713	7.4	8,641	1.7	397	0.1	99,160	20.0
EU28	112,253	22.6	194,870	39.2	176,528	35.5	13,160	2.6	496,811	100.0
B. Thresholds based on national medians										
2005										
CORE	23,030	4.7	99,727	20.6	56,202	11.6	2,503	0.5	181,462	37.4
PERI	25,099	5.2	55,843	11.5	43,572	9.0	3,500	0.7	128,014	26.4
EUNEA	12,971	2.7	33,647	6.9	24,514	5.1	2,062	0.4	73,194	15.1
NEU15	19,079	3.9	45,721	9.4	33,701	7.0	3,717	0.8	102,218	21.1
EU28	80,179	16.5	234,938	48.5	157,989	32.6	11,782	2.4	484,888	100.0
2015										
CORE	27,613	5.6	95,277	19.2	59,866	12.0	3,364	0.7	186,120	37.5
PERI	27,752	5.6	55,180	11.1	45,841	9.2	3,358	0.7	132,131	26.6
EUNEA	12,875	2.6	37,358	7.5	27,424	5.5	1,745	0.4	79,402	16.0
NEU15	18,005	3.6	45,661	9.2	33,394	6.7	2,101	0.4	99,161	20.0
EU28	86,245	17.4	233,476	47.0	166,525	33.5	10,568	2.1	496,814	100.0

Source: Authors' elaboration on data from EU-SILC CROSS UDB 2005–2017 (version of October 2017), excluding Croatia; equivalized disposable household income; modified OECD equivalence scale; distribution among individuals; incomes in PPSs. *CORE*: Austria, Belgium, Finland, France, Germany, Luxembourg, the Netherlands; *PERI*: Greece, Ireland, Italy, Portugal, Spain; *EUNEA*: Denmark, Sweden, the UK; *NEU15*: Bulgaria, Cyprus, Czech Republic, Estonia, Hungary, Latvia, Lithuania, Malta, Poland, Romania, Slovakia, Slovenia.

at-risk-of-poverty rate would be significantly lower, around 17% of the EU population in either year. In 2005, core and periphery countries would account for 29% and 31% of EU low-income individuals, respectively, against 24% for new accession countries. In 2015, the corresponding shares would fall to 21% for new accession countries, but it would rise to 32% for both core and periphery countries. This is a neat example of Atkinson's observation (1995: 71) cited in the introduction: using the EU-wide threshold, the at-risk-of-poverty rate clearly improves as a consequence of taking into account 'the relative growth rates of different member countries'.

The EU-wide perspective has implications not only for the 'size' of income-defined social classes and for their developments over time, but also, and perhaps more importantly, for the identities of poor and rich people beyond their residence country. For example, with EU-wide threshold, in 2005, more than 27% of European children (aged 0–17 years) lived in low-income households against 24% based on national income thresholds. By 2015, progress in the reduction of child poverty turns out to be stronger on the basis of the EU-wide threshold (down to 25%) than on the basis of national thresholds (stable at 24%).

Focusing on the European Union as a whole helps underscore important fault lines. While similar population categories achieve comparable levels of well-being across countries, others fare very differently. This can be seen by comparing the relative equivalized income positions of selected sociodemographic categories and their changes relative to the overall EU between 2005 and 2015. Sociodemographic categories are identified from educational achievement, age, employment status, and country-group of residence, where all characteristics refer to the household's head. Figure 2.10 plots the changes in the ratios of the group-specific deciles to the overall median against their initial values in 2005, for each group (i.e., a sociodemographic category in a country group).[11] Points in the northeast quadrant indicate that the group-specific deciles were above the overall median to start with and, over the period, moved farther away from the overall median. On the contrary, points in the southwest quadrant indicate that the group deciles were below the overall median at the beginning of the period and fell further below it over time; points in the two other quadrants indicate a convergence towards the median during the period. Visually, an upward (downward) sloping curve means that the group-specific distribution became more

---

11 Let m_t be the overall median real equivalized income at time t, and q_t^{dc} the d-th decile of the distribution of real equivalized income *within* sociodemographic group c at time t. The ratios $p_t^{dc} = (q_t^{dc}/m_t)$ indicate the position of group c's distribution relative to the overall distribution, as summarized by its median value, and $\Delta^{dc} = (p_t^{dc}-p_s^{dc})$ says by how much this *relative* position changed between time s and t. For example, consider people living in households whose head has high education (i.e., at least a high school degree, *HS*). In 2005, the overall EU median real equivalized income was 13,548 euros; the 5th decile of the income distribution for these educated heads in CORE countries was about 17,240 euros, 27.2% higher than the overall median, hence $p_{2005}^{5,HS,CORE} = (17,240/13,548) = 1.272$. In 2015, the overall median rose to 14,681 euros, and the 5th decile of highly educated heads in CORE countries rose to 20,127 euros, yielding $p_{2015}^{5,HS,CORE} = (20,127/14,681) = 1.371$. As a result, $\Delta^{5,HS,CORE} = 1.371 - 1.272 = 0.099$, which indicates a rise of 10 percentage points in the ratio $p_t^{5,HS,CORE}$.

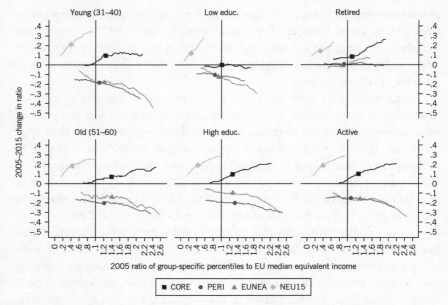

Figure 2.10 Relative equivalized incomes dynamics in EU28 country groups (2005–2015). *Source:* Authors' elaboration on data from EU Statistics on Income and Living Conditions (EU-SILC) CROSS UDB 2005–2017 (version of October 2017), excluding Croatia; equivalized disposable household income; modified OECD equivalence scale; distribution among individuals; incomes in purchasing power standards (PPSs). *CORE*: Austria, Belgium, Finland, France, Germany, Luxembourg, the Netherlands; *PERI*: Greece, Ireland, Italy, Portugal, Spain; *EUNEA*: Denmark, Sweden, the UK; *NEU15*: Bulgaria, Cyprus, Czech Republic, Estonia, Hungary, Latvia, Lithuania, Malta, Poland, Romania, Slovakia, Slovenia. Markers single out group-specific medians, where group indicates a population category in a country group.

(less) unequal over time, whereas a flat one suggests that the relative positions did not change; the position of the curve in the space informs instead on the position of the group relative to the overall median. For each group-specific curve, the marker in Figure 2.10 singles out the 2005 group-specific median.

With the exceptions of those with low education levels and the retired, the broad patterns are rather similar across groups. In periphery and in non-EA EU15 countries the position of these groups relative to the overall EU distribution has worsened, more so for higher initial income levels; in core and new accession countries, instead, they have generally climbed the distribution while, at the same time, recording an increase in within-group inequality. Only among the low-educated have residents in core countries just maintained their relative positions. These patterns are broadly absent in the group of retirees' households whose incomes are plausibly more insulated from cyclical macroeconomic developments. While in PERI and EUNEA countries retirees' households have virtually kept their positions, in NEU15 countries they have significantly improved their relative conditions, as have other groups; a significant upgrade has been also achieved by rich retirees' households in CORE countries. This evidence confirms the divergent patterns within the EA, with income gaps among specific groups, which in some cases were already sizeable in 2005, becoming more marked during the following decade.

To sum up, the evidence in this section shows that casting national income distributions into a wider EU perspective leads to different assessments of the current situation and of the progress made with respect to social targets such as the at-risk-of-poverty rate. It also highlights how the patterns of income convergence across Member States are not the same for all categories of residents; incomes of some population groups, typically young and active persons in the labour market, have fared much more differently both within and across countries than those of other groups (elderly and retired). It therefore suggests that there is room for a better integration of regional and social policies that take jointly into account the personal and the national dimension.

2.6 CONCLUSION

Sixty-two years have passed since the European project started with the signature of the Treaty of Rome; 26 years since the establishment of the European Union sanctioned the free movement of goods, services, people, and money among all member countries; 20 years since the euro became the common currency. Yet the European project is facing hard times. The divergent economic performance of Northern and Southern economies following the sovereign debt crisis of 2011, the strengthening of populist and anti-European parties, the political disagreement on how to cope with the refugee crisis, and the British withdrawal from the Union after the referendum held in 2016 are unambiguous symptoms of the increasing difficulty to push forward integration.

These difficulties should be put into a broader historical context. In this chapter we have adopted an explicit European perspective to assess how the distribution of well-being has evolved among Europeans since the start of the integration process. We have measured income distribution in the European Union as if it was a single country rather than taking it to be the average of national values.

Our analysis has ascertained a few facts.

- Average living standards have improved considerably, in terms of both much higher income levels and lower time spent at work; while no causal link can be easily established, economic progress went along with European integration.
- Average differences among people living in different countries narrowed, at least until the mid-2000s (macroeconomic convergence).

- Within most countries, income inequality declined up to the mid-1980s, then started to increase, although the timing, size, and persistence of this rising tendency vary across countries.
- As a result of the macroeconomic convergence and the prevailing U-shaped profiles of national inequality, the EU15-wide income distribution narrowed until the mid-1980s; the subsequent pattern is less clear, but the economic turmoil around 2010 pushed inequality up, mainly because of the divergence between the core and the periphery of the EA. The EU28-wide inequality has instead remained on a descending trend, driven by the macroeconomic convergence of new accession countries.
- Around 2015, incomes appear to be more unevenly distributed in the United States than in the European Union, and especially so in the EA, thanks to the more redistributive European tax-and-benefit systems; aside from annual fluctuations, the increase in EU15-wide inequality in the past decade parallels that observed in the United States.

In brief, the EA income inequality has tended to grow as integration has deepened and in particular since the adoption of the common currency. However, the parallel trend of inequality in the United States and the similar patterns in Sweden and Finland, two countries which differ in terms of participation in the monetary union, hint that the story may be more complicated. Our brief review of the inequality literature underlines the importance of national policy choices, such as those aimed at stimulating economic growth and keeping public finances under control through, for example, more flexible labour markets and more limited government redistribution. These policies started to be implemented before the deepening of the integration process and also in countries not necessarily involved in it, although sharing the common EU policy framework might have sustained the process.

The European perspective provides further insights. For example, based on the standard practice of setting national poverty thresholds, the number of low-income Europeans is estimated to have increased from 80 million to 86 million between 2005 and 2015. With a common EU-wide threshold, the measured number of low-income people would turn out to be substantially higher but would have also shown a fall from 122 million to 112 million during the same period. Thus, using a common European benchmark would signal some progress in reducing the at-risk-of-poverty rate rather than the deterioration shown by standard measures. The change in perspective naturally leads to a reassessment of who belongs to certain segments of the income distribution and, in turn, to a reconsideration of the association between individual characteristics and socio-economic status such as, for example, being at risk of poverty.

All this has to do with the *analytical* insights that can be derived from adopting the European perspective. Our main contention is that the reason for taking this perspective is *foundational*, as it follows naturally from the rationale of European integration.

Deep political motivations are traditionally seen as lying at the roots of the project of European integration initiated in the aftermath of World War II—'the response to the trauma and demons of the two halves of the twentieth century' (Fabbrini, 2015: 3). As recently stated, 'A complete EMU is not an end in itself. It is a means to create a better and fairer life for all citizens, to prepare the Union for future global challenges and to enable each of its members to prosper' (Juncker, 2015: 2). However, superior motivations aside, the core of the project has constantly been the much more mundane formation of a common market. Even recently, the Four Presidents' Report (Van Rompuy, 2012) and the Five Presidents' Report (Juncker, 2015) attempted to revive the integration project by outlining interventions almost exclusively in the economic sphere. Once more the economic objectives appear to prevail on the social dimension. As Sen noted long ago, it is surprising how these instrumental objectives overshadow the underlying 'bigger objectives that involve social commitment to the well-being and basic freedoms of the involved population' (1996: 33).

In fact, the social dimension has not been missing from the European policy discourse. An EU social policy has existed for decades. It has taken diverse forms: an extensive and long-standing activity of regulation in various fields (labour law, working condition, safety at the workplace, gender equality, etc.), a limited redistribution through various community programmes (e.g., the European Social Fund, the European Globalization Adjustment Fund), and a mutual evaluation of national policies through the open method of coordination (Daly, 2006; Falkner, 2010). The Lisbon European Council of 2000 declared the strategic goal of 'greater social cohesion' and the commitment to taking steps 'to make a decisive impact on the eradication of poverty' (Council of the European Union, 2000). Ten years later, the Europe 2020 strategy has gone even further by making poverty reduction a priority, with a well-defined quantitative target to be achieved by 2020 (European Commission, 2010). The income quintile ratio is among the overarching indicators used to monitor social progress. In November 2017, the EU leaders gathered at the Social Summit for fair jobs and growth in Gothenburg proclaimed the European Pillar of Social Rights expressing 'principles and rights essential for fair and well-functioning labour markets and welfare systems in 21st century Europe' (European Parliament, Council of the European Union and European Commission, 2017: 8).

Nevertheless, the improvement of the well-being of European citizens is seen as flowing naturally from achieving the economic targets of the single market. This view not only underlies documents such as the Five Presidents' Report but also informs the whole policy discourse, a good example being the primacy attributed to raising employment among the policies to combat poverty, despite the little association observed between household jobless rates and relative income poverty ratios.[12] Once the conditions for a properly functioning single European market are laid down, the attainment of social objectives is entirely left to national policies, subject to limitations due to EU membership. Even the mutual surveillance mechanism is much softer than the one envisaged for macroeconomic imbalances. As explained by the European Commission, the Macroeconomic Imbalance Procedure 'endeavours to both avoid the accumulation of unsustainable trends or vulnerabilities and ensure a proper adjustment of existing imbalances' in order to preserve *macroeconomic stability*: 'The main rationale for a supra-national surveillance mandate builds on the fact that macroeconomic imbalances and economic policies in one country have relevance also for other Member States' (2016: 7–8). There is no corresponding supranational attempt to preserve *macrosocial stability*.

It could be argued that the separation between the supranational economic dimension and the national social dimension was the only practicable way of pushing forward European integration, given the diversity of EU Member States' societies and institutions. On the other hand, this approach is bound to reinforce an intrinsic tension between economic integration and nation-based welfare states. As observed by Ferrera, 'based as it is on the logic of economic opening, European integration is programmatically geared towards the expansion of individual option and choices, often challenging those closure conditions that sustain social solidarity [i.e., a clearly demarcated and cohesive community]. Therefore, it is no surprise that ordinary citizens remain 'nationalist' when asked about the latter and express a preference for keeping the EU away from this sphere' (2005: 2). Moreover, this separation is likely to indirectly back up views that the EU integration process is to be blamed for growing economic insecurity and inequalities, for instance, because of the limits imposed on national governments in carrying out independent fiscal policies. These are commonly held views in the political conjuncture of the late 2010s, but they contributed to slow the approval of the European constitution already in the early 2000s. As presciently noted by Bertola, the risk is that 'economic integration may be politically unsustainable if it results in less generous inequality-preventing independent social policies but does not foster the higher productivity which deregulation promises when markets work well' (2010: 362).

Forgoing the hierarchical separation between economic and social dimensions and taking a supranational view of the EU social condition could ease these tensions. This approach would better capture not only the narrative of European integration but also the spirit of Article 2 of the Treaty of Lisbon, the constitutional basis of the European Union, according to which the Union 'shall promote economic, social and territorial cohesion, and solidarity among Member States'. Consistently with this view, in this chapter, we have adopted the EU-wide approach to the measurement of inequality and poverty. It is a way to deal with the

---

12   See de Beer (2007), Cantillon (2011), de Graaf-Zijl and Nolan (2011), Vandenbroucke and Vleminckx (2011) and Marx et al. (2012).

decoupling between macroeconomic convergence and inequality.[13] It is admittedly a short step, but it signals a radical change in perspective to evaluate progress toward greater social cohesion.

ACKNOWLEDGEMENTS

Earlier drafts of this chapter were presented at the 56th Annual Conference of the Italian Economic Association (Naples, 22 October 2015), the Department of Economics and the European Union Centre of Excellence of Dalhousie University (Halifax, Nova Scotia, 12 February 2016), the book-project workshop 'Europe Volume – Global Trends in Income, Wealth, Consumption, Wellbeing and Inequality' (Paris, 20 April 2017), the 35th IARIW General Conference (Copenhagen, 20–25 August 2018), the 3rd Workshop of the EC's Community of Practice on Fairness 'Income Inequality and Its Policy Determinants – Beyond a MS-Level Analysis' (Brussels, 11 September 2018), and the workshop 'Economic and Social Inequality in Europe' (Ravenna, 12 October 2018). In addition to participants in these meetings, we are indebted to Georg Fischer, Marco Magnani, Wiemer Salverda, Robert Strauss, Roberto Tedeschi, and John Verrinder for many valuable comments. We thank Luis Ayala Cañon, Zsombor Cseres-Gergely, Stefano Filauro, Fabrice Murtin, Andrew Sharpe, and Francesco Vercelli for sharing their estimates with us, and Wim Bos for explanations about the Dutch official inequality statistics. The views expressed here are solely those of the authors; in particular, they do not necessarily reflect those of the Bank of Italy or the Eurosystem.

REFERENCES

Aaberge, R., Langørgen, A., and Lindgren, P. (2010). The impact of basic public services on the distribution of income in European countries. In A. B. Atkinson and E. Marlier (eds.), *Income and living conditions in Europe* (pp. 329–344). Luxembourg: Publications Office of the European Union.

Alvaredo, F., and Saez, E. (2009). Income and wealth concentration in Spain from a historical and fiscal perspective. *Journal of the European Economic Association, 7*(5), 1140–1167.

---

13 In his agenda for a reformed European cohesion policy, prepared for the Commissioner for Regional Policy, Barca suggested to partially overcome this decoupling by bringing together social and territorial objectives into a 'territorialized social agenda', which is 'focused on individuals but aware that their well-being and the effectiveness of any intervention depend on the place where they live' (2009: XIII).

Anand, S., and Segal, P. (2008). What do we know about global income inequality? *Journal of Economic Literature, 46*(1), 57–94.

Anand, S., and Segal, P. (2015). The global distribution of income. In A. B. Atkinson and F. Bourguignon (eds.), *Handbook of income distribution (Vol. 2A) (pp. 937–979)*. Amsterdam: Elsevier.

Anand, S., and Sen, A. K. (2000). The income component of the human development index. *Journal of Human Development, 1*(1), 83–106.

Anderson, G., Pittau, M. G., Zelli, R., and Thomas, J. (2018). Income inequality. cohesiveness and commonality in the euro area: A semi-parametric boundary-free analysis. *Econometrics, 6*(2), art. 15.

Andrews, B., Palesch, N., and Thomas, J. (2015). *Estimation of EU-comparable poverty-related variables in the United States, 1995–2014*. CSLS Research Reports, 2015–12. Ottawa: Centre for the Study of Living Standards.

Atkinson, A. B. (1995). Poverty, statistics and progress in Europe. In A. B. Atkinson (ed.), *Income and the welfare state. Essays on Britain and Europe*: 64–77. Cambridge: Cambridge University Press.

Atkinson, A. B. (1996). Income distribution in Europe and the United States. *Oxford Review of Economic Policy, 12*(1), 15–28.

Atkinson, A. B. (1997). Bringing income distribution in from the cold. *Economic Journal, 107*(441), 297–321.

Atkinson, A. B. (1998). *Poverty in Europe*. Oxford: Blackwell.

Atkinson, A. B. (2003). Income inequality in OECD countries: Data and explanations. *CESifo Economic Studies, 49*(4), 479–513.

Atkinson, A. B. (2008). *The changing distribution of earnings in OECD countries*. Oxford: Oxford University Press.

Atkinson, A. B. (2013). Ensuring social inclusion in changing labour and capital markets. European Commission, Directorate-General for Economic and Financial Affairs. Economic Papers 481.

Atkinson, A. B. (2017). *Monitoring global poverty. Report of the Commission on Global Poverty*. Washington, DC: World Bank.

Atkinson, A. B., Guio, A.-C., and Marlier, E. (2017). Monitoring the evolution of income poverty and real incomes over time. In A. B. Atkinson, A.-C. Guio and E. Marlier (eds.), *Monitoring social inclusion in Europe* (pp. 65–88). Luxembourg: Publications Office of the European Union.

Atkinson, A. B., and Micklewright, J. (1983). On the reliability of income data in the Family Expenditure Survey 1970–1977. *Journal of the Royal Statistical Society*, Series A, *146*(1), 33–53.

Atkinson, A. B., and Micklewright, J. (1992). *Economic transformation in Eastern Europe and the distribution of income*. Cambridge: Cambridge University Press.

Ayala Cañon, L. (2016). La Desigualdad en España: Fuentes. Tendencias y Comparaciones Internacionales. Fedea, Estudios sobre la Economía Española 2016/24.

Bach, S., Corneo, G., and Steiner, V. (2009). From bottom to top: The entire income distribution in Germany. 1992–2003. *Review of Income and Wealth,* 55(2), 303–330.

Bach, S., Corneo, G., and Steiner, V. (2013). Effective taxation of top incomes in Germany. *German Economic Review, 14*(2), 115–137.

Barca, F. (2009). *An agenda for a reformed cohesion policy. A place-based approach to meeting European Union challenges and expectations.* Independent Report prepared at the request of Danuta Hübner, Commissioner for Regional Policy.

Bargain, O. (2012). The distributional effects of tax-benefit policies under new labour: A decomposition approach. *Oxford Bulletin of Economics and Statistics,* 74(6), 856–874.

Beblo, M., and Knaus, T. (2001). Measuring income inequality in Euroland. *Review of Income and Wealth, 47*(3), 301–320.

Becker, I. (1997). Die Entwicklung von Einkommensverteilung und Einkommensarmut in den alten Bundesländern von 1962 bis 1988. In I. Becker and R. Hauser (eds.), *Einkommensverteilung und Armut. Deutschland auf dem Weg zur Vierfünftel-Gesellschaft?* (pp. 43–61). Frankfurt: Campus.

Becker, I., Frick, J. R., Grabka, M. M., Hauser, R., Krause, P., and Wagner, G. G. (2003). A comparison of the main household income surveys for Germany: EVS and SOEP. In R. Hauser and I. Becker (eds.), *Reporting on income distribution and poverty* (pp. 55–90). Berlin-Heidelberg: Springer.

Beckfield, J. (2006). European integration and income inequality. *American Sociological Review, 71*(6), 964–985.

Beckfield, J. (2009). Remapping inequality in Europe: The net effect of regional integration on total income inequality in the European Union. *International Journal of Comparative Sociology, 50*(5–6), 486–509.

Behr, A., and Pötter, U. (2010). What determines wage differentials across the EU? *Journal of Economic Inequality, 8*(1), 101–120.

Belfield, C., Blundell, R., Cribb, J., Hood, A., and Joyce, R. (2017). Two decades of income inequality in Britain: The role of wages, household earnings and redistribution, *Economica, 84*(334), 157–179.

Benczúr, P., Cseres-Gergely, Z., and Harasztosi, P. (2017), *EU-wide income inequality in the era of the Great Recession.* JRC Working Papers in Economics and Finance 2017/14; Luxembourg: Publications Office of the European Union

Bertola, G. (2010). Inequality, integration, and policy: Issues and evidence from EMU. *Journal of Economic Inequality, 8*(3), 345–365.

Biewen, M. (2000). Income inequality in Germany during the 1980s and 1990s. *Review of Income and Wealth, 46*(1), 1–19.

Biewen, M., and Juhasz, A. (2012). Understanding rising income inequality in Germany. 1999/2000–2005/2006. *Review of Income and Wealth, 58*(4), 622–647.

Biewen, M., Ungerer, M., and Löffler, M. (2017). Why did income inequality in Germany not increase further after 2005? *German Economic Review, 20*(4), 471–504.

Blomgren, J., Hiilamo, H., Kangas, O., and Niemelä, M. (2014). Finland: Growing inequality with contested consequences. In B. Nolan, W. Salverda, D. Checchi, I. Marx, A. McKnight, I. G. Tóth, and H. G. van de Werfhorst (eds.), *Changing inequalities and societal impacts in rich countries: Thirty countries' experiences* (pp. 222–247). Oxford: Oxford University Press.

Boix, C. (2004). The institutional accomodation of an enlarged Europe. *Friedrich Ebert Stiftung. Europäische Politik, 6*, 1–9.

Bonesmo Fredriksen, K. (2012). *Income inequality in the European Union.* OECD Economics Department, Working Paper 952.

Bönke, T., and Schröder, C. (2014). European-wide inequality in times of the financial crisis. *Journal of Income Distribution, 23*(3-4), 7–34.

Bontout, O., Fulvimari, A., Salanauskaite, L., and Vaalavuo, M. (2016). Convergence and divergence in the E(M)U and the role of employment and social policies. In European Commission (ed.), *Employment and Social Development in Europe 2016* (pp. 45–80). Luxembourg: Publications Office of the European Union.

Bourguignon, F. (2015). Appraising income inequality databases in Latin America. *Journal of Economic Inequality, 13*(4), 557–578.

Brandolini, A. (1999). The distribution of personal income in post-war Italy: Source description, data quality, and the time pattern of income inequality. *Giornale degli economisti e Annali di economia, 58*(2), 183–239.

Brandolini, A. (2007). Measurement of income distribution in supranational entities: The Case of the European Union. In S. P. Jenkins and J. Micklewright (eds.), *Inequality and poverty re-examined* (pp. 62–83). Oxford: Oxford University Press.

Brandolini, A. (2008). Coesione sociale e distribuzione del reddito tra i cittadini dell'Unione Europea. In C. Gnesutta, G. M. Rey, and G. C. Romagnoli (eds.), *Capitale industriale e capitale finanziario nell'economia globale* (pp. 241–267). Bologna: Il Mulino.

Brandolini, A., and Carta, F. (2016). Some reflections on the social welfare bases of the measurement of global income inequality. *Journal of Globalization and Development, 7*(1), 1–15.

Brandolini, A., Gambacorta, R., and Rosolia, A. (2018). Inequality amid stagnation: Italy over the last quarter of a century. In B. Nolan (ed.), *Inequality and inclusive growth in rich countries: Shared challenges and contrasting fortunes* (pp. 188–220). Oxford: Oxford University Press.

Brandolini, A., and Rosolia, A. (2016). The euro area wage distribution over the crisis. In A. B. Atkinson, A.-C. Guio, and E. Marlier (eds.), *Monitoring social Europe* (pp. 317–332). Luxembourg: Publications Office of the European Union.

Brandolini, A., Rosolia, R., and Torrini, R. (2012). The EU-wide earnings distribution. In J. A. Bishop and R. Salas (eds.), *Inequality, mobility and segregation: Essays in honor of Jacques Silber (Research on Economic Inequality, Vol. 20)* (pp. 205–235). Bingley: Emerald.

Brandolini, A., and Smeeding, T. M. (2009). Income inequality in richer and OECD countries. In W. Salverda, B. Nolan, and T. M. Smeeding (eds.), *The Oxford handbook of economic inequality* (pp. 71–100). Oxford: Oxford University Press.

Cantillon, B. (2011). The paradox of the social investment state: Growth, employment and poverty in the Lisbon era. *Journal of European Social Policy, 21*(5), 432–449.

Caselli, F., Centeno, M., Novo, A., and Tavares, J. (2016). The challenge of European inequality. In F. Caselli, M. Centeno, and J. Tavares (eds.), *After the crisis: Reform, recovery, and growth in Europe* (pp. 171–193). Oxford: Oxford University Press.

Corneo, G., Zmerli, S., and Pollak, R. (2014). Germany: Rising inequality and the transformation of Rhine capitalism. In B. Nolan, W. Salverda, D. Checchi, I. Marx, A. McKnight, I. G. Tóth, and H. G. van de Werfhorst (eds.), *Changing inequalities and societal impacts in rich countries. Thirty countries' experiences* (pp. 271–298). Oxford: Oxford University Press.

Council of the European Union. (2000). *Presidency Conclusions.* Lisbon European Council 23–24 March 2000.

Daly, M. (2006). EU social policy after Lisbon. *Journal of Common Market Studies, 44*(3), 461–481.

Darvas, Z. (2016). Some are more equal than others: New estimates of global and regional inequality. Bruegel, Working Paper 8.

Dauderstädt, M., and Keltek, C. (2011). Immeasurable inequality in the European Union. *Intereconomics, 46*(1), 44–51.

Deaton, A. (2005). Measuring poverty in a growing world (or measuring growth in a poor world). *Review of Economics and Statistics, 87*(1), 1–19.

de Beer, P. (2007). Why work is not a panacea: A decomposition analysis of EU-15 countries. *Journal of European Social Policy, 17*(4), 375–388.

de Graaf-Zijl, M., and Nolan, B. (2011). Household joblessness and its impact on poverty and deprivation in Europe. *Journal of European Social Policy, 21*(5), 413–431.

Delhey, J., and Kohler, U. (2006). From nationally bounded to pan-european inequalities? On the importance of foreign countries as reference groups. *European Sociological Review, 22*(2), 125–140.

de Vos, K., and Zaidi, M. A. (1999). Poverty measurement in the European Union: Country-specific or union-specific poverty lines? *Journal of Income Distribution, 8*(1), 77–92.

de Vries, K., and Erumban, A. A. (2017). *Total economy database. A detailed guide to its sources and methods.* Mimeo. New York: The Conference Board.

Eriksson, I., and Pettersson, T. (2000). Income distribution and income mobility: Recent trends in Sweden. In R. Hauser and I. Becker (eds.), *The personal distribution of income in an international perspective* (pp. 158–175). Berlin: Springer.

Eurofound. (2015). *Recent developments in the distribution of wages in Europe*, prepared by E. Fernández-Macías and C. Vacas-Soriano. Luxembourg: Publications Office of the European Union.

European Commission. (2010). *Europe 2020. A strategy for smart, sustainable and inclusive growth.* COM(2010) 2020 final.

European Commission. (2016). *The macroeconomic imbalance procedure: Rationale, process, application: A compendium.* Directorate-General for Economic and Financial Affairs, European Economy, Institutional Paper 039. Luxembourg: Publications Office of the European Union.

European Parliament, Council of the European Union and European Commission. (2017). *European Pillar of Social Rights.* Luxembourg: Publications Office of the European Union.

Eurostat. (2012). *Eurostat-OECD Methodological Manual on Purchasing Power Parities.* Luxembourg: Publications Office of the European Union.

Eurostat. (2017). Income and living conditions (ILC). Reference Metadata in Euro SDMX Metadata Structure (ESMS). Compiling agency: Eurostat, the statistical office of the European Union. Last updated 17 October 2017. https://ec.europa.eu/eurostat/cache/metadata/en/ilc_esms.htm.

Fabbrini, S. (2015). *Which European Union? Europe after the euro crisis.* Cambridge: Cambridge University Press.

Fábián, Z., Gábos, A., Kopasz, M., Medgyesi, M., Szivós, P., and Tóth, I. G. (2014). Hungary: A country caught in its own trap. In B. Nolan, W. Salverda, D. Checchi, I. Marx, A. McKnight, I. G. Tóth, and H. G. van de Werfhorst (eds.), *Changing inequalities and societal impacts in rich countries. Thirty countries' experiences* (pp. 322–345). Oxford: Oxford University Press.

Fahey, T. (2007). The case for an EU-wide measure of poverty. *European Sociological Review, 23*(1), 35–47.

Fahey, T., Whelan, C. T., and Maître, B. (2005). *First European quality of life survey: Income inequalities and deprivation.* European Foundation for the Improvement of Living and Working Conditions. Luxembourg: Office for Official Publications of the European Communities.

Falkner, G. (2010). European Union. In F. G. Castles, S. Leibfried, J. Lewis, H. Obinger, and C. Pierson (eds.), *The Oxford handbook of the welfare state* (pp. 293–305). Oxford: Oxford University Press.

Feenstra, R. C., Inklaar, R., and Timmer, M. P. (2015). The next generation of the Penn World Table. *American Economic Review, 105*(10), 3150–3182.

Ferrera, M. (2005). *The boundaries of welfare: European integration and the new spatial politics of social protection.* Oxford: Oxford University Press.

Ferrer-i-Carbonell, A., Ramos, X., and Oviedo, M. (2014). What can we learn from past decreasing inequalities? In B. Nolan, W. Salverda, D. Checchi, I. Marx, A. McKnight, I. G. Tóth, and H. G. van de Werfhorst (eds.), *Changing* inequalities and societal impacts in rich countries. Thirty countries' experiences (pp. 616–640). Oxford: Oxford University Press.

Filauro, S. (2018). The EU-wide income distribution: Inequality levels and decompositions. Luxembourg: Publications Office of the European Union.

Filauro, S., and Parolin, Z. (2019). Unequal unions? A comparative decomposition of income inequality in the European Union and United States. Journal of European Social Policy, 29(4), 545–563.

Förster, M. F. (2005). The European social space revisited: Comparing poverty in the enlarged European Union. Journal of Comparative Policy Analysis, 7(1), 29–48.

Frémeaux, N., and Piketty, T. (2014). France: How taxation can increase inequality. In B. Nolan, W. Salverda, D. Checchi, I. Marx, A. McKnight, I. G. Tóth, and H. G. van de Werfhorst (eds.), Changing inequalities and societal impacts in rich countries: Thirty countries' experiences (pp. 248–270). Oxford: Oxford University Press.

Fritzell, J., Bacchus Hertzman, J., Bäckman, O., Borg, I., Ferrarini, T., and Nelson, K. (2014). Sweden: Increasing income inequalities and changing social relations. In B. Nolan, W. Salverda, D. Checchi, I. Marx, A. McKnight, I. G. Tóth, and H. G. van de Werfhorst (eds.), Changing inequalities and societal impacts in rich countries: Thirty countries' experiences (pp. 641–665). Oxford: Oxford University Press.

Fuchs-Schündeln, N., Krueger, D., and Sommer, M. (2010). Inequality trends for Germany in the last two decades: A tale of two countries. Review of Economic Dynamics, 13(1), 103–132.

Goedemé, T., and Collado, D. (2016). The EU convergence machine at work: To the benefit of the EU's poorest citizens? JCMS: Journal of Common Market Studies, 54(5), 1142–1158.

Goedemé, T., and Rottiers, S. (2011). Poverty in the enlarged European Union: A discussion about definitions and reference groups. Sociology Compass, 5(1), 77–91.

Goedemé, T., Trindade, L. Z., and Vandenbroucke, F. (2019). A Pan-European perspective on low-income dynamics in the European Union. In B. Cantillon, T. Goedemé, and J. Hills (eds.), Decent incomes for all: Improving policies in Europe (pp. 56–82). Oxford: Oxford University Press.

Grabka, M. M., Goebel, J., and Schupp, J. (2012). Has income inequality spiked in Germany? DIW Economic Bulletin, 2(12), 3–14.

Guio, A.-C. (2005). Material deprivation in the EU. Eurostat, Statistics in focus, Population and Social Conditions, 21. https://ec.europa.eu/eurostat/web/products-statistics-in-focus/-/KS-NK-05-021.

Gustafsson, B., and Palmer, E. (1997). Changes in Swedish inequality: A study of equivalent income, 1975–1991. In P. Gottschalk, B. Gustafsson, and E. Palmer (eds.), Changing patterns in the distribution of economic welfare: An international perspective (pp. 293–325). Cambridge: Cambridge University Press.

Gustafsson, B., and Uusitalo, H. (1990). Income distribution and redistribution during two decades: Experiences from Finland and Sweden. In I. Persson (ed.), *Generating equality in the welfare state: The Swedish experience* (pp. 73–95). Oslo: Norwegian University Press.

Heidenreich, M., and Härpfer, M. (2011). On the measurement of 'immeasurable inequality'. Comment on the article by Michael Dauderstädt and Cem Keltek in Intereconomics No. 1/2011. *Intereconomics, 46*(2), 106–108.

Heidenreich, M., and Wunder, C. (2008). Patterns of regional inequality in the enlarged Europe. *European Sociological Review, 24*(1), 19–36.

Hoffmeister, O. (2009). The spatial structure of income inequality in the enlarged EU. *Review of Income and Wealth, 55*(1), 101–127.

Jäntti, M., Riihelä, M., Sullström, R., and Tuomala, M. (2010). Trends in top income shares in Finland. In A. B. Atkinson and Thomas Piketty (eds.), *Top incomes: A global perspective* (pp. 371–447). Oxford: Oxford University Press.

Jenkins, S. P. (1995). Accounting for inequality trends: Decomposition analyses for the UK, 1971–86. *Economica, 62*(245), 29–63.

Jenkins, S. P. (1996). Recent trends in the UK income distribution: What happened and why? *Oxford Review of Economic Policy, 12*(1), 29–46.

Jenkins, S. P. (2020). Perspectives on poverty in Europe. Following in Tony Atkinson's Footsteps, *Italian Economic Journal, 6*(1), 129–155.

Jenkins, S. P., Brandolini, A., Micklewright, J., and Nolan, B., with the assistance of Basso, G. (2013). The Great Recession and its consequences for household incomes in 21 countries. In S. P. Jenkins, A. Brandolini, J. Micklewright, and B. Nolan (eds.), *The great recession and the distribution of household income* (pp. 33–89). Oxford: Oxford University Press.

Johnson, P., and Webb, S. (1993). Explaining the growth in UK income inequality: 1979–1988. *Economic Journal, 103*(417), 429–435.

Juncker, J.-C. in close cooperation with Tusk, D., Dijsselbloem, J., Draghi, M., and Schulz, M. (2015). *Completing Europe's economic and monetary union.*

Kahanec, M., Guzi, M., Martišková, M., and Siebertová, Z. (2014). Slovakia and the Czech Republic: Inequalities and convergences after the velvet divorce. In B. Nolan, W. Salverda, D. Checchi, I. Marx, A. McKnight, I. G. Tóth, and H. G. van de Werfhorst (eds.), *Changing inequalities and societal impacts in rich countries: Thirty countries' experiences* (pp. 567–592). Oxford: Oxford University Press.

Kangas, O. E., and Ritakallio, V.-M. (2007). Relative to what?: Cross-national picture of European poverty measured by regional, national and European standards. *European Societies, 9*(2), 119–145.

Letki, N., Brzeziński, M., and Jancewicz, B. (2014). The rise of inequalities in Poland and their impacts. When politicians don't care but citizens do. In B. Nolan, W. Salverda, D. Checchi, I. Marx, A. McKnight, I. G. Tóth, and H. G. van de Werfhorst (eds.), *Changing inequalities and societal impacts in rich countries: Thirty countries' experiences* (pp. 488–513). Oxford: Oxford University Press.

Lindner, P. (2015). Factor decomposition of the wealth distribution in the euro area. *Empirica, 42*(2), 291–322.

Maddison, A. (2001). *The world economy: A millennial perspective.* Paris: Organisation for Economic Co-operation and Development.

Maquet, I. (2015). *High and rising inequalities: What can be done about it (at EU level)?* In collaboration with E. Meyermans and M. Duiella, Analytical Web Note 6. Luxembourg: Publications Office of the European Union.

Marx, I., Vandenbroucke, P., and Verbist, G. (2012). Can higher employment levels bring down relative income poverty in the EU? Regression-based simulations of the Europe 2020 target. *Journal of European Social Policy, 22*(5), 472–486.

Milanovic, B. (2005). *Worlds apart: Measuring international and global inequality.* Princeton: Princeton University Press.

Morrisson, C., and Murtin, F. (2004). *History and prospects of inequality among Europeans.* Mimeo, provided by the authors.

Muffels, R., and Nelissen, J. (1997). The distribution of economic well-being in the Netherlands, its evolution in the 1980s and the role of demographic change. In P. Gottschalk, B. Gustafsson, and E. Palmer (eds.), *Changing patterns in the distribution of economic welfare: An international perspective* (pp. 265–292). Cambridge: Cambridge University Press.

Nolan, B., and Whelan, C. T. (2011). *Poverty and deprivation in Europe.* Oxford: Oxford University Press.

Papatheodorou, C., and Pavlopoulos, D. (2014). Income inequality in the EU: How do member states contribute? *International Journal of Social Economics, 41*(6), 450–466.

Pereira, J., and Galego, A. (2018). Inter-country wage differences in the European Union. *International Labour Review, 157*(1), 101–128.

Perugini, C., and Pompei, F. (2016). Employment protection and wage inequality: Within education groups in Europe. *Journal of Policy Modeling, 38*(5), 810–836.

Pijoan-Mas, J., and Sánchez-Marcos, V. (2010). Spain is different: Falling trends of inequality. *Review of Economic Dynamics, 13*(1), 154–178.

Piketty, T. (2003). Income inequality in France, 1901–1998. *Journal of Political Economy, 111*(5), 1004–1042.

Rodríguez-Pose, A., and Tselios, V. (2009). Mapping regional personal income distribution in Western Europe: Income per capita and inequality. *Finance a úvěr-Czech Journal of Economics and Finance, 59*(1), 41–70.

Roine, J., and Waldenström, D. (2008). The evolution of top incomes in an egalitarian society: Sweden, 1903–2004. *Journal of Public Economics, 92*(1–2), 366–387.

Salverda, W. (2017). *Top incomes and income inequality in the Netherlands: The first 100 Years 1914–2014*: What's next? Mimeo. AIAS, University of Amsterdam. https://wid.world/document/top-incomes-income-and-wealth-inequality-in-the-netherlands-the-first-100-years-1914-2014-whats-next-wid-world-wp-2-2019/

Salverda, W., de Graaf-Zijl, M., Haas, C., Lancee, B., and Notten, N. (2014). The Netherlands: Policy-enhanced inequalities tempered by household formation. In B. Nolan, W. Salverda, D. Checchi, I. Marx, A. McKnight, I. G. Tóth, and H. G. van de Werfhorst (eds.), *Changing inequalities and societal impacts in rich countries: Thirty countries' experiences* (pp. 459–487). Oxford: Oxford University Press.

Sen, A. K. (1996). Social commitment and democracy: The demands of equity and financial conservatism. In P. Barker (ed.), *Living as equals* (pp. 9–38). Oxford: Oxford University Press.

Smeeding, T. M., and Rainwater, L. (2004). Comparing living standards across nations: Real incomes at the top, the bottom, and the middle. In E. N. Wolff (ed.), *What has happened to the quality of life in the advanced industrialized nations?* (pp. 153–183). Northampton: Elgar.

SOEP Group. (2015). *SOEP 2013 – SOEPmonitor Individuals 1984–2013 (SOEP v30)*. SOEP Survey Papers 284 (Series E). Berlin: DIW/SOEP.

Solt, F. (2016). The standardized world income inequality database. *Social Science Quarterly, 97*(5), 1267–1281.

Szulc, A. (2006). Poverty in Poland during the 1990s: Are the results robust? *Review of Income and Wealth, 52*(3), 423–448.

Troitiño Cobas, A. (2007). Income inequality in the EU15 and member countries. In J. Bishop and Y. Amiel (eds.), *Inequality and poverty (Research on economic inequality, Vol. 14)* (pp. 119–136). Bingley: Emerald.

Uusitalo, H. (1989). *Income distribution in Finland. The effects of the welfare state and the structural changes in society on income distribution in Finland in 1966–1985,* Studies 148. Helsinki: Central Statistical Office of Finland.

Vacas-Soriano, C. (2018). The 'Great Recession' and low pay in Europe. *European Journal of Industrial Relations, 24*(3), 205–220.

Van Rompuy, H. in close collaboration with Barroso, M. J., Juncker, J.-C., and Draghi, M. (2012). *Towards a genuine economic and monetary union.*

Vandenbroucke, F., and Vleminckx, K. (2011). Disappointing poverty trends: Is the social investment state to blame? *Journal of European Social Policy, 21*(5), 450–471.

Vercelli, F. (2018). *The evolution of inequality and social cohesion in Europe: 1957–2014.* Banca d'Italia, Occasional Papers n. 526.

Wang, J., Caminada, K., Goudswaard, K., and Wang, C. (2018). Income polarization in European countries and Europe wide, 2004–2012. *Cambridge Journal of Economics, 42*(3), 797–816.

Whelan, C. T., and Maître, B. (2009a). Europeanization of inequality and European reference groups. *Journal of European Social Policy, 19*(2), 117–130.

Whelan, C. T., and Maître, B. (2009b). The 'Europeanisation' of reference groups. A reconsideration using EU-SILC. *European Societies, 11*(2), 283–309.

Whelan, C. T., and Maître, B (2010). Comparing poverty indicators in an enlarged European Union. *European Sociological Review, 26*(6), 713–730.

APPENDIX 2.1 DATA SOURCES AND MEASUREMENT DEFINITIONS

We draw national accounts data from three sources: the Conference Board Total Economy Database (version November 2018), the Penn World Table (version 9.0), and the Eurostat website (Tables nama_10_gdp, nama_10_pe, nasa_10_nf_tr; January 2019). The first two sources contain GDP estimates expressed in international dollars whose real value is comparable across times and countries thanks to the use of PPPs. PPPs account for differences in price structures across countries and generally raise measured living standards in poorer countries, where labour-intensive nontradable services are typically cheaper than in rich countries. PPP indices differ in their underlying methodology, which in turn reflects alternative ways of summarizing the bilateral price comparisons between all pairs of countries. Maddison (2001) and the Conference Board apply the *EKS method*, named after Eltetö, Köves, and Szulc (de Vries and Erumban, 2017), whereas the Penn World Table favours the *GK method*, named after Geary and Khamis (Feenstra et al., 2015). These methodological differences can account for the diverse aggregate patterns revealed by the two sources (compare Figure 2.2 with Figure 2.A1 in this Appendix).

The EKS method is also applied by Eurostat (2012) to provide the conversion rates from national currencies to an artificial common currency labelled Purchasing Power Standard (PPS). Incomes in PPS are normalized in such a way that they have the purchasing power of 1 euro in the average of the European Union (or some specific EU subgroup). Eurostat releases PPP indices for various national account aggregates, including GDP and HFCE. The PPP index for HFCE might be preferable for real income comparisons across persons because it measures purchasing power in terms of consumption goods and services, while GDP covers items, such as in-kind transfers for education and healthcare, which are generally not included in the household disposable income as measured in surveys (Smeeding and Rainwater, 2004). PPP indices adjust for cross-country differences in price levels but not for their changes over time. Hence, we convert nominal household incomes to real values in two steps. First, we adjust for cross-country price-level differences by dividing all nominal values in national currency by the annual PPP for HFCE for the EU28. Second, we deflate these adjusted nominal values by the annual HFCE implicit deflator (covering also NPISH) for the EU28 to express all values at the 2010 prices for the whole EU28

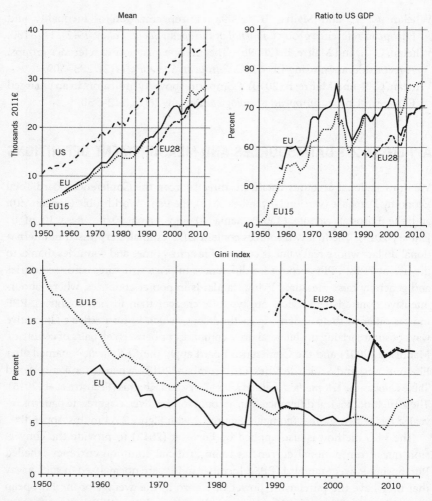

Figure 2.A1 Real gross domestic product (GDP) per capita in EU, EU28, EU15, and United States (1950–2015).

Source: Authors' elaboration on data from Penn World Table, version 9.0. The figures for West Germany in 1958–1990 are obtained by rescaling the total for Germany based on separate figures for West and East Germany from the Conference Board Total Economy Database™, May 2016. Real GDP is obtained by applying the GK method; original values in millions of 2011 US$ at chained purchasing power parities are converted into 2011 euros by multiplying for the exchange rate in 2011 (0.719€/$). EU: totals for actual EU member countries; EU15: totals for the 15 countries that formed the EU in 1995–2003; EU28: totals for the 28 countries that form the EU since July 2013. The vertical lines indicate the changes in EU membership. All estimates are population-weighted values.

(as in Brandolini and Rosolia, 2016). PPPs are drawn from Table prc_ppp_ind in the Eurostat website.

The distributions of real incomes in the EU countries are calculated on data from the EU-SILC public use file CROSS UDB 2005–2017, version of October 2017. This release covers all 28 Member States. However, to maximize time coverage, we exclude Croatia, which joined the project only in 2010, and we approximate the missing data for Bulgaria, Malta, and Romania in 2005 by duplicating the wave for 2006 (after deflating all income values by the change between 2005 and 2006 in the national nominal household disposable income per capita). Hence, our EU28 aggregate actually refers to 27 countries. The income reference period is the whole calendar year preceding the interview in all countries except Ireland, where it is the 12 months immediately prior to the interview, and the United Kingdom, where it is the calendar year of the interview. While for Irish data there is no straightforward solution, for British data we depart from the Eurostat practice of reporting information from the same wave, and we take the previous wave (as in Filauro, 2018; Filauro and Parolin, 2019).

We focus exclusively on equivalized total disposable income (variable HX090), which accounts for age-related changes in needs and economies of scale in consumption by applying the modified Organisation for Economic Cooperation and Development (OECD) scale recommended by Eurostat. This scale assigns value 1 to the first adult, 0.5 to any other person aged 14 or older, and 0.3 to each child younger than 14. We attribute the equivalized household income to all persons living in the household. Household income is the sum of the incomes received by all household members less tax on income and social insurance contributions, regular taxes on wealth, and regular interhousehold cash transfer paid. In detail, income includes gross cash, near-cash and non-cash employee income; gross cash profits or losses from self-employment (including royalties); interests, dividends, profit from capital investments in unincorporated business; pension from individual private plans; social benefits (unemployment benefits, old-age benefits, survivors' benefits, sickness benefits, disability benefits, education-related allowances, family- and children-related allowances, housing allowances, and social exclusion not elsewhere classified); income from rental of a property or land (excluding imputed rents on owner-occupied dwellings); and regular interhousehold cash transfers received.

To convert nominal incomes to real values, we apply the same two-step procedure described earlier for aggregate data. First, taking into account that the variable HX090 in the EU-SILC user database is expressed in euros, we divide it by the annual Price Level Index (PLI) for HFCE instead of the PPP index. The PLIs are calculated by dividing the PPPs by the current nominal exchange rates and express the price level of each country relative to the EU28. As with the PPPs, the PLIs are drawn from Table prc_ppp. Second, we deflate these adjusted nominal values by the annual HFCE implicit deflator (covering also NPISH) for the EU28 to express all values at the 2010 prices for the whole EU28.

The impact of these adjustments on income levels and their changes is shown in Figure 2.A2. Each panel reports the GICs for different price adjustments for

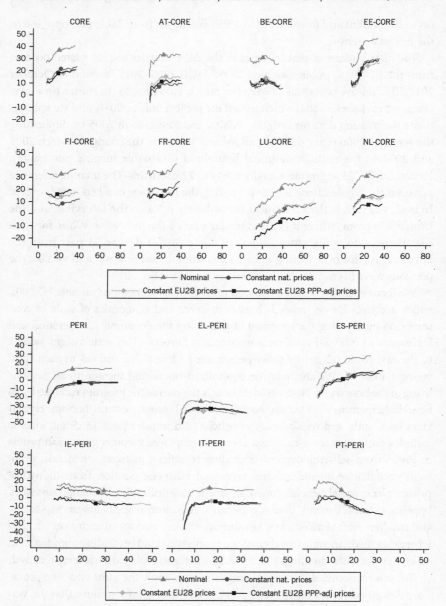

Figure 2.A2 Growth incidence curves for country groups and Member States (2005–2015).
Source: Authors' elaboration on data from EU Statistics on Income and Living Conditions (EU-SILC) CROSS UDB 2005–2017 (version of October 2017), excluding Croatia. The figure displays, for each country or country group, the percentage cumulated growth rates between 2005 and 2015 (y-axis) for every percentile of the distribution of equivalized disposable household income among individuals against their value (in purchasing power standards) in 2005 (x-axis); only percentiles 3 to 97 are reported. CORE: Austria, Belgium, Finland, France, Germany, Luxembourg, the Netherlands; PERI: Greece, Ireland, Italy, Portugal, Spain; EUNEA: Denmark, Sweden, the UK; NEU15: Bulgaria, Cyprus, Czech Republic, Estonia, Hungary, Latvia, Lithuania, Malta, Poland, Romania, Slovakia, Slovenia.

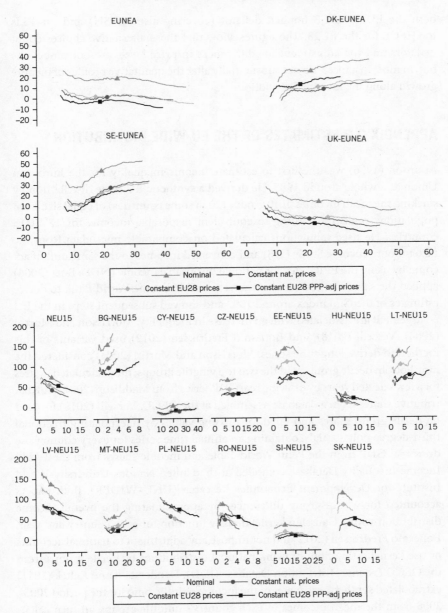

Figure 2.A2 Continued

each country or group of countries. We report the cumulated growth rates of equivalized incomes between 2005 and 2015 in nominal terms (unadjusted), adjusted for the national HFCE implicit deflator (covering also NPISH), adjusted for the EU28 HFCE implicit deflator (covering also NPISH), and adjusted for both the EU28 HFCE implicit deflator (covering also NPISH) and the PLIs for HFCE for the EU28. The figures show that these alternative choices about deflators and the adjustment for differences in price levels are not innocuous but, in most instances, do not substantially alter the qualitative profiles of income growth along the income distribution.

APPENDIX 2.2 ESTIMATES OF THE EU-WIDE DISTRIBUTION

Atkinson (1996) was the first to estimate income inequality for the European Union as a whole around 1985. He derived a synthetic EU-wide distribution by stacking the mean incomes of 40 groups (20 in some countries) of equal size from populations ranked according to equivalent disposable income, for 12 EU15 countries. He used tabulations calculated on comparable microdata from the Luxembourg Income Study (LIS) and converted incomes to the same unit of account by using the PPP index for national disposable income (NDI). Boix (2004) applied the same method to tabulations assembled at the World Bank to derive estimates of the Gini index around 1993 and showed subsequent steps in the EU enlargement are associated with an increase in inequality. Morrisson and Murtin (2004), Vercelli (2018), and Bonesmo Fredriksen (2012) used variants of this method to derive long time series. Morrisson and Murtin (2004) considered the nine bottom decile groups and the two top vingtile groups; they calculated figures for a few selected years by drawing real GDP series from Maddison (2001) and distributive shares from a database assembled at the OECD. Vercelli (2018) focused on decile group shares and filled for missing values by interpolating fractional third-degree polynomials, obtaining an annual time series for every country; he drew real GDP from the Penn World Table and income shares from the World Income Inequality Database compiled at the United Nations University-World Institute for Development Economics Research (UNU-WIDER). Both papers accounted for within-group differences by approximating the overall income distribution with a Gaussian kernel density function for each country and year. Bonesmo Fredriksen (2012) did not impose any adjustment to national accounts or use kernel estimation, drawing national distributions by decile groups from the OECD Income Distribution Database (IDD). Dauderstädt and Keltek (2011) extrapolated synthetic estimates of the income quintile ratio for the period 2005–2008 from the mean incomes of each country's quintile groups, in turn calculated from deciles drawn from EU-SILC. Darvas (2016) applied a parametric version of the synthetic approach. He estimated national income distributions by calibrating two-parameter distributions with the observed values of the mean and Gini index. He considered both deterministic and stochastic estimates of lognormal, Pareto, and Weibull distributions for a total of nine sets of estimates, which turned out to be very similar each other. He drew the Gini index from the Standardized World Income Inequality Database (SWIID) of Solt (2016) and adjusted mean values to real GDP per capita series from the World Economic Outlook database of the International Monetary Fund (IMF WEO). Table 2.A1 reports the available synthetic estimates and summarizes their main characteristics (only a selection of Vercelli's annual figures is included).

The alternative approach of estimating the EU-wide income distribution directly from microdata is more recent because it requires the availability of a suitable database. The collection of cross-nationally comparable microeconomic information for all EU countries started with the European Community Household Panel (ECHP), an input-harmonized annual longitudinal survey conducted by national statistical agencies from 1994 to 2001 under Eurostat coordination. In the early 2000s, the ECHP was replaced by the EU-SILC, which has since collected income microdata using a decentralized output-harmonized approach. EU-SILC provides the EU reference source for comparative statistics on income distribution and social exclusion at the European level, particularly in the context of the EU monitoring of progress towards greater social cohesion. Comparable information obtained by ex-post standardization of existing national surveys is also contained in the long-established LIS database used by Atkinson (1996), but its coverage by country/year is too sparse for a comprehensive estimation of EU-wide statistics. Last, since around 2013, the Eurosystem's Household Finance and Consumption Survey (HFCS) collects output-harmonized microdata on households' assets and liabilities as well as gross incomes in EA countries.

The first estimates of the EU/EA distribution based on microdata relied on the ECHP data possibly integrated with the LIS data (Beblo and Knaus, 2001; Brandolini, 2007, 2008; Troitiño Cobas, 2007; Rodríguez-Pose and Tselios, 2009) or on the LIS data alone (Beckfield, 2009; Hoffmeister, 2009). The EU-SILC data are the basis for all recent studies (Heidenreich and Härpfer, 2011; Bönke and Schröder, 2014; Papatheodorou and Pavlopoulos, 2014; Maquet, 2015; Caselli et al., 2016; Benczúr et al., 2017; Filauro, 2018; Filauro and Parolin, 2019; Anderson et al., 2018; Wang et al., 2018), including our own estimates in this chapter. Table 2.A2 reports available estimates and summarizes their main characteristics.

In addition to these studies, the literature has also focused on poverty (Atkinson, 1995, 1998; de Vos and Zaidi, 1999; Förster, 2005; Fahey et al., 2005; Fahey, 2007; Kangas and Ritakallio, 2007; Whelan and Maître, 2010; Goedemé and Rottiers, 2011; Goedemé and Collado, 2016; Jenkins, 2020; Goedemé et al., 2019), earnings distributions (Behr and Pötter, 2010; Brandolini et al., 2012; Eurofound, 2015; Brandolini and Rosolia, 2016; Perugini and Pompei, 2016; Pereira and Galego, 2018; Vacas-Soriano, 2018), and wealth distributions (Lindner 2015).

For both the synthetic and direct approaches, it should be borne in mind that the adjustment to national accounts may be important. Grossed-up income estimates derived from sample surveys tend to differ from the corresponding

Table 2.A1 Synthetic estimates of the Gini index in EU15 and EU28, 1960–2016

Authors	Atkinson 1996	Boix 2004	Morrisson Murtin 2004	Dauderstädt Keltek 2011	Bonesmo Fredriksen 2012		Darvas 2016			Vercelli 2018
Income concept	Disposable	Not specified	Disposable	Disposable	Disposable	Disposable	Disposable	Market	Disposable	Mostly disposable
Equivalence scale	Square root	Per capita	Square root	Modified OECD	Square root	Square root	Not specified	Not specified	Modified OECD	Various
Welfare unit	Individual	Individual	Individual	Individual	Individual	Individual	Not specified	Not specified	Individual	Mostly individual
Conversion rate	PPP (NDI)	PPP	PPP (GDP)	Market exchange rate	PPP	Market exchange rate	PPP	PPP	PPP	PPP (GDP)
Source of national distribution data	LIS, data for 20/40 quantile groups	Database assembled by Milanovic at World Bank	Database assembled at OECD, data for 9 bottom decile groups and 2 top vingtile groups	Eurostat estimates on deciles based on EU-SILC	OECD IDD, data for decile groups	OECD IDD, data for decile groups	SWIID and Eurostat (2014–15)	SWIID and Eurostat (2014–15)	Eurostat estimates based on EU-SILC	WIID, data for decile groups
Adjustment to national accounts	none	None	Real GDP per capita from Maddison (2001)	None	None	None	Real GDP per capita from IMF WEO	Real GDP per capita from IMF WEO	None	Real GDP per capita from PWT

Notes	Data from various years around indicated year; index estimated from decile group shares	Estimates for quintile ratio	Data from various years around indicated year	Data from various years around indicated year	Based on national log-normal distributions estimated from Gini index and mean	Based on national log-normal distributions estimated from Gini index and mean	Based on national log-normal distributions estimated from Gini index and mean	Missing observations estimated by fractional polynomials of 3rd degree
EU15	Excl. AT DK EL		Excl. East DE until 1990	Excl. AT BE ES IE PT				
1960								0.471
1965								0.448
1970			0.320					0.421
1975								0.387
1980			0.299	0.278				0.369
1985	0.292				0.302	0.463		0.351
1988					0.300	0.463		0.349
1989					0.300	0.464		0.338
1990			0.301		0.302	0.467		0.353
1991			0.306		0.304	0.473		0.344
1992					0.307	0.479		0.353
1993		0.342						0.357
1994					0.308	0.484		0.350

(continued)

Table 2.A1 Continued

Authors	Atkinson 1996	Boix 2004	Morrisson Murtin 2004	Dauderstädt Keltek 2011	Bonesmo Fredriksen 2012	Darvas 2016		Vercelli 2018
1995			0.303		0.291	0.308	0.486	0.347
1996						0.307	0.485	0.343
1997						0.305	0.484	0.339
1998						0.305	0.485	0.336
1999						0.305	0.485	0.336
2000					0.307	0.305.	0.487	0.333
2001						0.305	0.488	0.329
2002						0.305	0.489	0.353
2003						0.305	0.490	0.351
2004						0.305	0.492	0.351
2005					0.306	0.305	0.492	0.337
2006						0.307	0.495	0.333
2007						0.308	0.496	0.340
2008					0.312	0.309	0.499	0.345
2009						0.310	0.503	0.341
2010						0.312	0.508	0.342
2011						0.315	0.510	0.348
2012						0.317	0.512	0.343
2013						0.319	0.516	0.344
2014						0.319	0.515	0.350

	EU28	Excl. HR	Excl. HR BG (2005–2006) RO (2005–2006)	Excl. HR BG (2005–2006) RO (2005–2006)	Excl. BG HR EE LT LV MT RO	Excl. BG CY EE HR LT LV MT RO
2015						0.320
2016						0.319
						0.515
1988	0.472					0.329
1989	0.474					0.330
1990	0.480					0.338
1991	0.490					0.349
1992	0.499					0.356
1993	0.505	0.399				0.358
1994	0.509					0.358
1995	0.511					0.356
1996	0.509					0.353
1997	0.508					0.352
1998	0.509					0.352
1999	0.510					0.352
2000	0.511					0.351
2001	0.512					0.350
2002	0.511					0.347
2003	0.510					0.344
2004	0.510					0.341

(continued)

Table 2.A1 Continued

Authors	Atkinson 1996	Boix 2004	Morrisson Murtin 2004	Dauderstädt Keltek 2011	Bonesmo Fredriksen 2012		Darvas 2016		Vercelli 2018
2005							0.339	0.509	
2006							0.337	0.509	
2007							0.334	0.508	
2008					0.328	0.354	0.332	0.508	
2009							0.331	0.511	
2010							0.333	0.515	0.353
2011							0.334	0.515	0.354
2012							0.335	0.517	0.351
2013							0.335	0.519	0.352
2014							0.334	0.518	0.352
2015							0.333	0.517	0.352
2016							0.330		0.348

Source: Authors' elaboration.

Table 2.A2 Direct estimates of the Gini index in EU15, EU28, and EA, 1980–2015

Authors	Beblo Knaus 2001	Troitiño Cobas 2007	Brandolini 2007				Beckfield 2009	Hoffmeister 2009	Rodríguez-Pose and Tselios 2009	Heidenreich Härpfer 2011	Bonke Schroeder 2014
Income concept	Disposable	Disposable	Disposable	Disposable	Disposable	Disposable	Disposable	Disposable	Disposable	Disposable	Disposable
Equivalence scale	Modified OECD	Modified OECD	Modified OECD	Modified OECD	Modified OECD	Modified OECD	OECD	Square root	None	Modified OECD	Modified OECD
Welfare unit	Individual	Individual	Individual	Individual	Individual	Individual	Individual	Individual	Individual	Individual	Individual
Conversion rate	PPP	PPP	PPP (HFCE)	PPP (GDP)	PPP (GDP)	market exchange rate	PPP (GDP)	PPP (HFCE)	market exchange rate	PPP	PPP
Source of national distribution data	ECHP, LIS	ECHP	ECHP, LIS	ECHP, LIS	ECHP, LIS	ECHP, LIS	LIS	LIS	ECHP	EU-SILC	EU-SILC
Adjustment to national accounts	None	None	None	Adjusted to household net disposable income	None	None	None	None	None	None	None

(continued)

Table 2.A2 Continued

Authors	Beblo Knaus 2001	Troitiño Cobas 2007	Brandolini 2007	Beckfield 2009	Hoffmeister 2009	Rodríguez-Pose and Tselios 2009	Heidenreich Härpfer 2011	Bonke Schroeder 2014
Notes	Estimates for Theil index			Data from various years around indicated year; top/bottom coded incomes	Estimates for mean logarithmic deviation	Only individuals with positive income below 90th percentile; estimates shown only in chart	Excl. Zero incomes; top/bottom coded incomes	Top/bottom coded incomes
EU15		Excl. LU AT SE FI		Excl. EL PT	Excl. PT	Excl. FN NL		
1980				0.393				
1993		0.345						
1994		0.336						
1995		0.330						
1996		0.324	0.317					
1997			0.315					
1998			0.316					
1999			0.310					
2000		0.310	0.296	0.330	0.313	0.291	0.294	

	Excl. BG CY HR LT LV MT RO	Excl. BG CY HR LT LV MT RO	Excl. BG CY HR LT LV MT RO	Excl. BG CY HR LT LV MT RO	Excl. BG CY CZ HR LV LT MT PT SK RO	Excl. MT	Excl. BE BG HR IE MT RO
2001							
2002							
2003							
2004							
2005							
2006							
2007							
2008							
2009							
2010							
2011							
2012							
2013							
2014							
2015							
EU28							
2000	0.334	0.328	0.317	0.378			0.327
2004							
2005							
2006							

(continued)

Table 2.A2 Continued

Authors	Beblo Knaus 2001	Troitiño Cobas 2007	Brandolini 2007	Beckfield 2009	Hoffmeister 2009	Rodríguez-Pose and Tselios 2009	Heidenreich Härpfer 2011	Bonke Schroeder 2014
2007								
2008							0.347	
2009								
2010								
2011								0.311
2012								
2013								
2014								
2015								
EA								EA12 excl. BE IE
1996								
2000			0.293					
2004			0.290					0.297
2005			0.288					
2006				0.307				
2007								
2008								
2009								
2010								

2011											0.317	
2012												
2013												
2014												
2015												
Income concept	Disposable	Disposable	Disposable	Market	Disposable	Disposable	Disposable, incl. Imputed rents	Market	Disposable	Disposable	Disposable	Disposable
Equivalence scale	Modified OECD	Not specified	OECD	OECD	Modified OECD	Modified OECD	Modified OECD	Modified OECD	Modified OECD	Square root	Modified OECD	Modified OECD
Welfare unit	Not specified	Not specified	Individual	Individual	Individual	Individual	Individual	Individual	Not specified	Not specified	Individual	Individual
Conversion rate	PPP	Not specified	Fixed euro conversion rates	Fixed euro conversion rates	PPP (actual individual consumption)	PPP (GDP)	PPP (GDP)	PPP (GDP)	PPP (HFCE)	PPP	PPP (HFCE)	Market exchange rate
Source of national distribution data	ECHP, EU-SILC	EU-SILC	ECHP, EU-SILC	ECHP, EU-SILC	ECHP, EU-SILC	EU-SILC	EU-SILC	EU-SILC	EU-SILC	EU-SILC	EU-SILC	EU-SILC
Adjustment to national accounts	None	None	None	None	None	None	None	None	None	None	None	None

(continued)

Table 2.A2 Continued

Authors	Beblo Knaus 2001	Troitiño Cobas 2007	Brandolini 2007	Beckfield 2009	Hoffmeister 2009	Rodríguez-Pose and Tselios 2009	Heidenreich Härpfer 2011	Bonke Schroeder 2014
Notes	Top/bottom censored distribution	UK wave realigned	UK wave realigned	UK wave realigned	Estimated with mixture distribution techniques; only positive incomes	Excl. non-positive income; estimates for polarization indices	UK wave realigned; BG(2005), MT(2005), RO(2005) estimated	UK wave realigned; BG(2005), MT(2005), RO(2005) estimated
EU15								
1980								
1993								
1994								
1995								
1996	0.300		0.306					
1997			0.308					
1998			0.306					
1999			0.304					
2000			0.305					
2001								
2002								
2003								

Year	Excl. CY HR MT LU	Excl. CY MT LU	Excl. HR	Excl. MT (2006) HR (2006–2008)	Excl. MT (2006) HR (2006–2008)	Excl. MT (2006) HR (2006–2008)	Excl. BG ES FR GR HR IT LV MT PT RO	Excl. HR	Excl. HR
2004			0.306				0.303	0.315	
2005			0.301				0.309	0.319	
2006			0.305				0.313	0.321	
2007			0.306				0.313	0.319	
2008	0.294						0.310	0.316	
2009			0.303				0.316	0.322	
2010			0.309				0.317	0.323	
2011			0.312				0.318	0.326	
2012			0.311				0.319	0.327	
2013			0.311				0.320	0.329	
2014			0.315				0.322	0.330	
2015									
EU28									
2000									
2004									
2005							0.361	0.404	
2006			0.347	0.359	0.344	0.540	0.362	0.403	
2007			0.346	0.359	0.343	0.532	0.362	0.400	
2008			0.342	0.354	0.343	0.532	0.356	0.390	
2009			0.338	0.349	0.338	0.536	0.352	0.390	
2010			0.339	0.350	0.339	0.541	0.353	0.391	

(continued)

Table 2.A2 Continued

Authors	Beblo Knaus 2001	Troitiño Cobas 2007	Brandolini 2007			Beckfield 2009	Hoffmeister 2009	Rodríguez-Pose and Tselios 2009	Heidenreich Härpfer 2011	Bonke Schroeder 2014
2011			0.341	0.350	0.338	0.540			0.353	0.391
2012			0.339	0.350	0.338	0.544			0.353	0.394
2013	0.38	0.44	0.338	0.349	0.337	0.543			0.351	0.394
2014			0.339	0.349	0.336	0.542			0.351	0.395
2015									0.349	0.394
EA		EA12 excl. LU	EA12 excl. LU	EA19 excl. MT (2006)	EA19 excl. MT (2006)		EA19 excl. MT		EA19 excl. HR	EA19 excl. HR
1996			0.41							
2000			0.37							
2004										
2005							0.385		0.307	0.321
2006				0.315	0.299				0.317	0.331
2007				0.318	0.305				0.319	0.331
2008				0.314	0.302		0.400		0.316	0.327
2009				0.314	0.303				0.316	0.327
2010				0.319	0.307				0.321	0.333
2011				0.319	0.306		0.404		0.321	0.333
2012				0.322	0.310				0.326	0.339
2013	0.325	0.332	0.392	0.325	0.311				0.328	0.341
2014				0.323	0.309		0.421		0.327	0.340
2015									0.325	0.339

Source: Authors' elaboration.

aggregates from national accounts. These discrepancies are due in part to underreporting and sampling errors in surveys and in part to conceptual differences (e.g., Atkinson and Micklewright, 1983, for the UK; Brandolini, 1999, for Italy; Atkinson et al., 2017, for EU countries). For instance, national account aggregates often include the disposable income of NPISH since separate accounts are only available in some countries; they cover incomes of persons living permanently in institutions (hostels, nursing homes for the elderly, military bases, etc.), who are excluded from sample surveys; they include imputed rents on owner-occupied housing whose amount is significant in many EU countries but is not incorporated in the survey income definition. The alignment of survey data to mean incomes from national accounts is common in the literature on global income inequality, and, until recently, the statistical department of the UN Economic Commission for the Latin America and Caribbean region adjusted survey data by income category based on their shortfalls relative to sector accounts to enhance cross-national comparability (Bourguignon, 2015). These adjustments allow studying within-country distributions without altering the country ranking provided by the national accounts. On the other hand, they overlook that national accounts are intrinsically different from survey data: 'the differences in coverage and definition between [national accounts] and surveys mean that, even if everything were perfectly measured, it would be incorrect to apply inequality or distributional measures which are defined from surveys, which measure one thing, to means that are derived from the national accounts, which measure another' (Deaton, 2005: 17). As shortfalls of survey totals relative to national accounts values are negatively correlated with real income levels across countries, the alignment of household-level data to aggregate statistics is likely to reduce measured EU-wide inequality.

3

INCOME AND LABOUR MARKET DEVELOPMENTS AND SOCIAL OUTCOMES IN GERMANY AND FRANCE

Lucia Granelli, Balázs Pálvölgyi, and Johannes Ziemendorff

3.1 INTRODUCTION

This chapter discusses differences and similarities between France and Germany, exploring income, poverty, and inequality developments, as well as the key determinants of these outcomes in particular labour market institutions. These are the two largest economies of the European Union (EU), accounting for 36% of the EU28's gross domestic product (GDP) in 2018[1] and 49% of the Euro Area's (EA) GDP. Together they have acted as motors of European integration and share many features of a social market economy. Still, the structure of their economies and their social models differ considerably, meriting closer attention.[2]

---

1 This equals 43% of the EU27's GDP after the departure of the United Kingdom from the EU.

2 This comparison follows a number of studies that have taken a similar approach of comparing directly the German and French economies, albeit with different perspectives. Enderlein and Pisany-Ferry (2014) take a policy-oriented perspective by proposing priority areas for reforms and investment in the two countries as well as at the EU level. Piketty (2017) focusses on explaining the similarities and differences of Germany and France in terms of labour productivity and GDP per capita, also relative to some other advanced economies. Lallement (2017) identifies the strengths and weaknesses of the German economy by comparing key macroeconomic indicators to those of France and the EA average. Praet (2018) uses the divergent developments of Germany and France to illustrate the emergence of macroeconomic imbalances in

Lucia Granelli, Balázs Pálvölgyi, and Johannes Ziemendorff, *Income and Labour Market Developments and Social Outcomes in Germany and France* In: *Europe's Income, Wealth, Consumption, and Inequality.* Edited by: Georg Fischer and Robert Strauss, Oxford University Press (2021). © Oxford University Press. DOI: 10.1093/oso/9780197545706.003.0003

While GDP per capita has been traditionally higher in Germany than in France, it converged between 1995 and 2005. However, after 2008, incomes in Germany increased more; a development recently interrupted by the 2018 slow-down of especially the manufacturing sector in the global economy (see Section 3.2). The labour market, and underlying labour market institutions, played a key role in income developments (Section 3.3). These institutions also played a key role in explaining why labour market outcomes improved more in Germany while social outcomes, such as at-risk-of-poverty indicators, have stayed more favourable in France (Section 3.4). Following an increasing trend in unemploy-ment since the early 1970s in Germany, the early 2000s saw a turnaround, but these years were also marked by increasing labour market vulnerability, wage re-straint, and an emerging low-wage sector. By the 2010s, the constantly improving labour market situation started to have a positive influence also on some social indicators in Germany. On the contrary, the labour market in France continued to face difficulties: while the two countries both had an unemployment rate of 7.8% in 2008, it was about 9% in 2018 and still above 8% in 2019 in France, while it was about one-third of that in Germany (Bosch, 2011). Interestingly, social outcomes remained remarkably stable and similar. In regard to current policies, future social developments will likely reflect economic patterns which seem to be more cyclical in Germany than in France—one of the conclusions of Section 3.5.

3.2 ECONOMIC DEVELOPMENT IN GERMANY AND FRANCE

In this chapter, we use per capita income (defined as GDP per inhabitant) as an indi-cator for economic performance, and we analyse the divergence between Germany and France, through a decomposition of productivity developments. The fact that the German labour market involves a larger proportion of the population across all age groups contributes importantly to a higher GDP per capita.

While both France and Germany are industrialized, high-income economies, a longer term perspective shows that there have always been episodes when one country performed better than the other in terms of GDP per capita (Figure 3.1). Starting from 72% of German GDP per capita (PPS) in 1960, the French economy caught up with the West German economy until reaching 80–85% in the 1980s. As the less developed East Germany joined West Germany, French GDP per capita jumped to 87% of the GDP per capita of the unified Germany[3]

EMU. This following comparison builds mainly on two chapters from Cléaud et al. (2019), providing an updated and focused presentation on social developments.

3 At the same time, total GDP of France dropped from 83% of Germany's to 71%. Looking at the full period, in France, the population increased steadily from about 47 million in 1960 to 58 million in 1989 and 67 million in 2018. The West German population increased from 55 million in 1960 to 62 million in 1989; unified Germany

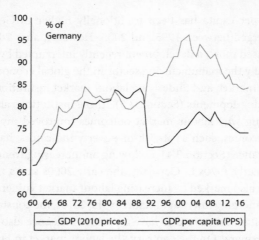

Figure 3.1 Gross domestic product (GDP) (in constant prices) and GDP per capita (in purchasing power standards [PPS]) in France in % of Germany (1960–2018).
(1) GDP in constant prices is at 2010 reference levels.
(2) GDP per capita is GDP at current prices per head of population in PPS.
(3) 1960–1990 data relate to West-Germany only.
Source: European Commission.

and continued to gain ground between 1995 and 2002, climbing to about 96% of German GDP per capita in 2002. During that latter period, Germany was often labelled 'the sick man of Europe' due to its weak economic performance that was reflected in low growth and high unemployment. However, economic hardship at the same time created momentum for taking difficult decisions on far-reaching and partly painful reforms (the Hartz reforms) that enabled economic adjustments; this was combined with increasing reliance on traditional labour market institutions such as the short-time work arrangement *Kurzarbeit* and working time accounts. After the mid-2000s, GDP per capita has been increasing more in Germany than in France, bringing down the ratio of French to German GDP per capita to about 84% in 2018. Thus, in a longer term perspective, the current gap in per capita GDP could be a return to the post-unification situation, when Germany's per capita GDP exceeded that of France by 3,800 European currency units (ECU) in 1995. Still, the French economy tends to follow a more stable path, and the 2018 slowdown in the global economy showed that this income difference is not a steady state: France's GDP per capita expanded in 2018 and 2019 more than that of Germany (Table 3.1), which tends to be more exposed to the global cycle. As long as the global economy remains weak, this pattern is expected to continue (European Commission, 2019a).

---

had a population of 80 million in the first years of the 1990s, which increased to nearly 83 million in 2018.

Table 3.1 Gross domestic product (GDP) per capita average growth rate (in volume terms)

	1996–2005	2006–2017	2018–2019
DE	1.2	1.5	08
FR	1.7	0.6	1.5
EU28	2.2	1.0	1.5
EA 19	1.8	0.7	1.4

Source: Ameco, European Commission.

The observed income trends are not explained by higher aggregate productivity levels or dynamics in either country. In volume terms, Germany has had a similar hourly productivity *growth* (Figure 3.2). On the other hand, in nominal terms, France's productivity *level* was higher over the period 1999–2015 (Figure 3.3). The difference peaked at close to 8% just before the 2008 financial crisis. Since then, hourly productivity growth has declined in both countries, but Germany has been catching up, to regain a slight advantage as of 2016.[4]

Productivity per employee does not explain diverging incomes, as it has been persistently lower in Germany compared to France. Hours worked per employee are approximately 11% lower in Germany than in France. This difference in hours worked per employee is mainly a reflection of a higher share of part-time

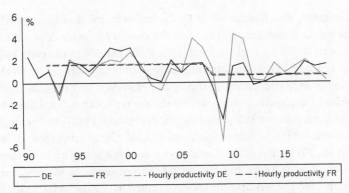

Figure 3.2 Annual gross domestic product (GDP) per capita growth and average hourly labour productivity growth.
Chain linked volumes. The continuous lines show annual GDP changes, and the straight dashed lines show the average productivity increase in the periods 1992–2007 and 2008–2019. The average increase in productivity was somewhat higher in Germany in 1992 to 2007 (1.8% vs. 1.7% in 1992–2007), while it was 0.6% for both countries in 2008–2019.
Source: Eurostat, author's calculations.

---

4 Hourly productivity growth declined from 1.8% in Germany and 1.7% in France on average from 1991 to 2007 to 0.7% in Germany and 0.6% in France since 2009.

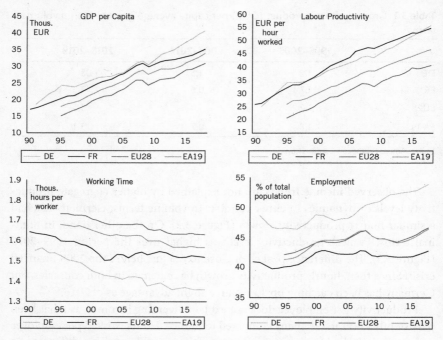

Figure 3.3 Main drivers of per capita gross domestic product (GDP).
Source: Eurostat, authors' calculations.

jobs in Germany, which is not offset by the higher number of hours worked per employee by those working full-time in the country (Costes et al., 2015). This ratio has been widening over the long term. From just 5% in the early 1990s, the difference reached 11% at the current juncture. In both countries, hours worked per employee were decreasing in the 1990s. However, this decrease had a different cause in the two countries. While the decrease can be explained by a reduction in the hours worked per employee occupying a full-time job in France, it is accounted for by the intensified development of part-time jobs in Germany (Costes et al., 2015). The incidence of part-time work is higher in Germany not only among older workers, but also among prime agers. As of 2000, the hours worked stabilized in France, while they continued to decline in Germany (Figure 3.3). By contrast, labour markets in the two countries have developed markedly differently. In particular, the unemployment rates diverged significantly between Germany and France since the financial crisis (Figure 3.4). In both countries, the unemployment rate stood at 7.4% in 2008, after which it declined markedly in Germany, reaching 3.4% in 2018, while it has been hovering around 9–10% since 2012 in France and only started to decline from mid-2015 onwards.

Moreover, the activity rate is higher in Germany than in France. This gap has substantially widened between 2003 and 2010, from +2.4 percentage points to +6.4 percentage points, remaining broadly at that level since. This divergence is

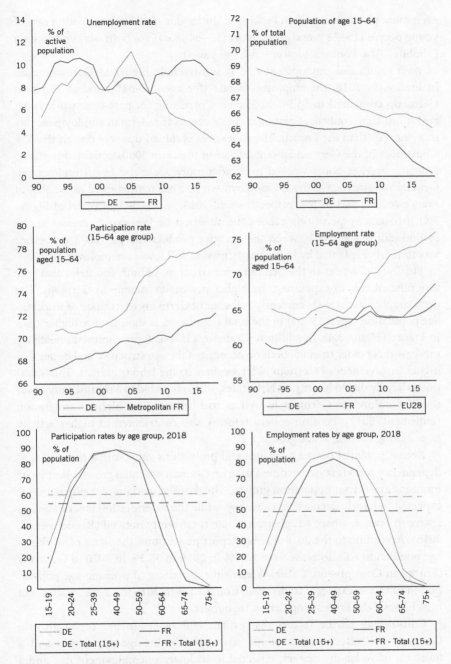

Figure 3.4 Labour market performance.
Source: Labour Force Survey, Eurostat, authors' calculations.

even more pronounced when looking at the labour market participation rate of young people (15–24 years) and seniors (55–64 years), for both women and men (Thubin, 2014; Figure 3.4 lower left-hand panel).

As a result, the employment rate is substantially higher in Germany than in France. In 2018, the employment rate (for ages 15–64) stood at 75.9% in Germany, compared to 65.9% in France. Correcting for part-time work to arrive at full-time equivalent employment discounts the German employment rate more heavily than the French. The data series obtained this way reveals that the adjustment of the German labour market in the early 2000s consisted partly in reducing average hours worked to avoid a more acute rise in unemployment. Generally, however, Germany's employment rate has tended to be above that of France (65.2% and 61.5%, respectively, in 2018; see mid-right panel of Figure 3.4). In some respects this echoes the situation in Western Germany in the second half of the 1980s, when the negative productivity gap vis-à-vis France was similarly explained by higher participation and lower unemployment.

Finally, differences in the demographic structure of both countries also play a significant role in explaining the higher per capita income in Germany. The demographic structure is currently in favour of Germany as its share of working-age population (aged 15–64) in the total population is significantly higher than in France (Figure 3.4). In addition, Germany's labour force comprises relatively more workers older than 65, both on account of the age structure and because of higher involvement of German older workers in the labour market. This situation is largely due to lower past birth rates, which have led to a significantly lower share of children in Germany as well as, to a lesser extent, higher immigration (Lallement, 2017). Pension system reforms also contributed to higher activity rates among the senior age groups.

Recent potential output estimates and projections suggest that the (old-age) dependency ratio is set to become a drag on German potential growth, despite its immigration-driven population growth. The share of working-age population is expected to largely decrease in Germany, while the deterioration is set to be less severe in France, where a higher birth rate is currently noticed (Baquero et al., 2015). According to the 2018 Ageing Report projections, the share of working-age population will decrease from 65.7% in 2016 to 55.3% in 2070 in Germany (European Commission, 2018a). Meanwhile, the share of working-age population in France is expected to decrease from 62.6% in 2016 to 57.3% in 2070, not least because the French population is younger.

Considering all the factors that explain differences in per capita growth, Germany benefitted from a higher share of working-age population and a more inclusive labour market, reflected in its lower unemployment rate and a higher participation rate (Figure 3.5). These factors more than compensated for the higher incidence of part-time employment and the resulting lower hours worked per worker in Germany. The lower capital-to-labour ratio of Germany with respect to France, implying that Germany relies on a more labour intensive

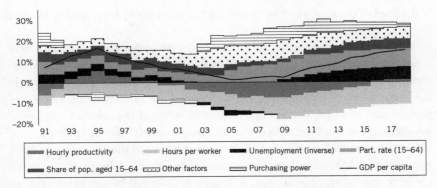

Figure 3.5 Decomposition of the per capita gross domestic product (GDP) difference.
Source: Eurostat, Ameco, European Commission.

production, is at the same time combined with higher total factor productivity and has therefore not resulted in a persistent productivity disadvantage.

3.3 LABOUR MARKET INSTITUTIONS AS DRIVERS OF DIFFERENT ECONOMIC AND SOCIAL OUTCOMES

The different labour market outcomes explored in the previous section, notably the high employment rate in Germany, reflect considerable differences in French and German labour market institutions. In a nutshell, in France, industrial relations have traditionally been regulated by the state through laws, while in Germany, the system of industrial relations was shaped by a more flexible social dialogue on the basis of higher trade union membership rates (Visser, 2019), collective bargaining of trade unions, and co-determination of works councils at firm level. The following sections explore these factors more in detail.

3.3.1 Collective Bargaining

In France, collective bargaining is characterized by a very high coverage rate of collective agreements and the presence of a hierarchy between the norms established by law, those set at sector-level, and those at firm-level agreement (Hancké, 2001). In France, the coverage rate of collective agreements is estimated to be higher than 90% of the workforce. Hence, almost all employees are covered by sectoral wage agreements. Some first attempts at decentralization of sectoral bargaining started from the early 1980s ('Auroux laws'), but the *principle of favourability* that forbids company agreements from providing less favourable provisions than higher level agreements (i.e., the provisions set by law or by sector-level agreement), was maintained. Recent reforms redefined the scope of sector-level and firm-level agreements, giving more space to collective bargaining at the level of the firm while not inverting the principle of favourability (France Stratégie, 2018a,b).

By contrast, German firms have a higher degree of flexibility to deviate from a negotiated agreement than their French peers, including from agreements concerning sectoral wages. First, in Germany, collective sectoral agreements are binding only when an employer is a member of the corresponding employers' association.[5] If a firm decides not to be a member of the relevant employers' association, that firm can either negotiate wages individually or opt for a firm-level agreement with a trade union. As a consequence of this flexibility, in 2018, only 46% of German employees were covered by sectoral collective agreements, 8% by firm-level agreements, and 46% were not covered by any agreement, although half of those (51%) were employed by firms declaring their wages to be in line with collective agreements[6] that they did not officially subscribe to (Kohaut, 2019). Second, since the mid-1990s, social partners have increasingly agreed on including flexible elements in collective agreements.[7] In 2005, 75% of establishments covered by collective bargaining made use of one or more opening clauses within the agreements. A small share of these opening clauses addressed basic pay, while most of them allowed for derogations of other working conditions, such as working time.

The differences in the collective bargaining mechanisms are likely to have led to different wage developments, thereby contributing to dissimilar unit labour cost and cost-competitiveness dynamics in the two countries, notably before the crisis.[8] Figure 3.6 concentrates on the period when unit labour costs diverged between Germany and France, reflecting the 'great wage moderation' in Germany. It shows that, in France, unit labour costs have grown at an average rate of 2.0% per year between 2002 and 2008 and then decelerated to 1.2% after 2008. By contrast, in Germany, unit labour costs have decreased at an average of 0.1% per year before 2008 and then increased at 1.9%.

The different unit labour cost dynamics in France and Germany do not depend on different productivity patterns, but are due to different wage developments. The contribution of productivity to the evolution of the cost of labour has been similar in the two countries both in 2002–2008 (0.9% for both) and in 2009–2019 (0.6% in France; 0.3% in Germany). The different unit labour cost dynamics in the two countries rather depend on the development of employees' compensations. In nominal terms, these increased at an average rate of 2.9%

---

5   Theoretically, employees also have to be members of trade unions negotiating an agreement, although employers would typically extend signed agreements also to employees not members of any trade union (Thorsten, 2018).

6   Those firms have adjusted their pay to the collectively agreed wages without officially subscribing to the agreement.

7   Dustmann et al. (2014) offer a good overview of how the German system allowed for a higher degree of flexibility.

8   For an overview of empirical evidence, see OECD (2018).

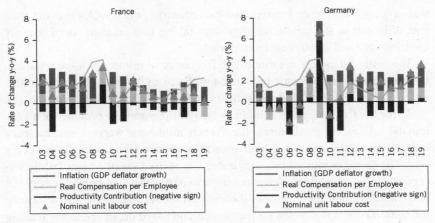

Figure 3.6 Unit labour cost evolution and decomposition.
Source: Ameco, European Commission.

per year in France and 1.1% in Germany in 2002–2008. They then decelerated to the level of 1.7% per year in France but accelerated to 2.5% in Germany in 2009–2019. These divergences remain, even when looking at the development of employees' compensations in real terms. Real compensations per employee remained stable (0.1%) in Germany, while they grew at 0.8% in France in 2002–2008. After the crisis, real employees' compensations broadly kept the same pace of development in France (0.9%, albeit most recently suppressed) and started growing in Germany (1.0%).

The wage-setting framework also has an impact on the wage distribution of the two countries. While France has more uniform wages, Germany has higher wages for skilled and highly skilled workers and lower wages for unskilled workers, leading to a wider wage distribution. The wage distribution of the two countries has become somewhat more similar after Germany introduced a national minimum wage in 2015, yet the relationship appears overall unchanged.

In the EU economic policy coordination process, the European Semester, the European Commission emphasized in the 2018 and 2019 Country Reports (2018b, 2019b) that the German collective bargaining system is not well constructed for reducing wage dispersion and for increasing the level of wages to support domestic demand and advocated more effective tools for extending of collective bargaining.

3.3.2 Minimum Wages (Level and Mechanism) and Wage Responses to Inflation (Indexation)

A statutory general minimum wage was introduced in Germany in 2015, although it has been present since 1950 in France. As of 1 January 2019, the minimum wage in France was at €10.03 and at €9.19 in Germany. However, there was no major difference between the two countries when looking at the total cost of labour at the minimum wage after taking into account social security contributions and labour cost reductions.[9]

The main differences are due to the frequency of minimum wage revisions, the presence of an automatic indexation mechanism, the role of the committee overseeing minimum wage developments, and the government's decision margin.

As for the frequency of minimum wage revisions and the presence of an automatic indexation mechanism, the French minimum wage is automatically indexed to inflation and real wage growth of certain labour categories[10] every year. The German minimum wage, instead, is revised every 2 years (while, exceptionally, an interim revision was announced in advance not only for 2019 but also for 2020), and the revision—theoretically—does not follow any automatic indexation rule. It is decided on past trends and based on an economic reading of a broad set of macroeconomic variables.[11]

Given the absence of an automatic rule for the minimum wage indexation, the role of the committee overseeing minimum wage developments is stronger in Germany than in France. In Germany, this committee is composed of representatives of social partners who have the power to decide by how much to change the statutory minimum wage. Experts on the subject are also members of this committee, but with an advisory role only, as they take no part in the decision to change the value of the minimum wage. In contrast, in France, a committee of independent experts (mainly economists) is in charge of publishing an annual report which discusses the opportunity to raise the minimum wage above the minimum revaluation rate. The social partners are consulted but are not formally part of the committee.

Last, whereas in Germany the government can only express its agreement or disagreement with the indexation proposed by social partners, in France the government can decide to adopt ad hoc increases in the level of the minimum wage. The decision of the government is not subject to any condition and can be taken even in the case of a negative opinion issued by the committee of experts.

Noting that it is still early days, there is little evidence of spillovers of the German minimum wage (or its increases) to other wage groups so far, while the

---

9 For a more comprehensive summary, see European Commission (2016a).

10 Only the average hourly real wage of employees and clerks (*salaire horaire moyen des ouvriers et des employés*) is taken into account for the automatic indexation of the minimum wage. Its annual growth rate is multiplied by a coefficient equal to 0.5 to avoid excessively fast minimum wage development.

11 Practically, social partners agreed on a working rule that quasi-automatically ties future increases of the minimum wage to past increases in the negotiated wages. As overall wage dynamics have exceeded that of negotiated wages since 2014, and as negotiated wages have reacted only to a small extent to increases in inflation, this quasi-indexation may have had so far a mitigating effect on minimum wage dynamics in a context of increasing labour market tightness.

indexation of the French minimum wage has been found to translate into overall wage increases (Lestrade, 2017). In France, because the minimum wage is often used as a starting point in collective agreements, minimum wage increases may raise other wage levels up to the eighth decile of the wage distribution.[12] These spillover effects are larger on the lowest decile and decrease over the wage distribution, thereby leading to a reduction of wage dispersion across individuals. In Germany, the relatively recent introduction of the minimum wage does not yet allow us to robustly assess the presence of possible spillovers.

The International Monetary Fund (IMF) suggested in its 2019 Article IV report that the German authorities encourage robust wage growth in their public communications, adding that, given the tightness of the labour market and the moderate level of the minimum wage, stronger increases in the minimum wage could also be contemplated at their next revision (IMF, 2019).

3.3.3 Working Time

In Germany, the impact on unemployment of the 2008–2009 recession was partly mitigated by the widespread diffusion of working time accounts translating into a large(r) number of workers who experienced a decline in worked hours without losing their job. As shown by Burda and Hunt (2011), employment losses during the 2008–2009 crisis were much smaller than during the previous four recessions (1973–1975, 1979–1982, 1991–1993, 2001–2005). For example, between 1973 and 1975, employment fell for 11 quarters and by 4.3%, whereas in 2008–2009 employment decreased only for two quarters and by 0.5%.

While in both countries working time flexibility agreements can be signed at firm level,[13] the significantly smaller drop in employment during the last crisis was possible thanks to a wider diffusion of working time accounts in Germany than in France, and thanks to a more flexible legal framework and other methods of reducing hours per worker (such as the short-time accounts or *Kurzarbeit*) that accompanied these schemes in Germany. In Germany, therefore, the fall in economic activity was mostly absorbed by a reduction in working time (−3.4%

---

12 See Arpaia and Van Herck (2017); Aeberhardt et al. (2016); Fougère et al. (2016).

13 Working time standards are based on European regulations, both in Germany and France. In France, the labour code sets a working week of 35 hours and leaves the possibility for firms to bargain arrangements that are more flexible. For example, firms can define the standard working time in hours per year or calculate executives' working times in terms of working days per year rather than working hours per week. In Germany, the distribution of working hours is decided by the employer, with worker representatives having co-determination rights when works councils are in place at firm level. Collective bargaining over working time takes place mainly at the sectoral level, with sectoral-level agreements defining monthly or weekly working time, number of holidays, and hours of shift or night work. Opening clauses are usually present in this kind of collective agreements to leave firms with some flexibility for adapting sector-level agreements to firms' specific conditions.

in hours worked per head between 2008 and 2009), which took the shape of a decrease in overtime hours (25% of the total reduction in working time), short-time working schemes (29%), working time accounts (21%), and a temporary cut in working time by other kinds of collective agreement (25%) (Fréhaut, 2012a). In France, instead, the 2008 crisis had a larger negative impact on employment, and the fall in economic activity was mainly cushioned by a decrease in tempo-rary contracts (Ananian, Debauche, and Prost, 2012), as temporary employment dropped by 7.6% in France and only by 0.7% in Germany. This drop was stronger in the manufacturing sector, where temporary employment fell by 19.8% in France (and by 3.6% in Germany) between the 2008-Q1 and 2009-Q1. In the services sector, the drop in temporary employment was less severe, although it decreased by 9.3% in France, while it increased by 3.9% in Germany. Working time accounts hence played a minor role in mitigating the 2008 crisis in France; in 2010, 51% of German employees had access to a working time account versus only 12% in France (Delpech et al., 2016; Burda and Hunt, 2011) notably due to the complexity of the French short-time working scheme (Fréhaut, 2012b).

The part-time employment rate is higher in Germany than in France, al-though part-time employment has steadily increased over time in both coun-tries.[14] While France and Germany post broadly similar actual average working times per worker, this similarity hides a higher proportion of part-time wage-earning jobs in Germany (Costes et al., 2015). In 2017, indeed, the part-time employment rate was at 26.9% in Germany, 8.8 percentage points higher than in France, although a smaller proportion of part-time workers describe it as an involuntary choice (in 2017, 42% of part-time employment was involuntary in France, while this share was only 10.6% in Germany). In both countries, this form of employment is generally more widespread among women and parents with young children. The definition of part-time work is slightly different in the two countries. In France, part-time work is defined as working less than 35 hours per week (Sainsard, 2014). The applicable working time is then determined through collective agreement, although part-time working contracts require a minimum of 24 hours per week by law.[15] In Germany, part-time contracts do not require a minimum number of hours per week and are generally defined as having a shorter regular weekly working time with regard to comparable

---

14 The gender gap in part time employment in Germany is twice that in France. This means that in France, women participate more equally in the labour market, while Germany is now struggling to move in this direction.

15 The minimum of 24 hours' work per week can be waived under certain circumstances. Notably, for any contracts entered into on or after 1 July 2014, employees must be offered at least 24 hours' work per week unless stated otherwise in the rele-vant Collective Bargaining Agreement or in the case of a written request from an employee that can be justified by his or her personal commitments or if he or she wishes to work elsewhere at the same time. For more detail, see https://www.employmentlawworldview.com/france-new-laws-on-part-time-contracts

full-time contracts. Similar rules apply to fixed-term contracts and temporary-agency work, although these rules are more flexible in Germany than in France for both kinds of contracts.[16]

3.3.4 Employment Protection Legislation

While employment protection legislation (EPL) is applicable to any worker in France, it only applies if the worker is employed in an establishment with more than 10 employees in Germany. Other employment relationships can be terminated by the employer (and employee) without any justifying reason. Moreover, both countries provide trial periods during which an EPL is not applied. While for Germany this is always 6 months, it varies between 2 and 4 months in France (2 months for blue-collar and white-collar workers, 3 months for supervisors and technicians, and 4 months for managers).

The level of legally granted employment protection for individual and collective dismissals is relatively comparable for permanent employment contracts (with more flexibility in Germany, in particular for collective dismissals), whereas there is a significant gap for fixed-term contracts. France and Germany rank among the member countries of the Organisation for Economic Cooperation and Development (OECD) (and EU) with the strong(est) regulations of dismissal for open-ended contracts in an international comparison. However, there are some important differences.

When looking at the set of measures developed by the OECD to gauge the level of employment protection across countries (Table 3.2 for details), the French EPL for temporary forms of employment is much higher (index of 3.1 in France vs. 1.9 in Germany, for 2019). This category comprises two parts—fixed-term contracts and work-agency employment—with the difference mostly due to a much stricter regulation of fixed-term contracts and, to a smaller extent, by the regulation of temporary-agency work.

The difference in the EPL indicator for fixed-term contracts likely explains a substantial part of the flexibility-gap between the two labour market regimes.

---

16 The maximum duration established by law is shorter in France than in Germany, both for fixed-term contracts and temporary-agency work. In France, fixed-term contracts can last for a maximum period of 18 months in principle, but in practice they are used for a time span of 9 to 24 months. In addition, fixed-term contracts can be renewed only twice, and the same rules apply to temporary-agency work, with the exception of sectors concerned with 'contrats d'usage' and seasonal contracts for which highly flexible rules apply, feeding into observed segmentation. In Germany, fixed-term contracts without objective limitation reasons can last for up to 2 years. Within this period, the contract may be extended not more than three times. There are no legal provisions on the duration of fixed-term contracts justified by objective reasons. The duration depends on the objective reason for fixing the term. Successive fixed-term contracts justified by objective reasons are possible, but there is a misuse control by the labour courts.

Table 3.2 The Organisation for Economic Cooperation and Development (OECD) indicators on Employment Protection Legislation (2019)

	Protection of permanent workers against individual and collective dismissals	Protection of permanent workers against (individual) dismissal	Specific requirements for collective dismissal	Regulation on hiring temporary forms of employment
France	2.7	2.4	3.3	3.1
Germany	2.3	2.2	2.6	1.9

Scale from 0 (least restrictions) to 6 (most restrictions).
Source: OECD.

The significant difference regarding the regulation of fixed-term contracts is due to the maximum duration of successive contracts being relatively short and the valid reasons for these contracts being rather limited in France. As Germany and France are both countries with relatively rigid regulations on permanent contracts, hiring of temporary workers and termination of fixed-term contracts represent an overwhelming share of gross worker flows (Jahn and Rosholm, 2012). In France, in particular, 78% of hires and 71% of separations in 2011 were due to the start or end of a fixed-term contract, and these figures appear broadly stable across age classes and time judging from the degree of duality of the French labour market remaining high over time.[17]

Another major difference is the legal handling of EPL cases by the courts, which constitutes an important element of termination costs for firms and thus negatively influences their decision to hire additional workers. While Germany has highly specialized labour courts that deal with EPL cases, France has been reforming the functioning of labour tribunals and labour processes starting from 2014, in order to make labour courts more specialized and trials periods shorter. A lower proportion of cases appealed and faster decisions were made in the German case as of 2013. Moreover, decisions by the German labour courts over the years have established a de facto 'price list' for compensation to be paid in case of unlawful dismissals, thereby contributing to more reliable expectations for employers and employees and less appeals to court decisions. Such a grid of compensations has been introduced in France thanks to the latest reform of the labour law. To prevent termination cases going to court, France introduced a formalized scheme of termination by mutual agreement in 2008 (*rupture conventionnelle*), extended to the case of collective dismissals in 2017. The agreement is subject to a cooling-off period, after which the employee is at least entitled to standard severance pay and unemployment benefits. However,

---

17   See Paraire (2012). For the evolution over time of the 2011 statistics, see Milin (2018).

neither the agreement nor its official approval prevent the employee from subsequently taking a case to court alleging that the agreement was not made voluntarily, notably in the case of previous conflicts between the employer and employee.

3.3.5 Industrial Action and Disputes

In France, the right to strike is guaranteed by the Constitution, and it applies to all employees whether or not there is a trade union involved. Though it is an individual right, it has to be exercised collectively. In other words, it is necessary for several employees to decide, together, that they will stop working as a means of achieving work-related demands. One employee alone cannot strike except within the framework of a national strike. Moreover, strikers (in normal strikes) have to raise issues that are related to the terms and conditions of their employment (for instance, related to wages, working conditions, or restructuring).

By contrast, while the German constitution secures the right to take industrial action, there is no guaranteed individual right to strike, so political or general strikes are considered to be unlawful. Moreover, there is no law governing the regulation of strikes. Thus, the regulation of industrial conflict has been effectively left to the courts. Case law has been developed by the Federal Labour Court in subsequent rulings. The fundamental principle governing disputes is that industrial action must pursue an aim that can be regulated by collective agreements. Therefore, only unions have the right to call strikes. Moreover, industrial actions are only lawful in the context of collective bargaining. Strikes cannot be called once a collective agreement is in place because they contain peace clauses that prohibit industrial action while they are in force (so-called *Friedenspflicht*).

When comparing the two regimes, it appears that the regulation of industrial actions is more stringent in Germany than in France, resulting in significantly more strike days in France. When looking at the number of working days lost per 1,000 employees, the German average was estimated at 20 days per year between 2006 to 2015, while the French private sector (including SOEs) had to deal with an average of 132 days, so more than six times as many days.[18]

3.3.6 Youth Unemployment, Active Labour Market Policies, Vocational Education and Training

Youth unemployment is higher in France than in Germany, especially for low-skilled workers.[19] In 2018, the unemployment rate for young people aged between 15 and 24 years was equal to 20.7% in France and 6.2% in Germany, respectively, 5.5 percentage points above and 9 percentage points below the EU28

---

18 See Hans Boeckler Stiftung—WSI Tarifarchiv.

19 More discussion of unemployment and long-term unemployment in France and Germany is provided in a separate note of this project.

average of 15.2% (see Figure 3.7). These figures were higher for workers having the lowest levels of skills. Notably, youth unemployment rates were three times as high in France as in Germany for workers having up to lower secondary education (ISCED 0–2) only. The picture is similar for youth not in education, employment, or training (NEET) but with smaller gaps: their share is low in Germany (5.9% in 2018), higher in the EU28 (10.5%), and even higher in France (11.1%). Neither youth unemployment rates nor NEET figures are strongly influenced by the definition of youth, and in particular by the age category taken into account for defining youth, which can range either between 15 and 24 years or between 15 and 29 years.

Also, youth unemployment can be linked to the different approach and governance of the vocational education and training systems, where two main differences are at play. First, the combined approach is used in Germany, in which theoretical teaching is always coupled with training embedded in a real-life work environment. This 'dual system' of vocational education and training is the result of the close cooperation between firms (mainly of small and medium size) and public vocational schools and is regulated by law. By contrast, in France, this link between theory and practice is not always ensured; the possibility to match the theoretical teaching often depends on the students' ability to find training corresponding to the subjects taught *ex-catedra*. The second difference is the strict alliance between the federal government, the federal states (*Länder*), and companies to ensure that the training provided is recognized nationwide and documented with certificates issued by the chamber of industry and commerce or the chamber of crafts and trades. In France, the law 'for the freedom to choose

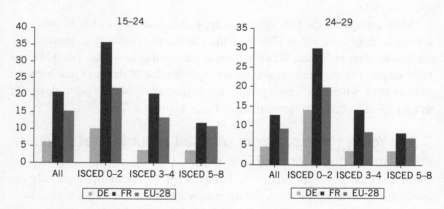

Figure 3.7 Youth unemployment rate by age and education level (2018).
The International Standard Classification of Education (ISCED) is a statistical framework for organizing information on education maintained by the United Nations Educational, Scientific and Cultural Organization (UNESCO). An ISCED level between 0 and 2 corresponds to less than primary, primary, and lower secondary education; between 3 and 4 to upper secondary education and postsecondary nontertiary education; between 5 and 8 to tertiary education.
Source: Labour Force Survey, Eurostat.

one's professional path' adopted in 2018 has entirely changed the functioning and governance of the French vocational training system, making it closer to the German system. Regions have lost their competence in the field of apprenticeship: training centres will now be financed by the former collection organisms (OPCA; renamed *operators of competences* [OPCO]), which are linked to professional branches. Therefore, professions now play a direct role in the definition of apprenticeship curricula. The central state has a direct role in the administration of OPCOs, while regions have begun to collaborate with OPCOs in the definition of the vocational training strategy in their area. Companies can now more easily create their own training centres to meet their skill needs, while the new regulating agency (France Compétences) will ensure the quality of certification and the match between training offer and demand.

3.3.7 Reform Adjustment

The differences between the French and the German labour market institutions are also reflected in a different approach to reform. Indeed, the more decentralized the wage-setting process, politically, the more easier it may be to reform it. As a result, while reforms adopted in Germany have been less frequent but characterized by a wider scope, labour law in France is a field where only a step-by-step approach to reform seems possible.

In Germany, the fact that larger numbers of employees were kept in jobs during the 2008 downturn is often seen as the result of the structural employment policies put in place since 2003 (Ziemann, 2010). After having gone through the 'Hartz reforms' in the mid-2000s,[20] labour market reforms in Germany in the past few years included introducing a statutory general minimum wage (2015), facilitating the extension of sectoral collective agreements (including amendments to labour court procedures), and tightening the rules on temporary agency work. While the motivation of the 'Hartz reforms' was mainly to deregulate institutions and increase incentives to take up work after the sluggish labour market performance at the beginning of the 2000s,[21] increased vulnerability of workers followed, suggesting that increasing labour market pressures beyond a certain level may be socially unsustainable. Hutter et al. (2019) identified a clear role of the Hartz reforms for the labour market upswing through increasing matching efficiency, fostering job creation, and strengthening search intensity. However, it also led to intensifying downward wage pressure. The latest set of reforms was motivated to protect workers from unfair situations and improve the functioning of the collective bargaining system.

---

20 For recent discussion of the 'Hartz reforms' and their (limited) impact on the German labour market, see Burda and Hunt (2011) as well as Odendahl (2017).

21 Burda and Seele (2016) show that the Hartz reforms induced important increases of labour supply after 2003.

At the same time, France has embarked on a series of reforms since 2008, promoting the introduction of a 'flexicurity system'. In particular, the reforms enacted by the *El Khomri law*, adopted in July 2016, provide employers with more incentives to hire on open-ended contracts because they introduced the so-called *offensive agreements* through company-level agreements that can modify the working conditions and remunerations of employees to maintain or increase employment. The same law also continued the previous series of reforms redefining dismissal procedures (2008, individual dismissal; 2013, collective dismissal; 2014, labour court reform) by enlarging the concept of individual dismissal to include economic reasons. Equally, the El Khomri law paved the way for the reduction in the number of industrial sectors from 700 to 200 and the reform of the Labour Code initially planned by August 2018 and then anticipated in September 2017. The latter redefined the relationship between firm- and sector-level agreements to enlarge the field of collective bargaining, simplify representative institutions within firms, and redefine *prud'homial indemnities* in terms of worker seniority. All these reforms have been accompanied by a progressive reinforcement of professional transitions. Since 2011, the *professional securing contract* supports workers in getting back to work by setting up specific accompanying and training measures and grants. Furthermore, a personal training account was introduced in 2014 to provide training rights directly attached to active people in the private sector throughout their careers. The personal training account has been encompassed in the personal activity account since January 2017. This personal activity account is accessible to all, including civil servants, unemployed, and self-employed. It allows them to have access to all the rights acquired throughout their career in terms of both training and retirement. The 2018 reform of the vocational education and training system has changed the way in which training rights stored in personal training accounts are measured, passing from points to euros.

3.4 SOCIAL OUTCOMES

Labour market developments are key determinants of the distribution of market income. This section reviews differences in unemployment rates, part- and full-time employment, share of low-wage earners, and in-work poverty.

As observed in Sections 3.2 and 3.3, the unemployment gap between France and Germany has widened significantly since the outbreak of the economic and financial crisis. The French unemployment rate developed in parallel with that of Germany at the beginning of the 1990s. Thereafter it decreased almost steadily, falling below the German rate in 2002 (also as a result of the impact of the crisis in Germany in the early 2000s). However, an ongoing wage moderation and the labour market reforms adopted in Germany during that period (including the 'Hartz reforms'), along with other factors, explained in the previous section,

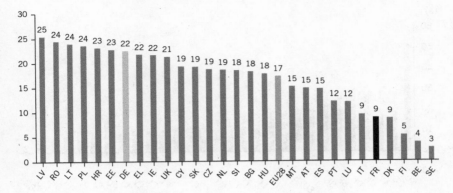

Figure 3.8 Share of workers who earn low hourly wages in the EU (2014).
Low-wage earners are defined as those employees (excluding apprentices) earning two-thirds
or less of the national median gross hourly earnings in that particular country. The Structure of
Earnings Survey (SES) is done every 4 years; the latest data available are for 2014.
Source: Structure of Earnings Survey, Eurostat.

have contributed to a sustained decline in German unemployment since then. By contrast, the economic and financial crisis that broke out in 2008 reversed the previous years' positive trend in French unemployment. As a consequence, the unemployment rate in France was at 8.9% of the labour force, 5.6 percentage points higher than in Germany by the fourth quarter of 2019.

Labour market incomes are considerably more unequal in Germany, partly due to a higher dispersion of hourly wages. This is reflected in the higher incidence of low-paid work—the share of workers who earn less than two-thirds of the national median of gross hourly wages—which is about double in Germany than in France. This relationship is confirmed both from detailed data for companies with at least 10 employees (Figure 3.8) and income surveys. Current levels reflect a considerable change compared to the past—at the beginning of 1990s, the incidence of low-paid work was similarly low in France and Germany (OECD, 1996), while it increased to about double as much in Germany by the mid 2000s (Bosch, 2009).[22] Labour market institutions are key determinants for the distribution of labour market income. As explained earlier, differences in these institutions are reflected in income disparities. As discussed there, the wage-setting framework in Germany and changes between the mid-1990s and mid-2000s—the decentralization of collective bargaining and the Hartz reforms—contributed to a wider wage distribution in Germany than in France.

A high share of part-time work also contributes to higher inequality of labour market incomes in Germany. While in 2000 the share of part-time in employment was similar in France and in Germany, later the share of part-time work increased only marginally in France, where the share is now below the EU

22 For a recent overview, including a longer term perspective, see OECD (2019).

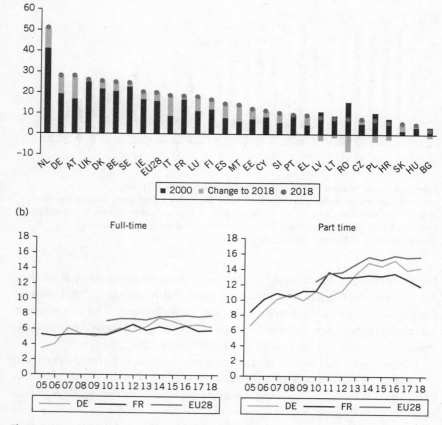

Figure 3.9 (a) Share of part-time employees among all employees. (b) In-work poverty by working time.
Source: (a) Labour Force Survey, Eurostat; (b) EU Statistics on Income and Living Conditions (EU-SILC), Eurostat.

average; by contrast, the increase was considerable in Germany, in particular in the beginning of the 2000s (panel a of Figure 3.9). Similar considerations can be derived when looking at temporary employment, with the difference that France features a higher percentage of temporary out of total employees (in 2017, 17.9% in France and 12.9% in Germany).

Together, a relatively high share of low hourly wages and part-time employment results in a higher in-work poverty rate in Germany. The share of workers who are at risk of poverty increased in the past decade in both France and Germany. However, while in France the increase amounted to about 2 percentage points and the in-work poverty rate remained below the EU average, in Germany it increased by more than twice as much, reaching the EU average.

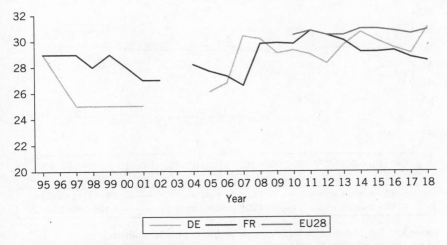

Figure 3.10 Gini coefficients for total disposable household income including pensions.
Source: EU Statistics on Income and Living Conditions (EU-SILC), Eurostat.

By working time, the in-work poverty rate of part-time workers increased more strongly in Germany (panel b of Figure 3.9).

3.4.1 Disposable Income Inequality and Poverty

Apart from market incomes, taxes, transfers, and subsidies can play a crucial role to assuage market-income inequality and mitigate poverty. Although crucial, market income is only one of the elements behind the overall income distribution and social outcomes thereof. The evolution of unemployment is key to explain differences in income distribution and poverty rates between Germany and France. In addition, tax and public transfer schemes can also have a considerable impact in shaping the income distribution (Haget and Montel, 2016).

Measured as Gini indicators counted from internationally comparable EU Statistics on Income and Living Conditions (SILC) data, Germany and France have had similar levels of income inequality, below the EU average. While Germany became markedly more unequal in the decade preceding the 2008 crisis, in the case of France, disposable income inequality has been largely stable since the early 1980s or even declined in the mid-1990s (OECD, 2008). A limited increase in overall income inequality can be observed during the years following the crisis, mainly related to the increase in unemployment after 2008 (see Figure 3.10). For Germany, EU SILC survey data suggest some oscillation of income inequality in the 2010s, but at higher levels than in the past, with the Gini indicator jumping to 31.1 in 2018, reversing a slight reduction that took place after 2014, the period when the statutory general minimum wage was introduced. The same picture emerges from S80:S20 ratios. The overall trend is confirmed by the German national Socio-Economic Panel (SOEP) survey, which suggests

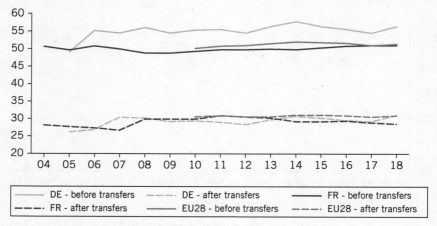

Figure 3.11 Gini of disposable income inequality, before and after transfers.
(1) Figure shows Gini coefficients of equivalized disposable income before social transfers, including pensions in social transfers.
(2) Transfers include pensions.
(3) Break for France in 2008.
Source: EU Statistics on Income and Living Conditions (EU-SILC), Eurostat.

that, between 1991 and 1999, the Gini indicator was stable at around 25, after which it jumped to 29 by 2005, followed by a slight reduction until 2009 to 28, before rising towards its historical peak, with a level of 29.5 in 2016 (Grabka and Goebel, 2018; Spannagel and Molitor, 2019).

Even if the unemployment rate in Germany declined to well below the French one, income inequality before transfers remains higher in Germany. Market income inequality, before considering the implications of social transfers and pensions, was higher in Germany than in France, with Gini levels of about 56 and 51, respectively, in the two countries in 2018 (Figure 3.11). France is about at the EU average, while Germany is among the EU countries with the highest Gini before transfers. After transfers, disposable income inequality has recently been at about a Gini of 29 for both, even if the 2018 data suggest an increase in Germany. Pensions play an important role in the redistributive system in both countries: the Gini coefficients before pension distribution of about 50–55 are reduced to about 35 (36.6 in Germany and 34.9 in France in 2018) and other social transfers reduce inequality further to Ginis of around 29.

Aggregate measures of disposable income inequality are slow moving indicators and, in Germany, mask important changes. While in France low, median, and high disposable incomes increased similarly since 1995, in Germany there were considerable divergences (Figure 3.12). In Germany, low incomes increased more than median incomes in the late 1990s, while in the 2000s they lagged considerably behind. In addition, while in the 2000s high-income earners in Germany kept pace with income increases in France, there emerged

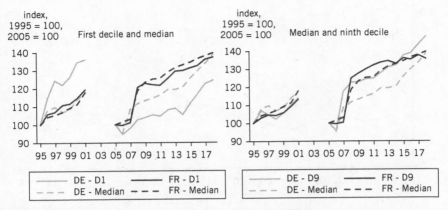

Figure 3.12 Disposable income at the first and the ninth decile and at the median income. Due to discontinuity of European Community Household Panel, 2002–2003, data missing for these years and break in series.
Source: European Community Household Panel, EU Statistics on Income and Living Conditions (EU-SILC), Eurostat.

a considerable gap for median-income earners, with the median German ones growing considerably less than the median French disposable income earners.

The total rate of households at risk of poverty in Germany has persistently exceeded that in France since 2006 (while in Germany it has oscillated around 16%, in France it has remained close to 13%). The steady decline in unemployment in Germany was thus accompanied by a more limited decline in the risk of poverty after 2014. Despite the sizeable reduction in unemployment, the total rate of households at risk of poverty[23] in Germany has persistently exceeded that in France since 2006 (Figure 3.13), and no convergence is observed. The German national SOEP survey gives a more nuanced picture of historical developments: it suggests that the at-risk-of-poverty rate oscillated around 11% in 1991–1999, then rapidly increased to around 14% by 2004, remaining around 15% during the financial crisis; between 2013 and 2015, it increased from 15% to close to 17% (Grabka and Goebel, 2018).

The overall higher impact of the tax benefit system in reducing relative poverty is mainly explained by larger social expenditure in France. While the share of social spending in total public spending is very similar in both countries,[24] the level of public expenditure as percentage of GDP in France significantly outweighs that in Germany (Herndon et al., 2013). The higher impact of social

---

23 At-risk-of-poverty rate is measured as the share of the population with equivalized disposable income, after taxes and social transfers, below 60% of the national median equivalized disposable income. The median equivalized disposable income is the total income available for spending or saving, divided by the number of household members weighted by their age.

24 See also Section 3.1.

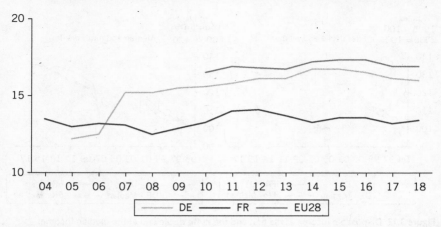

Figure 3.13 At-risk-of-poverty rates (share of population with less than 60% of mean equivalized income, after social transfers).
Source: Eurostat, EU Statistics on Income and Living Conditions (EU-SILC).

public spending on relative poverty reduction in France is consistent with the findings in Chen et al. (2018).[25] The labour market reforms in this regard could also help explain part of the increase in the at-risk-of-poverty rate observed in 2006 and 2007 in Germany, including those for aged between 18 and 24, and the subsequent overall upward trend despite the sizeable reduction in unemployment. While relative poverty increased more in Germany, key measures of absolute poverty developed similarly in the two countries. Severe material deprivation has declined in both countries by a similar extent (Figure 3.14).

3.4.2 Intergenerational Income Differences

Social implications in terms of inequality are also different across generations and cohorts between Germany and France. Disparities in unemployment rates for young and middle-aged workers have accentuated since 2008. Youth and middle-age unemployment was higher in France until the early 2000s (Figure 3.15). The gap declined significantly for young workers in the early years of the century. However, the gap started to widen again after the outbreak of the crisis due to the increase in youth unemployment in France, whereas it continued to decline in Germany. For older workers (those aged between 55 and 64), the divergent trends are even more salient. While the unemployment rate of French older workers used to be less than half of their German counterparts until 2006,

---

25   Chen et al. (2018) also find evidence of a positive relationship between long-term unemployment and the level of poverty. However, they also find that higher labour market flexibility tends to increase absolute poverty. These two findings appear somewhat contradictory though in that long-term unemployment tends to be negatively correlated with labour market flexibility.

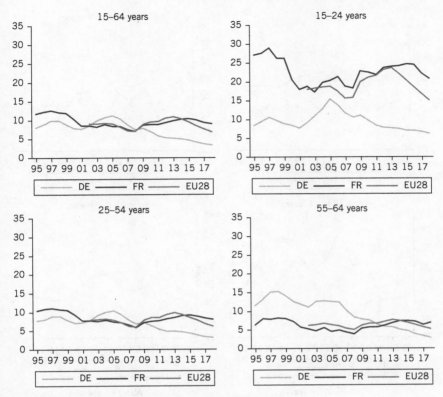

Figure 3.14 Severe material deprivation, by age group.
Source: EU Statistics on Income and Living Conditions (EU-SILC), Eurostat.

the latter has steadily declined since then to fall below the French rate in 2012. In this regard, recent reforms of pension and pre-retirement schemes in France have increased the retirement age and tightened the conditions for early retirement since the beginning of 2004, thereby leading workers to remain longer on the labour market even if they are unemployed. For example, at the end of 2017, 66.3% of 50- to 64-year-olds are active, employed, or unemployed: that is a +1.1 percentage point over 1 year (DARES, 2018).

The better unemployment performance of Germany since 2007 has not always translated into better social outcomes across all age groups. Between 2005 and 2007, income inequality as measured by Gini coefficients rose in all age groups in Germany despite the decline in unemployment rates (Figure 3.16), which might be due, at least in part, to the labour market reforms implemented between 2003 and 2005. Since 2007, however, no systematic trend is observed for the total and those older than 55, as income inequality has remained roughly stable. This contrasts with the steady decline in unemployment rates also observed for older workers. However, young workers between 18 and 24 of age, and to a lesser

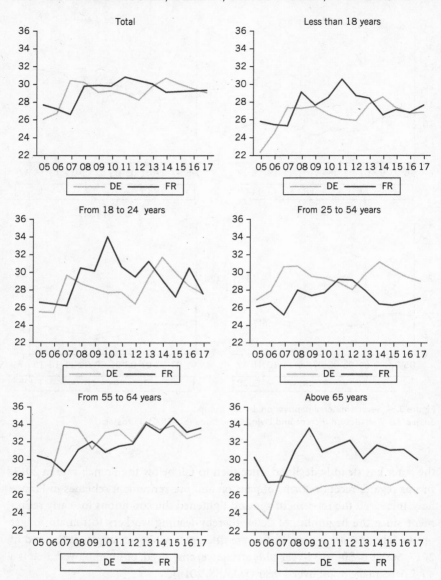

Figure 3.15 Unemployment rates, by age groups.
Source: Labour Force Survey, Eurostat.

extent those aged between 25 and 54, seem to have benefited from the aftermath of the labour market reforms in that a significant decline in Gini coefficients was observed between 2007 and 2012.

In France, the increase in income inequality has gone hand in hand with the pick-up in unemployment. A significant increase was observed in 2008 for all age groups. Following the improvement of the economic setting as of 2013, income

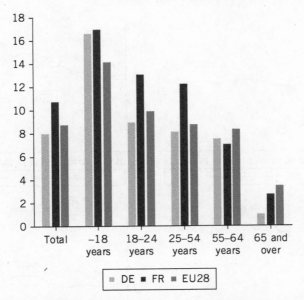

Figure 3.16 Gini coefficients by age group for total disposable household income including pensions.
Ad-hoc extraction request.
Source: EU Statistics on Income and Living Conditions (EU-SILC), Eurostat.

inequality dwindled for those younger than 54, whereas it rose slightly for those between 55 and 64 years of age and remained broadly stable for the elderly.

The share of the middle-aged and the elderly at risk of poverty in France is lower than in Germany, whereas the opposite is true for the young (Figure 3.17). The at-risk-of-poverty rate among those younger than 18 in France is about 4 percentage points higher than in Germany. This gap has widened in recent years, which may be related, at least in part, to a more advanced demographic ageing in Germany. This has resulted in relatively smaller cohorts at younger ages and, consequently, a relatively smaller number of children to care for.[26] Moreover, the widening gap between the respective unemployment rates also seems to have played a role. A similar picture emerges for those aged between 18 and 24: they tend to display higher at-risk-of-poverty rates in France, which is also linked to the higher youth unemployment rate (Figure 3.15) and to the fact that, in most cases, they are not entitled to the main social benefit, the Revenu de Solidarité Active (RSA). At the same time, the labour market reforms

---

26 The at risk of poverty situation for those younger than 18 highly depends on the family situation. According to Eurostat data, about one-third of the children who live in a single-parent family are at risk of poverty in both countries (33.2% in Germany, 32.6% in France, compared to 35.3% in the EU, in 2017), which is more than two times than the at-risk-of-poverty rate in the whole population.

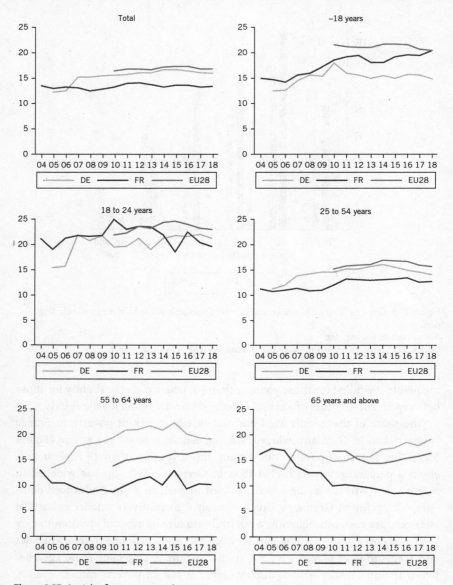

Figure 3.17 At-risk-of-poverty rates, by age group.
Source: EU Statistics on Income and Living Conditions (EU-SILC), Eurostat.

in Germany implemented in 2003–2005 made unemployment benefits less generous for the young and enhanced active labour market policies also for this age group. Demographic ageing and smaller younger cohorts meant for young adults less competition on the labour market, contributing to easier school-to-work transitions (in addition, school-to-work transitions have traditionally been easier in Germany, helped by the traditionally well-working dual education/ apprenticeship system). All this resulted in especially good labour market performance for the young in recent years, which led to a broadly stable at-risk-of-poverty rate for individuals aged 18–24, which contrasts to the overall increase for the other age groups. However, for those older than 25, at-risk-of-poverty rates have been persistently higher in Germany, even if the unemployment rate is lower for this group. It becomes especially sizeable for older workers (between 55 and 64 years old), where at-risk-of-poverty rates have widened markedly since 2004 and remain at some 9 percentage points higher in Germany. This also reflects that the Hartz reforms closed early retirement pathways by restricting duration of unemployment benefits, thus forcing older workers to stay on the labour market longer while those nevertheless leaving employment face strong reductions of income. Interestingly, this trend has gone hand in hand with a sizeable decline in the German unemployment rate among older workers, whereas the opposite has been witnessed in France, also due to the increase in the legal retirement age. As a result, the German unemployment rate of older workers has fallen well below the French one.

The gap between at-risk-of-poverty rates for people older than 25 is possibly linked to more generous work and housing welfare benefits existing in France. Those benefits protect the income of inactive or unemployed people and guarantee a minimum income for working people. Indeed, while young workers face similar poverty risks in the two countries, prime-age and older workers have a higher poverty risk in Germany (Figure 3.18). A similar picture emerges for the at-risk-of-poverty rate for the elderly. Higher at-risk-of-poverty rates are observed in Germany since 2007, with the gap even widening in recent years to reach 9.9 points in 2018. In the case of France, however, the risk of relative poverty has shown a steady decline since the outbreak of the crisis, which reflects that their incomes were better protected than those still of working age and the high minimum benefits for elderly people.

The reduction of at-risk-of-poverty rates in France by social transfers and benefits outweighs that in Germany in all age groups considered (Figure 3.19). The social transfer-benefit system reduces the total at-risk-of-poverty rate by 10.8 and 8.0 percentage points in France and Germany, respectively. While the larger corrections in the two countries take place within the youngest cohorts, namely those below 18 years of age, the more pronounced discrepancies are observed for those aged 25–54.[27] Accordingly, the higher youth at-risk-of-poverty rate in France seems more likely linked to higher youth unemployment and high

27 A word of caution is required to interpret data on the reduction in at-risk-of-poverty rates by benefits and transfers. The higher reduction in at-risk-of-poverty rates in certain age groups might just reflect initial at-risk-of-poverty rates (i.e., before socials transfers and benefits) higher for those age groups, rather than social transfer-and-benefit systems targeting more specific groups or populations.

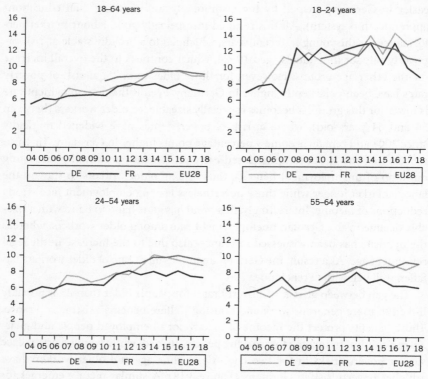

Figure 3.18 In-work poverty: Share of workers who are at risk of poverty, by age group.
Source: EU Statistics on Income and Living Conditions (EU-SILC), Eurostat.

poverty risk for single-parent families. Severe material deprivation by age group shows similar patterns to those observed with the at-risk-of-poverty rate (Figure 3.19). While Germany fares markedly better in severe material deprivation of those younger than 25 and somewhat better for the prime working age population, for elder workers (aged 55–64) it is worse than in France. Severe material deprivation for the elderly (aged 65 or older) is similarly low in the two countries.

3.4.3 Regional Income Disparities

An additional dimension of income inequality is the one concerning different parts of a country, so that regional disparities may be assessed in parallel to inequality considerations at an individual level (Rodríguez-Pose, 2018; Rosés and Wolf, 2018). What follows sheds light on the evolution over time of the distribution of GDP and income per capita measured at regional level.[28] It also shows

---

28 Some words of caution are needed when applying to data the results of literature showing that regional disparities may be assessed in parallel with inequality considerations at the individual level. For example, the definition of a regional

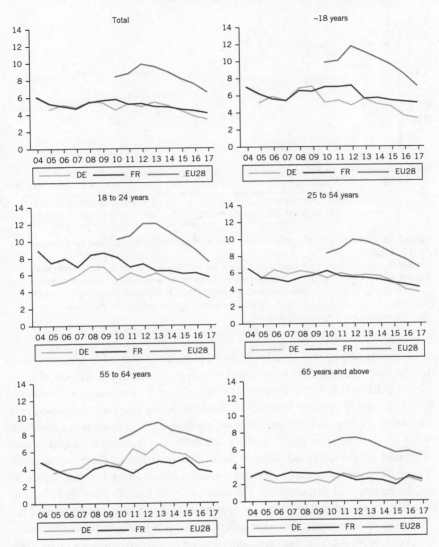

Figure 3.19 Reduction in at-risk of poverty rates by benefits and transfers (pension not considered as transfers here) (2018).
Source: EU Statistics on Income and Living Conditions (EU-SILC), Eurostat.

how the evolution of regional disparities is accompanied by differences in GDP per capita growth rates, employment outcomes, and the role of the local administration at regional level.

---

aggregate may be less homogeneous than the one at the individual level, making comparisons between two regional entities more difficult to interpret than a comparison between two different individuals.

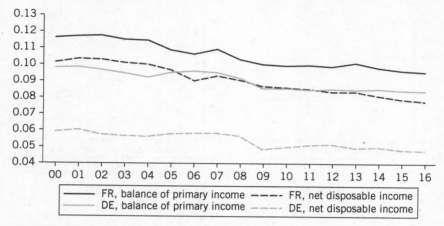

Figure 3.20 Evolution of Gini coefficients by Nomenclature of Territorial Units for Statistics (NUTS) 2 regions.
The NUTS classification is a hierarchical system for dividing up the economic territory of the EU at three different levels (NUTS 1, 2, and 3, respectively, moving from larger to smaller territorial units). Notably, NUTS 1 are major socioeconomic regions, NUTS 2 are basic regions for the application of regional policies, and NUTS 3 are small regions for specific diagnoses.
Source: Eurostat, authors' calculations.

Inequality among regions is lower in Germany and has steadily decreased over time in both countries, both regarding primary and disposable income (Figure 3.20). Gini coefficients for regional inequality have a lower value in Germany, both when using primary income (i.e., income before taxes and subsidies) and disposable income (i.e., income after taking into account taxes and subsidies). Although decreasing in both countries, the difference between Gini coefficients calculated on primary and disposable income is larger in Germany than in France. This indicates that taxes and subsidies play a more important role in equalizing regional disparities in Germany than in France, possibly reflecting the stronger role played in Germany by subnational governments (Figure 3.21).

The decrease in regional income inequalities has been accompanied by a similar evolution of the GDP per capita distribution in the two countries up to 2008. Since then, the poorest regions in Germany started to develop relatively faster. Regional disparities in terms of GDP per capita are below the OECD average in both France and Germany. However, changes in these disparities have taken opposite directions over time, in particular after the last financial crisis. Figure 3.20 shows the evolution of the first and the last decile, as well as the median of the regional GDP per capita distribution. Between 2000 and 2008, GDP per capita has increased in a quite homogenous way in most of the regions under analysis. In both France and Germany, regions belonging to the first decile of the distribution were developing faster than the others, with poorest regions in France growing even faster than in Germany. At the same time, GDP per capita of regions belonging to the tenth decile of the distribution were growing hand in hand

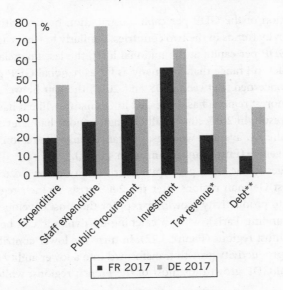

Figure 3.21 Subnational government role in public finances (2017).
* 2016 data, ** 2015 data
Source: OECD, OECD Regional Outlook 2016, authors' calculations.

with the median. After 2008, the development of those regions falling into the first decile of the distribution outpaced the rest of German regions. A widening gap opened up between France and Germany for the median regions. The richest regions in France had a more sustained development than in Germany up to 2013, with a peak in their GDP per capita in 2016. This remarkable concentration of GDP per capita distribution to the richest regions in 2016 in France reflects the evolution of GDP per capita concentrated to two regions (Île de France and Hauts-de-Seine), which significantly outperformed that of all others.

These indicators do not capture significant variations in purchasing power due to regional differences in housing costs. This is particularly felt in the larger cities where the affordability of housing can become an important factor to consider. Although the so-called *housing cost overburden rate* (i.e., the proportion of the population spending more than 40% of disposable income on housing costs) is declining in both countries, it remains well above the EU average in Germany (standing at 14.5% compared to 10.4% for the European Union in 2017). Whilst the housing cost overburden rate was less than half of the EU average in France, house price developments differ markedly across the country and have been more pronounced in the larger cities, notably in Paris. Even if house price increases do not appear to cause any macro or financial stability risks in either of the countries at present, they could point to persistent gaps in housing supply and may constitute an obstacle for mobility of labour across sectors and regions, especially at the lower end of the wage scale.

The evolution of the GDP per capita distribution occurs with different labour productivity trends in the two countries. Similarly to what can be observed in terms of GDP per capita at the national level, the last financial crisis had a stronger impact in France than Germany as far as regional GDP per capita dynamics are concerned. Between 2008 and 2013, the gap between the 20% of richest and poorest regions has decreased in Germany, while it has increased in France. As a result, in 2015, almost all German regions had a level of GDP per capita above the EU average, whereas, in France, only five regions were in line with the EU average (European Commission, 2018c).

Such changes in the GDP per capita distribution mirror a catch-up process for the poorest German regions after the 2008 crisis. French regions struggle to contribute to productivity growth, except for the most developed one (Ile de France, surrounding Paris), while a catching-up dynamic can be observed in Germany for most regions (Figure 3.22). In turn, the lower contribution to national labour productivity growth transformed into a lower ability to contribute to the national GDP growth for most of the French regions, while the highest

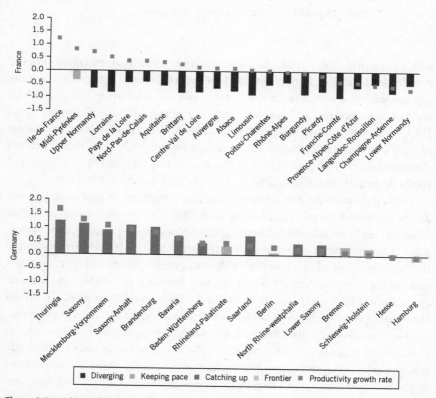

Figure 3.22 Labour productivity growth by regions (2000–2016).
Source: OECD, authors' calculations.

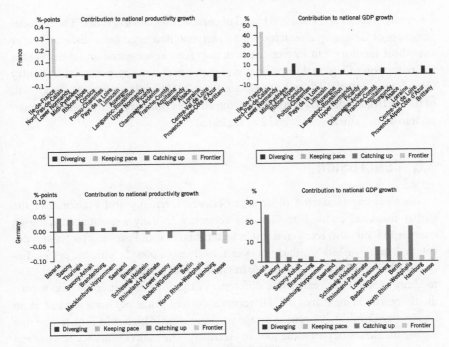

Figure 3.23 Catching-up trends among regions (2000–2016).
The contribution of a region is defined as the difference between the national annual average labour productivity growth rate and the annual average labour productivity growth rate for all regions but the one indicated.
Source: OECD, authors' calculations.

contribution to national GDP growth stemmed from catching-up regions in Germany (Figure 3.23).

The catch-up process for the least developed German regions in recent years was largely driven by two main factors: (1) their geographical proximity to more dynamic regions in Eastern Europe and (2) the different regional structure of the two economies. As for the first factor, between 2008 and 2015, GDP per head increased relative to the EU average in all regions in the central and eastern Member States. Proximity, integrated supply chains, and other trade links to catching-up eastern EU economies may have spilled over in the form of higher GDP per capita growth in German regions. As for the second factor, an alternative explanation to such differences in the catch-up process is constituted by the different regional structures in the two countries. The Regional Competitiveness Index[29] points to the existence of a broader constellation of competitive regions in

---

29 The Regional Competitiveness Index (RCI) is designed to capture the different dimensions of competitiveness for Nomenclature of Territorial Units for Statistics (NUTS) 2 regions and is the first measure to provide an EU-wide perspective on this. The 2016 edition follows the two previous ones published in 2010 and 2013 (Annoni

Germany versus Paris's isolated island of competitiveness in France. The regional structure of Germany, characterized by metropolitan aggregates dislocated over the whole territory, but interconnected, may have represented an advantage for the reduction of regional disparities and the overall development of the country (Henderson, 2000; Frick and Rodríguez-Pose, 2018) while, in France, the growth of the metropole of Paris is still outpacing all other, more recently created metropolitan areas (Dherbécourt and Le Hir, 2016).[30]

3.5 CONCLUSION

Income per capita started to diverge between Germany and France after the global financial crisis. The German economy initially experienced a much sharper fall, but also recovered much faster than that of France, after having developed more or less similarly between 1991 and 2008. In current prices, between 2005 and 2018, the difference in GDP per head increased from about €330 to almost €5,800 per year. These differences cannot be explained by labour productivity which, measured in GDP terms at current prices per hour worked, is no longer significantly different. Average working time is higher in France due to a higher incidence of part-time jobs in Germany. The main difference lies instead in the performance of the labour market.

In contrast to France, there was a rise in the employment rate and a sizeable fall in unemployment in Germany. The unemployment rate was identical in 2008 (at 7.8% of the labour force) in the two countries. While it increased until 2016 to more than 10% in France, slowly declining thereafter to about 8.5%, it fell continuously in Germany to just over 3% in 2019 (see Figure 3.24). Differences are even more pronounced for the young and long-term unemployed. The employment rate was still similar in 2005 (at around 70% of population aged 20–64 years) and has remained broadly stable in France, while it increased to almost 80% in Germany (79.9% in 2018). The EU28 saw 73.2% in 2018. The higher labour

---

and Kozovska, 2010; Dijkstra et al., 2011; Annoni and Dijkstra, 2017). All three are built on the same approach as the Global Competitiveness Index of the World Economic Forum (World Economic Forum, 2017, 2018). The 2016 index is based on 74 mostly regional indicators covering the 2012–2014 period, though with a number of indicators for 2015 and 2016. The index is based on a definition of regional competitiveness from the perspective of both firms and residents (Dijkstra et al., 2011).

30 Recent literature puts into question the 'Williamson hypothesis' on the existence of an inverted U-shaped relationship between regional agglomeration and GDP growth (Brülhart and Sbergami, 2009). The growth of the services sector has transformed metropolitan cities into growth engines (Combes, 2000; Díez Minguela and Sanchís Llopis, 2018; Rosés et al., 2015), in turn reshaping the inverted U-shaped relationship found in previous literature into an N-shaped relationship between regional disparities and development (Lessmann and Seidel, 2017).

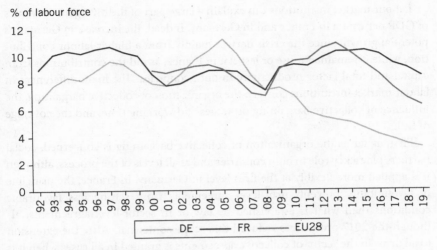

Figure 3.24 Unemployment rate (1991–2019).
Source: Ameco, European Commission.

market participation and employment rates suggest that the German labour market has significantly more outreach.

Considering the long term, Germany and France have always seen episodes when one country performed better than the other in terms of income and per capita income developments. France had been catching up to West Germany between 1960 and 1974, but this process stalled until German unification had a statistical effect on the relative income levels. Then, after a period of buoyant growth in Germany in the years following unification, France regained economic ground between 1995 and the mid-2000s. Thereafter, however, France has been falling behind, and incomes have risen relatively faster in Germany.

The two economies have fundamentally different growth models that have evolved gradually over time. Germany's postwar economic growth model is strongly based on exports, particularly of manufactured goods. In addition to substantial non-price factors, Germany has regularly made price competiveness gains through relatively low inflation. This model was briefly interrupted by unification, which required higher investment and caused higher inflation. In contrast, GDP growth in France has traditionally relied on domestic demand, driven by its sizeable public sector and a lower household saving rate. In addition, France's large public sector has helped to smooth economic cycles. While Germany has performed better in recent years, its growth model is more volatile, reflecting in part its exposure to the global economic cycle. France has traditionally a steadier path, but at a cost of pressure on public finances and a persistently higher unemployment rate. It is clear that both growth models have displayed different shortcomings.

Labour market institutions can explain a large part of the divergent dynamics of GDP per capita in France and in Germany. Indeed, the increase in Germany's potential growth since the crisis derives mainly from a higher labour contribution, while it remained more or less flat in France, as did the contributions from capital and total factor productivity in both countries. The main differences in labour market institutions concern the organization of collective bargaining, the influence of collective bargaining on wages and working time, and the coverage of EPL.

First, as far as the organization of collective bargaining is concerned, social partners play a key role in both countries and at all levels of the process, although it is applied more flexibly at the firm level in Germany. In France, the principle of favourability prevents firm-level agreements from setting less favourable conditions than what is established by law or in sector-level agreements, although the 2017 ordinances reduced this scope somewhat. Also, the extension to all firms in the sector of collective agreements is granted in all cases when it is requested by social partners. By contrast, the extension of collective agreements is rarely requested by social partners in Germany, and firms can decide whether to be part of sector-level agreements. Another key difference is that, in Germany, employee participation in the management of larger companies is the norm, with representatives of workers sitting on company supervisory boards. This practice, the so-called *Mitbestimmung* (or co-determination), has allowed for a better alignment of the interests of employers and employees, and it encourages consensus-seeking. Furthermore, works councils allow employee representatives to participate in the management decisions that directly affect them, such as social and personnel matters.

Second, collective bargaining also has a different influence on wages and working time in the two countries. Germany's higher flexibility, including through working time accounts and short-time work arrangements (*Kurzarbeit*), has allowed firms to reduce working hours in bad times, to a larger extent. This helped Germany to avoid a large drop in employment during the 2008 crisis. While these instruments have been in effect for some time, their use expanded considerably. *Kurzarbeit* was created in 1924, and already in 1999 about 30% of employees were using working time accounts; however, the state support for *Kurzarbeit* was expanded during the 2008 crisis, and the number of workers using working time accounts has been expanding over time, almost doubling to close to 60% by 2016 (Ellguth et al., 2018). These adjustments also allowed a more flexible reaction of wages to economic shocks. Notably, wage dynamics in Germany tend to adapt to avoid, at least to some extent, sudden erosions of the country's cost competitiveness in the aftermath of an external shock. Moreover, there seem to be less severe spillovers from minimum wage increases in Germany than in France due to the higher level of the French minimum wage (relative to the median wage) and the so far cautious increases in Germany, although this should not be overinterpreted given the relatively short time period that has elapsed since Germany introduced a minimum wage in 2015.

Third, the level of EPL is higher in France for fixed-term contracts, and there are fewer (and quicker) labour court disputes in Germany than in France. On the other hand, EPL is relatively similar in France and Germany for individual and collective dismissals for the traditional permanent employment contract.

Fourth, smaller differences can also be observed in other labour market institutions. The unemployment insurance and pension systems in the two countries have somewhat different features. Furthermore, the focus and governance of the vocational education and training system seem to offer a more effective answer to youth unemployment in Germany than in France, although there has been some convergence in performance.

The differences in labour market institutions have translated into differences in labour market and social outcomes. In simplified terms, the higher degree of flexibility allowed the German economy to weather the crisis better. This was due to a more flexible collective bargaining system that allowed more adjustment in work time patterns and in wages, where the interests of employees and the companies were more aligned through the involvement of workers in the management through co-determination (*Mitbestimmung*) and there was a scope for firm-level agreements to secure jobs (*Beschäftigungspakte*). Within-company flexibility was enhanced by state support, such as higher state subsidies to the short-term work arrangement scheme (*Kurzarbeit*). In contrast, a lower degree of labour market and company internal flexibility in France forced firms to adjust more through cuts in employment, notably by reducing temporary jobs. Hysteresis effects and other features of the French labour market (high minimum wage relative to median income, weak apprenticeship system, industrial relations where trade unions have paid less attention to factoring in the impact of wage developments on the economy at large) have made it more difficult for those who lost their jobs during the crisis to return to the regular labour market.

However, the higher resilience and flexibility of the German labour market comes at the price of higher market income inequality and poverty across individuals, age groups, and geographic areas. While flexibility has enabled a higher employment rate overall, market outcomes show more wage inequality and in-work poverty in Germany than in France. These considerably more unequal labour market incomes in Germany are due to a higher inequality of hourly wages, higher variation in hours worked, and a higher share of part-time work.

In terms of labour market opportunities, however, Germany has performed better. Despite the higher wage inequality and at-risk-of-poverty rate in Germany, labour market opportunities appear considerably better than in France. Standard indicators of market income inequality only take into account people in employment. For example, involuntary fixed-term employment has been on a divergent trend in the two countries, reaching 1.7% of the active population in Germany and 9.8% in France, in 2018. However, unemployment is also a major form of labour market inequality that results in essentially no market income. Major changes in the economic structure of a country might also lead to prolonged unemployment periods for groups of workers and long-lasting consequences on the productivity and potential growth of a country. When looking at the differences between France and Germany, however, these hysteresis phenomena do not seem to have a large explanatory power so far, although it cannot be excluded that it may have an impact on human capital in the longer term.

Overall, the distribution of disposable income (i.e., after redistribution) is similar in Germany and France. The inequality of market income is considerably higher in Germany than in France; however, after transfers, disposable income inequality was similar in both countries. There are some signs of increasing inequality in Germany, but an early conclusion may be premature. If pensions are not considered social transfers, the Gini coefficients of disposable income before transfers would be closer for the two countries. Apart from pensions, the tax benefit system in France plays a more important role in correcting at-risk-of-poverty situations, whilst requiring higher social expenditure than in Germany, not least because of the higher unemployment rate. Irrespective of their levels, the reduction of at-risk-of-poverty rates achieved by social transfers and benefits in France outweighs that in Germany.

By age group, the distribution of income and at-risk-of-poverty rates makes for a mixed picture. Interestingly, the share of middle-aged and elderly at risk of poverty is lower in France than in Germany, even if the unemployment rate is lower for this group in Germany. However, for those younger than 25, a more uneven income distribution and higher at-risk-of-poverty rates can be observed in France, mainly related to a higher youth unemployment rate combined with restricted access to the main means-tested benefits. Along with the higher population share of this group in France, this relative disadvantage may help to explain emerging social tensions. Moreover, for those older than 55, income inequality in France is higher in spite of significantly lower at-risk-of-poverty rates. This is mainly explained by a relatively generous social system for relatively poorer elderly households in France. Consequently, income appears to be more evenly distributed in France than in Germany only for those aged 25–54.

Across regions, inequalities in GDP per capita are relatively low by international comparison and have steadily decreased over time in both France and Germany. Income inequality is relatively lower in Germany and is accompanied by a faster catching-up in the poorest regions. Similarly to the national level, different regional trends could be observed in the two countries after the 2008 crisis, with the gap between the 20% of the richest and poorest regions decreasing in Germany while trending up in France until 2013 and thereafter stabilizing. In Germany, this reflects factors such as the proximity to more dynamic regions in

Eastern Europe and a more decentralized regional structure with more growth centres. While these are interconnected and located across the country, which contributes to the reduction of regional disparities, many of them may lack a critical mass to be centres of excellence competing with innovations at a global level. In contrast, French regions still struggle to contribute to (productivity) growth, except for Paris (or Île de France) which has a scale that results in strong positive and negative ('Marshallian') externalities. These data do not capture variations in purchasing power due to regional variations in housing costs that are particularly felt in the larger cities, where affordability of housing can become an important factor to consider. Labour productivity represents an important element to explain such trends and mirrors different labour market outcomes and roles by local authorities. An open question here is whether a more centralized territorial structure, as in France, or a more decentralized structure, as in Germany, is more supportive of medium to long-term growth for the country as a whole.

Concluding overall, the gap between the two growth models and the resulting differences in social outcomes appears to be narrowing. The 2010s saw a series of social measures in Germany also making the labour market more inclusive. While in the 2000s there may have been a tradeoff between employment growth and employment quality, in the 2010s, both employment levels and employment quality improved. The introduction of the statutory general minimum wage in 2015 is a case in point. Wage increases exceeded inflation and productivity growth, while economic growth has been increasingly relying on domestic demand. The earlier observed increases in disposable income inequality, income poverty, and in-work poverty appear to have largely halted or at least slowed, while unemployment remains low. This result is mirrored by a lower regional income inequality accompanied by a faster catching-up in the poorest regions. At the same time, in France, unemployment has started to decline and a series of reforms have increased the flexibility of its labour market and reduced benefit generosity. While these reforms will likely contribute to adjustment, social unrest, such as the so-called *gilets jaunes* demonstrations, show that it is important to consider both the economic and social impact of reforms undertaken. Relatively favourable developments in France during previous years (1990s) and in Germany during the 2010s recall that there is no predestination in economic and social development and that policies can make a difference. Societies and economies change and adapt over time—while adaptation may also necessitate corrections later, moving the pendulum in the other direction. Looking further ahead, increased uncertainty in global trade, automation, and the transformation need of the labour market and of social protection will undoubtedly test different aspects of both models.

ACKNOWLEDGEMENTS

The authors were working for the European Commission when preparing this paper. Opinions expressed are those of the authors and do not necessarily reflect the view of the European Commission. This article draws on Cléaud et al. (2019), and the authors are thankful for their joint work to Guillaume Cléaud, Francisco de Castro Fernández, Jorge Durán Laguna, Anne Jaubertie, Carlos Maravall Rodriguez, Diana Ognyanova, Tsvetan Tsalinski, and Kai-Young Weißschädel, as well as Annika Eriksgaard and Martin Hallet. The authors thank Manfred Bergmann, Annika Eriksgaard, Georg Fischer, Martin Hallet, Carlos Martinez-Mongay, Magdalena Morgese Borys, Moisés Orellana, Wiemer Salverda, and Robert Strauss for their comments.

REFERENCES

Aeberhardt, R., Givord, P., and Marbot, C. (2016), *Spillover effect of the Minimum wage in France: An unconditional quantile regression.* Working Papers 2016-05. Paris: Center for Research in Economics and Statistics.

Ananian, S., Debauche, E., and Prost, C. (2012). *L'ajustmenet du marché du travail français pendant la crise de 2008–2009.* Dares Analyses no. 40. Paris: Ministry of Work, Employment, and Development.

Annoni, P., and Dijkstra, L. (2017). Measuring and monitoring regional competitiveness in the European Union. In Huggins, R. (ed.), *Handbook of regions and competitiveness: Contemporary theories and perspectives on economic development* (pp. 49–79). Cheltenham, UK: Edward Elgar.

Annoni, P., and Kozovska, K. (2010). *EU Regional Competitiveness Index 2010, EUR 24346 EN—2010, European Commission.* Luxembourg: Publications Office of the European Union.

Arpaia, A., and Van Herck, K. (2017). Wage distribution spill-overs from minimum wage increases in France, Analytical Web Note no. 1/2017, European Commission. DG Employment, Social Affairs and Inclusion.

Bosch, G. (2009). Low-wage work in five European countries and the United States. *International Labour Review, 148*(4), 337–356.

Bosch, G. (2011). The German labour market after the financial crisis: Miracle or just a good policy mix. In Vaughan-Whitehead, D. (ed.), *Work inequalities in the crisis, evidence from Europe* (pp. 243–277). Cheltenham, UK: Edward Elgar.

Brülhart, M., and Sbergami, F. (2009). Agglomeration and growth: Cross-country evidence. *Journal of Urban Economics, 65*(1), 48–63.

Burda, M. C., and Hunt, J. (2011). What explains the German labour market miracle in the Great Recession. Brookings Papers on Economic Activity. Bronking Institution Press. Spring 2011, pp. 273–319.

Burda, M. C., and Seele, S. (2016). No role for the Hartz reforms? Demand and supply factors in the German labor market, 1993–2014. SFB 649 Discussion Paper, no. 2016-010, Economic Risk. Humboldt University, Berlin, Germany.

Chen, T., Hallaert, J-J., Pitt, A., Qu, H., Queyranne, M., Rhee, A., . . . Yackovlev, I. (2018). Inequality and poverty across generations in the European Union. IMF staff discussion note 18/01. https://www.imf.org/en/Publications/Staff-Discussion-Notes/Issues/2018/01/23/Inequality-and-Poverty-across-Generations-in-the-European-Union-45137.

Cléaud, G., de Castro Fernández, F., Laguna, J. D., Granelli, L., Hallet, M., Jaubertie, A., . . . Weißschädel, K. Y. (2019). Cruising at different speeds: Similarities and divergences between the German and the French economies (no. 103). Directorate General Economic and Financial Affairs (DG ECFIN). Brussels: European Commission.

Combes, P.-P. (2000). Economic structure and local growth: France, 1984–1993. *Journal of Urban Economics, 47*(3), 329–355.

Costes, T., Rambert, L., and Saillard, E. (2015 January). Temps partiel et partage du travail: Une comparaison France/Allemagne. *Trésor-Eco 141.*

DARES. (2018 July). *Emploi, chômage et population active en 2017: Nouvelle accélération de l'emploi salarié privé et amplification de la baisse du chômage.* DARES analyses, no. 031. Paris: Ministry of Work, Employment, and Development.

Delpech, Q., Garner, H., Guézennec, C., and Naboulet A. (2016). Collective bargaining and internal flexibility: A Franco-German comparison. France Stratégie, Document de travail N°2016-02, février.https://www.strategie.gouv.fr/sites/strategie.gouv.fr/files/atoms/files/collective_bargaining_and_internal_flexibilty-26-02-2016.pdf.

Dherbécourt, C., and Le Hir, B. (2016). Dynamiques et Inégalités Territoriales. Enjeux, France Stratégie Projet 2017–2027. https://www.strategie.gouv.fr/publications/20172027-dynamiques-inegalites-territoriales.

Díez Minguela, A., and Sanchís Llopis, M. T. (2018). *Regional income inequality in France: What does history teach us?* Working Papers in Economic History (WP 18-01). Madrid: Universidad Carlos III de Madrid.

Dijkstra, L., Annoni, P., and Kozovska, K. (2011). A new European Regional Competitiveness Index: Theory, methods and findings. DG Regional Policy Working Papers WP02/2011. Brussels: European Commission.

Dustmann, C., Fitzenberger, B., Schönberg, U., and Spitz-Oener, A. (2014). From sick man of Europe to economic superstar: Germany's resurgent economy. *Journal of Economic Perspectives, 28*(1), 167–188.

Ellguth, P., Gerner, H. D., and Zapf, I. (2018). Arbeitszeitkonten in Betrieben und Verwaltungen: Flexible Arbeitszeitgestaltung wird immer wichtiger (no. 15/2018). IAB-Kurzbericht.

Enderlein, H., and Pisani-Ferry, H. (2014) Rapport–Réformes, investissement et croissance : un agenda pour la France, l'Allemagne et l'Europe, France

Stratégie, November 2014, https://www.strategie.gouv.fr/publications/reformes-investissement-croissance-un-agenda-france-lallemagne-leurope.

European Commission. (2016a). *Labour market and wage developments in Europe, 2016.* Directorate-General for Employment, Social Affairs and Inclusion. Brussels: European Commission.

European Commission. (2018a). *The 2018 ageing report: Economic and budgetary projections for the EU Member States (2016–2070).* Institutional Paper 079. Brussels: European Commission.

European Commission. (2018b). *Country report Germany 2018.* Brussels: European Commission.

European Commission. (2018c). *Seventh report on economic, social and territorial cohesion.* Brussels: European Commission.

European Commission. (2019a). *European economic forecast, autumn 2019.* European Economy Institutional Paper 115. November 2019. Brussels: European Commission.

European Commission. (2019b). *Country report Germany 2019: Including an in-depth review on the prevention and correction of macroeconomic imbalances.* SWD(2019) 1004. Brussels: European Commission.

Fougère, D., Gautier, E., and Roux, S. (2016, 28 May). The effect of minimum wage on wage bargaining at the industry level: Evidence from France. VoxEu blog. https://voxeu.org/article/effect-minimumwage-wage-bargaining-industry-level-evidence-france

France Stratégie. (2018a). Comité d'évaluation des ordonnances relatives au dialogue social et aux relations de travail. Séance plénière vendredi 22 juin 2018. Synthèse des présentations. https://www.strategie.gouv.fr/sites/strategie.gouv.fr/files/atoms/files/1-_ordonnances_synthese_des_resultats_enquetes.pdf

France Stratégie. (2018b). Evaluation des ordonnances relatives au dialogue social et aux relations de travail. Note d'étape sur les travaux du comité d'évaluation, 18 Décembre 2018. https://www.strategie.gouv.fr/publications/evaluation-ordonnances-relatives-dialogue-social-aux-relations-de-travail-note-detape

Fréhaut, P. (2012a). Chômage partiel, activité partielle, Kurzarbeit: Quelles différences entre les dispositifs publics français et allemand? *Trésor-Eco 107*, November 2012.

Frick, S. A., and Rodríguez-Pose, A. (2018). *Change in urban concentration and economic growth. World development (Vol. 105[C])* (pp. 156–170). Amsterdam: Elsevier.

Garbinti, B., Goupille-Lebret, J., and Piketty, T. (2017). Accounting for Wealth Inequality Dynamics: Methods, Estimates and Simulations for France (1800–2014). CEPR Discussion Papers 11848, C.E.P.R. Discussion Papers.

Grabka, M. M., and Goebel, J. (2018). Income distribution in Germany: Real income on the rise since 1991 but more people with low incomes. *DIW Weekly Report, 8*(21), 181–190.

Haget, R., and Montel, O. (2016, Dec). *Les dépenses en faveur de l'emploi et du marché du travail en 2014.* DARES résultats, no. 072. Paris: Ministry of Work, Employment, and Development.

Hancké, B. (2001). Revisiting the French model: Coordination and restructuring in French industry. In P. A. Hall and D. Soskice (eds.), *Varieties of capitalism: The institutional foundations of comparative advantage* (pp. 307–337). Oxford: Oxford University Press.

Hans Boeckler Stiftung. WSI Tarifarchiv. https://www.boeckler.de/wsi-tarifarchiv_64142.htm

Henderson, V. J. (2000). The effects of urban concentration on economic growth., NBER Working Papers, 10.3386/w7503. Cambridge, MA: National Bureau of Economic Research.

Herndon, T., Ash, M., and Pollin, R. (2013). *Does high public debt consistently stifle economic growth?* A critique of Reinhart and Rogoff. Political Economy Research Institute Working Paper no. 322. Amherst: University of Massachusetts.

Hutter, C., Klinger, S., Weber, E., and Trenkler, C. (2019). Which factors are behind Germany's labour market upswing? IAB-Discussion Paper no. 20/2019, Institute for Employment Research, Nuremberg, Germany. ttps://EconPapers.repec.org/RePEc:iab:iabdpa:201920.

IMF. (2019). *Article IV consultation report on Germany.* IMF Country Report no. 19/213. Washington, DC: International Monetary Fund.

Jahn, E., and Rosholm, M. (2012). Is temporary agency employment a stepping stone for immigrants? *Economics Letters, 118,* 225–228.

Kohaut, S. (2019). Tarifbindung: Weiterhin deutliche Unterschiede zwischen Ost-und Westdeutschland. *IAB-Forum,* 22 May 2019.

Lallement, R. (2017). Les mutations socioéconomiques en Allemagne: Bilan et perspectives. France Stratégie document de travail no. 2017–04. https://www.strategie.gouv.fr/sites/strategie.gouv.fr/files/atoms/files/dt-2017_allemagne-ok.pdf.

Lessmann, C., and Seidel, A. (2017). Regional inequality, convergence, and its determinants: A view from outer space. *European Economic Review, 92*(C), 110–132.

Lestrade, B. (2017). *L'introduction du salaire minimum en Allemagne: Un premier bilan.* Notes du Cerfa, no. 136. Paris: Ifri.

Milin, K. (2018). *CDD, CDI: Comment évoluent les embauches et les ruptures depuis 25 ans?* Dares Analyses, no. 026, 2018. Paris: Ministry of Work, Employment, and Development.

Odendahl, C. (2017). *The Hartz myth: A closer look at Germany's labour market reforms.* London: Center for European Reform.

OECD. (1996). *Employment outlook 1996: Earnings inequality, low-paid employment and earnings mobility* (chapter 3). Paris: OECD Publishing, Paris.

OECD. (2008). *Growing unequal?: Income distribution and poverty in OECD countries.* Paris: OECD Publishing.

OECD. (2016). *OECD regional outlook 2016: Productive regions for inclusive societies.* Paris: OECD Publishing. http://dx.doi.org/10.1787/9789264260245-en

OECD. (2018). *OECD employment outlook 2018.* Paris: OECD Publishing. https://doi.org/10.1787/empl_outlook-2018-en

OECD. (2019). *Under pressure: The squeezed middle class*. Paris: OECD Publishing. https://doi.org/10.1787/689afed1-en

Paraire, X. (2012). *Les mouvements de main-d'oeuvre en 2011: Une rotation élevée dans le tertiaire*. Dares Analyses-Dares Indicateurs, no. 2012–071. Paris: Ministry of Work, Employment, and Development.

Praet, P. (2018). Improving the functioning of Economic and Monetary Union: Lessons and challenges for economic policies. Speech at the NABE Symposium. Madrid, 16 April 2018. https://www.ecb.europa.eu/press/key/date/2018/html/ecb.sp180416.en.html

Rodríguez-Pose, A (2018). The revenge of the places that don't matter (and what to do about it). *Cambridge Journal of Regions, Economy and Society, 11*(1), pp. 189–209.

Rosés, J. R., and Wolf, N. (2018). *Regional economic development in Europe, 1900–2010: A description of the patterns*. CEPR Discussion Paper no. 12749. https://EconPapers.repec.org/RePEc:cpr:ceprdp:12749.

Rosés, J. R., Sanchís Llopis, M. T., and A. Díez Minguela. (2015). Regional inequality in France: The dynamic role of structural change, 1860–2010. Mimeo. https://afse2015.sciencesconf.org/61881/document

Sainsard, J.-M. (2014). France: New laws on part-time contracts. Employment Law Worldview. https://www.employmentlawworldview.com/france-new-laws-on-part-time-contracts/

Spannagel, D., and Molitor, K. (2019). Einkommen immer ungleicher verteilt. Wirtschafts- und Sozialwissenschaftliches Institut, WSI-Verteilungsbericht no. 53. https://www.nomos-elibrary.de/10.5771/0342-300X-2019-6-440/einkommen-immer-ungleicher-verteilt-wsi-verteilungsbericht-2019-volume-72-2019-issue-6.

Thorsten, S. (2018). *The role of extension in German collective bargaining, in collective agreements: Extending labour protection*. S. Hayter, and J. Visser (eds.). Geneva: ILO.

Thubin, C. (2014). Le décrochage du PIB par habitant en France depuis 40 ans: pourquoi? *Trésor-Eco* 131.

Visser, J. (2019). Data base on institutional characteristics of trade unions, wage setting, state intervention and social pacts, 1960–2019. (ICTWSS v 6.1.) Amsterdam: Amsterdam Institute for Advanced Labour Studies (AIAS), University of Amsterdam. http://www.uva-aias.net/nl/ictwss.

World Economic Forum. (2017). *The global competitiveness report*. Cologny, Switz: World Economic Forum.

World Economic Forum. (2018). *The global competitiveness report*. Cologny, Switz: World Economic Forum.

Ziemann, V. (2010). What explains the resilience of employment in Germany? *Trésor-Eco 79*.

4

LIVING STANDARDS IN SOUTHERN EUROPE OVER THE LONG RUN

Manos Matsaganis

This chapter reviews how material conditions improved in Italy, Spain, Portugal, and Greece over many decades from the postwar period to the onset of the Eurozone crisis and the Great Recession; how Southern Europe lost ground in the 2010s (at least until the time of writing); and how changes in living standards were distributed between different population groups. The chapter unfolds in 15 short sections. Section 4.1 sets the scene by briefly discussing similarities and differences between the four countries. Section 4.2 recounts how life in Southern Europe was transformed since the mid-20th century, in terms of the economy but also of health and education. Section 4.3 analyses gross domestic product (GDP) growth in the four countries. Section 4.4 looks at changes in consumption; Section 4.5 in investment. Section 4.6 describes developments in labour productivity; Section 4.7 in employment. Section 4.8 turns to education attainment; Section 4.9 to health levels. Section 4.10 traces changes in social spending. Section 4.11 reviews the evidence on income inequality, Section 4.12 in poverty and social exclusion. Section 4.13 presents estimates of levels of wealth and its distribution. Section 4.14 discusses survey results on life satisfaction. Section 4.15 concludes.

Manos Matsaganis, *Living Standards in Southern Europe over the Long Run* In: *Europe's Income, Wealth, Consumption, and Inequality.* Edited by: Georg Fischer and Robert Strauss, Oxford University Press (2021). © Oxford University Press.
DOI: 10.1093/oso/9780197545706.003.0004

4.1 SOUTHERN EUROPE AS A CONSTRUCT

Does it make sense to speak of 'Southern Europe' as a distinct group of countries, similar to each other?[1] The historical and cultural differences (or overlapping similarities) are clear: Italy became a republic in 1946; in the other three countries, democracy was not restored until the 1970s, in Portugal and Spain (which, of course, remains a constitutional monarchy) after several decades of authoritarian rule. Italy and Portugal were founding members of NATO in 1949; Greece joined shortly later (in 1952), Spain not until 1982. Portugal and Greece remain centralized, while Italy and Spain have, since the 1970s, devolved powers to the regions, with tensions occasionally flaring up, most recently with the emergence of the Catalan Question. Spain remained neutral in both World Wars, Portugal in World War II, while Italy and Greece briefly fought on opposite sides in 1940–1941 (and Italy was part of the Axis powers occupying Greece in 1941–1943). Italy, Spain, and Portugal are all predominantly Catholic; Greece is Orthodox. Italy and Greece are Mediterranean, Portugal is Atlantic, Spain is both.

On the other hand, all four countries are obviously located in Europe's southern periphery, a fact whose geopolitical implications were made evident once again by mass immigration and the 2015 refugee crisis. Moreover, political legacies were similar, with strong communist and other radical parties on the Left, especially during the Cold War, long episodes of socialist-led governments since the 1980s, and conservative rather than market liberal parties on the Right.

EU membership has played an important part in the modern history of Southern Europe. Italy was one of the six original signatories of the 1957 Treaty of Rome that gave birth to the European Communities (EC), precursors of the European Union. Greece joined the EC in 1981, Spain and Portugal in 1986; in all three, accession was seen as a prerequisite to each country becoming 'a normal European country'; that is, a stable democracy, an advanced economy, and a cohesive society. EU membership came with more tangible benefits, too, often in the shape of financial support for projects to boost infrastructure, reduce regional disparities, and support vulnerable groups.[2] Moreover, all four countries are part of the Euro Area (EA) and were all hit hard by its recent crisis: Greece and Portugal were officially bailed out by a EU-International Monetary Fund

---

1   See Baumeister and Sala (2015). On the transition to democracy in Greece, Spain and Portugal, see Gunther et al. (1995).

2   The direct contribution of EU funding to the national economies was higher in Portugal, Greece, and Spain than in all other Western European countries. In Portugal, 'cohesion finding' (under the European Social Fund, the European Regional Development Fund, and the Cohesion Fund) amounted to 1% of gross national income (GNI) in the 1980s, 2.3% in the 1990s, 1.8% in 2000–2006, and 1.9% in 2007–2013. In Greece, it was 0.6% of GNI in the 1980s, 1.7% in the 1990s, 1.4% in 2000–2006, and 1.6% in 2007–2013. In Spain, EU funding reached 0.3% of GNI in the 1980s, 0.9% in the 1990s, 0.9% in 2000–2006, and 0.5% in 2007–2013. See European Commission (2014: 179–182).

(IMF)-European Central Bank (ECB) 'Troika' in 2010 and 2011 respectively, while the largest economies of Italy and Spain became subject to softer forms of conditionality.

4.2 THE *LONGUE DURÉE*

From a contemporary viewpoint, living standards in Portugal, Spain, Greece, and large parts of Italy in the aftermath of World War II could only be described as low.[3] In Portugal and Greece, real GDP per capita in 1950 (adjusted for differences in prices) was less than a quarter of what it was in the United States; in Spain it was 27%, in Italy 42%. In that same year, real GDP per capita in Germany (not exactly prosperous herself, pre-*Wirtschaftswunder*) was just over half that in the United States (i.e., significantly higher than in Italy and about twice as high as in the other three countries).[4] See Figure 4.1.

In other respects, too, life in Southern Europe was hard.[5] In 1950, 7% of all infants in Italy and Spain died before they reached their first birthday. In 1955, when that figure had fallen to 5% in both countries, infant mortality in Greece was 4%, while in Portugal 9%. By comparison, in 2016, infant mortality in Afghanistan (the poorest country in the world) was 4.3%, while in the four countries of Southern Europe it was around 0.3%.[6]

In terms of adult illiteracy, UNESCO estimated it to be 10–15% in Italy around 1950, 15–20% in Spain, 25–30% in Greece, and 40–45% in Portugal.[7] By comparison, the relevant figures in 2011 (latest census year in most countries) had fallen to 1% in Italy, 2% in Spain, 3% in Greece, and 6% in Portugal. (In Afghanistan, the adult illiteracy rate in 2011 was 68%.)[8]

In 1950, large numbers of workers were still employed in agriculture: 33% of the labour force in Italy; 42% and 44%, respectively, in Spain and Portugal; and as many as 57% in Greece.[9] As agriculture declined as a provider of jobs, employment

---

3   On the (economic) history of Southern Europe, see Broadberry and O'Rourke (2010), Eichengreen (2008), Judt (2005), especially chapter 16 'A time of transition'. In terms of single-country studies, on Italy see Ginsborg (2003, 2007), Salvati (2000). On Spain, see Pérez-Díaz (1999), Guillén and León (2011). On Portugal, see Royo (2018), Fishman (2014). On Greece, see Iordanoglou (2008).

4   Real GDP per capita in 2011 US dollars (US$) 2011 benchmark (suitable for cross-country growth comparisons, rgdpnapc). See Maddison Project Database 2018 (https://www.rug.nl/ggdc/historicaldevelopment/maddison/releases/maddison-project-database-2018).

5   See also OECD (2014).

6   See UNICEF, Child mortality estimates (http://www.childmortality.org/).

7   See table 9 in UNESCO (1957: 42).

8   See UNESCO eAtlas of Literacy (https://tellmaps.com/uis/literacy/#!/tellmap/ -601865091).

9   See table 13.1 in Broadberry and O'Rourke (2010: 335).

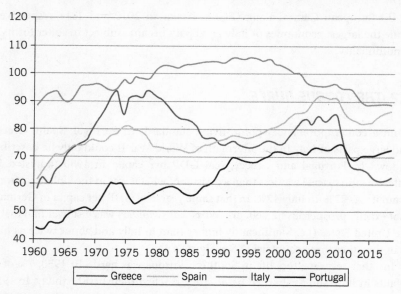

Figure 4.1 Gross domestic product (GDP) per capita.
GDP at current market prices per head of population in purchasing power standards
(EU15 = 100).
Source: AMECO Eurostat (HVGDPR).

in industry started to grow. At its peak in the mid-1970s, it accounted for 28% of
the civilian workforce in Italy, 25% in Portugal, 23% in Spain, 19% in Greece.[10]
Employment in services continued to expand, reaching 62% of all workers in
Italy and Spain, 61% in Greece, and 51% in Portugal at the end of past century.[11]

Living standards improved enormously over the next six decades. Just before
the outbreak of the Eurozone crisis, relative real incomes per capita in Italy had
been 96% of the average level for the EU15 (i.e., the group of member states
before the Eastern enlargements of 2004), down from 106% in 1995. In Spain,
relative real incomes peaked at 92% of the EU15 (in 2007), in Greece at 85% (in
2009), and in Portugal at 75% (in 2010). The Eurozone crisis dealt a serious blow
to all four countries: real incomes per capita relative to the EU15 fell by 6 percentage points in Portugal (in 2010–2012), by 7 in Italy (in 2009–2016), by 10
in Spain (in 2007–2013), and by as many as 24 percentage points in Greece (in
2009–2016).[12]

---

10 See table 2.11 in OECD (1999: 43). In Portugal and in Greece employment in manu-
facture peaked in the late 1980s, having increased by around 1 percentage point since
the mid-1970s.
11 See table 2.12 in OECD (2001: 41).
12 See AMECO Eurostat: Gross domestic product at current market prices per head of
population (HVGDPR).

Still, in spite of recent setbacks, Southern Europe remains relatively rich: all four countries are classified as 'advanced economies' while, of course, Italy is a member of the G7 (the group of 'major advanced economies').[13]

4.3 GDP GROWTH

Against the general trend of steady growth until the onset of the recent crisis, the economic history of Southern Europe following World War II has followed rather a different pattern in each country.[14] As the *miracolo economico* took off, the Italian economy grew as fast as the West German one (on average 5.0% per year in 1950–1973). When *les trente glorieuses* ended, and in the context of greater political and industrial strife than in most other industrialized countries, economic activity slowed down. The average annual rate of growth fell steadily, to 3.0% between the two oil shocks (1973–1979), 2.3% in the 1980s, 1.2% from the fall of the Berlin Wall to the launch of the Euro (1989–1999), and 1.2% again in the first decade of the common currency, until the outbreak of the Great Recession (1999–2008).

The rest of Southern Europe followed a different trajectory. In Spain, it was U-shaped: the average annual rate of growth fell from 5.6% in 1950–1973 to 1.2% in 1973–1979; it then rose to 2.3% in 1979–1989, remained at 2.3% in 1989–1999, and increased further to 3.5% in 1999–2008. Similarly, in Greece, the rate of growth slowed from 6.2% in 1950–1973 to 2.6% in 1973–1979, remained sluggish in 1979–1989 (1.2%) and in 1989–1999 (1.4%), then climbed to 3.5% in 1999–2008. In Portugal, growth rates were broadly similar to the other two countries in 1950–1979 (5.5% in 1950–1973, 1.0% in 1973–1979), slightly higher over the following two decades (2.9% in 1979–1989, 2.7% in 1989–1999), and significantly lower from the introduction of the Euro to the Great Recession (1.4% in 1999–2008).

As is well known, the Eurozone crisis was harshest in Greece, wiping out a cumulative 26.3% of total output in 2008–2013. GDP declined significantly, though by less, in Spain (−8.9%), in Portugal (−7.8%), and in Italy (−7.6%). Since then, the economy started to recover, more strongly so in Spain (+11.5% in 2013–2017) and in Portugal (+7.1%) than in Italy (+3.3%) and in Greece (+1.6%).

---

13 See IMF (2017) and World Bank (2017).

14 For 1950–1973, See table 12.2 in Broadberry and O'Rourke (2010: 301). Table 2.2 in Eichengreen (2008: 17) provides identical estimates for Italy and Greece and slightly higher (by 0.2 percentage points) for Spain and Portugal. The sources cited are Groningen Growth and Development Centre, Total Economy Database (Broadberry and O'Rourke) and Maddison (Eichengreen). For 1973–1999, table 3.2 in OECD (2000: 48). For 1999–2017, Eurostat – GDP and main components (output, expenditure and income) [nama_10_gdp].

156 EUROPE'S INCOME, WEALTH, CONSUMPTION, AND INEQUALITY

Over the past decade or so (2008–2017), the compound annual rate of growth was −3.2% in Greece, −0.5% in Italy, −0.1% in Portugal, and +0.2% in Spain. In cumulative terms, the size of the economy in Greece was still 25.1% lower in 2017 than it had been in 2008. In Italy the figure was −4.5%; in Portugal −1.3%; only in Spain had GDP surpassed its pre-crisis level (+1.6%).

In the nearly two decades since the launch of the common currency, the compound average annual rate of growth was a respectable 1.8% in Spain, but a rather disappointing 0.6% in Portugal, 0.3% in Italy, and 0.1% in Greece.[15]

4.4 CONSUMPTION

Over the long run, the growth in final consumption expenditure (on the part of governments and households as well as nonprofit institutions serving households) closely matches that in GDP.[16] In the short run, under the permanent income hypothesis (Friedman, 1957), individuals wish to spread their consumption smoothly over their lifetime, which implies that household consumption rises more slowly than income when the times are good, but also falls more slowly than income when times are bad. Similarly, for stabilization purposes, governments wishing to balance their budget over the business cycle will act countercyclically (i.e., raise taxes and/or cut spending in a boom and cut taxes and/or raise spending in a bust). On the whole, the data seem to be only partly consistent with the permanent income hypothesis.

During the first decade of the common currency (1999–2008), the annual rate of growth in final consumption expenditure in the EA as a whole fell short of that in GDP (by 1.7% vs. 2.0% per year, respectively). In Southern Europe, only in Italy did consumption rise more slowly than GDP (by 1.0% vs. 1.2% per year, respectively). In Portugal, where GDP growth was relatively sluggish (1.4% per year), consumption increased faster (1.8%). In Spain and Greece, where GDP rose fastest (by 3.5% per year), the annual rate of growth in consumption was higher still (3.6%).

During the Eurozone crisis, when austerity ruled and fiscal policies tended to be pro-cyclical, in the EA as a whole the negative growth in consumption was slower than that in GDP (−1.7% vs. −2.0% per year, respectively). In Southern Europe, this pattern was borne out in Greece (−5.4% vs. −5.9% per year) and in Italy (−1.2% vs. −1.6%); in contrast, consumption decreased faster than total output in Spain (−1.9% vs. −1.8%) and especially in Portugal (−2.0% vs.

---

15 See Eurostat—GDP and main components (output, expenditure and income) [nama_10_gdp], Gross domestic product at market prices. No data for Southern European countries before 1995 in the Eurostat database.

16 See Eurostat—GDP and main components (output, expenditure and income) [nama_10_gdp], Final consumption expenditure.

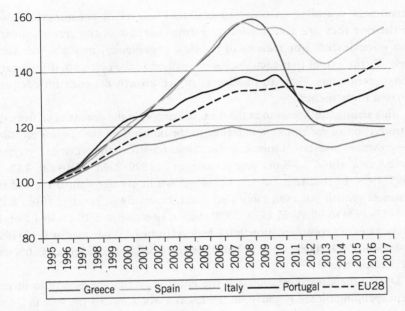

Figure 4.2 Consumption.
Final consumption expenditure, chain linked volumes (1995 = 100).
Source: Eurostat (nama_10_gdp).

−1.6%), the figures indicating annual growth rates in consumption versus GDP respectively.

In more recent years, when Southern European economies stabilized and tentatively started to recover, consumption again rose more slowly than total output (in the EA as a whole: by 1.5% vs. 1.9% per year). In the case of Spain, the difference was even greater (2.1% vs. 2.8% per year). In Greece, in 2014 and again in 2017, the economy registered a positive rate of growth, but consumption continued to fall (except in 2014). In Portugal and in Italy, consumption rose by marginally more than GDP (1.8% vs. 1.7% and 0.9% vs. 0.8%, respectively).

Over the nearly two decades since the launch of the Euro, these differences cancelled out, with average annual rates of growth in consumption deviating by 0.1% or less from those in GDP (see Figure 4.2).

4.5 INVESTMENT

Investment, or 'gross fixed capital formation', follows a different logic.[17] In a recession, cash-strapped households find it less painful to postpone

———————————

17 See Eurostat –GDP and main components (output, expenditure and income) [nama_10_gdp], Gross fixed capital formation.

investment spending in order to maintain a level of consumption close to the one they are accustomed to. Firms (because of the credit squeeze) and governments (for reasons of political expediency) may also act similarly. To the extent that such decisions really do take place, their long-term consequences are likely to be dire as future growth depends on adequate current investment.[18]

This assumption seems to fit the data. In Europe, in the decade or so from the introduction of the common currency to the outbreak of the Great Recession, the growth in investment spending was slower relative to the previous 5 years: in the EA as a whole, 2.3% per year on average in 1999–2008, relative to 4.1% in 1995–1999. In Southern Europe, the slowdown in average annual rates of investment growth was even more significant, especially in Portugal (from 9.2% in 1995–1999 to −0.4% in 1999–2008), and in Greece (from 10.4% to 4.2%). In Spain, rates of investment growth fell by less (from 7.1% per year in 1995–1999 to 4.9% in 1999–2008), while in Italy they remained low throughout (3.0% and 2.1%, respectively).

During the Great Recession and the Eurozone crisis, the growth in investment spending turned negative (in the EA as a whole, −3.3% per year in 2008–2013). Disinvestment was even greater in Southern Europe: −5.7% per year in Italy, −8.3% in Spain, −8.7% in Portugal, and as much as −17.3% in Greece. Cumulatively, the decline in investment spending in real terms in 2008–2013 can only be described as enormous: −15.4% in the EA as a whole, −25.5% in Italy, −35.0% in Spain, −36.5% in Portugal, and an almost incredible −61.3% in Greece.

In 2013–2017, investment growth resumed somewhat: 3.3% per year in the EA, above average in Spain (4.9%) and Portugal (4.6%), below average in Italy (1.6%) and Greece (1.4%). Nevertheless, the recent growth in investment has not made up the earlier decrease. In Spain, real investment spending in 2017 was roughly the same as in 2002. In Italy (1998) and Portugal (1996), the retreat in investment turned the clock back by 20 years. In Greece, investment spending in 2017 remained 12% below its 1995 level.

Southern Europe suffers from severe underinvestment. While it is true that much of the investment pre-crisis may have been misallocated (as witnessed by the emblematic case of the hundreds of thousands of holiday homes built along Spain's Mediterranean coast still lying vacant many years later), there is little doubt that disinvestment of that scale can only bode ill for Southern Europe's future growth prospects.

---

18 See Perez and Matsaganis (2018) for a discussion of falling public investment in Southern Europe under austerity and its implications.

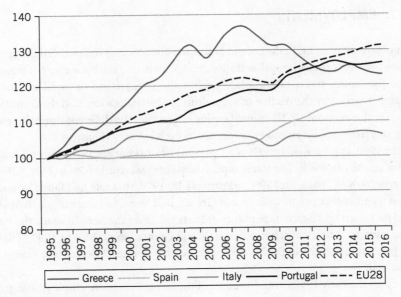

Figure 4.3 Labour productivity.
Real labour productivity per hour worked, chain linked volumes (1995 = 100).
Source: Eurostat (nama_10_lp_ulc).

4.6 LABOUR PRODUCTIVITY

Since the mid-1990s, the growth in real labour productivity per hour worked in Southern Europe was below average (i.e., relative to that in the European economy as a whole), with Greece up until 2011 being a partial exception.[19] The case of Italy is the most extreme: real labour productivity per hour worked was only 6% higher in 2016 than it had been in 1995 (compared to 31% in the EU28). Spain's position improved somewhat (16% in 1995–2016) thanks to a surge since 2008. Portugal's trajectory was closest to the EU average (Figure 4.3).

Labour productivity to a considerable extent depends on technological innovation and moves in tandem with investment in physical capital, so the low productivity growth in recent years partly reflects disinvestment, as just discussed. On the other hand, labour productivity by definition improves when GDP (the numerator) rises faster than employment or, when as here productivity is defined in hourly terms, than the number of hours worked (the denominator).

---

19   See Eurostat—Labour productivity and unit labour costs [nama_10_lp_ulc].

4.7 EMPLOYMENT

Employment patterns in the second half of the 20th century in Southern Europe as elsewhere were shaped by urbanization, emigration, and the mass entry of women into the labour force, taking place against the background of rapid economic change marked by the decline of agriculture, industrialization, and the transition to a service economy.[20] Their overlapping effects and the different timing in each country help explain employment trends in each country (Figure 4.4).

In 1960, approximately 60% of all persons of working age in Southern Europe were actually in work. The total employment rate was nearly 63% in Italy, 62% in Greece, 60% in Spain, and 58% in Portugal. By 1970, that rate had fallen by more than 6 percentage points in Italy and Greece, had remained unchanged in Spain, and had risen by 7 percentage points in Portugal. Over the next 20 years, the total employment rate hardly changed in Italy and Greece (about 55% in 1990), fell by 10 percentage points in Spain, and increased by another 7 percentage points in Portugal.[21]

From the early 1990s until the onset of the Great Recession, employment grew throughout Southern Europe. In Spain, where labour market reform permitted the creation of millions of temporary jobs, the total employment rate went from 46% in 1994 to 66% in 2007. In Greece, it rose from 53% in 1993, to 61% in 2008. In Italy from 51% in 1995, to nearly 59% in 2007. In Portugal, where employment rates remained above the EU average, they peaked at 69% in 2001.

The crisis was a serious setback. In 2008–2013 employment rates declined by 3 percentage points in Italy, 7 in Portugal, 10 in Spain, and by as many as 13 percentage points (to less than 49%, an all-time low) in Greece. By comparison, the employment rate for the European Union as a whole fell by a mere 2 percentage points or less. In recent years, employment picked up everywhere in Europe (in the EU28, by 2.5 percentage points in 2013–2016). In the South, the magnitude of the increase in the total employment rate ranged from less than 2 percentage points in Italy to almost 5 percentage points in Spain and Portugal. On the whole, employment in Southern Europe remained below pre-crisis levels, most significantly so in Spain and especially Greece.

One of the features of the recent crisis throughout Europe and beyond was that it destroyed disproportionally more jobs previously held by male workers (most typically in construction). As a result, the gender gap in employment

---

20 For 1960–1999, see table 2.14 in OECD (1999: 44) and table 2.13 in OECD (2001: 42). For 1993–2017, Eurostat—Employment and activity by sex and age—annual data [lfsi_emp_a].

21 Looking at the period for which figures are available from both sources (1993–1999), and assuming that Eurostat estimates are more reliable, OECD data overestimated the employment rate for Portugal (by more than 5 percentage points in 1996 and 1997) and underestimated it for Spain (by 1–2 percentage points).

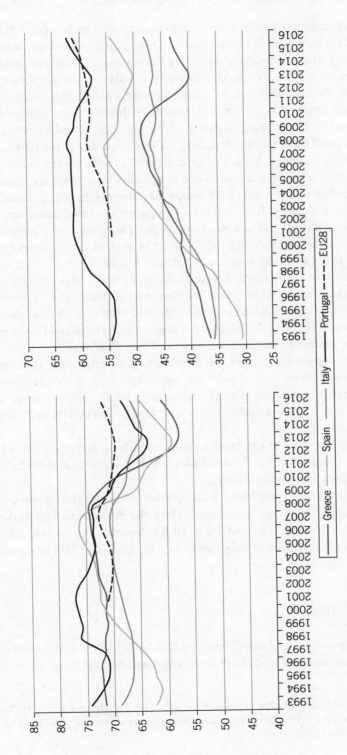

Figure 4.4 Employment rates.
Percentage of total population from 15 to 64 years (resident population concept—LFS). Left-hand panel: males; right-hand panel: females.
Source: Eurostat (lfsq_egan).

narrowed dramatically in 1993–2013: from 35 to 18 percentage points in Greece, from 33 to 18 in Italy, from 32 to 9 in Spain, and from 20 to 6 percentage points in Portugal. The partial jobs recovery since 2013 did not much change that pattern.

Employment rates are, of course, affected by population changes, driven by patterns of fertility and migration. While the former has been falling steadily, the latter has been subject to rather complex fluctuations. Immigration into Southern Europe peaked in 2007 in Spain (at 21.4 per 1,000 population), and Italy (9.1), in 2000 in Portugal (7.6), and in as early as 1991 in Greece (at nearly 15 per 1,000 population). During the recent crisis, immigration fell to a trickle (to less than 2 per 1,000 population in Portugal, around 5 or 6 in the other three countries), though it may have picked up again since 2015, also in the context of the refugee crisis.

In contrast, emigration from Southern Europe has increased rather significantly. In Spain, the relevant rate rose from 0.6 per 1,000 population in 2003 to 11.4 in 2013. In Portugal, from 0.5 in 2006 to 5.1 in 2013. In Greece, from 3.5 in 2006 to 11.2 in 2012. In Italy, from 0.9 in 2007 to 2.4 in 2015.

In the context of the economic downturn, falling fertility, and net emigration, total population declined throughout Southern Europe, although to a varying degree and length of time across countries. Overall, relative to 10 years earlier, the population in 2017 had shrunk by more than 2% in Portugal and Greece and had grown by around 4% in Spain and Italy (+2.7% in the EU28).

In view of population changes, job losses during the crisis were more dramatic in absolute terms than employment rates might suggest. Counting from peak to trough, the number of employed workers fell by 25% in Greece (in 2008q3–2013q4), by 18% in Spain (in 2007q3–2013q1), and by 15% in Portugal (in 2008q2–2013q1).

In terms of numbers of employed workers, the job recovery post-crisis (in 2013–2017) offset two-thirds of earlier losses in Italy and Portugal, about half in Spain, and a mere one-fifth in Greece.

The rise of part-time employment implies that job losses during the crisis were more significant in terms of hours worked. The proportion of all workers who are in part-time jobs, around 5% in all four countries in the mid-1980s, went up to more than 18% in Italy, nearly 16% in Spain, and 10% or more in Portugal and Greece.

4.8 EDUCATION

Employment patterns differ significantly by skill level.[22] In 2016, about 85% of university graduates aged 25–64 were in work in the European Union as a whole,

---

22 Eurostat—Employment rates by sex, age and educational attainment level (%) [lfsa_ergaed]. Eurostat – Population by educational attainment level, sex and age (%)—main indicators [edat_lfse_03].

against a general employment rate of 73%. The 'college premium' (in terms of employment) was also between 11 and 12 percentage points in Portugal and Greece, 13 in Spain, and 15 percentage points in Italy.

While that looks high, it is important to note that the employment rate differential between those with university degrees and the general population is on the decline. In 1992, it was 20 percentage points in Greece, 21 in Portugal, 24 in Italy, and 25 percentage points in Spain.

Of course, part of the reason for the declining college premium in employment is that, while the supply of workers with degrees expanded everywhere, the demand for their skills has not always kept pace. For instance, in Italy the employment rate of graduates in the 25–64 age group fell from more than 84% in 1993 to less than 80% in 2009–2016. In Portugal, it decreased from 93% in 1992 to just over 80% in 2013 (it has bounced back since, to 85% in 2016). In Spain and Greece, it peaked in 2007 (at 85% and 83%, respectively), fell sharply during the crisis, and went up slightly more recently; in 2016, it was 80% in Spain and 70% in Greece, relative to around 80% in both countries in 1992. In contrast, in the European Union as a whole, the employment rate of those with university degrees has fluctuated within a narrow range (between 83% and 85%) over the past two decades.

Since the early 1990s, mass access to tertiary education has raised the supply of workers with university degrees quite spectacularly: throughout Southern Europe, younger population cohorts number far more graduates than in the past. In 1992–2016, the proportion of population aged 25–34 who have completed tertiary education grew from 7% to 26% in Italy, from 14% to 35% in Portugal, from 19% to 41% in Greece, and from 21% to 41% in Spain. The corresponding figure for the EU15 was 39% in 2016 (up from 20% in 1995). See Figure 4.5.

Women did better: their share with tertiary degrees among those aged 25–34 has risen faster than that of men over the past 20 years. In the EU15, the gender difference in that age group went from almost zero in 1995 to 9 percentage points in 2016. In Southern Europe, the gap grew from 1 percentage point to 12 in Italy, from 2 to 14 in Greece, from 3 to 12 in Spain, and from 6 to 16 percentage points in Portugal.

4.9 HEALTH

While mass access to tertiary education (especially for women) can be seen as a marker of progress, the same goes for improvements in health.[23] In

---

23 Eurostat—Life expectancy by age and sex [demo_mlexpec]. Eurostat—Infant mortality [demo_minf]. Eurostat—Self-reported unmet needs for medical examination by sex, age, main reason declared and income quintile [hlth_silc_08].

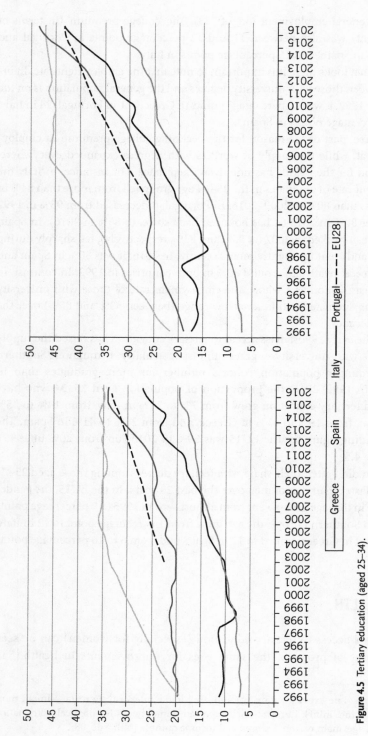

Figure 4.5 Tertiary education (aged 25–34).
Percentage of total population from 25 to 34 years with tertiary education (ISCED11 levels 5–8). Left-hand panel: males; right-hand panel: females.
Source: Eurostat (edat_lfse_03).

1960–1964, out of every 1,000 infants born alive in Portugal, 77 died before they reached their first birthday. In 2010–2014, that share had fallen to 3 in 1,000, same as in Spain and Italy (from 34 and 41, respectively, half a century earlier). In Greece, the infant mortality rate declined from 39 in 1,000 live births in 1960–1964 to 3.5 in 2010–2014. Infant mortality in the EU28 has been higher, although it has converged to the level of Southern Europe more recently.

The same pattern can be observed in terms of life expectancy. People live longer throughout Europe (and beyond), but differences between the four countries, and between Southern Europe and the rest of the European Union, have narrowed significantly in recent years. In 1961, life expectancy at birth was just over 72 years in Greece, compared to less than 63 years in Portugal. In 2015, it had risen to 81 years in both countries. Italy and Spain did even better: 83 years in 2015 (up from around 76 in 1985). In all four countries, life expectancy at birth was above the EU average (Figure 4.6).

In 2015, women lived about 5.5 years longer than men in Greece and Spain (and in the EU28 as a whole). In the same year, the gender gap in life expectancy was more than 6 years in Portugal and less than 5 years in Italy. Everywhere, that gap grew until the early 1990s (later in Greece), then narrowed somewhat.

Improvements in health are often credited less to advances in medicine than to behavioural factors (and, in developing countries, to improvements in material conditions). Nonetheless, the availability and quality of healthcare obviously still matters and can make a difference to health outcomes. On the whole, universal access to good healthcare irrespective of income is seen as a key achievement (or, at the very least, aspiration) of the European Social Model. The available evidence confirms that this is true to a large extent: responses to the EU-Statistics on Income and Living Conditions (SILC) survey show that the proportion of Europeans reporting that they did not obtain the healthcare they needed because they could not afford it was around 2% (although it rose to 4% for those in the poorest 20% of the population).

The evidence for Southern Europe is more mixed. In Spain, unmet need for healthcare because 'too expensive' was virtually zero even for poorer households (and remained virtually zero during the Eurozone crisis). In Portugal, it fluctuated around the EU average. In Italy, it went from 4% in 2008 to more than 6% in 2015 in the general population, and from 9% to 15% in the poorest 20%. In Greece, the proportion of those reporting that they could not afford the healthcare they needed rose from 4% in 2008 to 11% in 2015 as a whole, and from 7% to 17% in the poorest 20% of the population.

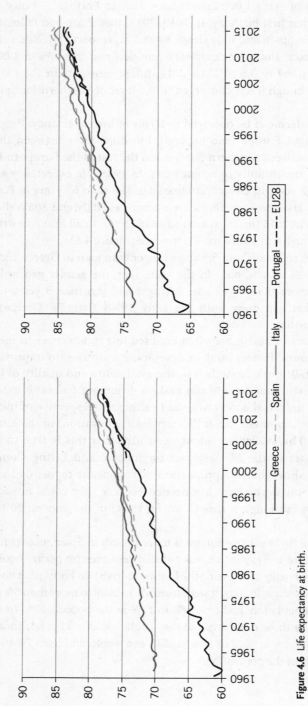

Figure 4.6 Life expectancy at birth.

Life expectancy by age and sex. Left-hand panel: males; right-hand panel: females.

Source: Eurostat (demo_mlexpec).

4.10 SOCIAL SPENDING

Welfare state building in Italy unfolded gradually over several decades since World War II.[24] In contrast, in the other three countries, it gathered speed in the 1980s, marked by the electoral victories of the socialists within a few years from the restoration of democracy. In 1980, social spending was less than 10% of GDP in Portugal and Greece, 15% in Spain, and just over 17% in Italy. By 2010, it had risen to around 24% of GDP in Portugal and Greece, 26% in Spain, and nearly 28% in Italy (Figure 4.7).

During the crisis, GDP declined faster than social expenditure throughout Southern Europe. Still, under austerity, social spending moved cyclically (i.e.,

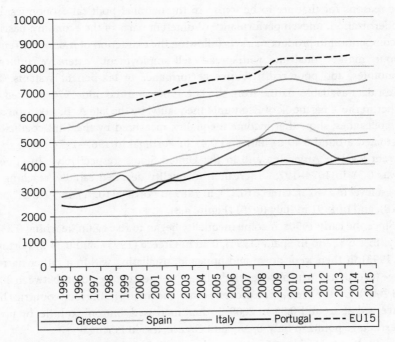

Figure 4.7 Social expenditure.
Euro per inhabitant (at constant 2010 prices).
Source: Eurostat (spr_exp_sum).

---

24 For 1995–2015, see Eurostat—Expenditure: main results [spr_exp_sum]. For 1980-2016: OECD Social Expenditure Dataset—Aggregated data. Note that the two sources adopt different definitions of what constitutes social expenditure, so results tend to differ. For instance, in 1995, social spending as a share of GDP in Greece and Portugal was about 2 percentage points lower according to the OECD than it was according to Eurostat, while in Italy it was 1.4 percentage point lower. In 2015, the difference in estimates was nearly zero for Greece and Italy, +0.6 in Portugal, and −1.2 in Spain (i.e., the OECD reported a higher figure than Eurostat).

it decreased just as the need for social protection was at its highest). Funding cuts affecting social programmes were most significant in the case of Greece, where total social expenditure per inhabitant in constant prices fell by 20% in 2009–2013. Social spending per capita in real terms fell by almost 8% in Spain over the same period, by 5% in Portugal (in 2010–2012), and by more than 3% in Italy (in 2010–2013).

4.11 INCOME INEQUALITY

The income distribution has been more unequal in Southern Europe than elsewhere in the European Union, with the exception of parts of Eastern Europe.[25] The reasons for that are to be found in the national political economies: late modernization, uneven performance of different parts of the economy, barriers to competition in product markets (allowing the extraction of monopoly rents), labour market dualism, widespread self-employment, extensive informal economies, and poor redistributive performance of tax-benefit systems. The oldest data available, dating from the late 1960s and the mid-1970s, pieced together in the 'Chartbook of Economic Inequality' by the late A. B. Atkinson and his colleagues, show that income inequality, measured by the Gini coefficient, fluctuated around 0.40 in Italy and 0.45 in Portugal in 1967–1973 (close to its current level in Argentina and in the United States, respectively). In Greece, it was 0.38 in 1974–1975. Thereafter, inequality declined rapidly, reaching its lowest level in 1982 in Greece (0.31), in 1989 in Portugal (0.31), in 1990 in Spain (0.28), and in 1991 in Italy (0.29) (Figure 4.8).

Since the early 1990s, income inequality began to rise again, reaching 0.33 in Italy (in 1993) and in Spain (1996), 0.35 in Greece (1995), and 0.39 in Portugal (in 1993). It then went down and up again, oscillating within a rather narrow range (except in Portugal, where it declined by 4 percentage points between 2005 and 2009). On the eve of the Eurozone crisis, inequality in the four countries had converged at around 0.33 in 2009. It then increased, but only a little: by up to 2 percentage points in Italy, Spain, and Greece; less in Portugal.

According to the latest Eurostat estimates, all four Southern European countries were clustered together near the top of the EU income inequality league table, ranking 5th to 8th, with a Gini score of between 0.02 and 0.04 above the EU average (almost 0.31 in 2016). Among all member states, the Gini coefficient

25 On Italy, Spain, and Portugal in 1967–2014, see Atkinson et al. (2017). On Greece, Gini coefficient in 1974–1994: Mitrakos and Tsakloglou (2012); top 1% share in 1967–2013: Chrissis and Koutentakis (2017). On the EU, Gini coefficient in 1995–2016: Eurostat—Gini coefficient of equivalized disposable income—EU-SILC survey [ilc_di12]. On the EU, S80/S20 ratio in 1995–2016: Eurostat—S80/S20 income quintile share ratio by sex and selected age group—EU-SILC survey [ilc_di11].

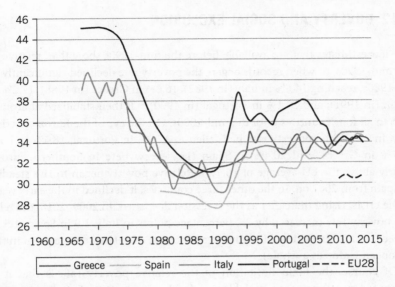

Figure 4.8 Inequality.
Gini coefficient (× 100).
Source: Atkinson et al. (2017), Mitrakos and Tsakloglou (2012), Eurostat (ilc_di12).

was now higher only in Bulgaria, Lithuania, Romania, and Latvia—and, in the latter two countries, only very slightly so.

Eurostat estimates of the income quintile ratio (S80/S20) reveal similar trends. In 1995, inequality as measured by the ratio of the income earned by the richest 20% divided by that earned by the poorest 20% was highest in Portugal (7.4), followed by Greece (6.5), then Italy and Spain (both 5.4). From the mid-1990s to the early 2000s, the ratio fell in all four countries, to between 4.8 (Italy) and 6.4 (Portugal). In 2009, the indicator ranged from 5.3 in Italy to 5.8–6.0 in the other three countries. The S80/S20 ratio increased in 2010–2014 in Portugal, but then fell again, and was lower in 2016 (5.9) than it had been in 2008 (6.1). In the other three countries, the trend was clearly upwards during the crisis: to 6.3 in Italy, and 6.6 in Spain and Greece, relative to 5.2 in the EU28 (in 2016).

Recent estimates, made available by the contributors to the 'Chartbook of Economic Inequality', reveal that the (gross) income share of the richest 1% of the population fell significantly until the early 1980s: in Italy, from 7.5 in 1974 to 6.3 in 1983; in Portugal, from 7.9 in 1976 to 4.0 in 1981; in Greece, from 11.4 in 1967 to 5.4 in 1984. It then climbed up again: in Italy, to 9.9 in 2007; in Portugal, to 9.8 in 2005; in Greece, to 8.0 in 2005; in Spain, to 9.1 in 2006 (from 7.5 in 1981, when records began). In the late 2000s, the share of the top 1% in gross income declined somewhat in Italy (to 9.4 in 2009), Spain (to 8.1 in 2010), and in Greece (to 6.5 in 2007). More recent estimates are still unavailable, except for Greece, where the share of the top 1% is estimated to have risen to 7.8 in 2013.

4.12 POVERTY AND SOCIAL EXCLUSION

The few estimates that are available before the mid-1990s show that, relative to the mid-1970s, or when records began, the poverty rate declined significantly in the 1980s, reaching 14.6% in Italy (in 1982), 16.6% in Greece (in 1988), 17.2% in Spain (in 1991), and 20.1% in Portugal (in 1990).[26] It then stabilized at around 20% in all four countries until the mid-2000s. On the eve of the Eurozone crisis (say, in 2009), the poverty rate had fallen to 17.9% in Portugal, 18.4% in Italy, 19.7% in Greece, and 20.4% in Spain (i.e., everywhere in Southern Europe clearly above the EU average of 16.4%). Relative poverty began to rise steadily in Spain from 2007 on. In the other three countries, it declined in the early years of the crisis, rising thereafter as the recession deepened. In 2009–2016, the relative poverty rate increased by 2.2 percentage points in Italy, 1.9 in Spain, 1.5 in Greece, and 1.1 in Portugal (relative to an increase of 1.0 percentage point in the European Union as a whole).

Of course, the main limitation of the relative poverty rate is that it is computed by reference to a variable threshold, equal to 60% of median income. Nevertheless, when income change is rapid, people tend to compare their situation not only to that of others in society (the rationale behind focusing on relative poverty), but also to their own situation before the rapid income change occurred. 'Anchoring' the poverty threshold at an earlier point in time may therefore give a better sense of the actual deterioration in living standards. The proportion of population with income below 60% of the 2008 median, adjusted for inflation, rose very steeply in 2010–2014 throughout Southern Europe, most so in the case of Greece (from 18% to 48%), but also significantly increasing in the other three countries: 31% in Spain, 25% in Italy, and 24% in Portugal.

Eurostat estimates suggest that, just before the Eurozone crisis broke out, the share of population at risk of either poverty or social exclusion or both (a 'Europe 2020 indicator') had fallen to around 23% in Spain, 25% in both Italy and Portugal, and 28% in Greece. During the worst years of the crisis, that indicator rose significantly by 3 percentage points in Portugal (in 2011–2014), 5 in Italy (in 2009–2016), 6 in Spain (in 2007–2014), and more than 8 in Greece (in 2009–2014). In 2016, the indicator stood at 25.1% in Portugal, 27.9% in Spain, 30.0% in Italy, and 35.6% in Greece. In the European Union as a whole, the proportion of people at risk of poverty or social exclusion remained lower than in

---

26 On Italy, Spain, and Portugal, in 1967–2014: Atkinson et al. (2017) 'The Chartbook of Economic Inequality'. On Greece, poverty rate in 1974–1994: Mitrakos and Tsakloglou (2012). On the EU, poverty rate in 1995–2016: At-risk-of-poverty rate by poverty threshold, age and sex—EU-SILC survey [ilc_li02]; poverty or social exclusion in 2003-2016: People at risk of poverty or social exclusion by age and sex [ilc_peps01].

Southern Europe: it went up a little at first, from 23.8% in 2010 to 24.8% in 2012, then down again to 23.5% in 2016.

In the European Union as a whole, women had a higher rate of poverty or social exclusion in 2016, the gender differential being about 2 percentage points. That was also true in Southern Europe, except for Spain, where it was about the same for both men and women. Otherwise, the rate of poverty or social exclusion in 2016 was above average for children below the age of 16 (by 2.4 points in the EU28). That was also true for Southern Europe, by between 0.7 (Greece) and 3.8 percentage points (Spain). Perhaps surprisingly, the elderly suffered significantly less poverty or social exclusion than the general population throughout the European Union (18.2% or 5.3 percentage points less in 2016), with the rate for men older than 65 being as low as 15.0%. Once again, Southern Europe followed that pattern: in 2016, the poverty or social exclusion rate for the elderly in Greece and Spain was about 13.5 percentage points lower than it was for the general population; in Italy 6.8, in Portugal 3.3 percentage points. The gender differential was unfavourable to women: in 2016, it was between 5 and 6 percentage points higher in Italy, Greece, Portugal, and the EU28, although only 1 point higher in Spain.

4.13 WEALTH

Comparable figures on levels of wealth and its distribution in the EA have only been made available recently, when results from the first two waves of the Eurosystem Household Finance and Consumption Survey were released by the European Central Bank in 2013 and 2016, respectively.[27] The key stylized facts from the survey may be summarized as follows.

To start with, mean net wealth per household was above Eurozone average in Spain and Italy and below average in Greece and Spain. Between the first and the second waves, when mean net wealth per household fell only slightly in the EA as a whole, the relative position of Italy and Greece deteriorated significantly. (In Italy, mean net wealth per household went from 19% above Eurozone average in 2011 to only 1% in 2015. In Greece, the gap widened: mean net wealth per household went from 36% below Eurozone average in 2009 to 53% in 2014.) In Spain and Portugal, the change in relative position was less dramatic. (In Spain, mean net wealth per household moved from 27% above Eurozone average in 2008–2009 to 23% in 2011–2012. In Portugal, mean net wealth per household actually inched closer to the Eurozone average: from 31% lower in 2010 to 30% lower in 2013.)

Wealth is known to be distributed more unequally than income. As a matter of fact, the Gini coefficient for the EA as a whole was 0.68 in 2009, and 0.69 in 2014.

---

27   See European Central Bank (2016).

(The values of the Gini coefficient of the income distribution for the same group of countries in the same years were 0.30 and 0.31, respectively.) Figures for Southern Europe show that the distribution of wealth there was slightly less unequal than in the EA as a whole, even though more unequal than before (especially in Greece and, to a lesser extent, in Portugal and Spain). According to the latest estimates, the Gini coefficient was 0.60 in Italy, Spain, and Greece, and 0.68 in Portugal.

If net wealth is zero or negative at the low end of the distribution, as is likely the case, alternative statistics such as P80/P20, comparing the net wealth of the respective percentiles, may give a better indication of inequality. In the EA as a whole, between waves one and two of the Eurosystem Household Finance and Consumption Survey, the P80/P20 increased only a little, from 40.1 to 41.0. In Spain, where that ratio was lowest, it increased from 7.0 to 7.7. In Greece, where the wealth distribution was also less unequal than average to start with, the ratio rose steeply from 14.7 to 21.7. In Portugal, it went from 16.6 to 25.9. In Italy, from 20.9 to 30.1.

Overall, the values of the P80/P20 ratio confirm that wealth was less unequally distributed in Southern Europe than in the rest of the EA and that wealth inequalities increased during the recent crisis.

How can it be that the distribution of wealth remains less unequal in Southern Europe than elsewhere in the Eurozone, when we know that the opposite is true with respect to the distribution of income? To a large extent, the answer to that question is to be sought in the higher rates of home ownership (the most significant asset for most households) in Southern Europe, especially before mortgage finance transformed housing markets and increased owner occupation rates elsewhere in Europe. For instance, in 2016, the proportion of population living in owner-occupied housing was 78% in Spain, 75% in Portugal, 74% in Greece, and 72% in Italy, compared to 69% in the European Union as a whole. Back in 1980, the distance separating Southern Europe from other Member States was even greater: in the EU15, the share of owner-occupied dwellings in Greece (75%) and Spain (73%) was only surpassed by that in Ireland (76%), with Italy (59%) and Portugal (52%) not far behind.[28]

4.14 LIFE SATISFACTION

How does it all add up? Since the whole point of economic growth is to improve the human lot, one might ask whether and to what extent the undeniable

---

28   For the latest figures, see Eurostat—Distribution of population by tenure status, type of household and income group [ilc_lvho02]. For the 1980 figures, see table 3.4 in National Agency for Enterprise and Housing (2003: 39). (No information provided for the EU average.) Note that the denominator is dwellings stock in 1980 and total population in 2016.

material progress of Southern Europe from the devastations of the mid-20th century to the present day has led to its peoples being 'happier'.[29]

This is not the right place to discuss the complex relationship between living standards and life satisfaction, or indeed happiness, except for remarking that, as Adam Smith had noted almost two and a half centuries ago, it is changes in income and wealth, rather than levels, that are most likely to produce changes in subjective well-being.[30]

Unfortunately, life satisfaction (and happiness) statistics for the countries under examination here have only started to be made available relatively recently. Results from the European Quality of Life Survey, carried out since 2003 by The European Foundation for the Improvement of Living and Working Conditions, show that mean values on a 0–10 scale fell continuously over the period in Greece, especially between 2007–2008 and 2016 (from 6.6 to 5.3 for life satisfaction and from 7.4 to 6.0 for happiness). In Spain, mean scores fell less dramatically from 2011–2012 to 2016 (life satisfaction: from 7.5 to 7.0; happiness: from 7.8 to 7.3). In Italy, mean scores fell most significantly between 2003 and 2007–2008 (i.e., before the crisis) and stood in 2016 at 6.6 for life satisfaction and 6.8 for happiness. Finally, in Portugal, in spite of the Eurozone crisis, mean scores increased steadily since 2003 and stood at 6.9 and 7.5 for life satisfaction and happiness respectively, in 2016. Overall, the latest estimates show that Portugal and Spain were clustered close to the EU average, Italy fairly lower, and Greece a lot lower.

Life satisfaction measures from the Gallup World Poll, as reported by the Organisation for Economic Cooperation and Development (OECD), confirm the general picture—except for Portugal, with mean scores that remained stable since the mid-2000s, but at significantly lower levels (5.2 in 2014-2016, same as Greece, compared to the OECD-33 average of 6.5).

4.15 CONCLUSION

Living standards in Southern Europe largely converged to the EU average until the eve of the Eurozone crisis (except in Italy, where they peaked in the

---

29 See Eurofound (2013, 2018); life satisfaction measures from the Gallup World Poll cited in OECD (2017).

30 'It deserves to be remarked, perhaps, that it is in the progressive state, while the society is advancing to the further acquisition, rather than when it has acquired its full complement of riches, that the condition of the labouring poor, of the great body of the people, seems to be the happiest and the most comfortable. It is hard in the stationary, and miserable in the declining state. The progressive state is in reality the cheerful and the hearty state to all the different orders of the society. The stationary is dull; the declining melancholy' Smith (1776: I.8.42).

mid-1990s). All four countries then lost ground relative to other Member States. Thereafter, their destinies diverged: in Greece, the fall was greatest and the recovery most timid; in Italy, the decline was slow but steady; in Portugal and Spain, the economy turned the corner in 2012 and 2013, respectively, and started to bounce back, gradually closing the gap with the rest of the European Union.

Can convergence continue in Spain and Portugal and resume in Italy and Greece? The answer to that question will hinge on a variety of factors, internal and external, closely related to each other. External factors include the ability of policymakers at European level to rebalance macroeconomic governance so that both core and periphery Member States can prosper. Internal factors mainly concern political instability. In the aftermath of the Eurozone crisis, Southern Europe (with the exception of Portugal) has been the theatre of a series of convulsions, starting from the confrontation between an anti-austerity government in Greece and the country's European partners in 2015, followed by the outbreak of the Catalan question in Spain in 2017, culminating in the rise to power of a populist Eurosceptic coalition in Italy in 2018. The successful resolution of those crises in a manner that preserves the integrity of the European Union, and the return of a milder political climate within each country, none of which can be taken for granted, will be crucial for the prosperity of Southern Europe in the years to come.

ACKNOWLEDGEMENTS

Financial support under the Reconciling Economic and Social Europe (REScEU) project, coordinated by Maurizio Ferrera (University of Milan) and funded by the European Research Council (Advanced Grant no. 340534), is gratefully acknowledged.

REFERENCES

AMECO. Annual macro-economic database of the European Commission's Directorate General for Economic and Financial Affairs. https://ec.europa.eu/info/business-economy-euro/indicators-statistics/economic-databases/macro-economic-database-ameco/ameco-database_en

Atkinson A. B., Hasell J., Morelli S., and Roser M. (2017). *The chartbook of economic inequality*. The Institute for New Economic Thinking. Oxford: Oxford University Press.

Baumeister, M., and Sala, R. (2015). *Southern Europe? Italy, Spain, Portugal, and Greece from the 1950s until the present day*. Frankfurt, New York: Campus Verlag.

Broadberry, S. N., and O'Rourke, K. H. (2010). *Cambridge economic history of modern Europe (Vol. 2)*. Cambridge: Cambridge University Press.

Chrissis, K., and Koutentakis, F. (2017). From dictatorship to crisis: The evolution of top income shares in Greece (1967–2013). Presented at 1st WID.world Conference. Paris School of Economics, 14–15 December.

European Commission. (2014). *Sixth report on economic, social and territorial cohesion. Investment for jobs and growth. Promoting development and good governance in EU regions and cities*. Brussels: European Commission.

European Central Bank (ECB). (2016). *The Household Finance and Consumption Survey: Results from the second wave. Statistics Paper Series 18*. Frankfurt: European Central Bank.

Eichengreen, B. (2008). *The European economy since 1945: Coordinated capitalism and beyond*. Princeton, NJ: Princeton University Press.

Eurofound. (2013). *Quality of life: Trends 2003–2012*. Dublin: European Foundation for the Improvement of Living and Working Conditions.

Eurofound. (2018). *European Quality of Life Survey 2016*. Dublin: European Foundation for the Improvement of Living and Working Conditions.

Fishman, R. M. (2014). Democracy and markets: Notes on a twenty-first century paradox. In D. Brinks, M. Leiras, and S. Mainwaring (eds.), *Reflections on uneven democracies: The legacy of Guillermo O'Donnell* (pp. 106–120). Baltimore, MD: Johns Hopkins University Press.

Ginsborg, P. (2003). *A history of contemporary Italy: Society and politics, 1943–1988*. Basingstoke: Palgrave Macmillan.

Ginsborg, P. (2007). *L'Italia del tempo presente: Famiglia, società civile, Stato (1980–1996)*. Torino: Einaudi.

Guillén, A. M., and León M. (2011). *The Spanish welfare state in European context*. Surrey/Burlington, VT: Ashgate.

Gunther, R., Diamantouros, N., and Puhle, H.-J. (1995). *The politics of democratic consolidation: Southern Europe in comparative perspective*. Baltimore, MD: Johns Hopkins University Press.

International Monetary Fund. (2017). *World economic report*. Washington, DC: International Monetary Fund.

Iordanoglou, C. H. (2008). *The Greek economy in the longue durée (1954–2005)*. Athens: Polis (in Greek).

Judt, T. (2005). *Postwar: A history of Europe since 1945*. London: Penguin Press.

Mitrakos, T., and Tsakloglou, P. (2012). Inequality, poverty and social welfare in Greece: From the restoration of democracy to the current economic crisis. In *Social policy and social cohesion in Greece in conditions of economic crisis* (pp. 23–63). Athens: Bank of Greece (in Greek).

National Agency for Enterprise and Housing. (2003). *Housing statistics in the European Union 2003*. Copenhagen: National Agency for Enterprise and Housing.

Organisation for Economic Cooperation and Development (OECD). (1999). *Historical Statistics 1960–1997*. Paris: OECD.

Organisation for Economic Cooperation and Development (OECD). (2000). *Historical Statistics 1970–1999*. Paris: OECD.

Organisation for Economic Cooperation and Development (OECD). (2001). *Historical Statistics 1970–2000*. Paris: OECD.

Organisation for Economic Cooperation and Development (OECD). (2014). *How was life? Global well-being since 1820*. Paris: OECD.

Organisation for Economic Cooperation and Development (OECD). (2017). *How's life? Measuring well-being*. Paris: OECD.

Perez S. A., and Matsaganis M. (2018). The political economy of austerity in Southern Europe. *New Political Economy, 23*(2), 192–207.

Pérez-Díaz, V. (1999). *Spain at the crossroads: Civil society, politics, and the rule of law*. Cambridge, MA: Harvard University Press.

Royo, S. (2018). The legacies of revolution: Path-dependence and economic performance in Portugal. *Portuguese Studies, 34*(1), 86–103.

Salvati, M. (2000). *Occasioni mancate: Economia e politica in Italia dagli anni '60 a oggi*. Bari: Laterza.

Smith, A. (1776). *An inquiry into the nature and causes of the wealth of nations*. (Originally published in Glasgow.)

UNESCO. (1957). *World illiteracy at mid-century: A statistical study*. Paris: The United Nations Educational, Scientific and Cultural Organisation.

World Bank. (2017). *World development report*. Washington, DC: International Monetary Fund.

5

INCOME, WEALTH, EMPLOYMENT, AND BEYOND

CENTRAL AND EASTERN EUROPE

Márton Medgyesi and István György Tóth

5.1 INTRODUCTION

This chapter looks at trends in Central and Eastern European (CEE) countries, exploring both convergence between these countries and the centre of the
European Union on the one hand and comparative inequality trends within some
of the CEE economies on the other. The region covered in the chapter includes
the three Baltic States (Estonia, Latvia, and Lithuania), the four Visegrad countries (Czech Republic, Hungary, Poland, Slovakia), and Slovenia, Romania, and
Bulgaria.[1] For time series data, the period covered stretches from the beginning
of the 1990s until the most recent available year. The aim of this chapter is to answer the following questions:

- What patterns of income convergence and inequality developments can
  be identified for CEE countries that experienced a transition from non-
  democratic regimes and centrally planned economies to competitive
  markets and representative democracies?
- What kind of similarities and dissimilarities can be identified among
  these developments?

---

1 Although it would have been interesting, and very special, the analysis of the case of
   the German Democratic Republic falls outside the scope of this chapter.

Márton Medgyesi and István György Tóth, *Income, Wealth, Employment, and Beyond* In: *Europe's Income, Wealth,
Consumption, and Inequality.* Edited by: Georg Fischer and Robert Strauss, Oxford University Press (2021).
© Oxford University Press. DOI: 10.1093/oso/9780197545706.003.0005

- Do the observed countries form a homogenous country grouping at any part of our observation period?
- What kind of similarities and dissimilarities can we identify with regard to the drivers behind societal changes in these countries?

The historic and social development of the countries studied in this chapter show important similarities. They have in common, for example, the socialist legacy,[2] two or three waves of institutional adaptation processes, and three major economic shocks for most of them.

As a first institutional change, the transition from command to market economy and from dictatorship to liberal democracy must be examined. All these CEE countries abandoned communism and adopted democracy and a market economy around 1990. As Kornai (2006) describes, these countries experienced a transition that was unique in world history in the sense that it was a peaceful and at the same time remarkably fast process (which took 10–15 years) moving in the main direction of the economic and political institutions of Western civilization. This process has not come about without sacrifices, however: as the first of the shocks, the CEE economies experienced structural shocks and the resulting recessions at the beginning of the transition process. Gross domestic product (GDP) shrunk by double digits in 1991 in almost all CEE countries, and the recession continued until the middle of the decade. The Baltic States were particularly heavily affected during this period. In the second half of the 1990s, the majority of transition countries recovered from recession and enjoyed growth rates above the European Union (EU) average during the period preceding EU accession. Nevertheless, as a second shock, most (though not all) of these countries were also affected by the crisis in Russia at the end of the 1990s.

The second large institutional adaptation process was linked to the accession to the European Union. The Central European transition countries (Poland, the Czech Republic, Slovakia, Hungary, and Slovenia) and the three Baltic States (Estonia, Lithuania, and Latvia) became members of the European Union in 2004; Bulgaria and Romania joined in 2007. Within this process a great deal of legal harmonization to the EU *acquis* had to be completed, with similar procedures but varying extents of harmonization for the various countries and various fields. The five smaller countries of the 10—Estonia, Latvia, Lithuania, Slovakia, and Slovenia—have also joined the Eurozone, taking a large step towards a more complete integration of their economies into the European Union.

---

2   Characterized, in economic terms, by severe shortages, miserable service deliveries, queuing, full but very inefficient employment, very low levels of human capital investments, obsolete and uncompetitive economic structures, etc. The elimination of the so-called shortage economy, was, however, very speedy in most cases. (See the account by Kornai [1995] for Hungary).

The transition paths have also displayed important differences that had a deep impact on outcomes in terms of income growth and inequality. The first is the historical heritage these countries brought with them into the process. For example, the Czech Republic and Slovenia had a level of economic development much closer to the levels of the EU15 countries—a fact that goes back in history, much before the socialist times. The CEE countries also differed in their economic structures, educational distribution, and in their ethnic heterogeneity as well.

And there were important differences in the transition process itself. In some of the countries, the reforms have been faster, while other countries have adopted a more gradual approach. Poland was, at least at the beginning, an example of the 'shock therapy' approach, with a sudden release of price and currency controls, withdrawal of state subsidies, and immediate trade liberalization.[3] In countries like Slovenia, Hungary, or Romania reforms were introduced more incrementally. Reform strategies also differed in complementarity/substitutability of reforms, their possible reversibility in view of needed adjustments, and the sustainability of their political economic conditions (Marangos, 2005).

The privatization strategies adopted were also different early on (between 1990 and 1995). For example, the Czech Republic, Latvia, and Lithuania used primarily voucher-based distributional mechanisms in the privatization process. In Estonia and Hungary, state-owned capital was privatized to outsiders with the large participation of foreign investors, while in Bulgaria a smaller role of foreign capital was observed. In Poland, Romania, and Slovenia the main privatization method was employee buy-out, while in Slovakia management buy-out was most important (World Bank, 2000).[4]

Overall, despite the broad similarities between institutional structures of liberal democracy and market economy, the chosen economic and social policies and institutions adopted in CEE countries differed to a significant extent (Myant and Drahokoupil, 2011; Bohle and Greskovits, 2012; Cerami and Vanhuysse, 2009). Bohle and Greskovits (2012) identify four types of capitalism in the CEE countries. According to their theory, the Baltic States are examples of a neoliberal institutional setup as they have small welfare states and relatively weak employee

---

3 The so-called *Balczerowicz-plan* (a fast acceptance and implementation of 10 core laws about privatization and fiscal, monetary, and labour policies and institutions) brought a relatively larger shock but then a fairly quick GDP recovery. Afterwards the Polish economic policy also became more eclectic and incremental.

4 The actual country experiences were, however, more eclectic than can be reflected in a typology like this. Poland, for example, also had a (relatively short-lived) 'voucher privatization' programme. Many government-owned enterprises were merged into a few 'investment funds', and buy options were made available at a low price to a broad circle of Poles. Given that these shares were small in value, the take-up was not robust, and a quick concentration on secondary markets started—resulting larger piles of stock in the hands of banks and specialized investors.

representation and protection. At the other extreme lies neo-corporatist Slovenia in which employee interest representation mechanisms are much stronger and welfare state programmes are more extensive and redistributive. The central European countries (cases of 'embedded neoliberalism') can be found somewhere between the liberal and the neo-corporatist institutional setup. They have quite substantial welfare provision and the significant influence of representatives of social interests. A fourth type is defined as a 'nonregime' (e.g., Romania and Bulgaria) where the conflicting objectives cannot be balanced, leading to social and political instability.[5]

In addition, as a recent development, one can also observe a diversion from the general European path (into which all the above types can still broadly fit) in the case of at least two countries: first Hungary, in 2010, then Poland, in 2015, started diverging from the liberal democratic development paths by constraining checks and balances, limiting media freedom and the independence of the judiciary, instituting autocratic tendencies in these countries, and prompting fierce clashes between their countries and the European mainstream. János Kornai (2015) calls this a U-turn in Hungarian development, mentioning that recentralization in public administration, renationalization in the economy, and setbacks with respect to the overall checks and balances cannot but be understood as a step backwards on the path that earlier characterized the transition.

In what follows, we compare developments in these countries by focussing on economic convergence to EU15 countries, on distributional issues, and on population well-being and satisfaction.

5.2 ECONOMIC DEVELOPMENT AND INCOME CONVERGENCE TO THE EU15

5.2.1 Trends of Economic Convergence

First, the convergence trends of CEE countries are described in terms of GDP per capita. As Figure 5.1 shows, all CEE countries have managed close the gap to average GDP levels of EU15 countries over the quarter of a century between

---

5   In a different classification, Myant and Drahokoupil (2011) classify the whole postcommunist group (CEE, SEE, and Commonwealth of Independent States [CIS] countries) into five categories, from which the currently observed 10 belong either to FDI-based (second-rank) market economies (V4 plus Slovenia) or to peripheral market economies (the Baltic republics, Romania, and Bulgaria). The remaining five categories are the 'oligarchic or clientelistic capitalisms' (a larger part of the CIS region); 'order states' (other CIS states that underwent only very limited reforms); and remittance- and aid-based economies (a number of low-income countries in Eastern Europe and CIS).

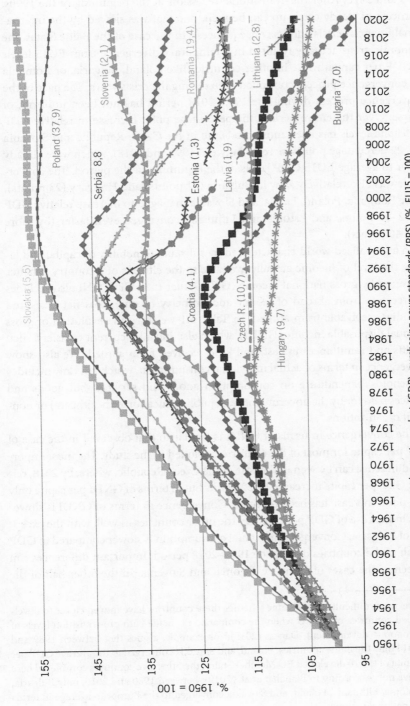

Figure 5.1 Evolution of relative per capita gross domestic product (GDP), purchasing power standards (PPS) (%, EU15 = 100).

Source: Ameco database, European Commission, table HVGDPR, accessed 2020.03.30.

1993 and 2018. After the 'transitional recession' at the beginning of the 1990s, a process of steady catch-up can be seen, one that was slowed by the international financial crisis and its consequences.[6] In the case of the Baltic States, the economic crisis actually resulted in a temporary divergence from EU15 levels of GDP per capita, while in other countries like Poland, Bulgaria, or Romania the convergence process continued even during the crisis years. The pace of the convergence process during the 1993–2018 period has not been uniform, of course. Over the entire period, the percentage point increase in relative GDP per capita levels has been more moderate in the Czech Republic and Slovenia (19–22 percentage points increase between 1993 and 2018), which were already closer to average EU15 GDP levels at the beginning of the period. The convergence was also relatively slow in Bulgaria (11 points) and Hungary (23 points), while Romania, Poland, Latvia, and Slovakia managed to increase relative GDP by 32–39 points, and Estonia and Lithuania converged even faster (by more than 40 points).

In a globalized world characterized by substantial mobility of capital and labour, the level of income actually available to the citizens of a country is better measured by gross national income (GNI) rather than GDP. GNI also includes net receipts from abroad of labour and property income, plus net taxes and subsidies receivable from abroad. In Table 5.1 we show the evolution of gross national disposable income (GNDI), which also includes current transfers, such as gifts and remittances in cash and kind received from abroad. We also show convergence in terms of actual individual consumption, which not only includes households' expenditure on consumption goods and services, but goods and services paid for by the government (e.g., public education or healthcare) or non-profit organizations.

The convergence in terms of GNDI is similar to that observed in the case of GDP per capita for most of the countries included in the study. The most important difference can be seen in the case of the Czech Republic, where, by 2018, relative GDP per capita increased by 22 points but in terms of GNDI per capita only a 16-point increase has been detected. Convergence in terms of GNDI is slower than in the case of GDP per capita in the other countries as well, with the exception of Bulgaria. Convergence in actual consumption is slower compared to GDP in half of the countries during the 1995–2018 period. Important differences can be seen in the cases of Hungary, Estonia, and Slovenia. In the other half of the

---

6   It is more difficult to determine whether these countries have moved closer to developed countries of the EU when the comparison is made with pre-transition levels of economic development. Darvas (2015), for example, argues that between 1989 and 2014 only the Baltic countries, Poland, and Slovakia converged to the average GDP per capita of the 10 developed EU Member States; the other five countries considered here have not. According to Blanchet et al. (2019), between 1980 and 2015, only Bulgaria, Estonia, Lithuania, Poland, and Slovakia converged to the European average in terms of national income.

Table 5.1 Evolution of relative income and consumption (% relative to EU15)

	GDP per head of population, (PPS: EU15 = 100)				Gross national disposable income per head of population (PPS: EU15 = 100)				Actual individual consumption (PPS: EU15 = 100)			
	1993	2000	2008	2018	1993	2000	2008	2018	1995	2000	2008	2018
Bulgaria	36	24	38	48	37	25	38	49	36	27	41	52
Czech Rep.	63	62	76	85	63	61	71	80	58	57	65	77
Estonia	30	36	62	77	32	35	60	76	32	36	58	69
Latvia	26	31	53	65	27	32	54	65	31	33	53	65
Lithuania	31	32	57	75	33	33	57	75	33	38	65	83
Hungary	43	45	56	66	44	43	53	64	47	47	55	60
Poland	34	41	50	66	34	41	50	64	38	45	55	71
Romania	24	22	46	60	25	23	47	60	28	25	48	66
Slovenia	62	68	81	81	62	69	79	80	66	67	73	74
Slovakia	39	43	64	72	39	44	63	70	39	44	62	68

Source: GDP, GNDI from AMECO database (tables HVGDPR, HVGTPR) accessed 30 March 2020. AIC from Eurostat database (table prc_ppp_ind, accessed 2020.03.30). First data point on GNDI in the case of Bulgaria is from 1995.

countries, convergence in terms of consumption moved more quickly towards EU15 average levels than in the case of GDP. The difference is most important in the case of Bulgaria, Poland, and Lithuania, where the increase in the relative level of consumption was 4–5 points higher than in the case of GDP per capita.

Econometric studies that investigate real economic convergence between the CEE countries and the rest of Europe confirm that CEE countries have converged to more developed countries of Europe. Studies of beta convergence are based on the estimation of growth regressions that investigate the relationship between the longer term growth rate of an indicator (e.g., per capita GDP at PPP) and its 'initial' relative level (controlling for other factors). A significantly negative regression coefficient (beta) of initial development level indicates the existence of beta convergence, meaning that the growth rate of underdeveloped countries (regions) is higher than that of developed countries (regions).

Studies analysing the transition/pre-accession period generally show that CEE countries have managed to reduce the gap with EU15 countries after the years of transitional recession (Kornai, 2006) in the early 1990s. Kočenda, Kutan, and Yigit (2006) studied real convergence for eight CEE countries (Romania and Bulgaria are not included) in the pre-accession period. They found evidence that strong convergence is taking place towards the EU core and periphery countries. Convergence towards the core countries accelerated around 2000 in the Czech Republic, Hungary, and the Baltic countries. Studying growth regressions on quarterly data for the period 1995–2005, Reza and Zahra (2008) have confirmed the existence of absolute beta convergence with the EU15 for the whole CEE group. Próchniak and Witkowski (2013) also find beta convergence in per capita GDP among EU countries during the 1993–2010 period. Their results show faster convergence regarding the EU27 (5% per year) than among the EU15 countries (3%), which suggests a faster catch-up in the case of CEE countries.

An interesting issue is whether convergence has accelerated after accession to the European Union. Próchniak and Witkowski (2013) divide the time period studied into three subperiods (1993–1998, 1998–2004, 2005–2010) but do not find significant difference in the pace of convergence between the subperiods, suggesting no acceleration in convergence after joining the European Union. Similarly, Andersen et al. (2019) have not found significant effects of EU membership on economic growth. Contrary to these findings, Böwer and Turrini (2010) find a significant impact of EU accession on the growth performance of CEE countries in a panel analysis after controlling for a series of institutional factors. This result thus suggests that EU accession per se had an impact on growth, and the growth-enhancing effect of EU accession was not only working through the promotion of institutional convergence. Their analysis also showed that EU accession had a growth-enhancing effect especially for those countries that had relatively low initial income levels, weak institutional quality, and lower degrees of financial development. Similar results were obtained by Campos et al. (2014). Those authors estimated the effect of accession to the European Union by constructing synthetic counterfactuals and found that EU accession has increased economic growth in most CEE countries covered by the study (Romania and Bulgaria were not included). The biggest increase in growth rates was found in the Baltic States (2–3 percentage points per years), and growth rates of Slovenia, Hungary, and the Czech Republic have increased by 1 percentage point.

5.2.2 Determinants of Growth in CEE Countries

There is an extensive literature of determinants of growth in transition countries (for reviews of the early studies, see Svejnar [2002] and Campos and Coricelli [2002]). In growth accounting exercises, economic growth can be the result of an increase in the quantity of production factors (capital and labour) used in an economy or an increase in the productivity of the process by which the production factors are transformed into output. In the following sections, the developments in growth components will be presented, first by reviewing main trends in the evolution of the labour force and capital.

5.2.2.1 Population Trends and Structure

As Figure 5.2 shows, population growth declined considerably after 1990 in most of these countries. In the case of countries like Slovakia, Poland population growth decreased after the systemic change, while in a number of countries population has been actually declining during the decades following transition.

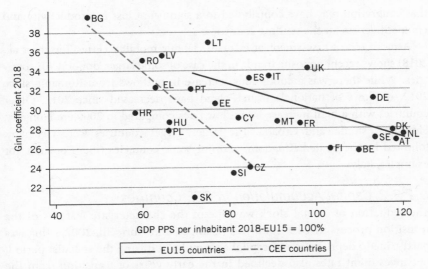

Figure 5.2 Trends of total population in Central and Eastern European (CEE) countries, 1950 = 100 (population size in 2019, millions, in brackets).
Source: Authors' calculations based on United Nations (2019). Population estimates from UN Population Division, Department of Economic and Social Affairs, last revision August 2019.

The decline of the Hungarian population started in 1980, followed by very significant drops in Bulgaria, Romania, and the three Baltic States after the systemic change. The source of the decline comes basically from two sources. First, there is a natural loss, due to the significant drop in total fertility rates and the still high mortality in most countries. However, outward migration has also increased almost everywhere. The target of this migration was, in the vast majority of cases, somewhere out of this region (EU15 countries, other European countries, and outside Europe, mostly the United States). A notable exception is the migration of ethnic Hungarians from Romania to Hungary, mostly in the first half of the 1990s (contributing to a slowdown of the decline in the Hungarian population at the time).

Atoyan et al. (2016) estimated that emigration numbers were about an annual ½% to 1% of the 1990s population in the CEE countries, and emigration has tended to speed up after various waves of EU expansion in 2004 and 2007. According to their calculations, the cumulative emigration flows amounted to some 8% of the 1990 population of the respective countries. This has significantly reduced population growth where—from demographic reasons—it existed or worsened the process where there was already a decline for demographic reasons. Given that emigrants tended to be (on average) younger and more highly educated than their home populations, emigration tended to exacerbate a shortage of high-skilled labour and, as such, constituted a brain drain that and has lowered potential growth in CEE. Atoyan et al. (2016) also argue that emigration may have contributed to a significant loss in productivity and competitiveness for the sending countries.

A more recent assessment of intra-EU labour mobility (Fries-Tersch et al., 2018) shows recent opposite trends in the case of some larger 'donor' CEE countries. While there was a continuous increase in outflows from Romania since 2012, outflows of nationals from Poland have decreased since 2012. Other countries with a high increase in outflow rates compared to 2009 are Hungary, Slovenia, Estonia, and Croatia. The largest target countries were Germany, followed by the United Kingdom, and, for some countries (like Romania, for example), Italy.

5.2.2.2 Capital Accumulation in CEE Countries

The reduction of capital stock was one of the characteristic features of the transition process in CEE countries (Campos and Coricelli, 2002). This was partly due to depreciation of capital accumulated during the socialist period, but investment rates also declined in the early years of transition from the very high levels characteristic of centrally planned economies. According to a study by the European Investment Bank (EIB) (Bubbico et al., 2017), between 1995 and 2015, overall gross fixed capital formation (GFCF) in the five CEE countries has fluctuated between 20% and 25% of GDP at levels slightly higher than the EU28 average. Investment declined during the crisis years from the pre-crisis peak of around 25% to just above 20% of GDP in 2013. In the Baltic States, Bulgarian and Romanian GFCF evolved with stronger cyclical fluctuations: before the crisis, the investment rate went up to 33–35% of GDP and then it dropped below 20% in the Baltic States and to 25% in the south-eastern countries (Bubbico et al. 2017).

Before the economic crisis, private capital inflows (i.e., cross-border loans, foreign direct investment, and others) were exceptionally high in the CEE region, even by historical standards (Becker et al., 2010). As a result, private investment as a share of national income was (well) above the EU average. The saving rate was low by international comparison, lagging behind the investment rate—often considerably so. This implies that, during the prosperous period between 1995 and 2007, rapid physical capital accumulation in CEE countries was to a large extent financed by external resources. With the onset of the crisis, however, foreign private capital inflows declined sharply, which resulted in a drop in the share of private investment in GDP, by as much as 15 percentage points in some countries. Moreover, there is very little sign of recovery, and the share of private investment is still below the EU average in most CEE countries (Bubbico et al., 2017).

Another important source of capital formation was public investment, which has been significantly higher in the CEE region than in the EU28. Following the crisis, public sector investment changed little in CEE but declined in the Baltics and South-Eastern European (SEE) countries. Public investment has recovered after the crisis, especially in CEE countries, largely as a result of disbursement of EU funds.

5.2.2.3 Components and Determinants of Economic Growth

Studies decomposing economic growth into the role of its components (accumulation of capital, labour, and increases in productivity) unanimously show that labour accumulation has played a relatively small role in economic growth in Eastern European countries (World Bank, 2008; Burda and Severgnini, 2009; Dombi, 2013; Levenko et al., 2017; Kónya, 2018). Decomposing the contribution of labour into that of employment, working hours and human capital Kónya (2018) finds small positive contribution of increases in employment and human capital and a small negative contribution of hours in case of the Visegrad countries in the period 1998–2014.[7]

On the other hand, studies report different results about the role played by capital accumulation and productivity growth. According to the World Bank (2008) or the European Bank for Reconstruction and Development (EBRD) Transition Reports (2013, 2017) economic convergence of transition countries is mainly driven by increasing total factor productivity (TFP), and capital accumulation had a relatively smaller effect. Market reforms helped to increase productivity by improving the inefficient use of capital and labour under central planning. Consequently, the region's economies caught up to levels of productivity that would normally be expected at similar level of development. The increase in productivity has slowed in the CEE countries after the crisis. Between 2008 and 2014, the contribution of TFP growth to GDP growth has been negative in the Central European and Baltic countries (EBRD, 2017).

Other studies, however, find a more important role for capital accumulation. For example, results from Levenko et al. (2017) suggest that the growth of physical capital played an important role during the period between 1995 and 2016, although it was not the main source of growth. In case of countries like the Czech Republic and Slovakia, however, the contribution from capital growth is more than one-half of average output growth. Findings from Kónya (2018) on the Visegrad countries suggest that although increases in TFP were the main driver of growth in the 1998–2014 period, capital accumulation also played a role. Dombi (2013), on the other hand, concludes that capital accumulation was the main driving force of growth in CEE countries.

According to Falcetti et al. (2006) studies of the early transition years identified three main type of factors as determinants of economic growth. Differences in the country's initial conditions (e.g., skill level of the population, duration

---

7   Using a different method for calculating the stock of human capital Leeuwen and Földvári (2013) conclude that human capital accumulation was an important factor in economic growth during the period between 1994 and 2005 in the Visegrad countries, Romania and Bulgaria.

of communism) have been found to explain variations in subsequent development. Credible macroeconomic stabilization programmes were also shown to be a necessary condition for growth. Third, most early studies argued that reforms were beneficial for growth. Reforms studied included price or trade liberalization, privatization, and also institutional reforms that addressed characteristics of corporate governance, competition policy, or financial institutions. The later literature—taking into account endogeneity of reforms and multicollinearity among different measures of reform—however, has found the relation between reform and growth less robust (Falcetti et al., 2006).

Later studies also demonstrated the importance of other factors such as trade openness, technology transfer, and institutional quality. For example, Kutan and Yigit (2009) studied the convergence of CEE countries in labour productivity during the period between 1995 and 2006. According to their modelling framework, productivity growth is the result of domestic innovation or technology transfers from more developed countries. They demonstrate that variables related to technology transfer from more developed countries (like foreign direct investment [FDI]) have an important effect on productivity growth. Among variables related to domestic innovation, human capital had a significant positive effect on productivity growth, while R&D had no effect. The analysis also shows that the increase in productivity is higher when the productivity gap is larger, which suggests convergence in technical efficiency. Using industry-level data over the 1995–2005 period, Bijsterbosch and Kolasa (2010) also find that FDI had a significant and positive effect on labour productivity in CEE countries (Bulgaria and Romania not included). They also show that the effect of FDI on productivity seems to be increasing with absorptive capacity of the industry (measured by productivity differentials vis-á-vis the Euro Area) and with levels of human capital.

Some studies have directly analysed the impact of the institutional context. For example, Schadler et al. (2006) analyse the growth experience of the new Member States and other emerging market countries and find that institutional quality is an important determinant of growth in addition to income levels, population growth, and investment. Havrylyshyn and van Rooden (2003) have found that the importance of the quality of the institutional environment was increasing over time. In the same time their analysis finds a stronger effect of economic liberalization measures on economic growth compared to measures of the quality of the institutional environment.

As we have seen before, many studies find acceleration of economic growth in CEE countries after accession to the European Union. One possible channel through which this could happen is cohesion policy. There is no wide consensus among researchers on the effects of cohesion policy on regional growth and convergence (see, e.g., Crescenzi and Giua, 2017, for a review).[8] Some studies use

---

8 This is partly due to the methodological difficulties inherent in studying the effect of such policy instruments (Crescenzi and Giua, 2017). First, cohesion policy includes

a regression framework and try to take into account specificities of the socio-economic environment where the programme has been implemented, such as institutions, interaction of cohesion policy with other instruments, or variables of the local political economy. Other approaches try to identify the net effect of cohesion policies by comparing data on actual outcomes to a counterfactual which shows the outcomes that would have been observed in the absence of that policy. For example, Becker et al. (2013) use a regression discontinuity design and exploit the GDP threshold in the definition of Objective 1 regions. Regions that were eligible for cohesion funds show higher growth rates compared to similar regions which were just above the GDP threshold and did not receive cohesion funds.

5.2.2.4 Wage Convergence Before and After the Crisis

The increase in levels of productivity brought about increasing wages during the transition process. Oblath et al. (2015) show by econometric analysis that before the crisis, increases in labour costs were higher in countries with lower initial levels of labour costs. They also conclude that convergence stopped during the crisis years. Galgóczi (2017) reaches similar conclusions: he finds that wage increases also slowed after the crisis in most of the countries in the region, with the exception of Estonia, Lithuania, and Bulgaria. In the Czech Republic, Poland, and Slovakia, wage increases were moderate until 2016. In Slovenia, wages stagnated, while in Romania and Hungary decline in real wages were observed.

Despite the significant convergence over the 1995–2015 period, wages in CEE countries tend to be significantly lower than in the EU15 countries. Whether wages in CEE countries are too low relative to productivity levels is an issue of debate. Galgóczi (2017) argues that wages could be increased in CEE countries without putting cost competitiveness in danger. Oblath et al. (2015) argue, however, that relative real labour costs roughly correspond to relative productivity levels in the European Union. On the other hand, they agree that wages net of taxes and social security contributions are indeed relatively low in CEE countries. They argue that relatively low levels of net wages in CEE countries might be explained by the relatively high per capita real level of government services provided to households.

---

very different interventions in different local socioeconomic contexts. In addition, EU financial resources are meant to be additional to national resources, which makes the effect of EU financing difficult to separate. There might also be important spill-over effects and indirect effects of the policy which are difficult to capture. It matters greatly what measures of cohesion policy are used in the analysis: for example, committed funds might be different from the money actually spent on the programme.

5.3 EVOLUTION OF INCOME INEQUALITY IN CEE COUNTRIES

Despite the significant convergence of CEE countries to the EU core since the transition not everyone has benefitted equally from the results of economic growth. The following sections discuss the evolution and main drivers of income inequality and poverty in the region. A major data source on income inequality used in this section is derived from the GINI project (for more information on this project, see Salverda et al. [2014] and Nolan et al. [2014]; on the database, see Tóth [2014]). The research design of GINI included in-depth case studies for the 30 participant (European and non-European) countries, and, fortunately, all of our target countries in this chapter are represented.[9]

For Gini coefficients, the preferred income concept, in accordance with recommendations (see Canberra Group, 2011) generally accepted by the inequality research community, is the net disposable household income, equivalized to take differences in household size and composition into account. This is consistent with common practice in the measurement of income inequality and poverty by the European Union. The income sharing unit is the household, whereas the unit of analysis for the computation of various indices is the individual member of the household. Household resources are assumed to be shared among household members, and a correction for economies of scale in the household is assumed and implemented by means of equivalization. For this historic time series, there is no preferred equivalence scale applied, leaving open the choice between the increasingly common square root of the number of persons in the household, the modified Organisation for Economic Cooperation and Development (OECD) scale that takes the number of adults versus children in the household into account, or a national set of equivalence scales.[10] Applying a strictly uniform scale would have required access to micro data in all countries, and we did not have this access.

---

9 Each study (available in Nolan et al., 2014) was undertaken by a team of national experts, including leading figures of the profession internationally and nationally. For some of the variables, it was possible to create a systematic collection of indicators, and the resulting database was proved to provide a very useful starting point for further development into a new and extensive set of data on inequality in a major rich country grouping in general but also in CEE in particular, with a real value added compared to existing inequality datasets (for more information, see Tóth, 2014).

10 In the GINI project, where the data collection was carried out via thematically harmonized country case studies, full comparability with regard to the equivalence scales could not have been achieved. However, this does not cause any serious problems for the inequality measures (unlike for poverty comparisons, where it could be a problem for assessing poverty rates of families with various sizes).

5.3.1 Trends in Income Inequality

To show the 'big picture' of inequality trends in CEE countries, Table 5.2 presents countries in terms of their inequality levels during four different parts of the period scrutinized here: 1980–1984, 1996–2000, 2006–2010, and 2014–2018. To smooth out measurement uncertainties and cyclical trends, values for the Gini coefficient are averaged for these periods.

As shown in Table 5.2, CEE countries for which data were available for the pre-transition era (Table 5.2 shows 1980–1984 figures, averaged for the period) all appeared in the lowest inequality group, having a Gini value lower than 0.25 Although the reliability of the income distribution statistics for periods of socialism is sometimes questioned, the impression of the seemingly homogenous low-inequality group remains. The classical collection of inequality data for the regions by Atkinson and Micklewright (1992) is consistent with all these findings.

While the group of CEE countries was very homogenous during the 1980s, at least as far as differences in their inequality levels are concerned, the first half of the 1990s saw remarkable changes leading to great divergence in their inequality. This resulted from the evolution from a seemingly uniform country grouping stagnating behind the Iron Curtain, with Gini figures between 0.20 and 0.25, to a very heterogeneous group with Gini figures ranging from 0.23 to 0.37. This means that, by the time these countries joined the European Union in the 2000s, they already represented different inequality regimes (see, e.g., Medgyesi 2008, Tóth and Medgyesi, 2011). A cluster of six countries—Estonia, Lithuania, and

Table 5.2 Average inequality levels (Gini coefficient values) of Central and Eastern European (CEE) countries during four periods between 1980 and 2018

Gini coefficients	1980–1984	1996–2000	2006–2010	2014–2018
>0.350		Estonia, Romania,	Latvia, Lithuania, Romania,	Bulgaria, Lithuania, Latvia, Romania
0.301 to 0.350		Hungary, Latvia, Lithuania, Romania,	Bulgaria, Estonia, Poland	Estonia
0.251 to 0.300		Poland	Hungary	Hungary, Poland
Up to 0.250	Bulgaria, Czech Republic, Estonia, Hungary, Latvia, Lithuania, Slovakia	Czech Republic, Slovakia, Slovenia	Czech Republic, Slovakia, Slovenia	Czech Republic, Slovakia, Slovenia
No data	Romania, Slovenia			

Source: For the period 1980–2010 GINI project database, see more details in Table A1. For 2006–2018 Eurostat Database. In the case of the period 2006–2010, the countries are assigned to identical groups based on the two datasets.

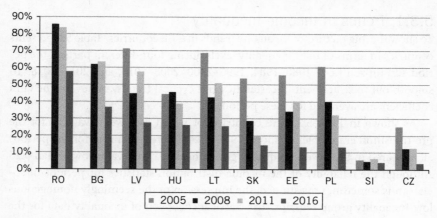

Figure 5.3 Gross domestic product (GDP) per capita (EU28 = 100) and inequality in equivalent household income (2018).
Note: Ireland, Luxembourg omitted from the graph.
Source: Gini:Eurostat database, GDP:Ameco database

Latvia, on the one hand, and Bulgaria, Romania, and Hungary, on the other— experienced a large (more than 10 Gini points) increase in inequality in just a few years, while in the other group consisting Czech Republic, Slovakia, Poland, and Slovenia the increase of inequality was much smaller. The general pattern of rising inequalities during this period in CEE countries has been confirmed in other studies using different data and different inequality indices. For example, Blanchet et al. (2019) demonstrated based on data from the World Inequality Database[11] that the increase in the income share of the top 10% of society was the steepest in the Eastern European region during the period between 1985 and 2015.

5.3.2 Levels of Income Inequality and Poverty 25 Years After Transition

To compare the most recent average income and inequality of these countries, Figure 5.3 presents Gini indices of disposable equivalent incomes of households together with relative GDP levels. Among the CEE countries Latvia, Lithuania, and Romania appear to be in the group with highest inequality levels (more than 0.35 of Gini value), while the Czech Republic, Slovakia, and Slovenia remained in the most equal end (still having a Gini in the value range lower than 0.25). There is clearly a large difference between the levels of economic development in the EU15 and CEE countries, while the internal variance of inequality levels is similar in the two subgroups of the European Union. Income inequality is

---

11   These data have been compiled on the basis of household surveys, fiscal data, and national accounts.

relatively strongly and negatively related to GDP per head across the observed EU countries. The slope of the relationship is negative for both the EU15 countries and the new Member States. Inequality in net household wealth is much higher than in the case of income in these countries as well. Brzezinski et al. (2019) report Gini indices between 0.49 (in Slovakia) and 0.79 (in Latvia) with values in the 0.60–0.70 range for Estonia, Poland, and Hungary.

Behind differences in inequality levels of net household income we can find differences in market income inequality and differences in the inequality-reducing effect of government redistribution. Market income inequality among the working age (16–64 years old) is not especially high in the transition countries. EU countries with the highest levels of market income inequality are Southern European countries (Greece, Spain, Portugal) and also Ireland. The three Baltic States and Bulgaria and Romania have high levels of net income inequality mainly because of a low level of inequality reducing the effect of government redistribution, which decreases the Gini index by 14–16% only. Slovenia, on the other hand, has a similar level of market income inequality but this is combined with the highest degree of inequality reducing effects from government transfers (38%). The low level of inequality in Slovakia and the Czech Republic is not only the result of government redistribution (21–28%) but also of a relatively low level of market income inequality (0.33–0.35 instead of 0.4 in other CEE countries).

When using relative income poverty measures people with low incomes are identified in comparison to other citizens of the country. Using the 60% of median equivalized income as a poverty threshold, we have a picture that is similar to the case of inequality: the Baltic States together with Bulgaria and Romania have relatively high income poverty rates compared to other EU Member States, with percentage of poor equal to or higher than 22%. Relative income poverty in Poland is close to the EU28 average (17.3% in 2016), while in other CEE countries it is lower than that. Countries with a higher rate of relative income poverty generally have deeper poverty as well; that is, the poor on average are further away from the poverty threshold (see Lelkes and Gasior, 2018). Outliers to this general tendency are Slovakia, Bulgaria, and Romania where the relative poverty gap is higher than would be predicted on the basis of their poverty rate, while in the case of the Baltic States the reverse is true.

Measures of economic inequality and relative income poverty show relative differences between individuals, households, and various social groups of a given country. However, a joint cross-country comparison of relative economic development and convergence can be more balanced with the study of poverty rates, where the poverty threshold in a given year is identical across countries. This can be done via the establishment of an all-European poverty rate (with the assumption of a pan-European income distribution). The share of the population below the all-European poverty line would then jointly show inequality within countries in the context of the relative economic differences

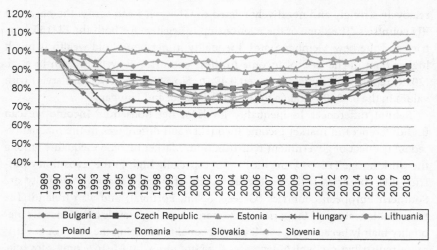

Figure 5.4 Percentage of people with incomes lower than 40% of the EU15 median income (2006–2016).
Source: Authors' calculation based on EU-SILC UDB 2006, 2009, 2012, 2017.

between countries. This is shown for CEE countries in selected years on Figure 5.4, taking 40% of the EU15 median income as the poverty threshold in every country.

From the cross-country comparisons, it is seen that by taking 40% of the EU15 median income[12] as the poverty threshold, the majority of the Romanian and more than one-third of the Bulgarian population would belong to the low-income category even in 2016. It can also be seen that during the decade following accession to the European Union, poverty rates declined in all countries, showing catch-up by the CEE countries (for similar results, see Goedeme and Collado, 2016). Between 2005 and 2016, the poverty rate declined the most in the case of Poland. The only cases when poverty rates (based on EU15 median) increased were during the crisis years in the case of the Baltic countries, but this rise has proved temporary: after 2011, poverty rates declined. Even during the years of the economic crisis, the percentage of the poor defined on an EU-wide poverty threshold has declined in some CEE countries, most importantly in Poland and Slovakia. The convergence of CEE countries can also be seen in the development of non–income-based poverty indicators, such as the severe material deprivation rate proposed by Eurostat (see, e.g., Calvert and Nolan, 2012).

---

12 The EU15 median income is calculated from microdata of the EU15-wide income distribution that was created from the EU-SILC database (with PPP adjustment). The 40% threshold was selected (instead of 50% or 60%) to avoid close to 100% poverty in case of the lower income CEE countries.

5.3.3 Explanations of Inequality Change: Similar Driving Forces During the Transition Process

In addition to country-specific studies, some studies have presented comparative analyses of changes in inequality in Eastern European countries since the beginning of the transition process. For a very careful analysis of trends in earlier years of transition, see Flemming and Micklewright (1999). Milanovic (1999), the World Bank (2000), and Mitra and Yemtsov (2006) give an in-depth analysis of the driving forces behind the evolution of income inequalities in these countries. Perugini and Pompei (2015) review evidence on trends and drivers of inequality, while Heyns (2005) reviews aspects of increasing inequalities such as those related to gender, age, region of residence, etc. Some studies use an inequality decomposition framework to uncover driving forces behind inequality change (e.g., Milanovic 1999), while others such as Bandelj and Mahutga (2010), Milanovic and Ersado (2012), or Aristei and Perugini (2015) analyse determinants on country-panel data. Studies on the determinants of inequality change during the early years of transition point to the role of declining employment, increasing wage inequality, increasing role of capital income, and the declining inequality-reducing effect of government taxes and transfers.

During the economic recession in the early transition years, employment decreased dramatically in CEE countries, while unemployment and inactivity were on the rise (see Figure 5.5). The income situation of households which lost employment deteriorated tremendously, and this gave rise to a form of inequality previously unknown to them: namely, inequality between those in employment and those working age people who were out of the labour market. Employment recovered to some extent in most of the CEE countries after the transformational recession: during the growth years between the end of the 1990s until the recession struck in 2009, most countries have seen increasing employment rates. But still in 2014, the employment ratio is considerably lower than at the beginning of the transition process.

Moreover, inequalities between those in employment were also rising during the first phase of transition. As described by Rutkowski (2001), at the beginning of the transition period the Gini coefficient of earnings inequality fell in the 0.16–0.27 range in these countries. In the first half of the 1990s, inequality of earnings increased by 4–6 Gini points. During the second half of the decade, earnings inequality continued to increase in six out of nine countries covered by the data (Table 5.3).

One important factor in increasing earning disparity was an increasing wage premium for educated labourers (e.g., Rutkowski, 2001). In the Czech Republic, the wage premium of tertiary education (compared to those with primary education) increased from 38% to 58%[13] between 1988 and 1992 (Večerník,

---

13 Estimates from Mincer-regressions.

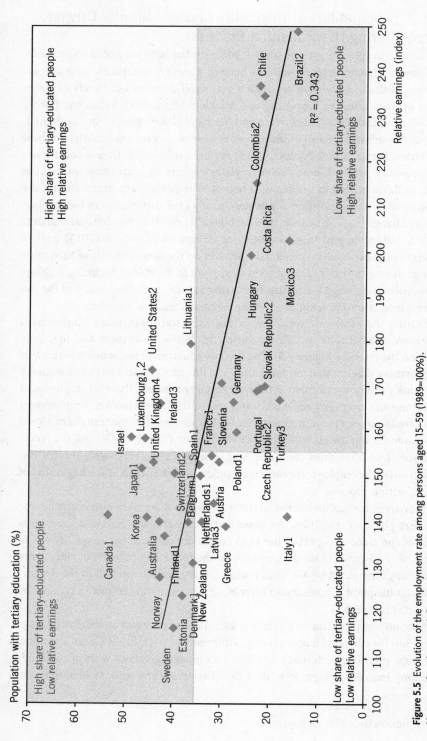

Figure 5.5 Evolution of the employment rate among persons aged 15–59 (1989=100%).

Note: employed rate is defined as employed persons as % of the population of the same age.

Source: For period 1989–2000 Transmonee 2016 database, UNICEF, for period 2000–2018 Eurostat database (table lfsa_ergaed, accessed 30/03/2020).

Table 5.3 Evolution of earnings inequality in Central and Eastern European (CEE) countries during the 1990s (Gini coefficients)

	1989–1990	1993–1994	1998–1999
Bulgaria	0,213	0,250	0,292[a]
Czech Republic	0,198	0,257	0,258
Estonia	0,250	nd.	0,380
Latvia	0,249[c]	0,282	0,331
Lithuania	n.d.	0,391	0,353
Hungary	0,268	0,315	0,349[b]
Poland	0,205	0,257	0,293
Romania	0,156	0,229	0,357
Slovenia	0,222	0,273	0,306

[a] Data from 1996.
[b] Data from 1997.
[c] Data from 1991.
Monthly wages (and bonuses) of full-time employees based on company surveys. nd, no data. Data are from the first available year in the given interval.
Source: Rutkowski (2001), based on data from UNICEF, Transmonee database.

2001) and then increased further to 74% by 1996. Sakova described a similar increase in the case of Slovakia (Sakova, 1996). In Slovenia, men with tertiary degrees earned 72% more than those with a primary degree in 1987, and the wage premium increased to 94% by 1991 (Orazem and Vodopivec, 1997). In Hungary, the wage premium of men with tertiary degrees (base: upper secondary) increased from 51% to 82% between 1986 and 1992 (Kertesi and Köllő, 2002). In Poland, the return to 1 year of schooling increased from 5% to 7.3% (Rutkowski, 2001).

The role of education as a driving force behind inequality change can be analysed in the frame of supply and demand for skills. The latter is driven by technology change because new technologies require higher skills while, depending on the availability (supply) of higher skills in the market, the premium for higher education may be larger or smaller. In the CEE countries the importance of education in determining employment opportunities and wages was rising despite the significant expansion of education that occurred. We illustrate this increase in supply of skilled labour by comparing the share of higher educated individuals in older cohorts (55- to 74-year-olds in 2016) with a similar share in younger cohorts (25- to 54-year-olds since 2016); this shows the following:[14]

---

14 Data for these calculations come from Eurostat http://ec.europa.eu/eurostat/statistics-explained/index.php/File:Share_of_the_population_by_level_of_educational_attainment,_by_selected_age_groups_and_country,_2016_(%25).png

- The share of the higher educated among the older cohorts is the highest in the three Baltic States (34.6%, 26.7%, and 24.6% in Estonia, Lithuania, and Latvia, respectively) while it is the lowest in Romania (8.5%), followed by Slovakia (13.6%), Poland (14.1%), and the Czech Republic (14.2%).

- The difference in higher education attainment rates between the two cohorts (which can be considered an indicator of the dynamics of higher education expansion in the observed countries) is shown to be the largest in Poland (33.9% as compared to 14.1%) and in Romania (19.8% as compared to 8.5%).

- However, despite the assumed high growth rates in Romania, the share of the higher educated in the 25- to 54-year-old age group is still the lowest in Romania (when compared to the rest of the CEE countries).

- With the spectacular change in Poland (and a slightly smaller change in Slovenia), the share of higher educated in Poland and Slovenia is now relatively close to the level in the Baltic States (rates ranging between 34% and 43% in this five-country group), with Slovakia, Czech Republic, Hungary, and Bulgaria in the range of 25–30% and Romania still lagging behind with a rate of 19.8%.

Increasing wage premium in a context of an increasing supply of skilled labour suggests that in these countries demand for skilled labour has been increasing rapidly. The relative demand for skilled labour increased during the period of structural changes and transformational recession, and also during the period of economic growth that followed. Foreign direct investment brought about a significant technological modernization of production processes. Technological change increased demand for young educated labour, while employment prospects worsened for the poorly educated and older cohorts with obsolete human capital (Figure 5.6).

Overall, in 2015, the wage premium for skilled labour tends to be highest among the CEE countries in Hungary, the other three Visegrad countries, and Slovenia, where the share of the higher educated is relatively low (in the range of 20–30%). At the same time, in case of the two Baltic States represented in the figure (Latvia and Estonia) the share of the higher educated is higher and the wage premium for them is lower than in the other countries.[15]

---

15 Mysiková and Vecernik (n.d.) found that returns to education are higher in the new Member States than in the old. However, while in the old Member States they found the expected negative relationship between education returns and the proportion of tertiary-educated in the active population; this relationship was not confirmed in CEE countries. Rather, in CEE, it was the job vacancy rate that had a significant negative impact on returns to tertiary education.

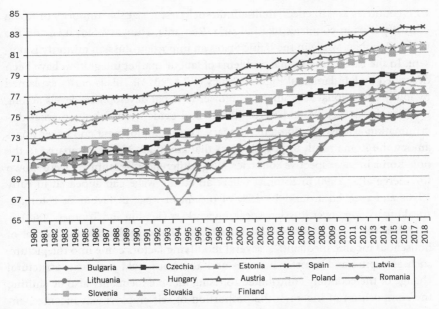

Figure 5.6 Relative earnings of tertiary-educated workers and their share of the population (2015: 25- to 64-year-olds with income from employment; upper secondary education = 100). Tertiary education includes short-cycle tertiary, bachelor's, master's, doctoral, or equivalent degrees.
1) Year of reference differs from 2015. Refer to the source table for details.
2) Index 100 refers to the combined ISCED levels 3 and 4 of the educational attainment levels in the ISCED 2011 classification.
3) Earnings net of income tax.
Source: OECD (2017: table A6.1).

Regression-based decompositions of income inequality between households also show that, in general, the CEE countries cluster among those where education plays a relatively important role in defining household inequality (Medgyesi, 2014). In Bulgaria, Hungary, and Romania, the variance of incomes explained by education is around 20% markedly higher than in countries with a much better education composition of the population (Sweden, Denmark, or Austria). In addition to these three outstanding shares variance explained by education, most CEE countries belong to the league where the role of education in inequality is central.

Labour market differences were not only increasing by educational attainment, but region and ethnicity have also become important variables of differentiation. Regional development proved to be uneven in the CEE countries. Alcidi et al. (2018) highlight that despite significant convergence of CEE countries to the EU core, regional dispersion remained high. This suggest that outstanding growth performance of certain regions (e.g., around the capital cities) drives up the national average and hides very poor growth in other regions. Many of the

CEE countries are, in effect, multiethnic societies. A sizeable minority of Roma ethnicity lives in countries like Bulgaria, Romania, Hungary, Slovakia, and the Czech Republic, while in the Baltic States an important Russian minority is present. In the case of the Roma, problems of labour market integration have been described by Fundamental Rights Agency (FRA, 2014). This is partly explained by lower educational attainment and lower regional development levels among the Roma, but Kertesi and Kézdi (2011) find evidence of labour market discrimination against the Roma in Hungary. Lower employment and lower wages among the Roma result in poverty rates that are much higher compared to the non-Roma in the respective countries. Wage differences by ethnicity were shown to emerge after 1990 in Estonia, where an ethnic wage gap appeared in early 1990s and reached around 10–15% of the mean wage in favour of Estonian-speaking workers over Russian-speaking workers (Leping and Toomet, 2008).

When the focus of analysis is shifted from the wage distribution to that of household income inequalities, several modifying factors come into the picture, such as capital and transfer incomes and also household structure. Structural change of the economy contributed to rising income inequality also by shifting the composition of incomes: the proportion of self-employment incomes, entrepreneurial incomes, and capital incomes has risen, while the share of labour income has fallen.

During this 20-year period, the share of wages in GDP has been declining the most in Poland and Hungary, but Estonia and Latvia also experienced declining trends. Studies show that the share of wages in GDP is lower in CEE countries compared to the Eurozone countries (see Podkaminer, 2013; Galgóczi, 2017). Although this is true on average, there are significant differences between the countries of the region. In Slovenia, the wage share declined between 1995 and 2015, but it remains the highest by far in the region, also exceeding the Euro Area average. The high wage share in Slovenia may reflect that country's particularly low level of FDI and also its unique system of corporatist labour management. Romania is also a special case because the wage share is much lower than elsewhere—and does not really seem to be declining consistently.

This fall in the wage share was partly due to the decrease in employment, but also to the emergence of the private sector (World Bank, 2000). The removal of legal restrictions on private ownership and entrepreneurship has led to the emergence of new small, private firms in industry and services. Privatization of formerly state-owned firms has resulted in the formation of national economic elites of corporate business owners. This has contributed to increasing income inequality since self-employment and entrepreneurial income is more unevenly distributed than wages. Moreover, these activities often depend on an individual's access to assets (property, but also information), which thus reinforces initial inequalities.

After the years of consolidation and economic growth that followed the transitional recession period, the CEE countries had to face economic recession at the end of the past decade. The economic crisis that started in 2008 also brought about changes in income inequality. When analysing the potential la- bour market drivers of inequality change during the years of the economic crisis, Brzezinski (2018) found that in explaining the increase of Gini between 2008 and 2012 (statistically significant for Bulgaria, Estonia, Hungary, and Slovenia), it was the falling full-time employment rate that played the biggest role. It was shown to be responsible for some 60–80% of market income Gini change in general, less for Hungary. The shift towards increased part-time em- ployment during the recession had instead an inequality decreasing effect, if any.

5.3.4 DIFFERENCES OF COUNTRY EXPERIENCES OF INEQUALITY DEVELOPMENTS

Decline in employment, increasing wage inequalities, increasing educational wage premia, and the increasing role of property income were common driving forces of inequality change in CEE countries in the early years of the transition process. Despite these common forces there have been differences in policies (e.g., speed of reforms, welfare state arrangements) and outcomes of different countries, which we summarize here.

Among the Baltic countries, Estonia and Lithuania underwent the largest rise in inequality, with a close to 13-point Gini increase in Estonia over just 2 years between 1990 and 1992—and an almost 10-point Gini increase in Lithuania between 1990 and 1993. Several factors make these extreme changes more plausible than they might seem at first sight. The most fundamental differ- ence between these countries' stories concerns the speed of the transition to a market economy. Masso et al. (2014) emphasize that the transition was excep- tionally fast in Estonia—and followed by the largest inequality increase among the three countries. The differences in speed of privatization and liberalization were reflected in labour market developments, although the largest unemploy- ment shock occurred in Latvia, whose highest level of industrialization in the Soviet era led to major shocks in redundancies when transforming to a market economy. Finally, its exceptionally low educational premium before the transi- tion (with the higher educated at only 108% of the national average wage while the lower educated were at 97%) was changed by an exceptionally fast differ- entiation of pay by education in the first half of the 1990s. Equally interesting, though, is the divergence between the inequality paths of the three countries after they had reached their local peaks. While in Estonia a consistent inequality decline occurred, Lithuania witnessed a continued increase albeit at a reduced pace. Latvia, as opposed to the other two Baltic States, has climbed rather gradu- ally from the position of being one of the most equal European countries in 1990 to the most unequal by 2010 (see Masso et al., 2014). In fact, in the second half of the 1990s, Estonia had the highest inequality in Europe; at the end of the past decade, however, Latvia took the lead.

The cluster of transition countries following a second inequality trajectory covers the Czech Republic, Poland, Slovakia, and Slovenia. The cases of Slovenia and the Czech Republic deserve special attention. These two countries were able to avoid large inequality shocks throughout the transition process.[16] To understand the immediate reasons, one has to understand the economic and social policies adopted and as well as the way transition has proceeded. In Slovenia, low inequality is largely attributable to the relatively efficient tax and social policy measures in redistributing incomes (Filipovic Hrast and Ignjatovic, 2014). In the Czech Republic, the role of tax and transfer policies can also be emphasized (Kahanec et al., 2014): the transfers of the pension system for the older population and taxes for the working-age population. For Poland, the transition resulted in an inequality increase, but the magnitude of 5 Gini points remains relatively modest by 'eastern standards' (Letki et al., 2014). Slovak development parallels the Czech one, albeit with a break in the series that lifted inequality on a higher level (Kahanec et al., 2014).

Both in Bulgaria and (to a lesser extent) in Romania, the increase in inequality has taken place in two waves. In Bulgaria, the dynamics of this process derive from a complex interplay of GDP growth and decline, incomes and pension policies, and migration, as described by Tsanov et al. (2014). The peculiar pattern of Romania is associated with nontransparent privatization practices, state capture, corruption, and shadow economy activities,[17] together with the effects exerted by migration on inequality; at the same time, social policies are inefficient in tackling increases in inequality (Precupetu and Precupetu, 2014).

The Hungarian story of inequality development is different from the rest, as is the country's transition. Given that the transition, at least in terms of liberalization of the economy, started earlier than in other countries (Tóth, 2008; Fábián et al., 2014), the transition shock seems to be smaller, at least for the final outcomes in inequalities. Overall, the increase of inequality was relatively smaller in Hungary. On the one hand, there were strong forces working towards inequality increase: tough bankruptcy laws resulted in major job destruction, there was an insufficient job supply for low-skilled workers, and badly designed active labour market policies did not prevent marginalization of the low-educated masses. On the other hand, various social policies, most

---

16 There is a series break in Slovenia between 2004 and 2005—with no effect on trends. (see figure 2 in Filipovič Hrast and Ignjatović, 2014).

17 Normally, the shadow economy should not directly appear in net incomes, of course. However, if there is an over-time variation in the way the various surveys can capture these items, then this volatility can be reflected in the inequality trends as well.

notably passive labour market instruments, social assistance, and early retirement provisions, provided some shelter for those at the lower end of the labour market. The combined effect was a smoother increase of inequality in the short run and very low-level employment equilibrium (due to a massive financing of inactivity) in the long run.

5.4 CONVERGENCE IN WELL-BEING

In earlier sections, we reviewed trends in average income and the distribution of income in CEE countries over the past 25 years. In this section, we describe evolution and convergence in terms of well-being indicators. First, we describe the evolution of distributionally adjusted mean income, then we discuss the evolution of life expectancy and subjective life satisfaction in CEE countries.

5.4.1 Distributionally Adjusted Income Growth

The report by Stiglitz et al. (2009) proposes to take into account distributional changes when evaluating social progress. We compare the evolution of average household income with indicators of social progress that are sensitive to the distribution of income as well. From the various potential measures (see Jenkins, 2012), we chose an indicator of distributionally adjusted mean income. (This index can be expressed as the product of real mean income and an index of income equality that lies between 0 and 1. This means that an increase in income inequality will reduce the growth in the distributionally adjusted mean, while a reduction will increase it. In the case of the index proposed by Amartya Sen, the equality index used in the formula is 1 minus the Gini coefficient.)

Table 5.4 compares change in GDP per capita and change in the Sen index in selected periods. Differences in the change of the two indicators arise in periods when there is an important change in income inequality. For example, in the early transition years (1990–1996), GDP per capita declined in seven of the CEE countries and, at the same time, inequality increased, which caused a greater fall in the value of the Sen index compared to that of GDP per capita. Since the mid-1990s, differences between the evolution of the two indicators are moderate, since in most of the countries changes in income inequality were small. The most important exceptions are Romania and Latvia in the 1996–2004 period, Bulgaria in the 2004–2008 period, and Bulgaria and Lithuania in the last period studied. In these cases, inequality increased during periods of economic growth, and thus the increase in the Sen index is smaller than in the case of the GDP per capita. Interestingly, in some cases (e.g., Estonia between 2004 and 2008) inequality actually declined, so the Sen index increased more than GDP per capita.

Table 5.4 Change in gross domestic product (GDP) per capita and Sen index (%, beginning of period = 100%)

	Change in GDP per capita (%, beginning of period = 100%)						Change in Sen index (%, beginning of period = 100%)					
	1990–1996	1996–2004	2004–2008	2008–2012	2012–2018	1990–2018	1990–1996	1996–2004	2004–2008	2008–2012	2012–2018	1990–2018
Bulgaria	85	134	134	102	122	190	79	138	117	106	111	151
Czech Rep.	100	121	121	97	117	167	97	115	127	97	119	163
Estonia	81	171	125	98	121	207	68	174	132	96	124	186
Hungary	89	140	110	95	126	165	84	140	114	93	123	154
Latvia	55	183	138	97	126	170	49	169	136	100	126	143
Lithuania	63	171	138	102	130	195	54	172	133	106	120	157
Poland	117	138	122	114	124	278	109	136	122	116	130	272
Romania	96	128	136	97	134	215	87	117	138	100	131	184
Slovakia	96	133	135	104	118	212	88	131	139	102	125	205
Slovenia	101	136	119	90	116	173	94	138	120	90	117	164

Source: For 1990–2008 real GDP at constant 2011 national prices (in mil. 2011US$) and population data from Penn World Tables 9.0. For 2008–2018, GDP per capita (at constant 2010 US$ prices) from World Development Indicators. Data for Gini index of income inequality for 1990–2008, GINI project database (see Table 5.A1 for details) and for the 2008–2018 period Eurostat database. The Sen index is calculated as GDP per capita*(1-Gini).

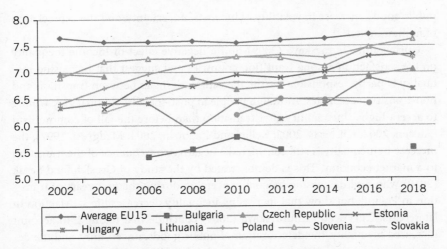

Figure 5.7 Evolution of life expectancy at birth in Central and Eastern European (CEE) countries and selected EU15 countries.
Source: European Commission, Eurostat database, table demo_mlexpec, accessed 2020.04.02.

5.4.2 Life Expectancy

Figure 5.7 shows the evolution of life expectancy in CEE countries. The figure shows that the period of transformational recession has halted the process of increasing life expectancy in many transition countries. In the Baltic States life expectancy dropped dramatically (by 5–7 years) during the 1987–1994 period, but Romania, Bulgaria, Hungary, Poland, and Slovakia also have seen episodes of declining life expectancy during this period. Since the mid-1990s, life expectancy has been growing in CEE countries, but convergence to EU15 countries seems to take place only in the case of Slovenia and Estonia (after the mid-1990s). In the case of other CEE countries the increase in life expectancy seems to be similar or lower when compared to EU15 countries, which is shown by the stability of the life expectancy gap.

5.4.3 Life Satisfaction

Life satisfaction in CEE countries declined sharply during the years of the transformational recession (Easterlin, 2009). After these early transition years, high unemployment and the cutback of welfare programmes resulted in slow recovery of life satisfaction despite improving GDP. Multivariate studies comparing transition countries with OECD countries show the existence of a 'happiness gap': individuals living in transition countries show significantly lower levels of life satisfaction even after controlling for a large set of determinants of life satisfaction, such as gender, age, income, etc. (see Guriev and Zhuravskaya, 2009; Gruen and Klasen, 2012). Guriev and Zhuravskaya (2009) discuss several potential causes of the happiness gap, such as increased inequality, deterioration of public goods, increase in volatility of incomes, uncertainty, and the depreciation of human capital.

Guriev and Zhuravskaya (2009) find a negative effect of income inequality on life satisfaction among transition countries and suggest that increasing inequality is partly responsible for the life satisfaction gap between transition and non-transition countries. Although people in post-socialist countries are willing to accept higher inequalities after transition than before the fall of communism (Austen, 2002; Gijsberts, 2002; Kelley and Zagorski, 2004; Medgyesi, 1997), the increase in inequality is still considered a negative consequence of the transition to a market economy. This is demonstrated by the study of Grosfeld and Senik (2010) who find decreasing inequality aversion during the first years of transition in Poland, but show that increasing inequality decreases life satisfaction in later years. Guriev and Zhuravskaya (2009) conclude that taking into account increased inequality, the deterioration of public goods, uncertainty, and the depreciation of human capital explain lower levels of life satisfaction in transition countries.

More recent studies have reported a decreasing life satisfaction gap between the East and the West. Večerník and Mysíková (2015) concluded that

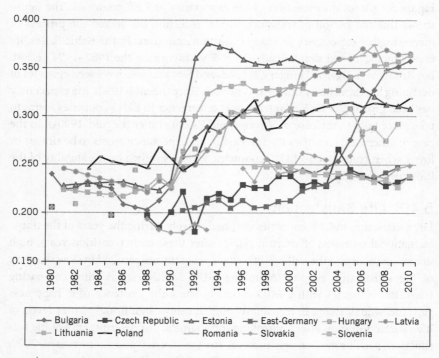

Figure 5.8 Evolution of average happiness in Central and Eastern European (CEE) countries. *Source:* Authors' calculation from European Social Survey. Figures represent unadjusted country averages of happiness measured on a 0–10 scale.

life satisfaction, due to stagnation in old Member States and improvement in the new Member States, converged, although the findings drawn from different surveys in the post-crisis period do seem somewhat inconsistent. Guriev and Melnikov (2017), in a more recent paper, also confirm the closure of the 'transition happiness gap', which is also shown for the second half of the period studied in Figure 5.8.

5.5 CONCLUSION

The period since 1990 has been one of intense social change in CEE countries. These countries abandoned the socialist system and adopted the political and economic institutions of the Global West in two steps, first during the transition years and then with accession to the European Union. CEE countries experienced two major recessions during this period, first during the early years of transition and then during the economic crisis of 2009. Despite these periods of recession, CEE countries managed to reduce their disadvantage compared to EU15 countries in many aspects.

A key common feature of the pre-crisis growth model in countries of the region was deep economic and institutional integration with the European Union. Prior to the crisis, countries enjoyed significant capital inflows, with FDI being the most important component. The capital stock was upgraded, with more productive assets allowing for technology transfers to CEE countries. The resulting higher incomes generated more domestic demand and domestic investment. The EU provided an important anchor for the institutional development of these countries and was not only a major source of private capital but also of public investment via the cohesion funds contributed to the economic development of the region.

This development process is not, however, without tensions. Inequality increased in all CEE countries during the early years of transition. While certain regions (e.g., capital cities), sectors (e.g., dominated by multinationals), and social groups (the young, more educated) were able to reap the benefits of the development process, other groups were left behind. The crisis exacerbated these tensions as unemployment increased and government transfers were cut by austerity programmes. Frustration in social groups more affected by the crisis increased, and this was exploited by populist parties.

There were important differences between the experiences of CEE countries. Some of the more successful countries in terms of income convergence—the Baltic States—were also those with the biggest increase in income inequality. Slovakia and Poland, on the other hand, were able to achieve high levels of GDP growth without an excessive increase in income inequality. The Czech Republic and Slovenia, which were relatively more developed at the start of the transition process, recorded slower convergence to EU15 levels of income but recorded only moderate increases in inequality during the period studied. We conclude that large social transformations (like the socioeconomic transition in CEE countries) have had very significant effects on inequality developments. However, the magnitude of the impact depends heavily on country-specific factors.

Although the CEE countries seem to have returned to the path of convergence after the economic crisis, these countries face important problems which might constrain future growth. Emigration and low fertility will result in a decline of the active age population, while the percentage of dependent populations is likely to increase in the future. Levels of FDI and private investment remain at a low level since the crisis, which might also threaten future growth prospects. Increasing economic growth via raising productivity will also be more difficult as these countries are now closer to the productivity frontier.

One possible avenue to sustain development is to make growth more inclusive. Investment and productivity increase should also reach to less developed regions of the country and less developed sectors of the economy (e.g., the small and medium-sized enterprise [SME] sector). Human capital investment must be increased, especially in social groups (e.g., the Roma) that have difficulties integrating into the labour market. Development of early childhood education and care institutions should help the labour market integration of women with small children. EU funds have to be channelled to investments in human capital and productive infrastructure with long-term benefits, and serious efforts should be made to constrain the possibilities of rent-seeking and corruption.

ACKNOWLEDGEMENTS

The authors wish to thank Georg Fischer, Robert Strauss, Michal Brzezinski, Iryna Kyzyma, Mihály Laki, Péter Mihályi, Wiemer Salverda, Krzysztof Zagórski, and Jiři Večerník for their comments on an earlier draft. They bear no responsibility for this text, however.

REFERENCES

Alcidi, C., Núñez Ferrer, J., Di Salvo, M., Pilati, M., and Musmeci, R. (2018). Income Convergence in the EU: A tale of two speeds. *CEPS Commentary*, 9 January 2018, 1-7.

Andersen, T. B., Barslund, M., and Vanhuysse, P. (2019). Join to prosper? An empirical analysis of EU membership and economic growth. *Kyklos, 72*, 211–238. https://doi.org/10.1111/kykl.12200

Aristei, D., and Perugini, C. (2015). The drivers of personal income inequality in transition, and the role of reform approaches. In C. Perugini and F. Pompei (eds.), *Inequalities during and after transition in Central and Eastern Europe* (pp. 41–58). London: Palgrave Macmillan.

Atkinson, A. B., and Micklewright, J. (1992). *Economic transformation in Eastern Europe and the distribution of income.* Cambridge: Cambridge University Press.

Atoyan, R., Christiansen, L., Dizioli, A., Ebeke, C., Ilahi, N., Ilyina, A. . . . Zakharova, D. (2016). Emigration and its economic impact on Eastern Europe. Staff Discussion Note SDN/16–07. International Monetary Fund.

Austen, S. (2002). An international comparison of attitudes to inequality. *International Journal of Social Economics, 29,* 218–237.

Bandelj, N., and Mahutga, M. C. (2010). How socio-economic change shapes income inequality in post-socialist Europe. *Social Forces, 88*(5), 2133–2162.

Becker, S. O., Egger, P. H., and von Ehrlich, M. (2013). Absorptive capacity and the growth and investment effects of regional transfers: A regression discontinuity design with heterogeneous treatment effects. *American Economic Journal: Economic Policy, 5*(4), 29–77.

Becker, T., Daianu, D., Darvas, Z, Gligorov, V., Landesmann, M., Petrovic, P., . . . Di Mauro, B. W. (2010). Whither growth in Central and Eastern Europe? Policy lessons for an integrated Europe. *Bruegel Blueprint Series, XI.*

Blanchet, T., Chancel, L., and Gethin, A. (2019). How unequal is Europe? Evidence from Distributional National Accounts, 1980–2017. WID.world Working Paper 2019/6. World Inequality Lab, https://wid.world/document/bcg2019-full-paper/.

Bohle, D., and Greskovits, B. (2012). *Capitalist diversity on Europe's periphery.* Ithaca, NY: Cornell University Press.

Böwer, U., and Turrini, A. (2010). EU accession: A road to fast-track convergence? *Comparative Economic Studies, 52*(2), 181–205.

Bijsterbosch, M., and Kolasa, M. (2010). FDI and productivity convergence in Central and Eastern Europe: An industry-level investigation. *Review of World Economics, 145*(4), 689–712.

Brzeziński, M. (2018). Income inequality and the Great Recession in Central and Eastern Europe. *Economic Systems.* https://doi.org/10.1016/j.ecosys.2017.07.003

Brzeziński, M., Salach, K., and Wronski, M. (2019). *Wealth inequality in Central and Eastern Europe: Evidence from joined household survey and rich lists'* data. Warsaw: University of Warsaw, Faculty of Economic Sciences. Working Papers no. 9/2019 (294).

Bubbico, R. L., Gattini, L., Gereben, Á., Kolev, A. Kollár, M., and Slacik, T. (2017). Wind of change: Investment in Central, Eastern and South Eastern Europe. EIB Economics Dept., Luxembourg.

Burda, M. C., and Severgnini B. (2009). TFP growth in old and new Europe. *Comparative Economic Studies, 51,* 447–466.

Calvert, E., and Nolan, B. (2012). Material deprivation in Europe. GINI Discussion Paper no. 68. Amsterdam: Amsterdam Institute for Advanced Labour Studies (AIAS).

Canberra Group. (2011). *Canberra Group handbook on household income statistics* (2nd ed.). Geneva: UN Economic Commission for Europe. https://www.unece.org/fileadmin/DAM/stats/groups/cgh/Canbera_Handbook_2011_WEB.pdf.

Campos, N. F., and Coricelli, F. (2002). Growth in transition: What we know, what we don't and what we should. *Journal of Economic Literature, 40*(Sept 2002), 793–836

Campos, N. F., Coricelli, F., and Moretti, L. (2014). *Economic growth and political integration: Estimating the benefits from membership in the European Union using the synthetic counterfactuals method.* DP no. 8162. Bonn: IZA.

Cerami, A., and Vanhuysse, P. (eds.) (2009). *Post-communist welfare pathways. Theorizing social policy transformations in Central and Eastern Europe.* London: Palgrave Macmillan

Cornia, G. A. (1994). Income distribution, poverty and welfare in transitional economies: A comparison between Eastern Europe and China. *Journal of International Development, 6*(5), 569–607.

Crescenzi, R., and Giua, M. (2017). Different approaches to the analysis of the EU Cohesion Policy: Leveraging complementarities for evidence-based policy learning. In P. Berkowitz, J. Bachtler, T. Muravska, and S. Hardy (eds.), *EU cohesion policy reassessing performance and direction.* Regions and Cities book series (pp. 21–32). London: Routledge.

Darvas, Z. (2015). The convergence dream 25 years on. Bruegel Institute. https://www.bruegel.org/2015/01/the-convergence-dream-25-years-on/

Dombi, Á. (2013). The sources of economic growth and relative backwardness in the Central Eastern European countries between 1995 and 2007. *Post-Communist Economies, 25*(4), 425–444.

Easterlin, R. A. (2009). Lost in transition: Life satisfaction on the road to capitalism. *Journal of Economic Behavior & Organization, 71*(2), 130–145.

European Bank of Reconstruction and Development (EBRD). (2013). *Transition report 2013.* London: European Bank for Reconstruction and Development.

European Bank of Reconstruction and Development (EBRD). (2017). *Transition report 2017.* London: European Bank for Reconstruction and Development

Fábián, Z., Gábos, A., Kopasz, M., Medgyesi, M., Szivós, P., and Tóth, I. G. (2014). Hungary: A country caught in its own trap. In Nolan, B., Salverda, W., Checchi, D., Marx, I., McKnight, A., Tóth, I. G, and van de Werfhorst, H.(eds.), *Changing inequalities and societal impacts in rich countries: Thirty countries' experiences* (pp. 322–345). Oxford: Oxford University Press.

Falcetti, E., Lysenko, T., and Sanfey, P. (2006). Reforms and growth in transition: Re-examining the evidence. *Journal of Comparative Economics, 34*(3), 421–445.

Flemming, J. S., and Micklewright, J. (1999). Income distribution, economic systems and transition. In A. Atkinson, and F. Bourguignon (eds.), *Handbook of income distribution (Vol. 1)* (pp. 843–918). Amsterdam: Elsevier Science.

Filipovic Hrast, M., and Ignjatović, M. (2014). Slovenia: An equal society despite the transition. In B. Nolan, W. Salverda, D. Checchi, I. Marx, A. McKnight, I. G., Toth, and H. van de Werfhorst (eds.), *Changing inequalities & societal impacts in rich countries: Thirty countries experience* (pp. 593–615). Oxford: Oxford University Press.

FRA (2014). *Poverty and employment: the situation of Roma in 11 EU Member States Roma survey – Data in focus*. European Union Agency for Fundamental Rights, Vienna.

Fries-Tersch, E., Tugran, T., Rossi, L., and Bradley H. (2018). *2017 annual report on intra-EU labour mobility: Final report January 2018*. Brussels: European Commission DG EMPL Directorate D—Labour Mobility.

Galgóczi, B. (2017). Why central and eastern Europe needs a pay rise? Working Paper 2017.01 Brussels: European Trade Union Institute.

Gijsberts, M. (2002). The legitimation of income inequality in state-socialist and market societies. *Acta Sociologica, 45*, 269–285.

Goedemé, T., and Collado, D. (2016). The EU convergence machine at work: To the benefit of the EU's poorest citizens? *JCMS: Journal of Common Market Studies, 54*(5), 1142–1158.

Grosfeld, I., and Senik, C. (2010). The emerging aversion to inequality: Evidence from subjective data. *Economics of Transition, 18*, 1–26.

Gruen, C., and Klasen, S. (2012). Has transition improved well-being? *Economic Systems, 36*(1), 11–30.

Guriev, S., and Melnikov, N. (2017). Happiness convergence in transition countries. EBRD Working Paper No. 204. http://www.ebrd.com/documents/oce/happiness-convergence-in-transition-countries.pdf.

Guriev, S., and Zhuravskaya, E. (2009). (Un)happiness in transition. *Journal of Economic Perspectives, 23*(2), 143–168.

Havrylyshyn, O., and van Rooden, R. (2003). institutions matter in transition, but so do policies. *Comparative Economic Studies, 45*(1), 2–24.

Heyns, B. (2005). Emerging inequalities in Central and Eastern EU. *Annual Review of Sociology, 31*(1), 163–197.

Jenkins, S. P. (2012). Distributionally-sensitive measures of national income and income growth. LSE Growth Commission. London: London School of Economics.

Kahanec, M., Guzi, M., Martišková, M., and Siebertová, Z. (2014). Slovakia and the Czech Republic: Inequalities and convergences after the Velvet Divorce. In B. Nolan, W. Salverda, D. Checchi, I. Marx, A. McKnight, I. G. Toth, and H. van de Werfhorst (eds.), *Changing inequalities & societal impacts in rich countries: Thirty countries experience* (pp. 569–592). Oxford: Oxford University Press.

Kelley, J., and Zagorski, K. (2004). Economic change and the legitimation of inequality: The transition from socialism to the free market in Central-East Europe. *Research in Social Stratification and Mobility, 22*, 319–364.

Kertesi, G., and Kézdi, G. (2011). Roma employment in Hungary after the postcommunist transition. *Economics of Transition, 19*(3), 563–610.

Kertesi, G., and Köllő, J. (2002). Economic transformation and the revaluation of human capital: Hungary 1986–1999. In A. De Grip, J. Van Loo, and K. Mayhew. (eds.), *The economics of skill obsolescence*. Research in Labour Economics Vol. 21 (pp. 235–273). Amsterdam: Elsevier Science.

Kočenda, E., Kutan, A. M., and Yigit, T. M. (2006). Pilgrims to the Eurozone: How far, how fast? *Economic Systems, 30*(4), 311–327

Kónya, I. (2018). *Economic growth in small open economies: Lessons from the Visegrad countries*. London: Palgrave Macmillan

Kornai, J. (1995). Eliminating the shortage economy: A general analysis and examination of the developments in Hungary. *Economics of Transition, 3*(1), 13–37, and *3*(2), 149–168.

Kornai, J. (2006). The great transformation of Central Eastern Europe: Success and disappointment. *Economics of Transition, 14*(2), 207–244.

Kornai, J. (2015). Hungary's U-turn. *Capitalism and Society, 10*(1), 1–24.

Kutan, A. M., and Yigit, T. M. (2009). European integration, productivity growth and real convergence: Evidence from the new member states. *Economic Systems, 33*(2), 127–137.

Lelkes, O., and Gasior, K. (2018). Income poverty in the EU: What do we actually measure? Empirical evidence on choices, underlying assumptions and implications (based on EU-SILC 2005–2014). In R. Carmo, C. Rio, and M. Medgyesi (eds.), *Reducing inequalities* (pp. 75–96). London: Palgrave Macmillan.

Leping, K-O., and Toomet, O. (2008). Emerging ethnic wage gap: Estonia during political and economic transition *Journal of Comparative Economics, 36*, 599–619.

Letki, N., Brzeziński, M., and Jancewicz, B. (2014). The rise of inequalities in Poland and their impacts: When politicians don't care but citizens do. In B. Nolan, W. Salverda, D. Checchi, I. Marx, A. McKnight, I. G. Toth, and H. van de Werfhorst (eds.), *Changing inequalities & societal impacts in rich countries: Thirty countries experience* (pp. 488–513). Oxford: Oxford University Press.

Levenko, N., Oja, K., and Staehr, K. (2017). *Total factor productivity growth in Central and Eastern Europe before, during and after the global financial crisis.* Working Paper Series 8/2017. Tallin: Eesti Pank.

Marangos, J. (2005). A political economy approach to the neoclassical gradualist model of transition. *Journal of Economic Surveys, 19*(2), 263–293.

Masso, J., Espenberg, K., Masso, A., Mierina, I., and Philips, K. (2014). Between economic growth and social justice: Different inequality dynamics in the Baltic States. In B. Nolan, W. Salverda, D. Checchi, I. Marx, A. McKnight, I. G. Toth, and H. van de Werfhorst (eds.), *Changing inequalities & societal impacts in rich countries: Thirty countries experience* (pp. 96–125). Oxford: Oxford University Press

Medgyesi, M. (1997). A kereseti egyenlőtlenségekkel kapcsolatos attitűdök alakulása a rendszer-váltás kapcsán. *Szociológiai Szemle, 7*(4), 87–107.

Medgyesi, M. (2008). Income distribution in European countries: First reflections on the basis of EU-SILC 2005. In I. G. Tóth (ed.), *Tarki European Social Report 2008* (pp. 89–106). Budapest: TARKI.

Medgyesi, M. (2014). *Components of income inequality and its change in EU countries, 2004–2010.* ImPRovE Discussion Paper no. 14/01. Antwerp: Herman Deleeck Centre for Social Policy, University of Antwerp.

Milanovic, B. (1999). Explaining the growth in inequality during the transition. *Economics of Transition, 7*(2), 299–341.

Milanovic, B., and Ersado, L. (2012). Reform and inequality during the transition: An analysis using panel household survey data, 1990–2005. In G. Roland (ed.), *Economies in transition: The long-run view* (pp. 84–108). London: UNU-Wider and Palgrave Macmillan.

Mitra, P., and Yemtsov, R. (2006). *Increasing inequality in transition economies: is there more to come?* Policy Research Working Paper Series 4007. Washington, DC: The World Bank.

Myant M. R., and Drahokoupil, J. (2011). *Transition economies: Political economy in Russia, Eastern Europe, and Central Asia.* Hoboken, NJ: Wiley.

Nolan, B., Salverda, W., Checchi, D., Marx, I., McKnight, A., Tóth, I. G., and van de Werfhorst, H. (2014). *Changing inequalities and societal impacts in rich countries: Thirty countries' experiences.* Oxford: Oxford University Press.

Oblath, G., Palócz, É., Popper, D., and Valentinyi, Á. (2015). *Economic convergence and structural change in the new member states of the European Union.* DP 2015/44. Budapest: Institute for Economics, Hungarian Academy of Sciences.

Orazem, P. F., and Vodopivec, M. (1997). Value of human capital in transition to market: Evidence from Slovenia. *European Economic Review, 41*, 893–903.

Perugini, C., and Pompei, F. (2015). Income distribution. In J. Hölscher and H. Tomann (eds.), *Palgrave dictionary of emerging markets and transition economics* (pp. 458–476). London: Palgrave Macmillan.

Podkaminer, L. (2013). *Development patterns of Central and East European Countries in the course of transition and following EU accession.* Research Reports no. 388. Vienna: Vienna Institute for International Economic Studies (WIIW).

Precupetu, I., and Precupetu, M. (2014). Romania: High rising inequality over two decades of post-communist transformation. In B. Nolan, W. Salverda, D. Checchi, I. Marx, A. McKnight, I. G. Toth, and H. van de Werfhorst (eds.), *Changing inequalities & societal impacts in rich countries: Thirty countries experience* (pp. 541–568). Oxford: Oxford University Press.

Próchniak, M., and Witkowski, B. (2013). Real β-convergence of transition countries robust approach. *Eastern European Economics, 51*(3), 6–26.

Reza, R. and Zahra, K. T. (2008). Evaluation of the Income convergence hypothesis in ten new members of the European Union. A Panel Unit Root Approach. *Panoeconomicus, 55*(2), 157–166.

Rutkowksi, J. (2001). *Earnings inequality in transition economies of Central Europe: Trends and patterns in the 1990s.* Social Protection Discussion Paper Series no. 0117. Washington, DC: World Bank, Social Protection Unit, Human Development Network.

Sakova, S. (1996). Changes and differences in earnings structures. Unpublished thesis, Budapest: Central European University.

Salverda, W., Nolan, B., Checchi, D., Marx, I., McKnight, A., Tóth, I.G., and van de Werfhorst, H. (2014). *Changing inequalities in rich countries: Analytical and comparative perspectives.* Oxford: Oxford University Press.

Schadler, S., Mody, A., Abiad, A., and Leigh, D. (2006). *Growth in the Central and Eastern European countries of the European Union.* International Monetary Fund, Occasional papers No. 252. Washington, DC.

Stiglitz, J. E., Sen, A., and Fitoussi, J.-P. (2009). *Report by the Commission on the Measurement of Economic Performance and Social Progress.* Paris: Commission on the Measurement of Economic Performance and Social Progress.

Szulc, A. (2000). Economic Transition, poverty and inequaity: Poland in the 1990s. *Statistics in Transition, 4*(6), 997–1017.

Svejnar, J. (2002). Transition economies: Performance and challenges. *Journal of Economic Perspectives, 16*(1), 3–28.

Tóth, I. G. (2008). The reach of transition in Hungary: Assessing the effects of economic transition on income distribution, 1987–2001 In L. Squire and J. M. Fanelli (eds.), *Economic reform in developing countries: Reach, range and reason* (pp. 3–34). GDN Series. Cheltenham, UK: Edward Elgar Publishing.

Tóth, I. G. (2014). Revisiting grand narratives of growing income inequalities: Lessons from 30 country studies. In B. Nolan, W. Salverda, D. Checchi, I. Marx, A. Mcknight, I. G. Tóth, and H. G. van de Werfhorst (eds.). *Changing inequalities and societal impacts in rich countries: Thirty countries' experiences* (pp. 11–47). Oxford: Oxford University Press.

Tóth I. G., and Medgyesi, M. (2011). Income distribution in new (and old) EU member states. *Corvinus Journal of Sociology and Social Policy, 2*(1), 3–33.

TransMonee (2004). A database of socio-economic indicators for CEE/CIS/Baltics, Florence : UNICEF International Child Development Centre. Online database: http:// www.unicef-irc.org/databases/transmonee/.

TransMonee (2005). A database of socio-economic indicators for CEE/CIS/Baltics. Florence : UNICEF International Child Development Centre. Online database: http://www.unicef-irc.org/databases/transmonee/.

Tsanov, V., Ivanova, P., Panteleeva, S., and Bogdanov, B. (2014). Bulgaria: Rising inequality in the period of transition and restrictive incomes policy. In B. Nolan, W. Salverda, D. Checchi, I. Marx, A. McKnight, I. G. Toth, and H. van de Werfhorst (eds.), *Changing inequalities & societal impacts in rich countries: Thirty countries experience* (pp. 152–171). Oxford: Oxford University Press.

United Nations, Department of Economic and Social Affairs, Population Division (2019). World population prospects 2019. Online Edition. Rev. 1. https://population.un.org/wpp/.

Van Leeuwen, B., and Földvári, P. (2013). Capital accumulation and growth in Central Europe, 1920–2006. *Eastern European Economics, 51*(5), 69–93.

Večerník, J. (2001). *Earnings disparities in the Czech Republic: Evidence of the past decade and cross-national comparison.* Working paper no. 373. Ann Arbor, MI: William Davidson Institute.

Večerník, J., and Mysíková, M. (2015). GDP and life satisfaction in European countries: Focus on transition. *Post-Communist Economies, 2*(2), 170–187.

World Bank. (2000). *Making transition work for everyone: Poverty and income inequality in Europe and Central Asia.* Washington, DC: World Bank.

World Bank. (2008). *Unleashing prosperity: Productivity growth in Eastern Europe and the former Soviet Union.* Washington, DC: World Bank.

APPENDIX

Table 5.A1 Sources for inequality data on Central and Eastern European (CEE) countries in GINI project database

Country	Reference (see details in reference list)	Data source	Note
Bulgaria	Tsanov et al. (2014)	1980–2010: SWIID, Version 3.1.	Equivalent net income per household member.
Czech Republic	Kahanec et al. (2014)	1988: Atkinson and Micklewright (1992); 1989–1994 Cornia (1994); 1995–2002 Transmonee (2004), 2003 Transmonee (2005), 2005–2010 country team calculations based on EU-SILC; 2004: LIS	Units of analysis is household (after 1993) or person (up to 1992). Household income equivalized since 2005. Income defined as disposable (monetary disposable income before 1989).
Estonia	Masso et al. (2014)	1981–2010: SWID	Disposable equivalized household income.
Hungary	Fábián et al. (2014)	1982, 1987: Hungarian Central Statistical Office income survey; 1992, 1995, 1996: Hungarian Household Panel; 1999–2009: TÁRKI Household Monitor, EU-SILC	
Latvia	Masso et al. (2014)	1981–2010: SWID	Disposable equivalized household income.
Lithuania	Masso et al. (2014)	1981–2010: SWID	Disposable equivalized household income.
Poland	Letki et al. (2014)	1983–1989: Atkinson and Micklewright (1992), 1990–1992: Szulc (2000), 1993–2010: Brzezinski et al. (2019)	Before 1989: per capita incomes, then equalized household incomes. Original OECD equivalence scale, which assigns the weight of 0.7 to every adult household member beyond the first one and the weight of 0.5 to every child. Two breaks in the series: in 1993 and in 1997.
Romania	Precupetu and Precupetu (2014)	1990–2009: NIS	

Table 5.A1 Continued

Country	Reference (see details in reference list)	Data source	Note
Slovakia	Kahanec et al. (2014)	1980, 1985, 1988 Atkinson and Micklewright (1992); 1989–1992: Cornia (1994); 1993: Milanovic (1999), 1996–2002: Transmonee (2004); 2003: Transmonee (2005); 2005–2010 calculations by the GINI team of Slovakia, based on EU-SILC	Unit of analysis is person, income defined as disposable income (monetary disposable income before 1989). Household income equivalized since 2005.
Slovenia	Filipovic Hrast and Ignjatović (2014)	1997–2010: SORS	Disposable net household income. Before 1997: there is no official data on Gini coefficients.

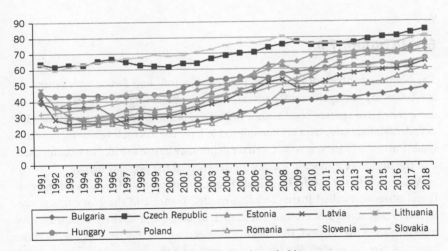

Figure 5.A1 Evolution of the Gini index of equivalent household income
Source: Tóth (2014), based on GINI project database, see more details in Table 5.A1.

6

RISING INEQUALITY IN THE EGALITARIAN NORDICS

Erling Barth, Kalle Moene, and Axel West Pedersen

6.1 INTRODUCTION

The Nordic countries of Denmark, Finland, Norway, and Sweden are renowned for following an egalitarian path as they combine wage compression and a comprehensive welfare state with a high exposition to global competition. For decades, all four countries are considered to have the lowest levels of income inequality and the highest levels of welfare generosity in the world. No wonder then, that the notion of a specific society model entered the popular debate.

What should the model be called? People in Sweden and influential international observers called it the 'Swedish model'. Danes and the Norwegians preferred to talk about a 'Scandinavian model', insisting that all three countries were basically alike. In the end, the name converged to the shorter and maybe more accurate 'Nordic model'. The implicit quarrel over the geographic pointer in the name may be misplaced. Nobody actually created the model by intelligent design. It evolved, exhibiting a seemingly self-enforcing egalitarian development path in small open economies with strong social organizations.

When reliable comparative micro-data on income distribution started to become available from the mid-1980s,[1] the new data confirmed the image of Nordic egalitarianism.[2] Not only did the Nordic countries show low initial levels of income inequality and poverty, they also seemed to be unaffected by the trends

---

1 Of particular importance was the establishment of Luxembourg Income Study (LIS).
2 See Smeeding et al. (1990) and Atkinson et al. (1995).

Erling Barth, Kalle Moene, and Axel West Pedersen, *Rising Inequality in the Egalitarian Nordics* In: *Europe's Income, Wealth, Consumption, and Inequality.* Edited by: Georg Fischer and Robert Strauss, Oxford University Press (2021).
© Oxford University Press. DOI: 10.1093/oso/9780197545706.003.0006

towards increasing inequality and higher unemployment observed in other countries at the time, particularly the United States and the United Kingdom.

Three major developments have recently changed income and inequality in all member countries of the Organisation for Economic Cooperation and Development (OECD): (1) new labour-saving technologies; (2) more migration and integration in the world economy and, in particular, the 'China shock'[3] that followed from the entrance of China in the world market; and (3) a series of crises, notably the financial crisis from 2008, and the early 1990 crisis that hit Finland and Sweden severely.

The Nordic model should be well suited to face such challenges. It ensures against the impact of shocks and gives employers an edge in the technological race. The egalitarian wage distribution speeds up the process of creative destruction. High levels of public spending on education and training provide an adaptive workforce. Coordinated wage bargaining emphasizes the needs of the internationally exposed industries when wages are set for all sectors.[4]

Yet the Nordic countries also have experienced rising income inequality, and they have all been affected by economic crises and periods with soaring unemployment rates. The Nordic countries have also tried to recalibrate their social security systems with a view to limiting expenditure growth and improving labour market incentives.

Since institutions differ and details matter, we need to explore more precisely how the Nordic countries have changed as they responded to the same challenges that other countries also faced. In particular, we want to know if their responses might have raised inequality at bottom of the income distribution. Have the Nordic countries coped with the economic and financial problems by reinforcing direct and indirect redistribution of income from the worst off to the better off? And, if so, have they done it to the same extent in all four countries?[5]

The model is no doubt under pressure. Unions become weaker, and export-led wage-setting is difficult to maintain as employment in the exposed industries shrinks. Outsourcing and immigration tend to increase wage dispersion, eroding one of the success features of the Nordic model. A higher dispersion of market incomes also tends to diminish the political demand for social insurance, weakening the second key feature of the Nordic model. Rising inequality combined with retrenchments in social insurance have been prevalent in OECD countries since the mid-1980s.[6] The question is whether the Nordic countries are approaching international inequality levels and joining in the race to the bottom in taxation and welfare spending?

---

3   As coined by Autor et al. (2016).
4   All these aspects are further discussed in Barth, Moene, and Willumsen (2014).
5   Due to data limitations, our analysis covers only the four larger Nordic countries: Denmark, Finland, Norway, and Sweden.
6   See Barth and Moene (2014, 2016).

To answer these questions, we take a closer look at recent developments in income and inequality in each of the Nordic countries. We explore whether rising inequality at least partly can be the result of an erosion of the two pillars of the Nordic model: generous welfare state arrangements and wage compressing labour market institutions. In his last book, Tony Atkinson (2015) suggested that too little redistribution was the root of the recent rise in inequality among OECD countries. Zooming in on the low-income tail of the income distribution, we find support for the claim that social security retrenchment is indeed contributing to more dispersion of household incomes in the Nordic countries.

Before we defend this claim, we set the stage with a summary of past developments in the Nordic countries, emphasizing that they consist of small, open, and rich economies exposed to a high level of international competition. None of them was among the countries hardest hit by the financial crisis. Yet all of them have had their doses of macroeconomic shock. It seems, however, that the comprehensive welfare state and the highly coordinated wage setting system have been able to dampen the worst consequences that other countries have experienced.

Overall, the Nordic countries still have high employment rates, generous welfare states, and low wage differentials. In the concluding remarks, we briefly discuss the viability of these characteristics of the Nordic model in the light of the increasing inequality that we document.

6.2 INCOME, PRODUCTIVITY, AND CRISIS

The Nordic countries are similar, but not identical.

All four countries are small open economies. They rely heavily on international trade. Export as a share of gross domestic product (GDP) is 54% in Denmark, 38% in Finland and Norway, and 45% in Sweden (OECD Factbook, 2014). The total population is small, slightly more than 27 million people (Grunfelder et al 2020), with 5.8 million in Denmark, 5.5 million in Finland, 5.3 million in Norway, and 10.2 million in Sweden.

All four countries are among the richest countries in Europe. Figure 6.1 shows the development in per capita income (measured in constant purchasing power parities) from 1985 to 2017. In 2015, Finland was at the average of EU15, with Denmark and Sweden well above, and Norway even higher, even when we disregard the direct contribution from the oil sector (mainland Norway, dashed line).

All four countries have coordinated wage setting in the labour market. The separate histories of wage bargaining in each country differ somewhat. It is rather parallel in Sweden and Norway with strong labour unions and employers' associations, formed in the late 1800s and early 1900s, and with an export-led wage coordination established during the crisis in the 1930s. The system has remained intact except for a short period after 1983, when Swedish employers

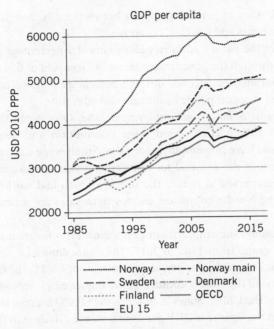

Figure 6.1 Per capita income in US dollars purchasing power parities (1985–2017).

withdrew from the central negotiations—only to recentralize the system a few years later. Denmark had developed a similar slightly less coordinated system earlier and more gradually than Sweden and Norway. Finland was on a more dramatic historical path with its civil war and the early defeats of the social democratic labour movement at the end of that war. Finland did not establish coordinated wage bargaining before the end of the 1940s.

All four countries have high levels of public expenditures. Table 6.1 shows general government revenues as per cent of GDP and also how the revenue is spent, in per cent of GDP, on health, education, and social insurance. The last column

Table 6.1 Government revenues and public expenditure on health, education, and social protection in per cent of GDP

	Denmark	Finland	Norway	Sweden	OECD average	Diff
Government revenues as % of GDP	54.8	56.9	48.8	50.2	43.8	8.9
Health	8.6	7.2	8.4	7.0	6.5	1.3
Education	7.0	6.3	5.5	6.5	5.3	1.0
Social protection	23.6	25.6	19.4	20.9	16.5	5.9

Figures from OECD public expenditure data base.

shows the difference in percentage points between the (unweighted) average of the Nordic countries and the OECD average.

Accordingly, the Nordic countries allow almost 9 percentage points more of their GDP go through the government sector. A large part of this additional revenue is spent on socialprotection, almost 6 percentage points. The Nordic countries also spend more on public healthcare and education.

All four countries have high employment rates. One might think, however, that countries with a compressed wage distribution and generous welfare spending should have low employment rates. Small wage differences could be expected to reduce the demand for low-skill workers, and a generous welfare state could be expected to reduce the supply of marginal workers. This is not the case for the Nordic countries: employment rates are among the highest in world.

Figure 6.2 shows the employment population ratio for men and women of the 25–64 age group from 1985 to 2017. The figure shows higher employment rates for men in Denmark, Norway, and Sweden compared to the OECD average. Among women, all the Nordic countries have higher employment rates than the OECD average. The United States is closer to the OECD average than the Nordic countries. As in the figure for GDP per capita, we see a decline in the early 1990s, in particular for Finland and Sweden. Throughout, Sweden and Norway have the highest employment rates. Sweden and Norway also saw a smaller decline in employment during the financial crisis, while Denmark took a larger hit. All countries have seen increasing employment rates after the crisis, with the exception

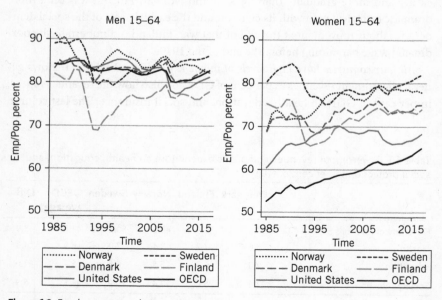

Figure 6.2 Employment population ratio, per cent.

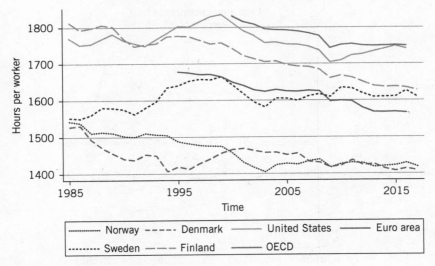

Figure 6.3 Annual hours per worker (1985–2017).
Note: Data extracted on 24 Jun 2018 05:01 UTC (GMT) from OECD Stat.

of Norway, most likely due to a modest rise in unemployment following a fall in oil prices in 2014.

All four countries have low or declining levels of hours worked. Employment rates may hide large differences in hours per worker. Figure 6.3 shows hours per worker for the same time period. Denmark and Norway have fewer annual hours per worker than the other countries—and in particular compared to the high level in the United States. Finland has seen a steady decline in hours per worker during the whole period. Combining these patterns with the GDP per capita measures observed in Figure 6.1 provides us with a picture of labour productivity in the four Nordic countries measured as production per hour. Figure 6.4 shows the development compared to the United States (US = 100). Denmark and Norway display the highest level of productivity and mainland Norway has been more productive than the United States since 2004, with Denmark following after 2013. Both countries converged back to the US level by 2017. It appears that both Denmark and Norway have spent some of their productivity gain on reduced hours while at the same time keeping employment rates high.

All four countries have faced periods with macroeconomic problems. In the period 1970–1990, Denmark was somewhat of a Nordic outlier with high, persistent unemployment rates and large deficits both on the state budget and in the balance of trade. The unemployment rates in Figure 6.5 clearly show how in particular Finland and Sweden suffered record-high unemployment rates in the early 1990s. After a decade of recovery, all four countries were again negatively affected by the downturn in 2003, before the unemployment rates converged to a very low level in years just before the advent of the financial crisis in 2008.

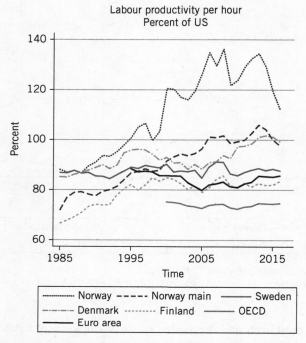

Figure 6.4 Labour productivity per hour (1985–201): Per cent of US level.

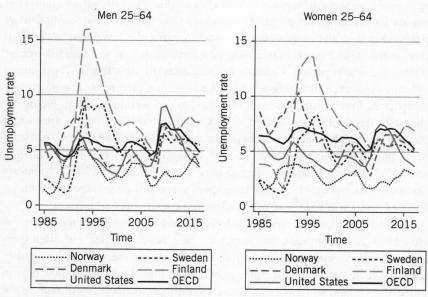

Figure 6.5 Unemployment rates (aged 25–64).
Source: Data extracted from OECD.Stat.

The financial crisis hit all four countries, with Norway as a partial exception. In the decade that passed after the onset of the financial crisis, both Norway and Sweden have done relatively well in terms of economic growth and employment and unemployment rates, whereas both Denmark and Finland have been struggling with sluggish economic growth. Norway experienced a recent relatively modest increase of unemployment in 2014 as a result of a fall in oil prices.

6.3 TRENDS IN INCOME INEQUALITY

With these structural features as a background, we are now ready to compare how the Nordic countries perform as inequality rises in the rest of Europe. It is important to note that different data sources available are not perfectly aligned for various conceptual and methodological reasons. We thus explore the developments using several sources and methodologies. Figure 6.6 presents data provided by the OECD. It shows that inequality in disposable income is on the rise in all Nordic countries, although from a lower level than in most other countries. The rise in inequality is particularly high in Sweden and lowest in Denmark and Norway.

Figure 6.7 is based on data from the so-called Chartbook of Economic Inequality, that in turn is based on national sources showing time-series on inequality in disposable household income. Compared to the OECD data, the Chartbook data build on less systematic efforts to standardize the measurement across countries. Yet the internal consistency of the time-series for each country should be high. Figure 6.7 gives the more detailed time trends where the starting point in 1985 is set equal to 100 for all countries.

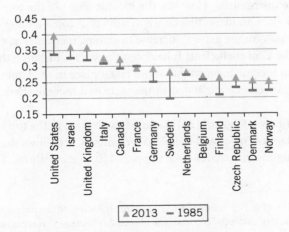

Figure 6.6 Gini inequality in equalized disposable household income. Selected OECD countries 1985 and 2013.
Source: OECD Income distribution database.

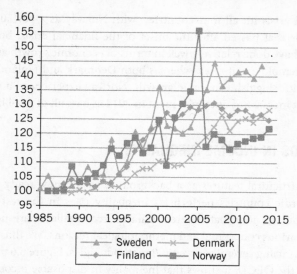

Figure 6.7 Inequality trends in the Nordic countries. Gini inequality in disposable equivalent household income (1987 = 100).
Source: The Chartbook of Economic Inequality. National data sources.

Apart from the Norwegian blip in 2005 (connected to a reform that implied higher tax rates on dividends[7]), the Nordic countries show similar patterns of inequality in household disposable income, with some nontrivial differences in magnitudes. Inequality went up in Sweden by almost 45% from the initial level in 1987, while the increase is smaller in the three other countries, ranging from 22% in Norway to 28% in Denmark, with Finland in between at 25%.

In recent years there has been considerable interest in changes at the very top of the income distribution. How has the income share of the top 1% changed, and what role does an increasing concentration of income among these top income earners play for the general increase in income inequality as measured, for instance, by the Gini coefficient? It has been shown, for instance, that almost all the increase in income inequality that has taken place in the United States over the past 30 years can be attributed to the increased income share going to the top 1%.

In a recent paper, Søgaard (2018) compares changes in the top income share between the United States and the Nordic countries. He shows the well-known U shape in top income shares over the past 110 years, with the United States

---

7   In anticipation of the tax reform firms ttemporarily increased the payment of dividends that are registered as capital income. The blip comes because this is registered as a high increase in capital incomes. The blip, is not an indication of a real increase in the level of capital income. Hence, the blip does not represent any fundamental change in the distribution of incomes.

Table 6.2 Change in top 1% income shares in percentage points, the contribution of this change to the overall Gini coefficient, and actual (observed) change in the Gini coefficient

Country	Period	Increase in top income share	Contribution to the Gini coefficient	Actual change in the Gini coefficient
USA	1980–2014	9.5	6.6	7.7
Denmark	1985–2015	3.4	2.9	7.6
Finland	1981–2014	3.2	2.6	4.2
Norway	1986–2011	3.4	2.8	3.7
Sweden	1980–2013	3.2	2.6	10.9

Source: Søgaard (2018: 77); see also Atkinson and Søgaard (2016).

currently having 20% of total income going to the top 1% and with the Nordic countries moving well below 10% to the top 1%. He calculates the approximate contribution to the Gini coefficient of top income shares in the respective countries.[8] By comparing these calculated contributions to Gini inequality and the actual, observed changes in the Gini coefficients, it is possible to indirectly assess the role played by increasing top income shares in explaining the general increase in Gini inequality. The results are shown in Table 6.2 for the United States and the four Nordic countries.

We see that the rise in the income share going to the top 1% is rather similar in all four Nordic countries (between 3.2 and 3.4 percentage points) and equals only about one-third of the corresponding rise in top income shares observed in the United States over the past 30 years (9.5 percentage points). In the United States, this rise in top income shares itself corresponds to an increase in Gini inequality of 6.6 Gini points, which is only slightly below the actual, observed increase in Gini inequality of 7.7 points over the same period. By contrast, the rise in top incomes explains much less of the total increase in inequality among the four Nordic countries. This is particularly so for Sweden, where the contribution from increased top income shares is estimated at 2.6 Gini points, while the actual, observed increase in overall inequality amounts to 10.9 Gini points.

It seems safe to conclude from this that increasing income inequality in the Nordic countries is not exclusively a matter of increasing top income shares.

To gain additional insights, we turn to micro-data to discuss changes in the degree of redistribution and in the contribution to overall inequality from different income components. We use two data sources: Luxembourg Income Studies

---

8 To approximate the contribution to total inequality by the top 1% income share Søgaard uses the following formula: $G \approx G_{99} + (1 - G_{99})S$, where S is the top 1% income share and G_{99} is the income inequality measured on the remaining 99% of the population.

Table 6.3 Gini inequality: household disposable income per person (general population and population aged 30–59)

	Denmark			Finland			Norway			Sweden		
	1995	2004	2013	1995	2004	2013	1995	2004	2013	1995	2005	2013[a]
General population	0.208	0.218	0.245	0.210	0.260	0.255	0.231	0.274	0.243	0.213	0.228	0.250
Age 30–59	0.190	0.199	0.229	0.213	0.258	0.249	0.213	0.257	0.236	0.201	0.221	0.231

[a]The figures for Sweden for 2013 are calculated from EU_SILC. Household disposable income per equivalent household member (EU-equivalence scale).

Source: Luxembourg income study (LIS).

(LIS) and the European Union's Statistics on Incomes and Living Conditions (EU-SILC). We need to combine these two data sources because we want to cover a long time period, from the mid-1990 to the mid-2010s, and EU-SILC is only available from 2004, while unfortunately, there is currently no LIS data for Sweden after 2005.

Table 6.3 shows the development in Gini inequality of equivalent disposable income from 1995 to 2013. With the exception of the numbers for Sweden in 2013, the numbers are calculated on LIS data.[9] Consistent with the pattern of Figure 6.7, all the countries have experienced an increase in inequality over the period. Finland and Norway have a higher increase between 1995 and 2004, while Denmark and Sweden are catching up with a high increase in the last period. The intra-Nordic differences in inequality trends that we saw in Figures 6.6 and 6.6 are less pronounced in the LIS and SILC data although the ranking is roughly similar, and we lack a satisfactory explanation for this observation. One should note that the relative high inequality score for Norway in 2004 is related to the even more pronounced spike we saw in Figure 6.7 for 2005, and, as discussed earlier, it should be interpreted as somewhat artificial.

Consider also the bottom row of Table 6.3. It shows that the widening of income inequality is happening also within the 30–59 age group in all the Nordic countries. Clearly, therefore, rising inequality in disposable household income is not only a result of changes in the age composition of the population or a decline in living conditions among the young or the elderly. It represents real changes in the allocations of relative income to different groups in society with implications for measures of poverty as well.

To focus on developments in the lower part of the income distribution, we have also, in Table 6.4, calculated relative poverty rates using the EU

---

9   To compare, we also calculated the figures for Sweden for 2005 using the EU-SILC data. The numbers were very close to the LIS data, 0.231 for the general population and 0.219 for those aged 30–59 in 2005.

Table 6.4 At-risk of poverty rates by age group: relative poverty (poverty threshold = 60% of national median, EU equivalence scale)

	Denmark			Finland			Norway			Sweden		
	1995	2004	2013	1995	2004	2013	1995	2004	2013	1995	2005	2013[a]
General population	9.6	10.6	10.4	7.1	11.8	12.9	11.4	11.0	11.9	9.1	9.7	14.8
Age 30–59	3.9	5.1	5.8	5.1	7.8	9.4	5.4	6.1	8.3	4.6	6.4	10.2

Source: Luxembourg income study (LIS). Swedish figures for 2013 are calculated from EU-SILC.

'at-risk-of-poverty' indicator, where individuals are classified as poor if their household income is below 60% of the national median in a particular year.

Overall poverty rates have risen in all four countries, with the exception of Norway. Not surprisingly, the poverty pattern follows the general pattern of income inequality closely, and a substantial part of the rising inequality is, in fact, located at the bottom of the income distribution. Again, we find a similar pattern among individuals of 'prime-age' (30–59 years).

Obviously, the finding of increasing relative income poverty does not necessarily mean that the absolute income standards of the lower deciles have deteriorated, and cross-national differences do not accurately reflect differences in real living standards.

The relative poverty threshold is by far the highest in real terms in Norway, where the increase in the median real incomes has been the largest over the past two decades. Therefore, the stability of relative poverty rates in Norway indicates an increase in the real incomes of the least privileged strata of the population. Also in Denmark, relative poverty rates have remained rather low and stable over time, but here real incomes are much lower than in Norway and hardly any improvements have taken place over the past decade. By contrast, the very substantial increase in relative poverty rates in Sweden must be seen in light of the fact that median incomes also have increased over the past decade. So, while the lowest income deciles are lagging behind, their absolute income levels have not declined.

These points are borne out in the Appendix Table 6.A1, where we show poverty rates for the Nordic countries when the poverty threshold is anchored at the level of median incomes received in Sweden in 2004. According to this measure, poverty rates are dramatically lower in Norway compared to the other three countries and rapidly declining over time. According to this measure, 'absolute' poverty is also on the decline in Sweden and Finland over the past decade, but not in Denmark.

Consistent with our interest in inequality, we find the pattern and trajectory of relative income poverty worth noting. It raises questions about how successful the welfare state actually is. Do the Nordic countries fail, more than before, to reach the poor and alleviate their situation of relative deprivation with social assistance and social security benefits?

We should also fill out the picture with some observations on the tendency of increasing wealth concentration at the other end of the income distribution. Measuring richness is similar to measuring poverty. The head count measure of poverty informs us about the number of people with an income lower than a certain threshold called the 'poverty line'. In the same way, we can look at the number of extremely wealthy people, the number of people with a wealth beyond a certain threshold called the 'richness line'. To measure wealth as the relative number of wealthy people in the population—the head count measure of richness—should be as natural as measuring the relative number of poor people. In practice, of course, it is not obvious where the richness line should be set, just as it is not obvious where the poverty line should be. There is no objective distinguishing line, neither for poverty nor for richness.

To illustrate the head count measure of richness in the Nordic countries relative to others, we can use Forbes list of billionaires. It uses an implicit richness line of wealth equal to US$1 billion. According to this measure, the United States has 1.7 billionaires per million inhabitants, Denmark 0.9, Finland 0.9, Norway 2.0, Sweden 2.4. The head count measure of billionaires in other European countries is in the range of 0.5 to 1.3 per million inhabitants: for instance, Spain has 0.4, Italy 0.6, France, 0.7, the UK 0.8, and Germany 1.2. So, compared to the rest of Europe, there are more billionaires relative to the population in all the Nordic countries.

As seen, Norway and Sweden have even more billionaires relative to the population than United States. This feature is more thoroughly discussed in Moene (2016) who provides further evidence on the relative number of super rich using different richness lines and different data sources. No doubt, the wealthiest persons in the United States are far richer than the wealthiest persons in the Nordic countries. For example, the 0.1% richest in the United States get 11% of total national income, while the 0.1% richest in Norway get 2.5% of the national income. Our basic point is about the level of the head count measure of richness. Relatively speaking, the upper class in the Nordic countries seems to be larger than in most other countries—an indication that Nordic equality has special features that allow a rather larger fraction of the population to become super rich.

6.4 DEVELOPMENTS IN SOCIAL SECURITY AND LABOUR MARKET INSTITUTIONS

Since the mid-1980s, the social security systems of the Nordic countries have undergone significant changes. While all the Nordic countries used to provide a level of income security in case of sickness, unemployment, disability, and old age that was clearly more generous than the level offered on average by the other OECD countries, this is no longer the case to the same degree. Figure 6.8 shows the development over time in the average net replacement rates offered to an average full-time worker in the core social security programmes—sickness benefits, unemployment benefits, and old age pensions.

In the mid-1980s, all four Nordic countries scored much higher than the average among the non-Nordic OECD countries. Social security was particularly generous in Sweden, with an average net replacement rate of 78%. Norway came second with an average score of 73%, followed by Denmark with 66%, and Finland with 63%. From 1985 to 2010, the relative generosity of social security has declined in all of the Nordic countries except for Norway, while it appears to have remained stable on average in the non-Nordic OECD countries. The drop in generosity is particularly strong in Sweden, with a decline of 18 percentage points, followed by Denmark (12 percentage points), and Finland (7 percentage points). In 2010, these three countries are still above the OECD average in terms of social security generosity, but the differences are smaller than before. The trajectory for Norway is distinctly different, with a stable net replacement rate at about 75%—in other words, at 22 percentage points above non-Nordic OECD average.

Figure 6.8 does not capture all aspects of the developments in social security over the past three decades. We know from other sources, however, that the generosity of minimum protection (social assistance schemes) shows a similar development (see Kuivalainen and Nelson, 2012). In all the Nordic countries, including Norway, policymakers have in the past decades become

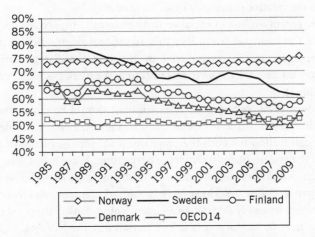

Figure 6.8 Average net compensation rates in core social security programs for workers with an average full-time wage. The four Nordic countries compared to the average of 14 non-Nordic OECD countries.
Average over sickness benefits, unemployment benefits, standard old age pensions, and minimum old age pensions.
Source: Comparative Welfare Entitlements Dataset 2.

more concerned about combating welfare dependency and ensuring that all possibilities for labour market integration are exhausted before social security benefits are granted to individuals in the economically active age brackets. As a result, not only the relative generosity of benefits has been reduced to a varying degree, but also the criteria for receiving benefits have been tightened and activation measures have been put in place in an effort to reinforce a work-first strategy. For Sweden, Ferrarini et al. (2012) have documented the development towards reduced generosity and a more limited access to social security.

We believe therefore that a more comprehensive account would produce a similar picture as that shown in Figure 6.8: Sweden has the largest negative change in generosity and access to social security; Finland and Denmark have a more modest change from a lower level than in Sweden, while Norway has almost no change.

It is hardly a coincidence that the most dramatic decline in Sweden took place during and just after the profound economic crises at the beginning of the 1990s. Also in Finland, the decline appears to have gained momentum in the aftermath of the deep economic crisis of the early 1990s, when automatic stabilisers during the crisis resulted in an increase in public debt. It is further worth noting that in both Sweden and Finland, the periods of retrenchment align with periods of increasing wage inequality (see Figure 6.10). Norway, in contrast, has maintained healthy state finances for at least two reasons. The country has suffered only relatively mild economic setbacks over this 30-year period; and it has benefitted from oil revenues since the 1980s. Its healthy finances have in turn made it easier to maintain the relative generosity of social security.

The more recent decline in social security generosity in Sweden started before the onset of the financial crisis. It is to a significant degree driven by changes in the system of taxation introduced by the non-socialist government that reduced taxes on labour income in an effort to make work pay (see Pedersen and Finseraas, 2013).

The tendencies of welfare state retrenchment should be considered in connection with changes within the other cornerstone of the Nordic model: the high degree of organization for both the employee and employer sides of the labour market and the system of collective wage bargaining. Wage bargaining and coordination between the social partners are still strong features of the Nordic countries, as shown in Figure 6.9. However, in Denmark, Finland, and Sweden, union density has been in steady decline. In Sweden, union density dropped from more than 85% to near 65%. Norway is the outlier among the Nordics, with a steady but lower union density, showing only a modest decline from 57% to 52%. The collective coverage of the wage settlements has been steadier than union density, with only a modest decline in Sweden and Norway.

The social organization of all workers is important for income at the bottom of the pay scale and for the support of welfare spending. Could it be that these

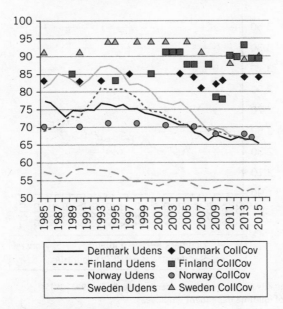

Figure 6.9 Union density and collective coverage.
Source: Data from OECD.Stat.

institutional developments are partly responsible for the simultaneous increase in inequality, and, if so, what is most important for the worst-off groups: the decline in earnings or the retrenchment of welfare spending?

6.5 THE SOURCES OF INCREASING INEQUALITY

To explore the possible importance of social security and changes in the distribution of pay and transfers, we now turn to a decomposition of the change in Gini inequality. What is the contribution to this change of changes in the different components of total disposable income: gross labour earnings (wages and self-employment income), income from capital, public transfers, or income taxes (a negative component in disposable income)?

The decomposition uses the so-called natural decomposition of the Gini coefficient. A key role is played by the *concentration coefficient*. The concentration coefficient is a pseudo-Gini coefficient, with the important difference that the ranking of the different income sources is decided by total disposable income, even when calculated on specific components of total disposable income. The concentration coefficient for a given component can be further decomposed into the product of the proper Gini coefficient for this component and a measure of correlation between this component and total disposable income (Lerman and Yitzhaki, 1985).

Figure 6.10 Inequality in gross earnings (decile 9/decile 1) (1995–2015).
Gross earnings of full-time dependent employees.
Source: Data from OECD.Stat.

Appendix Table 6.A3 provides the full decomposition of total inequality in 1995 and 2013. At each point in time the overall pattern is similar in all countries. Earnings and capital income contribute positively to inequality in total income, while social transfers and taxes are redistributive and contribute to reducing inequality. Gross labour earnings constitute the dominant positive component (making up between 110% and 130% of total disposable income), and it generally has a concentration coefficient that clearly exceeds the Gini coefficient for disposable income. This means that earnings are by far the most important positive contribution to total inequality. Income from capital is more highly concentrated, but the contribution to inequality from this income source is rather modest because capital income takes up a relatively small share of total disposable income (in the area of 5% in all countries at both time points). Social transfers are redistributive throughout because they are disproportionately distributed towards the poorer segments of the population. Taxes are also redistributive, resulting from a combination of a positive concentration coefficient and a negative share in total income.

We can extend the simple decomposition of the Gini coefficient to analyse changes in Gini inequality between two periods. Table 6.5 presents the decomposition of changes in Gini inequality in total disposable income for prime age adults (aged 30–59) in each of the Nordic countries between 1995 and 2013 (the formula used for decomposing income inequality changes over time is given in Appendix 6.1).

Table 6.5 Decomposition of change in inequality between 1995 and 2013 (aged 30–59)

Denmark	Contribution to change 1995–2013		
	From changes in the share of the component	From changes in the concentration of the component	Total contribution to change
Gross earnings	0.000	0.039	**0.041**
Capital income	−0.002	−0.005	−0.007
Transfers	0.027	−0.014	**0.014**
Taxes	0.006	−0.019	−0.012
Disposable income			**0.036**
Finland	**Contribution to change 1995–2013**		
Gross earnings	0.004	0.002	**0.005**
Capital income	0.003	−0.002	0.001
Transfers	0.047	−0.023	**0.027**
Taxes	0.014	−0.012	0.000
Disposable income			**0.034**
Norway	**Contribution to change 1995–2013**		
Gross earnings	−0.004	0.045	**0.041**
Capital income	0.000	0.007	0.007
Transfers	−0.019	0.013	**−0.007**
Taxes	−0.001	−0.018	−0.019
Disposable income			**0.022**
Sweden	**Contribution to change 1995–2013**[a]		
Gross earnings	0.005	−0.009	**−0.004**
Capital income	0.000	0.009	0.009
Transfers	0.048	−0.016	**0.033**
Taxes	0.008	−0.015	−0.008
Disposable income			**0.031**

[a]Swedish figures for 2013 are calculated from EU-SILC. Income measures are defined per equivalent household member (EU-equivalence scale).
Source: Luxembourg income study (LLIS).

Consider the first column: if an income component is more concentrated than disposable income, and its share in total disposable income goes up, the result is increased inequality in disposable income. For components that are less concentrated than total disposable income, an increase in the share contributes to lower inequality. Hence, the first column gives an estimate of the contribution from changes in the share that a component takes up in total disposable income to the change in the overall Gini coefficient.

Consider then the second column: if a positive income component becomes more concentrated over time, it contributes to increased inequality in disposable income. If a negative component, such as taxes, becomes more concentrated, it contributes to reduced inequality.

Consider finally the third column: summing the first and second columns gives us the total contribution of each component to the observed change in the Gini of disposable income, and the sum of the contributions from each component is equal to the overall change in Gini inequality between the two time points.

The overall picture is clear. Even though the magnitudes of the increases were similar in the four countries over this period, the sources of the increase were quite different. In Denmark and Norway, increased inequality in gross earnings gave the largest contribution to the increase in the Gini of disposable income. Earnings inequality contributed close to nothing in this period to the change in inequality in Finland and Sweden, where retrenchments in the system of social transfers stood for the largest contribution to the increase in the Gini. In Denmark, changes in transfers contributed to increased inequality, albeit to a smaller degree.

In Denmark, overall inequality in total disposable income increased by 0.036 points. The most important impetus comes from a stronger concentration of gross labour earnings, which alone is responsible for a contribution to change of 0.041 Gini points. On top of that comes a contribution of 0.014 Gini points from changes in social transfers, which is the net effect of a decline in the share of transfers (contributing 0.027 Gini points) and an increase in the concentration coefficient for transfers (contributing −0.014 Gini points). Changes in the incidence of taxes contribute moderately to decrease inequality (−0.012 Gini points), while changes in capital incomes (primarily lower concentration) contribute modestly to decrease inequality (0.007 Gini points).

In other words, social transfers have become slightly more redistributive, but their share in the incomes of prime age adults has declined, adding up to a modest inequality increasing effect. Changes in both capital income and taxes point in the direction of decreased inequality, and they help to contain the inequality-increasing impetus from changes in earnings and transfers.

Turning to Finland, we see a somewhat different pattern, even though the scope of change in the overall Gini coefficient is about the same (at 0.034). Here, a relatively strong decline in the share taken up by social transfers in disposable household income is the main source of increasing overall inequality among prime age adults. The lower share taken up by social transfers gives an inequality increasing contribution of 0.047 Gini points. At the same time, however, social transfers have become more strongly concentrated among the poorest section of the population, and this means that the total net effect of changes in social transfers is reduced to 0.027 Gini points. Changes in the other income components play only a marginal role.

The pattern is again very different in Norway. As with Denmark, gross labour earnings contribute to an increase in inequality of 0.041 Gini points. Yet Norway is the only country where changes in social transfers have not led to an increase in inequality but instead to a modest decline. Taxes have also alleviated the impact of higher gross earnings inequality.

Finally, the Swedish pattern is rather similar to Finland. The main contribution to increased inequality in disposable income comes from social transfers. The higher inequality, arising from changes in social transfers, is associated with a considerable decline in the share taken up by social transfers in the income packages of prime age adults. Since transfers tend to compress the earnings distribution, this decline goes together with higher inequality in disposable income. The gross effect is 0.048 Gini points, but it is modified by a stronger concentration of social transfers among the lowest income brackets, resulting in a net effect of 0.033.

In Denmark and Norway, we find an impetus for higher inequality from a higher concentration of earnings, while this is not the case for Sweden and Finland. This corresponds reasonably well with the pattern in wage inequality over the same period, as shown in Figure 6.10, showing the ratio between the 9th decile and the 1st decile of the gross earnings distribution among full-time workers. Between 2000 and 2015, we find the largest increase in Norway and Denmark; a positive, but smaller increase in Finland; and a flat or slightly decreasing earnings ratio in Sweden. It appears that the early 1990s was a period of wage compression in Finland, whereas in Sweden the large increase in the earnings ratio occurred between 1985 and 2000.

In all countries with the exception of Norway, a distinct part of the rise in income inequality seems to stem from changes in social transfers. This is particularly visible for Sweden, where the increases due to retrenchments in transfers are larger than the total increase in disposable income inequality. Changes in capital income did not amount to much in these data.

Finally, in Table 6.6, we examine the household incomes of the bottom 20% of the gross labour earnings distribution. The pattern is clear for Denmark, Finland, and Sweden, with a strong decline in the average transfer to the bottom 20% over this period, measured in per cent of median gross income in the population. At the same time, relative level gross labour earnings received by the bottom 20% has increased somewhat. Yet the growth in earnings for this group does not compensate for the loss in transfers. All in all, the average disposable income of the bottom 20% among prime age adults has declined relative to the median disposable income of the population as a whole, and the poverty rates at the bottom of the gross earnings distribution have gone up.

Norway displays a rather different pattern: here we see a rise in transfers and a decline in labour earnings, with an overall reduction as the end result. Poverty rates at the bottom quintile have increased in Norway as well, but more modestly than in Finland and Sweden.

Table 6.6 Household incomes received by the lowest earnings quintile, population aged 30–59

	Denmark			Finland			Norway			Sweden		
	1995	2004	2013	1995	2004	2013	1995	2004	2013	1995	2005	2013[a]
Relative mean Transfers[b]	51.7	45.9	45.7	56.5	42.9	39.7	34.8	45.8	41.1	59	48.5	28.2
Relative mean Earnings[b]	14.7	17.1	16.4	9.3	15.6	16.7	27.2	18.8	18.1	12.8	15.3	27.6
Relative mean disp income[c]	79.1	73.1	71.1	78.8	72.7	66.1	75.3	74.3	67.4	80.8	73.9	60.5
Poverty rate	18.7	26	28.4	22.6	39.3	45.1	26.2	28.9	37.6	19.3	30.2	50.0

[a] Swedish figures for 2013 are calculated from EU-SILC. Income measures defined per equivalent household member (EU-equivalence scale).

[b] In per cent of median gross income in general population.

[c] In per cent of median disposable income in general population.

Source: Luxembourg Income Study.

Even though there are some divergences across the Nordic countries, it is clear that there are important changes in the generosity of the Nordic welfare state, with convergence movement in the direction of how social protection works in other OECD countries. The consequences are particularly evident for the worst-off groups that used to fare relatively well in the Nordic countries as defenders of the Nordic model would be proud to point out.

6.6 CONCLUSION

The Nordic countries are small, open economies renowned for combining egalitarian labour market institutions and comprehensive welfare states with highly productive and competitive economies. As we have seen, the Nordic countries continue to perform comparatively well in terms of labour force participation and employment rates, and in the general level of prosperity, productivity, and economic growth. Even if each of the Nordic countries has experienced economic recessions and periods with sluggish economic growth, they have—at least so far—shown a remarkable ability to recover and return to a persistent growth path. While we do see increasing income inequality in the Nordic countries and increasing relative income poverty, it generally happens in the context of overall economic growth. While some segments tend to fall behind in relative terms, they do not often suffer absolute declines in material well-being.

One of the keys to the Nordic success story is that labour earnings compression and generous welfare states appear to reinforce each other. Barth and Moene (2016) labelled this the 'equality multiplier', where equality creates more equality.

But the multiplier can also be expected to work in the opposite direction. When inequality of labour earnings goes up, the generosity of the welfare states comes under pressure. Crises tend to reinforce this 'inequality multiplier' because a majority of both voters and politicians feel that they cannot afford generous welfare states in periods of low income and large insurance pay outs. This mechanism can help us understand why Denmark, Finland, and Sweden are trimming down their welfare spending, while Norway has not yet implemented the same level of retrenchment.

The Nordic countries still feature low levels of income inequality relative to other countries. The latest decades have shown, however, that factors that tend to increase the dispersion in market incomes are felt in the Nordic countries as well.

The underlying forces that tend to erode wage equalizing institutions in the labour market are at work here as well. These factors, together with economic downturns, put pressure on the generosity of their welfare states. Retrenchment of the social transfers weakens the bargaining power of low-paid workers, which in turn may fuel further inequalities in market incomes as well.

As we have shown, inequality of disposable household income has been on the rise in the Nordic countries over the past 30 years. This rise came at different times and with somewhat different intensities. Sweden has had the highest and most consistent growth in inequality overall, while Finland had a particularly large growth from 1995 to 2000. Norway, in contrast, had an increase in inequality for the whole period from 1985 to 2005, but the rise in Denmark was particularly strong between 2000 and 2005. In all the Nordic countries, with the partial exception of Sweden, it seems that growth in income inequality has tapered out somewhat in the past decade.

Similar increases in inequality have occurred in most OECD countries. Coming from a low level of inequality, the Nordic countries have not yet caught up with inequality in the rest of the world. The Nordic countries remain among the most egalitarian. Yet the period since 1990 has demonstrated that even with earnings compressing wage bargaining and high welfare state spending, the Nordic economies are susceptible to some of the same underlying forces that have raised inequality in the rest of the developed world.

The rise in inequality of disposable income is associated with both more inequality in gross labour earnings and a retrenchment of the social transfers. In Sweden, the rise in the inequality of labour earnings came early, most likely because of the dismantling of the centralized bargaining system in the early 1980s. Denmark and Norway followed suit in the late 1990s and early 2000s, without much change in the bargaining system. In Finland, the growth in earnings inequality followed a period of compression in the early 1990s.

What is to be blamed: the rise in earnings inequality or the retrenchment of the welfare state? The answer is both. From a descriptive point of view, it is fair to say that from 1995 to 2015, the rise in gross labour earnings inequality provided a *major impulse* to inequality in disposable income only in Denmark

and Norway. In Finland and Sweden, the retrenchments in the generosity of social transfers were the main impulse behind the rise in inequality of disposable
income. Denmark, actually, had both a major rise in earnings inequality and a
major decline in welfare generosity. The concurrent occurrence of an increase
in gross earnings inequality and a decline in welfare generosity is not a big surprise, and most likely the two developments feed on each other. This pattern has
been evident in many other European countries as well, among those that have
experienced a process of institutional reciprocity where higher gross earnings
inequality contributed to lower political demand for welfare generosity, which in
turn fuelled more earnings inequality (Barth and Moene, 2014).

Why do we have these differences across countries that are so similar? Finland
and Sweden came out of a severe crisis, and leading politicians accepted the idea
that their countries could no longer afford such generous welfare spending. Their
views gained support from considerable parts of the population. Decisive voter
groups may have felt that they were lagging behind in the average income rise
and that they could not afford the high taxes needed for high public spending.
The voters may have felt that the welfare state was in competition with other
pressing needs for higher disposable incomes. A more general decline among the
social democratic parties may have added to this momentum.

The formation and development of the Nordic model has been one of gradual
adaptations rather than of large big-jump transformations. Dissolving the model
may mirror its rise. Yet history also teaches us that most of the planned funerals
of the Nordic model of the past have been cancelled because the old man, after
all, was still alive.

One reason why the Nordic model is not yet dead is that the Nordic countries
enjoy high levels of trust and social cohesion within and across groups, with the
encompassing organizations of both workers and employers. This potential for
collective action stabilizes their economic and political systems. It may also act
as a countervailing power against the rising inequality that we now see. Thus, to
understand whether Nordic egalitarianism is actually dissolving or not, it may
not be enough to observe, as we have done here, that the arrows are pointing in
the wrong direction according to the main historical emphasis of the model. Any
investigation of the possible decline of the model has to start from the success of
the arrangement that may also give inspiration to self-correction today.

Much of the behaviour of the organizations is still anchored in a common
understanding of what is the real economic situation (via routine consultations)
and what are the required responses to achieve common goals. On the individual
level, many people still follow the social ethos of making his or her contribution
to society, in full expectation that others do the same. This kind of consonance,
cooperation,cooperation| and reciprocity may again stabilize the model. Yet in
the age of welfare retrenchment and union decline, many people doubt that the
arrangement will work equally well in the future as it has done in the past.

ACKNOWLEDGEMENTS

Funding from the Norwegian Research Council projects no. 257603 and 227072 is gratefully acknowledged.

REFERENCES

Atkinson, A. B. (2015). *Inequality: What can be done?* Harvard: Harvard University Press.

Atkinson, A. B., Rainwater, L., and Smeeding, T. M. (1995). *Income distribution in OECD countries. Evidence from the Luxembourg Income Study.* Paris: OECD.

Atkinson, A. B., and Søgaard, J. E. (2016). The long-run history of income inequality in Denmark. *Scandinavian Journal of Economics, 118*(2), 264–291.

Autor, D. H., Dorn, D., and Hanson, G. H. (2016). The China shock: Learning from labor market adjustment to large changes in trade. *Annual Review of Economics, 8*, 205-240.

Barth, E., and Moene, K. O. (2014). When institutions reciprocate: Turning European social models around. In J. E. Dølvig and A. Martin (eds.), *European Social models from crisis to crisis: Employment and inequality in the era of monetary integration* (chapter 10). Oxford: Oxford University Press.

Barth, E., and Moene, K. O. (2016). The equality multiplier: How wage compression and welfare empowerment interact. *Journal of the European Economic Association, 14*(5), 1011–1037.

Barth, E., Moene, K. E., and Willumsen, F. (2014) The Scandinavian Model – an interpretation. *Journal of Public Economics, 117*, 60–72.

Esping-Andersen, G. (1990). *Three worlds of welfare capitalism.* Cambridge: Polity Press.

Ferrarini, T., Nelson, K., Palme, J., and Sjöberg, O. (2012). Sveriges socialförsäkringar i jämförande perspektiv. En institutionell analys av sjuk-, arbetsskadeoch arbetslöshetsförsäkringarna i 18 OECD-länder 1930 till 2010. SOU (S 2010:04)

Grunfelder, F. et al. (2020). State of the Nordic Region 2020. Nord 2020:001. Nordic Council of Ministers. https://doi.org/10.6027/NO2020-001.

Hoffmann, R. (2013). How to measure the progressivity of an income component. *Applied Economics Letters, 20*, 328–331.

Jäntti, M. (2017). Income inequality and income poverty across time: The Nordic countries in comparative perspective.

Korpi, W. (1989). Power, politics, and state autonomy in the development of social citizenship: Social rights during sickness in eighteen OECD countries since 1930. *American Sociological Review*, 309–328.

Kuivalainen, S., and Nelson, K. (2012). Eroding minimum income protection in the Nordic countries. In J. Kvist et al. (eds.), *Changing social equality. The Nordic welfare model in the 21st century.* Bristol: Policy Press.

Lerman, R. I., and Yitzaki, S. (1985). Income inequality effects by income source: A new approach and applications to the United States. *Review of Economics and Statistics, 67*, 151–156.

Moene, K. O. (2016). The social upper class under social democracy. *Nordic Economic Policy Review, 2016*(2), 245–261.

OECD (2014), *OECD Factbook 2014: Economic, Environmental and Social Statistics*, OECD Publishing, Paris, https://doi.org/10.1787/factbook-2014-en.

Pedersen, A. W., and Finseraas, H. (2013). Arbeidsbetingede stønader—liberale virkemidler i arbeidslinjas verktøykasse. *Søkelys på arbeidslivet, 30*(4), 335–355.

Smeeding, T., et al. (eds.). (1999). *Poverty, inequality and income distribution in comparative perspective: The Luxembourg Income Study.* Hertfordshire: Harvester Wheatsheaf.

Sørgaard, J. E. (2018). *Top incomes in Scandinavia: Recent developments and the role of capital income. Nordic Economic Policy Review 2018: Increasing income inequality in the Nordics.* Copenhagen: Nordic Council of Ministers.

APPENDIX 6.1 A PROCEDURE FOR DECOMPOSING CHANGES IN THE GINI COEFFICIENT OVER TIME

It is well known that the Gini coefficient for total disposable household income (G) at time t can be decomposed according to the following formula, where C_k is a so-called concentration coefficient for the kth component and S_k is the share in the total income package taken up by the same component:

$$G_t = \sum s_{kt} C_{kt}$$

The concentration coefficient is a pseudo-Gini coefficient, with the important difference that the ranking of income units is decided by total disposable income. The concentration coefficient can be further decomposed as the product of the Gini coefficient proper for this component and a measure of correlation between this component and the total income package (Lerman and Yitzhaki, 1985).

If a component is negatively correlated with the distribution of total disposable income, it will have a negative concentration coefficient, and this means that it contributes to reduce overall inequality—unless we are talking about a component with a negative share (like income tax).

It has been pointed out that the 'natural' decomposition of the Gini coefficient in its most simple form has serious weaknesses. A uniform transfer to all income units will appear to make no contribution (either positive or negative) to overall inequality since the concentration coefficient will be zero. In reality, of course, a uniform transfer is highly equalizing, but this effect will only show up indirectly as a decrease in the shares taken up by the other inequality enhancing income components and hence a decrease in *their* contributions to overall inequality. In order to overcome this problem, the formula can be extended to give the elasticity of overall inequality with respect to marginal changes in the size of each specific component (Lerman and Yitzhaki, 1985).

The 'natural' decomposition of the Gini coefficient can also be extended to provide a decomposition of changes in total Gini inequality between two time points $(G_1\text{-}G_2)$ according to the following formula (Hoffman, 2013):

$$\left[\frac{1}{2}(C_{k,1}+C_{k,2})-\frac{1}{2}(G_1+G_2)\right]\Delta s_k +\frac{1}{2}(S_{k,1}+S_{k,2})\Delta C_k$$

Also this formula overcomes the weakness of the natural decomposition by capturing the redistributive effects of expanding a uniform income component (and the inegalitarian implications of a corresponding cut back).

The first part of the expression measures the role played by changes in the relative size of the component. It says that an increase in the share of income component will contribute to increasing inequality if the concentration coefficient for this component is higher than the overall Gini coefficient. The second part measures the contribution to the overall change from changes in the concentration of the component. It says that any increase in the concentration of a component will lead to higher level of inequality in total income—unless we are talking about a negative income component (read: a tax)—and that the size of the contribution depends on the relative size of the component.

APPENDIX 6.2
TABLES

Table 6.A1 Absolute poverty (poverty rates using a poverty threshold anchored in median incomes in Sweden 2004)

	Denmark		Finland		Norway		Sweden	
	2004	2013	2004	2013	2004	2013	2004	2013
General population	4.0%	4.8%	11.5%	6.6%	3.8%	2.1%	9.1%	5.4%
Age 30–59	2.3%	2.7%	7.6%	5.5%	1.9%	0.7%	5.6%	4.0%

Poverty thresholds adjusted for country specific inflation rates.
Source: EU-SILC.

Table 6.A2 Gini inequality in market income, gross income (including transfers) and disposable income (net of taxes); difference from income component to the next; household income per member

	Denmark				Finland			
	1995		**2013**		**1995**		**2013**	
	Level	Change	Level	Change	Level	Change	Level	Change
Market income	0.350		0.361		0.399		0.382	
Gross income	0.232	−0.118	0.262	−0.099	0.263	−0.136	0.292	−0.090
Disposable income	0.190	−0.042	0.229	−0.033	0.213	−0.050	0.249	−0.043
	Norway				Sweden			
	1995		**2013**		**1995**		**2013**	
	Level	Change	Level	Change	Level	Change	Level	Change
Market income	0.321		0.370		0.369		0.328	
Gross income	0.247	−0.074	0.276	−0.094	0.238	−0.131	0.264	−0.064
Disposable income	0.213	−0.034	0.236	−0.040	0.201	−0.037	0.231	−0.033

Source: Luxembourg Income Study and EU-SILC (Sweden 2013). Income measures defined per equivalent household member (EU-equivalence scale).

Table 6.A3 Decomposition of inequality in disposable income 1995 and 2013 (aged 30–59)

	Per cent of disposable income	Concentration coefficient	Contribution	Per cent of disposable income	Concentration coefficient	Contribution
Denmark	**1995**			**2013**		
Gross labour earnings	123.23	0.300	0.379	125.59	0.331	0.417
Capital income	5.46	0.584	0.032	4.94	0.480	0.024
Transfers	24.32	−0.235	−0.057	18.46	−0.299	−0.055
Taxes	−56.01	0.290	−0.162	−48.99	0.325	−0.160
Disposable income	100.00	0.191		100.00	0.225	
Finland	**1995**			**2013**		
Gross labour earnings	109.92	0.338	0.371	111.90	0.341	0.382
Capital income	5.90	0.632	0.037	6.54	0.613	0.040
Transfers	29.61	−0.117	−0.035	16.89	−0.216	−0.036
Taxes	−45.44	0.353	−0.160	−35.33	0.389	−0.137
Disposable income	99.99	0.213		100.00	0.248	
Norway	**1995**			**2013**		
Gross labour earnings	116.66	0.283	0.330	111.96	0.322	0.361
Capital income	5.70	0.561	0.032	5.56	0.695	0.039
Transfers	14.49	−0.208	−0.030	19.48	−0.131	−0.026
Taxes	−36.86	0.324	0.120	−37.10	0.376	−0.139
Disposable income	99.99	0.213		99.99	0.235	
Sweden	**1995**			**2013**		
Gross labour earnings	111.82	0.313	0.350	117.66	0.305	0.359
Capital income	5.03	0.373	0.019	5.17	0.548	0.028
Transfers	27.25	−0.121	−0.033	14.30	−0.196	−0.028
Taxes	−44.10	0.306	−0.135	−37.12	0.344	−0.128
Disposable income	100.00	0.201		100.01	0.231	

Source: Luxembourg Income Study and EU-SILC (Sweden 2013). Income measures defined per equivalent household member (EU-equivalence scale).

7

INEQUALITY IN INCOME, WEALTH, AND CONSUMPTION TRENDS IN THE WESTERN BALKANS

Zsóka Kóczán and Sara Savastano

This chapter examines the evolution of inequality and poverty in the Western Balkans[1]—a region still coping with incomplete transition and the legacies of the boom-bust cycle, as most clearly reflected in still-high unemployment rates. The chapter thus presents trends in inequality in the context of the broader context of persistent unemployment and perceptions of high and rising inequality. It is fundamentally a story of transition, the process, still unfinished, of transition

---

1 Throughout the chapter, Western Balkans refers to Albania, Bosnia and Herzegovina, Croatia, North Macedonia, Montenegro, and Serbia (of the former Yugoslav republics, Slovenia is excluded here as it has from the start—not least because of its proximity to its western neighbors Austria and Italy—followed a different path). Where data are available Kosovo will be analyzed separately. The New Member States of the European Union are subdivided into Central Europe (the Czech Republic, Hungary, Poland, the Slovak Republic, and Slovenia); the Baltics (Estonia, Latvia, and Lithuania), and South Eastern Europe (Bulgaria and Romania). 'Emerging Europe' includes the New Member States and the Western Balkans economies. The overview of macroeconomic developments draws on the authors' previous work in Murgasova et al., (2015), the sections on the analysis of inequality trends and drivers draw on Koczan (2016), and the discussion of spatial disparities draws on the African Development Bank (AfDB), the Asian Development Bank (ADB), the European Bank for Reconstruction and Development (EBRD), and the Inter-American Development Bank (IDB) (2019). The authors are very grateful to Alexander Plekhanov for sharing the data underlying Figures 7.9 and 7.10 from EBRD (2017).

Zsóka Kóczán and Sara Savastano, *Inequality in Income, Wealth, and Consumption Trends in the Western Balkans*
In: *Europe's Income, Wealth, Consumption, and Inequality.* Edited by: Georg Fischer and Robert Strauss,
Oxford University Press (2021). © Oxford University Press. DOI: 10.1093/oso/9780197545706.003.0007

from a system with an 'employer of last result' and resulting job security, to one with income gains for some parts of the population, but widening inequality and increasing uncertainty, translating into reform fatigue and general feelings of discontent with the process of transition.

7.1 HISTORICAL CONTEXT: STALLED CONVERGENCE

Emerging Europe has undergone a major economic transformation over the past 25 years. Most countries experienced the U-shaped path of economic performance that has become a 'stylized fact' of transition countries, with initial drops in output followed by recovery in the second half of the 1990s. The path of transition in the Western Balkans (used here to refer to Albania and former Yugoslavia, excluding Slovenia) has, however, been particularly uneven and more complicated than in the rest of Emerging Europe. The path of gross domestic product (GDP) resembled more a 'W-shape': recovery, followed by reversal, and then recovery again (Sanfey and Cviić, 2010).

Albania was nearly completely autarkic at the time it began to open up from its self-imposed isolation in 1991. Political fracturing of Yugoslavia, conflict, civil unrest, and sanctions dominated the 1990s. Physical capital was destroyed, and trade—which had been high within the Yugoslav Federation—collapsed. Most economies experienced severe recessions at some stage: −28% in Albania in 1991, −8% in Croatia in 1993, −11% in Serbia in 1999, and −8% in North Macedonia in 1993.[2] As in other transition economies, inflation rose quickly, following price liberalization, substantial increases in administered prices, exchange rate devaluations, and, in some cases, passive monetary financing of growing fiscal deficits. Consumer price inflation reached more than 225% in Albania in 1992; after hyperinflation earlier in the 1990s, it was still in high double digits in Serbia and Montenegro by the end of the decade.

Following the conflict-ridden 1990s, the countries of the Western Balkans set out to comprehensively rebuild and reform their economies. They opened up to global trade and became increasingly export-oriented, expanded the role of the private sector, dismantled regulations that stifled business development, and began to build institutions needed to support a market system. The result of these efforts has been robust economic growth, a significant rise in incomes and living standards, and enhanced macroeconomic stability.

After 2000, the Western Balkan countries enjoyed sustained economic growth up until the global financial crisis. While growth rates showed some heterogeneity across countries (Albania grew rapidly from a low base; growth picked up

---

2 Based on the International Monetary Fund (IMF)'s World Economic Outlook. Data coverage is, however, patchy; there may have been worse recessions during the 1990s for which there are no official data.

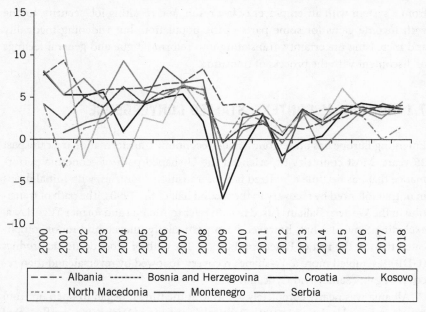

Figure 7.1 Per capita gross domestic product (GDP) growth (%).
Source: International Monetary Fund, World Economic Outlook, and authors' calculations.

somewhat later in Serbia, Kosovo, and North Macedonia because of conflicts; Montenegro stood out later with high growth rates associated with a real estate boom; see Figure 7.1), the entire region experienced a period of high growth before the financial crisis. With average economic growth across the region exceeding 5% per year during 2000–2008, income per capita increased significantly and partially closed the gap with the standards of living of Europe's advanced economies. During this pre-crisis period, real GDP per capita in the region increased by more than 40% on average, riding the tide of deeper financial and trade integration with the rest of Europe, high capital inflows, rapid credit expansion, and productivity growth (Murgasova et al., 2015). Poverty fell sharply—both in absolute numbers and in depth.[3]

---

3   The following sections rely on the headcount and the poverty gap from the World Bank as standard measures of poverty. The headcount is the per cent of the population living in households with consumption per person below the poverty line. The poverty line used in this section is $US38 per month, corresponding to the World Bank $US1.25 per day extreme poverty line (in 2005 purchasing power parity [PPP], as proposed by Ravallion et al., 2009). The poverty gap is the mean distance below the poverty line as a proportion of the poverty line. While the headcount provides an estimate of the number of poor, the poverty gap provides an additional metric of the depth of poverty. Poverty rates at national poverty lines are considerably higher, in the order of magnitude of 15–30%.

While the boom years resulted in significant gains in terms of incomes and living standards, the New Member States caught up with Advanced EU economies significantly more quickly at similar stages of transition, in part due to closer physical distance of the New Member States to Europe's core, allowing some of them to integrate into the German supply chain, but also because of the slower development of the private sector in the Western Balkans (Murgasova et al., 2015). Rapid growth also brought uneven benefits, and the early 2000s saw large increases in inequality.

7.1.1 Structural Transformation

The sequence of early structural reforms was similar to that in the New Member States: price liberalization and reforms to trade and foreign exchange systems preceded privatization and were followed only later by reforms to governance and competition policy. However, the pace of reforms was quite different, and the Western Balkans have not progressed as far as the New Member States along some reforms, in particular privatization (Figure 7.2).

One notable feature of the early transition period was the unique economic system, known as 'market socialism', that was in place in the former Yugoslavia well before the 1990s, where heavy reliance on administrative controls coexisted with a vibrant private sector of small and medium-sized enterprises (SMEs) without Soviet-style central planning (Boughton, 2012). Albania, on the other hand, started the transition process as an isolated and autarkic state with virtually no elements of a market economy, but it made swift progress, particularly in trade and foreign exchange liberalization, where reforms went further than in the rest of the Western Balkan states as early as 1992.

Despite a difficult decade, by 1999, the Western Balkans as a group had reached a fairly advanced stage of transition (measured by a value of 3 or higher for the Transition Indicators of the European Bank for Reconstruction and Development [EBRD]) in the areas of price liberalization, trade and foreign exchange, and small-scale privatization by 1999, trailing the New Member States by only a few years. However, other reforms, such as large-scale privatization, were delayed. Yugoslavia's 'socially owned' system of enterprise ownership (in contrast to state ownership in centrally planned economies elsewhere) posed additional challenges to large-scale privatization (Murgasova et al., 2015).

There was considerable variation across countries (privatizations started later in Bosnia and Herzegovina and Serbia and Montenegro) as well as sectors: privatizations in the banking, telecommunications, and in some cases energy sectors generally moved ahead, but large public enterprises in historically important industries—such as metals, shipyards, utilities, and railways—proved particularly difficult to privatize. Stalled privatizations often reflected large social opposition, high short-run costs, and few serious bidders. Corporate governance and enterprise restructuring of former state-owned enterprises remained

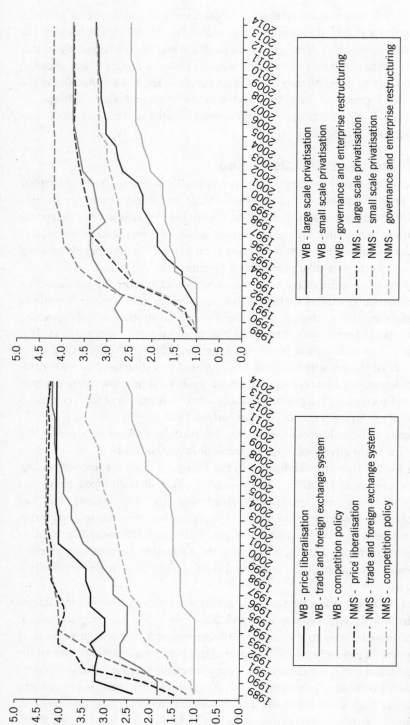

Figure 7.2 Transition indicators in the Western Balkans and the New Member States.
Western Balkans excludes Kosovo due to data limitations. simple averages across countries.
Source: EBRD and authors' calculations.

a challenge across the region, and state support often continued (Murgasova et al., 2015).

The process of structural transformation also began to stall in the mid-2000s and remains incomplete (EBRD, 2013; Murgasova et al., 2015). Some of this fatigue can be explained by increasing difficulties in pushing through reforms, especially those with significant short-run costs and with benefits coming only later, in a context where there is a sense that reforms have underdelivered and that the spoils of growth have benefited only a few. While European Union (EU) accession provided an important incentive for reforms in the New Member States, in the Western Balkans such prospects are more distant and uncertain and thus also weigh on reform momentum.

7.1.2 Crisis and Aftermath

By the time of the global financial crisis, growth in the Western Balkans was driven more by ample global liquidity and unsustainable capital inflows than by real progress on economic reforms. Unemployment rates were extremely high, remaining above 20% in several countries even at the height of the pre-crisis boom.

The boom years ended abruptly in 2009, and per capita GDP growth has largely stalled since then. Most of the region experienced dips in growth not only in 2009, but also in 2012 and, in the cases of Croatia and Serbia, again in 2014.

Growth remains lacklustre in the region. The end of a period of rapid global growth unmasked problems associated with stalled transition in the Western Balkans, and external conditions have also weighed on growth because growth in the Euro Area—a key export market for the region—has been weak, creating a less than supportive external environment for the Western Balkan states.

Income convergence has stalled. The Western Balkan countries lag well behind the New Member States in terms of economic transformation and income levels, which are around one-third of those in Advanced EU economies (Figure 7.3). At currently projected growth rates, Western Balkan economies will only close a small fraction of the gap with Advanced EU economies' income per capita levels by 2030. Slow growth also hinders the creation of much-needed employment opportunities to absorb the large surplus of unutilized labour in the region. Labour market liberalization in the context of weak job creation and rising inequality might thus not deliver the expected beneficial effects in terms of more and better jobs.

7.1.3 A Lack of Jobs

Persistent unemployment represents a unique regional challenge both in its importance and magnitude. The region was unable to generate significant employment gains during the boom years and registered large job losses during the global crisis. In 2008, at the tail end of the growth spurt, the unemployment rate in the region still averaged almost 20% (Figure 7.4). Employment levels tell an equally disappointing story, hovering between 40% and 45% on average

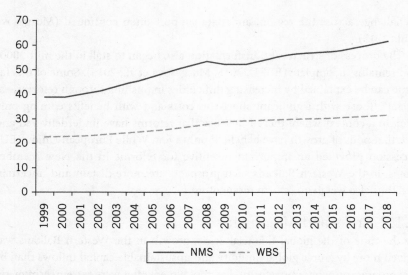

Figure 7.3 Per capita gross domestic product (GDP) as a per cent of average EU15 per capita GDP (PPP).
Sources: International Monetary Fund, World Economic Outlook, and authors' calculations.

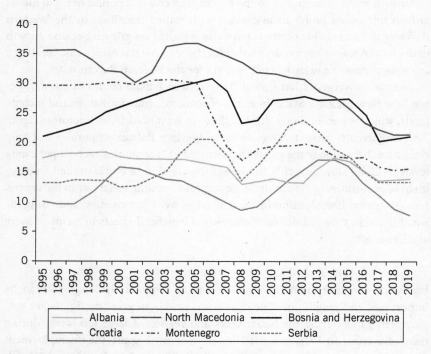

Figure 7.4 Unemployment rates (per cent of 15+ population).
Source: ILO modelled estimates.

since 2000, a full 10 percentage points lower than in the New Member States. Employment is particularly low among women and the young, strikingly so in Bosnia and Herzegovina and Kosovo (Murgasova et al., 2015).

The New Member States— and particularly the Baltics— experienced large cyclical swings of both employment and unemployment during the 2000s, but in a qualitatively different context of markedly lower unemployment and higher employment. In contrast, workers in the Western Balkans failed to significantly benefit from employment gains during the boom years while still registering significant job losses in the aftermath of the crisis (International Labour Organization, 2012). Atoyan et al., (2015) highlight the persistence of unemployment in the Western Balkans regardless of cyclical conditions—in sharp contrast with larger and statistically significant responses found in most Central European and Baltic economies.

Skill gaps have also been particularly severe in the Western Balkans, as in, and in some cases more so than, in the Baltics or Central Europe (Murgasova et al., 2015). In some countries, the legacy of self-management and social ownership has contributed to labour market rigidity, de facto protection for insiders, and resulting labour market duality (Kuddo, 2013).

Household-level survey evidence for Serbia shows that low-skill sectors have been especially affected by job losses during the global financial crisis. The same evidence also points to the 'freezing' effect of the crisis on labour market mobility, with the movement of workers between employment, unemployment, and inactivity dropping significantly, thus restricting opportunities for economically inactive populations to rejoin the workforce.

While substantial labour market reforms have been undertaken, particularly in the areas of flexibility of wage determination and redundancy costs, increased labour market flexibility in the Western Balkan countries is a recent phenomenon and may not manifest itself in improved labour market outcomes unless it is accompanied by a more meaningful pick-up in activity.

One reason for worse labour market outcomes and persistently high unemployment in the region could be that while in the New Member States the infusion of capital from abroad (especially via greenfield foreign direct investment [FDI]) played a key role in developing new businesses or even new sectors and provided a chance for workers dismissed from declining sectors or areas to be reabsorbed by new economic activities, delayed transition and low FDI put the Western Balkans at a disadvantage in diversifying away from traditional sectors (Kovtun et al., 2014).

The region not only received less FDI than the New Member States, even controlling for country characteristics, the investment flows that did arrive were mostly related to privatizations (greenfield investment was only marginal), biased towards consumption rather than investment, and concentrated in nontradable service sectors (such as financial intermediation and real estate) and thus did little to generate employment, improve productivity growth, or boost exports

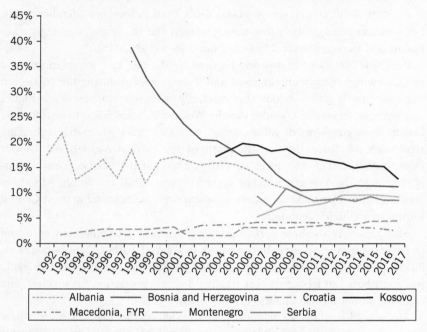

Figure 7.5 Remittances (per cent of gross domestic product [GDP]).
Sources: International Monetary Fund, World Economic Outlook, World Bank, and authors' calculations.

(Demekas et al., 2005, European Commissi,on 2009; Dukić and Bodroža, 2011; Žugić, 2011, Estrin and Uvalić, 2014; Kovtun et al., 2014), though it has held up better in recent years than in the New Member States.[4]

Remittances continue to constitute an important alternative source of income for many households in the Western Balkans and can help somewhat offset other income shocks (Figure 7.5). As a unique characteristic of the region, pensions also often constitute the most stable income flow of the household.

7.1.4 Trends in Inequality

At the start of the transition process, income inequality was low by international standards. It has, however, increased subsequently as a result of globalization trends compounded by the transition to market economies.

Inequality rose sharply in the 1990s: during the early years of the transition process, newly created markets placed a premium on new skills—such as business acumen—as well as political connections. This resulted in a sharp divergence in wages, with upward and downward adjustments in wages for large sections of the population (EBRD, 2017). In most countries, privatizations of

---

4 Most FDI and portfolio flows come from the EU15, especially Austria, Germany, Greece, Hungary, and Italy.

large companies—as opposed to privatizations of SMEs—also contributed to the rise in inequality and, in particular, the concentration of wealth among the very rich.

As the boom years of the early 2000s brought steady increases in incomes, poverty fell sharply—both in terms of absolute numbers, as measured using the headcount, and depth, as measured using the poverty gap. Mean consumption, however, remained far below that in Central and Eastern Europe. Rapid growth also brought uneven benefits, and the early 2000s continued to see large increases in inequality (as measured using the Gini index) driven by increases at the top (Figure 7.6). While in absolute terms everyone appears to have been made better off, disparities increased as the share of the top rose relative to the share of the bottom.

Inequality continued to increase until 2005 across the region, although after 2005 the share of the top decile declined in Albania, Bosnia and Herzegovina, and Serbia and, to a lesser extent, in Montenegro, but continued to increase in Croatia and North Macedonia, with corresponding trends in inequality.[5] This could be driven by the fact that Croatia and North Macedonia were at a somewhat more advanced stage of transition already; in particular, privatizations may have allowed the top to reap more of the benefits of large capital inflows and growth. Poverty continued to fall across the Western Balkans up to the financial crisis.

Poverty, however, has increased since 2008, though with significant variation across countries and to a lesser extent than in the New Member States. Albania and Montenegro have seen the sharpest increase in poverty since the global financial crisis, although poverty in Serbia also increased. Wage reductions, and importantly, a loss of remittances served to transmit the economic slowdown across Europe to poverty levels in the Western Balkans.

Inequality fell as a result of the crisis, mostly driven by a decline in incomes at the top. At the peak of inequality in the early 2000s, the Western Balkans were more unequal than Central and South-Eastern Europe, and, although the overall pattern was similar, inequality peaked earlier in Central and Eastern Europe. By 2010, inequality in the Western Balkans and the New Member States was broadly comparable (Figure 7.7).

The World Bank defines shared prosperity (Table 7.1) as the growth in the income or consumption of the bottom 40% of the income distribution, a measure of whether and how quickly prosperity is shared among the poor. It captures two key elements, economic growth and equity: without sustained economic growth, poor people are unlikely to increase their living standards; however, growth is not enough by itself and improvement in the shared prosperity indicator requires

---

5 Increasing inequality in Croatia could be driven by rapid financial integration resulting in fast growth of the financial industry and corresponding increases in the incomes of those employed in the sector.

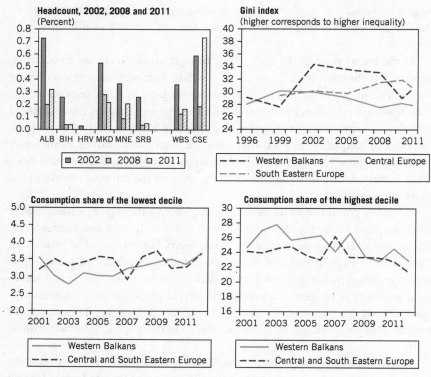

Figure 7.6 Poverty, inequality, and consumption shares.
Some year-on-year fluctuations (for instance in 2007 and 2009) can be explained by changes in the sample as data are not available for all countries, for all years. CSE refers to Central and South Eastern Europe.
Source: Koczan (2016).

growth to be inclusive of the less well-off (World Bank, 2016). During the period 2008–2012, the growth in income (or consumption) of the most vulnerable population was negative for all countries in the region except North Macedonia. Mean per capita consumption levels are two or three times higher than standard poverty line levels; however, consumption levels are low for the bottom 40% of the population: average daily per capita consumption is US$6.2, equivalent to less than US$200 per capita per month. This average conceals significantly higher levels in Croatia, Montenegro, and Serbia, and close to half their levels in Albania and North Macedonia.

The Europe 2020 strategy promotes social inclusion, in particular through the reduction of poverty, by aiming to lift at least 20 million people out of the risk of poverty and social exclusion. Eurostat provides indicators of the share of people at risk of poverty or severely materially deprived or living in households with very low work intensity. 'At risk of poverty' refers to people with an equivalized disposable income below the risk-of-poverty threshold, which is set at 60% of the

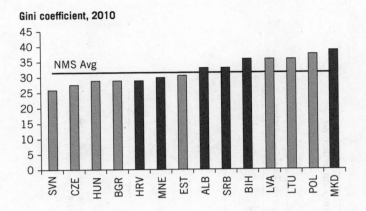

Gini coefficient, 2010

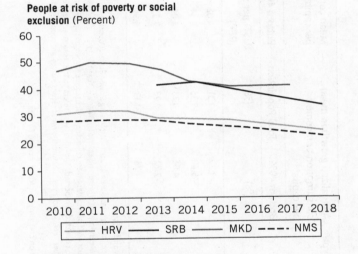

People at risk of poverty or social exclusion (Percent)

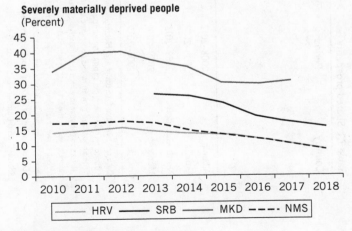

Severely materially deprived people (Percent)

Figure 7.7 Inequality, risk of poverty, and deprivation.
Source: Koczan (2016), Eurostat, and authors' calculations.

Table 7.1 Shared prosperity

Country	Period[c]	Type[d]	Annualized growth in mean consumption or income per capita[a,b]		Mean consumption or income per capita[a]	
			Bottom 40%	Total Population	Bottom 40%	Total Population
			(%)	(%)	USD per day (PPP)	
Albania	2008–2012	c	-1.22	-1.31	4.08	7.41
Croatia	2009–2012	i	-5.40	-5.35	8.44	17.24
North Macedonia	2009–2013	i	4.98	0.73	4.08	9.74
Montenegro	2009–2014	c	-2.72	-2.27	7.53	14.51
Serbia	2008–2013	c	-1.73	-1.13	6.96	12.7

Data not available for Bosnia and Herzegovina and Kosovo.

[a] Based on real mean per capita consumption or income measured at 2011 Purchasing Power Parity (PovcalNet).

[b] The annualized growth rate is computed as (Mean in year 2/Mean in year 1)∧(1/(Year 2 − Year 1)) − 1.

[c] Refers to the year in which the underlying household survey data were collected and, in cases for which the data collection period bridged two calendar years, the first year in which data were collected is reported. The initial year refers to the nearest survey collected 5 years before the most recent survey available; only surveys collected between 3 and 7 years before the most recent survey are considered. The final year refers to the most recent survey available between 2011 and 2015.

[d] Denotes whether the data reported are based on consumption (c) or income (i) data.

Source: Global Database of Shared Prosperity.

national median equivalized disposable income (after social transfers). Material deprivation covers indicators relating to economic strain and durables: severely materially deprived people have living conditions severely constrained by a lack of resources, such that they experience at least 4 out of 9 following deprivations items: they cannot afford to (1) pay rent or utility bills; (2) keep their home adequately warm; (3) face unexpected expenses; (4) eat meat, fish, or a protein equivalent every second day; (5) a week's holiday away from home; (6) a car; (7) a washing machine; (8) a colour TV; or (9) a telephone. People living in households with very low work intensity are those aged 0–59 living in households where the adults (aged 18–59) work 20% or less of their total work potential during the past year. The share of people at risk of poverty and social exclusion and the share of severely materially deprived people also remains somewhat higher in the Western Balkans than in the New Member States, especially in the poorer southern countries of the region (Figure 7.7).[6]

7.1.5 Drivers of Inequality

The shifts seen in income patterns over the past two-and-a-half decades reflect both broader globalization trends and experiences unique to the region—a legacy of the sharp increase in wage inequality and deep recessions seen in the early years of the transition process, as well as the very fast shift from manufacturing- and agriculture-based economies to a more service-oriented model.

As in the New Member States, the transition process also involved an unprecedented shift from an economic model favouring manufacturing and agriculture to a more service-oriented structure. On average in the transition region, the share of services in GDP jumped from less than 40% in 1990 to almost 60% today. Mirroring this, the average share of agriculture in GDP has halved, falling from around a quarter in the early 1990s to around 12% today. While other emerging market economies, such as China, have undergone similar shifts, the pace of the structural change seen in the early years of the transition process was unparalleled.

The dynamics of inequality and poverty are also closely linked to labour market developments in the region. Looking at simple scatter plots, there is a striking correlation between unemployment and inequality, even more so in the Western Balkans than in the New Member States (Figure 7.8). This raises the question whether government policies, and in particular social safety nets, are successful in mitigating the impact of shocks, in particular on the poor who appear to be harder hit.[7] Regression results (as documented in Koczan,

---

6   Data are unfortunately not available for other countries in the Western Balkans, and data coverage in earlier years is limited.

7   Household-level surveys in Bosnia and Herzegovina suggest that it is the 45–54 age group which is at the highest risk of poverty, and more so in rural areas—likely linked to difficulties of this group in finding re-employment (Cojocaru and Ruggeri Laderchi, 2013).

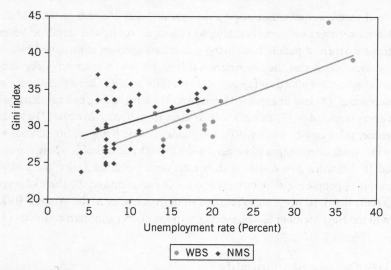

Figure 7.8 Correlation between unemployment and inequality.

2016) confirm that unemployment has a highly significant impact, increasing inequality and the share of the top and reducing the share of the bottom, suggesting that the poor may be more likely to become unemployed and/or that the social safety net may not provide effective insulation against shocks (or at least to a lesser extent for the poor).

At first sight, privatizations also appear to have a negative effect, increasing inequality and the share of the top while reducing the share of the bottom and increasing poverty. However, this effect is channelled through its impact on unemployment.[8] Once differing unemployment rates are controlled for, small-scale privatizations appear to be pro-poor, possibly capturing the development of entrepreneurship and a private sector (Koczan, 2016).

The Western Balkans are characterized by relatively low inequality in education: primary, secondary, and some tertiary education are free, and, other than at the tertiary level, private schooling is rare, with the overwhelming majority attending state schools. Pre-primary school enrolment, which (other than tertiary education) is likely to have the most variation, does not appear to have a significant impact on poverty or inequality, probably explained by equal access at successive stages, a legacy of the socialist system. What governments spend on, however, matters. Goods and services expenditure, likely acting as an overall

---

8   Note that an increase in unemployment measured at the country level could have an ambiguous impact on inequality (and poverty) depending on whether unemployment increases more among the top or the bottom of the income distribution.

stimulus to the economy, is significantly pro-poor, reducing inequality, the share of the top quintile, and poverty (Koczan, 2016).

7.2 PERSISTENT DISSATISFACTION

Across all of Emerging Europe, transition has been associated with uncertainty and worry, about issues ranging from fear of losing one's job to being unable to pay higher electricity bills. The transition from planned to market economies was far from smooth, especially in the early years. The social, economic, and physical costs of those reforms were so substantial that men and women born at the start of the transition process are an average of around 1 centimeter shorter than those born just before or after that period (EBRD, 2017). It is no wonder, then, that most people in the transition region were, until recently, less happy than people with similar income levels elsewhere in the world (EBRD, 2017).

However, the effects of transition seem to have been more traumatic and persistent in the Western Balkans, and nostalgia appears to be more prevalent here than in other former communist regions (Sanfey and Cviić, 2010). It is striking that even in 2006 (following years of high growth and before the global crisis began to affect the region), more than half of the population in the Western Balkans thought they were worse off than they were in 1989 (compared with around 35% in the New Member States). A mere 11% thought they were better off (compared with around a third in the New Member States). This dissatisfaction appears to be strongest in the former Yugoslav republics, where people overwhelmingly believe that the economic and political situations were better under the old regime.[9]

Large parts of the electorate feel that they have not benefited from the growth seen in the past two and a half decades. In many countries, average growth rates—the ones typically reported in the press and used by policymakers—simply do not apply to significant sections of the population. EBRD (2017) highlighted that, in the transition region as a whole, average income growth corresponds to the experience of someone in the top 27% of the income distribution. In contrast, 23% of people are actually worse off today than they were in 1989, while a further 33% have experienced income growth below the G7 average, implying that only 44% of all men and women in post-communist countries have enjoyed total

---

9 Though such estimates should be treated with great caution given data limitations and uncertainties about prices and exchange rates, real GDP per capita roughly doubled between 1989 and 2006 in Croatia and Kosovo, increased less than 1.5-fold (if at all) in Albania, Bosnia and Herzegovina, North Macedonia and Montenegro, and was still below its 1989 level in Serbia in 2006. Albanians tend to regard transition in a much more positive light, remembering the bleak economic conditions and oppressive political regime that prevailed up to the end of the 1980s (Sanfey and Cviić, 2010).

income growth that is higher than the average for the G7 economies. This means that more than half of all people in the transition region have not seen their earnings converge with those of people living in richer countries. These numbers are even more striking for the Western Balkans: between 62% and 76% of Western Balkans populations experienced below-average growth; income remains below 1989 levels for the entire populations of Montenegro and Serbia, around 61% of the population of North Macedonia and 38% in Bosnia and Herzegovina. Only Croatia has seen significant growth above G7 averages, pointing to some convergence (Figure 7.9).

Figure 7.10 shows cumulative income growth since 1989 by income decile. Since the 1990s, these curves have shifted upward as growth has benefited (almost) all deciles of the income distribution. However, the lines also became steeper (in some cases starkly), pointing to increases in inequality as the poor experienced much weaker growth than the well-off. Consistent with Figure 7.9, these lines suggest that the entire distributions of Montenegro and Serbia are worse off than they were in 1989, as are the bottom 40% and 60%, respectively, in Bosnia and Herzegovina and North Macedonia.

In this context, it is not surprising that people are also overwhelmingly of the view that inequality levels are high and rising. In all countries in the region, the percentage of people who believe that inequality has risen over the past 4 years exceeds the percentage who believe it has fallen (EBRD, 2017). Such perceptions of inequality tend to matter more than officially reported figures when it comes to social conflict and backlashes against reforms, according to recent studies. It is people's perception of their own economic situation that matters most when it comes to support for government policies, and this perception may, to a significant extent, be influenced by people's views of opportunities open to them— more so than by average measures of economic performance such as output or unemployment.

7.3 SPATIAL DISPARITIES

Spatial disparities are also increasing: urban and rural areas as well as small and large cities are increasingly diverging. Historically, countries in Emerging Europe were characterized by high urbanization rates relative to their level of development, though with more dispersed settlement patterns and a greater role of secondary cities, with populations less concentrated in large urban agglomerations than in many other emerging markets. Concentration, however, increased in the transition years of the 1990s as structural shifts required changes in cities' economies as well.

Capital cities and large urban centres found themselves in a privileged position, attracting investment in banking, retail, and information-based technologies, thus sustaining more stable labour markets. Some secondary cities

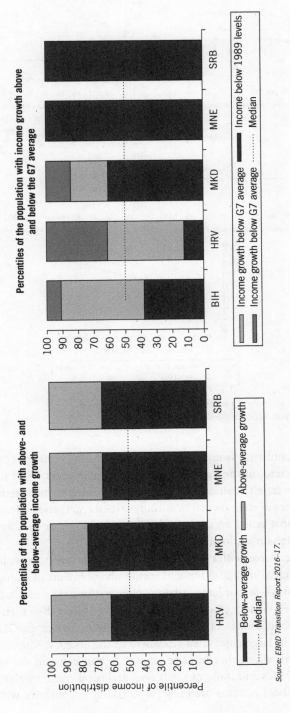

Figure 7.9 Income growth by percentiles of the population (1989–2016).
Sources: EBRD Transition Report 2016–2017.

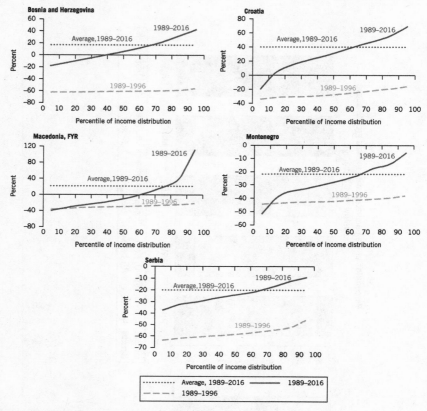

Figure 7.10 Cumulative income growth since 1989 by income decile.
Source: EBRD Transition Report 2016–2017.

also managed to shift away from traditional manufacturing industries to service-oriented urban economies and gained economic attractiveness. Most secondary cities were, however, left behind. Highly concentrated employment centres were hit hard by closures of state-owned or socially owned enterprises. Many smaller cities and those that relied on a single, dominant employer or industry turned into pockets of high unemployment and poverty.

This divergence across cities has continued more recently because improved technologies—such as digitalization and major advancements in transport and telecommunications—favour large, urban agglomerations. As a result, the share of output produced in large cities has been rising even faster than their share of their countries' populations. As in advanced economies, per capita GDP is significantly higher in large cities than elsewhere in the country. Moreover, GDP growth is also typically higher in large cities. The gap between the economic fortunes of large cities and those of small ones and rural communities has thus been widening. These patterns are especially striking in countries with low or

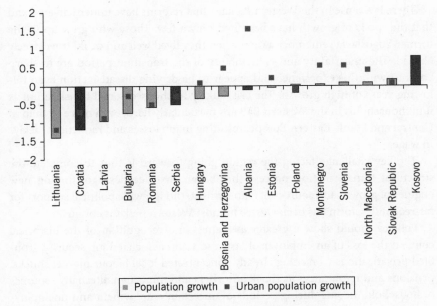

Figure 7.11 Population and urban population growth (2017) (%).
Source: World Bank, World Development Indicators, and authors' calculations.

even negative population and urban population growth (Figure 7.11). In Serbia more than 70% of cities are shrinking. In Albania, despite rapid urban population growth, more than 80% of cities are shrinking as a result of increasing concentration (AfDB, ADB, EBRD, and IDB, 2019).

7.4 CHALLENGES AHEAD

Across the region, governments are dealing with the legacies of the past, including an incomplete transition. While the role of the state—acting as a stimulus to the domestic economy and as an employer—has shrunk, the development of the private sector is often lagging, as reflected in high unemployment rates.

The reform process had largely stalled by the mid-2000s and was left incomplete, a victim of reform fatigue, a difficult political economy, vested interests, and disillusionment with the way some reforms were executed. The process of accession to EU membership—arguably the main catalyst of reforms in the New Member States—remains a distant prospect for most of the Western Balkans. Today, the region lags well behind the New Member States in terms of structural transformation and the development of the private sector, weighing not only on growth, but also notably on employment, and making it more difficult to share income gains more broadly.

There is a sense in the Western Balkans that reforms have underdelivered and that the spoils of growth have benefited only a few. Those who grew up in the former Yugoslavia remember a time when they lived well and could travel freely abroad. The uncertainty and vulnerability of the transition period are in sharp contrast with this experience and appear to be driving dissatisfaction even following years of high growth. The crisis likely further worsened the situation as it hit households in the Western Balkans particularly hard, even more so than in Central and South-Eastern Europe, resulting in job losses and reductions/delays in wages.

The key challenge facing the region going forward is thus to complete the structural transformation process that began two decades ago, finding new engines of growth and sources of employment, though wide political support for far-reaching reform has been elusive in most Western Balkans countries.

Policies should show a greater awareness and recognition of the historical context: the loss of an employer of last resort and associated job security, troubled privatizations worsening already concentrated local labour market shocks, pensions and remittances as shock absorbers and important alternative sources of household income during periods of uncertain employment and unemployment, and a lagging development of the private sector.

Policies should also recognize that country-level aggregates may mask very different local experiences—not just across urban and rural areas, but also across cities of different sizes— with urban decline constituting a particularly difficult challenge and one that, in the past, was largely confined to advanced economies.

REFERENCES

African Development Bank, Asian Development Bank, European Bank for Reconstruction and Development and Inter-American Development Bank (2019). *Creating livable cities: Regional perspectives.* Manila: Asian Development Bank.

Atoyan, R., Jankulov, I., and Van Rooden, R. (2015). The quest for jobs. In Murgasova, Z. Ilahi, N., Miniane, J., Scott, A., Vladkova-Hollar, I., and an IMF Staff Team (eds.), *The Western Balkans: 15 years of economic transition* (pp. 33–39). IMF Regional Economic Issues Special Report. Washington, DC: IMF.

Boughton, J. M. (2012). Tearing Down Walls: The International Monetary Fund 1990-1999. Washington, DC: IMF.

Cojocaru, A., and Ruggeri Laderchi, C. (2013). Social exclusion in Bosnia and Herzegovina. In C. Ruggeri Laderchi and S. Savastano (Eds.), *Poverty and exclusion in the Western Balkans: New directions in measurement and policy* (pp. 71–98). New York: Springer.

Demekas, D. G., Horváth, B., Ribakova, E., and Wu, Y. (2005). *Foreign direct investment in Southeastern Europe: How (and how much) can policies help?* IMF Working Paper, No. 05/110. Washington, DC: IMF.

Dukić, M., and D. Bodroža (2011). Foreign direct investment attraction in Western Balkan countries: A case study from Serbia. International Scientific Conference: Young ScientistsNitra, Slovak Republic.

Estrin, S., and Uvalić, M. (2014). FDI into transition economies: Are the Balkans different? *Economics of Transition, 22*(2), 281–312.

European Bank for Reconstruction and Development (EBRD). (2013). *Stuck in transition: Transition Report 2013.* London: European Bank for Reconstruction and Development.

European Bank for Reconstruction and Development (EBRD). (2017). *Transition for all: Equal opportunities in an unequal world, Transition Report 2016–17.* London: European Bank for Reconstruction and Development.

European Commission. (2009). *The Western Balkans in transition.* Directorate-General for Economic and Financial Affairs, Occasional Paper No. 46. Brussels: European Commission.

International Labour Organization. (2012). *Global employment trends: Preventing a deeper job crisis.* Geneva: International Labour Organization.

Koczan, Z. (2016). *Being poor, feeling poorer: Inequality, poverty and poverty perceptions in the Western Balkans.* IMF Working Paper, No. 16/31. Washington, DC: IMF.

Kovtun, D., Meyer-Cirkel, A., Z. Murgasova, D. Smith, and S. Tambunlertchai (2014). Challenges and solutions for fostering job creation in the Balkans. In Schindler, M., Berger, H. Bakker, B., and Spilimbergo, A. (eds.), *Jobs and growth: Supporting the European recovery* (pp. pp. 125–150). Washington: International Monetary Fund.

Kuddo, A. (2013). *South East Europe Six: A comparative analysis of labor regulations.* Technical Note (August). Washington: World Bank.

Murgasova, Z., Ilahi, N., Miniane, J., Scott, A., Vladkova-Hollar, I., and IMF Staff Team (2015). *The Western Balkans: 15 years of economic transition.* IMF Regional Economic Issues Special Report. Washington, DC: IMF.

Ravallion, M., Chen, S., and Sangraula, P. (2009). Dollar a day revisited. *World Bank Economic Review, 23,* 163–184.

Sanfey, P., and Cviić, C. (2010). *In search of the Balkan recovery.* London: Hurst.

World Bank. (2016). *Poverty and shared prosperity 2016: Taking on inequality.* Washington, DC: World Bank.

Žugić, J. (2011). Foreign direct investment and global economic crisis in the Western Balkans. *Journal on European Perspectives of the Western Balkans, 1*(4), 69–90.

8

ECONOMIC GROWTH, INCOME DISTRIBUTION, AND SOCIAL EXCLUSION IN TURKEY

Anıl Duman and Alper Duman

8.1 INTRODUCTION

The worsening of income inequality across many countries and the slowdown in economic performance after the financial crisis shifted the focus of policy discussion towards the relationship between growth and distribution. There are various approaches in the literature examining how rising national incomes and economic performance can affect well-being in general and disadvantaged groups in particular (Ravallion and Chen, 2003; Dollar and Kraay, 2002; White, 2012). While the importance of high growth rates is undeniable, it has been also shown that policies that ensure a wide distribution of the benefits of growth are crucial for reducing poverty (White and Anderson, 2001; Lopez, 2004). Hence, policies that stimulate economic activity and provide all groups with greater access to markets and resources can generate both higher growth and lower inequality levels. This chapter investigates the inclusiveness of the Turkish growth experience and to what extent the country has been successful in fostering economic performance along with higher material and social well-being.

To this end, we first overview the long-term economic and political developments since the 1980s in Turkey. We take a long-term perspective as changes in polices and institutions impact on economic and social outcomes often with considerable lags. Then we examine the degree of income and institutional convergence between Turkey and European Union (EU) as well as trends in inequality and poverty. Turkey implemented various development strategies from the onset of the

Anıl Duman and Alper Duman, *Economic Growth, Income Distribution, and Social Exclusion in Turkey* In: *Europe's Income, Wealth, Consumption, and Inequality.* Edited by: Georg Fischer and Robert Strauss, Oxford University Press (2021).
© Oxford University Press. DOI: 10.1093/oso/9780197545706.003.0008

Republic, and integration into world markets has always been an important part, but increasingly so in the 1990s, similar to other less-developed countries. In that sense, the EU accession process and catching up can be viewed as one of the many attempts to achieve economic development. Due to reasons of data availability, we emphasize the post-2000 period in the analysis of income distribution and well-being. Our findings reveal major advancements in the standard of living in Turkey due to both higher average incomes and also to policies and international standards adopted in the early 2000s. Nevertheless, in the most recent era, there have been significant setbacks for certain groups in terms of regulatory environment, equality of opportunity, and access to markets and resources. Although there has been progress made in the overall distribution of income and other aspects of social inclusion, the persistently high inequality and poverty levels in Turkey can be taken as signs of weakness of inclusive growth and its sustainability. We argue that the exclusion of certain groups from the labour market, the lack of educational opportunities for the socioeconomically disadvantaged groups, and regional disparities are potential barriers to further growth and social inclusion.

8.2 ECONOMIC AND POLITICAL DEVELOPMENTS IN TURKEY

In the 1960s and 1970s, the Turkish government pursued an import substitution strategy to catch up with the gross domestic product (GDP) per capita levels of the United States and European countries.[1] However, firms barely managed to improve their competitiveness in the international markets and mostly focused on the well-protected domestic markets for their profitably. Additionally, imports of capital and intermediate goods remained very significant even during the import substitution industrialization era. Consequently, a balance of payment crisis at the end of the 1970s forced Turkey to change track. In the early 1980s, many developing countries switched from inward-oriented growth and industrialization strategies to more export-oriented and liberal programmes, either at their own discretion or under the conditionalities enforced by the International Monetary Fund (IMF) and the World Bank. China can be considered within the first group, and several Latin American countries, which opened-up their economies around the same time, in the second group. In the Turkish context, the change was partly voluntary and partly due to external pressure (Schick and Tonak, 1987; Arıcanlı and Rodrik, 1990; Boratav, 2009).

Immediately after the 1980 Coup, the military government started the current account liberalization process, moving from import substitution to export orientation. By the mid-1980s, import quotas were mostly removed, tariffs were reduced, and generous incentives were offered to exporters; thus trade

---

1   A brief overview of the governments, development strategies, and outcomes is provided in the Appendix.

liberalization has been almost completed. Nevertheless, the real success of rising exports depended on a strategy that required devaluation of the currency, dramatically suppressed domestic demand, and cuts in real wages (Boratav, 2009). Focusing on international competitiveness implied lower unit costs, which could be brought about by decreasing real wages in tradable sectors. Reducing agricultural support and introducing value-added tax in 1985 constrained domestic demand and thus allowed greater amounts of manufactured goods to be exported. In terms of foreign trade, these policies were effective, at least until the 2000s. Trade liberalization was followed by capital account liberalization and the convertibility of the Turkish lira (TL) in 1989. Capital account liberalization freed the movement of financial flows into and out of the country. Foreign exchange controls on capital outflows were removed, and both the current and capital accounts were completely liberalized. Capital account liberalization was concomitant to domestic financial market liberalization. Interest rate controls were abandoned in public banks, and foreign firms were allowed to operate in Turkish financial markets. These developments, accompanied by decreasing constraints on domestic financial markets, considerably transformed the Turkish economy. Figure 8.1 presents the performance of the Turkish economy between 1980 and the 2000s.

Since the completion of financial liberalization in 1989, the Turkish economy has been subject to a series of shocks and crises, mostly associated with boom–bust cycles of capital flows. This can also be seen from the erratic GDP growth performance after the opening of the capital account, as shown in Figure 8.1. Booms have been generally driven by an increase in capital flows, and, when these declined, the process was reversed, causing a parallel reduction in domestic demand. It can be said that, throughout the period, there has been an increase in

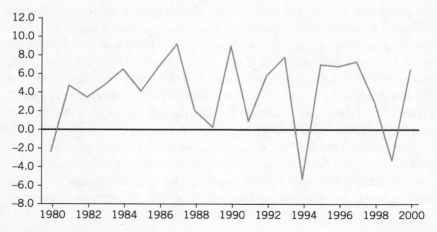

Figure 8.1 Gross domestic product (GDP) growth before 2000s.
Source: TURKSTAT.

the financial flows and growth of the economy. At the same time, import dependency of exports became a structural feature in the Turkish economy. As well as industrial sectors, the service sectors, such as construction and trade, have high imported input requirements (Duman and Özgüzer, 2012). Hence, overall, the Turkish economy became highly fragile in this period due to excessive reliance on capital inflows as well as imports.

The following decade of the 1990s was punctuated by the economic crises of 1994 and 2001 and characterized by relatively frequent changes in governments, particularly towards the end of the 1990s. During the 1980s, there had been only three Prime Ministers under two governments; the 1990s saw six Prime Ministers and six coalition governments with intense electoral competition and the return of the 1970s-style populism undermining macroeconomic stability. Discretionary favours, directed credits through the increasingly bloated public-sector banks, and rampant corruption exemplified the governance model of the 1990s and eventually led to the economic and political collapse of 2001 (World Bank, 2014). After the severe financial crisis in 2001, the Turkish economy experienced a rapid recovery, growing on average by 6.8% annually until 2008. However, since then, there have been major fluctuations, which can be considered a sign of inherent weakness of the development model adopted. Figure 8.2 shows the GDP growth rate between 2001 and 2016, and it can be seen that the average performance fell significantly after 2011.

Economic success in the early 2000s was largely the outcome of structural changes, greater integration into the world economy, and productivity increases. For instance, with 3% annual total factor productivity (TFP) growth between 2002 and 2006, Turkey outperformed many developing and developed countries in international rankings (Atiyas and Bakis, 2013). High productivity growth was

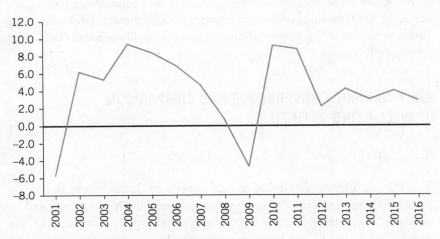

Figure 8.2 Gross domestic product (GDP) growth in Turkey.
Source: TURKSTAT.

mainly due to the structural transformation of employment from agriculture to manufacturing and services, which also had significant implications for labour markets. The underlying dynamics evolved around a continuous rural–urban migration pattern, in which the rate of urbanization increased from 59% in 1990 to 75% in 2015. Urbanization has contributed to domestic demand since urban incomes are on average almost three times higher than rural incomes. Moreover, after the 2001 crisis, the country's banking sector was heavily restructured and a series of regulations were adopted to manage risks prudentially. In this period, EU negotiations also contributed to the institutional framework of the country due to harmonization of many laws and regulations with EU standards. At the same time, Turkey improved its current account balance through exports to European markets. Last, unprecedented levels of foreign direct investment (FDI) entered the Turkish economy, reaching a historical peak in 2006, with net FDI inflows around 3.8% of GDP (World Bank, 2014).

As can be seen from Figure 8.2, the remarkable growth trajectory came to an end in 2008. Although the slowdown was partly a result of the global crisis and the sharp decline in exports to the EU countries, Turkey's internal weaknesses also played a large role (Acemoğlu and Üçer, 2015). First of all, the productivity gains in the earlier years disappeared, and both TFP and labour productivity stagnated after 2007; TFP was even estimated to be negative in all three sectors between 2007 and 2011 (Atiyas and Bakis, 2013). Labour market problems including low female labour force participation (LFP) the sizable in-formal sector, and the low-educated workforce began to slow the economic per-formance of the country after 2008. Despite strong growth rates in 2010 and 2011, the economy on average grew by only 3.4% in the period from 2009 to 2015. Moreover, Turkey's external deficit significantly worsened over time as Turkey lost its attractiveness for FDI in the post-crisis era. Rising inflation has been another threat to macroeconomic stability and equitable resource allo-cation. In the following section, we examine socioeconomic developments in Turkey within the EU context and discuss in more detail the factors behind its volatile performance.

8.3 ECONOMIC CONVERGENCE AND COMPARISON OF WELL-BEING WITH EU

8.3.1 Income and Institutional Convergence

8.3.1.1 Economic Performance of Turkey in Comparison to EU

Turkey and the European Union are in an engagement which may not end in marriage. Whatever the outcome of that engagement process turns out to be, the fates of Turkey and EU are interdependent. The EU economy is a major trade partner and the biggest investor in Turkey, and around 50% of all Turkish exports are destined for EU countries. Moreover, EU countries contribute 70% of total FDI stock in Turkey. Also, Turkey has recently become the key country for managing migrant flows into and out of EU countries. The long-lasting relationship started with the Ankara association agreement of 1959. In 1987, Turkey applied for membership to the European Economic Community, and, 10 years later, it was considered eligible for a negotiations process. Turkey joined the Customs Union in 1995, but integration with EU has slowed since then. Official accession negotiations, which were formally started in 2005, are currently at a standstill. Most of the issues regarding Turkey's accession troubles lie in its social and political institutions. With regards to economic indicators, the country is at par, if not superior relative to a number of current Member States that joined after 2000. Unfortunately, the much faster completion of application and acceptance processes for these states only served to increase the anti-EU sentiments within Turkey and weakened the negotiations further.

According to the World Bank, the Turkish economy has been exemplary and outperformed its peers over the past decades (World Bank, 2014). It managed to raise its share of global GDP from 0.6% in 1980 to 1.1% in 2016, and its growing middle class offers a lucrative emerging market for European firms. Taking a longer term view, from 1980 onwards, the economic convergence becomes more visible. As can be seen from Figure 8.3, in purchasing power parity (PPP) terms, Turkey's GDP per capita has risen from 18% of the EU average in 1980 to 33% in 2015. The partial success in convergence has been marked by highly volatile economic growth rates, as described in the previous section. Turkey's annual average GDP per capita growth rate was 2.8% for the period of 1960 to 2016, as

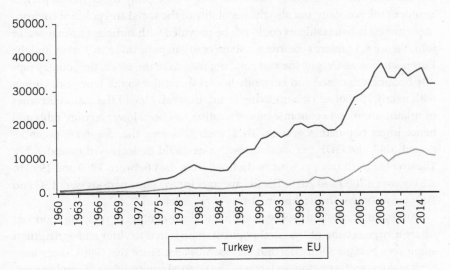

Figure 8.3 Income convergence between Turkey and EU (GDP PPP).
Source: World Development Indicators.

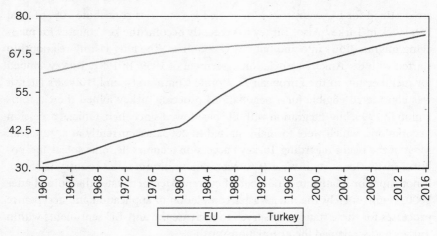

Figure 8.4 Convergence in urbanization (share of urban population in total, %).
Source: World Development Indicators.

opposed to EU's 2.29%. However, the standard deviations are dramatically different; 3.89 for Turkey, but merely 1.8 for the European Union. The institutional, social, and political stability of EU continues to ensure a smooth growth performance compared to Turkey, albeit at a slightly slower pace.

There are a number of reasons why the Turkish economy has been able to partially catch up with other European countries. The most striking convergence has been in terms of urbanization. As late as the 1980s, Turkey had a semi-rural economy, and the shift of people and resources from rural to urban areas marked a great transformation which paved the way for not only the dynamic performance of the economy, but also the instability of the social and political environment as new urban residents could not be provided with sufficient formal-sector jobs. Figure 8.4 presents the average share of urban population in Turkey and the European Union. Despite the vast rural population in the 1960s, the country rapidly became urbanized and currently has levels similar to the European Union, with nearly 75% of all citizens living in urban areas. One of the main outcomes of urbanization and economic modernization has been lower fertility rates and hence lower population growth. Thus, even achieving the long-term potential growth rate, the GDP per capita growth rate could be increased considerably. The average birth rate per woman declined from 4.44 between 1960 and 1999 to 2.23 between 2000 and 2015. The EU averages for the same periods were 1.98 and 1.53; nevertheless, the decline in Turkey is remarkable.

Turkey's urbanization process is similar to those of other developing countries where a large section of the rural population migrated to cities and agricultural employees became industrial and service workers. Since the 1980s, there have been major transformations in terms of the sectoral composition of employment. As can be seen from Table 8.1, the share of agricultural employment, previously

Table 8.1 Sectoral employment and employment status in Turkey (% of total employment)

	1985	1990	1995	2000	2005	2010	2015
Sectoral Employment							
Agriculture	46.9	46.8	44.1	36	25.5	23.3	20.6
Industry	25.3	20.3	22.1	24	27.2	27.7	27.2
Services	27.8	32.9	33.8	40	47.3	49.1	52.2
Employment Status							
Wage earners	40.4[a]	39	41.6	48.6	57	61	66.3
Employers	3.5[a]	4.5	5.4	5.1	5.5	5.3	4.5
Self-employed	25.9[a]	26.4	24.5	24.7	23.4	20.1	16.3
Unpaid family workers	30.2[a]	30.1	28.5	21.6	14.1	13.6	12.9

[a] Figures are for 1988.
Source: TURKSTAT.

more than 46%, diminished significantly to almost 20% in 2015. Industrial employment was stable and currently stands at 27.2%. On the other hand, service employment began to gain importance in the Turkish economy, with its share rising from 27.8% in 1985 to 52.2% in 2015. In 2015, wage earners constituted more than 66% of all employed people in Turkey, whereas the unpaid family workers' share declined from more than 30% in the mid-1980s to 12.9% in 2015.

Moreover, the dramatic increase in exports as a share of GDP in Turkey until 2001 can be seen from Figure 8.5. In that year, exports of goods and services peaked at 26% of GDP, compared to 34% in the same year for EU states: a

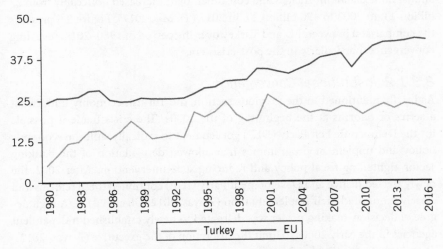

Figure 8.5 Export of goods and services (% of gross domestic product [GDP]).
Source: World Development Indicators.

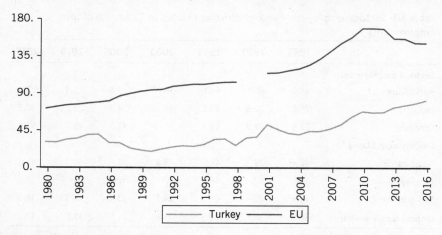

Figure 8.6 Financial deepening (total private credit to gross domestic product [GDP] ratio, %). *Source:* World Bank (2017a).

difference of 8%. Considering that, in 1980, the gap was as much as 20 percentage points, the degree of convergence is remarkable. After 2001, however, the momentum in Turkey slowed and the gap widened, mainly due to domestic and global crises disproportionately affecting the export sector. Last, after the capital account liberalization, financial services in Turkey developed significantly and domestic credit as percentage of GDP rose steadily from slightly less than 31% in 1980 to more than 81% in 2016. Levels have been always higher in the European Union, but the rate of growth in Turkey was much more rapid. As an example, households' access to finance has been dramatically extended, and previously almost nonexistent mortgages and consumer loans increased noticeably from 22 billion TL in 2002 to 470 billion TL in 2017 (TCMB, 2017). Figure 8.6 presents the comparison between EU and Turkey over the period of 1980–2016, revealing convergence, particularly in the post-crisis era.

8.3.1.2 *Institutional Convergence*

As briefly mentioned in the previous section, the Turkish economy underwent a series of reforms at the beginning of the 2000s. The crisis made it possible for the Democratic Left Party (DLP) government to radically shift the economic policy and implement programmes that allowed deregulation of the banking sector, tightening fiscal policy and reducing state intervention. After 2002, the newly elected Justice and Development Party (JDP) continued these reforms and closely monitored their implementation (Atiyas, 2012; Ülgen, 2013). A high degree of decision-making power was delegated to newly established independent agencies in the early 2000s to limit the discretion of the executive (Atiyas, 2012). They include the Public Procurement Authority, Energy Market Regulatory Authority, and Banking Regulatory and Supervision Agency among others.

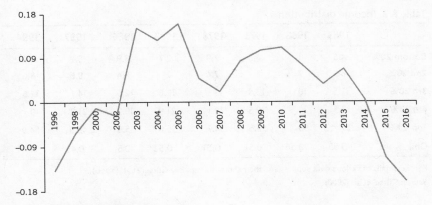

Figure 8.7 Rule of Law Index in Turkey.
Source: World Bank (2017b).

These were created to ensure enforcement of best practice to keep the governing of Turkish public and private markets in line with internationally compatible rules. Together with economic institutions, there has been a shift towards more comprehensive and inclusionary policymaking. For example, the property rights for non-Muslim religious foundations were improved, trade union rights were enhanced, bans on strikes were removed, and individuals were allowed to apply to the Constitutional Court when their freedoms of fundamental rights had been violated (Acemoğlu and Üçer, 2015). The reforms continued during the late 1990s and early 2000s, when the global crisis prompted improvements in institutional quality in Turkey.

There were two main benefits of the EU accession process. On the one hand, it contributed to attract sizable FDI to the country, especially during the first term of JDP government. On the other hand, EU rules and regulations were used as signals of state capacity, and a certain degree of institutional convergence was achieved at this time. However, as Figure 8.7 shows, in recent years, most of this progress has been reversed. The authoritarian turn in Turkish politics caused a decline in the Rule of Law Index, and, currently, Turkey stands at the same level as in 1996, indicating the accumulated losses in institutional quality. Moreover, voice and accountability[2] and control of corruption have deteriorated significantly after 2008. Indeed, the greatest gap between Turkey and EU has appeared in measures of voice and accountability despite the initial convergence in the first decade of the century. Given the importance of these areas for equality of opportunity in a society, it can be said that the deterioration in governance had

---

2   The Worldwide Governance Indicators project measures voice and accountability by looking at the perceptions of citizens in terms their participation in selecting the government, freedom of association, freedom of expression, and freedom of the media in a country.

Table 8.2 Income distribution

	1963	1968	1973	1978	1983	1986	1987	1994
Bottom 20%	4.5	3	3.5	2.9	2.7	3.9	5.2	4.9
2nd 20%	8.5	7	8	7.4	7	8.4	9.6	8.6
3rd 20%	11.5	10	12.5	13	12.6	12.6	14.1	12.6
4th 20%	18.5	20	19.5	22.1	21.9	19.2	21.2	19
Top 20%	57	60	56.5	54.7	55.8	55.9	49.9	54.9
Gini	0.55	0.56	0.51	0.51	0.52	0.5	0.43	0.49

For the details of various data sources and their shortcomings, see Gürsel et al. (2000).
Source: Gürsel et al. (2000).

a greater impact on economically and socially disadvantaged groups. This effect is examined in detail later.

8.3.2. Trends in Income Distribution and Well-Being
8.3.2.1 Income Inequality

The military rule that followed the 1980 coup transformed not only the political structure but also economic and social relations. A few studies examine Turkish income inequality before the 1980s, but their findings are highly clouded by issues of measurement and comparability. Table 8.2 presents income inequality measures for Turkey between 1963 and 1994. Until the late 1980s, distribution of income in Turkey was highly skewed and the share of the poorest 20% steadily decreased. A substantial improvement was achieved between 1983 and 1987, which can be mainly attributed to the growth in real wages that were heavily suppressed in the years immediately following the coup. Real wages fell nearly 50% between 1979 and 1984 due to austerity policies demanded by IMF stand-by agreements and also due to a ban on trade union activities by the military government (Ar, 2007; Sönmez, 2001). In 1984, a number of the restrictions against labour organizations were lifted, bringing a recovery in real wages, although they still lagged behind productivity increases (Boratav, 2009). Moreover, the newly elected civil government undertook a variety of initiatives such as public housing, cheap credit options, and social assistance programmes to enhance income distribution (DPT, 1989).

Even though these developments reduced inequality in the country as a whole, it persisted due to migration from rural to urban areas as a result of unfavourable policies towards the agricultural sector and competitiveness based on cheap labour. In addition to the current account openness that the Turkish government implemented in the post-coup era, it also liberalized the capital account in 1989. This move has arguably destabilized the Turkish economy via public sector overborrowing, overvaluation of currency, and a rapid increases in labour costs due to high inflation (Kepenek and Yentürk, 2011). Despite the growing macroeconomic imbalances, the governments maintained their populist policies through the 1989–1994 era, which resulted in massive crisis and economic contraction. The Gini coefficient rose to 0.49 in 1994, and nearly 50% of the increase can be attributed to a rise in interest incomes, whereas all the other factor incomes worked in the opposite direction (Gürsel et al., 2000).

The Turkish economy was highly unstable as it became more dependent on short-term capital flows and real-sector investment shrank due to lucrative financial rents. Consequently, there was a meltdown in the banking sector and currency devaluations in 2000 and 2001, giving way to extensive programmes designed and supported by IMF. There were three pillars of the agreement: public sector finance reform; social security, privatization, and restructuring of agricultural sector; and monetary policy anchored in nominal exchange rates (BSB, 2006). Changes in each of these areas had substantial effects on inequality and poverty. The real wages in the public sector declined by 27% and in the manufacturing sector by 20% during the crisis years of 2000 and 2001 (Ar, 2007). The rising tax burden on productive sectors such as industry led to unemployment and thus higher levels of poverty. Also the dismantling of public and social safety nets made the urban poor more vulnerable, increasing the risk of social exclusion.

This picture changed in the first half of the 2000s, as macroeconomic stability and growth coupled with improved social welfare programmes reduced income inequality and poverty. As can be seen from Table 8.3, economic inequality in Turkey declined noticeably until 2008.[3] The Gini fell from 0.44 in 2002 to 0.405 in 2008, a major achievement in such a short period. This also holds for the S80/S20 income quintile ratio; the ratio decreased from 10.8 in 2002 to 9.3 in 2008. Overall, the share for the poorest 20% of the population of the national income rose more than the share of the richest 20%. However, Turkey's income distribution was still much more unequal than EU countries on average, in terms of both the Gini coefficient and S80/S20 ratio, even considering the positive developments after 2002. On average, the European Union displayed a Gini of 0.309 in 2008, along with a ratio of 5 for lowest and highest quintile income shares. Some members, such as Bulgaria and Romania, as well as accession countries like Serbia and Macedonia, have Gini coefficients comparable to Turkey. In terms of the S80/S20 ratio, Serbian inequality is even more severe and Romania is very close to the Turkish level. Hence, prospects for a catch-up in terms of greater economic equality and resource allocation to the most disadvantaged segments of the population were limited at best.

After 2008, reductions in inequality have been less pronounced in Turkey, as can be seen from Figure 8.8. Indeed, inequality peaked in 2009 due to the

---

3 The spike in 2006 is due to the change in the data source used for calculating Gini coefficients in Turkey. While previously Household Budget Surveys were utilized, in 2006, TURKSTAT began to use Household Income and Living Conditions Survey to harmonize its data collection with that of the EU.

Table 8.3 Income distribution by quintiles

	Bottom 20%	2nd 20%	3rd 20%	4th 20%	Top 20%	Gini
2002	5.29	9.81	14.02	20.83	50.05	0.44
2003	6.00	10.28	14.47	20.93	48.32	0.42
2004	6.04	10.69	15.22	21.88	46.17	0.4
2005	6.05	11.08	15.83	22.60	44.44	0.38
2006	5.80	10.47	15.17	22.12	46.48	0.43
2007	6.38	10.93	15.44	21.79	45.46	0.41
2008	6.39	10.87	15.4	22	45.34	0.41
2009	6.18	10.72	15.26	21.85	46	0.42
2010	6.5	11.09	15.62	21.91	44.87	0.40
2011	6.5	11	15.5	21.9	45.2	0.40
2012	6.5	11	15.6	22	45	0.40
2013	6.6	10.9	15.4	21.8	45.2	0.40
2014	6.5	11	15.6	22.2	44.7	0.39
2015	6.29	10.85	15.54	22.02	45.3	0.40
2016	6.26	10.63	15.19	21.62	46.29	0.40

Source: TURKSTAT.

economic contraction, with a Gini coefficient of 0.415 according to TURKSTAT and Gini coefficient for the same year was 0.442 according to EUROSTAT figures. The global financial crisis seriously affected the country in terms of both lower export revenues from particularly European countries and a sharp fall in capital flows (Rodrik, 2012). Once growth recovered, the Turkish income

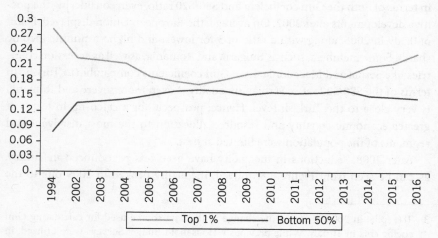

Figure 8.8 Income inequality.
Source: World Wealth and Income Database.

inequality saw another decline, but in 2016, the Gini coefficient returned to its pre-crisis level at 0.404. Figure 8.8 presents the share of top 1% households versus the share of bottom 50% households in national income over time. There were major improvements in the incomes of the bottom segment until the mid-2000s, and its share rose from 7.9% in 1994 to 16.2% in 2007. Since then, there has been a steady decline for the bottom 50%, which is accompanied by an increase in the incomes of the top 1%. In 2016, the top 1% of the population in Turkey received more than 23.4% of the national income, surpassing what they had at the beginning of the 2000s. The advancement in distribution was therefore temporary, and, after 2008, the gap began to get larger again.

The functional distribution of income is important for inequality dynamics. As the labour share decreased in most of the developed countries, inequality of income has worsened (Atkinson and Bourguignon, 2015). First, real wage growth in Turkey generally could not catch up with productivity gains, for which the minimum wage is a case in point. Officially, about 5 million receive the minimum wage, and a large proportion of workers are earning only slightly above that level. Hence, the minimum wage can serve as benchmark to gauge the standard of living of Turkish employees. Over the period of 1974–2014, real GDP per capita is estimated to have increased by 97% (Yüncüler and Yüncüler, 2016). If the minimum wage had kept pace with the GDP per capita growth, it would be expected to be 90% above its current level. This indicates the lack of statutory interventions by the government to advance the well-being of the majority of employees.

Labour markets and well-being are very closely associated in Turkey, similar to many other countries, particularly given the low level and coverage of non-market safety nets. Labour markets are among the most crucial determining factors of income distribution and poverty in Turkey. As mentioned in earlier sections, there was a dramatic upsurge in wage employment, and share of agriculture declined steadily since the 1980s. However, these developments were not accompanied by a proportional growth in the labour share. Figure 8.9 presents the distribution of national income between labour and capital, and it is puzzling that labour has been losing, despite the larger number of people becoming wage earners. The reduction in the labour share in Turkey is higher than in other emerging markets. Between 1995 and 2012, it has been estimated that Turkish wage earners as a group saw a decrease of nearly 17%, while the ratio in Mexico was 10%, and in Brazil approximately 2% (OECD, 2015). Since lower labour shares can have a negative impact on personal income inequality, the downward momentum in total wage bill can be considered a reason that distribution is so unequal. Moreover, the real average wages have persistently fallen throughout the 2000s in comparison to the 1990s, which can be taken as another labour market factor contributing to inequality and poverty.

Differences in non-wage incomes are also important for high inequality in Turkey, and the non-wage components form nearly 50% of total household

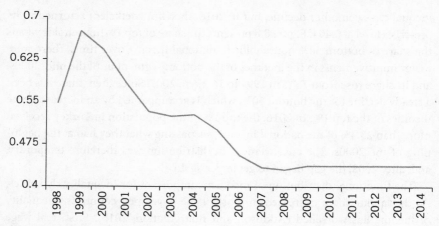

Figure 8.9 Labour share (% of gross domestic product ([GDP]).
Source: Penn World Tables.

income. Table 8.4 shows the growth rates of different types of incomes in three periods.[4] As can be observed, average total individual income rose by 1.15% annually between 1987 and 1994, whereas the labour income increased by 6.8%. The greatest change in this era was seen in interest incomes, with an average rise of 29.7%. In the next period, between 2002 and 2007, the growth rate of total income was higher, around 7.1%, and labour incomes rose by 7.4% per annum. Total income growth declined after 2007 to 2.4%, and a similar trend was observable for labour income, which increased only by 3.7%. The most remarkable change between pre- and post-2007 years in Turkey occurred with respect to average interest income. While in the first era the mean interest income declined significantly, by 13.4%, afterwards it recovered immediately and grew by 45.6% between 2007 and 2011.

Table 8.4 Annual growth rates of income types

	1987–1994	2002–2007	2007–2011
Total income	1.15	7.1	2.4
Labour income	6.8	7.4	3.7
Entrepreneurial income	−2.1	5.7	4.8
Interest income	29.7	−13.4	45.6
Transfers	1.2	6.2	3.2

Source: Authors' own calculations based on TURKSTAT data and Selim et al. (2014).

---

4   The table is indicative only because the survey structure after 2002 is different from the earlier period, and a direct comparison is difficult to make.

A possible factor behind this spectacular growth in interest after 2007 is rising indebtedness, especially from the corporate and household sectors. The interest rates increased considerably after the 2008 crisis, and higher borrowing boosted returns to capital owners (Duman and Duman, 2013). Additionally, financial assets are distributed in a dramatically unequal way in Turkey, where half of all bank deposits are held by only 120,000 people. Considering that total bank deposits accounted for 80% of GDP in 2016, the income accruing to these deposits presents a potentially large income basis. The real interest rates were above many other emerging markets in the 2000s, and the difference grew even greater after the 2008 global crisis. Coupled with the extremely skewed allocation of bank deposits among households and individuals, the higher interest rates in the late 2000s played a major role in the growth of inequalities in Turkey.

In addition to interest incomes, rental income due to unequal distribution of private housing is also important in Turkey. The real house price index in Turkey reached 122 in 2016, while the real estate market value decreased to 96.3 in the EU region over the same period (Figure 8.10). The construction boom after the global crisis of 2008, coincided with steeply rising real estate prices in many cities of Turkey and enabled property owners to increase their rental income and wealth dramatically. Unsurprisingly, the home ownership rate is lowest among the bottom quintile, indicating the limited gains from the real estate boom. Mass public housing projects failed to bring prices down and were only partially successful in producing affordable housing for poorer segments. Rents increased massively in major cities that continue to be prime migration destinations, and this issue was not addressed by policies to control the increase in rents. Overall, high interest rates and increasing rents caused the record level of indebtedness for low-income households in the 2000s, which tilted functional income distribution further against labour incomes.

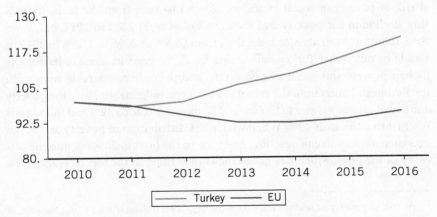

Figure 8.10 Real House Price Index.
Source: OECD Stats.

Table 8.5 Selected poverty and social exclusion indicators for Turkey

	2006	2007	2008	2009	2010	2011	2012	2013	2014	2015
Poverty rate	66.4	64.4	63.9	63.9	65.7	63.8	61.3	51.2	41.6	41.3
1st quintile	100	100	100	100	100	100	100	100	100	100
5th quintile	24	23.8	24.2	23.9	25.5	23.7	19.4	11.3	8.1	5.2
Severe deprivation rate	60.4	58.8	57.7	56.7	59.3	57.9	55	43.8	29.3	30.3
1st quintile	91.6	89.9	88.4	85.9	87.5	88.9	86.7	83.4	65.6	68.5
5th quintile	19.3	19.7	20	19.6	20.9	19.7	16	7.4	4	1.3

Source: EUROSTAT.

8.3.1.2 Poverty, Social Spending, and Redistribution

Data unavailability makes it difficult to compare Turkish inequality and poverty rates to European countries before the 2000s. Nevertheless, the few existing studies reveal that Turkey's income distribution was much more skewed than in European countries at the time. Portugal ranked at the top with a Gini coefficient of 0.371 in 1995, well below the one in Turkey, and various other measures show similar results (Rodrigues, 1999; Gürsel et al., 2000). Poverty rates in Turkey, on the other hand, are akin to several European countries. Indeed, Greece and Portugal displayed higher rates of poverty than Turkey in the 1990s, measured as 50% of median income. In the two former countries, 16.5% and 18% of their population were considered as poor, respectively, while Turkish rate was around 15.9% (Gürsel et al., 2000). However, it should be noted that if purchasing power is taken into account, deprivation is much more severe in Turkey than either Portugal or Greece whose median income is nearly three times higher.

Table 8.5 presents various indicators of poverty and deprivation in Turkey between 2006 and 2015. The first half of the table shows the percentage of people at risk of poverty or social exclusion.[5] As can be seen from the table, there is slow decline in the poverty and social exclusion from 2006 to 2012, but, since then, there has been a major reduction, from 66.4% in 2006 to 41.3% in 2015. It should be noted that Turkey ranked first for all the years in terms of having the highest poverty and social exclusion rate, and the only comparable country in the European Union until the recent era has been Bulgaria. In 2015, the poverty and social exclusion rates in Greece and Romania exceeded 35% and in Bulgaria reached to more than 40%. When we look at distribution of poverty and social exclusion across income quintiles, everyone in the bottom 20% fall into the category of the poor, which has not changed over time. In the top 20%, there is a

---

5   At risk of poverty or social exclusion (AROPE) is an indicator estimating the sum of persons who are either at risk of poverty, severely materially deprived, or living in a household with very low work intensity.

significant decline from a 24% poverty and social exclusion rate in 2006 to 5.2% in 2015. Nonetheless, these proportions are larger than in most EU Member States and hint at the greater risks of falling into poverty and social exclusion in Turkey even for people at the top income quantile.

The severe material deprivation indicator is based on the inability to pay for at least four listed items in a living conditions survey.[6] From Table 8.5, it becomes clear that, in Turkey, a substantial proportion of citizens are unable to afford basic consumption goods and services needed for quality of life. In 2006, the severe material deprivation rate was 60.4%, many percentage points above the EU average, and even worse than the highest Member State, Latvia, with 31.3%. Although, there was a reduction in severe material deprivation to 30.3% in 2015, convergence to European living standards is slow and a large section of Turkish people still lack the means to pay for a number of basic goods and services. The situation is more serious for the lowest income quintile since more than 90% were severely deprived in 2006, slowly declining to 68.5% in 2015. For the top quintile, the progress is more evident and only 1.3% of this group lack funds for the listed goods and services in 2015. In the same year, on average, 22% of EU citizens from the bottom and less than 1% of EU citizens from the top quintiles of income distribution were subject to severe material deprivation. Bulgaria had higher proportions of impoverishment for almost the entire period.

One of the main factors limiting Turkey's convergence in terms of income distribution and poverty is the public transfer and tax system. Social spending and progressive taxation are found to be positively related to economic equality and poverty alleviation across countries and over time (Atkinson et al., 1995; Kenworthy, 2011; Nolan and Marx, 2009). The countries with generous social protection and associated tax policies manage to reduce market inequalities, and one way to show this relationship is to compare pre-tax and transfer and post-tax and transfer indicators for income dispersion and deprivation. Table 8.6 presents the difference between Gini coefficients and relative poverty rates for Turkey before and after social transfers for the years 2006–2015. As can be understood from the table, public policy was successful in reducing both inequality and poverty, and over time their effectiveness increased. For instance, the Gini coefficient in Turkey was 0.502 in 2015, if social transfers including pensions were not considered. This ratio went down to 0.419 after transfers were taken into account, which means an 8.3-point decline in inequality. A similar effect is observable for poverty rates in 2015, where the pre-transfer share of 32% fell to 16.6% with government transfers.

The effectiveness of social transfer and tax policies in Turkey improved partly due to greater spending levels. Also, a number of reforms, especially in health

---

6 These items are to pay their rent, mortgage, or utility bills; to keep their home adequately warm; to face unexpected expenses; to eat meat or proteins regularly; to go on holiday; and to own a television set, a washing machine, a car, or a telephone.

Table 8.6 Reduction in inequality and poverty (2006–2015)

	Reduction in Gini	Reduction in poverty
2006	5.9	12.1
2007	5.8	12.5
2008	6.2	13.6
2009	6.6	13.8
2010	7.5	15.1
2011	7	14.4
2012	7.1	14.3
2013	7.4	15.6
2014	7.9	16.3
2015	8.3	16.6

Source: Authors' calculations based on EUROSTAT data.

and education, were undertaken in the 2000s to make public services more equitable and improve quality. The government also launched various programmes to provide social assistance and in kind benefits, as well as conditional cash transfers to the poor, the disabled, and families of soldiers serving compulsory military service (World Bank, 2014). As a result, social policy coverage increased significantly, and, with support from publicly funded health and education services, improvements were seen in the living standards of underprivileged groups. Nonetheless, the achievements are modest compared to EU countries. For EU states, the average reduction in Gini coefficient after social transfers is around 20 points and the average drop in poverty rate is nearly 28 percentage points. While market incomes are more skewed and a greater proportion is materially deprived than in Turkey before government intervention, European countries have been more successful in correcting these failures with tax and transfer policies.

This is partly due to the relatively low levels of social spending in Turkey despite recent improvements. Figure 8.11 shows total public expenditure in Turkey and the countries of the Organisation for Economic Cooperation and Development (OECD) from 1980 onwards. Turkish public spending as a percentage of GDP grew substantially from 4% to 13.5% during this era; however, this is well below the OECD average, rising from nearly 15% in 1980 to 21% in 2014. A big part of social disbursements go to pensions, but the pension system is tied to formal employment. Given the large share of the informal sector, many people are left out, and social security coverage is limited despite the expansion of spending (Buğra and Keyder, 2006). Thus, the Turkish government has not been able to reduce inequality and poverty as much as other European countries via social expenditures.

There are no administrative data by which to evaluate the impact of taxes on individual well-being and social welfare. The tax system in Turkey has a few

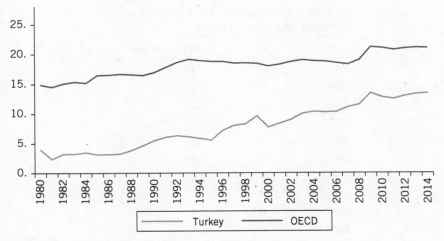

Figure 8.11 Social spending % of gross domestic product (GDP).
Source: OECD Stats.

shortcomings with regards to the extent of tax evasion and a high share of indirect taxes. Over time, total tax revenues in Turkey rose, reaching 30% of GDP as of 2015, which is in line with OECD averages. However, taxes on corporate income, profits, and capital gains constitute less than 6% of all tax revenue while more than 44% of the proceeds are derived from taxes on goods and services (OECD, 2017a). In addition, the share of indirect taxes has increased, particularly after 2002, whereas revenue from taxes income, profits, and other sources of direct taxation lost weight in the same period. Tax composition and social inequalities are closely related, as the burden of excise tax payments falls on the lower income groups due to larger shares of their budgets allocated to goods and services. The impact of the value-added tax and private excise tax is 2.5 times greater for the poorest centile in comparison to richest (Zenginobuz et al., 2010). Hence, the taxation system, with its reliance on indirect taxes and its narrow base, is one of the factors hampering income distribution and impairing the living conditions of disadvantaged segments. The next section particularly looks at groups that suffer most from the lack of inclusionary policies and the end of trickle-down economics by the mid-2000s.

8.4 SOCIAL EXCLUSION IN TURKEY

8.4.1 Labour Market Disparities

While there have been improvements in the average incomes in Turkey, there are still major discrepancies across social groups. Female LFP and employment opportunities are persistently lower in Turkey, which puts women in a more

Table 8.7 Gender gap in labour force participation (LFP) and unemployment rates

	LFP	Unemployment
2000	47.1	−0.3
2001	45.8	−1.2
2002	43.7	−1.3
2003	43.8	−0.6
2004	47	0.2
2005	47.3	0.7
2006	46.3	1.2
2007	46.2	1
2008	45.6	0.9
2009	44.5	0.4
2010	43.2	1.6
2011	42.9	2.1
2012	41.5	2.3
2013	40.7	3.2
2014	41	2.9
2015	40.1	3.4
2016	39.5	4.1

Source: Authors' calculations based on TURKSTAT data.

vulnerable position than men. Table 8.7 shows differences in LFP and unemployment rates for men and women in Turkey. It can be seen that not only are women less likely to become wage earners, they also are subject to higher levels of unemployment. Despite an improvement in the LFP rate for females between 2000 and 2016, the gap remains sizable. For example, LFP of women was around 26.5% in 2002 and only increased to 32.5% in 2016; yet male LFP was on average nearly 70% for the entire period. Unpaid family workers were mainly women, and, after agricultural shedding, these had difficulty finding jobs in cities due to low skills and insufficient childcare service (Goldin, 1994; Mammen and Paxson, 2000). It should be noted that female LFP in the Turkey is not only the lowest among European states, but the gender gap is high even for emerging market economies. For example, the participation rates were around 44% in South Africa and 43.7% in Mexico in 2016 (World Bank, 2017a). Moreover, women on average earn almost 15% less than men in similar jobs, which is higher than the OECD average. Female workers are also given lower quality jobs; in 2014, it was found that 48% were employed in the informal sector, compared 29% for men (OECD, 2016).

The unemployment rate was more severe for women, and the percentage difference between women and men peaked in 2016, with 4.1 points. Although women in Turkey were subject to lower levels of unemployment at the very beginning of the 2000s, this trend was reversed in 2004. The gender gap persists in employment rates among the younger cohorts, thus suggesting that the younger female labour market participants are experiencing negative conditions due to both their gender and age (Duman, 2014). Last, unemployment among university graduates is much higher than the national average for both genders, but there is still a considerable difference between men and women, suggesting that even highly educated female workers in Turkey are not well protected against labour market risks. Given the importance of the labour market for individual well-being, the lack of participation and employment opportunities puts women in a disadvantaged position in Turkey.

Another widely disadvantaged segment in Turkish labour markets are the informal sector employees. Economic composition in Turkey is quite distinctive from the rest of Europe in terms of the high degree of dualization attributable to formal and informal sectors. At the beginning of the 2000s, the informal sector represented slightly more than 50% of all employment in Turkey, falling to 33% in 2016, as can be seen from Figure 8.12. The biggest drop was achieved in rural employment. However, there was also a decline in informal employment in urban sites and nonagricultural sectors between 2000 and 2016. Even though informality appears to be higher than EU averages, Turkey is at par with economies that have comparable income levels, such as Mexico, Bulgaria, and Romania (Elgin and Schneider, 2013). The decrease in the share of informal sector jobs contributes positively to income distribution since informal sector wages are typically much lower than the formal ones. However, informality is still much more common among female and younger workers, which aggravates earning inequalities among individuals with similar labour market characteristics. The

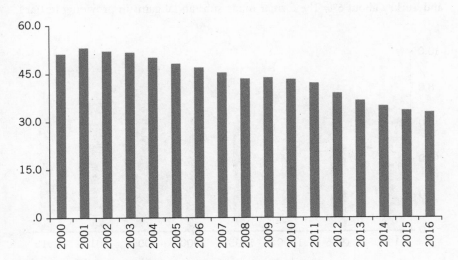

Figure 8.12 Informal employment in Turkey (% of total employment).
Source: TURKSTAT.

main reason for a higher share of women in the informal sector continues to be unpaid family employment. For younger workers, the barriers to enter into the labour market and the greater risk of unemployment are among the key factors (Tansel and Kan, 2011). Last, as mentioned earlier, the bulk of social transfers in Turkey are pensions, which require formal labour market attachment; thus, informal employees are excluded.

8.4.2 Access to Education and Educational Outcomes

One of the main determinants of income is human capital, and the key qualification for this is education. Turkey has steadily upgraded the human capital of its population and its labour force. Currently, enrolment in primary education is almost universal, and the gender gap has disappeared at this level. In secondary education, enrolment rates have almost doubled, from 38% in 1998 to 67% in 2012, and the gender differences were cut from around 9 to just 1.5 percentage points (World Bank, 2014). Average years of education have increased from less than 4 years in 1980 to almost 8 years in 2015, as can be observed from Figure 8.13. Nevertheless, it is still considerably behind the EU average and some of its peers, such as Poland, where average length of education for the entire population has almost reached 10 years, thus leaving Turkey a long way to go if it is to catch up.

Since the major attempts to upgrade the educational attainment occurred recently, the performance of older generations is still comparatively low. For instance, obligatory education up to 12 years was only introduced in 2013. Higher education has become more accessible and expanded dramatically after 2002. However, the outcome is still not as successful as in European counterparts. Both Poland and Turkey started from very low bases in 1997: Poland at 10% and Turkey about 6%. The former made substantial gains in providing tertiary

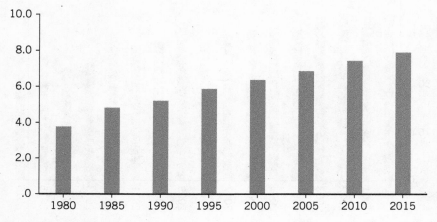

Figure 8.13 Educational attainment.
Source: Lee and Lee (2016)

education for the relevant age groups, while Turkey lagged significantly behind. By 2016, the proportion of 24- to 35-year-olds participating in university education was nearly 45% in Poland as opposed to 30% in Turkey (OECD, 2017b). Also, the returns to university education have been declining in Turkey, especially for women, although there are still gains to additional years of schooling (Tansel, 2016). Equally importantly, the unemployment rate among university graduates is higher than that of lower secondary school graduates. For example, in 2016, the unemployment rate among tertiary educated workers was 12%, higher than that of less educated employees. Another major problem related to youth lies in the high rates of inactivity, since about 30% of 15- to 29-year-olds are neither in employment nor in education and training (NEET) in Turkey. Figure 8.14 presents the share of NEET for both the entire age group and for females. It can be immediately seen that there is an improvement in terms of share of youth in education or employment since 1997. The ratio was almost 38% for the total group, but for women, it was extremely high, around 59%. In 2016, the shares declined to 28.2% and 41.5%, respectively. The current figures of NEET in Turkey are similar to those of some other European countries, such as Greece and Spain, which saw dramatic rises after 2008 financial crisis. However, the proportion of the young female population that is NEET in Turkey is still extremely high despite a decline over the years. In addition to being a female, residing in Eastern and South Eastern regions of Turkey and belonging to the poorest households greatly increase the likelihood of youth being in NEET.

Intergenerational mobility in education is low in Turkey, which ranks second lowest among OECD countries, with 66% of survey participants having the same educational attainment as their parents. In other words, Turkey has the lowest intergenerational social mobility among OECD countries, except for Slovakia. The outlook becomes even bleaker when we consider that, among this group,

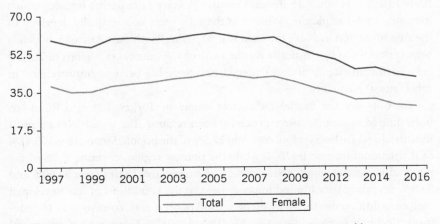

Figure 8.14 Not in employment, education, or training (NEET) 15- to 29-year-olds.
Source: OECD Stats.

Turkey already has the lowest level of mean educational attainment among the OECD sample (Aslankurt, 2013). Finally, access to education is quite unequal among different income groups. It has been shown that, on average, the poorest 20- to 24-year-old cohort has 5.1 years of education in Turkey and the richest, 11.56 years (United Nations, 2017). The schooling gap is much smaller for other middle-income countries, where the bottom earning groups generally receive more years of education. Obviously, poor households can afford schooling far less than the richer households, and free public education alone is not sufficient to compensate for the private expenditures. There is also an enormous gap in terms of performance among different high schools and universities (Eğitim Reformu Girişimi, 2017). Thus, children of richer households not only access educational facilities more easily but also enjoy far better quality. Last, after graduation, finding a job in the labour market still predominantly involves social networks, again giving richer households major advantages.

8.4.3 Regional Divergence

As mentioned earlier in the chapter, rural-to-urban migration in Turkey had important labour market consequences, which translated into sectoral transformation of the economy and, to a certain extent, diminished informality. Nonetheless, the sizable and persistent regional differences in income inequality and poverty remain. A number of reasons are offered to shed light on the growth variances within the country, such as uneven distribution of public investments, inadequate human capital, and sectoral composition (Çelebioğlu and Dall'erba, 2010; Tansel and Güngör, 2000; Deliktaş et al., 2008). Provinces with a mean income of more than 18,909 TL in 2015 are heavily concentrated in North-Western and Western regions of Turkey. The Eastern and South-Eastern regions, on the other hand, had the lowest levels of mean income, between 8,089 TL and 11,695 TL. The gap between the richest (Ankara) and the poorest (Diyarbakır) cities was 2.8 times in 2015. Figure 8.15 displays relative poverty rates across regions, which indicates a similar picture. While less than 3% were economically deprived in the Aegean region in 2016, the ratio was 33.5% in South East Anatolia, which is heavily populated by ethnically Kurdish citizens. A number of regions in Turkey have been consistently underprivileged, and there has been no improvement in this regional inequality.

Not only are the spatial differences ample in Turkey, but also there has been limited economic convergence between regions. The wealthiest and most industrialized Turkish region, covering 27.5% of the population, received 58.46% of the national income in 2004, while the poorest region, covering 8.2% of the population, received only 4.8%. In 2014, the respective shares were 58.99% and 5.08%, revealing very limited improvement in the conditions of less developed regions. Additionally, the share of the second poorest area, consisting of 16 provinces, declined from 5.32% to 5.13% (Özkul, 2017). There have been several attempts made at regional development by the Turkish government during the

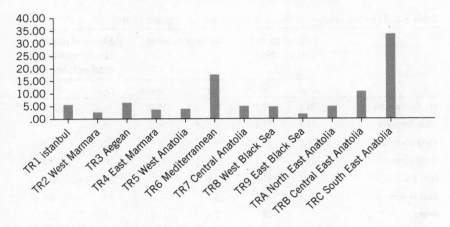

Figure 8.15 Poverty rates across regions (2016).
Source: TURKSTAT.

period from 2002 and 2016; however, the allocation of investments was uneven, and, as a result, the programmes had very limited success in reducing spatial disparities. Between 2012 and 2015, the JDP government invested 309 billion TL nationally, and the wealthiest region, including Istanbul, took the lion's share of 35%. This was followed by other developed regions in Western Turkey, leaving the least developed region with a mere 5% of all supported investments (Sönmez, 2016). The incentive mechanism was not effective, as investments in the poorest regions have been discouraged for security reasons emanating from the Kurdish conflict. Hence, the lower income regions are trapped in a vicious cycle of under-investment and lack of economic opportunities, leading to the outward migration of young and relatively skilled workers.

Table 8.8 provides a number of labour market indicators across Turkish regions, and it can be seen that there are rampant spatial differences. While the average unemployment rate was 10.1% for Turkey, in Southeast Anatolia, Istanbul, the Mediterranean, and Central Anatolia, the risk of unemployment was greater. In addition, more serious gender inequalities in labour markets exist in several regions. For instance, LFP for men is higher than for women across Turkey, but the gender gap is much larger in South East Anatolia. As well as the staggeringly low participation rate of female workers, less than 20%, they are also subject to greater chances of job loss in the region. The unemployment rate for the small proportion of working women in Southeast Anatolia is around 19%, which is well above any other group. Moreover, the share of unpaid family workers in total employment varies across regions, and, in a number of places, it accounts for half of all female employees. In Northeast Anatolia more than 66% of women and 41% of men are unpaid family workers, suggesting that they are unable to benefit from public services related to labour market contributions.

Table 8.8 Selected labour market indicators across regions (2016)

	Labour force participation		Unemployment		Share of unpaid family workers in total employment	
	Male	Female	Male	Female	Male	Female
Mediterranean	70.4	31.7	10	15.8	19.6	27.7
West Anatolia	73.8	31.2	7.9	14.5	8.5	14.5
West Black Sea	69.5	37.2	6.7	9.3	30.5	55.7
West Marmara	71.3	35.3	5.2	11	20.3	29.2
East Black Sea	67.7	41.3	4.6	4.4	30.5	39
East Marmara	72.3	31.7	8.3	13.6	10	16.4
Aegean	71.4	37.1	7.3	12.9	18.4	31.1
Southeast Anatolia	69	19.5	18.6	18.9	18.3	26.8
Northeast Anatolia	68.5	32.4	5.2	4.4	41.2	66.5
Central Anatolia	72.1	29.7	8.5	15	24	45.5
Middle East Anatolia	65.1	26.5	9.2	8.7	26.3	53.8
Istanbul	77.4	35.5	11.8	17.3	0.8	2.9

Source: TURKSTAT.

In addition to rural-to-urban migration in Turkey, there were episodes until the end of the 1980s when considerable numbers left the country to work mainly in Europe. This pattern changed first with migrants entering Turkey from ex-Soviet countries, some of whom chose to stay and work in the informal sector. There is no official figure indicating the size of this group, but the total number of immigrants is argued to reach almost 1 million (Toksöz et al., 2012). Syrian migrants form the biggest migrant community, with 2.5 million as of 2015, and in certain provinces they have become the majority. Only 6,000 have work permits; however, employment rates are much higher in the informal sector. Syrians are often employed in agriculture and the construction and garment industries at wages below native averages and without social security coverage (Erdoğan and Ünver, 2015). Native Turkish unskilled employees, particularly women, faced higher unemployment and lower earnings due to Syrian migration (Del Carpio and Wagner, 2015). Given that the already disadvantaged segments of the population—less-educated, females, and younger workers—suffer disproportionately from the influx of migrants to Turkey, the income inequality and poverty are expected to grow as a result.

8.5 CONCLUSION

Turkey has successfully transformed its inward-looking and largely agricultural economy in the past 35 years into an export-oriented and urban-based economy.

The transformation has been achieved mostly in periods of dramatic reform embedded in business and political cycles. Nevertheless, there has only been partial success in terms of income convergence to EU standards. The biggest contributor to this success has been the structural change in the economy, shifting resources from agriculture into industry and services. The concomitant process of urbanization also enabled governments to deliver better public services. The Customs Union agreement in 1995 and the EU candidate application in 1999 increased international integration, thus enhancing the growth performance of the Turkish economy. The macroeconomic stability and institutional improvement after the 2001 crises led to an acceleration in the convergence process.

Income inequality improved partially, and poverty rates have declined, especially until 2008. However, convergence to EU standards is not easy to observe in these indicators. Moreover, the institutional backlash after the 2008 global crisis, as well as the recent structural weaknesses of the Turkish economy, has thrown doubt on the sustainability of Turkish growth performance. High inflation and unemployment rates, a low female labour participation rate, continued informality, and high NEET levels among youth are some of the structural weaknesses to be overcome in the near future. The dependency on foreign capital inflows, coupled with the lack of state capacity in terms of fostering well-paid employment for the younger generation, upgrading the human capital of the labour force, and improving regional inequality mean that it will be challenging even to maintain the partial success of growth and convergence to the European Union.

REFERENCES

Acemoğlu, D., and Üçer, M. (2015). *The up and downs of Turkish growth, 2002–2015: Political dynamics, the European Union and the institutional slide.* NBER Working Paper, No. 21608. Cambridge, MA: National Bureau of Economic Research.

Aldan. A., and Yüncüler. G. (2016). Real wages and the business cycle in Turkey. *TCMB Working Paper*, No. 1706, Ankara.

Ar, K. N. (2007). *Küreselleşme Sürecinde Türkiye'de Ücretlerin Gelişimi.* Ankara: Kamu-İş Yayınları.

Arıcanlı, T., and Rodrik, D. (1990). *Political economy of Turkey: Debt, adjustment and sustainability.* Cambridge, MA: Harvard University Press.

Aslankurt, B. (2013). Intergeneration mobility in education. http://www.tepav.org.tr/upload/files/1361799155-7.Intergenerational_Mobility_in_Education_How_Does_Turkey_Compare.pdf

Atiyas, İ. (2012). Economic institutions and institutional change in Turkey during the Neoliberal Era. *New Perspectives on Turkey, 14*, 45–69.

Atiyas, İ., and Bakış, O. (2013). *Aggregate and sectoral TFP growth in Turkey: A growth accounting exercise*. REF Working Paper, No. 2013-1, Istanbul.

Atkinson, A., and Bourguignon, F. ed. (2015). *Handbook of income distribution (Vol. 2A)*. Amsterdam: Elsevier.

Atkinson, A., and Bourguignon, F. ed. (2015). *Handbook of income distribution (Vol. 2B)*. Amsterdam: Elsevier.

Atkinson, A., Rainwater, L., and Smeeding, T. (1995). *Income distribution in OECD countries*. OECD, Paris.

Boratav, K. (2009). *Türkiye İktisat Tarihi*. Ankara: İmge Kitabevi.

BSB. (2006). BSB İktisat Grubu. http://www.bagimsizsosyalbilimciler.org/ Yazilar_BSB/BSB2006_Final.pdf

Buğra, A., and Keyder, Ç. (2006). The Turkish welfare regime in transformation. *Journal of European Social Policy*, *16*(3), 211–228.

Çelebioğlu, F., and Dall'erba, S. (2010). Spatial disparities across the regions of Turkey: An exploratory spatial data analysis. *Annals of Regional Science*, *45*, 379–400.

Del Carpio, X. V., and Wagner, C. M. (2015). *The impact of Syrian refugees on the Turkish labour market*. Policy Research Working Paper, No. 7402. Washington, DC: World Bank.

Deliktaş, E., Önder, O., and Karadağ, M. (2008). The spillover effects of public capital on the Turkish private manufacturing industries in the geographical regions. *Annals of Regional Science*, *43*, 365–378.

Dollar, D., and Kraay, A. (2002). Growth is good for the poor. *Journal of Economic Growth*, *7*, 195–225.

DPT. (1989). Altıncı Beş Yıllık Kalkınma Planı. http://www.dpt.gov.tr/ PortalDesign/PortalControls/WebIcerikGosterim.aspx?Enc=83D5A6FF03C 7B4FC1D20ECF6C1940897

Duman, A. (2014). *Labour market institutions, policies, and performance: Flexibility and security in Turkey*. EAF Report, No. 14-01. İstanbul: Koç University.

Duman, A., and Duman, A. (2013). *Household debt in Turkey: The critical threshold for the next crisis*. 1st World Keynes Conference: Attacking the Citadel Conference Proceeding, Izmir.

Duman, A., and Özgüzer, G. (2012). Input-output analysis of rising imports in Turkey. *Ekonomik Yaklaşım*, *23*(84), 39–54.

Eğitim Reformu Girişimi. (2017). Eğitim İzleme Raporu, 2016–2017. http:// www.egitimreformugirisimi.org/egitim-izleme-raporu-2016-17/ on

Elgin, C., and Schneider, F. G. (2013). *Shadow economies in OECD Countries: DGE vs. MIMIC approaches*. Bogazici University Department of Economics Working Papers, No: 2013/13. Istanbul: Bogazici University.

Erdoğan, M., and Ünver, C. (2015). *Türk İş Dünyasının Türkiye'deki Suriyeliler Konusundaki Görüş, Beklenti ve Önerileri*. Ankara: TİSK.

Goldin, C. (1994). The U-shaped female labour force function in economic development and economic history. NBER Working Paper, No. 4707. Cambridge, MA: National Bureau of Economic Research.

Gürsel, S., Levent, H., Selim, R., and ve Sarıca, Ö. (2000). *Bireysel Gelir Dağılımı ve Yoksulluk: Avrupa Birliği ile Karşılaştırma*. TÜSIAD Report, No. 2000–12, Istanbul.

Kenworthy, L. (2011). *Progress for the poor*. Oxford: Oxford University Press.

Kepenek, Y., and Yentürk, N. (2011). *Türkiye Ekonomisi*. İstanbul: Remzi Kitabevi.

Lee, J.-W., and Lee, H. (2016). Human capital in the long-run. *Journal of Development Economics, 122,* 147–169.

Lopez, J. H. (2004). *Pro-poor growth: A review of what we know (and of what we don't know)*. Washington, DC: World Bank.

Mammen, K., and Paxson, C. (2000). Women's work and economic development. *Journal of Economic Perspectives, 14*(4), 141–164.

OECD. (2015). *The labour share in G20 Economies*. Paris: OECD.

OECD. (2016). The *employment outlook*. Paris: OECD.

OECD. (2017a). Revenue Statistics. https://stats.oecd.org/Index.aspx?DataSetCode=REV

OECD. (2017b). Education at a Glance. http://www.oecd.org/edu/education-at-a-glance-19991487.htm

Özkul, İ. (2017). Bölgesel eşitsizlik azalmadı sadece geri iller arası denge değişti. *Dunya.com.* http://www.dunya.com/kose-yazisi/bolgesel-esitsizlik-azalmadi-sadece-geri-iller-arasi-denge-degisti/345057

Ravallion, M., Chen, S., and Sangraula, P. (2007). *New evidence on the urbanization of global poverty*. World Bank Policy Research Working Paper, No. 4199. Washington, DC: World Bank.

Rodrigues, C. F. (1999). *Income distribution and poverty in Portugal*. CISEP, ISEG/Universidade Técnica de Lisbao. Lisbon: Universidade Técnica de Lisbao.

Rodrik, D. (2012). The Turkish economy after the crisis. *Ekonomi-Tek, 1,* 41–61.

Schick, I., and Tonak, A. ed. (1987). *Turkey in transition*. Oxford: Oxford University Press.

Sönmez, M. (2001). *Gelir Uçurumu, Türkiye'de Gelirin Adaletsiz Bölüşümü*. İstanbul: Om Yayınevi.

Sönmez, M. (2016). Regional inequalities in Turkey not easing. *Hurriyet Daily News.* http://www.hurriyetdailynews.com/regional-inequalities-in-turkey-not-easing-.aspx?pageID=238&nID=99507&NewsCatID=344

Tansel, A. (2016). *Returns to education in Turkey: IV estimates from a developing country*. Economic Research Forum Working Paper, No. 23. Giza: Economic Research Forum.

Tansel, A., and Güngör, A. D. (2000). *Provincial Inequalities in School Enrollments in Turkey*. Economic Research Forum Working Paper, No. 2003. Giza: Economic Research Forum.

Tansel, A., and Kan, E. O. (2011). *Labour mobility across the formal/informal divide in Turkey: Evidence from individual level data.* MPRA Paper, No. 35672. Munich: Munich Personal RePEc Archive.

TCMB. (2017). Finansal Hesaplar Raporu. http://www.tcmb.gov.tr/wps/wcm/connect/49207310-0b03-4872-b51c-299f24b8d82c/2017-I.%C3%87eyrek.pdf

Toksöz, G., Erdoğdu, S., and Kaşka, S. (2012). *Irregular labour migration in Turkey and situation of migrant workers in the labour market.* Stockholm: International Organization for Migration.

Ülgen, S. (2013). *The political economy of reform in Turkey and its relevance for the Arab world.* Mimeo. Washington, DC: World Bank.

United Nations. (2017). Global education report. http://www.education-inequalities.org/indicators/eduyears?sort=mean&dimension=wealth_quintile&group=all&age_group=eduyears_20&countries=all

White, H., and Anderson, E. (2001). Growth vs. redistribution: Does the pattern of growth matter? *Development Policy Review, 19*(3), 167–289.

White, W. R. (2012). Policy debate: How do you make growth more inclusive? In L. de Mello and M. A.Dutz (eds.), *Promoting inclusive growth: Challenges and policies* ((pp. 279–283). Paris: OECD Publishing.

World Bank. (2014). *Turkey's transitions: Integration, inclusion, institutions.* Washington, DC: World Bank.

World Bank. (2017a). World Development Indicators. http://data.worldbank.org/indicator/BX.KLT.DINV.WD.GD.ZS?end=2015&locations=TR&start=1999

World Bank. (2017b). Worldwide Governance Indicators. http://databank.worldbank.org/data/reports.aspx?source=worldwide-governance-indicators

WID. (2017). World Income Database. http://wid.world/country/turkey/

Zenginobuz, Ü., Adaman, F., Gökşen, F., Savcı, Ç, and Tokgöz, E. (2010). *Vergi, Temsiliyet ve Demokrasi İlişkisi Üzerine Türkiye'de Vatandaşların Algıları.* Istanbul: Açık Toplum Vakfı.

APPENDIX 8.1
OVERVIEW OF ECONOMIC AND POLITICAL DEVELOPMENTS
IN TURKEY

Period	Government	Economic Strategy	Balance of Payments	Growth	Distribution
1960–1980	Democratic Party Republican People's Party Justice Party	Import substitution	Deficit	High	High inequality
1980–1983	Military rule	Domestic and international market liberalization	Deficit (but declining)	Low	High inequality
1984–1989	Motherland Party	Export-led	Deficit (but declining)	Moderate	High inequality
1989–1998	Coalition governments	Customs Union	High deficits	Moderate	Increasing inequality
1999–2001	Coalition governments	Crisis	High deficits	Low	Declining inequality
2002–2007	Justice and Development Party	Washington Consensus and EU candidacy	Deficits (increasing exports)	High	Declining inequality
2008–	Justice and Development Party	Authoritarian/ Populist	High deficits	Moderate	Increasing inequality

9

EDUCATION, INCOME, AND INEQUALITY IN THE EUROPEAN UNION

Anneleen Vandeplas

9.1 INTRODUCTION

Educational attainment has risen considerably across Europe over the past century. Most countries in Europe had introduced compulsory schooling laws by 1900. Over the first half of the 20th century, up to the 1960s and 1970s, the length of compulsory schooling was steadily extended (see, e.g., Garrouste, 2010; Gathmann et al., 2015). Rising educational attainment not only resulted from policy changes. Strong productivity gains, economic growth, and the development of welfare states supported rising living standards in the postwar period and freed up more time for study.[1] Moreover, structural changes in the economy, such as the shift from agriculture to manufacturing, generated a demand for more highly skilled workers. At the same time, the strong development of human capital over this period was a key driver of the observed productivity increases, so causality runs in both directions (Schultz, 1961; Arrow, 1962; Lucas, 1988).

Nevertheless, several countries in the European Union (EU) continue to show substantial gaps in upper secondary attainment, a level that is widely considered

---

1 The period from 1948–1973 (from the end of the war until the oil crisis which triggered a recession) is sometimes also referred to as the 'Golden Age of economic growth' (Vonyó, 2008).

Anneleen Vandeplas, *Education, Income, and Inequality in the European Union* In: *Europe's Income, Wealth, Consumption, and Inequality.* Edited by: Georg Fischer and Robert Strauss, Oxford University Press (2021). © Oxford University Press.
DOI: 10.1093/oso/9780197545706.003.0009

among policymakers as the minimum for successful integration in the labour market and society as a whole (Section 9.2.1). Moreover, strong variation in the level of foundation skills is observed among tertiary graduates in different countries, pointing at remaining challenges in terms of quality of the provided education (Section 9.2.2).

Ongoing economic and societal changes are set to exacerbate the negative consequences of remaining education and skills gaps. Broadly observed processes such as skills-biased technological change and deroutinization are reinforcing the role of educational attainment as a driver of employment and living standards (Section 9.3). While labour productivity is positively related with tertiary attainment among the workforce, it is more strongly related to the share of high-skilled jobs in the economy. This suggests that, to realize the benefits of higher attainment, educational attainment must coincide with the acquisition of relevant skills—hence quality matters—and economic policies, institutions, and investments which foster the creation of jobs that effectively use these skills.

The strengthening nexus between education and life outcomes calls more loudly than ever for providing equal educational opportunities to every individual if we are to safeguard social mobility, a crucial dimension of societal fairness. While social mobility is difficult to measure, the available proxies do not seem to point toward a general deterioration in equality of educational opportunities over the past 15 years. A majority of countries in Europe have seen tertiary attainment become more accessible and less contingent on parental background as a result of the expansion of tertiary attainment (Section 9.4.1). Beyond opportunities for initial education, access to learning opportunities for adults is essential as well. Strikingly, adult learning opportunities tend to be scarcer in those societies with the strongest penalty (in terms of labour market outcomes) for low qualifications (Section 9.4.2).

Educational outcomes—and their links with labour market outcomes—come about through a complex interplay of factors. Many of the differences across Member States in terms of educational attainment can be traced back to the structures of their education systems, their economies, and the interactions between these. Broader policy settings also play an important role (Section 9.5). The complementarity between different institutions—not only within the world of education, but also in those governing labour markets, business investment, and social protection policies—shows how deeply engrained education systems are in societal structures, values, and norms. This complicates the transferability of institutions from one setting to another. At the same time, the ongoing changes witnessed in Europe's labour markets today highlight the importance of keeping education policies flexible and up to date to provide effective responses to changing skills demands and to support the growth of incomes and living standards in the coming decades.

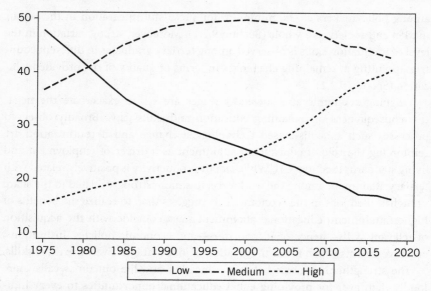

Figure 9.1 Trends in educational attainment in the EU28 (30–34 age group).
Educational attainment of the 30–34 age group in early years was approximated by attainment of older age groups in 2005. For instance, attainment of the 30–34 age group in 1975 was approximated by attainment of the 60–64 age group in 2005.
Source: EU Labour Force Survey (LFS).

9.2 TRENDS IN EDUCATIONAL ATTAINMENT

9.2.1 Educational Attainment

Educational attainment has expanded swiftly over the past century in Europe. Whereas in 1975, almost half of the EU population aged 30–34[2] had left school without an upper secondary school degree, by 2018, this share declined to fewer than one-sixth (Figure 9.1). Over the same period, the proportion of tertiary graduates in the same age group has gone up from around 15% to 40%. As educational attainment increased, the share of medium-qualified individuals first rose, until around 2000, on the back of a declining share of individuals with low attainment.[3] It then levelled off and saw a decline again as a result of increasing tertiary attainment.

---

2 The age group 30–34 is used as a reference age cohort here as it is a group that is old enough to ensure that most individuals have finished education but young enough to be relevant to explore recent developments in education and training systems. It is also the reference group for tertiary education attainment in the EU's Social Scoreboard.

3 This chapter will refer to individuals who do not hold an upper secondary degree (i.e., qualifications at ISCED-level 2 or less) as low-qualified or individuals with low educational attainment. Medium-qualified individuals are defined as those with an upper secondary degree or a postsecondary, non-tertiary degree (ISCED levels 3 and 4); and highly qualified individuals are those with a tertiary degree (ISCED 5 and above).

An important driving force behind the educational expansion was the increasing length of compulsory schooling. This is likely to have reduced the additional cost of staying in school until completing upper secondary school (Breen et al., 2009a). Still, in most European countries, compulsory schooling age does not yet stretch until the typical age of completing upper secondary education, which means that regulations allow most youngsters in Europe to leave school before obtaining their upper secondary qualification.[4] Hence, non–policy-related factors are likely to have played a role as well. According to Breen et al. (2009a), improving living conditions have enabled children from working class families to improve their health and nutrition, thereby creating more favourable conditions for education, and education reforms have reduced the cost of education and risks of failure. Another and perhaps even more important reason is the changing structure of the economy: the decline of agriculture and the rise of manufacturing and service sectors requiring workers with higher skills levels has generated substantial (lifetime) private benefits of pursuing higher educational attainment.[5]

The rise in attainment (at both the lower and upper end) is visible across all countries, albeit with considerable variation in the speed of change. Germany features among the slowest changers: while it was one of the best performers in attainment in 1975, it has seen less progress since then. Today, it has become a more median performer in the EU28 context in terms of attainment. At the other end of the spectrum, countries such as Greece, Cyprus, Poland, and Ireland, which started out from relatively low attainment levels in 1975, have exhibited relatively fast increases in attainment over time.

Still, low-qualified individuals still make up more than one-quarter of the 30–34 age group in Italy in 2018, and more than one-third in Portugal, Spain, and Malta. This is especially concerning in view of the unfavourable life outcomes that tend to be associated with low qualifications. Over the next 30 years (throughout which these adults are expected to remain in the labour market), demand for low-qualified labour is expected to decline further in line with theories of skill-biased technological change and deroutinization, as will be discussed in more detail in Section 9.3. At the other end of the spectrum, low attainment in the 30–34 age group is below 7% in Poland, the Czech Republic, Slovenia, Lithuania, and Croatia.

Cyclical effects can have a notable influence on attainment rates. In the runup to the 2008 economic crisis, the economic boom in Italy and Spain slowed (and

ISCED refers to the International Standard Classification of Education, the reference international classification for organizing education programs and qualifications by levels and fields.

4   Exceptions include Austria, Belgium, Germany, the Netherlands, and Portugal (since 2009).

5   These will be discussed in more detail in Section 9.3.

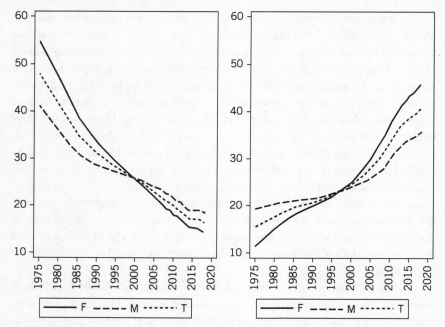

Figure 9.2 Trends in educational attainment across Europe (1975–2018).
The left bar (1) shows educational attainment of 30–34 age group in 1975, the right bar
(2) shows attainment in 2018. Countries are sorted in order of increasing low attainment
in 2018. Educational attainment of the 30–34 age group in early years was approximated by
attainment of older age groups in 2005.
Source: Author's calculations based on Labour Force Survey (LFS) data.

even reversed) the previously declining trend in low attainment as attractive job
opportunities lured some youngsters out of school. Since the crisis, educational
attainment has started to increase again, and further improvements are also
observed among younger age groups.

Progress over the past 10 years has been worryingly slow in countries such as
Denmark and Bulgaria in spite of a still relatively high incidence of low educational
attainment in the 30–34 age group (around 17%). In Romania, the incidence of low
attainment has even doubled (from 12% to 24%) over the past 20 years.

Tertiary attainment among 30- to 34-year-olds ranges from less than 30% in
Romania and Italy to more than 50% in Lithuania, Luxembourg, Cyprus, Ireland,
and Sweden.[6] It is generally low in countries with high shares of low-qualified

---

6 Note that, in some cases, educational attainment figures result from differences in educational system structures. For example, in Germany, almost 30% of graduates from
   postsecondary training graduate with a postsecondary degree that is not recognized
   as a tertiary qualification, even though they typically require 3–4 years of further education and training (school- and work-based), of which 2 years are full-time at an
   educational institution, meaning that the line between postsecondary non-tertiary on

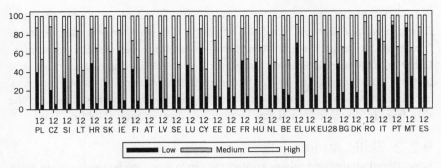

Figure 9.3 Trends in educational attainment in the EU28 (30–34 age group), by gender: (a) share of population without an upper secondary qualification; (b) share of population with a tertiary degree.
Educational attainment of the age group 30–34 in early years was approximated by attainment of older age groups in 2005.
Source: EU Labour Force Survey (LFS).

individuals (except for in Spain), but it is not always high in countries with low shares of low-qualified individuals. For example, tertiary attainment is around 30% in the Czech Republic, Slovakia, and Croatia, which at the same time have less than 10% low-qualified people in the 30–34 age group. The latter countries tend to have high shares of vocational education and training graduates, re-flecting, among other factors, a relatively strong economic orientation towards the manufacturing industry.

The past 50 years have seen a remarkable reversal in gender patterns of edu-cational attainment (Figure 9.3). Whereas, prior to 1995, women in their early thirties tended to be less qualified than men, in the 21st century, the odds turned around and a growing divergence in educational attainment can be observed be-tween men and women, both at the bottom (lack of upper secondary attainment) and at the top (tertiary attainment). The smallest gap is observed in Germany, where, until 2016, men in the 30–34 age group still outperformed women in ter-tiary attainment.[7]

Over time, views on gender roles have become increasingly egalitarian in Europe. Some studies show that, already in the 1950s and 1960s, girls tended to earn better grades at school than boys of similar cognitive ability (Buchmann et al., 2008). Nevertheless, female students tended to quit school earlier than

---

the one hand and tertiary degrees (e.g. 'professional bachelor degrees') on the other hand can be thin.

7 One of the reasons is that a substantial share of women hold qualifications to work in the nonprofit sector (social, care, educational, and medical professions). In Germany, qualification standards for such professions are often at the nontertiary level, in con-trast with most other European countries where a tertiary degree is required (see, e.g., Powell and Solga, 2011; Haasler and Gottschall, 2015) (cfr. Footnote 6).

did male students. As stigma for women working out of the house gradually disappeared, and as their likelihood of continuing employment after marriage increased, the returns to educational attainment improved steadily for women. Other factors have also played a role, such as the delayed age of marriage and birth of first child (due to the widespread introduction of contraceptives), antidiscrimination laws and government intervention to enforce these, and the shift from informal to formal care by qualified professionals (Goldin, 2006).

9.2.2 Skills Attainment

Educational attainment relates strongly to but is not a perfect measure of skills attainment. Yet skills are more difficult to assess than educational attainment, and this is reflected in poor data availability. Some relevant lessons can be drawn from recent skills surveys by the Organisation for Economic Cooperation and Development (OECD), such as the Programme for International Student Assessment (PISA) and the Programme for the International Assessment of Adult Competences (PIAAC), which include direct tests of foundation skills such as literacy and numeracy. Foundation skills are considered a critical base for further learning and therefore considered relevant proxies for broader skills endowments.[8] PISA assesses the mathematics, reading, and science foundation skills of 15-year-olds on a triannual basis and was carried out for the first time in 2000. PIAAC was set up more recently. Its first round of data collection took place over the period 2008–2013 and assessed the numeracy, literacy, and problem-solving skills of the adult population (aged 16–65).

Both surveys reveal a considerable variation in skills proficiency across individuals of similar age and educational attainment in different countries.[9] While some countries in the European Union are among the global top performers (e.g., the Netherlands and Estonia) in terms of median mathematics proficiency of 15-year-olds, other countries (such as Romania and Bulgaria) lag behind substantially (Figure 9.4). Poland made a great leap forward over the past 15 years, to land among the top of the league in Europe in 2018. At the same time, it is important to note that student performance varies more strongly within than across countries.

---

8   At the same time, these proficiency measures are, of course, not fully comprehensive—they are more likely to reflect 'fluid' intelligence (cognitive ability) than 'crystallized' intelligence (accumulated knowledge). They are also not informative of job-specific skills. In general, 'fluid' intelligence is considered to decline with age, while 'crystallized' intelligence is considered to increase with age (Horn and Cattell, 1967). At the same time, a higher level of fluid intelligence provides a better foundation for the accumulation of crystallized knowledge.

9   For example, PIAAC shows that while young adults (25–39) in Ireland and Poland have high educational attainment compared to other Member States, their numeracy proficiency is among the lowest when individuals of all educational attainment levels are considered jointly (see later discussion).

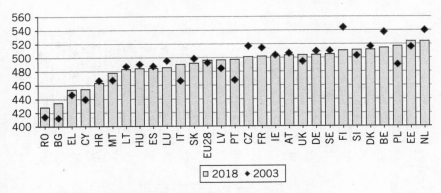

Figure 9.4 Median mathematics scores among 15-year-olds.

No 2003 data available for SI, EE, LT, RO, HR, BG, UK, MT, CY. For these countries, the earliest available data are used instead: 2006 (SI, EE, LT, RO, HR, BG, UK), 2009 (MT), 2012 (CY). *Source:* OECD Programme for International Student Assessment (PISA) survey.

There is a broad (albeit not full) correspondence between well-performing countries in PISA and well-performing countries in PIAAC. Scandinavian countries, the Netherlands, and Belgium perform quite well in both surveys. Greece and Cyprus perform weakly in both. Estonia and Spain are examples of countries that perform well in terms of the mathematics proficiency of their 15-year-olds but less so for tertiary graduates. A possible explanation is that the quality of their education system is improving over time. A similar message derives from the comparison of graduate skills levels over time (over different age cohorts). At the same time, less progress seems to have been achieved over the past 15 years for 15-year-olds in these two countries.

On average in the EU, the mathematics skills of 15-year-olds have improved slightly over time. Results of successive rounds of the PISA survey show that mathematics skills of 15-year-olds strengthened in around half of EU Member States over 2003–2018, but they worsened in the other half (Figure 9.4). Some countries that were initially among the worst performers made a great leap forward (e.g., Bulgaria, Italy, and Portugal). However, there were also some countries that already showed relatively weak skills performance in 2003 and saw a further deterioration in mathematics proficiency over the considered period (e.g., Luxembourg and Slovakia). As the Member States that performed weakly in 2003 made more progress on average than those with a solid performance in 2003, in all, some convergence in average mathematics skills levels is observed.

PIAAC data are currently only available as a cross-section, which is why variation over age cohorts is sometimes used as a proxy for variation over time. Figure 9.5 singles out tertiary graduates across three age groups (25–39, 40–54, and 55–64) and shows that, on average, numeracy scores of younger tertiary graduates are higher than those of older graduates. This generational gradient is

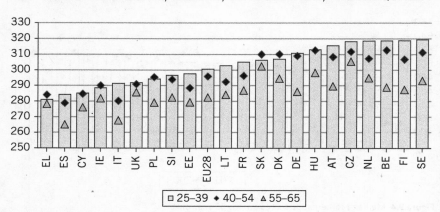

Figure 9.5 Median numeracy score among tertiary graduates, different age cohorts.
Source: OECD Programme for the International Assessment of Adult Competencies (PIAAC)
Survey (Round 1: 2008–2013). Data for Greece, Lithuania, and Slovenia are based on PIAAC
Round 2 (2012–2016); data for Hungary Round 3 (2017).

particularly pronounced for tertiary graduates in Finland, Lithuania, Italy, and
Belgium. On the other hand, hardly any difference is observed between generations in Greece, the United Kingdom, and Slovakia.

The presence of a generational gradient may reflect improvements in the
quality of education, but it may just as well reflect the result of skills dynamics
over the lifecycle as a result of atrophy, depreciation, and so on (de Grip, 2006).
Intuitively, even if the quality of education (in the sense of its effectiveness in
promoting numeracy foundation skills acquisition) would remain constant over
time, older generations are still likely to have lower skills levels than young generations because of these dynamics. Recent studies that try to disentangle the impact of ageing from cohort effects suggest that literacy proficiency declines with
age (especially after 45) but is also often lower on average for younger age cohorts
than for older ones (Flisi et al., 2019; Barrett and Riddell, 2016). For numeracy,
structural trends over cohorts are less clear.

Skills attainment is not necessarily higher for tertiary graduates in countries
with less tertiary attainment.[10] On the one hand, skills attainment of young tertiary graduates is relatively low for those countries with the highest rates of tertiary attainment (Cyprus and Ireland) and above the EU average for countries
with relatively low shares of tertiary graduates (the Czech Republic, Slovakia,
and Germany). On the other hand, Italy combines the lowest tertiary attainment
rate with relatively weak proficiency scores of young tertiary graduates, while
the Netherlands, Finland, Belgium, and Sweden combine relatively high tertiary
attainment rates with high average numeracy among tertiary graduates. These

---

10 Some have argued that educational expansion reduces the 'average quality' of
graduates (see, e.g., Beblavý et al., 2015; Galindo-Rueda and Vignoles, 2005).

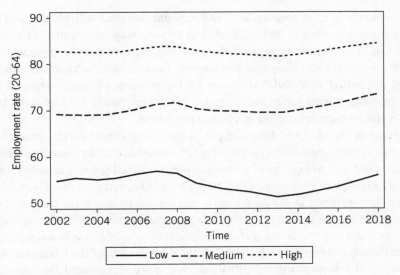

Figure 9.6 Employment rate trends in the EU28 (20–64 age group).
Source: EU Labour Force Survey (LFS).

countries also report relatively high mathematics proficiency among the broader
population of 15-year-olds (Figure 9.4).

9.3 EDUCATIONAL ATTAINMENT AND SOCIOECONOMIC OUTCOMES

9.3.1 Educational Attainment and Employment

Educational attainment shows a strong positive association with an individual's
probability of employment. On average in the EU28, the employment rate of low-
qualified individuals stood at 56% in 2018 (Figure 9.6). The employment rates of
medium- and highly qualified individuals were considerably higher, at 73% and
85%, respectively. Contributing factors include the higher relative demand and
the higher opportunity cost of not working for higher qualified individuals, as
well as the fact that it is typically easier for higher qualified individuals to take up
jobs with lower skills requirements than the other way around. High-qualified
individuals may also be more mobile across sectors and countries and therefore
have access to a larger labour market (Mauro and Spilimbergo, 1999; Persyn,
2017).[11]

Over recent decades, low-qualified individuals have lost some ground in the
labour market relative to medium-qualified individuals. Whereas the difference

---

11 Unfortunately, the analysis on this topic is severely constrained by lack of data (see,
    e.g., Martí and Ródenas, 2007).

in employment rates between low- and medium-qualified individuals stood at 14 percentage points in 2002, it peaked at 18 percentage points in 2014 to decline again to 17 percentage points by 2018. Employment rates of low-qualified individuals have also increased less strongly than for other attainment groups over the period 2002–2018: they rose by 1 percentage point as compared to 4 percentage points for medium- and 2 percentage points for high-qualified individuals in spite of starting out from a lower level.

Some of the observed trends might be caused by cohort effects: given that younger generations have generally higher educational attainment than older generations, the average age of a low-qualified individual of today is higher than the average age of the low-qualified 10 years ago. On average, in the EU28, 45% of the low-qualified in the 20–64 age group are older than 50 (as compared to 40% in 2002), and these tend to have lower employment rates than younger age groups. Data indicate however that this cohort effect explains only a small part of the change. Among younger cohorts, the deterioration of the labour market position of low-qualified individuals is even more pronounced than among older cohorts, adding to the evidence that education and skills have, over the past 10 years, indeed become stronger determinants of labour market outcomes.

Ongoing structural changes such as globalization and technological change have played a major role. The general shift of employment and labour demand away from low-skilled jobs and jobs with a higher routine content is now well-documented. The *skills-biased technological change* hypothesis argues that new technologies are substitutes for low-skilled labour and complements for high-skilled labour, so that the introduction of these technologies raises demand for skills (see, e.g., Bound and Johnson, 1992; Katz and Murphy, 1992). The *routine-biased technological change* hypothesis, which is based on a more granular investigation of the task content of declining jobs, asserts that employment mostly moves away from tasks with a higher routine content as these are easier to outsource or automate (see, e.g., Autor et al., 2003, 2006; Goos et al., 2009). Both theories predict a rising gap in labour market outcomes between lower-skilled and high-skilled individuals as empirical analysis finds a higher routine-intensity among lower-skilled jobs (e.g., Marcolin et al., 2016; Nedelkoska and Quintini, 2018; Pouliakas, 2018). Increasing returns to skills are likely to put upward pressure on wage dispersion (e.g., Krueger, 1993; Autor et al., 1998; Katz and Autor, 1999; Acemoglu, 2002a, 2002b), unless policy measures are put in place to mitigate these pressures.

The impact of these longer term trends was accelerated and exacerbated by the 2008–2011 financial crisis, which affected the manufacturing and construction sectors more than the services sector. The construction sector was hit strongly as many countries[12] were in the midst of a construction boom in 2008, which then

---

12 Most prominently Cyprus, Greece, Spain, Portugal, Ireland, and the Baltics; see Kiss and Vandeplas (2015, fig. 24).

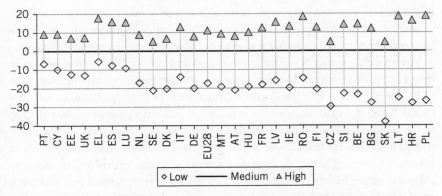

Figure 9.7 Relative employment rates across attainment groups (aged 20–64, 2018). Countries are sorted according to the distance (in percentage points) between employment rates of low- and highly qualified individuals. The white diamonds show the difference (in percentage points) between employment rates of low- and medium-qualified individuals; the grey triangles show the difference (in percentage points) between employment rates of highly and medium-qualified workers.
Source: EU Labour Force Survey (LFS).

burst as the crisis hit. Employment in manufacturing had already been on a long-term decline in many EU countries before the crisis,[13] but the crisis accelerated job destruction in already struggling industries (Havlik, 2014). These changes have hit low-qualified men strongly. By 2018, employment rates of low-qualified individuals were just about to reach their pre-crisis peak again, while medium-qualified individuals had already reached the pre-crisis peak in 2016 and have shown further improvements since then.

In some countries the gaps are considerably larger than in others. Notably, the employment rate gap between low- and highly qualified individuals exceeds 40 percentage points in Poland, Croatia, Lithuania, and Slovakia. At the other end of the spectrum, the employment rate gap between the low- and highly qualified is below 20 percentage points in Portugal.

The large employment rate gaps in countries in Central and Eastern Europe are noteworthy. Imbalances in the demand and supply of skills are quite common in the context of transition economies. Dramatic changes in the structure of the economy since the breakdown of the Soviet Union in 1990 and the accession to the European Union of former Soviet countries in 2004 (2007 for Bulgaria and Romania)[14] have triggered a growing demand for highly qualified

---

13 Over the period 1980–2007, the share of employment in manufacturing declined by around one-third or more in most EU countries, mostly in favour of employment in market services (van Ark et al., 2012).

14 According to Havlik (2015), structural change, implying a strong shift from agriculture and industry to services, was much more pronounced in the Baltics and in Bulgaria and Romania than in other countries such as the Czech Republic, Slovakia, and Slovenia; most of these changes occurred prior to 2000.

individuals.[15] The supply of skills is usually slower to adapt as most of the education and training that individuals undertake happens before they enter the labour market, where they spend several decades after leaving initial education.

Another factor that is intrinsically related and cannot be disentangled from the previous issue is that, in most of these countries (with the notable exception of Bulgaria), the share of low-qualified individuals in the population is very low (below 10%).[16] As the share of the population without upper secondary degree in the population becomes very small, its composition may worsen, in the sense that a larger share of individuals in this group are constrained by multiple, often complex barriers (health problems, disabilities, social exclusion) to sustainable integration into the labour market. At the same time, stigma and prejudice against low-qualified labour is likely to strengthen. This implies by no means that policymakers cannot act to make labour markets more inclusive. For instance, in Estonia, the share of low-qualified individuals is below 10% and yet low-qualified persons have relatively good employment rates (66%).

Employment rate disparities across educational attainment groups are more pronounced for women than for men. On average in the EU28, the employment rate gap between low- and highly qualified individuals is 36 percentage points for women and 22 for men in 2018. The most extreme case is Malta, where this employment rate gap is as high as 47 percentage points for women and only 12 percentage points for men. A possible reason is the stronger persistence of traditional breadwinner–housewife patterns among families with less-qualified women. Low-qualified women are more prone to inactivity traps as their participation tax rates[17] are usually higher given the wide presence of fiscal support schemes for dependent mothers across Europe, the often significant cost of childcare, and the higher incidence of low earnings among low-qualified women once they enter the labour market (due to working at low wages and/or working fewer hours). Data from the Structure of Earnings Survey indeed reveal that, in 2014, 21% of female employees in the EU28 were working at low wages[18] as compared to 13% of male workers. The gender gap in part-time employment stood at 23 percentage points on average in the EU28 in 2018. The share of part-time employment declines with educational attainment, especially for women.

---

15 Peracchi (2006) documents the increasing returns to education in the transition to a market economy.

16 Note that the 25–64 age group is considered here, as a large share of individuals remains in initial education until the age of 25.

17 The participation tax rate is a measure of the financial incentives to take up a job. It quantifies how much of the first dollar earned will be taxed away or lost in terms of means-tested government support.

18 'Low wages' are defined as two-thirds or less of the national median gross hourly earnings.

9.3.2 Educational Attainment and Aggregate Labour Productivity

Human capital theory asserts that education and training have a positive impact on productivity (see, e.g., Schultz, 1961; Lucas, 1988). Not only formal schooling matters in this context, but also on-the-job and other types of informal or nonformal training. The impact that education and training have on productivity critically depends on their quality and the skills an individual accumulates as a result of them. Whereas Becker (1964) mostly emphasizes the direct role of human capital as a production factor necessary for the operation of complex machinery as well as for the development of new products and processes and to adopt innovations from other countries, Nelson and Phelps (1966) focus on the importance of human capital for individuals' capacity to adapt to changing working environments (e.g., in response to technological change).

Some have argued against these theories, asserting that the positive correlation between educational attainment and productivity reflects the higher innate ability of individuals, such that education merely has a signalling value (e.g., Arrow, 1973; Spence, 1973, 1974). While a few empirical studies have found evidence in favour of the signalling hypothesis (e.g., Brown and Sessions, 1999; Psacharapolous, 1979), others have in contrast pointed at a substantial impact of education on productivity (e.g., Chevalier et al., 2004; Layard and Psacharopolous, 1974; Groot and Oosterbeek, 1994; Kroch and Sjoblom, 1994; Johnes, 1998; Dickson, 2013).

Macro-level data suggest a positive correlation between tertiary attainment and labour productivity (Figure 9.8) across countries in the European Union. This correlation remains if time series data are considered rather than a cross-section. Still, there is quite a lot of variation around the fitted linear relationship, indicating that other factors matter as well for labour productivity. For instance, labour productivity is more strongly correlated with the proportion of high-skilled jobs in the economy than with the level of tertiary attainment (Figure 9.8). This suggests that strengthening labour productivity not only requires a well-educated labour force, but also jobs that are able to effectively use their skills. The match between individuals' qualifications and their jobs has received ample attention in the literature and is discussed in more detail in the next section.

9.3.3 Under- and Overqualification

Aggregate productivity is higher if workers' skills are well-matched with their jobs. If workers' attainment is beyond what is strictly required for their job, they still have a productivity benefit from their additional education but not as much as they would in a job that fully utilizes their skills (van der Velden and Bijlsma, 2019). If workers' attainment is below what is required for their job, this may also result in lower productivity than what would be achievable without these skills gaps.

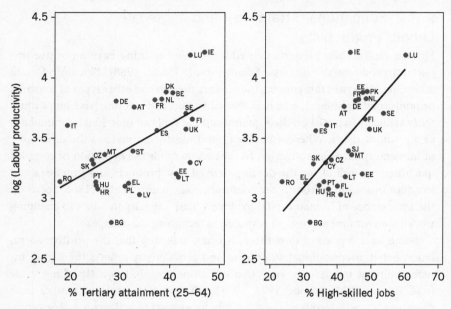

Figure 9.8 Linear fit between productivity and (A) tertiary attainment (B) proportion of highly skilled occupations.
Highly skilled jobs are jobs classified under ISCO 1-digit codes 1–3 (according to ILO, 20147).
Tertiary attainment is measured as the share of individuals holding a tertiary degree (ISCED levels 5–8) in the 25–64 age group. Both are based Labour Force Survey (LFS) data, available through Eurostat. Data on labour productivity are based on national accounts data, measured as log(GDP per hour worked in PPP). The R^2adj-values of the linear models are, respectively, 0.32 and 0.45.
Source: Vandeplas and Thum-Thysen, 2019

A proliferating literature has addressed the issue of 'on-the-job' mismatch. It mostly considers 'overqualification', notably, the incidence of workers with higher qualifications than those strictly required to do their job; and 'underqualification', which concerns workers with lower qualifications than those required to do their job effectively. Unfortunately, the measurement of over- and underqualification is no panacea, in particular because it is hard to pin down what is the right qualification for a job.[19]

---

19 Not only are formal qualifications very coarse measures of job-relevant skills because they do not account for nonformally or informally acquired skills, but the occupation-related information that is available at the individual level is typically also not sufficiently precise and may cover a range of different jobs with different skills requirements. Another option is to use self-reported data by individuals, but this has been criticized for being overly subjective. Different ways to measure skills mismatch on the job have produced substantially diverging results that are only weakly correlated with each other. See, e.g., Kiss and Vandeplas (2015) or Asai et al. (2020) for a critical discussion of different methodologies.

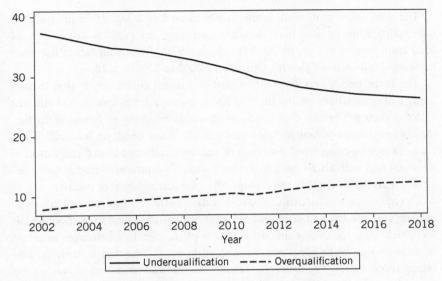

Figure 9.9 Trend in underqualification and overqualification in the EU28.
Underqualification and overqualification are expressed as a per cent of total employment in the
20–64 age group. The calculation methodology is described in the text.
Source: Labour Force Survey (LFS) data.

A rough methodology to measure over- and underqualification that allows for cross-country comparison in an EU context is to use the job classification methodology proposed by International Labour Organization (ILO, 2014)[20]: jobs classified at the International Standard Classification of Occupations (ISCO) levels 1–3 require workers who are highly qualified, jobs at ISCO 4–8 require workers who are medium-qualified, and elementary jobs (ISCO 9) do not require workers to have any qualification.[21] As a result, overqualification concerns highly qualified workers with a job at ISCO 4–9 and medium-qualified workers with a job at ISCO 9. Conversely, underqualification concerns medium-qualified workers with a job at ISCO 1–3 and low-qualified workers with a job at ISCO 1–8.[22]

---

20 While the clear advantage of this method is that it is simple to apply based on frequently collected data and allows for cross-country comparison, its drawback is that it imposes rigid assumptions, notably that qualification requirements are the same for all jobs within an ISCO 1-digit category, and that these are the same across time and across countries.

21 ISCO 1-digit categories are specified as follows: 1, Managers; 2, Professionals; 3, Technicians and associate professionals; 4, Clerical support workers; 5, Service and sales workers; 6, Skilled agricultural, forestry and fishery workers; 7, Craft and related trades workers; 8, Plant and machine operators, and assemblers; 9, Elementary occupations.

22 This methodology is also used and discussed in more detail (including in terms of its advantages and limitations vis-à-vis other methods) in Kiss and Vandeplas (2015).

The data show that, while underqualification has a higher incidence than overqualification, it has been steadily declining since 2002—from 37% of total employment to 26% by 2018 (see Figure 9.9). Overqualification has been increasing (albeit more slowly), from 8% in 2002 to 12% in 2018.

The main policy concern with regard to underqualification is that it risks being a drag on labour productivity as it may mean that workers are less efficient at doing their job or that they would be slower in adopting or fostering the further improvement of new technologies. On the other hand, underqualification could as well be considered the result of successful labour market integration of low-qualified individuals, and, from that perspective, be considered as more desirable than the case where the low-qualified are unemployed or inactive.

Overqualification, in turn, can to some extent be the result of rational decision-making at the individual or household level. Some individuals may choose a job for which they are overqualified because it offers certain advantages in terms of wage or non-wage benefits as compared to other jobs that fit their qualification levels better. For example, Frank's (1978) 'differential overqualification theory' argues that women are often constrained in their job search by their husband's job choice.[23] By facing a 'smaller' labour market than men, they have a higher chance of being overqualified.[24] The argument that spatial mobility constraints lead employees to accept a job with lower formal requirements has broadly been accepted in the economic literature (e.g., Reichelt and Abraham, 2017). Furthermore, Sicherman (1991) suggests that some workers may accept jobs for which they are overqualified as a 'stepping stone' towards better work; that is, with a view to receiving on-the-job training and experience needed for future jobs. Similarly, recent immigrants or mobile workers might accept jobs with lower formal requirements temporarily whilst building up the necessary language skills for a more demanding job.

Some employers may prefer to hire overqualified workers[25] as they want to promote innovation and decentralized decision-making.[26] Individuals tend to

---

23 Notably, Frank (1978) argues that women are often 'tied stayers' or 'tied movers', as they have to stay in a certain area or move to a certain area where their husband has found a job. Note that, at the time of his writing, men were typically better educated and had higher earning power than women. This difference is slowly fading away by now. Still, optimizing job decisions in a couple is bound to be subject to more constraints than optimizing individual job decisions.

24 These predictions have been empirically tested by McGoldrick and Robst (1996) and Büchel and Battu (2003). While the former rejected its validity, the latter did find some evidence that higher commuting distances strongly reduce the probability of being overqualified and that individuals living in rural areas run a higher risk of being overeducated.

25 See, e.g., Verhaest et al. (2018).

26 See, e.g., Blundell et al. (2016) who consider decentralized decision-making as a skills-biased innovation.

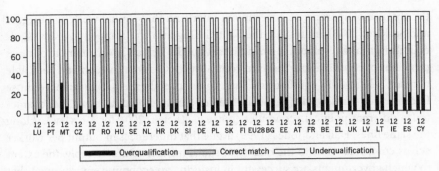

Figure 9.10 Underqualification/overqualification (% total employment, aged 20–64, 2018).
Source: Author's calculations based on EU Labour Force Survey (LFS) data; countries sorted in ascending order of overqualification in 2018.

undertake education not only to expand their labour market opportunities, but also to some extent for personal development and fulfilment.[27] Some reports of overqualification can also result from measurement error: there is some evidence that workers with lower levels of skills than the average for their qualification level are more likely to be overqualified for their jobs (Asai et al., 2020).

The increasing incidence of overqualification has in some countries raised concerns about the expansion of higher education and the potential inability of the labour market to absorb the increasing supply of tertiary educated workers. In general, overqualification is indeed observed to be positively correlated with the share of tertiary attainment in a country. However, it is not so that higher attainment is necessarily accompanied by more overqualification. The positive cross-country correlation between overqualification and tertiary attainment is driven by those countries with very low tertiary attainment and hardly any overqualification as a result. Among the countries with high tertiary attainment, there no longer is a significant correlation between tertiary attainment and overqualification. The reason is that, in some countries, growing tertiary attainment has coincided with a correspondingly strong growth in jobs with higher skills requirements, while in other countries the growing number of tertiary graduates has seemingly not been absorbed into higher skilled jobs, resulting in overqualification (see also Vandeplas and Thum-Thysen, 2019). Different factors may be at play here, including policy-related ones such as quality assurance in education, but also economic institutions and business regulations allowing for firm entry, growth, sectoral reallocation, policies supporting labour mobility and innovation, and investment in tangible and intangible capital.

In this context, Redding (1996) has highlighted the complementarities between investment in human capital and in research and development, giving rise to the existence of multiple equilibria, including a possible 'low skills' trap in

---

27 See, e.g., Green and Henseke (2016).

the absence of appropriate government intervention. Seminal work by Finegold and Soskice (1988) argues that the United Kingdom was trapped in a 'low skills equilibrium' as a result of the unwillingness of the British government to address problems of coordination; this is in contrast with Germany, which had been able to reach a 'high skills equilibrium'. Since then, several papers have nuanced those findings and analysed the particular mix of jobs and qualifications that characterize different political economies (see, e.g., Thelen, 2004 for a review). Along the same lines, Hall and Jones (1999) argue that differences in output per worker across countries relate to the quality of social infrastructure; notably, the extent to which governments are successful in fostering an economic environment that 'supports productive activities, encourages capital accumulation, skill acquisition, invention and technology transfer'. More recently, Colonna (2017) indicates the existence of low skills traps in Italy.

In those countries where overqualification is widespread, labour market demand for highly qualified individuals tends to be weak, suggesting that highly qualified individuals mostly take up jobs with lower qualification requirements because there are no other jobs available. At the same time, labour market outcomes for low- and medium-qualified individuals are usually even weaker, suggesting that there is still a strong rationale for pursuing a tertiary degree.

Countries with higher levels of overqualification typically have lower levels of underqualification (Figure 9.10). Spain, Cyprus, and Ireland are marked exceptions, with relatively high rates of overqualification in combination with relatively high rates of underqualification. This reflects a polarized attainment level among their workforces (a high incidence of low and of high qualifications), while many jobs in these countries still require a medium qualification level.

9.3.4 Educational Attainment and Wages

Not only are there significant differences in labour market status across different attainment groups; once individuals find a job, there are also substantial differences in the wages they earn. The returns to education vary considerably across countries.

To explain this, contrasting theories have been proposed regarding the impact of educational expansion on the returns to education. On the one hand, studies assuming a finite demand for graduates have predicted that the returns to education would decline as supply increased. Similar arguments have been built based on signalling and screening theories (see Section 9.3.2), which predict that an expansion of supply dilutes the signalling value of education and as a result also the returns to education. On the other hand, theories of skill-biased technological change have argued that technological change is complementary to skills, raising the demand for high-skilled workers and reducing the demand for lower skilled workers (Goldin and Katz, 2008). This could explain why, in many countries, the returns to education have increased rather than declined over the past decades. It underlines the role of the structure of the economy (which is no doubt itself

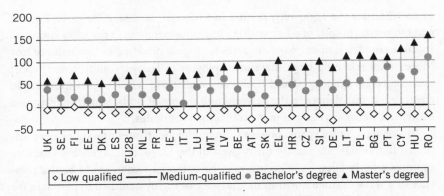

Figure 9.11 Differences in average hourly earnings by educational attainment (as percentage point difference relative to medium-qualified employees) (2014).
The Structure of Earnings Survey (SES) data cover companies with at least 10 employees in Industry, construction and services (B-S) (except O: public administration, defense, compulsory social security). Countries are sorted according to the size of the gap between the lowest (low-qualified) and the highest (master's degree) hourly earnings.
Source: Structure of Earnings Survey (SES) 2014.

impacted by trends in human capital development) as a driver of the returns to education.

The most recent structure of earnings survey shows that, on average in the EU28, medium-qualified employees earn around 15% more than low-qualified ones. Employees with a bachelor's degree earn up to 62% more than low-qualified employees; those with a master's degree earn almost double the hourly wage of low-qualified employees, on average.[28]

Figure 9.11 shows the relative wages for low- and highly qualified workers relative to workers with a medium qualification. The largest wage premium for a tertiary degree is observed in a set of Central and Eastern European countries (Romania, Hungary, Bulgaria, Poland, and Lithuania), but also in Cyprus and Portugal. Most of these (except for Lithuania and Cyprus) have a relatively low level of tertiary attainment. The lowest wage premium is observed in countries with generally higher levels of tertiary attainment (United Kingdom, Sweden, Finland, Denmark, Estonia, and Spain).

Several factors could contribute to this negative association between the share of tertiary attainment and the wage premium corresponding to a tertiary degree. First, low tertiary attainment could result in demand for tertiary graduates exceeding supply, thus generating upward wage pressure. This could be a possible

---

28 For the sake of simplicity, we refer in this chapter to individuals with a short-cycle tertiary degree or a bachelor's or equivalent degree (ISCED 2011 levels 5 and 6) as 'individuals with a bachelor's degree' and to individuals with a master's, a doctoral, or an equivalent degree (ISCED 2011 levels 7 and 8) as 'individuals with a master's degree'.

explanation for the high wage premia in Romania, Hungary, Bulgaria, Poland, and Lithuania (in spite of relatively high tertiary attainment in the latter country). In these countries, unemployment rates for highly qualified individuals are low. Moreover, a relatively large share of employers in Hungary and Poland report skills shortages (Vandeplas and Thum-Thysen, 2019).[29] These observations could again reflect imbalances in the demand and supply of skills, which were argued earlier to be characteristic of many transition economies.

In Portugal and Cyprus, however, unemployment rates among tertiary educated individuals are among the highest in the EU28. Still, a tertiary graduate captures a fairly large wage premium. One potential reason could be the presence of a skills mismatch within the category of highly qualified individuals; for instance, if there is a shortage of a certain type of highly qualified individuals and a surplus of others. However, Portugal and Cyprus are among those countries where the share of employers reporting shortages is the lowest. Another tentative explanation could be that a relatively large share of tertiary graduates works in the public sector, where wage setting does not necessarily follow market mechanisms. Data suggest that Portugal is indeed among the countries with the largest share of tertiary educated employees working in the public sector (and especially the education sector), and there is an above average public sector wage premium. In Cyprus, the share of tertiary educated employees working in the public sector is not so high, but the public sector wage premium is among the highest in the EU28.[30]

At the other end of the wage distribution, wage penalties for not having an upper secondary degree are most pronounced in Germany, Slovakia, and Austria, all countries with a very low proportion of low-qualified individuals. Therefore, possible adverse composition and stigma effects may contribute to higher wage penalties for individuals with a low qualification (as discussed earlier). At the same time, as the proportion of workers with a tertiary degree is relatively low as well (and the proportion of individuals with a non-tertiary post-secondary degree is high in Germany), the medium-qualified population may as well benefit from positive composition effects,[31] resulting in higher wages for medium- relative to low-qualified workers.

Wage inequalities between low- and highly qualified individuals tend to be larger for men than for women. This difference is particularly pronounced in Hungary, Germany, Bulgaria, Slovakia, the Czech Republic, and Austria where men with a master's degree earn up to three times the wages of low-qualified

---

29 Based on the share of firms reporting that their business is constrained by shortages of labour in the European Business survey.

30 Based on Structure of Earnings (2014) wage data by sector.

31 Note, for instance, that in each of these countries, employees in the healthcare sector tend to hold a medium qualification, while in the EU on average employees in the healthcare sector are more likely to hold a tertiary degree.

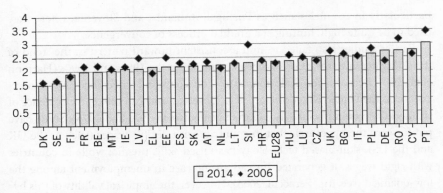

Figure 9.12 Ratio between hourly wages of professionals (ISCO 2) and elementary occupations (ISCO 9).
No data available for HR; 2010 instead, 2014 data are used for EL.
Source: Eurostat based on Structure of Earnings Survey.

men. The corresponding ratio for women stands around 2.5. All these countries have above average gender pay gaps for highly qualified workers (around 25–30%). The positive correlation between gender pay gaps and (male) wage dispersion has been highlighted earlier by Kahn (2015).

Unfortunately, as a result of changes in educational classifications between the Structure of Earnings Survey 2006 and 2014, it is not possible to directly compare relative wages for different educational groups over time. One way to circumvent this challenge is to compare relative wages for different occupational groups over time. Occupational levels are often correlated with education levels. Figure 9.12 shows the hourly wage of professionals (mostly highly qualified individuals) relative to the hourly wage of elementary occupations (with the highest proportion of low-qualified individuals) over time.

If we use this ratio as a proxy for the 'skills premium',[32] the data show that the relative skills premium has remained remarkably constant over the considered period. In 2014, it is lowest in Denmark, Sweden, Finland, and France, where professionals earn less than twice as much as workers in elementary occupations, and highest in Portugal, Cyprus, Romania, and Germany, where professionals earn 2.5–3 times as much as workers in elementary occupations.[33] In the EU average, the skills premium has remained relatively stable over 2006–2014. It increased in Germany and Greece. Relative wages for professionals have declined

---

32 Note that it only measures one dimension of the skills premium: if tertiary graduates become less likely over time to find a job that requires higher skills, this can also reduce the skills premium without affecting the wage differential between occupations.

33 While the ranking of some countries changes between Figure 9.12 and Figure 9.13, both figures consistently show a relatively low skills premium in Denmark, Estonia, Finland, France, Ireland, and Sweden; and a relatively high one in Cyprus, Germany, Poland, Portugal, and Romania.

particularly in countries such as Portugal, Romania, and Slovenia, where they used to be quite high, hinting at a gradual process of convergence.

Earlier studies also failed to find a consistent upward pattern in the trend of the skills premium for most European countries in the 1980s and 1990s (Harmon et al., 2001; Bernardi and Ballarino, 2016; Gottschalk and Smeeding, 1997). An exception is the United Kingdom (see, e.g., Devereux and Fan [2011] for evidence of rising skills premiums for UK cohorts born between 1970 and 1975). Some have put forward the hypothesis that in countries with flexible wages (such as the UK and the US), skill-biased technology has raised skills premia; while in countries with rigid wages, it generated instead an increase in unemployment among the low-qualified (see, e.g., Peracchi, 2006). However, the empirical validity of this hypothesis has been questioned. While unemployment rates may be higher, activity rates are also higher in the European Union, so that eventually employment rates of the low-qualified are not so different. Other mitigating factors that may have counteracted the rise in skills premia in European countries are the fast increase in supply of tertiary graduates (such as in Ireland), redistributive tax-benefit systems, and collective bargaining practices and other wage setting institutions.

When comparing Figure 9.7 and Figure 9.11, some broad trends emerge: in countries such as Denmark, Sweden, Spain, Estonia, and UK, there are considerably less inequalities across individuals of different educational attainment levels in labour market status as well as in wages earned than on average in the EU28. On the other hand, in Central and Eastern European countries such as Romania, Bulgaria, Hungary, the Czech Republic, Slovakia, and Lithuania, there are substantial disparities in labour market outcomes (in terms of both employment rates and wages) across educational attainment groups. As mentioned earlier, this provides some suggestive evidence of imbalances in skills supply and demand in the latter countries which could be linked to the ongoing process of transition in these countries. Structural differences in the set-up of education systems across Member States may also contribute to the observed differences. However, the prominence and effectiveness of policies facilitating the labour market integration of vulnerable individuals varies strongly across countries as well (see, e.g., Section 9.4.2).

9.3.5 Educational Attainment and Poverty

Because low-qualified individuals have lower chances of employment and are expected to earn lower wages, they are also more likely to live in poverty. The poverty measure used in this section is the number of people in the 18–64 age group at risk of poverty as a share of the total population, a measure of relative poverty.[34] Whereas around 8% of highly qualified individuals are considered to live

---

34 A household is considered to be at risk of poverty if it has an equivalized disposable income below the at-risk-of-poverty threshold, which is set at 60% of the national median equivalized disposable income after social transfers.

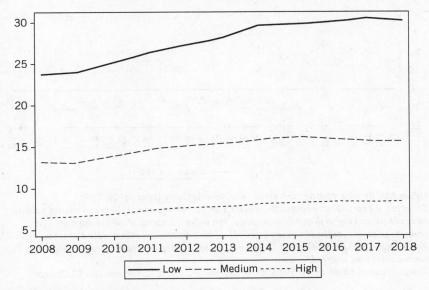

Figure 9.13 At-risk-of-poverty rate by educational attainment, EU28.
Source: Eurostat based on EU Statistics on Income and Living Conditions (EU-SILC) survey.
Croatia is included in EU aggregate only as of 2013 but does not have a significant impact on
the data.

in relative poverty, the figure is twice as high for medium-qualified individuals
(16%) and almost four times as high for low-qualified individuals (30%) in 2018
(Figure 9.13).[35]

Over the period 2008–2018, relative poverty has increased across all educational attainment groups in the EU28, but more so for low than for high attainment groups. While relative poverty started to increase around the onset of the
2008 crisis for medium- and highly qualified individuals, relative poverty among
low-qualified individuals was already on a rising trend before the crisis.

With regard to cross-country variation, the countries with the highest discrep-
ancy in poverty rates between high- and low-qualified individuals are Romania,
Bulgaria, Lithuania, and Croatia (see Figure 9.14). In Romania, this is mostly
the result of high inequality in hourly earnings; in Bulgaria and Lithuania, the
problem is exacerbated by strong differences in the probability of employment
across educational attainment groups. While Lithuania and Croatia are among

---

35 It is important to note that poverty is a concept that is defined at the household level,
while educational attainment is defined at the individual level. As a result, individuals'
poverty status will not only depend on their own employment status but also on the
employment status of other household members and/or the number of dependents
they have. As such, societal phenomena such as assortative matching (where low-
qualified individuals are more likely to marry other low-qualified individuals) will
exacerbate the poverty gradient across qualification groups.

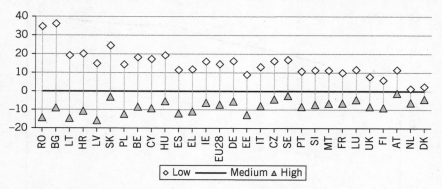

Figure 9.14 Relative poverty rates across attainment groups (aged 18–64, 2018).
Countries are sorted according to the distance (in percentage points) between relative poverty
rates of low- and highly qualified individuals. The white diamonds show the difference (in
percentage points) between poverty rates of low- and medium-qualified individuals; the
grey triangles show the difference (in percentage points) between poverty rates of high- and
medium-qualified workers.
Source: Eurostat based on EU Statistics on Income and Living Conditions (EU-SILC) survey.

the countries with the lowest incidence of low attainment in Europe, Bulgaria
and Romania are among the countries with higher proportions of low-qualified
individuals.

At the other end of the spectrum, the incidence of poverty is relatively similar
across individuals of different educational attainment in countries where wage
and employment rate differentials across attainment groups are not so strong
(such as Denmark, for instance).

9.3.6 Nonpecuniary Returns to Education

Education is also observed to be positively correlated with health, trust in
politicians and institutions, altruism/positive reciprocity, and life satisfaction outcomes. For example, Murtin et al. (2017) find, based on data from
17 OECD countries, that the gap in life expectancy between individuals with
low and high educational attainment is around 8 years for men and 5 years
for women at the age of 25.[36] Empirical analysis suggests that the extension of compulsory schooling laws over the early to mid-20th century has
reduced the likelihood of reporting to be in poor health, unemployed, or
unhappy for those students who were obliged to stay longer in school as
compared to those that were not subject to the policy (Oreopoulos, 2007).
Other strands of the literature have found positive correlations between
educational attainment on the one hand and social capital and trust in

---

36 The difference in life expectancy for men aged 25 is more than 11 years in Latvia,
   Poland, the Czech Republic, Hungary, and Estonia, and less than 5 years in Portugal
   and Italy.

institutions on the other hand (LaPorta et al., 1997; Helliwell and Putnam, 2007) and with interpersonal trust and participation in volunteering activities (Vera-Toscano et al., 2017; OECD, 2019). This highlights the wider benefits of investment in education for individual and societal well-being beyond economic outcomes.

9.4 EQUALITY OF OPPORTUNITY IN EDUCATION

Education is widely considered a powerful tool for fighting poverty and inequality. Some have even hailed it as 'the great equalizer' (e.g., Bernardi and Ballarino, 2016). Education is an important determinant of life outcomes such as employment and earnings, but also of health and happiness. It has been found to reduce wage and earnings inequality because it can act as a substitute rather than a complement for ability and raise the earnings potential of individuals with weaker innate ability (Brunello et al., 2009; Angrist and Krueger, 1991).

As a result, an issue of major policy concern is whether educational opportunities are distributed fairly and evenly across the population or whether, instead, educational attainment is strongly impacted by socioeconomic background. Some variation in these outcomes across individuals is unavoidable. However, if these outcomes are strongly linked to individuals' parental background, this raises concerns over inequality of opportunities, which may result in a lack of social mobility. If individuals are not able to realise their full potential because of restrictions imposed by societal structures, this has detrimental impacts on social inclusion and poverty reduction, but also on productivity and growth due to inefficiencies in the allocation of resources. This topic is related to the literature on inequality of opportunity, where various scholars have argued that policymakers should particularly focus on addressing that part of inequality of outcomes that arises from circumstances for which individuals cannot be held not responsible (e.g., Rawls, 1971; Sen, 1980; Arneson, 1989; Roemer and Trannoy, 2016; Almas et al., 2020).

9.4.1 The Impact of Parental Background on Skills and Qualifications

To investigate to what extent parental background matters in Europe for skills and qualifications, this section discusses the results of two empirical exercises. Notably, it explores the impact of parental background on skills of 15-year-olds based on PISA data—and how this has changed across subsequent survey rounds and on educational attainment based on PIAAC data—and how this has evolved across different age cohorts.

In the analysis of PISA data, the impact of parental background on mathematics performance is measured as the percentage point difference between the share of top-performing pupils from a 'strong' parental background and the

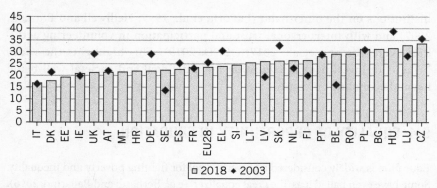

Figure 9.15 Gap (in percentage points) in probability of being a top performer in mathematics between pupils from strong and weak parental backgrounds.
The 2003 Programme for International Student Assessment (PISA) data are used as this is the first round available with solid data on mathematics skills. The 2000 PISA survey focused mostly on literacy. No 2003 data are available for SI, EE, LT, RO, HR, BG, MT. No microdata are available for CY. EU is calculated as the weighted average of the available EU countries.
Source: OECD PISA survey.

share that comes from a 'weak' parental background.[37] 'Top-performance' among pupils is defined as having a mathematics test score in the top quartile in their own country. Finally, 'strong' and 'weak' parental background are respectively defined as the top and bottom quartiles of a ranking based on parental education and occupational categories.[38]

On average, around 14% of 15-year-olds from a weak parental background perform in the top quartile in their country. For pupils from a strong parental background, this probability goes up to almost 40%. While skills acquisition patterns seem more egalitarian in Italy, Denmark, and Estonia, strong impacts of parental background are observed in the Czech Republic, Luxembourg, and Hungary.

At the EU level, these shares have hardly changed over 2003–2018, and, as a result, the impact of parental background on mathematics proficiency remained largely stable. At the same time, substantial changes (in both directions) can

---

37 We are well aware that the literature proposes a broad range of different ways to measure the impact of parental background on education outcomes. That different measures lead to different results is a fact that has been more broadly recognized in the inequality of opportunity literature (e.g., Ferreira and Peragine, 2016; Ramos and Van de gaer, 2016). The choice of the indicator has in this case been based mostly on its transparent and intuitive interpretation.

38 All surveyed 15-year-olds are first sorted (in ascending order) according to (a) highest parental education, (b) maternal education, (c) paternal education, (d) highest parental occupational status, (e) maternal occupational status, and finally (f) paternal occupational status. Observations with missing values for these variables are dropped from the analysis.

be observed at the individual Member State level, as shown in Figure 9.15. The impact of parental background declined markedly in five countries: Hungary, Slovakia, Greece, Germany, and the United Kingdom. In most of these countries, the impact was comparatively strong at the outset. With the exception of the Czech Republic, Poland, and perhaps Portugal, other Member States with a very strong impact of parental background on mathematics skills in 2003 achieved a substantial reduction in that impact by 2018. On the other hand, the influence of parental background became stronger in some other countries, with a notable increase in Sweden, Latvia, Finland, and Belgium—which had a particularly weak impact of background on proficiency in 2003. Hence, over time, some convergence can be observed in the impact of parental background on the mathematics' skills of 15-year-olds.

The indicator presents strong variation over time, with some Member States switching from best to worst performers (or the other way around) over a period of 15 years. Some of these improvements are likely to be the result of targeted policy action (e.g., in Germany); however, some of it is no doubt also due to the statistical properties of the indicator and measurement error. Therefore, it is important to focus mostly on broad patterns that remain consistent over time; for example, countries such as Hungary, Czech Republic, and Slovakia showing a stronger impact of background than countries such as Denmark and Sweden.

It is also important to note that the indicator of social mobility used here does not say anything about the general level of performance among 15-year-olds. In other words, a reduction in the gap (and hence an improvement in social mobility) is equally likely to arise from an improvement in performance among pupils from socioeconomically weaker backgrounds as from a deterioration in performance among pupils from socioeconomically stronger backgrounds. This is all the more relevant given that the average performance level declined over the concerned period in a number of countries, as shown in Figure 9.4.

A similar exercise can be carried out for educational attainment based on PIAAC data. As no time series are available, however, the analysis draws (as before in Section 9.2.2) on cross-sectional analysis, with the comparison over time proxied by a comparison over different age cohorts. In practice, we look at educational attainment across individuals from three age groups (25–39, 40–54, and 55–64), and we explore to what extent it is correlated with educational attainment of these individuals' parents. The impact of parental background on educational attainment is measured as the relative gap (in %) in tertiary attainment between individuals from a strong and those from a weak parental background. A strong (weak) parental background is defined as being in the top (bottom) quartile of a ranking of parental educational attainment.[39]

---

39 Unfortunately, no data on parental occupation are available in the PIAAC dataset.

First, in cross-country comparison and considering only the youngest age co-hort, lower tertiary attainment rates seem to coincide with a stronger impact of parental background on educational attainment. For example, parental attainment matters a lot for their children's tertiary attainment in Slovakia, Hungary, and Italy, where tertiary attainment is relatively low among 25- to 39-year-olds as compared to other Member States. The lowest impact of parental background is observed in the UK, Estonia, and Finland, where educational attainment is relatively high. Again, there are many exceptions to this broad pattern. Notably, Lithuania combines one of the strongest impacts of parental background on attainment with one of the highest tertiary attainment rates in the European Union. The strong impact of parental background on educational attainment in Italy is quite remarkable as well, given that we noted earlier that the impact of parental background on skills attainment of 15-year-olds in these countries is relatively weak. More generally, a comparison of Figure 9.15 and Figure 9.16 shows that equal opportunities at the level of 15-year-olds' skills attainment does not necessarily correlate with equal opportunities in terms of educational attainment. Some countries perform well (e.g., Estonia, United Kingdom, Sweden) or badly (e.g., Hungary, Czech Republic, and Slovakia) at both levels; on the other hand, Italy performs well at the skills attainment level but not in terms of tertiary attainment; and the opposite applies for Finland and Poland.

Then, if different age cohorts are compared to each other, data suggest that for younger generations in the European Union, tertiary attainment is less dependent on parental background than for older generations, especially in countries where tertiary attainment has expanded strongly (such as Ireland, Estonia, France, Slovenia, Poland). Typically, children from weaker parental backgrounds seem to have benefited more from the expansion of tertiary attainment (in

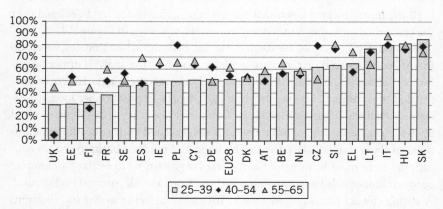

Figure 9.16 Relative gap in tertiary attainment rates between children of parents with stronger and weaker educational attainment, different age cohorts.
Source: OECD Programme for the International Assessment of Adult Competencies (PIAAC) Survey (Round 1: 2008–2013). Data for Greece, Lithuania and Slovenia are based on Round 2 (2012–2016); Data for Hungary are based on Round 3 (2017).

relative terms) than those from stronger parental backgrounds (who already had high rates of tertiary attainment). An exception is Lithuania, where the impact of parental background strengthened considerably across generations. While tertiary attainment remained relatively stable on average, it declined strongly for students from weaker parental backgrounds. Also in Slovakia, where the impact of parental background was already relatively high among older generations, this impact is even slightly stronger for the younger generation.

The finding that educational expansion has coincided with a widespread reduction on educational inequalities—in other words, the weakening of the relationship between educational attainment and socioeconomic background—is not new in the literature (see, e.g., Breen et al., 2009b; Arum et al., 2007). The literature finds more generally a decline in inequality in educational opportunities by social background (Bernardi and Ballarino, 2016). Of course, beyond education outcomes, there are other channels through which parental background can influence earnings. The literature has described, for instance, how parental support (at home and through networks) can help individuals to secure a better job (e.g., Knoll et al. 2017; Torche, 2015).

9.4.2 Inequalities in Lifelong Learning

The rising importance of skills in the labour market calls for adequate investments in human capital. This does not only concern equipping labour market entrants with strong cognitive and noncognitive skills through initial education, but also ensuring wide access to adult learning opportunities, to offer a second chance to those who did not succeed in initial education or to allow adults to reskill or upskill themselves, amongst other reasons to benefit from a wider set of employment opportunities.

At the level of initial education, clear patterns of rising attainment are observed as early school leaving rates are declining across the European Union. However, in spite of the increasing needs to keep skills up to date in today's rapidly changing economies, participation rates in adult learning have risen relatively slowly, from around 7% in 2000 to 11% in 2018 on average in the European Union.[40] Moreover, patterns of participation are typically skewed towards those who already have high levels of education and/or skills. Kilpi-Jakonen et al. (2015) find that, with a few exceptions, in most countries in the European Union, participation in adult learning tends to exacerbate existing educational inequalities rather than act as an equalizer.

Figure 9.17 shows that participation in adult learning by low-qualified (but also other) individuals is dramatically low in countries such as Romania, Croatia, and Bulgaria. Unfortunately, these are typically also countries where the largest gaps in socioeconomic outcomes are found for low-qualified workers (Section

---

40   This figure comes from Labour Force Survey data and refers to adults in the 25–64 age group reporting on their participation in training in the 4 weeks preceding the survey.

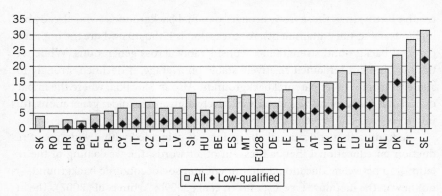

Figure 9.17 Participation in adult learning (25–64 age group, 2018).
The data reflect participation in education and training in the last 4 weeks. No data available on low-qualified for RO and SK.
Source: EU Labour Force Survey (LFS).

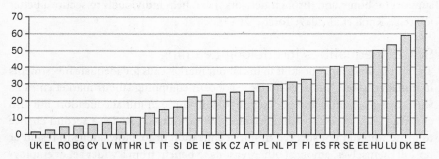

Figure 9.18 Participation rate in active labour market policies of those looking for work.
Data are expressed as the number of Active Labour Market Programme (ALMP) participants per 100 persons looking for work.
Source: European Commission: DG EMPL labour market policies database, latest available data (2017 or 2018 for most countries, 2014 for IT and 2009 for UK).

9.3). Moreover, in these countries, unemployed individuals also tend to receive less support in terms of active labour market policies (Figure 9.18), further exacerbating the 'low-skills-trap'.

9.5 DIFFERENCES ACROSS MEMBER STATES

The preceding considerations suggest substantial heterogeneity across Member States, not only with regard to the distribution of educational attainment, but also to the returns to educational attainment and inequality of opportunity in education. The determinants of these different outcomes are complex and point at important complementarities between the structure of education systems and labour markets, but also at the role of policies and institutions. In what follows, we briefly review some of the factors, without aiming at being exhaustive.

9.5.1 The Link Between Education Outcomes and the Returns to Education

Cross-country divergences in educational outcomes and returns to education have often been linked to differences in relative supply and demand for qualified workers. The preceding evidence provides some indications that human capital supply does respond to signals of human capital demand in the sense that those countries where labour market opportunities for the low-qualified workers are most scarce (such as Czech Republic, Slovakia, Bulgaria, and Poland) and financial incentives to finish at least upper secondary school are strong, individuals are more like to stay at school until they obtain at least an upper secondary degree. On the other hand, as mentioned earlier, there could be some endogeneity at play: the lower is the proportion of low-qualified adults, the stronger the stigma they experience might be in the labour market, resulting in more limited labour market opportunities.

Interestingly, while Denmark and Sweden used to be around Europe's best performers in the sense of having a low level of low-qualified adults in 2005, over the period 2005–2018, the proportion of low-qualified adults in these countries remained stagnant (or even increased slightly in Denmark) while other countries improved considerably. As a result, they are moving increasingly towards the EU28 average. The consequences of low achievement are, however, less dramatic than in other countries in the European Union, given the relatively good labour market outcomes for low-qualified workers.

One country that has made surprisingly little progress since 2005 as compared to other countries in the same region is Romania. This is all the more worrying as Romania has above-average employment gaps for low-qualified individuals, among the highest wage gaps for low-qualified workers (Figure 9.11), and, as a result, a strong correlation between educational attainment and poverty.

9.5.2 Structure of the Education System

The variation in educational attainment patterns results partly from differences in the structure of education systems across Member States. While education systems inspired by the Anglo-Saxon model are typically more focused on providing general training during compulsory schooling time, which can be complemented by academic tertiary education or more vocational-oriented training afterwards, education systems inspired by the Continental model tend to sort pupils into different streams (academic streams for those envisaging tertiary attainment and vocational streams for those envisaging a swift entry in the labour market) at a fairly young age. While some scholars have argued that the latter system is more likely to reduce social mobility and lead to unequal outcomes because parents with higher educational attainment are more likely to steer their children into academic tracks (e.g., Van de Werfhorst and Mijs, 2010; Schleicher and Zoido, 2016), there are also countries (such as the Netherlands and Finland) that follow the Continental model and still show relatively good outcomes in terms of equity.

Some scholars have argued that the structure of the education system is deeply engrained in the institutional setup of an economy, intertwined with societal values and norms, and complementary to structural features in other spheres of the economy such as labour market and product market regulations and should therefore be considered part of the 'social contract' in a country. Notably, Hall and Soskice (2001) posit that 'liberal market economies' (such as the UK and Ireland) are more likely to rely on markets for coordination. In such an environment, ensuring competition is important, and relatively loose product and labour market regulations provide sufficient flexibility to firms to hire, fire, and grow. Workers are less likely to stay in the same job for a long time and therefore benefit most from a good general training that is complemented by job-specific skills acquired on-the-job.

On the other hand, there are 'coordinated market economies' (of which Germany is the prime example, but Austria, Finland, the Netherlands, and Belgium also belong to this group) which rely more on strategic coordination between economic actors. The social contract establishes that workers receive more job-specific training and that they can expect to have the opportunity to stay in the same or a similar job for most of their career. This motivates firms to invest more extensively in worker's training (e.g., through apprenticeships). Stricter product and labour market regulations ensure that competition between firms does not crowd out coordination and that workers are better protected against dismissal. Typically, social safety nets are also better developed in coordinated market economies.

These institutional complementarities between different aspects of an economy are important to consider in policy discussions about the transferability of institutions from one country to another.[41] On the other hand, given the swift changes taking place in labour markets today as a result of progressive globalization and technological change, the lines between different 'models' are likely to become increasingly blurred (Hall and Gingerich, 2004), and transferable skills are gaining importance across Europe.

9.5.3 Patterns of Sectoral Specialization

Another important determinant of differences across Member States in the observed patterns of educational attainment is the structure of national

---

41 See, e.g., Beblavý et al. (2013) who arrive at similar conclusions based on an exploration of the complementarities between educational institutions and social protection institutions.

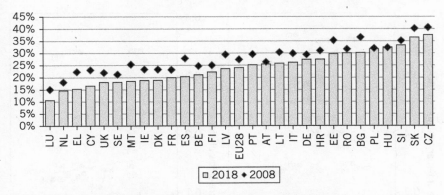

Figure 9.19 Employment share in industry and construction (2008 and 2018).
Industry and construction is defined as Statistical Classification of Economic Activities in
the European Community (NACE) sectors B–F. Employment is expressed as a share of total
employment.
Source: Eurostat, based on Labour Force Survey (LFS).

economies and in particular national patterns of sectoral specialization. In countries that are specialized in manufacturing, the demand for medium-qualified workers is likely to be higher than in those countries that are specialized in providing professional or business services where the demand for highly qualified workers is likely to be more prominent (see Figure 9.19).

As a result of important structural changes that are taking place triggered by globalization and technological change, significant shifts in patterns of skills demand are observed. Over time, the economic importance of the manufacturing sector (in particular in terms of employment) is declining across Europe (see also Section 9.3.1). The 2008 financial crisis sped up this process. At the same time, services are gaining in importance (see Kiss and Vandeplas, 2015, for more details). Still, strong differences persist in sectoral composition across Member States.

9.5.4 Policy Factors

Policy factors can have a marked impact on observed patterns of educational attainment as well. The level of public investment in education matters, but much less than one might expect. Most countries in the European Union still rely heavily on public spending to fund education. In a simple cross-sectional regression, public expenditures on education are only weakly correlated with tertiary attainment (with an R^2 of around 9%), and this correlation breaks down once variation across time is considered (in a fixed effects regression). The correlation between public expenditures and low attainment is not significant at all.[42] It is

---

42 One could argue that it is better to consider lagged data on expenditures; however, expenditures on education show relatively strong persistence over time and change relatively slowly.

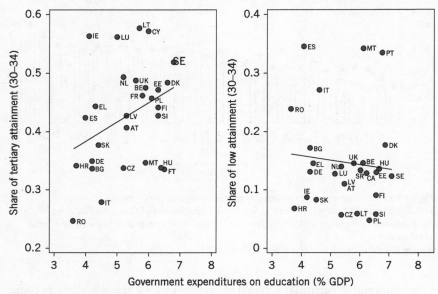

Figure 9.20 Relationship between government expenditures on education (2003) and educational attainment (30–34 age group) across the EU28 (2018).
Government expenditures were lagged by 15 years to reflect expenditures when the 30–34 age cohort was 15–19 years' old.
Source: Eurostat data (from COFOG).

more generally agreed in the literature that education outcomes depend more on *how money is spent* on education than on *how much is spent* (as long as basic financing conditions are satisfied) (see, e.g., Hanushek, 1986, 2003).[43]

The dimension of *how* money is spent concerns a wide range of different education policies that have an impact on educational outcomes and returns to education as well as on equality of opportunity in education. Important policies that have been referred to in the literature are high-quality early childhood education and care institutions, mechanisms to ensure teaching quality and provide support to children from vulnerable backgrounds, early school-leaving prevention policies, and so on. Schleicher and Zoido (2016) provide an overview of education policies that countries have implemented to address educational inequalities while emphasizing, however, that there are no 'one-size-fits-all' solutions.

Wider access to higher education can be facilitated through fair and effective policies regarding admission and tuition fees; but in many cases the decision of whether to pursue higher education is largely determined by what happens at earlier stages of education—in other words, academic performance in

---

43   This does not mean that the level of spending does not matter at all; see, e.g., Kirabo Jackson et al. (2016).

pre-primary, primary, and secondary schools and the aspirations and parental/ teacher support that emanate from there.

Policies outside of the education sector matter as well. One area where policies can matter is the tax-benefit system because it influences the relative private returns from (and hence the incentive to pursue) higher attainment. It not only counteracts inequality of earned income, but also offers insurance against unemployment and social protection in case of inactivity. High participation tax rates can generate poverty traps, especially for low-wage (often low-qualified) workers. Activation policies matter as well, especially those that improve matching and provide learning opportunities to adults (Lammers and Kok, 2019). Wage setting and employment protection institutions may also influence the labour market returns to education, as argued earlier.[44]

Another aspect is the regulation of qualification requirements to enter certain jobs. A considerable share of the population[45] is employed in the public sector, where occupations are more often regulated (in terms of educational requirements) than in the private sector. Especially in the education and (health) care sector, the quality of public services is often controlled through minimum qualification requirements in terms of educational qualifications. This can have an impact on the observed patterns of educational attainment. For example, minimum requirements for teachers and nurses vary across countries in terms of educational attainment (UNESCO, 2013).[46]

Policies can also influence demand for and utilization of skills by influencing how conducive the regulatory environment is to business investment and job creation. Policies affecting firm entry, firm growth, and firm exit can have an important impact on the efficiency of labour allocation across sectors and on the type of jobs that are created. If investment in knowledge-intensive industries is encouraged, tertiary educated graduates are more likely to find jobs that are in line with their qualifications, which will raise the returns to tertiary education.

9.6 CONCLUSION

This chapter has shown that education and skills are becoming increasingly important determinants of life outcomes in Europe. On the positive side, populations across Europe are upgrading their educational attainment, and educational attainment is less strongly linked to parental background than it was for previous generations. On the negative side, important gaps remain in educational

---

44 For a more detailed review of relevant policy factors, see Heckman and Jacobs (2011).

45 The share of public employment out of total employment ranged from 15% in Germany to 35% in Denmark in 2013 according to ILOSTAT figures.

46 Still, UNESCO (2013) observes a trend for programmes at lower levels of education to be gradually phased out.

attainment. Moreover, data suggest that skills attainment has not improved substantially over time. Furthermore, while lifelong learning is becoming increasingly important in today's fast-changing economies, the individuals who need it most may not always have access to adequate opportunities to upskill or reskill. Finally, the chapter highlights that education and labour market outcomes vary substantially across countries. The structure of national education systems is deeply engrained in the institutional setup of an economy, intertwined with societal values and norms, and complementary to other institutions—not only within the world of education, but also in those governing labour markets, business investment, and social protection policies, thus highlighting the challenges encountered when comparing educational outcomes between countries.

ACKNOWLEDGEMENTS

Opinions expressed in this paper are those of the author and do not necessarily reflect the view of the institutions to which she is affiliated.

REFERENCES

Acemoglu, D. (2002a). Technical change, inequality, and the labor market. *Journal of Economic Literature, 40*(1), 7–72.

Acemoglu, D. (2002b). Directed technical change. *Review of Economic Studies, 69*(4), 781–809.

Almas, I., Cappelen, A. W., and Tungodden, B. (2020). Cutthroat capitalism versus cuddly socialism: Are Americans more meritocratic and efficiency-seeking than Scandinavians? *Journal of Political Economy, 128*(5): 1753–1788. doi: 10.1086/705551

Angrist, J. D., and Krueger, A. B. (1991). Does compulsory school attendance affect schooling and earnings? *Quarterly Journal of Economics, 106*(4), 979–1014.

Arneson, R. J. (1989). Equality and equal opportunity for welfare. *Philosophical Studies, 56* (1), 77–93.

Arrow, K. J. (1962). The economic implications of learning by doing. *Review of Economic Studies, 29*, 155–173.

Arrow, K. J. (1973). Higher education as a filter. *Journal of Public Economics, 2*, 193–216.

Arum, R., Gamoran, A., and Shavit, Y. (2007). More inclusion than diversion: Expansion, differentiation, and market structure in higher education. In Y, Shavit, R. Arum, and A. Gamoran (eds.), *Stratification in higher education: A comparative study* (pp. 1–35). Stanford, CA: Stanford University Press.

Asai, K., Breda, T., Rain, A., Romanello, L., and Sangnier, M. (2020). *Education, skills and skill mismatch: A review and some new evidence based on the PIAAC survey.* Rapport IPP No. 26. Paris: Institut des Politiques Publiques.

Autor, D. H., Katz, L. F., and Kearney, M. S. (2006). The polarization of the US labor market. *American Economic Review, 96*(2), 189–194.

Autor, D. H., Katz, L. F., and Krueger, A. B. (1998). Computing inequality: Have computers changed the labor market? *Quarterly Journal of Economics, 113*(4), 1169–1214.

Autor, D. H., Levy, F., and Murnane, R. J. (2003). The skill-content of recent technological change: An empirical investigation. *Quarterly Journal of Economics, 118*(4), 1279–1333.

Barrett, G. F., and Riddell, W. C. (2016). *Ageing and literacy skills: Evidence from IALS, ALL and PIAAC.* IZA Discussion Paper 10017. Bonn: IZA.

Beblavý, M., Teteryatnikova, M., and Thum, A. (2015). *Does the growth in higher education mean a decline in the quality of degrees?* Centre for European Policy Studies Paper 10258. Brussels: Centre for European Policy Studies.

Beblavý, M., Thum, A.-E., and Veselkova, M. (2013). Education and social protection policies in OECD countries: Social stratification and policy intervention. *Journal of European Social Policy, 23*(5), 487–503.

Bernardi, F., and Ballarino, G. (eds.). (2016). *Education, occupation and social origin: A comparative analysis of the transmission of socio-economic inequalities.* London: Edward Elgar.

Blundell, R., Green, D.A., Jin, W. (2016). The UK Wage Premium Puzzle: How did a Large Increase in University Graduates Leave the Education Premium Unchanged? IFS Working Paper W16/01. Institute for Fiscal Studies, London, UK.

Bound, J., and Johnson, G. (1992). Changes in the structure of wages during the 1980s: An evaluation of alternative explanations. *American Economic Review, 82*(3), 371–392.

Breen, R., Luijkx, R., Müller, W., and Pollak, R. (2009a). Long-term trends in educational inequality in Europe: Class inequalities and gender differences. *European Sociological Review, 26*(11), 31–48.

Breen, R., Luijkx, R., Müller, W., and Pollak, R. (2009b). Nonpersistent inequality in educational attainment: Evidence from eight European countries. *American Journal of Sociology, 114*(5), 1475–1521.

Brown, S., and Sessions, J. G. (1999). Education and employment status: a test of the strong screening hypothesis in Italy. *Economics of Education Review, 18*(4), 397–404.

Brunello, G., Fort, M., and Weber, G. (2009). Changes in compulsory schooling, education and the distribution of wages in Europe. *Economic Journal, 119*(536), 516–539.

Büchel, F., and Battu, H. (2003). The theory of differential overqualification: does it work? *Scottish Journal of Political Economy, 50*(1), 1–16.

Buchmann, C., DiPrete, T. A., and McDaniel, A. (2008). Gender inequalities in education. *Annual Review of Sociology, 34,* 319–337.

Chevalier, A., Harmon, C., Walker, I., and Zhu, Y. (2004). Does education raise productivity, or just reflect it?. *Economic Journal, 114*: F499–F517.

Colonna, F. (2017). Chicken or the egg? Human capital demand and supply. *Politica Economica, 1,* 97–123.

de Grip, A. (2006). *Evaluating human capital obsolescence.* Working paper ROA-W-2006/2E. Maastricht: Research Centre for Education and the Labour Market, Maastricht University.

Devereux, P. J., and Fan, W. (2011). Earnings returns to the British education expansion, *Economics of Education Review, 30* (6), 1153–1166.

Dickson, M. (2013). The causal effect of education on wages revisited. *Oxford Bulletin of Economics and Statistics, 75*(4): 477–498.

Ferreira, F. H. G., and Peragine, V. (2016). Individual responsibility and equality of opportunity. In M. D. Adler and M. Fleurbaey (eds.), *The Oxford handbook of well-being and public policy* (pp. 746–784). Oxford: Oxford Handbook Online.

Finegold, D., and Soskice, D. (1988). The failure of training in Britain: analysis and prescription. *Oxford Review of Economic Policy,* 4(3), 21-53.

Flisi, S., Goglio, V., Meroni, E. C., and Vera-Toscano, E. (2019). Cohort patterns in adult literacy skills: How are new generations doing? *Journal of Policy Modeling, 41*(1), 52–65. https://doi.org/10.1016/j.jpolmod.2018.10.002

Frank, R. H. (1978). Why women earn less: the theory and estimation of differential overqualification. *American Economic Review, 68*(3), 360–373.

Galindo-Rueda, F., and Vignoles, A. (2005). The declining importance of ability in predicting educational attainment. *Journal of Human Resources, 40*(2), 335–353.

Garrouste, C. (2010). *100 years of educational reforms in Europe: A contextual database.* JRC Scientific and Technical Reports. Luxembourg: Publications Office of the European Union.

Gathmann, C., Jürges, H., and Reinhold, S. (2015). Compulsory schooling reforms, education and mortality in twentieth century Europe. *Social Science and Medicine, 127*(C), 74–82.

Goldin, C. (2006). The quiet revolution that transformed women's employment, education, and family. *American Economic Review, 96*(2), 1–21.

Goldin C., and Katz, L. F. (2008). *The race between education and technology.* Cambridge, MA: Harvard University Press.

Goos, M., Manning, A., and Salomons, A. (2009). Explaining job polarization in Europe: The roles of technology, globalization and institutions. *American Economic Review Papers and Proceedings, 99*(2), 58–63.

Gottschalk, P., and Smeeding, T. M. (1997). Cross-national comparisons of earnings and income inequality. *Journal of Economic Literature, 35*(2), 633–687.

Green, F., and Henseke, G. (2016). Should governments of OECD countries worry about graduate underemployment? *Oxford Review of Economic Policy*, 32(4), 514–537.

Groot, W., and Oosterbeek, H. (1994). Earnings effects of different components of human capital vs. screening, *Review of Economics and Statistics*, 76, 317–321.

Haasler, S. R., and Gottschall, K. (2015). Still a perfect model? The gender impact of vocational training in Germany, *Journal of Vocational Education & Training*, 67(1), 78–92, doi: 10.1080/13636820.2014.922118.

Hall, P. A., and Gingerich, D. W. (2004). *Varieties of capitalism and institutional complementarities in the macroeconomy: An empirical analysis*. Discussion Paper 04.5 Gottingen, GER: Max Planck Institute for the Study of Societies.

Hall, P. A., and Soskice, D. (2001). *Varieties of capitalism: The institutional foundations of comparative advantage*. Oxford: Oxford University Press.

Hall, R. E., and Jones, C. I. (1999). Who do some countries produce so much more output per worker than others? *Quarterly Journal of Economics*, 144(1), 83–116.

Hanushek, E. A. (1986). The economics of schooling: Production and efficiency in public schools. *Journal of Economic Literature*, 24(3), 1141–1177.

Hanushek, E. A. (2003). The failure of input-based schooling policies. *Economic Journal*, 113(485), F64–F98.

Harmon, C., Walker, I., and Westergaard-Nielsen, N. (2001). *Education and earnings in Europe: A cross country analysis of the returns to education*. Cheltenham, UK: Edward Elgar.

Havlik, P. (2014). *Structural change in Europe during the crisis*. FIW Policy Brief No. 22. Research Centre International Economics FIW, Federal Ministry for Digital and Economic Affairs, Vienna, Austria.

Havlik, P. (2015). Patterns of structural change in the new EU Member States. *Danube: Law and Economics Review*, 6(3), 133–157.

Heckman, J. J., and Jacobs, B. (2011). Policies to create and destroy human capital. In E. S. Phelps and H. W. Sinn (eds.), *Perspectives on the performance of the continental economies* (pp. 253–322). CESifo Seminar Series. Cambridge, MA: MIT Press.

Helliwell, J. F., and Putnam, R. D. (2007). Education and social capital. *Eastern Economic Journal*, 33(1), 1–19.

Horn, J. L., and Cattell, R. B. (1967). Age differences in fluid and crystallized intelligence. *Acta Psychologica*, 26, 107–129.

ILO. (2014). Skills mismatch in Europe. Statistics Brief, Department of Statistics, September 2014. International Labour Office, Geneva.

Johnes, G. (1998). Human capital versus sorting: New data and a new test. *Applied Economics Letters*, 5: 665–667.

Kahn, L. M. (2015). Wage compression and the gender pay gap. *IZA World of Labor 2015*, 150.

Katz, L. F., and Autor, D. H. (1999). Changes in the wage structure and earn-ings inequality. In O. Ashenfelter and D. Card (eds.), *Handbook of Labor Economics*, Vol. *3A* (pp. 1463–1555). North-Holland: Elsevier.

Katz, L. F., and Murphy, K. M. (1992). Changes in relative wages, 1963–1987: Supply and demand factors. *Quarterly Journal of Economics, 107*(1), 35–78.

Kilpi-Jakonen, E., Vono de Vilhena, D. and Blossfeld, H. (2015). Adult learning and social inequalities: Processes of equalisation or cumulative disadvantage?. *International Review of Education, 61*, 529–546. https://doi.org/10.1007/s11159-015-9498-5

Kirabo Jackson, C., Johnson, R. C., and Persico, C. (2016). The effects of school spending on educational and economic outcomes: Evidence from school fi-nance reforms. *Quarterly Journal of Economics, 131*(1), 157–218.

Kiss, A., and Vandeplas, A. (2015). *Measuring skills mismatch*. Analytical Webnote 7/2015. Brussels: European Commission.

Knoll, B., Riedel, N., and Schlenker, E. (2017). He's a chip off the old block—the persistence of occupational choices across generations. *Labour, 31*(2), 174–203.

Kroch, E., and Sjoblom, K. (1994). Schooling as human capital or a signal, *Journal of Human Resources, 29*: 156–180.

Krueger, A. (1993). How computers have changed the wage structure: Evidence from microdata, 1984–1989. *Quarterly Journal of Economics, 108*(1), 33–60.

Lammers, M., and Kok, L. (2019). Are active labor market policies (cost-)effec-tive in the long run? Evidence from the Netherlands. *Empirical Economics.* https://doi.org/10.1007/s00181-019-01812-3

LaPorta, R., Lopez-de-Silanes, F., Shleifer, A., and Vishny, R. W. (1997). Trust in large organizations. *American Economic Review Papers and Proceedings, 87* (2), 333–338.

Layard, R., and Psacharopolous, G. (1974). The screening hypothesis and the returns to education, *Journal of Political Economy, 82*, 985–998.

Lucas, R. E. (1988). On the mechanics of economic development. *Journal of Monetary Economics, 22*, 3–42.

Marcolin, L., Miroudot, S., and Squicciarini, M. (2016). *The routine content of occupations: New cross-country measures based on PIAAC, OECD trade policy papers 188.* Paris: OECD Publishing. http://dx.doi.org/10.1787/5jm0mq86fljg-en

Martí, M., and Ródenas, C. (2007). Migration estimation based on the labour force survey: An EU-15 perspective. *International Migration Review, 41*(1), 101–126.

Mauro, P., and Spilimbergo, A. (1999). How do the skilled and the unskilled re-spond to regional shocks? The case of Spain. *IMF Staff Papers, 46*(1), 1–17.

McGoldrick, K. M., and Robst, J. (1996). Gender differences in overeducation: a test of the theory of differential overqualification. *American Economic Review, 86*(2), 280–284.

Murtin, F., Mackenbach, J., Jasilionis D., and Mira d'Ercole, M. (2017). *Inequalities in longevity by education in OECD countries: Insights from new OECD estimates.* OECD Statistics Working Papers, 2017/02. Paris: OECD Publishing.

Nedelkoska, L., and Quintini, G. (2018). *Automation, skills use and training.* OECD Social, Employment and Migration Working Papers 202. Paris: OECD Publishing.

Nelson, R. R., and Phelps, E. S. (1966). Investment in humans, technological diffusion, and economic growth. *American Economic Review, 56*(1/2), 69–75.

OECD. (2019). The outcomes of investments in skills. In OECD (eds.), *Skills matter: Additional results from the Survey of Adult Skills.* Paris: OECD Publishing. https://doi.org/10.1787/1f029d8f-en

Oreopoulos, P. (2007). Do dropouts drop out too soon? Wealth, health and happiness from compulsory schooling. *Journal of Public Economics, 91,* 2213–2229.

Peracchi, F. (2006). Educational wage premia and the distribution of earnings: an international perspective. In: Hanushek, E.A., and Welch, F. (eds.) *Handbook of the Economics of Education,* Volume 1. Elsevier B.V.

Persyn, D. (2017). *Migration within the EU: The role of education, wage differences and cultural barriers.* JRC Technical Report JRC104494. Brussels: European Commission, DG Joint Research Centre, EUR 28286 EN. doi:10.2791/373605

Pouliakas, K. (2018). The risk of automation in EU labour markets. A skills-requirements approach. In T. Hogarth (ed.), *Economy, employment and skills: European, regional and global perspective in an age of uncertainty.* Rome: Quaderni Fondazione G. Brodolini, N.61.

Powell, J. W., and Solga, H. (2011). Why are higher education participation rates in Germany so low? Institutional barriers to higher education expansion. *Journal of Education and Work, 24*(1–2, S), 49–68.

Psacharopoulos, G. (1979). On the weak versus the strong version of the screening hypothesis. *Economics Letters, 4*(2), 181–185.

Ramos, X., and Van de gaer, D. (2016). Approaches to inequality of opportunity: Principles, measures and evidence. *Journal of Economic Surveys, 30*(5), 855–883.

Rawls, J. (1971). *A theory of justice.* Cambridge, MA: Harvard University Press.

Redding, S. (1996). The low-skill, low-quality trap: Strategic complementarities between human capital and R&D. *Economic Journal,* 106(435), 458–470.

Reichelt, M., and Abraham, M. (2017). Occupational and regional mobility as substitutes: a new approach to understanding job changes and wage inequality. *Social Forces, 95*(4), 1399–1426.

Roemer, J. E., and Trannoy, A. (2016). Equality of opportunity: Theory and measurement. *Journal of Economic Literature, 54*(4), 1288–1332.

Schleicher, A., and Zoido, P. (2016). Global equality of educational opportunity: Creating the conditions for all students to succeed. *Journal of Social Issues, 72,* 696–719.

Schultz, T. W. (1961). Investment in human capital. *American Economic Review*, *51*, 1–19.

Sen, A. (1980). Equality of what? In S. M. McMurrin (ed.), *The Tanner Lectures on human values (Vol. 1)* (pp. 195–220). Salt Lake City: University of Utah Press.

Sicherman, N. (1991). "Overeducation" in the labour market. *Journal of Labour Economics*, 9(2), 101–122.

Spence, M. (1973). Job market signalling. *Quarterly Journal of Economics, 87*, 355–374.

Spence, M. (1974). *Market signalling: Informational transfer in hiring and related screening processes*. Cambridge, MA: Harvard University Press.

Thelen, K. (2004). *How institutions evolve: The political economy of skills in Germany, Britain, the United States, and Japan. Cambridge*, UK: Cambridge University Press, 333 pp.

Thurow, L. C. (1975). *Generating inequality*. New York: Basic Books.

Torche, F. (2015). Analyses of intergenerational mobility: An interdisciplinary review. *The Annals of the American Academy of Political and Social Science, 657*(1), 37–62.

UNESCO. (2013). *ISCED Fields of Education and Training 2013 (ISCED-F 2013), Manual to accompany the International Standard Classification of Education 2011*. Montreal: UNESCO Institute for Statistics.

Van Ark, B., O'Mahony, M., and Timmer, M. P. (2012). Europe's productivity performance in comparative perspective: Trends, causes and recent developments. In M. Mas and R. Stehrer (eds.), *Industrial productivity in Europe: Growth and crisis* (pp. 65–92). Cheltenham: Edward Elgar Publishing.

Vandeplas, A., and Thum-Thysen, A. (2019). Skills Mismatch & Productivity in the EU. European Economy Discussion Paper 100, European Commission.

van der Velden, R., and Bijlsma, I. (2019). Effective skill: A new theoretical perspective on the relation between skills, skill use, mismatches, and wages. *Oxford Economic Papers, 71*(1), 145–165. https://doi.org/10.1093/oep/gpy028

Van de Werfhorst, H. G., and Mijs, J. J. B. (2010). Achievement inequality and the institutional structure of educational systems: a comparative perspective. *Annual Review of Sociology, 36*, 407–428. https://doi.org/10.1146/annurev.soc.012809.102538

Vera-Toscano, E., Rodrigues, M., and Costa, P. (2017). Beyond educational attainment: The importance of skills and lifelong learning for social outcomes. Evidence for Europe from PIAAC. *European Journal of Education, 52*(2), 217–231.

Verhaest, D., Bogaert, E., Dereymaeker, J., Mestdagh, L., and Baert, S. (2018). Do employers prefer overqualified graduates? A field experiment. *Industrial Relations, 57*(3), 361–388.

Vonyó, T. (2008). Post-war reconstruction and the Golden Age of economic growth. *European Review of Economic History, 12*(2): 221–241.

10

FROM SOCIAL PROTECTION
TO SOCIAL INVESTMENT

EUROPEAN RESPONSES TO GLOBALIZATION, TECHNOLOGICAL CHANGE, LABOUR MARKET FLEXIBILIZATION, AND MIGRATION

Olaf van Vliet, Vincent Bakker, and Lars van Doorn

10.1 INTRODUCTION

Welfare states play an important role in the daily life of European citizens. Traditionally, welfare states provided protection against income loss as a result of unemployment, disability, and old age. Recently, the enabling function of the welfare state has become more important. As a result of developments such as globalization and technological change, economies have become more dynamic and labour markets have become more flexible. Jobs in some sectors disappear whereas new jobs in other sectors are born. Hence, one of the main challenges for workers in the 21st century is how to smooth labour market transitions in order to adapt to increasing flexibility.

Welfare state programmes can play an important role in the transitions between jobs and sectors which workers are making increasingly more frequently during their careers. This enabling function requires a new type of welfare state, one that is focused on training and keeping human capital updated throughout throughout the working life. Such an approach requires so-called social investments which have been at the core of the European Union (EU) social policy agenda over the past decade. Yet welfare states have continuously

Olaf van Vliet, Vincent Bakker, and Lars van Doorn, *From Social Protection to Social Investment* In: *Europe's Income, Wealth, Consumption, and Inequality.* Edited by: Georg Fischer and Robert Strauss, Oxford University Press (2021).
© Oxford University Press. DOI: 10.1093/oso/9780197545706.003.0010

been under budgetary pressure over the past decades as a result of globalization affecting labour markets and because of increased expenditures on pensions and healthcare due to ageing populations. An important question related to such a transformation of the welfare state is how its redistributive function is affected and hence what the implications are for income inequality and poverty.

The aim of this chapter is to describe and analyse the challenges that European welfare states are confronted with in the first decades of the 21st century. First, we focus on the labour market effects of globalization and technological change. To date, the existing literature has been mainly focused on the question of what types of work will (dis)appear, for what types of workers, and in which sectors. Although this is an extremely relevant question, in this chapter, we propose to add another dimension to this debate. We expect that globalization and technological change also affect the type of contract that workers have. The share of nonstandard employment has grown over the past years, and we hypothesize that globalization and technological change have contributed to this trend. Furthermore, the results of this trend, job polarization and labour market flexibilization, will increase inequality between different groups on the labour market.

Another major trend that we discuss is the role of labour migration. Intra-EU immigration has grown slowly since Central and Eastern European (CEE) countries have joined the Union, but it is becoming an increasingly important feature of European labour markets and in the context of European welfare states. Subsequently, we discuss the implications of these trends and developments for European welfare states. Based on an empirical analysis, we show how European welfare states have evolved over time, and we examine to what extent social investment has become more important for them. Here, we update the existing literature with data for the years during and after the financial crisis, and we extend existing studies by including all 28 EU Member States. Furthermore, we demonstrate a novel way of correcting social expenditure data for the number of recipients in order to compare the generosity of new social programmes across countries and over time.

10.2 GLOBALIZATION AND TECHNOLOGICAL CHANGE

The economic literature considers globalization and technological change as two pivotal phenomena transforming European labour markets. However, given the comparable labour market effects of both forces, there has been a lively debate regarding the question of whether globalization or technological change is paramount in determining labour market outcomes (Iversen and Cusack, 2000). This debate is rooted in the methodological challenges associated with empirically disentangling these two effects from each other since both developments have taken place in the same period—namely about the past 30 years—and because they yield similar effects.

Only recently it has been acknowledged that it is not either globalization or technological change that matters, but that both developments have had an impact on the labour market. In several studies, David Autor and his co-authors have compared the labour market effects of Chinese imports with the labour market effects of technological change (Autor et al., 2013, 2015; Acemoglu et al., 2016). Based on data for the United States, they show that in sectors exposed to Chinese imports, employment declined because complete production lines disappeared as a result of these imports. In contrast, technological change lead mainly to polarization: the production line remained, but routine-intense work was replaced by machines. A growing number of studies that examined the employment effects of globalization and technological change across Europe find comparable results (Michaels et al., 2014; Balsvik et al., 2015; Thewissen and Van Vliet, 2019). In the next couple of paragraphs we elaborate on both phenomena and show how they have eventually resulted in the polarization of Europe's labour market.

10.3 THE INITIAL PROMINENCE OF SKILLS IN THE TRANSFORMING LABOUR MARKET

10.3.1 Globalization

Globalization can be understood as the process of economic, social, and political international integration. The economic, social, and political dimensions of globalization are closely related to each other, but, for the analysis of the impact of globalization on European labour markets, the economic dimension is the most relevant. This dimension entails the reduction or removal of international barriers as a result of which trade, capital, and migration flows between countries can increase. As a result, goods and services will be produced in those places in the world where they can be produced in the most efficient way. This leads to lower prices for consumers, which will increase welfare for a society as a whole (Fajgelbaum and Khandelwal, 2016).

At the same time, globalization will yield distributive effects within society. Based on a *Ricardo-Viner framework*, it can be expected that workers who work in sectors in which exports increase as a result of the reduction of trade barriers will benefit. In contrast, workers who work in sectors with increased imports will lose as the imports in fact replace their work (Samuelson, 1971; Sirgy et al., 2007; Walter, 2010). Based on another framework, the *Stolper-Samuelson model* (1941), it can be expected that the production factors that are relatively abundant will gain. Hence, when European countries engage in international trade, this generally means that products which are produced in labour-intensive manufacturing industries are imported from low-wage countries, which results in a lower domestic demand for low-skilled workers. At the same time, exports of knowledge-intensive products increase, which triggers firms to focus on increasing their productivity and hence on innovation. This results in a higher demand for high-skilled workers (Bloom et al., 2016). Over the past few decades, the process of globalization has accelerated rapidly across member countries of the Organisation for Economic Cooperation and Development (OECD) and across European countries in particular.

10.3.2 Technological Change

The literature initially assumed that technological change, like globalization, increased the relative demand for high-skilled workers. Inspired by the work of Tinbergen (1974, 1975), research explaining the rise in the relative wages of high-skilled workers vis-à-vis low-skilled workers throughout the 20th century argued that technological change is *skill biased* (Goldin and Katz, 2009). This bias is rooted in the assumption that technological improvements particularly augment the productivity of high-skilled workers resulting in a relative increase in the demand for high-skilled workers.

The wages of high-skilled workers are subsequently determined by the race between education and technological change (Katz and Murphy, 1992; Katz and Autor, 1999; Goldin and Katz, 2009; Acemoglu and Autor, 2010). If the growth of the relative supply of high-skilled workers stagnates, the upsurge in demand caused by technological change results in increased premiums[1] for high-skilled workers and thus wage inequality. In contrast, an equal increase in the supply and demand of high-skilled workers relative to low-skilled workers will result in skill-upgrading in terms of employment but does not affect the skill premium. While research showed that skill premiums particularly increased in the United Kingdom, this logic holds to a lesser extent for the other European countries, resulting in a more dispersed wage distribution (Davis, 1992; Berman et al., 1998; Fitzenbergen and Kohn, 2006; Atkinson, 2007).

10.4 EXPLAINING JOB POLARIZATION: SHIFTING THE FOCUS FROM SKILL TO ROUTINE

While the focus on skills just described has been quite successful in explaining labour market consequences for a long time, it is not able to offer an appropriate explanation for a rather recent labour market trend in advanced economies: job polarization (Goos et al., 2014; Gregory et al., 2016). This process entails an increase in the share of both high-skilled and low-skilled jobs and a simultaneous decrease in the share of middle-skilled jobs (Acemoglu and Autor, 2010). While the resulting U-shaped labour market was initially documented using

---

1   The wage of high-skilled workers relative to the wage of low-skilled workers.

data for the United States (Acemoglu, 1999), this pattern has also been reported for European countries (Goos et al., 2009, 2014; Michaels et al., 2014; Gregory et al., 2016).

To explain this trend, Autor et al. (2003) introduced the so-called *routine-biased technological change hypothesis*. In contrast to the skill-biased technological change hypothesis' emphasis on labour productivity, this hypothesis focusses on the nature of tasks.[2] More specifically, it assumes that digital capital (artificial intelligence, computers, and robots) is especially suited to perform routine-intense tasks characterized as procedural and rule-based (Acemoglu and Autor, 2010). Subsequently, it can be expected that jobs involving these types of tasks will be automated and might eventually become extinct. Research has shown that middle-skilled jobs in particular involve routine-intense tasks (Autor et al., 2006; Autor and Dorn, 2013; Goos and Manning, 2007; Goos et al., 2014). Examples in this regard are book-keepers, office clerks, and machine operators. The comparative advantage of digital capital in performing routine-intense tasks results in a lower demand for labour in these types of jobs, as a result of which the demand for middle-skilled workers decreases.

Figure 10.1 shows that the European labour market has indeed polarized: the shares of high- and low-paying jobs have relatively increased, while the share of middle-paying jobs decreased. We have grouped the jobs based on Goos et al. (2014), who use two-digit International Standard Classification of Occupations (ISCO) codes to rank occupations by their mean wage rank based on the European Statistics on Income and Living Conditions (EU-SILC).[3] For this figure we use aggregated country-level data. In this regard, we rely on data underlying the European Commission's Employment and Social Developments Review provided by the DG Employment, Social Affairs & Inclusions.

The clear trend of job polarization illustrated in Figure 10.1, the intensity of the process varies substantially per country. The share of middle-paying jobs

---

2   In this regard, a task is defined as a unit of work activity that produces output, both goods and services. Moreover, workers should be considered as individuals allocating their skills to different tasks depending on their comparative advantage and labour market prices (Roy, 1951; Acemoglu and Autor, 2010).

3   As a result, high-paying occupations include corporate managers; physical, mathematical, and engineering professionals; life science and health professionals; other professionals; managers of small enterprises; physical, mathematical, and engineering associate professionals; other associate professionals; and life science and health associate professionals. Middle-paying occupations include stationary plant and related operators; metal, machinery, and related trade work; drivers and mobile plant operators; office clerks; precision, handicraft, craft printing, and related trade workers; extraction and building trades workers; customer service clerks; machine operators and assemblers; and other craft and related trade workers. Finally, low-paying occupations include labourers in mining, construction, manufacturing, and transport; personal and protective service workers; models, sales persons, and demonstrators; and sales and service elementary occupations.

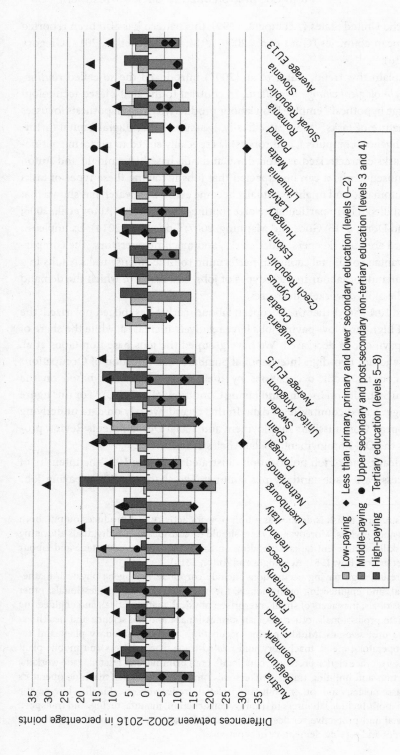

Figure 10.1 Job polarization and employment by educational attainment in Europe (2002–2016).
Educational attainment is coded according to ISCED 1997 for 2002 and ISCED 2011 for 2016. Data years for Romania are 2005 and 2016.

Source: European Commission DG Employment, Social Affairs & Inclusion (2018) and authors' own caluculations.

decreased quite dramatically in Luxembourg (21%), Ireland (19%), France (18%), Portugal (18%), and the United Kingdom (17%), whereas Poland experienced a decrease of only 5% in the share of middle-paying jobs. Moreover, this decrease in Poland was accompanied with a decrease in the share of low-paying jobs. Note that this variation is in line with the broader critique presented by some studies in relation to the importance of (labour market) institutions and culture in explaining labour market transformations (Oesch and Rodríguez Menés, 2011; Fernández-Macías and Hurley, 2017). The higher wages stemming from legal minimum wages and collective bargaining might for instance result in a higher share of high-quality and thus high-paying jobs (Grimshaw et al., 2014). Consequently, job polarization might be less pronounced. Institutions like employment protection or generous welfare state benefits could potentially have similar effects.

Another possible explanation for the polarization of the European labour markets is a shift in Europe's labour supply. This perspective assumes that employers take the characteristics of the supply of workers into account when deciding on production techniques that, in the end, determine the type of available jobs (Murphy and Oesch, 2018). Thus, the availability of a low number of low-skilled workers might decrease the demand for low-paying jobs as this incentivises employers to adapt their production process to the availability of a highly qualified supply of labour. The changes in employment by educational attainment presented in Figure 10.1 do not, however, support this argument. Although the number of high-skilled workers indeed increased, the supply of low-skilled workers increased in Denmarkt and Hungary only. While it should be noted that this does not mean that labour supply effects cannot account for the polarization of European labour markets, there are a least no clear trends that directly explain job polarization. Moreover, recent literature analysing the dissaperence of middle-skilled jobs support this finding (Green 2019).

10.5 INCREASED COMPETITION AT THE LOWER END OF THE LABOUR MARKET

In the previous paragraphs, we focussed on the effects of globalization and technological change, the ways in which both forces have shaped the demand for labour, and how this eventually resulted in job polarization in Europe. Next, we relate the process of job polarization to the increasing competition for low-skilled jobs. Middle-skilled workers faced with a lower demand for routine-intense tasks are forced to supply their labour to jobs involving either less or more complex tasks (Cortes 2016; Goos, 2018). We argue that without additional education or training it can be expected that the abilities of middle-skilled workers are better suited to less complex tasks. Consequently, job polarization will result in increased competition at the lower end of the labour market.

The employment shares of low-paying jobs for 2002 and 2016 presented in Figure 10.2 provide tentative support for this expectation.[4] In this figure we combine the data used for Figure 10.1 with individual-level data from the European Union Labour Force Survey (EU-LFS). This allows us to analyse changes in the share of each education group in low-paying jobs. Between 2002 and 2016 the share of middle-skilled workers employed in low-paying jobs increased across Europe. Note, that although a growing number of middle-skilled workers are on average employed in low-paying jobs (their share increased by 7%), there is a large variation between the countries. On the one hand, in countries like Portugal (194%), Spain (48%), and Italy (46%), the share of middle-skilled workers in low-paying jobs increased substantially. Denmark (−11%) and Sweden (−16%), on the other hand, experienced a decline in the share of middle-skilled workers in low-paying jobs.

10.6 FLEXIBLIZIATION OF THE LABOUR MARKET

Up to now, research has mainly analysed the impact of job polarization in relation to income distribution (Autor and Dorn, 2013; Goos et al., 2014; Cortes, 2016; Kurer and Gallego, 2019). The explicit link between job polarization and the type of employment contracts has not been analysed yet.[5] This is noteworthy given the shift towards flexible employment on most European labour markets. Moreover, this transition has sparked widely shared concerns regarding employment protection, social rights, training opportunities, and income inequality (ILO, 2016, 2019). The European Union also acknowledged the importance of these issues and addresses them in its Pillar of Social Rights.

We argue that the increasing flexiblization of European labour markets is partly the result of job polarization and in particular the increased competition for low-skilled jobs. Note that the number of middle-skilled workers employed in low-paying jobs increased in 16 out of 22 European countries between 2002 and 2016. Moreover, the share of middle-skilled workers holding low-paying jobs increased on average by 30% in these countries. Although purely descriptive, this provides empirical support for our argument that middle-skilled workers have shifted their labour supply to jobs characterized by less complex tasks, thereby increasing competition for low-skilled jobs.

---

4 Note, however, that this figure presents purely descriptive data. Consequently, these findings should be interpreted with some caution.

5 A notable exception in this regard is Peugny (2019), who showed that precarious employment (measured as the proportion of involuntary part-time jobs) mainly affected the lower skilled jobs in the service sector. Nevertheless, she does not explicitly analyse the link between job polarization and flexiblization.

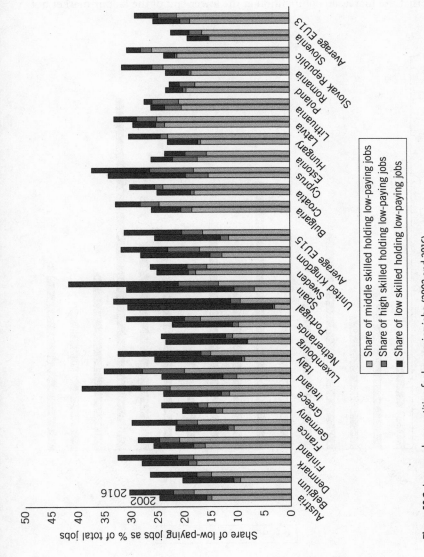

Figure 10.2 Increased competition for low-paying jobs (2002 and 2016).
Jobs were ranked based on Goos et al. (2014), who use two-digit ISCO codes to rank occupations by their mean wage rank based on EU Statistics on Income and Living Conditions (EU-SILC). Data years for Romania are 2005 and 2016.
Source: European Commission DG Employment, Social Affairs & Inclusion (2018) and EU-LFS.

As is shown in Figure 10.3, the share of non-standard employment (NSE) slightly increased in EU15 countries. In particular, the Netherlands and Luxembourg stand out with an increase of respectively 10 and 9 percentage points. Both countries are amongst the countries with a relatively high increase in the share of middle-skilled workers holding low-paying jobs. This might indicate that the increased competition at the lower end of the labour market not

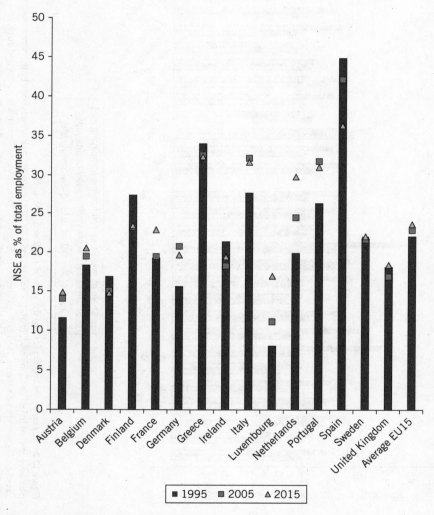

Figure 10.3 Labour market flexibilization in the EU15 (1995–2015).
In most studies NSE includes temporary employment, part-time, and on-call work; temporary agency work, and other multiparty employment relationships as well as disguised employment and dependent self-employment (Eurofound, 2019). Due to data limitations we have only included part-time work and self-employment.
Source: Eurostat Labour Market Database and authors' calculations.

only resulted in a stagnation of wage growth, but also resulted in competition amongst workers by type of contract. In contrast, in Denmark and Sweden, which did not experience an increase in the share of middle-skilled workers in low-paying jobs, the share of NSE remained relatively stable.

Figure 10.4, however, shows a slightly different story. Whilst the EU13 countries are generally characterized by a relatively stable share of middle-skilled workers in low-paying jobs, the share of NSE increased substantially in 9 out of 13 countries, with Hungary, Latvia, Lithuania, and Romania as the exceptions. For instance, Poland experienced an increase in NSE of almost 20 percentage points. Yet the share of middle-skilled workers holding low-skilled jobs dropped

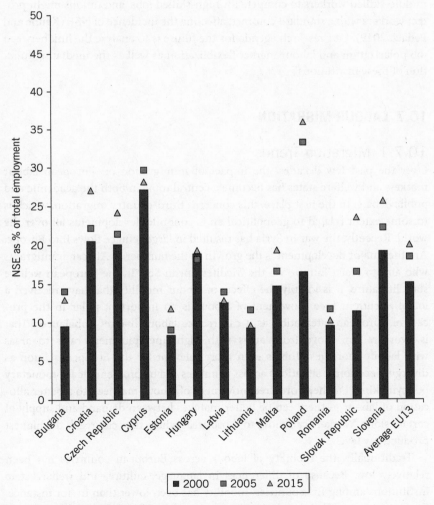

Figure 10.4 Labour market flexibilization in the EU13 (1995–2015).
Source: Eurostat Labour Market Database and authors' calculations.

in Poland with 6% in the same period. Although this finding seems to challenge our expectations, this result might also be caused by differences in the share of middle-skilled workers between EU13 and EU15 countries. In EU13 countries the average share of middle-skilled workers in low-paying jobs is 72% compared to 49% in EU15 counties. This difference might account for a different dynamic at the lower end of the labour market.

Moreover, it is important to emphasize the importance of labour market regulations and welfare state institutions. For instance, higher minimum wages might result in a higher demand for high-skilled workers (Grimshaw et al., 2014), strict employment protection and tax and transfer policies might provide incentives for employers to resort to NSE, education and training might enable middle-skilled workers to compete for high-skilled jobs, and unions might protect workers with a standard contract, affecting the incidence of NSE (Keune and Pedaci, 2019). Our research agenda for the future is to analyse the link between job polarization and labour market flexiblization as well as the mediating function of these institutions.

10.7 LABOUR MIGRATION

10.7.1 Migration Trends

Over the past few decades, the impact of immigration on European labour markets and welfare states has become a central topic in both the academic and public debate. In the first place, this concerns third-country migration, which is to some extent related to geopolitical and economic developments all over the world. Recently, the war in Syria has resulted in large refugee flows into Europe. Another major development is the growth in the number of African immigrants who aim to reach Europe via the Mediterranean Sea. In the European welfare state literature, it is mainly the effects of labour mobility that have received a lot of attention. Free movement of labour is an important pillar in the process of European integration as it can reduce labour market imbalances. That is, workers can move from areas with high unemployment rates to areas with labour shortages. This is even more relevant for the European Union as diverging economic situations across countries can be problematic for monetary policymaking. Furthermore, free movement of labour may lead to a better allocation of labour as there can be better matches between demand and supply of certain skills. Workers can move to those areas where they can reach the highest productivity levels.

Traditionally, the mobility of labour across European countries has been relatively low. Because of differences in language, culture, and welfare state institutions among EU countries, mobility has been lower than in, for instance, the United States. The rounds of enlargement of the EU in 2004, 2007, and 2013 with predominantly CEE countries have increased the flows of intra-EU labour migration. Given the differences in labour market conditions between Western and CEE countries, mainly with regard to employment and wages, it is predominantly mobility from east to west (Rojas-Romagosa and Bollen, 2018). Despite the attention paid to labour migration in both the public and academic debate, the coverage of labour migration in systematic empirical research has remained rather limited. An important reason for this is the lack of readily available data. In fact, most studies which are theoretically interested in European labour migration have used data on overall migration due to a lack of better data.

Recently, Fenwick and Van Vliet (2019) constructed an indicator for labour migration based on the EU Labour Force Survey (EU-LFS) microdata. These data are originally being used to generate insights into labour market trends such as unemployment rates, but they also contain information that can be used to construct trends in labour migration. We use these data in our analysis here. Fenwick and Van Vliet (2019) use information on country of birth and labour force status to identify labour migrants from CEE countries. They construct the indictor as a percentage of the labour force. Table 10.1 shows the volume of labour migration from CEE countries to Western European countries. Switzerland is included because it is a member of the Schengen Area, has a comparable economy and welfare state to the EU15, and is traditionally considered a country of notable immigration.

As shown in Table 10.1, labour migration from CEE countries to Western European countries has increased substantially since the enlargements of the European Union. Between 2004 and 2016, the average stock of labour migration has increased from 1% to 3.2% of the labour force. At the same time, it should be noted that this level is still far below the level of labour migration from Western European countries to other Western European countries; namely, on average 7.5% in 2016. Although the stock of CEE labour migration increased in all Western European countries, there is considerable variation. In Ireland, the stock of CEE migration has risen the sharpest. In 2016, more than 9% of the Irish labour force consisted of CEE immigrants. A likely explanation for this development is that Ireland was one of only three EU countries that did not impose labour market restrictions on immigrants from those countries that became EU Member States in 2004. Other countries with relatively large proportions of CEE immigrants are Austria and the United Kingdom. In contrast, in Portugal and France, only 0.3% and 0.7%, respectively, of the labour force consisted of CEE immigrants in 2016.

10.7.1.1 Policy Debate at the EU Level

To foster the mobility of labour, the European Union has adopted a number of policy initiatives aimed at removing institutional barriers (Eurofound, 2014). For instance, the limited portability of social rights is a relevant factor for the mobility of workers. In April 2014, the Directive (2014/50/EU) on minimum requirements for enhancing worker mobility between Member States by

Table 10.1 Labour migration from Central and Eastern to Western European countries, 2004–2016

	2004	2007	2010	2013	2016	Change 2004–2016
Austria	3.4	4.0	4.3	4.8	6.1	2.8
Belgium	0.5	0.7	1.7	2.2	2.6	2.2
Denmark	0.4	0.6	1.1	1.9	2.5	2.2
Finland	0.6	0.4	0.6	0.9	1.4	0.8
France	0.3	0.4	0.6	0.5	0.7	0.4
Germany	0.9	1.0	1.3	1.8	2.9	2.0
Greece	1.2	1.4	1.9	1.8	1.4	0.3
Ireland	3.3	9.7	9.2	9.4	9.4	6.1
Italy	1.2	1.8	3.4	3.9	4.3	3.0
Luxembourg	0.8	2.0	2.5	3.7	4.9	4.1
Netherlands	0.4	0.5	0.8	1.0	1.3	0.9
Portugal	0.2	0.3	0.4	0.4	0.3	0.1
Spain	1.8	3.0	3.6	3.3	3.5	1.8
Sweden	1.3	1.6	2.0	2.6	2.6	1.3
Switzerland	1.5	1.5	1.9	2.2	2.6	1.0
United Kingdom	0.6	2.3	3.3	3.7	5.4	4.8
Mean	1.0	1.9	2.4	2.7	3.2	2.3

CEE countries: Bulgaria, Croatia, Cyprus, Czech Republic, Estonia, Hungary, Latvia, Lithuania, Malta, Poland, Romania, Slovakia, Slovenia; immigration is expressed as a percentage of the labour force; for some countries data years are around 2005 (Ireland, 2004; Italy, 2004).
Source: Fenwick and Van Vliet (2019).

improving the acquisition and preservation of supplementary pension rights was adopted. In December 2016, the Directive (2016/2341/EU) on the activities and supervision of institutions for occupational retirement provision was adopted. As a broader policy agenda, the then President of the European Commission, Jean-Claude Juncker, presented the European Pillar of Social Rights in 2017. Part of this policy agenda deals with the coordination of social security systems within the European Union, which is aimed at protecting the social rights of workers when they move across the borders of EU Member States. As a concrete measure, the European Commission presented a proposal that extends the portability of unemployment benefits between Member States from 3 to 6 months. Early in 2019, it became clear that a majority of EU Member States would be in favour of this proposal but that the final decision-making would be left to the new European Parliament and European Commission, which were installed later that year.

A more direct type of measure to foster the mobility of labour migration is lifting labour migration restrictions. In the enlargement rounds since 2004, Western European countries had the possibility to impose temporary labour migration restrictions. For instance, workers from those countries which joined the Union in 2004 had direct access to the Irish, Swedish, and British labour markets, but could work in Austria, Germany, and Switzerland only since 2011 (Fenwick and Van Vliet, 2019). The rationale of these labour migration restrictions is that Western European countries could temporarily protect their domestic labour market. Given the differences in wages, Western European countries expected large inflows of workers from CEE countries and therefore substantial displacement on the labour market, which would harm native workers.

10.8 IMPLICATIONS FOR WELFARE STATES

Globalization, technological change, and migration yield not only employment effects. These developments may also affect welfare states in a more direct way. In the political economy literature, the debate on the relationship between economic openness and welfare state generosity has been centred around the supply and demand side of social protection (Van Vliet and Wang, 2019). With regard to the supply side of social protection, the *efficiency hypothesis* states that policymakers are inclined to cut tax burdens in order to facilitate attractive conditions for firms due to increasing competitiveness pressures in international markets. The budgetary pressure resulting from the lower tax revenues contributes to the reduction of the generosity of welfare state programmes (Garrett and Mitchell, 2001). In contrast, on the demand side, the *compensation hypothesis* states that economic globalization may lead to an increased demand from voters for social policy in order to compensate the increased labour market risks (Rodrik, 1998). Interestingly, a growing body of literature provides empirical support for the microlevel mechanisms of the compensation hypothesis (Scheve and Slaughter, 2004; Walter, 2017). Technological change can be expected to affect welfare state generosity via the compensation mechanism, too. The automation of jobs contributes to feelings of economic insecurity and hence to a higher demand for social protection (Iversen and Cusack, 2000).

The theoretical effects of migration on the provision of social welfare can also be classified along the lines of supply and demand. The possible displacement effects could lead to insecurity with regard to work and income among native workers, and this could result in a higher demand for social protection (Burgoon et al., 2012; Brady and Finnigan, 2014). At the same time, immigration may also affect the supply side of social policy. Solidarity among people is lower when they have fewer common linkages such as origin, language, and culture. Therefore, domestic workers would be less willing to pay taxes and social security contributions when immigrants are also entitled to social benefits (Alesina et al., 2001; Luttmer, 2001; Alesina and Glaeser, 2004; Eger, 2010).

Whether the demand-side effect or the supply-side effect dominates is hard to assess on purely theoretical grounds, and it is therefore more of an empirical question. A large body of literature with empirical studies on the relationship between globalization and social protection levels produces rather mixed results. Some studies reported negative effects on social protection levels (e.g., Busemeyer, 2009a), whereas other studies found evidence for positive associations (e.g., Hicks and Zorn, 2005) or even mixed effects (e.g., Brady et al., 2005). The mixed results in the literature partly reflect the variation in the selected countries and years and in the methodological approaches. A more substantive interpretation of the mixed results is that globalization affects welfare states via both the supply and demand sides. The resulting combination of budgetary pressure and an increased demand for social protection yields a dilemma for policymakers, one that has been called the *globalization dilemma* (Hays, 2009).

The empirical literature on the effects of immigration on social protection levels is younger. In an analysis of 18 OECD countries, Soroka et al. (2006) find evidence that suggests that the negative supply-side effect dominates. However, the results of the empirical study by Gaston and Rajaguru (2013) are not in line with this negative effect, and their results tend to suggest a positive association between immigrant and social expenditure. A recent study by Fenwick (2019) supports these results. Based on data for 16 European countries, she finds a positive association between immigration and welfare state effort, which is in line with the explanation that immigration contributes to a higher demand for social protection.

It can be expected that the effects of immigration vary across different welfare state programmes. The decrease in solidarity as a result of immigration will be smaller in the case of social insurance programmes, for which immigrants pay social contributions, than in the case of social security programmes, such as means-tested social assistance benefits, which are funded from general tax revenues (Boeri, 2010). In their empirical analysis of the cross-country variation in social expenditure on several welfare state programmes, Soroka et al. (2016) find that immigration is mainly negatively associated with unemployment benefits and active labour market policy. Fenwick and Van Vliet (2019) show that the effects of immigration not only vary across welfare state programmes, but that the effects are also dependent on the type of immigration. They find positive associations between labour migration from CEE countries and the generosity of several welfare state programmes in Western European countries. These results are in line with the argument that immigrants may pose labour market risks for native workers, which increases the demand for social protection. Interestingly, refugees are negatively associated with the generosity of unemployment benefits and positively associated with the generosity of social assistance benefits. An explanation for this finding might be that refugees are considered as 'less-deserving' of unemployment benefits but 'deserving' of social assistance benefits.

10.9 WELFARE STATE DEVELOPMENTS

To analyse the development of welfare states across Europe, we use data on public social expenditures.[6] The main public social policy areas considered are: old age; survivors; incapacity-related benefits; health; family; active labour market programmes; unemployment; housing; and 'other' social policy areas. Data are taken from the most recent version of the OECD (2019a) Social Expenditure Database (SOCX) and OECD (2019b) Labour Market Statistics. To guarantee consistency over time, increase the cross-country comparability of the data, and maximize the number of observations, some adjustments have been made. First, we have complemented the data with data from the OECD (2019c) Education Statistics for spending on pre-primary education, which have been included in SOCX since the introduction of ISCED 1997 (generally around 1998) only.[7] Second, some of the CEE member states of the EU are not members of the OECD (Bulgaria, Cyprus, Croatia, Malta, and Romania) or have been a member for a relatively short amount of time (Estonia, Latvia, Lithuania, Slovenia); as a result, statistics for these countries are not available from the OECD or for a relatively short time span only. In these cases, we have complemented the data with similar data from Eurostat.[8] An obvious limitation of social expenditure data is that

---

6   We do not focus on mandatory and voluntary private expenditures. Data on private social spending are deemed to be of lesser quality than public spending data (Adema and Fron, 2019). In addition, private social expenditures are almost exclusively confined to old-age, sickness, and health programmes (such as sickness benefits paid by employers to employees as mandated by law, mandatory pension contributions to private pension funds, and employment-related health plans), whereas the focus here is predominantly on new types of social policies. Moreover, voluntary private expenditures cannot be disaggregated to the same level of detail as public expenditures.

7   Expenditures on pre-primary education are included under SOCX category 5-2-1: in-kind spending for families on early childhood education and care. For years for which public expenditures on pre-primary education were not available from the same OECD database, data were estimated. This mainly refers to years before 1997. For the estimation, we used backward extrapolation based on the developments of public educational expenditure data from the UNESCO Institute for Statistics (UIS) or expenditures on educational institutions available from another OECD database. For almost all countries theses series are very strongly correlated to the public educational expenditure data available from the OECD (generally, $r \geq 0.99$). Furthermore, the corrections for differences in the compulsory age of entry into primary school implemented in SOCX (outlined in Annex I.1.4 of the SOCX 2019 Manual, see Adema and Fron, 2019) have been excluded because we are interested in total spending.

8   For European countries, SOCX data since around 1990 are based on data from the European System of integrated Social Protection Statistics (ESSPROS) provided by

developments do not only reflect deliberate policy changes, but that expenditures are also driven by cyclical and demographic trends such as unemployment and ageing of populations (Van Vliet, 2010; Jensen, 2011). Yet expenditure data offer a bird's-eye perspective which provides insight into long-term trends for a large number of countries. Furthermore, we also provide a descriptive analysis in which expenditures are corrected for the number of beneficiaries.

Table 10.2 shows developments in public social expenditure across 15 Western European countries, 13 CEE countries, and 4 non-EU countries for the period 1985–2015. On average, EU15 countries spent 25% of their gross domestic product (GDP) on welfare state programmes in 2015. This proportion is substantially lower in EU13 countries, where on average 18% of GDP was spent on social policies in 2015. The highest level of social expenditures can be observed in France, where in 2015 almost one-third of GDP was spent on welfare state programmes. With 14.6% of GDP, Romania was the country with the lowest social expenditures in 2015. In the United States, the proportion of GDP spent on social policy is comparable to the social expenditure level in the EU13.[9]

Against the background of globalization, technological change, and ageing of populations, the developments in social expenditure over time are particularly interesting. In the EU15, the EU13, and in the group of non-EU countries, the share of GDP devoted to social policy has on average increased over the past few decades. In the last couple of years, the high expenditures are probably partly caused by the high unemployment rates during the financial crisis. Yet also before 2010, the levels of social expenditures had been increased on average. Interestingly, there is substantial variation in the developments across countries. Over time, social expenditures have been increased in most of the

---

Eurostat. The definitions of social expenditures used by SOCX and ESSPROS are similar, but there are differences in coverage and categorization. ESSPROS data were converted to the SOCX format using Annex I.1.1 of the SOCX, 2019 Manual (Adema and Fron, 2019), which describes how to regroup ESSPROS items into SOCX using the example of Sweden in 2015. The latest edition of the ESSPROS manual (Eurostat, 2016) was used to identify schemes that classify as mandatory private or voluntary private for Bulgaria, Cyprus, Malta, and Romania. Data from the Croatian Bureau of Statistics (2019) was used for Croatia. As with SOCX data, OECD data on labour market programmes for European countries are also based on data from Eurostat. The only category for which substantial differences may exist concerns the first, 'public employment services (PES) and administration' (termed 'labour market services' by Eurostat) (OECD, 2018a). Statistics on education are usually obtained through the joint collection of education data by the UIS, the OECD, and Eurostat, referred to as UOE data. SOCX data on health expenditures are based on the OECD Health Statistics. For the five European countries not covered by SOCX, health expenditures are taken from ESSPROS.

9 This can partly be explained by the fact that private social expenditures, which account for roughly 40% of overall social expenditure—one of the highest among OECD countries—are not included.

Table 10.2 Public social expenditure (% GDP), 1985–2015

	1985	1990	1995	2000	2005	2010	2015	Change 1985–2015
Austria	23.2	23.2	26.4	25.9	26.1	27.7	27.7	4.4
Belgium	26.2	24.7	24.9	23.7	25.4	28.4	28.7	2.6
Denmark	19.9	22.3	25.3	24.0	25.4	28.9	28.9	9.0
Finland	21.7	23.3	28.9	22.6	23.9	27.2	30.1	8.4
France	25.9	24.9	29.1	27.7	28.8	31.1	31.9	6.0
Germany	20.0	19.1	25.3	25.5	26.4	26.1	25.0	5.1
Greece	15.4	15.7	16.6	17.8	19.9	24.9	25.3	9.9
Ireland	20.9	17.2	17.9	13.0	15.6	24.2	15.2	-5.7
Italy		21.0	21.4	22.6	24.1	27.0	28.4	
Luxembourg	18.9	18.3	19.9	18.7	22.8	23.1	22.1	3.2
Netherlands	23.8	24.0	22.4	18.7	20.1	17.6	17.6	-6.2
Portugal	10.5	12.3	16.1	18.5	22.3	24.5	24.1	13.6
Spain	17.3	19.4	21.0	19.4	20.6	25.1	24.7	7.3
Sweden	26.8	27.1	30.4	26.8	27.4	26.1	26.2	-0.6
United Kingdom	18.1	14.9	16.7	15.9	18.0	21.8	21.0	2.9
Mean EU15	20.6	20.5	22.8	21.4	23.1	25.6	25.1	4.5
Standard deviation	4.5	4.2	4.8	4.3	3.7	3.2	4.6	0.1
Coefficient of variation	0.22	0.21	0.21	0.20	0.16	0.13	0.18	-0.04
Bulgaria					14.8	16.8	17.6	
Croatia						20.3	20.7	
Cyprus					15.3	18.6	19.6	
Czech Republic			16.6	18.0	18.1	19.8	19.5	
Estonia				13.0	13.0	18.2	15.8	
Hungary				20.2	22.0	23.1	20.8	
Latvia				13.6	12.9	19.7	15.9	
Lithuania				15.0	13.7	19.4	15.9	
Malta					15.7	17.6	15.5	
Poland		21.1	22.2	20.5	21.0	20.7	20.3	
Romania				13.5	13.7	17.7	14.6	
Slovak Republic			18.7	17.6	15.8	17.9	17.7	
Slovenia				21.9	21.5	23.4	22.7	
Mean EU13				17.0	16.5	19.5	18.2	
Standard deviation				3.4	3.4	2.0	2.6	
Coefficient of variation				0.20	0.20	0.10	0.14	

(continued)

Table 10.2 Continued

	1985	1990	1995	2000	2005	2010	2015	Change 1985–2015
Non-EU								
Iceland		13.3	14.8	14.5	15.8	16.4	15.1	
Norway	17.2	21.6	22.5	20.4	20.7	22.0	24.8	7.6
Switzerland	13.5	12.2	14.2	14.0	15.7	15.3	16.1	2.6
United States	13.1	13.5	15.4	14.3	15.7	19.3	18.8	5.7

Total expenditures in current prices (millions of national currency) have been divided by GDP in current prices (millions of national currency) to obtain spending as a percentage of GDP; for some countries, data years are around 1985 (Denmark, 1986; Portugal, 1986), 1990 (Poland, 1991), 1995 (Belgium, 1994), 2000 (Estonia, 2003; Latvia, 2003; Lithuania, 2003; Romania, 2003; Slovenia, 2003), 2005 (Bulgaria, 2008; Cyprus, 2006; Malta, 2006), 2010 (Croatia, 2012) or 2015 (Croatia, 2014; Poland, 2014).

Source: OECD Social Expenditure Database; Eurostat ESSPROS Database; OECD Labour Database; European Commission DG Employment, Social Affairs & Inclusion Labour Market Policy Database; OECD Education and Training Database; Eurostat Education and Training Database; UIS Education Database; OECD National Accounts Database; authors' calculations.

countries. Within the EU15, only in Ireland, the Netherlands, and Sweden were social expenditures lower in 2015 than in 1985, with the sharpest decline in the Netherlands. The largest increase can be observed in Portugal where social expenditures have been increased from 10.5% of GDP in 1985 to 24.1% in 2015. Also within the EU13, social expenditures increased in most of the countries. Only in Malta, Poland, and the Slovak Republic have social expenditures declined as a percentage of GDP over time. In all four non-EU countries, social expenditures were increased.

Taken together, these trends indicate that in spite of budgetary pressure stemming from globalization and migration, social expenditures have not been decreased. In fact, most countries have increased the share of GDP spent on social policy. In the context of the debate about the impact of globalization, migration, and technological change, these findings lend support for the argument that economic insecurity stemming from structural labour market transformations has been compensated with higher public spending on welfare state programmes (Rodrik, 1998; Iversen and Cusack, 2000; Burgoon et al., 2012). Moreover, the development that countries have spent larger shares of their GDP on social policy is probably related to the increase in prosperity over the past decades (Meltzer and Richard, 1983), a catch-up effect. Interestingly, this increase in prosperity can be partly attributed to the same structural transformations.

Another notable pattern demonstrated by Table 10.2 is the trend of convergence. Between 1985 and 2010, the dispersion in social expenditures declined, indicated by the declines in the standard deviation and coefficient of variation. This indicates that, within the EU15, social expenditure levels converged. In earlier studies, in which this trend of convergence has been documented as well, it has been shown that this trend of convergence is stronger within the EU15 than in a broader group of OECD countries (Starke et al., 2008; Caminada et al., 2010; Van Vliet, 2010). For this reason, it has been argued in these studies that this EU-specific trend can be attributed, on the one hand, to European economic integration, which has progressed further than international economic integration in general. On the other hand, this EU-specific trend has been attributed to EU social policy initiatives, such as the European Employment Strategy and the Lisbon Strategy. Interestingly, an opposite trend can be observed from 2010 onwards. This trend of divergence seems to be related to the incidence of the financial crisis. The economic consequences of the crisis, for instance, in terms of unemployment and fiscal balance, varied across countries. For this reason, but also because of different political constellations, (social) policy responses to the crisis varied as well across countries (Starke et al., 2014; Raess and Pontusson, 2015). This has resulted in diverging social expenditures. A similar pattern can be observed in the EU13, where the dispersion in social expenditures has also increased since 2010. Moreover, the gap between the mean of the EU15 and the EU13 has not been narrowed over time. Earlier studies have shown that Western and Eastern European countries had not converged in terms of welfare state spending (Draxler and Van Vliet, 2010). Our data suggest that approximately a decade after the EU enlargements of 2004 and 2007, such a trend of convergence has still not occurred.

10.10 SOCIAL INVESTMENT

In response to the various challenges and developments just described, an academic discourse on the sustainability of the welfare state and future of social policy has developed since the 1990s. Several of these studies describe the rise of a so-called *new welfare state*, which 'puts the emphasis less on income replacement and more on the promotion of labour market participation through activation and investment in human capital' (Bonoli and Natali, 2012: 9). In comparison to the traditional, postwar welfare state, this entails a reorientation of social policies towards programmes aimed at activation and human capital development. The main objective thereof is increasing the carrying capacity of the welfare state by fostering labour market participation and preparing individuals for the new social risks of the service-based (knowledge) economy (Esping-Andersen, 2002; Armingeon and Bonoli, 2006; Bonoli, 2013; Hemerijck, 2013). Increased participation among women plays a central role within this While this increases the carrying capacity it simultaneously entails new social risks with regard to combining work and family. Instead of a safety net, the new welfare state provides a trampoline (Jenson and Saint-Martin, 2003) that involves policies aimed at preparing individuals, families, and societies to respond to such new social risks (Morel et al., 2012).

New social risks can be defined as 'the risks that people now face in the course of their lives as a result of the economic and social changes associated with the transition to a postindustrial society' (Taylor-Gooby, 2004: 2). These new risks include reconciling work and family life, single parenthood, having a frail relative, possessing low or obsolete skills, and insufficient social insurance coverage (Bonoli, 2006). In contrast, old social risks include unemployment, old age, ill health, sickness and disability, and the financial burden of raising children (Vandenbroucke and Vlemincx, 2011). From the perspective of the new welfare state, new social risks should be addressed by new welfare state programmes such as (child)care, family-friendly working-time arrangements, and education.

A second dimension of the new welfare state concerns an investment dimension, which is reflected in most of the new welfare state programmes (Vandenbroucke and Vlemincx, 2011). Whilst old social policies predominantly concern compensating benefits that protect individuals against old social risks associated with the loss of income, new social policies concern capacitating benefits that are aimed at preventing such risks from materializing as well as addressing new social risks (Häusermann, 2012; Hemerijck, 2013). Instead of passive benefits, the new welfare state allocates public resources to investments in human capital. Most of the new social policies are provided through services, which constitutes the third dimension (Vandenbroucke and Vlemincx, 2011). In line with this dimension, welfare states should become more service-oriented by prioritizing spending on in-kind benefits over spending on cash transfers.

A specific type of new welfare state that reflects these dimensions is the *social investment state*. This term was first coined by Antony Giddens (1998), who advocated a 'Third Way' that synthesises 'neoliberalism' and the postwar welfare state through a shift from protecting people against labour market risks to integrating them into the labour market and creating a society of 'responsible risk takers'. In order to achieve this, welfare expenditures ought to be concentrated on investments in human capital, and governments should emphasize life-long education: 'the guideline is investment in *human capital* wherever possible, rather than in the direct provision of economic maintenance. In place of the welfare state we should put the *social investment state*' (Giddens, 1998: 177, emphasis added).

Current and future challenges caused by globalization, technological change, the growth of the services sector, and demographic changes, such as job polarization, flexibilization, and the emergence of new social risks, and the implications for social policy associated with these challenges have also been acknowledged and documented in EU policies (European Commission, 2017). This has, for instance, resulted in the adoption of the European Pillar of Social Rights in 2017 and social investment explicitly being put on the European policy agenda. The Europe 2020 Strategy for smart, sustainable, and inclusive growth intends to lift at least 20 million people out of poverty and increase employment of the population aged 20–64 to 75% (European Commission, 2010). To help attain this target, the European Commission launched the Social Investment Package in 2013. In an era of economic crises and austerity, this package constituted a series of policy measures designed to address the growing risk of poverty and social exclusion. It provides a policy framework for redirecting national policies 'towards social investment throughout life, with a view to ensuring the adequacy and sustainability of budgets for social policies' by 'investing in social policies, services and cash benefits which both activate and enable' (European Commission, 2013: 4, 10).

Despite the positive effects ascribed to social investment in both the academic literature and EU policy documents, it has received substantial criticism. Realizing social inclusion through work may, for instance, not be feasible for vulnerable groups in society (Cantillon and Van Lancker, 2013). Given disappointing developments in poverty rates in relation to the Europe 2020 target, some scholars have questioned whether this focus on activation and employment has been at the expense of policies aimed at mitigating poverty and inequality (Cantillon, 2011; Vandenbroucke and Vlemincx, 2011; Van Kersbergen and Hemerijck, 2012). Empirical studies find limited support for such claims. Although shifts in expenditures from old to new welfare state programmes might be related to stagnating or increasing poverty rates in some European countries (Van Vliet and Wang, 2015), expansion of these new policies has not been at the expense of minimum income protection benefits (Noël, 2018). This phenomenon could potentially be explained by *Matthew effects*, whereby social benefits and services accrue to the middle and high-income classes.

Such Matthew effects have been identified for public childcare subsidies for children under 3 in Flanders (Ghysels and Van Lancker, 2011) and, to a somewhat lesser extent, for children under 6 in other European countries (Van Lancker and Ghysels, 2014).[10] They can predominantly be explained by supply-side issues such as limited availability and affordability, which means that a higher degree of government involvement and more spending could address their incidence (Van Lancker and Ghysels, 2016; Pavolini and Van Lancker, 2018). Bonoli and Liechti (2018) have also identified Matthew effects in relation to some active labour market policies (ALMPs). While these programmes generally focus on disadvantaged groups such as the low-skilled and migrants, they sometimes suffer from negative access bias by requiring preexisting skills.

---

10 Van Lancker and Ghysels (2014) do not find support for the assumption that expenditures on new policies (childcare and parental leave) crowd out spending on traditional policies (child benefits).

10.11 OPERATIONALIZING SOCIAL INVESTMENT

Given the new perspective on social policy and its relation to the economy that social investment entails, it has to a large extent been formulated in terms of the reallocation of expenditures on passive, compensating transfers to expenditures on activating and capacitating policies. While studies contrasting new capacitating social policies to old compensating social policies are abundant (Vandenbroucke and Vlemincx, 2011; Häusermann, 2012; Nikolai, 2012; Hemerijck, 2013; Kuitto, 2013; Ronchi, 2018), a univocal conceptualization of the policies that comprise social investment is absent in the literature. Nevertheless, broader definitions have been provided by some scholars. Social investment has, for example, been summarized as a future-oriented approach that aims to prepare, support, and equip individuals in a way that increases their chances to participate in the knowledge-based economy and reduces their future risks of income loss and poverty by creating, mobilizing, and preserving skills and human capital (Garritzmann et al., 2017: 36–39). Likewise, Hemerijck (2017) identifies three complementary functions of social investments over the life course: easing the 'flow' of labour market and life-course transitions, raising the quality of the 'stock' of human capital, and operating as stabilization 'buffer' by offering a safety net. These functions can, in turn, be linked to a broad range of policies that reflect these functions to different extents (De Deken, 2017).

Policies that have figured centrally in studies on social investment, both descriptive and empirical, are ALMPs and early childhood education and care (ECEC; henceforth childcare). While descriptive studies have linked a broad range of activating and capacitating welfare state programmes to different stages of the life course (Kvist, 2013; Kuitto, 2016), empirical studies have tended to concentrate on ALMPs and childcare only (Bonoli, 2013; Hemerijck et al., 2016; Noël, 2018). Others scholars have focused on aggregated groups of social policies. Some have, for example, distinguished traditional social protection from social investment by distinguishing between cash benefits and in-kind benefits (Ahn and Kim, 2015; Ronchi, 2018), whereas others have distinguished between groups of old and new social policies (Vandenbroucke and Vlemincx, 2011; Van Vliet and Wang, 2015). Nevertheless, some empirical studies based on a disaggregated spending approach have considered additional new social policies, such as education, maternity and parental leave, and residential care and home-help services (Nelson and Stephens, 2012; Taylor-Gooby et al., 2015; Bakker and Van Vliet, 2019; Kim and Ahn, 2020).

We closely follow Bakker and Van Vliet (2019) in classifying welfare programmes as social investments. Public expenditures on the following categories constitute total spending on new social policies: residential care and home-help services for the elderly; residential care, home-help services, and rehabilitation services for the sick, disabled, and incapacitated;

maternity and parental leave; early childhood education and care; home help and accommodation services for families with children; active labour market policies; and primary to tertiary education.

It has been debated whether spending on maternity and parental leave can be classified as investment-oriented given that this programme also reflects a compensatory function and is provided through cash benefits (Bonoli, 2013; De Deken, 2017). For that reason, Kuitto (2016), for example, groups this programme under compensating rather than social investment spending. The availability of maternity and parental leave increases the chance that people utilize the leave period and return to their pre-childbirth job once it ends (Klerman and Leibowitz, 1997), thereby stimulating continued labour market participation.[11] Moreover, it has been found that maternal care throughout children's first year of life can have a positive impact on their development (Berger et al., 2005; Baker and Milligan, 2010). Despite being provided as a cash benefit, these programmes do therefore reflect aspects of activation and human capital enhancement. Moreover, they address the new social risk of combining work and care, which has led several scholars to consider them as social investments or new social policies (Vandenbroucke and Vlemincx, 2011; Hemerijck, 2013; Taylor-Gooby et al., 2015).

Based on the aforementioned studies, we group traditional welfare state programmes that address traditional social risks by protecting against the loss of income, such as pensions, sickness benefits, unemployment benefits, and minimum income benefits, under old social policies.[12] This covers all cash pension benefits for people of old age, all cash benefits for survivors, all cash incapacity-related benefits, cash family allowances, all cash unemployment benefits, and all other cash benefits aimed at income maintenance.

10.11.1 Spending on Social Investment

Table 10.3 shows the development of public social expenditure on social investment-oriented new social policies and old social policies across all EU Member States and four non-EU countries for the period 1995–2015. In addition,

---

11 Several studies lend support for this claim and find positive employment effects associated with the provision of leave arrangements (Ruhm [1998] for European countries, Berger and Waldfogel [2004] for the United States, Baker and Milligan [2008] for Canada). Nevertheless, Lalive and Zweimüller (2009) found that a generous extension of parental leave from 1 to 2 years in Austria resulted in lower and delayed returns to work. If leave arrangements are too generous or long they might thus result in lower employment as a result of decreasing labour market attachment (see Akgunduz and Plantenga [2013] for a meta-analysis).

12 While unemployment benefits are generally considered compensatory by providing an income transfer to smooth consumption in case job loss occurs, they could also be seen as a job search allowance or tool to preserve or invest in skills that increase the prospects of finding a job. This latter view has mainly been reflected in the Varieties of Capitalism literature (e.g., Estevez-Abe et al., 2001).

Table 10.3 Spending on new and old social policies, 1995–2015

	New social policies (% GDP)			Old social policies (% GDP)			New / (New + Old) social expenditure ratio			
	1995	2005	2015	1995	2005	2015	1995	2005	2015	Change 1995–2015
Austria	7.4	6.7	7.3	23.9	23.6	24.7	24.0	22.1	22.9	−1.1
Belgium	6.5	7.2	8.1	22.7	22.8	25.5	22.8	24.0	24.1	1.3
Denmark	13.9	14.2	14.6	16.8	17.2	19.8	45.2	45.2	42.5	−2.6
Finland	11.1	9.3	11.3	22.9	18.8	22.8	32.7	33.1	33.1	0.3
France	8.9	7.5	7.8	24.3	24.7	27.7	26.8	23.4	21.9	−4.8
Germany	6.4	6.4	6.4	22.0	22.9	21.4	22.6	21.8	23.0	0.4
Greece	3.1	4.2	3.9	15.2	19.3	24.5	16.8	18.0	13.9	−3.0
Ireland	6.8	5.7	4.9	14.1	13.2	12.9	32.7	30.3	27.4	−5.3
Italy	4.9	5.1	5.0	20.4	22.5	26.0	19.5	18.6	16.0	−3.5
Luxembourg	5.0	6.2	6.2	18.4	19.5	18.4	21.5	24.0	25.3	3.8
Netherlands	7.0	8.0	8.1	19.4	16.5	13.9	26.5	32.7	37.0	10.5
Portugal	5.1	5.8	5.6	15.1	20.8	22.6	25.2	22.0	19.9	−5.3
Spain	5.2	5.7	5.6	19.4	17.9	22.4	21.1	24.1	19.9	−1.2
Sweden	14.0	13.0	13.7	20.7	19.0	16.5	41.6	40.7	45.2	3.6
United Kingdom	4.2	6.1	6.4	13.0	14.4	17.4	25.7	29.8	27.0	1.3
Mean EU15	7.3	7.4	7.7	19.2	19.5	21.1	27.0	27.3	26.6	−0.4
Standard deviation	3.3	2.8	3.2	3.7	3.4	4.5	8.0	7.9	9.2	1.2
Coefficient of variation	0.45	0.38	0.41	0.19	0.17	0.21	0.29	0.29	0.34	0.05
Bulgaria		5.3	5.0		12.6	15.2		29.5	24.9	
Croatia			5.8		16.4	18.1			23.7	
Cyprus		6.5	6.5	10.9	13.4	18.0		32.2	26.5	
Czech Republic	5.4	5.1	5.2	14.3	15.7	17.1	27.4	24.4	23.1	−4.3
Estonia		5.8	6.5	13.7	11.4	14.6		33.8	32.6	
Hungary	5.8	6.7	6.5	17.4	18.3	16.6	25.1	26.8	28.1	3.0
Latvia		5.8	6.8	13.1	10.9	13.0		34.8	34.2	
Lithuania		5.8	5.5	11.8	11.6	13.3		33.4	29.3	
Malta		6.5	6.0	12.1	13.9	13.4		31.6	31.1	
Poland	5.8	6.4	6.2	20.3	19.2	18.2	22.5	24.9	25.5	3.0
Romania		4.6	3.5	11.4	11.7	13.3		28.4	20.9	
Slovak Republic	5.9	5.1	5.9	16.5	13.9	15.7	26.2	26.7	27.3	1.1

Table 10.3 Continued

	New social policies (% GDP)			Old social policies (% GDP)			New / (New + Old) social expenditure ratio			
	1995	2005	2015	1995	2005	2015	1995	2005	2015	Change 1995–2015
Slovenia		6.7	5.9	20.3	19.7	20.6		25.4	22.4	
Mean EU13		5.9	5.8	14.7	14.5	15.9		29.3	26.9	
Standard deviation		0.7	0.9	3.4	3.1	2.4		3.7	4.1	
Coefficient of variation		0.12	0.15	0.23	0.21	0.15		0.13	0.15	
Non–EU										
Iceland	8.3	10.5	9.0	11.4	10.4	10.4	44.4	50.1	46.5	2.1
Norway	13.3	11.0	11.4	15.5	15.0	18.0	46.1	42.4	38.8	−7.3
Switzerland	6.3	7.0	6.8	12.3	13.2	13.3	33.8	34.5	33.7	−0.1
United States	4.7	5.1	4.9	13.9	14.4	17.3	25.5	26.6	22.2	−3.3

Total expenditures in current prices (millions of national currency) have been divided by GDP in current prices (millions of national currency) to obtain spending as a percentage of GDP; expenditures on new social policies exclude tertiary education in Luxembourg in 1995 and 2005; for some countries, data years for new social spending are around 1995 (Austria, 1997; Belgium, 1998; Sweden, 1997; United Kingdom, 1997; Hungary, 1999; Poland, 1997; Iceland, 1998), 2005 (Bulgaria, 2008; Cyprus, 2006; Malta, 2006), or 2015 (Denmark, 2014; Croatia, 2014; Estonia, 2013; Poland, 2014); for some countries, data years for old social spending are around 1995 (Cyprus, 2000; Estonia, 1999; Hungary, 1999; Latvia, 1997; Lithuania, 1996; Romania, 2000; Slovenia, 1996), 2005 (Bulgaria, 2008; Croatia, 2008) or 2015 (Poland, 2014).

Source: OECD Social Expenditure Database; Eurostat ESSPROS Database; OECD Labour Database; European Commission DG Employment, Social Affairs & Inclusion Labour Market Policy Database; OECD Education and Training Database; Eurostat Education and Training Database; UIS Education Database; OECD National Accounts Database; authors' calculations.

it shows the ratio of spending on new social policies as a share of total spending on both old and new policies. We have chosen to display data since 1995 because social investment has arisen throughout the 1990s and data for some of the spending categories are only available since then. In contrast to Table 10.2 the sum of new and old social policies excludes the categories 'other benefits in kind', funeral expenses for survivors, all housing benefits, and in-kind social assistance benefits, but additionally includes public expenditures on primary, secondary, and tertiary education.

On average, EU15 countries spent nearly 8% of GDP on new social policies in 2015, whereas they spent 21% of GDP on old social policies. Spending on new social policies hence comprises slightly more than 25% of total spending on old and new social policies. While social spending on both new and old social policies has on average increased between 2005 and 2015, the ratio of spending on new social policies to the sum of spending on new and old social policies has slightly decreased since 2005. EU13 countries spend considerably less on both new and old social policies. In 2015, they spent nearly 6% of GDP on new social policies and 16% of GDP on old social policies. While the average share of spending on new social policies in 2015 is comparable to 2005, spending on old social policies has increased relative to GDP. As a result, the ratio of spending on new social policies to spending on the sum of new and old social policies has fallen from approximately 29% to 27% of GDP. Although EU13 countries allocate less resources to social policies, the share of spending on new social policies is rather comparable to that of EU15 countries in 2015.

Nordic welfare states stand out as most generous spenders on new social policies relative to total spending on new and old social policies. This is to a large extent due to their strong orientation to the provision of social policy through services. In these countries, as well as in the Netherlands and Switzerland, spending on new social policies comprise 30% or more of total spending on new and old social policies. It is worth noting that the Baltic States and Malta realize nearly similar levels of relative spending on new social policies. In addition, the variability of relative spending levels on new social policies is much smaller in the new EU Member States than in the EU15, indicated by the lower standard deviations and coefficients of variation. In addition to the high levels of spending on new social policies in some of the countries just mentioned, this relatively high variability amongst EU15 countries is also attributable to the fact that the Mediterranean welfare states concentrate a substantially lower amount (less than 20%) of their social expenditures on new social policies. Moreover, these ratios have fallen in all of the Mediterranean welfare states over time. A potential explanation for this could be that these countries were hit relatively hard by the economic crises since 2008. On the one hand, this might have increased expenditures on old social policies, such as unemployment benefits. On the other hand, austerity measures might have involved cuts in expenditures on new social policies.

10.12 A DISAGGREGATED SPENDING APPROACH TO SOCIAL INVESTMENT

Although overall expenditure data provide insights into long-term trends, they do not enable one to identify the spending priorities of welfare states in terms of specific welfare state programmes. We therefore also use disaggregated expenditure data to examine long-term trends in specific programmes. We concentrate on the programmes that have figured most centrally in the literature on social investment and that are likely to offer the strongest responses to the challenges outlined earlier: social investment-oriented ALMPs, childcare, and education.

Table 10.4 presents public expenditures on ALMPs as a percentage of GDP for the same 32 countries over the period 1985–2015. The table shows that EU15 countries spend a substantially higher percentage of GDP on ALMPs than EU13

Table 10.4 Public expenditure on active labour market policies (ALMPs) (% GDP), 1985–2015

	1985	1990	1995	2000	2005	2010	2015	Change 1985–2015
Austria	0.28	0.31	0.37	0.50	0.60	0.81	0.73	0.46
Belgium	1.16	0.80	0.92	0.83	0.65	0.72	0.71	−0.45
Denmark	1.02	1.05	1.70	1.84	1.53	2.02	2.04	1.02
Finland	0.72	0.83	1.38	0.86	0.87	1.00	0.99	0.28
France	0.59	0.71	1.17	1.17	0.90	1.13	1.00	0.41
Germany	0.56	0.77	1.16	1.25	1.12	0.90	0.63	0.07
Greece	0.15	0.18	0.38	0.23	0.07	0.23	0.22	0.07
Ireland	1.02	1.03	1.30	0.78	0.61	0.90	0.56	−0.46
Italy		0.22	0.26	0.55	0.53	0.42	0.50	
Luxembourg	0.39	0.19	0.13	0.19	0.50	0.55	0.66	0.27
Netherlands	1.16	1.12	1.20	1.31	1.17	1.10	0.76	−0.41
Portugal	0.16	0.46	0.48	0.61	0.65	0.67	0.55	0.39
Spain	0.32	0.76	0.42	0.77	0.76	0.92	0.59	0.28
Sweden	1.95	1.54	2.08	1.63	1.10	1.10	1.25	−0.70
United Kingdom	0.44	0.38	0.26	0.21	0.38	0.38	0.19	−0.26
Mean EU15	0.71	0.69	0.88	0.85	0.76	0.86	0.76	0.05
Standard deviation	0.50	0.40	0.60	0.50	0.36	0.43	0.45	−0.05
Coefficient of variation	0.71	0.58	0.68	0.59	0.48	0.50	0.59	−0.12
Bulgaria					0.46	0.11	0.15	
Croatia						0.21	0.42	
Cyprus					0.08	0.28	0.15	
Czech Republic		0.16	0.12	0.18	0.23	0.32	0.43	
Estonia					0.07	0.07	0.22	0.21
Hungary		0.58	0.40	0.38	0.32	0.63	0.88	
Latvia					0.12	0.21	0.56	0.14
Lithuania					0.19	0.22	0.30	0.31
Malta						0.14	0.17	0.25
Poland				0.37	0.25	0.42	0.68	0.46
Romania						0.15	0.11	0.12
Slovak Republic			0.22	0.73	0.31	0.33	0.32	0.19
Slovenia					0.26	0.29	0.50	0.24
Mean EU13					0.24	0.34	0.30	0.06

(continued)

Table 10.4 Continued

	1985	1990	1995	2000	2005	2010	2015	Change 1985–2015
Standard deviation					0.13	0.19	0.21	0.08
Coefficient of variation					0.51	0.57	0.68	0.17
Non-EU								
Iceland		0.03	0.09	0.06	0.08	0.06	0.05	
Norway	0.58	0.88	1.22	0.60	0.72	0.62	0.52	−0.06
Switzerland	0.17	0.20	0.43	0.51	0.67	0.60	0.58	0.41
United States	0.27	0.21	0.17	0.15	0.12	0.13	0.09	−0.17

Total expenditures in current prices (millions of national currency) have been divided by GDP in current prices (millions of national currency) to obtain spending as a percentage of GDP; for some countries, data years are around 1985 (Denmark, 1986; Portugal, 1986), 1990 (Czech Republic, 1991; Hungary, 1992; Slovak Republic, 1991), 2000 (Estonia, 2003; Latvia, 2003; Lithuania, 2003; Slovenia, 2003), 2005 (Cyprus, 2006; Malta, 2006; Romania, 2006) or 2010 (Croatia, 2012).

Source: OECD Labour Database; European Commission DG Employment, Social Affairs & Inclusion Labour Market Policy Database; OECD Social Expenditure Database; OECD National Accounts Database; authors' calculations.

countries do. In 2015, EU15 countries on average spent 0.76% of GDP on ALMPs, whereas the average for the EU13 was 0.3%. Despite a somewhat volatile trend over time, with sharp increases in the second half of the 1990s and following the economic crisis, average spending levels have slightly increased in the EU15 over time. At the same time the variation in spending has decreased, which is mainly the result of substantial decreases among some of the more generous spenders such as Belgium, the Netherlands, and Sweden. Spending on ALMPs has hence converged to a higher level over time.

Even though expenditures on ALMPs constitute a substantially lower per cent of GDP in EU13 countries, spending has slightly increased over time in the majority of countries. The variation has, however, increased. This suggest that while some countries are modestly increasing their spending (e.g., the Czech Republic and Hungary), others have experienced substantial decreases, particularly in recent years (e.g., Latvia, Poland, and Slovenia). These statistics should, however, be interpreted with some caution, because expenditure-based indicators are fraught with limitations. They are, for example, unable to capture institutional characteristics of welfare programmes. In addition, variation in expenditures across or within countries may not only reflect policy preferences, but may also stem from different demographic compositions and economic trends such as ageing populations and unemployment (Jensen, 2011). If the main analytical interest actually lies in policy changes, expenditures have to be corrected for such trends. For that reason we also present 'effort' on specific programmes, which constitutes expenditures corrected for the number of recipients relative to GDP per capita in order to allow for comparison across countries and over time (cf. Vandenbroucke and Vlemincx, 2011; Ronchi, 2016; Bakker and Van Vliet, 2019).

Most of the existing studies have used the unemployment rate or number of unemployed as proxies to correct spending on ALMPs for the number of recipients (e.g., Van Vliet and Koster, 2011; Kuitto, 2016). The use of unemployment rates is, however, problematic as they are expressed as a share of the labour force. Labour force participation rates differ greatly across countries, to a large extent due to different rates of female participation. Moreover, since unemployment, inactivity, and employment together constitute the entire labour force, changes in other social policies such as early retirement, higher education or part-time work might affect the unemployment rate and thereby generate artificial changes in effort on ALMPs. Besides, not all ALMPs are designed to facilitate labour market participation by the unemployed. Programmes focused on sheltered employment or the provision of wage subsidies often provide alternatives to work for people who would otherwise not participate on the labour market, for instance due to reduced work capacity (Clasen et al., 2016). To provide a more accurate image of the generosity of ALMPs across countries, we correct spending on specific programmes for the number of participants in the respective programmes. These data are available from the 'Labour Market Programmes: Expenditure and Participants' dataset from the OECD Employment Database and the Labour Market Policy Database of the European Commission's DG for Employment, Social Affairs & Inclusion. Even though data on participant stocks are available since 1998 for most European countries, they have rarely been used in scholarly work.[13]

In Table 10.5 we present the development of public expenditure on two groups of ALMPs (cf. Bengtsson et al., 2017). Not all ALMPs similarly reflect social investment aspects. Bonoli (2010, 2012) distinguishes four groups of ALMPs based on the extent to which they reflect human capital investment and a 'pro-market employment orientation'. Two of them, *upskilling* and *employment assistance*, are considered social investment-oriented ALMPs. Upskilling entails human capital investment and 'facilitates labour market re-entry on the one hand, and impacts positively on productivity on the other' (Bonoli, 2012: 184). Employment assistance is aimed at removing obstacles to labour market participation and thereby constitutes 'a source of savings for the public purse, but it also reduces the duration of unemployment and hence its scarring effect on the beneficiary' (Bonoli, 2012: 183).

The former can be operationalized through expenditures on programmes included under the category 'training' in internationally comparative labour market programmes data. The latter category comprises the spending categories public employment services (PES) and administration, employment incentives

---

13   Cronert (2019) constitutes the sole exception.

Table 10.5 Public expenditure on active labour market policies (ALMPs) per participant (% GDP per capita), 2000–2015

	Training				Employment assistance			
	2000	2007	2015	Change 2000–2015	2000	2007	2015	Change 2000–2015
Austria	26.7	30.5	35.5	8.9	13.7	13.5	17.7	4.0
Belgium	24.4	17.3	12.6	−11.8	16.1	22.3	18.5	2.4
Denmark	71.0	37.1	59.2	−11.9	49.1	42.7	43.8	−5.3
Finland	37.9	41.4	37.7	−0.3	36.3	32.8	42.0	5.7
France	44.0	33.3	45.9	1.9	18.7	16.9	11.5	−7.2
Germany	54.5	27.8	16.8	−37.7	56.1	31.1	32.7	−23.5
Greece	13.1	41.0	15.3	2.2	8.9	39.5	22.4	13.5
Ireland	33.4	35.2	26.6	−6.7	16.6	14.8	12.7	−3.9
Italy	16.3	10.0	13.2	−3.1	14.8	16.1	19.2	4.4
Luxembourg	27.2	23.5	22.6	−4.6	8.7	11.5	11.4	2.7
Netherlands	13.4	12.9	8.6	−4.7	39.1	48.6	32.5	−6.6
Portugal	62.8	42.7	21.6	−41.2		18.1	13.5	−4.6
Spain	26.4	19.1	17.1	−9.4	8.4	4.8	8.1	−0.4
Sweden	76.2	67.7	41.8	−34.4	42.4	40.3	35.0	−7.3
United Kingdom	32.4	41.1			30.6	32.3		
Mean EU15	37.3	32.0	26.7	−10.6	25.7	25.7	22.9	−2.7
Standard deviation	20.3	14.6	15.0	−5.3	16.2	13.3	12.0	−4.2
Coefficient of variation	0.54	0.46	0.56	0.02	0.63	0.52	0.52	−0.11
Bulgaria		32.9	35.6		22.1	15.6	45.5	23.3
Croatia			55.4				37.0	
Cyprus		23.6	7.1			22.4	22.4	
Czech Republic	23.1	9.9	23.8	0.7	16.3	20.7	38.6	22.2
Estonia		34.7	39.6			6.1	19.2	
Hungary	30.6	42.7	42.9	12.4		15.2	24.0	
Latvia	42.8	42.0	46.3	3.5		39.2	18.5	
Lithuania	37.6	35.6	49.9	12.3		34.5	27.3	
Malta		7.2	12.5			29.6	17.3	
Poland		37.8	75.9			25.1	22.6	
Romania	39.0	14.2	2.0	−37.0	18.0	18.4	12.3	−5.8
Slovak Republic		40.4	25.0			13.3	17.7	
Slovenia	8.6	14.8	33.6	25.0		21.3	17.1	

Table 10.5 Continued

	Training				Employment assistance			
	2000	2007	2015	Change 2000–2015	2000	2007	2015	Change 2000–2015
Mean EU13		28.0	34.6	4.3		21.8	24.6	5.8
Standard deviation		13.3	20.7	8.0		9.3	9.9	6.9
Coefficient of variation		0.47	0.60	0.2		0.43	0.40	0.2
Non–EU								
Norway	47.4	32.8	35.3	−12.1	40.0	39.1	38.3	−1.6
Switzerland	57.6	46.5	43.9	−13.7	58.6	46.2	29.2	−29.3

Total expenditures in current prices (national currency) have been divided by the number of participants and this number was subsequently divided by GDP per capita (national currency) to obtain spending per participant relative to GDP per capita; participant stock data are not available for Iceland and the Unites States; for some countries, data years on training are around 2000 (Ireland, 1999; Luxembourg, 2001; Spain, 2003; Sweden, 2003; Czech Republic, 2002; Hungary, 2003; Latvia, 2003; Lithuania, 2003; Romania, 2003; Slovenia, 2003) or 2015 (Italy, 2014); for some countries, data years on employment assistance are around 2000 (Ireland, 1999; Spain, 2003; Czech Republic, 2003; Romania, 2003), 2007 (Malta, 2006) or 2015 (Italy, 2014; Slovenia, 2014).

Source: OECD Employment Database; European Commission DG Employment, Social Affairs & Inclusion Labour Market Policy Database; OECD National Accounts Database; authors' calculations.

(including job rotation schemes), sheltered and supported employment and re-habilitation, and start-up incentives. There are no participant data for PES and administration, however, because the expenditures included in this category re-late to participants in all the other programmes. Spending on this category is therefore not included in expenditures on employment assistance in Table 10.5.

Table 10.5 provides a much more nuanced picture than Table 10.4. While expenditures on ALMPs have risen in general, they have, on average, fallen per participant in training and employment assistance in EU15 countries. More in-terestingly, expenditures per participant in EU13 countries have increased to such an extent that these countries on average spent more relative to GDP per capita in 2015 than EU15 countries did. Within both country groups there are, how-ever, substantial differences between countries. While combining expenditure data with participant stocks might lead to better insights (Clasen et al., 2016), the data show a surprisingly volatile pattern for some countries. This raises some questions that require further investigation in order to determine whether this concerns an issue of data quality or whether countries have really altered the gen-erosity of their programmes to such extents. In addition, it should be stressed that changes in this indicator can be caused by multiple sources, including the level of expenditures, the number of participants, and the overall state of the economy.

Given the strong focus of the European social investment agenda on getting people out of poverty by moving them into work, Vandenbroucke and Vleminckx

(2011) argue that the 'active welfare state' might actually be a more accurate term than 'social investment state'. While the social investment state has gradually been developing since the 1990s, a more abrupt activation turn also occurred in the 1990s (Clasen, 2000; Raffass, 2017). Data on activation strategies in terms of benefit conditionality have only recently become available (Knotz and Nelson, 2019). Figure 10.5 presents the strictness of sanction rules for 14 European and 2 non-European countries in 1985 and 2012. It shows that sanction rules have gotten substantially tougher since 1985. According to Knotz (2018, 2019) this trend towards greater coercion in labour market policies can be explained through the adaption of rules and provisions in response to the emergence of new social risks, on the one hand, and the increased need for social protection in combination with limited resources during economic crises (such as those around 2000 and 2008), on the other. The only countries in which sanctions rules have been slightly relaxed over time are Denmark, France, and the Netherlands.

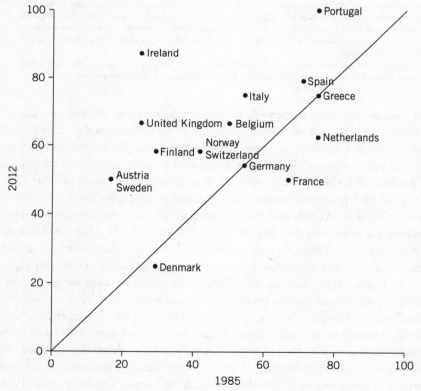

Figure 10.5 Strictness of sanction rules (1985–2012).
Original values have been multiplied by 100 to facilitate interpretation; data for the Netherlands are available since 1997 only; data are not available for Luxembourg, Central and Eastern European welfare states, Iceland, and the United States.
Source: Knotz and Nelson (2019) and authors' calculations.

10.13 EDUCATION

Together with ALMPs, policies focused on early childhood have figured most prominently in the literature on social investment. These policies cannot only be expected to increase labour market participation by enabling parents to reconcile work and family (see Akgunduz and Plantenga [2018] for a meta-analysis), but to stimulate cognitive development of children as well (Burger, 2010). In addition to education during early childhood, initial education and post-initial education during working life can both be expected to have a positive effect on the quality of a county's labour force. The modernization of education systems and expansion of lifelong learning programmes has been identified by the European Commission (2017) as one of the most important mechanisms to address the challenges that go hand in hand with globalization, technological change, and the growth of the services sector. The right to 'quality and inclusive education, training and life-long learning in order to maintain and acquire skills that enable [one] to participate fully in society and manage successfully transitions in the labour market' is even mentioned as very first in the European Pillar of Social Rights. Participation in education at a later age has become particularly relevant given that some jobs will become obsolete and the (routine-based) skills that go with them outdated. Workers are therefore confronted with the need to continuously adapt their skills or acquire new ones.

In Table 10.6 we show the development of public expenditure on education since 1995.[14] Educational expenditures can be distinguished into expenditures on core and peripheral educational goods and services, on the one hand, and expenditures on educational institutions and outside educational institutions, on the other. Public expenditures on education cover all of these categories (OECD, 2018b).[15] Data until 2011 are according to ISCED 1997, whereas data for 2012–2016 are according to ISCED 2011.[16] To guarantee comparability over time, spending data after 2011 exclude expenditures on ISCED 2011 level 01

---

14 Internationally comparative data on education spending by level are usually only available since the introduction of ISCED 1997. For that reason, the data we present with regard to education do not extend as far back in the past as data on social expenditure.

15 In addition to spending on teaching staff, school buildings, schoolbooks, and teaching materials this also includes, for example, spending on research and development; school meals; transport to schools; housing on campus; and public-to-private transfers such as loans for tuition and student living costs and subsidies for student living costs, reduced transport fares, private spending on school materials, and private tutoring.

16 The presented figures for Latvia (1995–2015) and Lithuania (2000–2015) are also according to ISCED 2011. Data according to this classification were provided retrospectively by the OECD, whereas data according to ISCED 1997 are not available from the OECD database used for the other OECD countries.

Table 10.6 Public expenditure on education (% GDP), 1995–2015

	1995	2000	2005	2010	2015	Change 1995–2015
Austria	6.1	5.6	5.2	5.7[b]	5.4	−0.7
Belgium		5.0	5.8	6.4	6.5	
Denmark	7.7	8.1	8.1	8.6[b]	8.8	1.0
Finland	6.5	5.7	6.0	6.5[b]	6.7	0.2
France	5.8	5.5	5.5	5.7	5.5	−0.3
Germany	4.5	4.3	4.4	4.9	4.6	0.1
Greece	2.9	3.3	4.0	3.6	3.6	0.7
Ireland	4.7	4.1	4.5	6.0	3.8	−0.9
Italy	4.3	4.4	4.2	4.3	4.1	−0.3
Luxembourg	3.6			4.3	3.9	0.3
Netherlands	4.8	4.6	4.8	5.5	5.3	0.6
Portugal	4.9	5.2	5.1	5.4	4.9	0.0
Spain	4.4	4.2	4.1	4.9[b]	4.2	−0.2
Sweden	7.1	6.8	6.5	6.5[b]	6.9	−0.1
United Kingdom	3.9	3.8	4.6	5.5	5.4	1.4
Mean EU15	5.1	5.0	5.2	5.6	5.3	0.2
Standard deviation	1.4	1.3	1.1	1.2	1.4	0.1
Coefficient of variation	0.27	0.25	0.22	0.21	0.27	0.00
Bulgaria	3.4	3.9	4.3	4.1	3.9	0.5
Croatia		3.7	4.0	4.3	4.4	
Cyprus	4.6	5.4	7.0	7.9	6.2	1.5
Czech Republic	4.0	3.7	3.9	4.1	5.8	1.7
Estonia	5.8	5.5	4.8	5.5	4.8	−1.0
Hungary	4.5	4.9	5.3	4.8	4.5	0.0
Latvia	6.0	6.2	4.8	5.1	5.3	−0.7
Lithuania	5.1	5.6	4.9	5.3	4.2	−0.9
Malta		4.5	6.6	6.7	5.1	
Poland	5.3	4.8	5.4	5.1	4.8	−0.5
Romania		2.9	3.5	3.5	3.1	
Slovak Republic		3.9	3.7	3.9	4.6	
Slovenia		5.8	5.7	5.5	4.6	
						0.0
Mean EU13		4.7	4.9	5.1	4.7	
Standard deviation		1.0	1.1	1.2	0.8	
Coefficient of variation		0.22	0.22	0.24	0.17	

Table 10.6 Continued

	1995	2000	2005	2010	2015	Change 1995–2015
Non–EU						
Iceland		6.4	7.4	7.0	6.9	
Norway	7.4	6.5	6.9	6.7[(b)]	6.9	−0.4
Switzerland	5.0	4.8	5.2	4.9	5.1	0.1
United States	5.1	4.7	4.9	5.3	4.8	5.0

Total expenditures in current prices (millions of national currency) have been divided by GDP in current prices (millions of national currency) to obtain spending as a percentage of GDP for most countries; for Bulgaria, Croatia, Cyprus, Malta, and Romania percentages were directly copied from Eurostat; the presented figures for Estonia (1995, 2000), Lithuania (1995), and Slovenia (2000) are estimates based on the development of percentages directly available from Eurostat.
To guarantee comparability over time spending on ISCED 2011 level 01 is excluded, because this category was not included in ISCED 1997; for Denmark and Lithuania, expenditures on ISCED 2011 level 01 cannot be distinguished from expenditures on level 02 and are hence included; the presented figure for Croatia (2015) concerns expenditures on public educational institutions, because public expenditures on education are not available after 2011;.
For some countries there is a break in the time series between 2011 and 2012 following the introduction of ISCED 2011 as a result of which spending on pre-primary education before and after 2011 cannot be compared (Austria, Denmark, Finland, Spain, Sweden, and Norway).
For most countries data according to ISCED 1997 are available since 1997 only (Austria, Denmark, Finland, France, Greece, Ireland, Italy, Luxembourg, Portugal, Spain, Sweden, and the United Kingdom); for some countries, data years are around 2000 (Croatia, 2002; Slovenia, 2001), 2010 (Greece, 2012; Luxembourg, 2012) or 2015 (Denmark, 2014; Croatia, 2014; Estonia, 2013; Slovak Republic, 2014).
Source: OECD Education Database; Eurostat Education and Training Database; OECD National Accounts Database; authors'own calculations.

(early childhood educational development). This constitutes a new category of early childhood education related to educational content for children in the age range of 0–2. This category did not exist under ISCED 1997, which only covered pre-primary education (designed for children from the age of 3 to the start of primary education; ISCED 1997 level 0; ISCED 2011 level 02).[17]

On average, expenditures on education as a per cent of GDP have increased in EU15 countries over time, although a drop can be observed after 2010 as a result of which the overall increase is rather small. As with social expenditures a trend of convergence can be observed until 2010, whereas a trend of divergence can be observed throughout more recent years. Again, Mediterranean countries are the lowest spenders on education among the EU15 whilst the Nordic countries stand out as the most generous spenders by allocating approximately 7% of their GDP

---

17 Currently, ISCED 01 programmes are in place in approximately half of the countries considered: Austria, Belgium (Flanders), Denmark, Finland, Germany, Greece, Italy, Spain, Sweden, the United Kingdom, Croatia, Cyprus, Estonia, Hungary, Latvia, Lithuania, Romania, Slovenia, Iceland, and Norway. For a country-by-country overview, see European Commission, Education, Audiovisual and Culture Executive Agency (EACEA) and Eurydice (2019).

to education. When excluding these countries, EU13 and the other EU15 countries display similar levels of education expenditure around 5% of GDP.

Despite moderate increases throughout the first decade of the 21st century, spending levels in EU13 countries in 2015 are comparable to those in 2000. Nevertheless, both the standard deviation and coefficient of variation have decreased over time. This convergence is mainly the result of the catch-up among some of the rather low spenders like Bulgaria, Croatia, the Czech Republic, and the Slovak Republic. With 3.1% of GDP, Romania was also the country with the lowest educational expenditures in 2015.

As with expenditure on ALMPs, we also provide spending figures per recipient. Instead of focusing on total education expenditure, we concentrate on expenditures for and of educational institutions (e.g., Busemeyer, 2009b). Specifically, we use expenditure on educational institutions per full-time equivalent (FTE) pupil or student as a share to GDP per capita, which provides an assessment of the investments made in each student, taking into account the relative wealth of countries (OECD, 2019d). As is customary in the literature, we distinguish between spending on pre-primary, primary, secondary (comprising lower secondary, upper secondary and post-secundary non-teriary education), and tertiary education (e.g., Garritzmann and Seng, 2016).[18]

For OECD countries these percentages are generally directly available for 2012–2016 for pre-primary education and 2005–2015 for primary and secondary education as well as tertiary education. Eurostat provides similar percentages for: primary and lower secondary; upper secondary, and post-secondary non-tertiary education; and tertiary education. Coverage for some countries extents back into the 1990s.[19] The OECD data were preferred over Eurostat data. The latter were only used for country-years not covered by the OECD data. For some country years, notably spending per FTE pupil enrolled in pre-primary education in 1995 and 2005, figures were calculated. This was done by dividing total expenditure on educational institutions at the respective level by the corresponding FTE enrolment. Next, expenditure per pupil or student was divided by GDP per capita.[20]

---

18 Note that spending on pre-primary education is not exactly the same as spending on childcare. In the SOCX data, childcare (ECEC) additionally includes spending on child (day)care and other pre-school services. Spending on pre-primary education, however, constitutes the lion's share of total spending on ECEC.

19 To obtain expenditures per FTE student in primary and secondary education, the two percentages were weighted by the relative shares of students enrolled in the two groups.

20 Note that expenditure and enrolment data often do not refer to the same period. The former usually refer to the calendar year (except for the United Kingdom and United States), whereas the latter generally refer to the calendar (pre-primary education only) or school year (usually September year$_{t-1}$ to August year$_t$). The OECD implements several adjustments on a country-by-country basis to ensure that student numbers

Table 10.7 shows that, on average, expenditures per pupil on pre-primary and primary and secondary educational institutions have increased in EU15 countries, whereas expenditures on tertiary educational institutions per student have somewhat decreased. In EU13 countries, expenditures per primary and secondary pupil have increased as well, but expenditures for pupils in pre-primary educational institutions and students in tertiary educational institutions decreased. Furthermore, it is worth noting that EU15 and EU13 countries on average invest rather similar shares of GDP per capita in their pupils and students. Nonetheless, spending on pupils in pre-primary education has traditionally been somewhat higher in the new EU Member States. There is, however, a lot of variation within these two groups of countries as well as within countries over time.

10.14 CONCLUSION

In this chapter, we presented the trends of globalization, technological change, and migration as three key challenges for European labour markets and welfare states in the 21st century. In particular globalization and technological change have been regarded as important sources of inequality between different groups in the labour market as these developments have been mainly beneficial for the employment opportunities and incomes of highly skilled workers. The more recent literature mainly considers the automation of routine-intense tasks as an important explanation for current labour market developments and in particular for the trend of job polarization. Whereas the existing literature has been mainly focused on the question of what types of work will (dis)appear, for what types of workers, and in which sectors, we argue that globalization and technological change, via job polarization, also affect the type of contract under which workers operate. The figures presented here show that the share of middle-skilled workers in low-paying jobs has increased in many European countries. At the same time, in many of these countries, the share of nonstandard employment has increased over time. Hence, we hypothesize that the increased competition for low-paying jobs is associated with the rise of nonstandard employment or, in other words, with labour market flexibilization. Interestingly, this hypothesis seems to have implications for both the policy agenda and the research agenda of the coming decade. For academic research, the implication would be that there is an additional outcome

---

coincide with the financial year (OECD, 2018b). Enrolment rates adjusted to the financial year are, however, only available since 2002 from the OECD and 2012 from Eurostat. These adjustment have therefore not been implemented in the calculations for the 1995 figures (and 2005 for Bulgaria, Croatia, Cyprus, Latvia, Lithuania, and Romania). Any biases associated with this are likely to be small as these calculations predominantly pertain to expenditure on pre-primary education, which generally uses headcounts instead of FTEs (OECD, 2018d).

Table 10.7 Expenditures on educational institutions per full-time equivalent (FTE) pupil or student by level (% GDP per capita), 1995–2015

	Pre–primary education (% GDP per capita)				Primary and secondary education (% GDP per capita)				Tertiary education (% GDP per capita)			
	1995	2005	2015	Change 1995–2015	1995	2005	2015	Change 1995–2015	1995	2005	2015	Change 1995–2015
Austria	19.0	18.7(b)	18.8	-0.1	31.0	27.2	27.8	-3.3	40.5	44.4	35.0	-5.5
Belgium	11.1	14.1	17.4	6.3	21.8	22.7	26.1	4.3	36.5	36.7	37.9	1.5
Denmark	22.1	15.3(b)	23.9	1.8	27.2	26.1	26.7	-0.5	44.5	43.5	32.5	-12.0
Finland	33.5	13.9(b)	25.2	-8.2	25.3	20.7	23.8	-1.5	53.0	38.5	41.7	-11.3
France	15.1	16.2	19.2	4.1	24.4	23.9	24.3	-0.1	31.6	36.6	39.7	8.1
Germany	17.1	17.9	20.4	3.3	25.1	22.1	22.5	-2.6	41.6	40.9	35.4	-6.2
Greece	–	–	19.6		11.9	20.9	23.1	11.2	20.0	24.7	15.3	-4.7
Ireland	12.4	13.3	12.7	0.4	15.0	15.8	12.6	-2.4	25.5	25.9	19.2	-6.3
Italy	11.7	16.3	17.1	5.4	22.3	23.6	24.6	2.3	23.4	24.2	30.8	7.4
Luxembourg	–	15.8	17.1		15.3	20.6	19.9	4.6	–	–	47.6	
Netherlands	13.3	15.8	16.7	3.4	18.6	20.6	21.9	3.2	50.2	40.9	38.5	-11.7
Portugal	6.0	15.2	24.1	18.1	18.8	24.7	28.9	10.1	40.6	42.3	39.9	-0.7
Spain	17.0	18.4(b)	18.9	2.0	21.8	22.7	23.5	1.7	32.8	35.5	36.2	3.4
Sweden	13.7	13.9(b)	29.5	15.8	25.2	22.5	22.9	-2.3	63.3	45.6	50.7	-12.6
United Kingdom	24.3	18.0	21.8	-2.5	16.2	24.6	26.9	10.7	36.3	44.1	64.1	27.8
Mean EU15	16.6	15.9	20.2	3.5	21.3	22.6	23.7	2.4	38.6	37.4	37.6	-0.9
Standard deviation	7.0	1.8	4.2	-2.8	5.3	2.7	3.9	-1.4	11.9	7.5	11.7	-0.2

	0.42	0.11	0.21	-0.21	0.25	0.12	0.16	-0.08	0.31	0.20	0.31	0.00
Coefficient of variation												
Bulgaria	27.6	25.6	25.0	-2.6	17.5	19.1	17.8	0.3	48.3	43.3	37.2	-11.1
Croatia		26.4	30.1			20.1	21.3			38.8	21.3	
Cyprus	11.0	15.8	16.9	5.9	25.8	31.8	39.6	13.9	59.9	41.6	41.1	-18.8
Czech Republic	17.2	15.1	14.8	-2.4	19.6	18.4	21.1	1.5	36.0	29.9	32.5	-3.5
Estonia		10.8	22.4			22.5	22.9			23.3	44.2	
Hungary	19.9	24.7	26.1	6.3	20.8	23.1	22.7	1.9	56.6	32.4	33.5	-23.1
Latvia	34.5	22.3	19.0	-15.5	24.6	24.1	22.4	-2.2	39.5	27.0	29.7	-9.8
Lithuania	37.6	22.6	19.1	-18.4	20.8	17.0	18.5	-2.3	49.1	31.3	33.7	-15.4
Malta		15.2	21.3			26.5	26.0		42.0	50.5	51.5	9.5
Poland	17.6	27.9	23.4	5.8	17.5	22.4	25.3	7.8	35.3	41.1	36.4	1.1
Romania		19.2	12.4			15.5	13.8			30.2	30.7	
Slovak Republic	15.8	17.3	19.6	3.8	13.1	16.7	22.8	9.7	42.2	35.2	53.6	11.4
Slovenia		47.1	24.9			29.5	26.7			35.8	32.4	
Mean EU13		22.3	21.1			22.1	23.2			35.4	36.8	
Standard deviation		9.1	4.9			5.0	6.1			7.5	8.9	
Coefficient of variation		0.41	0.23			0.23	0.26			0.21	0.24	

(continued)

Table 10.7 Continued

	Pre–primary education (% GDP per capita)				Primary and secondary education (% GDP per capita)				Tertiary education (% GDP per capita)			
	1995	2005	2015	Change 1995–2015	1995	2005	2015	Change 1995–2015	1995	2005	2015	Change 1995–2015
Non–EU												
Iceland	16.1	18.4	25.2	9.1	20.3	23.8	22.9	2.5	30.6	25.7	25.9	–4.7
Norway		10.9(b)	27.7			26.8	27.5		38.6	32.4	40.2	1.6
Switzerland	8.2	8.8	9.7	1.4	21.0	21.1	29.0	8.0	49.6	40.7	42.7	–6.9
United States	21.4	19.4	19.4	–2.0	21.3	22.7	22.5	1.2	56.2	54.8	53.6	–2.6

Expenditure concerns expenditure of and for public and private educational institutions from public, private and international sources; pre-primary education refers to ISCED 2011 level 01 (ISCED 1997 level 0) exclusively; primary and secondary education includes post-secondary non-tertiary education.

In Greece (until 2012) and Luxembourg (until 2008) expenditures on pre-primary education are included under primary education; underlined figures include expenditures on and pupils enrolled in pre-primary education.

Figures in italics were calculated by dividing expenditures in current prices (national currency) by the number of students enrolled in the respective level and subsequently relating this number to GDP per capita; the presented figures for Malta (2005) and Romania (2005) seem to overestimate expenditures, because they may include educational expenditures not allocated to a specific level.

For most countries expenditures on pre-primary educational institutions are not available for 1995 so that data for 1994 has been used instead (Austria, Belgium, Denmark, Finland, France, Ireland, Italy, Portugal, Spain, Sweden, United Kingdom, Czech Republic); for some countries, data years for expenditure on pre-primary education are around 1995 (Bulgaria, 1999; Cyprus, 1999; Hungary, 1997; Latvia, 1998; Lithuania, 1998; Poland, 1999; Slovak Republic, 1999; Iceland, 1998; Switzerland, 1999), 2005 (Luxembourg, 2008; Croatia, 2007; Malta, 2008; Switzerland, 2008) or 2015 (Denmark, 2014; Ireland, 2014; Croatia, 2014; Switzerland 2012).

For some countries, data years for expenditure on primary and secondary education are around 1995 (Luxembourg, 1996; Bulgaria, 1999; Cyprus, 1999; Hungary, 1996; Latvia, 1998; Lithuania, 1998; Poland, 1999; Slovak Republic, 1998; Iceland, 1998; Switzerland, 1999), 2005 (Luxembourg, 2008; Croatia, 2007; Switzerland, 2008) or 2015 (Denmark, 2014; Croatia, 2014; Switzerland 2012).

For some countries, data years for expenditure on tertiary education are around 1995 (Ireland, 1999; Italy, 1997; Bulgaria, 1999; Czech Republic, 1997; Hungary, 1997; Latvia, 1996; Poland, 1999; Slovak Republic, 1998; Iceland, 1998; Norway, 1999; Switzerland, 1999), 2005 (Croatia, 2007; Switzerland, 2008) or 2015 (Denmark, 2014; Croatia, 2014; Switzerland 2012). For some countries there is a break in the time series between 2011 and 2012 following the introduction of ISCED 2011 as a result of which spending on pre-primary education before and after 2011 cannot be compared (Austria, Denmark, Finland, Spain, Sweden, and Norway).

Source: OECD Education Database; Eurostat Education and Training Database; OECD National Accounts Database; authors' calculations.

variable in the analyses of globalization and technological change. In addition, job polarization and the rise of nonstandard employment may also have implications for market income distribution, which would be an interesting direction for future research. Moreover, the public policy debate regarding the consequences of globalization and technological change should not only be focused on the growth of certain sectors and the decline of other sectors, but it should also be focused on the trends in nonstandard employment and hence on the type of contract.

With regard to migration, the free movement of labour has been considered an important issue for European labour markets and welfare states. We have shown that, since 2004, the intra-EU labour migration from CEE countries to Western European countries has increased substantially. Free movement of labour is economically important for the European Union as it can reduce labour market imbalances, which is especially important for the functioning of the Eurozone. At the same time, it has been considered a challenge for welfare states as it might contribute to feelings of economic insecurity and erode solidarity, which forms the basis for the provision of social policy.

Subsequently, we have analysed developments in the provision of welfare state programmes across European countries. Interestingly, it turns out that, despite the budgetary pressure stemming from various sources, social spending has been increased in most European countries. However, in the 21st century, the main question will not be whether governments have increased or decreased their welfare state expenditures. Instead, the question will be whether and how the focus has been shifted from classical social protection to social investment in order to enable workers to adapt themselves to new labour market transformations. In the past decade, such welfare state reforms have been at the core of the EU agenda on social policy. Yet this policy agenda is not uncontroversial, as some fear that a shift of resources from social protection to social investment would reduce the redistributing capacity of welfare states and hence contribute to an increase of income inequality and poverty.

ACKNOWLEDGEMENTS

Financial support from Instituut Gak is gratefully acknowledged.

REFERENCES

Acemoglu, D. (1999). Changes in unemployment and wage inequality: An alternative theory and some evidence. *American Economic Review, 89*(5), 1259–1278.

Acemoglu, D., and Autor, D. (2010). *Skills, tasks and technologies: Implications for employment and earnings.* NBER Working Paper No. 16082. Cambridge: National Bureau of Economic Research.

Acemoglu, D., Autor, D., Dorn, D., Hanson, G., and Price, B. (2016). Import competition and the great US employment sag of the 2000s. *Journal of Labor Economics, 34*(S1), S141–S198.

Adema W., and Fron, P. (2019). *The OECD SOCX Manual—2019 Edition. A guide to the OECD Social Expenditure Database*. Paris: OECD.

Ahn, S.-H., and Kim, S.-W. (2015). Social investment, social service and the economic performance of welfare states. *International Journal of Social Welfare, 24*(1), 109–119.

Akgunduz, Y. E., and Plantenga, J. (2013). Labour market effects of parental leave in Europe. *Cambridge Journal of Economics, 37*(4), 845–862.

Akgunduz, Y. E., and Plantenga, J. (2018). Child care prices and maternal employment: A meta-analysis. *Journal of Economic Surveys, 32*(1), 118–133.

Alesina, A., and Glaeser, E. L. (2004). *Fighting poverty in the US and Europe: A world of difference*. Oxford: Oxford University Press.

Alesina, A., Glaeser, E. L., and Sacerdote, B. (2001). Why doesn't the United States have a European-style welfare state? *Brookings Papers on Economic Activity, 2*, 187–277.

Armingeon, K., and Bonoli, G. (eds.). (2006). *the politics of post-industrial welfare states: Adapting post-war social policies to new social risks.* London: Routledge.

Atkinson, A. B. (2007). The distribution of earnings in OECD countries. *International Labour Review, 146*(1), 41–60.

Autor, D., and Dorn, D. (2013). The growth of low-skill service jobs and the polarization of the US labor market. *American Economic Review, 103*(5), 1553–1597.

Autor, D., Dorn, D., and Hanson, G. (2013). The China syndrome: Local labor market effects of import competition in the United States. *American Economic Review, 103*(6), 2121–2168.

Autor, D., Dorn, D., and Hanson, G. (2015). Untangling trade and technology: Evidence from local labor markets. *Economic Journal, 125*(584), 621–646.

Autor, D., Katz, L. F., and Kearney, M. S. (2006). The Polarization of the US labor market. *American Economic Review, 96*(2), 189–194.

Autor, D., Levy, F., and Murnane, R. J. (2003). The skill content of recent technological change: An empirical exploration. *Quarterly Journal of Economics, 118*(4), 1279–1333.

Baker, M., and Milligan, K. (2008). How does job-protected maternity leave affect mothers' employment? *Journal of Labor Economics, 26*(4), 655–691.

Baker, M., and Milligan, K. (2010). Evidence from maternity leave expansions on the impact of maternal care on early child development. *Journal of Human Resources, 45*(1), 1–32.

Bakker, V., and Van Vliet, O. (2019). *Social investment, employment outcomes and policy and institutional complementarities: A comparative analysis across 26*

OECD countries. Department of Economics Research Memorandum 2019.01. Leiden: Leiden University Press.

Balsvik, R., Jensen, S., and Salvanes, K. (2015). Made in China, sold in Norway: Local labor market effects of an import shock. *Journal of Public Economics, 127*, 137–144.

Bengtsson, M., De la Porte, C., and Jacobsson, K. (2017). Labour market policy under conditions of permanent austerity: Any sign of social investment? *Social Policy & Administration, 51*(2), 367–388.

Berger, L. M., and Waldfogel, J. (2004). Maternal leave and the employment of new mothers in the United States. *Journal of Population Economics, 17*(2), 331–349.

Berger, L. M., Hill, J., and Waldfogel, J. (2005). Maternity leave, early maternal employment and child health and development in the US. *Economic Journal, 115*(501), 29–47.

Berman, E., Bound, J., and Machin, S. (1998). Implications of skill-biased technological change: International evidence. *Quarterly Journal of Economics, 113*(4), 1245–1279.

Bloom, N., Draca, M., and Van Reenen, J. (2016). Trade induced technical change? The impact of Chinese imports on diffusion, innovation, and productivity. *Review of Economic Studies, 83*(1), 87–117.

Boeri, T. (2010). Immigration to the land of redistribution. *Economica, 77*(308), 651–687.

Bonoli, G. (2006). New social risks and the politics of post-industrial social policies. In K. Armingeon and G. Bonoli (eds.), *The politics of post-industrial welfare states: Adapting post-war social policies to new social risks* (pp. 3-26). London: Routledge.

Bonoli, G. (2010). The political economy of active labor-market policy. *Politics & Society, 38*(4), 435–457.

Bonoli, G. (2012). Active labour market policy and social investment: A changing relationship. In N. Morel, B. Palier and J. Palme (eds.), *Towards a social investment welfare state? Ideas, policies and challenges* (pp. 181–204). Bristol: Policy Press.

Bonoli, G. (2013). *The origins of active social policy: Labour market and childcare policies in a comparative perspective*. Oxford: Oxford University Press.

Bonoli, G., and Liechti, F. (2018). Good intentions and Matthew effects: Access biases in participation in active labour market policies. *Journal of European Public Policy, 25*(6), 894–911.

Bonoli, G., and Natali, D. (eds.). (2012). *The politics of the new welfare state*. Oxford: Oxford University Press.

Brady, D., and Finnigan, R. (2014). Does immigration undermine public support for social policy? *American Sociological Review, 79*(1), 17–42.

Brady, D., Beckfield, J., and Seeleib-Kaiser, M. (2005). Economic globalization and the welfare state in affluent democracies, 1975–2001. *American Sociological Review, 70*(6), 921–948.

Breunig, C., and Busemeyer, M. R. (2012). Fiscal austerity and the trade-off between public investment and social spending. *Journal of European Public Policy*, *19*(6), 921–938.

Burger, K. (2010). How does early childhood care and education affect cognitive development? An international review of the effects of early interventions for children from different social backgrounds. *Early Childhood Research Quarterly*, *25*(2), 140–165.

Burgoon, B., Koster, F., and Van Egmond, M. (2012). Support for redistribution and the paradox of immigration. *Journal of European Social Policy*, *22*(3), 288–304.

Busemeyer, M. R. (2009a). From myth to reality: Globalisation and public spending in OECD countries revisited. *European Journal of Political Research*, *48*(4), 455–482.

Busemeyer, M. R. (2009b). Social democrats and the new partisan politics of public investment in education. *Journal of European Public Policy*, *16*(1), 107–126.

Busemeyer, M. R., and Garritzmann, J. L. (2017). Public opinion on policy and budgetary trade-offs in European welfare states: Evidence from a new comparative survey. *Journal of European Public Policy*, *24*(6), 871–889.

Busemeyer, M. R., and Neimanns, E. (2017). Conflictive preferences towards social investments and transfers in mature welfare states: The cases of unemployment benefits and childcare provision. *Journal of European Social Policy*, *27*(3), 229–246.

Caminada, K., Goudswaard, K., and Van Vliet, O. (2010). Patterns of welfare state indicators in the EU: Is there convergence? *Journal of Common Market Studies*, *48*(3), 529–556.

Cantillon, B. (2011). The paradox of the social investment state: Growth, employment and poverty in the Lisbon era. *Journal of European Social Policy*, *21*(5), 432–449.

Cantillon, B., and Van Lancker, W. (2013). Three shortcomings of the social investment perspective. *Social Policy and Society*, *12*(4), 553–564.

Clasen, J. (2000). Motives, means and opportunities: Reforming unemployment compensation in the 1990s. *West European Politics*, *23*(2), 89–112.

Clasen, J., Clegg, D., and Goerne, A. (2016). Comparative social policy analysis and active labour market policy: Putting quality before quantity. *Journal of Social Policy*, *45*(1), 21–38.

Cortes, G. (2016). Where have the middle-wage workers gone? A study of polarization using panel data. *Journal of Labor Economics*, *34*(1), 63–105.

Croatian Bureau of Statistics. (2019). *Social protection in the Republic of Croatia, 2017*. Zagreb: Croatian Bureau of Statistics.

Cronert, A. (2019). Unemployment reduction or labor force expansion? How partisanship matters for the design of active labor market policy in Europe. *Socio-Economic Review*, *17*(4), 921–946.

Davis, S. (1992). Cross-country patterns of change in relative wages. In O. J. Blanchard and S. Fischer (eds.), *NBER macroeconomics annual (Vol. 7)* (pp. 239–292). Cambridge, MA: MIT Press.

De Deken, J. (2017). Conceptualizing and measuring social investment. In A. Hemerijck (ed.), *The uses of social investment* (pp. 185–194). Oxford: Oxford University Press.

Draxler, J., and Van Vliet, O. (2010). European social model: No convergence from the east. *Journal of European Integration, 32*(1), 115–135.

Eger, M. A. (2010). Even in Sweden: The effects of immigration on support for welfare state spending. *European Sociological Review, 26*(2), 203–217.

Esping-Andersen, G. (ed.). (2002). *Why we need a new welfare state.* Oxford: Oxford University Press.

Estevez-Abe, M., Iversen, T., and Soskice, D. (2001). Social protection and the formation of skills: A reinterpretation of the welfare state. In P. A. Hall and D. Soskice (eds.), *The varieties of capitalism: The institutional foundations of comparative advantage* (pp. 145–183). Cambridge: Cambridge University Press.

Eurofound. (2014). *Labour mobility in the EU: Recent trends and policies.* Dublin: Eurofound.

Eurofound. (2019). *Labour market segmentation: Piloting new empirical policy analysis.* Dublin: Eurofound.

European Commission. (2010). *Europe 2020. A European strategy for smart, sustainable and inclusive growth.* Brussels: European Commission.

European Commission. (2013). *Towards social investment for growth and cohesion: Including implementing the European Social Fund 2014–2020.* Brussels: European Commission.

European Commission. (2017). *Reflection paper on the social dimension of Europe.* Brussels: European Commission.

European Commission. (2018). *Employment and social development in Europe: Annual Review 2018.* Brussels: European Commission.

European Commission, EACEA and Eurydice. (2019). *Key data on early childhood education and care in Europe: 2019 edition.* Luxembourg: Authors.

Eurostat. (2016). *European system of integrated social protection statistics—ESSPROS manual and user guidelines 2016 edition.* Luxembourg; Eurostat.

Fajgelbaum, P., and Khandelwal, A. (2016). Measuring the unequal gains from trade. *Quarterly Journal of Economics, 131*(3), 1113–1180.

Fenwick, C. (2019). The political economy of immigration and welfare state effort: Evidence from Europe. *European Political Science Review, 11*(3), 357–375.

Fenwick, C., and Van Vliet, O. (2019). *Immigration and EU welfare states: Does the type of migration matter?* Mimeo. Leiden: Leiden University Press.

Fernández-Macías, E., and Hurley, J. (2017). Routine-biased technical change and job polarization in Europe. *Socio-Economic Review, 15*(3), 563–585.

Fitzenberger, B., and Kohn, K. (2006). *Skill wage premia, employment, and cohort effects: Are workers in Germany all of the same type?* IZA Discussion Paper No. 2185. Bonn: Institute for the Study of Labor.

Garrett, G., and Mitchell, D. (2001). Globalization, government spending and taxation in the OECD. *European Journal of Political Research, 39*(2), 145–177.

Garritzmann, J., Häusermann, S., Palier, B., and Zollinger, C. (2017). The world politics of social investment. LIEPP Working Paper No. 64. Paris: Sciences Po.

Garritzmann, J. L., and Seng, K. (2016). Party politics and education spending: Challenging some common wisdom. *Journal of European Public Policy, 23*(4), 510–530.

Gaston, N., and Rajaguru, G. (2013). International migration and the welfare state revisited. *European Journal of Political Economy 29*(1), 90–101.

Ghysels, J., and Van Lancker, W. (2011). The unequal benefits of activation: An analysis of the social distribution of family policy among families with young children. *Journal of European Public Policy, 21*(5), 472–485.

Giddens, A. (1998). *The third way: The renewal of social democracy.* Cambridge, MA: Polity Press.

Goldin, C., and Katz, L. F. (2009). *The race between education and technology.* Cambridge, MA: Harvard University Press.

Goos, M. (2018). The impact of technological progress on labour markets: Policy challenges. *Oxford Review of Economic Policy, 34*(3), 362–375.

Goos, M., and Manning, A. (2007). Lousy and lovely jobs: The rising polarization of work in Britain. *Review of Economics and Statistics, 89*(1), 118–133.

Goos, M., Manning, A., and Salomons, A. (2009). Job polarization in Europe. *American Economic Review, 99*(2), 58–63.

Goos, M., Manning, A., and Salomons, A. (2014). Explaining job polarization: Routine-biased technological change and offshoring. *American Economic Review, 104*(8), 2509–2526.

Green, A (2019). *What is happening to middle skill workers.* OECD Social, Employment and Migration Working Papers NO. 230. Paris: OECD Publishing.

Gregory, T., Salomons, A., and Zierahn, U. (2016). *Racing with or against the machine? Evidence from Europe.* ZEW Discussion Paper No. 16-053. Mannheim: Leibniz Centre for European Economic Research.

Grimshaw, D., Bosch, G., and Rubery, J. (2014). Minimum wages and collective bargaining: What types of pay bargaining can foster positive pay equity outcomes? *British Journal of Industrial Relations, 52*(3), 470–498.

Häusermann, S. (2012). The politics of old and new social policies. In G. Bonoli and D. Natali (eds.), *The politics of the new welfare state* (pp. 111–132). Oxford: Oxford University Press.

Hays, J. C. (2009). *Globalization and the new politics of embedded liberalism.* Oxford: Oxford University Press.

Hemerijck, A. (2013). *Changing welfare states.* Oxford: Oxford University Press.

Hemerijck, A. (2017). Social investment and its critics. In A. Hemerijck (ed.), *The uses of social investment* (pp. 3–42). Oxford: Oxford University Press.

Hemerijck, A., Burgoon, B., Die Pietro, A., and Vydra, S. (2016). *Assessing social investment synergies.* Luxembourg: European Commissnio DG for Employment, Social Affairs and Inclusion.

Hicks, A., and Zorn, C. (2005). Economic globalization, the macro economy, and reversals of welfare: Expansion in affluent democracies, 1978–94. *International Organization, 59*(3), 631–662.

ILO. (2016). *Non-standard employment around the world: Understanding challenges, shaping prospects.* Geneva: ILO.

ILO. (2019). *Work for a brighter future.* Geneva: ILO.

Iversen, T., and Cusack, T. R. (2000). The causes of welfare state expansion: Deindustrialization or globalization? *World Politics, 52*(3), 313–349.

Jensen, C. (2011). Less bad than its reputation: Social spending as a proxy for welfare effort in cross-national studies. *Journal of Comparative Policy Analysis: Research and Practice, 13*(3), 327–340.

Jenson, J., and Saint-Martin, D. (2003). New routes to social cohesion? Citizenship and the social investment state. *Canadian Journal of Sociology, 28*(1), 77–99.

Katz, L., and Murphy, K. (1992). Changes in relative wages, 1963–1987: Supply and demand factors. *Quarterly Journal of Economics, 107*(1), 35–78.

Katz, L. F., and Autor, D. (1999). Changes in the wage structure and earnings inequality. In O. Ashenfelter and D. Card (eds.), *The handbook of labor economics* (pp. 1463–1555). Amsterdam: Elsevier.

Keune, M., and Pedaci, M. (2019). Trade union strategies against precarious work: Common trends and sectoral divergence in the EU. *European Journal of Industrial Relations.* doi: https://doi.org/10.1177/0959680119827182

Kim, S.-W., and Ahn, S.-H. (2020). Social investment effects of public education, health care, and welfare service expenditures on economic growth. *Asian Social Work and Policy Review. 14*(1), 34–44.

Klerman, J., and Leibowitz, A. (1997). Labor supply effects of state maternity leave legislation. In Blau, F., and Ehrenberg, R. (eds.), *Gender and family issues in the workplace* (pp. 68–85). New York: Russell Sage Foundation.

Knotz, C. (2018). A rising workfare state? Unemployment benefit conditionality in 21 OECD countries, 1980–2012. *Journal of International and Comparative Social Policy, 34*(2), 91–108.

Knotz, C. (2019). Why countries 'get tough on the work-shy': The role of adverse economic conditions. *Journal of Social Policy, 48*(3), 615–634.

Knotz, C., and Nelson, M. (2019). *The comparative unemployment benefit conditions and sanctions dataset.* Lund: Department of Political Science, Lund University.

Kuitto, K. (2016). From social security to social investment? Compensating and social investment welfare policies in a life-course perspective. *Journal of European Social Policy, 26*(5), 442–459.

Kurer, T., and Gallego, A. (2019). Distributional consequences of technological change: Worker-level evidence. *Research & Politics*, 6(1), 45–51.

Kvist, J. (2013). The post-crisis European social model: Developing or dismantling social investments? *Journal of International and Comparative Social Policy*, 29(1), 91–107.

Lalive, R., and Zweimüller, J. (2009). How does parental leave affect fertility and return to work? Evidence from two natural experiments. *Quarterly Journal of Economics*, 124(3), 1363–1402.

Luttmer, E. F. P. (2001). Group loyalty and the taste for redistribution. *Journal of Political Economy*, 109(3), 500–528.

Meltzer, A. H., and Richard, S. F. (1983). Tests of a rational theory of the size of government. *Public Choice*, 41(3), 403–418.

Michaels, G., Natraj, A., and Van Reenen, J. (2014). Has ICT polarized skill demand? Evidence from eleven countries over 25 years. *Review of Economics and Statistics*, 96(1), 60–77.

Morel, N., Palier, B., and Palme, J. (eds.). (2012). *Towards a social investment welfare state? Ideas, policies and challenges*. Bristol: Policy Press.

Murphy, E. C., and Oesch, D. (2018). Is employment polarisation inevitable? Occupational change in Ireland and Switzerland, 1970–2010. *Work, Employment and Society*, 32(6), 1099–1117.

Nelson, M., and Stephens, J. D. (2012). Do social investment policies produce more and better jobs? In N. Morel, B. Palier and J. Palme (eds.), *Towards a social investment welfare state? Ideas, policies and challenges* (pp. 205–234). Bristol: Policy Press.

Nikolai, R. (2012). Towards social investment? Patterns of public policy in the OECD world. In N. Morel, B. Palier and J. Palme (eds.), *Towards a social investment welfare state? Ideas, policies and challenges* (pp. 91–115). Bristol: Policy Press.

Noël, A. (2018). Is social investment inimical to the poor? *Socio-Economic Review*. doi: https://doi.org/10.1093/ser/mwy038

OECD. (2018a). Notes on the scope and comparability of data on labour market programmes. Paris: OECD.

OECD. (2019a). *Social expenditure database*. Paris: OECD.

OECD. (2019b). *Labour database*. Paris: OECD.

OECD. (2019c). *Education and training database*. Paris: OECD.

OECD. (2019d). *Education at a glance 2019*. Paris: OECD.

OECD. (2018b). *OECD handbook for internationally comparative education statistics 2018: Concepts, standards, definitions and classifications*. Paris: OECD.

Oesch, D., and Rodríguez Menés, J. (2011). Upgrading or polarization? Occupational change in Britain, Germany, Spain and Switzerland, 1990–2008. *Socio-Economic Review*, 9(3), 503–531.

Pavolini, E., and Van Lancker, W. (2018). The Matthew effect in childcare use: A matter of policies or preferences? *Journal of European Public Policy*, 25(6), 878–893.

Peugny, C. (2019). The decline in middle-skilled employment in 12 European countries: New evidence for job polarisation. *Research & Politics*, 6(1), 405–423.

Raess, D., and Pontusson, J. (2015). The politics of fiscal policy during economic downturns, 1981–2010. *European Journal of Political Research*, 54(1), 1–22.

Raffass, T. (2017). Demanding activation. *Journal of Social Policy*, 46(2), 349–365.

Rodrik, D. (1998). Why do more open economies have bigger governments? *Journal of Political Economy*, 106(5), 997–1002.

Rojas-Romagosa, H., and Bollen, J. (2018). *Estimating migration changes from the EU's free movement of people principle*. CBP Discussion Paper No. 385. The Hague: CPB Netherlands Bureau for Economic Policy Analysis.

Ronchi, S. (2016). *The social investment welfare expenditure data set (SIWE)*. GK SOCLIFE Working Paper No. 17. Cologne: Cologne University.

Ronchi, S. (2018). Which roads (if any) to social investment? The recalibration of EU welfare states at the crisis crossroads (2000–2014). *Journal of Social Policy*, 47(3), 459–478.

Roy, A. D. (1951). Some thoughts on the distribution of earnings. *Oxford Economic Papers*, 3(2), 135–146.

Ruhm, C. J. (1998). The economic consequences of parental leave mandates: Lessons from Europe. *Quarterly Journal of Economics*, 113(1), 285–317.

Samuelson, P. (1971). Ohlin was right. *Swedish Journal of Economics*, 73(4), 365–384.

Scheve, K., and Slaughter, M. J. (2004). Economic insecurity and the globalization of production. *American Journal of Political Science*, 48(4), 662–674.

Sirgy, M. J., Lee, D.-J., Miller, C., Littlefield, J. E., and Atay, E. G. (2007). The impact of imports and exports on a country's quality of life. *Social Indicators Research*, 83(2), 245–281.

Soroka, S., Johnston, R., and Banting, K. (2006). Immigration and redistribution in a global era. In S. Bowles, P. Bardhan, and M. Wallerstein (eds.), *Globalization and egalitarian redistribution* (pp. 261–288). Princeton: Princeton University Press and Russell Sage Foundation.

Soroka, S., Johnston, R., Kevins, A., Banting, K., and Kymlicka, W. (2016). Migration and welfare state spending. *European Political Science Review*, 8(2), 173–194.

Starke, P., Klaasch, A., and Van Hooren, F. (2014). Political parties and social policy responses to global economic crises: Constrained partisanship in mature welfare states. *Journal of Social Policy*, 43(2), 225–246.

Starke, P., Obinger, H., and Castles, F. G. (2008). Convergence towards where: In what ways, if any, are welfare states becoming more similar? *Journal of European Public Policy*, 15(7), 975–1000.

Stolper, W., and Samuelson, P. (1941). Protection and real wages. *Review of Economic Studies* 9(1), 58–73.

Taylor-Gooby, P. (ed.). (2004). *New risks, new welfare: The transformation of the European welfare state*. Oxford: Oxford University Press.

Taylor-Gooby, P., Gumy, J. M., and Otto, A. (2015). Can 'new welfare' address poverty through more and better jobs? *Journal of Social Policy, 44*(1), 83–104.

Thewissen, S., and Van Vliet, O. (2019). Competing with the dragon: Employment effects of Chinese trade competition in 17 sectors across 18 OECD countries. *Political Science Research and Methods, 7*(2), 215–232.

Tinbergen, J. (1974). Substitution of graduate by other labour. *Kyklos, 27*(2), 217–226.

Tinbergen, J. (1975). *Income differences: Recent research.* Amsterdam: North-Holland.

Van Kersbergen, K., and Hemerijck, A. (2012). Two decades of change in Europe: The emergence of the social investment state. *Journal of Social Policy, 41*(3), 475–492.

Van Lancker, W., and Ghysels, J. (2014). Who benefits from investment policies? The case of family activation in European countries. In B. Cantillon and F. Vandenbroucke (eds.), *Reconciling work and poverty reduction: How successful are European welfare states?* (pp. 212–237). Oxford: Oxford University Press.

Van Lancker, W., and Ghysels, J. (2016). Explaining patterns of inequality in childcare service use across 31 developed economies: A welfare state perspective. *International Journal of Comparative Sociology, 57*(5), 310–337.

Van Vliet, O. (2010). Divergence within convergence: Europeanization of social and labour market policies. *Journal of European Integration, 32*(3), 269–290.

Van Vliet, O., and Koster, F. (2011). Europeanization and the political economy of active labour market policies. *European Union Politics, 12*(2), 217–239.

Van Vliet, O., and Wang, C. (2015). Social investment and poverty reduction: A comparative analysis across fifteen European countries. *Journal of Social Policy, 44*(3), 611–638.

Van Vliet, O., and Wang, J. (2019). The political economy of social assistance and minimum income benefits: A comparative analysis across 26 OECD countries. *Comparative European Politics, 17*(1), 49–71.

Vandenbroucke, F., and Vleminckx, K. (2011). Disappointing poverty trends: Is the social investment state to blame? *Journal of European Social Policy, 21*(5), 450–471.

Walter, S. (2010). Globalization and the welfare state: Testing the microfoundations of the compensation hypothesis. *International Studies Quarterly, 54*(2), 403–426.

Walter, S. (2017). Globalization and the demand-side of politics: How globalization shapes labor market risk perceptions and policy preferences. *Political Science Research Methods, 5*(1), 55–80.

11

POPULATION AGEING AND FINANCING CONSUMPTION OF THE OLDER GENERATION IN THE EUROPEAN UNION

Agnieszka Chłoń-Domińczak

11.1 INTRODUCTION

The European population is ageing—in all European countries there is a growth in the number and proportion of older people in their populations. For some countries this phenomenon has already been observed for many decades, while for others it is a relatively new but quickly progressing development. In 2017, there are an estimated 962 million people aged 60 or older in the world, comprising 13% of the global population. The population aged 60 or older is growing at a rate of about 3% per year. Currently, the continent of Europe has the greatest percentage of population aged 60 or older (25%) (United Nations Department of Economic and Social Affairs Population Division, 2007: 11).

Simultaneously, fertility in all European countries is now below the level required for replacement of the population in the long run (around 2.1 births per woman, on average) and, in most cases, has been below the replacement level for several decades. Fertility for Europe as a whole is projected to increase from 1.6 births per woman in 2010–2015 to nearly 1.8 in 2045–2050. Such an increase, however, will not prevent a likely contraction in the size of the total population (United Nations Department of Economic and Social Affairs Population Division, 2007: 5).

The advance of population ageing as well as its future development also varies between European countries. In some, lower fertility and lower mortality has

Agnieszka Chłoń-Domińczak, *Population Ageing and Financing Consumption of the Older Generation in the European Union* In: *Europe's Income, Wealth, Consumption, and Inequality.* Edited by: Georg Fischer and Robert Strauss, Oxford University Press (2021). © Oxford University Press. DOI: 10.1093/oso/9780197545706.003.0011

already been observed for many decades. In others, the decline of fertility levels started in the 1990s, and the life expectancy is below the European average. In the future, these trends will continue, leading to an increased proportion of older people in the entire population (see Section 11.2).

Population ageing is an unprecedented phenomenon, one that requires an adjustment of public policies and a reshaping of the *intergenerational contract*. The notion of the intergenerational contract was first defined by Edmund Burke (1790) who, in his *Reflections on the Revolution in France*, stated that 'Society is indeed a contract. It is a partnership . . . not only between those who are living, but between those who are living, those who are dead, and those who are to be born.' It is since then used in the literature and understood as complex set of expectations and obligations underlying relations between generations and between age groups that exist in contemporary societies (Bengston and Achenbaum, 1993).

The demographic dividend experienced by European countries in the 20th century was used to introduce policies that led to a narrowing range of the economically active age through, among other factors, an extension of various routes towards earlier retirement as well as postponing the age of entering the labour market. As a result, currently, in all countries, the average borders of economically active age as assessed based on National Transfer Accounts (NTA) data differ from the standard borders of 20 and 65 years. Thus a larger share of the population relies on the incomes and taxes paid by those whose incomes are higher than their consumption levels. These patterns are also different for men and women. Women, who earn less and have lower labour market participation, also face longer periods of economic dependency when their incomes are below their consumption levels (Section 11.3.1).

For many years, the social protection systems in European countries evolved to provide significant financial protection for older people who retired from their economic activity. As a result, the current consumption of retired Europeans to a large extent relies on transfers they receive from public pension systems and is financed from contributions levied on earnings (Section 11.3.2). These incomes are also supplemented by consumption of savings or intergenerational transfers.

In the future, the current level of transfers might not be sustainable due to changing demographic conditions. Reforms of pension systems implemented by virtually all European countries are aiming at improving the financial sustainability of pension systems. According to the projections for expenditures on pensions in the future, developed under the auspices of the Ageing Working Group (AWG) and produced every 3 years, there is a shift in projection outcomes since 2015. Contrary to previous projections, after several years of increase, in the long-term, pension expenditure is likely to decline in relation to gross domestic product (GDP). This arises from pension systems becoming less generous in response to the projected population ageing (Section 11.4), which means that, in the future, pensions will only be provided for those of older ages, and their level in relation to wages will be smaller in many countries.

In the last section, I discuss the social challenges related to ensuring adequate means of consumption for older generations in the future. Following the reforms of the public pension systems, alternative sources of financing consumption for older ages will become more important, which means that the current working generations need to be more forward-looking with their long-term savings.

11.2 THE NEW DEMOGRAPHY OF EUROPE AND CHANGES IN THE POPULATION AGE STRUCTURE

The fall of fertility levels in all developed countries, observed since the 1960s, is attributed to a processes called the *second demographic transition*. It is characterized by a dramatic shift of norms towards progressiveness and individualism, which is moving Europeans away from marriage and parenthood. Cohabitation and out-of-wedlock fertility are increasingly acceptable. At the same time, the death rate remains at a low level (Lesthaeghe and van de Kaa, 1986; van de Kaa, 1987, 2002). As a result, the natural growth rate becomes negative. This negative natural growth rate is partially compensated by positive net migration rate.

Population ageing leads to changes in the population age structure. The fall of fertility and decline in the number of children first lead to an increased share of the working age population in the total population. This leads to a 'demographic dividend' contributing to the economic growth. In Europe, the demographic dividend started relatively early—in early 1960s—and its duration was one of the shortest in the world: less than 40 years (Mason et al., 2017), which is attributed to the early beginning of the second demographic transition (Figure 11.1).

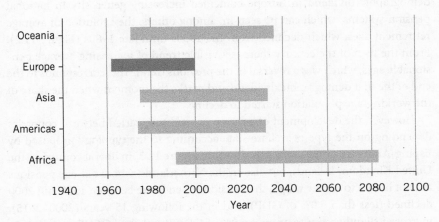

Figure 11.1 Start, duration, and end of the first demographic dividend by world region.
Source: Author's elaboration based on Mason et al. (2017).

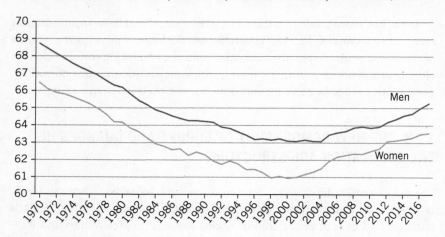

Figure 11.2 Average pensionable age in the OECD countries by sex (1970–2017).
Source: OECD Database on Average Effective Retirement Age.

The demographic dividend that was conducive to the expansion of social protection systems changed. Between 1980 and 2000 (i.e., in the second half of the period of the first demographic dividend), old-age and survivor pensions expenditure in the countries of the Organisation for Economic Cooperation and Development (OECD) grew from 5.5% to 6.6% of GDP. By 2014, this share further grew to around 8% of GDP. This means that the period of first demographic dividend in Europe was accompanied by the growth of expenditure on pensions. With the end of the demographic dividend, awareness grew of the necessity to reform pension systems.

The foreseen population ageing is one of the important drivers of pension reforms in the European Union (EU) in the past decades. The period of the first demographic dividend in Europe coincided increasing generosity in national pension systems, which can be seen in, among others, the evolution of average retirement ages, which declined from the 1950s until late 1980s (Figure 11.2). From the turn of the century there is a visible trend of increasing average pensionable ages, which was a reversal of the previous trend. This corresponds to the end of the first demographic dividend and marks the moment when the share of the working-age population started to decline.

However, the development of pension expenditure varied between countries depending on the type of welfare state according to the typology proposed by Esping-Andersen (1989), which is shown in Figure 11.3. In liberal countries (the United Kingdom, Ireland), but also in the Netherlands, where old-age pensions are not linked to earlier wages, the pension expenditure between 1980 and 2000 declined (less than 5.0% of GDP), and in the following 15 years (2000–2015), increased slightly again to around 6.0% of GDP (i.e., below OECD average). In Sweden (a country with a sociodemocratic welfare regime), pension expenditures

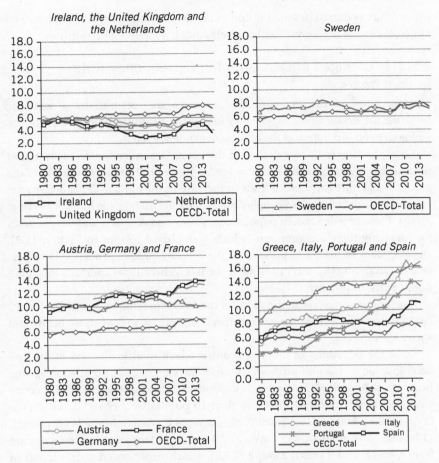

Figure 11.3 Old-age and survivor pensions expenditure in selected OECD countries (1980–2015, % gross domestic product [GDP]).
Source: Data from OECD.Stat.

in the middle of the demographic dividend period were slightly above the OECD average, but, since around 2000 (i.e., the end of the demographic dividend), they remain close to the OECD average.

Countries from continental Europe (France, Germany, Austria) characterize with above-average pension spending in the past four decades. While in Germany in past years the pension spending relative to GDP stabilized, in the other two countries it increased from around 12% to around 14% of GDP, which is almost double the EU average.

The fourth group of countries are those from Southern Europe (Greece, Portugal, Italy, Spain), where pension expenditure was rising from 1980s, with exception of Spain, where pension expenditure relative to GDP declined between 1996 and 2006 but started to rise again afterwards. The increase of pension expenditure occurred despite the end of the first demographic dividend, as well as despite one of the lowest fertility levels among the European countries.

11.2.1 Changes in Demographic Dependency Rate in Past Years

The outcomes of the demographic processes are captured by a synthetic measure: the *demographic dependency rate*. It can be divided into two parts: the young dependency rate and the old-age dependency rate.

Lower fertility leads to a decline in the young dependency rate, measured as the number of children and youth in aged 0–19 per 100 people in the 20–64 age group. Longer life expectancy leads to increase in the old-age dependency rate, calculated as the number of people 65 and older per 100 people in the 20–64 age group. These two dependent populations, young and old, have different sources for financing their consumption (which is discussed further in Section 11.3). Development of both components of the demographic dependency is important for analysing the sustainability of the intergenerational contract, including public pension systems.

One of the important foundations of the intergenerational contract is the relation between the three generations: working-age as well as those below and above working age.

Since the beginning of the 21st century, which marked the end of the first demographic dividend, European countries have experience population ageing. Between 2000 and 2015, the youth dependency rate declined in all EU countries. The largest declines (by more than 10 points) were observed in Cyprus (17.6 points), Poland (16.4 points), Slovakia (14.8 points), Malta (14.1 points), Lithuania (13.6 points), and Latvia (10.9 points). Many of these countries are from Central and Eastern Europe (CEE), which experienced a drastic fall in fertility levels after the economic transition; in other words, these countries quickly entered the phase of second demographic transition in the early 1990s (Figure 11.4).

In the same period, the old-age dependency rate increased in almost all EU countries, with the exception of Luxembourg. The largest increases were noted in Malta (9.9 points), Finland (9.8 points), Germany (8.6 points), and the Netherlands (8 points).

11.2.2 Changes in Demographic Dependency Rates in the Future

According to the 2015 Eurostat population projection (EUROPOP2015, Eurostat, 2015), the changes of EU countries' age structures will be characterized by the

2000

	YDR	OADR
SE	41.4	29.6
IT	31.7	29.1
EL	34.9	28.3
BE	39.6	28.1
FR	44.3	27.1
UK	43.0	26.8
ES	34.6	26.7
BG	37.3	26.5
PT	38.6	26.5
DE	41.9	26.0
AT	37.8	25.1
LV	42.6	24.8
EE	41.9	24.8
FI	40.8	24.5
HU	38.4	24.4
DK	38.5	24.1
LT	47.1	23.4
LU	39.8	23.3
SI	36.9	22.0
CZ	37.3	22.0
NL	39.4	21.9
RO	42.8	21.7
PL	48.1	20.5
MT	46.6	20.2
CY	53.8	19.4
IE	52.9	19.3
SK	46.4	18.8
EU	39.0	22.9

2015

	YDR	OADR
SE	39.3	34.0
IT	31.0	36.4
EL	32.7	35.1
BE	38.1	30.6
FR	43.3	32.3
UK	40.2	30.3
ES	32.1	30.0
BG	29.5	32.4
PT	32.8	33.8
DE	33.8	34.6
AT	31.7	29.8
LV	31.7	31.7
EE	33.8	30.9
FI	37.9	34.4
HU	31.7	28.7
DK	39.9	31.9
LT	33.5	30.8
LU	35.4	22.4
SI	30.9	28.5
CZ	31.3	28.5
NL	38.0	29.9
RO	33.8	27.4
PL	31.7	24.0
MT	32.5	30.1
CY	36.2	23.3
IE	48.0	22.1
SK	31.7	21.4
EU	34.8	31.4

Figure 11.4 Youth and old-age dependency rate in the EU countries (2000 and 2015).
YDR, youth dependency rate; OADR, old-age dependency rate.
Source: Author's analysis based on Eurostat population projection (EUROPOP2015).

stabilization of the youth dependency rates between 30 and 45 in most of the countries and further increases in the old-age dependency rate.

The largest increase in the old-age dependency rate between 2015 and 2040, exceeding 30 points, will be noted in Lithuania (32.3 points), and the rate will exceed 20 points in Spain, Greece, Portugal, Italy, Latvia, Slovenia, Romania, Poland, and Slovakia (Figure 11.5). Furthermore, between 2040 and 2080, the old-age dependency rate will increase in the range of 20–30 points in Cyprus, Poland, Slovakia, and Luxembourg.

As a result, by 2080, the EU average dependency rate will reach 98, which means that the ratio of youth and old-age generations to working age generations will be almost 1:1. The total demographic dependency, according to projections, will exceed 100 in Portugal (111), Greece (109), Poland (105), Italy (105), Slovakia (102), Bulgaria (101), and Germany (101). The level of demographic dependency will be the highest in Southern European as well as in CEE countries, which is related to the currently observed very low fertility levels in these Member States. The overall increase in old-age dependency rate will be the highest in countries from CEE, most notably Poland and Slovakia, which in the course of the 21st century will move from among the youngest to among the oldest in Europe.

	2040			2080	
	YDR	OADR		YDR	OADR
SE	43.0	41.0	SE	44.8	50.3
IT	30.4	61.8	IT	36.1	68.4
EL	29.9	63.0	EL	37.2	71.4
BE	40.1	44.0	BE	41.1	52.8
FR	45.6	50.1	FR	44.4	52.1
UK	40.7	42.4	UK	41.4	54.2
ES	38.3	59.1	ES	43.7	51.1
BG	33.4	51.8	BG	39.1	62.1
PT	29.1	59.7	PT	35.5	75.3
DE	36.4	54.1	DE	40.1	60.5
AT	34.6	46.0	AT	36.6	60.6
LV	38.3	56.6	LV	42.6	57.0
EE	36.4	46.4	EE	40.1	59.8
FI	38.2	47.7	FI	39.5	60.1
HU	35.5	45.0	HU	39.4	56.8
DK	40.8	43.7	DK	40.5	58.1
LT	36.1	63.1	LT	39.0	55.0
LU	36.3	35.6	LU	38.4	55.1
SI	34.2	52.5	SI	41.1	56.5
CZ	34.6	45.8	CZ	39.9	55.8
NL	41.1	48.5	NL	40.7	55.5
RO	36.6	49.5	RO	41.9	56.8
PL	31.4	45.8	PL	37.5	67.3
MT	35.4	45.1	MT	39.0	59.6
CY	27.0	37.3	CY	30.6	67.3
IE	42.6	40.7	IE	45.3	50.0
SK	32.2	42.5	SK	39.4	62.0
EU	37.2	50.8	EU	40.3	57.7

Figure 11.5 Youth and old-age dependency rate in the EU countries (2040 and 2080). YDR, youth dependency rate; OADR, old-age dependency rate.
Source: Author's analysis based on Eurostat population projection (EUROPOP2015).

11.3 ECONOMIC LIFE COURSE AND EFFECTIVE PRODUCTIVE AGE IN EUROPEAN COUNTRIES

The economic behaviour of individuals differs depending on their life course stages. During the period of childhood and youth, individuals consume more than they earn. This comprises private consumption in the household as well as public consumption, most notably of the education, which is also an investment in the human capital of individuals. Later, they enter a period of economic activity when, depending on individual choices as well as on family dynamics, individuals engage in work and receive income that finances their own consumption as well as that of other generations through private or public transfers. At the final stages of the life course, people retire from economic activity, and again, their consumption requires additional financing, which comes mainly from public sources such as cash transfers on pensions or healthcare benefits. The extent to which cohorts are able to finance their consumption allows one to assess the actual age span of economically active age that reflects, among other things, the socioeconomic situation of countries, as well as their institutions, including the design of their social protection systems. As Sanderson and Scherbov (2015) point out, demographic dependency or support ratios using fixed age limits were initially used as the best approximation available of the ratio of workers to nonworkers across many countries. In recent years, in a more data-rich environment, more accurate measures of economic dependency ratios are proposed using the data and projections on labour force participation rates.

In particular, the NTA approach (Lee and Mason, 2011) allows using generation accounts to estimate the age profiles of generations' consumption and labour income, as well as the resulting deficit/surplus at different stages of the life course.[1] Furthermore, this approach allows estimating the level of financing of the difference between consumption and income (i.e., the lifecycle deficit [LCD] from different [public and private] sources). The NTA approach is fully consistent with the national accounts. The NTA database was estimated for 25 European countries based on a harmonized dataset for 2010 (Istenič et al., 2017).[2]

11.3.1 Consumption, Labour Income, and Period of Economic Activity

The patterns of labour income and consumption vary both between countries and, more importantly, between sexes, which leads to differences in the age boundaries of economically active population. The normalized age profiles average for 25 EU countries for total population by sex as well as for the two countries with the shortest (Romania) and the longest (Sweden) range of economically active cohorts are shown in Figure 11.6.[3] In all countries, women have lower per capita labour income compared to men, while the level of consumption of both sexes is relatively similar. There are also differences between countries, which are related to the length of economic activity. In Sweden, the average labour income profile is shifted to the right, which results from the higher economic activity of generations aged 40 and older. The normalized per capita consumption levels are also different. As one can see in Romania, the consumption level relative to the labour income of those of prime age is higher than in Sweden. This means that the savings potential of the Romanian population is lower because a higher share of their income is used for consumption. This is due to the differences in the level of median equivalized income. For those in the 16–64 age group in 2010, it amounted to €2,128 in Romania and €20,155 (i.e., almost 10 times more) in Sweden. This means that the potential to accumulate additional long-term pension savings is smaller in Romania compared to Sweden or, in general, in countries with lower median equivalized income compared to those with higher median equivalized income, which influences pension policy.

---

1 For international comparability, the estimated age profiles are normalized using the average per capita labour income of cohorts aged 30–49. For details see United Nations Department of Economic and Social Affairs Population Division (2013).

2 The database was developed in the AGENTA project funded from the European Union's Seventh Framework Programme for research, technological development, and demonstration under grant agreement no. 613247.

3 The countries not covered by the estimates include Croatia, Luxembourg, the Netherlands, and Malta.

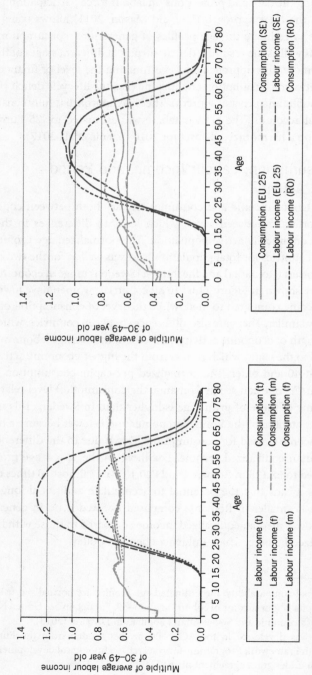

Figure 11.6 Normalized age profiles of consumption and labour income in Europe (2010). Values per capita, normalized by the average labour income of 30- to 49-year-olds.
Source: Istenič et al. (2017).

The NTA age profiles also allow identifying country-specific age ranges of economically active populations (Figure 11.7). In all countries, these values are different compared to the traditionally used limits (i.e., 20–65). Namely, for the average EU25 country, cohorts gain the ability to finance their own consumption on average at age 25 (men) and 31 (women), and they lose this ability at ages 60 and 52, respectively. This means that the range of economically active age is 21 years for women and 35 years for men. In two countries, Cyprus and Greece, according to the NTA estimates, women do not gain the ability to finance their own consumption at any age.

It should be noted that the span of economic activity in the NTA framework is much lower than the period of economic activity used for simulations of pension adequacy. Only in Sweden for men the exit age (64 years) is it close to the demographic NTA border.

Differences in labour income by age and an overall shorter period of economic activity mean that the total income over the life course of women is lower compared to men (*ceteris paribus*). The gender gap of total labour income, measured as the ratio of the sum of per-capital labour income by age relative to the income of workers of prime age (30–49 years) for women compared to the same

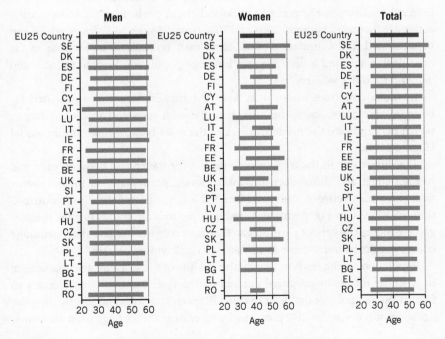

Figure 11.7 Limits of economically active age by country and sex (2010).
In Cyprus and Greece, women have higher consumption compared to their labour income in all age cohorts.
Source: Author's elaboration based on Istenič et al. (2017).

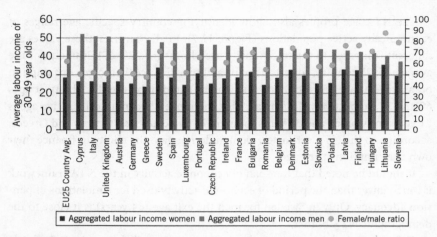

Figure 11.8 Labour income aggregated across ages by sex in the 25 European countries (2010). Labour income: left axis; Female/male ratio: right axis.
Source: Author's elaboration based on Istenič et al. (2017).

indicator for men is largest in Greece (women earn 48% of men's income over the life course) and smallest in Lithuania (women earn 88% of men's income).

Public policies as well as economic development affect the boundaries of economically active age. For example, in Poland, the upper limit of the economically active age increased between 2004 and 2016 from 53 years to 57 years, which can be attributed to the limitation of access to early retirement, an increase in the pensionable age, and a declining working-age population leading to increased demand for older workers.[4]

In those countries where men have the highest levels of aggregated labour income across ages, the difference between men and women is larger, which may indicate the predominance of the male breadwinner family model (Figure 11.8).

The differences in the total income during the life course between men and women affect also differences in pension levels, particularly in those systems with close links between wages and benefits (such as notional defined contribution (NDC) systems or points systems), leading to a significant gender pension gap. Reducing the gender pension gap therefore requires policies that encourage equalizing the labour income at all stages of employment careers.

Population ageing leads to the relative decline of the working age population; thus, in the future, to safeguard public pension systems, it will be necessary to further pursue policies that lead to extending working lives and lengthening the age span of economic activity, mainly by increasing the exit age from economic

---

4   NTA profiles for Poland for 2004, 2008, and 2012 were estimated in the project and estimates for 2016 were supported by the state budget funding for research.

activity. Another challenge, particularly for those countries with lower productivity levels, is to further improve productivity and wage levels in order to enhance the capacity for accumulating individual savings for old age, which will be needed to maintain consumption after retirement.

11.3.2 Economic Dependency and Financing Consumption of the Older Population

Differences in the levels of economic activity lead to different levels of economic dependency between countries. The application of fixed 'productive age' limits of 15 (or 20) and 64 years does not account for actual demographic, economic, and social circumstances. These measures don't take into account the consequences of rising life expectancy, including healthy life expectancy, that is increasing productive age limits beyond 64 years. Furthermore, a significant part of the population aged 15–25 is still inactive due to educational pursuits, and a considerable share of the population aged 64 and younger (especially older workers aged 55–64) is also inactive due to early withdrawal from the labour market.

There is a growing body of literature indicating the need to focus on economic dependency, rather than demographic, and providing suggestions of alternative measures of generational dependency. For example, Zamaro et al. (2008) propose an economic dependency ratio that measures the ratio between the population aged 0–14, 65 and older, and inactive shares of the population in the15–64 age group to the active population aged 15–64. Another example is the measure proposed by Sanderson and Scherbov (2010). Given the differences in life expectancy observed between populations, they proposed the *prospective old-age dependency ratio*. In this measure, the threshold of being 'old' is no longer fixed, but changes with the change in life expectancy and is based on a constant remaining life expectancy. It is assumed that people are old when remaining life expectancy in their age group is less than 15 years. Both approaches (Zamaro et al. [2008] and Sanderson and Scherbov [2010]) focus on the separation of different populations of 'consumers' and 'producers' using labour market and activity information.

The NTA approach adds to the demographic support measurement the quantitative extent of the economic characteristic; that is, estimated monetary flows of income, reallocations of economic resources across age, and consumption. Hammer, Prskawetz, and Freund (2014); Loichinger, Hammer, Prskawetz, Freiberger, and Sambt (2017); and Prskawetz and Sambt (2014) apply NTA profiles to estimate economic dependency ratios using flexible age limits of economically active population as well as consumption and labour income at different ages. Their results show that differences exist between the levels of economic and demographic dependency that are quite pronounced between countries.

Table 11.1 Demographic dependency ratio and economic National Transfer Accounts (NTA) dependency ratio for young age, old age, and total population (2010)

Country	Demographic dependency ratio			NTA dependency ratio		
	Young	Old	Total	Young	Old	Total
Austria	0.33	0.28	0.61	0.20	0.26	0.46
Spain	0.31	0.27	0.58	0.25	0.21	0.46
Slovenia	0.30	0.26	0.56	0.24	0.24	0.48
Sweden	0.40	0.32	0.72	0.26	0.22	0.48
Germany	0.31	0.34	0.65	0.19	0.31	0.50
Hungary	0.33	0.27	0.60	0.24	0.26	0.50
Finland	0.38	0.29	0.67	0.26	0.26	0.52
United Kingdom	0.40	0.28	0.68	0.27	0.26	0.53
Poland	0.32	0.22	0.54	0.28	0.26	0.54
France	0.42	0.29	0.71	0.26	0.29	0.55
Italy	0.31	0.34	0.65	0.26	0.34	0.60

Estimates for Poland for 2012, according to the national NTA database.

Source: Loichinger et al. (2017) with author' update for Poland based on the national NTA estimates.

NTA profiles for Poland were estimated in the project POLNTA 'Narodowy Rachunek Transferów oraz Narodowy Rachunek Transferów Czasu dla Polski' financed by the National Science Centre (UMO-2013/ 10/M/HS4/00466) and implemented by the Institute of Statistics and Demography at Warsaw School of Economics (SGH).

A comparison of the two dependency ratios—demographic[5] and NTA-based economic dependency—proposed by Loichinger et al. (2017) measures the value for selected EU countries is shown in Table 11.1.[6] The NTA dependency ratio measures the sum of the gap between consumption and labour income of young and old cohorts outside the range of economically active age divided by total labour income. It can be interpreted as the level of tax levied on wages needed to finance the LCD. As one can see, there are differences between countries with respect to the value of both indicators. Sweden has a high level of demographic dependency but at the same time a low level of economic dependency. Poland, on the contrary, has the lowest demographic dependency in the group of countries, whereas, at the same time, its economic dependency is one of the highest.

---

5   Relating the ratio of populations in the 0–19 and 65 and older age groups to the population at working age (i.e., 20–64).

6   The NTA method also allows other measures of economic dependency to be assessed based on the relationship between labour income and asset-based reallocations and consumption, or fiscal dependency that takes into account public transfers that are paid or received (see, e.g., Chłoń-Domińczak, Abramowska-Kmon, et al., 2016; Chłoń-Domińczak, Kotowska, et al., 2016; Lee and Edwards, 2002; Loichinger et al., 2017; Prskawetz and Sambt, 2014).

This shows that country-specific socioeconomic situation, combined with existing institutions, can influence economic outcomes.

The difference between consumption and labour income (i.e., the LCD) can be financed from three main sources: private transfers, public transfers, and asset reallocations (i.e., using savings to finance current consumption). The contribution of these three main transfers is different in the case of younger and older generations, which is shown in Figure 11.9.

The LCD of the young generation is financed from public and private transfers. Private transfers play a larger share in financing because parents are responsible for financing the private consumption of their children. Public transfers are linked to financing consumption on public education or healthcare. For the older generation, the dominant source of financing the LCD is public transfers, including cash benefits from the pension systems. The second important source is asset-based reallocations as seniors use their savings to finance consumption expenses, while private transfers received from other individuals (spouses, other family members, etc.) are insignificant. However, there are also differences between men and women in the direction of private transfers at older ages. Men are net payers of private transfers, while women are net receivers. This shows that, due to the higher income from pensions and earlier incomes from wages, men continue to share their assets and income with women after retirement.

Given the rising share of older cohorts in the population and the resulting increasing pressure for securing the financing of their consumption, the NTA database also allows assessing the contribution of public transfers in financing the LCD of cohorts older than 60 years (Figure 11.10). The contribution of net public transfers to the financing of the LCD for Europeans older than 60 in 2010 was at the level of 55%. This means that more than half of the difference between consumption and labour income was financed by benefits or services paid from public funds. Asset-based reallocations comprise 42% of the LCD of older population. The level and share of public transfers in financing the LCD of older people varies between countries. In relation to average labour income, it is the highest in Greece, Austria, and Slovakia, while the share is highest in Estonia and Austria. In all countries, there is a difference in the sign of private transfers: men are net payers and women are net receivers of private transfers. The largest relative payments are made by men in Luxembourg, Cyprus, and Greece, while the net transfers received by women are the highest in Bulgaria, Romania, and Spain.

As shown in Table 11.2, the share of public transfers in the total LCD of men 60 and older is higher compared to women (62% compared to 51% on average in the EU25 countries). In Austria, Greece, Italy, and Estonia almost the entire difference between consumption and the labour income of men is financed from public transfers. It is the smallest in Denmark, Ireland, and Luxembourg. In the first two countries, this can be linked to the structure of the pension system,

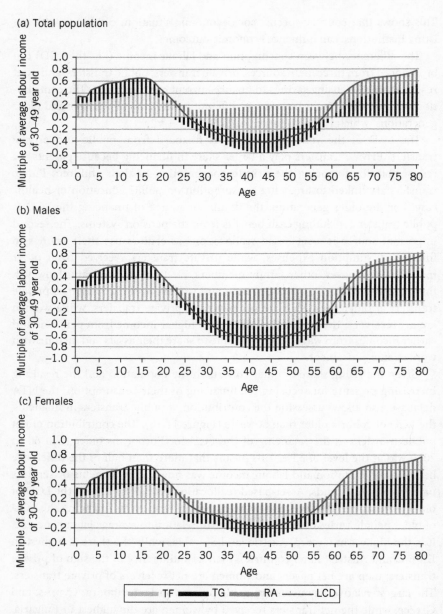

Figure 11.9 Lifecycle deficit, public and private transfers, and asset-based reallocations, average for EU25 countries (2010).
TF, total private transfers; TG, total public transfers; RA, asset-based reallocations.
Source: Author's elaboration based on Istenič et al. (2017).

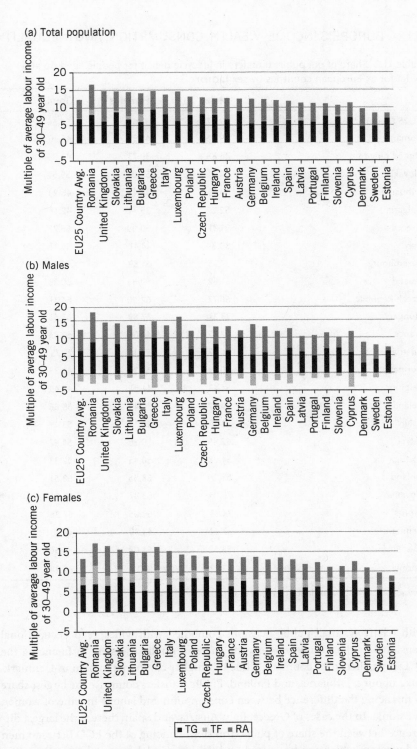

Figure 11.10 Total net public transfers, private transfers, and asset-based reallocations of cohorts aged 60 and older in the 25 European countries by sex (2010).
TF, total private transfers; TG, total public transfers; RA, asset-based reallocations.
Countries are presented in the order of total level of net transfers (TF + TG + RA).
Source: Author's elaboration based on Istenič et al. (2017).

Table 11.2 Share of net public transfers in lifecycle deficit for people aged 60 and older for 25 European countries by sex (2010)

	Males	Females	Total
EU25 Country Average	62.27	51.01	55.56
Romania	59.95	40.35	48.16
United Kingdom	45.88	39.73	42.08
Slovakia	66.21	56.09	59.61
Lithuania	40.73	48.42	46.23
Bulgaria	52.22	35.74	42.18
Greece	91.81	50.99	66.71
Italy	80.89	44.41	59.11
Luxembourg	37.75	51.89	46.76
Poland	61.62	59.65	60.36
Czech Republic	66.77	62.90	64.31
Hungary	73.31	57.89	63.55
France	58.42	48.06	52.35
Austria	94.38	56.16	71.75
Germany	50.94	38.30	43.25
Belgium	54.43	44.51	48.49
Ireland	39.67	39.49	39.66
Spain	72.76	40.73	53.49
Latvia	62.45	50.36	54.57
Portugal	54.28	50.45	52.33
Finland	68.26	68.55	68.51
Slovenia	76.94	63.87	68.95
Cyprus	74.33	62.05	67.28
Denmark	37.42	53.30	47.00
Sweden	58.69	55.08	56.56
Estonia	87.33	81.12	83.28

Source: Author's elaboration based on Istenič et al. (2017).

with relatively small public pensions combined with widespread occupational pensions. In the case of women, the share of public transfers in financing the LCD is smaller in 21 countries while it is higher compared to men in Denmark, Luxembourg, Lithuania, and Finland. Public transfers comprise the largest share in financing the difference between consumption and labour income of women in Estonia. In the cases of Greece, Italy, Austria, and Spain there is the largest difference between the share of public transfer financing of the LCD between men and women, which can be related to differences in labour market participation over the life course.

There are also differences in the share of asset-based reallocations (i.e., the use of private savings in various form) in the total net transfers received by cohorts 60 and older in the European countries. In countries where there are developed private pension schemes that provide pension income (Ireland, the United Kingdom, Denmark, Sweden), the share of asset-based reallocations in total transfers received is also high (respectively, 57.8%, 56.7%, 51.1%, 42.5%). Thus pension savings already are an important source for providing financial means for consumption in old age.

In the future, as indicated in the *Ageing Report 2018* (European Commission DG ECFIN, 2018), the role of asset-based reallocations in financing consumption in old age in Romania, Lithuania, Croatia, Estonia, and Latvia will increase, following the reforms of pension systems in these countries, with the mandatory funded components. There is also a visible gender divide. In all but four countries (Austria, Estonia, Greece, Italy), men have higher asset-based reallocations compared to women. This indicates that men have higher savings (including occupational and other private pensions) compared to women because they also have higher labour income over the life course.

In conclusion, today, economic dependency in many countries is higher than demographic dependency. This means that generations reach an ability to finance their consumption at an age older than 20 years, and they lose this ability at a younger age than 65 years. The consumption of the retired generation is to a large extent financed from received public transfers. This also means that the main instrument of intergenerational transfers for the older generations is public systems, including social insurance, healthcare, and long-term care provision. Reducing the generosity of pension systems (discussed in Section 11.4) can have an important impact on the future consumption of a retired generation, especially when compared to the consumption of the working age generation. Last but not least, differences in economic activity and labour income over the life course between men and women also lead to differences in received public transfers. This is corrected through private transfers: women aged 60 and older are net receivers and men are net payers of private transfers, which is particularly large in countries where the difference in the total per capita labour income across ages between men and women is the highest.

11.3.3 Inequality of Income and Pension Transfers

The differences in the public transfers between countries are only a part of those differences observed among pensioners in Europe. The design of pensions systems also results in inequalities of incomes. One of the applied measures of inequality is the *quintile ratio* (S80/S20). At the EU level, in past years, the quintile ratio for people who are younger than 65 remains above 5. Thus, those in the highest quintile have five times more income than those in the lowest quintile. In the case of Europeans aged 65 and older, this ratio remains slightly above 4.

Thus, income inequalities for pensioners are slightly lower than for younger generations.

The inequality of income varies between countries as well as between sexes. It is lowest in Czechia and Slovakia (less than 3), countries that have highly redistributive pension systems, while it is the highest in Portugal, Cyprus, and Italy. At the European level, there are 19 countries where income inequality for older women is lower compared to men and 8 countries where women experience higher income inequality (Table 11.3).

Income inequality changes over time, as presented in Table 11.4. Between 2010 and 2017, inequalities increased in 17 countries, particularly in the Baltic States (Latvia, Lithuania, Estonia), Hungary, and Luxembourg.

The inequality of pension income indicates that the life course differences in labour income affect also transfers received in old age. Pension systems only to some extent reduce these observed inequalities. Furthermore, recent changes in pension systems resulted in the increase of income inequality in people 65 years and older in the majority of European countries.

11.4 ADJUSTING TO DEMOGRAPHIC CHANGE: PENSION REFORMS AND THEIR POTENTIAL IMPACT ON CONSUMPTION AND LABOUR INCOME

The impact of population ageing on public finances and the future pension systems expenditure is monitored by the Economic Policy Committee (EPC) and its Working Group on Population Ageing (AWG). The Ageing Reports (European Commission DG ECFIN [2018] and earlier editions), published every 3 years, project, among other data, pension expenditures in Member States.

The overall pension spending relative to GDP increased between 2007 and 2016. This increase occurred during the financial and economic crisis, when, in most of the EU countries, the GDP level declined. At the same time, pension expenses were increasing as the pension adjustment mechanisms protect benefits from declining. The rise in the ratio between pension expenditure and GDP stimulated further reforms hoping to achieve the financial sustainability of pensions systems in the longer run with ageing populations.

As a result of these reform efforts, the projected trend of pension expenditure changed between the projections published in 2009 and 2012, when overall pension spending was increasing in the entire projection period, and those from 2015 and 2018, when after an increase of spending to around 2040 to 12.7% of GDP (according to the 2018 projection), the pension expenditure relative to GDP is projected to decline to reach the level observed around the initial projection year (Figure 11.11).

Table 11.3 S80/S20 income quintile share ratio by sex for people 65 years and older (EU-SILC survey, 2017)

	Total	Males	Females	Female/Male Ratio
European Union (current composition)	4.1	4.1	4.1	1.00
Czechia	2.4	2.2	2.4	1.09
Slovakia	2.4	2.4	2.4	1.00
Netherlands	3.0	3.2	2.8	0.88
Hungary	3.6	3.7	3.4	0.92
Finland	3.0	3.1	2.9	0.94
Belgium	2.9	3.0	2.9	0.97
Denmark	2.9	3.0	2.7	0.90
Malta	3.3	3.4	3.2	0.94
Estonia	3.7	4.1	3.4	0.83
Poland	3.5	3.3	3.5	1.06
Slovenia	3.4	3.2	3.5	1.09
Austria	3.7	3.6	3.8	1.06
Sweden	3.7	4.1	3.3	0.80
Ireland	3.9	4.1	3.7	0.90
Greece	4.2	4.2	4.1	0.98
Germany	3.9	4.0	3.6	0.90
Bulgaria	5.1	5.3	4.6	0.87
Spain	4.6	4.5	4.6	1.02
France	4.3	4.0	4.5	1.13
Lithuania	5.0	5.1	4.7	0.90
Romania	4.4	3.8	4.6	1.21
United Kingdom	4.5	4.4	4.5	1.02
Croatia	4.9	4.8	4.7	0.98
Latvia	4.8	5.2	4.6	0.88
Luxembourg	4.6	4.7	4.6	0.98
Italy	4.7	4.8	4.7	0.98
Cyprus	4.7	5.0	4.3	0.86
Portugal	5.4	5.6	5.2	0.93

Data for Ireland for 2016.

Source: EUROSTAT EU-SILC survey [ilc_di11], extracted on 15 January 2019.

Table 11.4 Change in income inequality between 2010 and 2017 (S20/S80 for 65 years and older)

Ratio of income inequality in 2017 compared to 2010					
Below 0.95	**0.95–0.99**	**1.00–1.04**	**1.05–1.09**	**1.10–1.19**	**1.20 and more**
BE	ES	CZ	UK	IT	LV
DK	NL	CY	RO	BG	EE
AT	FI	PL	PT	SE	HU
MT	IE	EL			LT
HR	FR	DE			LU
SI		SK			

Source: Author's analysis based on EUROSTAT EU-SILC survey [ilc_di11], extracted on 15 January 2019.

Thus pension reforms introduced during and after the financial crisis will contribute to declining expenditures on pensions despite demographic ageing. There are two major areas of pension reforms that contribute to the projected trends in pension expenditure. The first is the increase of the effective retirement age and the second is the reduction of the benefit ratio (i.e., the ratio between pension benefits and average wages). Both interventions are also likely to affect the future shape of the age profiles of labour income as well as the age profile of public transfers received by older generations. The latter further affects the need to finance consumption from other sources and/or the need to reduce consumption level relative to average wage.

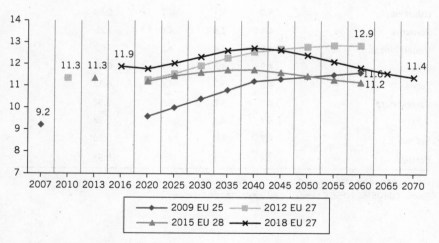

Figure 11.11 Projected pension spending in the EU Member States, reference year to 2060 (2070).
Source: Author's elaboration based on (European Commission DG ECFIN, 2018 and earlier editions).

11.4.1 Impact of Demographic Changes and Pension Reforms on the Long-Term Expenditure Levels

Population ageing will exert pressure on pension spending. If the current pension systems and therefore the age profiles of pension expenditure are not changed, the average pension expenditure would increase by 6.4 percentage points of GDP, ranging from almost 12 percentage points in Poland and Cyprus to slightly above 2 percentage points in Sweden.

Pension system reforms introduced in many EU countries offset the potential expenditure increase. This is estimated in the Ageing Reports by the decomposition of pension expenditure change into four components (European Commission DG ECFIN, 2018:77):

- The *dependency ratio effect* quantifies the impact of demographic changes; more precisely, the relative change in old age versus working age population. An increase in this ratio indicates a higher proportion of older individuals with respect to working age population (i.e., population ageing).
- The *coverage ratio effect* is defined as the number of pensioners of all ages to the population older than 65 years. The analysis of the coverage ratio provides information about how development of an effective exit age and the share of the population covered by the pension system influence pension spending.
- The *benefit ratio effect* indicates how the average pension (public pension spending divided by number of pensioners) develops relative to the average wage. It reflects the characteristics of the legal framework of pension systems concerning calculation and indexation rules.
- The *labour market effect* describes the effect labour market behaviour has on pension expenditure.

Figure 11.12 presents to what extent the effects of coverage ratio and benefit ratio offset the dependency ratio effect according to the estimates in the 2018 Ageing Report.

On average in the European Union, the coverage ratio effect compensates around a third of the estimated dependency ratio effect. The contribution of coverage ratio effect to offsetting the impact of demographic changes on pension expenditure is highest in Denmark, the Netherlands, Estonia, and Croatia. It is smallest in Malta and Sweden, which means that there are no expected changes in the effective exit age in these two countries. However, currently, the effective retirement age in Sweden is the highest among EU countries.

On average, the benefit ratio effect offsets around half of the projected dependency ratio effect. At the country level, the benefit ratio effect is higher than

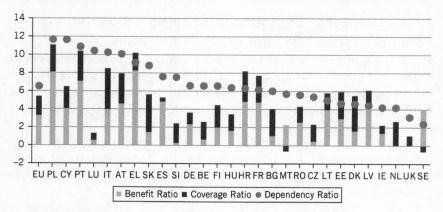

Figure 11.12 Decomposition of pension expenditure: dependency ratio effect vs. benefit and coverage ratio effects in the EU countries.
Source: Author's elaboration based on (European Commission DG ECFIN, 2018).

the dependency ratio effect in Sweden and Latvia and ranges between 75% and 100% in Greece, Lithuania, France, and Croatia.

Overall, in eight EU countries the changes in pension systems related to retirement age and benefit levels fully offset the impact of demographic change, and in six countries they compensate less than half of the impact of demographic change.

In those countries where pension benefits are linked to the lifetime wages and life expectancy at retirement age, an interplay occurs between the coverage ratio effect and benefit ratio effect. This can be illustrated by the example of Poland. The reversal of the increase in retirement age implemented in 2017 led to a reduced impact of the coverage ratio contribution to change in pension expenditure, while, at the same time, the impact of the benefit ratio contribution increased. The combined impact of the two effects remains exactly the same (Table 11.5).

11.4.2 Raising Effective Retirement Age

According to projections in the *Ageing Report 2018* (European Commission DG ECFIN, 2018), the average effective exit age from the labour market in EU countries will increase by 2 years for men and by 2.4 years for women.

The projected increases in the effective exit age from the labour market are the highest in those countries that introduced a link between retirement age and life expectancy: Italy, Finland, Portugal, Greece, Denmark, the Netherlands, Cyprus, and Slovak Republic. Such effect is, however, not projected in the case of Malta, where there is also a link of retirement age to changes in life expectancy (Figure 11.13). Higher than average increases are also projected in Hungary, France, and Belgium.

Table 11.5 Long-term pension expenditures in Poland: Summary of AWG projections

In % GDP	2009	2012	2015	2018
Base year pension expenditures	11.6	11.8	11.5	11.2
Base year:	2007	2010	2013	2016
2060 public pension expenditures	8.8	9.6	10.7	11.1
2060 FDC expenditures	1.9	1.3	0	0
Total 2060 expenditures	10.7	10.9	10.7	11.1
	2007–2060	2010–2060	2013–2060	2016–2060
Change in pension expenditures (% GDP)	−2.8	−2.2	−0.8	−0.1
Dependency ratio contribution	13.4	14.0	12.4	12.1
Benefit ratio contribution	−7.1	−8.7	−5.2	−7.3
Coverage ratio contribution	−6.3	−5.0	−5.2	−3.1

Source: Chłoń-Domińczak et al. (2020).

Reforms that lead to an increase in the effective retirement age lead to the extension of working lives and hence create a shift in the age profile of labour income to the right. This also means raising the upper limit of the effective productive age. As a result, the total LCD of older cohorts is likely to be reduced. As a result, the need to finance the consumption of the retired generation from both public and private transfers, as well as from asset reallocations, will be lower.

11.4.3 Reducing Pension Benefits

Another outcome of pension reforms in the European countries is change in future pension benefits. This affects the adequacy of future pensions. Principle 15 of the European Pillar of Social Rights underlines the importance of ensuring equal opportunities of men and women as well as adequate income in old age. There are several approaches to measure the levels of pensions currently and in the future. Individual benefits for specific types of workers who retire currently or in the future are captured by current and prospective theoretical replacement rates that are analysed every 3 years by the European Commission and Member States in Pension Adequacy Reports (European Commission, 2018) as well as by the OECD in the Pensions at a Glance series (OECD, 2017).

Another way to assess the adequacy of pension payments is the benefit ratio that captures the ratio between average pension and average wage for a given country. This indicator takes into account actual and projected levels of pensions based on employment and income characteristics of the population covered by the pension projections. Therefore, it captures also the important dimension of economic and labour market differences between countries.

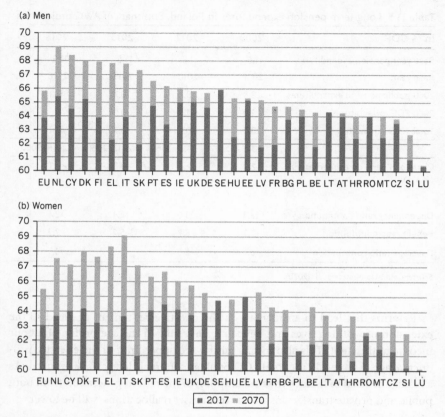

Figure 11.13 Average effective exit age from the labour market in the EU countries (2017–2070). *Source:* Author's elaboration based on (European Commission DG ECFIN, 2018).

Projections in the 2018 Ageing Report show that the benefit ratio is projected to decline in almost all EU countries (Figure 11.14). The average decline is 11 percentage points, while in Greece, Poland, Portugal, Cyprus, and Spain the benefit ratio, according to projections, will decline by more than 20 percentage points.

The projections show that in four countries—Latvia, Croatia, Lithuania, and Estonia——the benefit ratio by 2070 will be below 20 percentage points, but if pensions from mandatorily funded pension systems are added, the benefit levels will exceed this threshold in all countries with the exception of Latvia.

The benefit ratio effect indicates changes that shift the age profile of pension transfers downwards relative to the average wage levels. This can lead to either the necessity to increase the share of other sources (namely asset-based reallocations or private transfers) in financing the consumption of the retired

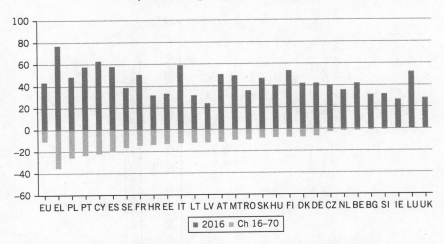

Figure 11.14 Benefit ratio and its projected change in the EU countries (2017–2070).
Source: Author's elaboration based on (European Commission DG ECFIN, 2018).

generation if the current consumption level is to be maintained or a potential reduction of relative consumption levels.

11.4.4 Pension Reforms and Lifecycle Deficit

As discussed earlier, pension reforms introduced in the European countries will have an impact on incomes, consumption, and transfers received by the older generation. The graphical representation of these potential changes and their impact on the per capita LCD is shown in Figure 11.15.

A higher retirement age combined with a longer working life shifts labour income to the right. As a result, the upper limit of productive age increases and the positive LCD appears at later age. A decline in benefit ratio can lead to reduced consumption for older people (relative to wages). As a result, the level of per capita LCD at older ages declines. A combination of these two changes leads to a sizeable reduction of accumulated LCD. .

Furthermore, the shift of the retirement age increases the accumulated surplus of labour income over consumption, which increases the potential of an average representative of the productive generation to finance the consumption of children or seniors through both public and private transfers. Increasing the upper limit of the productive age will also contribute to reducing the gap between economic and demographic dependency levels.

An important policy direction to reduce the LCD and increase the capacity to finance it from transfers (public and private) generated by the working-age generation is to increase labour income. This includes policies to increase labour

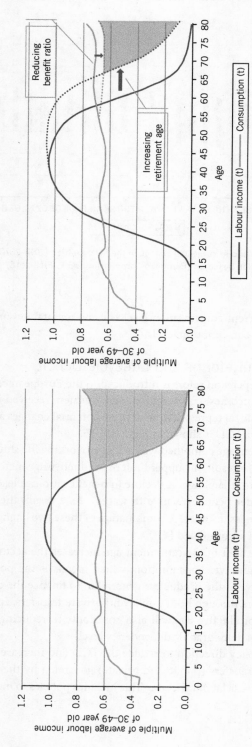

Figure 11.15 Pension reforms and lifecycle deficit of older cohorts.
Source: Author's elaboration.

force participation across the entire life course, but also a focus on improving the productivity of workers through investment in their human capital.

11.5 CONCLUSION

European countries are facing the challenge of population ageing and a declining demographic dividend. After almost four decades of harnessing the first demographic dividend, welfare systems and social policies need to adjust to a changing intergenerational balance.

NTA estimates for European countries allow one to quantify the most important challenges to the current intergenerational and intragenerational balance:

- Financing the LCD of older generations to a large extent from public transfers (mainly public pensions systems and healthcare)
- Financing the LCD of younger generations from private transfers (mainly from parents within household)
- A 'double burden' on the working-age generation, which finances the LCD of older generations via the public system (paying taxes) and finances the consumption of the young generation by private transfers; when, due to ageing, the tax on labor income increases, this affects consumption of both working-age and young generations
- A relatively short period of effective economic activity, particularly of women
- A gender gap in labour income and pension income and the resulting need of intragenerational transfers between men and women

Changes in the age structure of European populations mean that the current consumption and labour income age patterns are not sustainable. In the past decade, virtually all European countries changed their pension systems in order to meet the goal of financial sustainability.

The pressure of an increase in pension expenditure caused by demographic changes is offset by reducing pension transfers by changing benefit formulae or benefit indexation (around half of the demographic impact) as well as increasing the effective pensionable age (around a third of the demographic impact). Estimates of the impact of these two effects on projected pension expenditure indicates that those policy changes that lead to a reduction of benefit ratios are preferred over the policies that lead to raising retirement age. Thus, in the future, the amount paid per month as pension to the pensioner compared with the wages being earned will be reduced. As discussed before, reducing pensions relative to wages has lower impact on reducing LCD for older cohorts compared to extending working lives. However, raising retirement ages is seen by politicians as a more difficult policy intervention, one frequently not supported by society, as the recent reversal of retirement age increases in Poland shows.

Reforms of pension systems affect generational accounts. An increase of the effective retirement age leads to a lengthening of working lives and a shifting of the labour income age profile to the right, thus reducing the LCD. Increasing the upper limit of the productive age will also contribute to reducing the gap between economic and demographic dependency levels. A decline of the benefit ratio leads to a lowering of the level of public transfers (relative to wages) received by older generation. This can either result in maintaining the consumption levels when offset by increasing asset-based reallocations or reducing consumption levels. The latter will lead to a reduction of the LCD. As shown in Section 11.4, increasing the retirement age can lead to improving the intergenerational balance of the aggregated LCD of older generations and the lifecycle surplus of economically active generation by both reducing the period of the LCD and lengthening the age span of productive ages.

The generational accounts reveal social challenges related to ensuring adequate consumption for older generations in the future. Following reforms of the public pension systems, alternative sources of financing consumption at older ages will have to become more important, which means that the current working generations need to save more if they are to be able to finance their future consumption to a larger extent from asset-based reallocations.

Many challenges are linked to observed inequalities within generations. As discussed, in many countries, income inequalities of older people increase in time, following reforms of pension systems that tighten the link between lifetime earnings and pensions. There are also differences in the health status within generations, which lead to further inequalities in the total pension income received during pensioners' lives. Mortality differences interact with government programmes (e.g., pension systems) for the elderly and may reduce or even reverse the direction of income redistribution. As shown by Sanchez-Romero, Lee, and Prskawetz (2018) using the data from the United States, the widening of the longevity gap between the birth cohorts of 1930 and 1960 leads to much greater inequalities in pensions. This also requires the attention of European policymakers.

Last but not least, continuous efforts are needed to increase the lifetime labour income to improve the capacity of the working generations in the future to finance the LCD of both younger and older generations. These include two main directions of reforms. First, mobilizing the potential of inactive people of working age. This includes most importantly tapping the potential of women in the workforce. In all European countries, the span of women's productive age is much shorter compared to men, and, in some countries, an average woman is not able to earn sufficiently to finance her consumption at any age. Again, with population ageing, maintaining the status quo may not be sustainable. Increasing the economic activity of women is one of the most important policy challenges, particularly in Southern Europe and in CEE. A second important direction is investments in improving the human capital of future and current workers, which would lead to increases in productivity and, therefore, labour income.

ACKNOWLEDGEMENTS

Research included in this chapter was supported by the project POLNTA 'Narodowy Rachunek Transferów oraz Narodowy Rachunek Transferów Czasu dla Polski' that received funding from the National Science Centre (UMO-2013/10/M/HS4/00466) and was implemented by the Institute of Statistics and Demography at Warsaw School of Economics (SGH), the state budget funding for research in 2018.

Opinions expressed in this paper are those of the author and do not necessarily reflect the view of her institution.

REFERENCES

Bengston, V. L., and Achenbaum, W. L (eds.). (1993) *The changing contract across generations*. New York: Aldine de Gruyter.

Burke, E. (1790). *Reflections on the Revolution in France*. London.

Chłoń-Domińczak, A., Abramowska-Kmon, A., Kotowska, I. E., Łątkowski, W., and Qi, H. (2016). *Demographic developments and public finances in the past two decades in the EU countries*. AGENTA Project Deliverable 4.1. Warsaw.

Chłoń-Domińczak, A., Góra, M., Kotowska, I. E., Magda, I., Ruzik-Sierdzińska, A., and Strzelecki, P. (2020). The impact of lifetime events on pensions: Nonfinancial defined contribution schemes in Poland, Italy, and Sweden, and the point scheme in Germany. In Holzmann, R., Palmer, E., Palacios, R., and Sacchi, S. (eds). *Progress and Challenges of Nonfinancial Defined Contribution Pension Schemes: Volume 2. Addressing Gender, Administration, and Communication* (pp. 55–85). Washington, DC: World Bank.

Chłoń-Domińczak, A., Kotowska, I. E., Istenic, T., Sambt, J., and Hammer, B. (2016). Measruing the economic and fiscal challenges of population ageing. *AGENTA Project Policy Brief, 1*, 1–9. https://doi.org/10.1016/j.marpol.2008.04.002.governments.

European Commission. (2018). *Pension adequacy report 2018: Current and future income adequacy in old age in the EU. Volume 2—Country Profiles*. Luxembourg: Publications Office of the European Union. https://doi.org/10.2767/1907

European Commission DG ECFIN. (2018). *The 2018 ageing report. Economic and budgetary projections for the 28 EU Member States (2016–2070)*. European Economy Institutional Paper No. 079. https://doi.org/10.2765/615631

Eurostat. (2015), EUROPOP2015: European Population projections 2015-based.

Esping-Andersen, G. (1989). *The three worlds of welfare capitalism.* Oxford: Polity Press.

Hammer, B., Prskawetz, A., and Freund, I. (2014). Production activities and economic dependency by age and gender in Europe: A cross-country comparison. *Journal of the Economics of Ageing.* https://doi.org/10.1016/j.jeoa.2014.09.007

Istenič, T., Hammer, B., Šeme, A., Lotrič Dolinar, A., and Sambt, J. (2017). *European National Transfer Accounts.*

Lee, R., and Edwards, R. (2002). *The fiscal effects of population aging in the US: Assessing the uncertainties.* NBER/Tax Policy and the Economy (Vol. 16). Cambridge, MA: MIT Press. doi: 10.1162/089286402760173485%5Cn. http://ezproxy.lib.monash.edu.au/login?url=http://search.ebscohost.com/login.aspx?direct=trueanddb=bthandAN=7105524andsite=ehost-liveandscope=site

Lee, R. D., and Mason, A. (2011). *Population aging and the generational economy: A global perspective.* London: Edward Elgar.

Lesthaeghe, R., and van de Kaa, D. J. (1986). Twee Demografische Transities? [Two demographic transitions?] In R. Lesthaeghe and D. J. van de Kaa (eds.), *Bevolking: Groei en Krimp (Population: Growth and decline)* (pp. 9–24). Deventer: Van Loghum Slaterus.

Loichinger, A. E., Hammer, B., Prskawetz, A., Freiberger, M., and Wien, T. U. (2014). Dependency ratios: Present situation and future scenarios. (*74*).

Loichinger, E., Hammer, B., Prskawetz, A., Freiberger, M., and Sambt, J. (2017). Quantifying economic dependency. *European Journal of Population.* https://doi.org/10.1007/s10680-016-9405-1

Mason, A., Lee, R., Abrigo, M., and Lee, S.-H. (2017). *Support ratios and demographic dividends: Estimates for the world.* UN Population Division Technical Paper No. 2017/1. http://workspace.unpan.org/sites/Internet/Documents/UNPAN97453.pdf

OECD. (2017). *Pensions at a glance 2017: OECD and G20 indicators.* Paris: OECD Publishing. https://doi.org/10.1787/pension_glance-2013-en

Prskawetz, A., and Sambt, J. (2014). Economic support ratios and the demographic dividend in Europe. *Demographic Research, 30*(1), 963–1010. https://doi.org/10.4054/DemRes.2014.30.34

Sanchez-Romero, M., Lee, R. D., and Prskawetz, A. (2018). *Redistributive effects of pension schemes if individuals differ by life expectancy.* Presentation at the Conference 'The Economics of Ageing and Inequality', University of Hohenheim, Germany, 4–5 May 2018.

Sanderson, W. C., and Scherbov, S. (2010). Remeasuring aging. *Science, 10*(3295997), 1287–1288. https://doi.org/0.1126/science.1193647

Sanderson, W. C., and Scherbov, S. (2015). Are we overly dependent on conventional dependency ratios? *Population and Development Review, 41*(4), 687–708. https://doi.org/10.1111/j.1728-4457.2015.00091.x

United Nations Department of Economic and Social Affairs Population Division. (2007). *World population prospects: The 2017 revision, key findings and advance tables*. Working Paper. Geneva: UN.

United Nations Department of Economic and Social Affairs Population Division. (2013). *National transfer accounts manual: Measuring and analysing the generational economy*. Geneva: UN.

van de Kaa, D. J. (1987). Europe's second demographic transition. *Population Bulletin*, 42(1), 1–59.

van de Kaa, D. J. (2002). *The idea of a second demographic transition in industrialized countries*. Paper Presented at the Sixth Welfare Policy Seminar of the National Institute of Population and Social Security, Tokyo, Japan, 29 January 2002, 1–34.

Zamaro, G., Green, G., Tsouros, A., and Chiavon, E. (2008). A new model dependency ratio for European cities. *Italian Journal of Public Health*, 5(3), 217–227.

12

OLD AGE CARE

Slavina Spasova and Bart Vanhercke

12.1 INTRODUCTION: THE EUROPEAN UNION AS A LEADER IN LONG-TERM CARE PROVISION FOR THE ELDERLY

Long-term care (LTC) is considered to be an 'invisible' social welfare scheme for two reasons. First, in most European countries, LTC financing and provision are divided between healthcare and social care. Second, LTC relies heavily on unpaid care provided by relatives, mostly women, whose social rights are still 'at the fringe of social protection systems' (Bouget et al., 2017).

However, the position of LTC—under the policymakers' radar—is becoming increasingly financially and socially unsustainable, especially with regard to care for the frail elderly. LTC for the elderly has been the poor cousin of LTC provision and services, while LTC for disabled persons has received considerably more policy attention. Likewise, while research on LTC for disabled children and adults is well-developed (and, to some extent, for disabled persons), analysis of LTC for the elderly is lagging far behind (Torella and Masselot, 2010; Greve, 2017).

In several European countries, LTC policies for the elderly are changing in an attempt to respond to constantly growing demand (Spasova et al., 2018; Greve, 2017). Indeed, it is clear that LTC demand will continue to increase steeply with population ageing. The number of EU citizens aged 80 and older is projected to increase from 4.9% to 13% in the period, 2016–2070 (in the EU28). Consequently, public expenditure on LTC is expected to grow by 70% (from 1.6% to 2.7% of gross domestic product [GDP]) between 2016 and 2070 (EU28) (European Commission, 2018). Meanwhile the availability of informal carers is

Slavina Spasova and Bart Vanhercke, *Old Age Care* In: *Europe's Income, Wealth, Consumption, and Inequality.*
Edited by: Georg Fischer and Robert Strauss, Oxford University Press (2021). © Oxford University Press.
DOI: 10.1093/oso/9780197545706.003.0012

falling due to changing family patterns, women's increasing participation in the labour market, and the rise in pensionable ages (European Commission, 2018; Spasova et al., 2018). LTC provision is also a part of a 'wider agenda of recasting welfare states' to respond to 'new social risks' linked to, for instance, the combination of paid employment with childcare and/or care for the elderly, rather than 'old social risks' such as unemployment (Bonoli, 2005; Esping-Andersen, 2009; Taylor-Gooby, 2008). .

In this context, one of the most significant challenges for the future is access—ideally affordable and financially sustainable—to LTC provision for the elderly. There is a clear difference between Europe, as a leader in LTC provision, and the rest of the world, where large inequalities in public investment and access to LTC provision prevail between and within continents. There are indeed countries in Africa, Asia, and Latin America where LTC provisions are close to 'non-existent' (International Labour Organization [ILO], 2018).

Recent research (ILO, 2018)—as well as data from the World Health Organization (WHO) and the Organisation for Economic Cooperation and Development (OECD)—clearly flag that, in the European Union, Norway and Iceland are the leaders in LTC provision to the elderly compared to the rest of ·the world. Worldwide, in 2015, 906 million persons aged 60 and older were considered to be care-dependent, and by 2030, this number is expected to reach 1.4 billion (ILO, 2018). Europe, and in particular Eastern Europe, is the region with the highest old-age dependency ratio. In general, high-income countries have the highest dependency ratios for older persons (6.9%); this figure is halved for middle-income countries (3.7%) and is only 2.6% for low-income countries (ILO, 2018).

LTC provision for disabled people and the elderly is rare in most African, Latin American, and Asian countries. Even, for example, in Argentina, which is one of the most socially and economically developed countries in Latin America, only 2% of older people have the possibility of living in residential homes; by contrast, the values for Belgium are 8.8% (65+) and 24% (80+) (ILO, 2018). In Europe, and to some extent in Central Asia, leaves widespread. In the Americas, only 4 out of 33 countries provide paid leave (Canada, El Salvador, Nicaragua, and Peru) and only 2 countries (the Bahamas and the United States) provide unpaid leave. In this respect, it should be pointed out that home care services are less widely available than institutional care all over the world (ILO, 2018).

Attitudes and preferences also differ greatly around the world. Thus, in Western Europe a majority (65%) prefer care for older persons outside the family setting. Interestingly, in a country such as Turkey with a strong tradition of familialism,[1] the share of people preferring care outside the family is around 70%. By contrast,

---

1   Familialism is related to society models where care duties are traditionally provided by family and there are scarce publicly provided alternatives to this family care. For further discussion, see Saraceno (2004: 68–88); see also Bouget et al. (2017: 155–179).

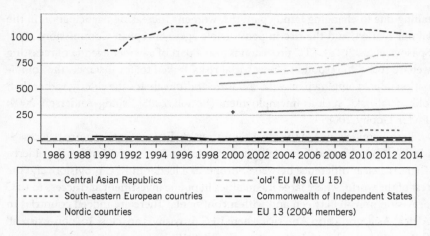

Figure 12.1 Nursing and elderly beds per 100,000 population.
Source: World Health Organization. Green: Nordic countries, purple: 'old' EU MS (EU15), dark blue: EU13 (2004 members),light blue: Member of the EU after May 2004 (EU13) red: South-eastern European countries, dark green: Central Asian Republics, orange: Commonwealth of Independent States.

in Eastern Asian countries, also characterized by strong familialism, 53% still primarily favour family responsibility (ILO, 2018).

WHO statistics on institutional care for the elderly (available only for Europe and Central Asia) present similar clear trends. Although the Nordic countries in Europe have reduced their number of beds over the past 20 years, they still score the highest, with 1,053 beds per 100,000 inhabitants. The lowest values are found in the Central Asian Republics[2] and the Commonwealth of Independent States,[3] with, respectively, 39 and 55 beds (2014) per 100,000 inhabitants. These are, unsurprisingly, followed by other countries with a strong familialist culture: in South-Eastern Europe[4] with 129 beds in, 2013 (Figure 12.1).

The EU average of 753 beds per 100,000 inhabitants is clearly boosted by the 'old' Member States (EU15), which have 860 beds per 100,000 inhabitants. By contrast, this figure is less than half in the 13 'new' EU Member States (2004 accession): 349 beds (2014) per 100,000 inhabitants. The EU countries register a slightly upwards trend (for more details see Section 12.2).

With regard to LTC expenditure, the inequalities between continents are even more striking, with a relatively clear-cut North–South divide. Available data

---

2   Kazakhstan, Kyrgyzstan, Tajikistan, Turkmenistan, and Uzbekistan

3   Azerbaijan, Armenia, Belarus, Georgia, Kazakhstan, Kyrgyzstan, Moldova, Russia, Tajikistan, Turkmenistan, Uzbekistan, and Ukraine.

4   South-Eastern Europe Health Network (SEEHN) Albania, Bosnia and Herzegovina, Bulgaria, Montenegro, the Republic of Moldova, Romania, Serbia, and the former Yugoslav Republic of Macedonia.

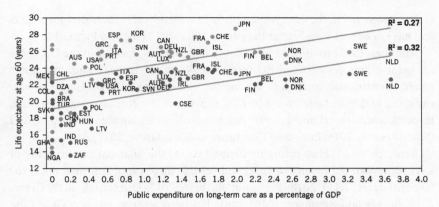

Figure 12.2 Public long-term care expenditure as a percentage of gross domestic product (GDP) and life expectancy at age 60 in 45 countries, by sex (2010–2015).
Source: International Labour Organization (ILO), 2018; Global Health Observatory, 2018.

show that the leaders in LTC expenditure (on both health and social LTC) are the Nordic European countries, followed by the EU Continental countries. African and Latin America countries spend the least, with values very close to zero (see Figure 12.2; ILO, 2018). They are followed by Asian countries, Australia, the United States, and Southern European and Eastern European Countries.

Available OECD data (only on the LTC health component) confirm the abovementioned trend and show that Nordic and Continental countries are also the countries with the highest increase in LTC spending over the past 28 years (Figures 12.3 and 12.4). The lowest expenditure on LTC outside Europe is in Australia (less than 0.2%), Costa Rica (0.1%), the United States (0.9%), and Korea

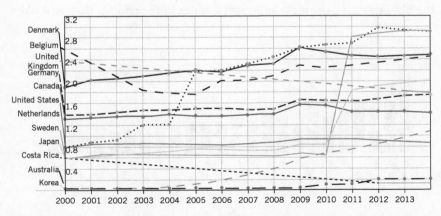

Figure 12.3 Evolution of long-term care (health) expenditure, share of gross domestic product (GDP) (2000, 2005, 2010, 2015).
Source: OECD Health Statistics 2017.

(1.2%). However, in the latter, expenditure has considerably increased since 2005 and has risen most steeply over the period 2005–2015 (see also Figure 12.3).

Although LTC provision is most developed and less unequal in the EU, there are great disparities between EU countries: Nordic countries—and, to a lesser extent, Continental countries—are among the leaders in providing relatively sufficient and affordable access to LTC provisions. By contrast, Southern and, in particular, Central and Eastern European countries lag significantly behind (Spasova et al., 2018; European Commission, 2016; Greve, 2017).

Research on LTC has primarily focused on (a) the financial sustainability of LTC provision, (b) quality of care, and (c) the situation of informal and professional carers (ILO, 2018; Bouget et al., 2016, 2017; Eurofound, 2015; Greve, 2017; Becker and Reinhard, 2018). Little has been written, by contrast, on the challenge of access to and affordability of formal services, be they home-based, community-based, or residential. In order to fill this research gap, the focus of our chapter is on access and affordability of LTC provision. We believe that the availability of affordable LTC provision is the condition *sine qua non* for socially and financially viable LTC systems, which should be considered as two sides of the same coin. For instance, the unavailability of LTC services jeopardizes the employment of carers, who, in turn, do not contribute to the labour market and social protection system (Bouget et al., 2017, 2016), thus impacting the financial sustainability of LTC schemes. Financially unsustainable LTC systems are then bound to lead to socially unequal outcomes.

Section 12.2 presents the main issues related to access to LTC for the elderly, such as financial sustainability, the role of informal care, and changing societal patterns. Section 12.3 discusses the core challenge of access to LTC for the elderly by presenting evidence on access to residential and home care services; it also outlines different models of institutionalization/deinstitutionalization. Finally, Section 12.4 focuses on how LTC schemes have been 'in the making' in the EU, presenting the most important features of the reforms that have taken

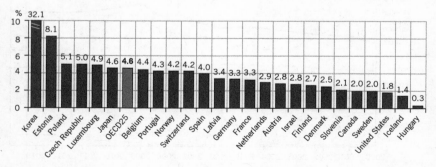

Figure 12.4 Annual growth rate in expenditure on long-term care (LTC) (health and social) by government and compulsory insurance schemes, in real terms, 2005–2015 (or nearest year). *Source:* OECD Health Statistics 2017.

place in Member States' LTC systems over the past 5 years. This chapter draws on a Synthesis Report written for the European Social Policy Network (ESPN) and uses original evidence from 28 national ESPN country reports on 'Challenges in Access to Long-Term Care'.[5] It also builds on secondary research regarding access to LTC for the elderly and presents Eurostat, OECD, and WHO data.

12.2 LONG-TERM CARE PROVISION AND EXPENDITURE IN THE EU: INEQUALITIES IN THE MOST EQUAL REGION IN THE WORLD

There are two types of superposed inequalities in access to LTC in the EU.[6] First are the aforementioned geographical inequalities in LTC among EU countries, as well as regional and rural disparities within a country. Second, there are inequalities in the countries' mix of LTC provision: home care versus residential care. In general, the availability and affordability of home-based services—enabling the elderly to live independently at home as long as possible—are a significant issue in national policy-making in several EU countries (Spasova et al., 2018; Greve, 2017).

This section provides a broad perspective on LTC provision, presenting the main trends related to access, quality, employment of carers, and financial sustainability of LTC within the European Union. Crucially, LTC is not a separate social protection scheme in the social security systems of the Member States. The only exceptions in this respect are Germany, Luxembourg, and the Belgian federated region of Flanders, which have social insurance-based LTC schemes. As mentioned before, LTC for the elderly relies mainly on informal carers. In general, LTC provision and funding are split horizontally and vertically (i.e., between healthcare and social care, as well as between territorial entities).

12.2.1 Types of LTC Provision in the EU

LTC for the elderly provided by health professionals is typically regulated and funded at the national level. Social care for the elderly, which includes care services that aim to help the care-dependent person to carry out activities of daily life (such as household tasks, eating, etc.), is funded and regulated at the national, regional, or local level and often as a mix between these three levels. When it comes to ensuring provision of social services, these are mostly the responsibility of subnational levels (regions and municipalities). For instance, home care is most often provided by the municipalities.

---

5   The Synthesis Report and (35) European country reports on 'Challenges in access to long-term care' can be downloaded from the European Commission website: https://ec.europa.eu/social/main.jsp?catId=738&langId=fr&pubId=8128&furtherPubs=yes

6   This Section largely draws on Spasova et al. (2018).

In some countries, *home care* is well-developed and is given priority over residential care (e.g., AT, DE, DK, ES, FI, FR, IS, LI, LU, NO, SE, SI). The Nordic countries in particular have made major efforts to make it easier for people to stay as long as possible in their own homes and to reduce the number of people living in institutions (e.g., DK, FI, IS, NL, SE). To enable the elderly to live independently as long as possible, and thus to prevent reliance on care services, some countries have emphasized prevention and rehabilitation (e.g., DE, DK, LU, PT, as well as, more recently, FR, UK/England, and Scotland).

In Southern European and Eastern European countries, home care services for the elderly are underdeveloped (e.g., EE, EL, HR, HU, RO, see Section 12.3). As a result, only a limited number of people in need of LTC can benefit from these services. In still other countries, important efforts have been made recently to strengthen home care (IE, HU, LV), often with support from European funds (e.g., BG, EL, EE, IT, LT, SI, RS).

Semi-residential care is care provided in an institutional setting for care-dependent persons who do not permanently reside in the institution. It includes centres where the frail elderly can be cared for only during the day or during the night. Day care is provided in nearly all countries, night care much less so (e.g., DK, BE, ES, MT).

Finally, all countries provide *residential care* (i.e., care provided in a residential setting for elderly people living in accommodation with permanent caring staff). It includes care facilities specifically for the elderly or incorporated into institutions for disabled people. Nordic and Continental countries typically have a well-developed residential LTC sector for the elderly. In many other countries, residential care facilities for the elderly are historically underdeveloped (e.g., EL, PL, RO, HR, MK, RS, TR); in still others, supply has been reduced as a result of deinstitutionalization policies. In many countries, demand for residential care exceeds supply (e.g., CY, EL, HU, LV, MK, MT, PT, RO, RS, TR). It should also be highlighted that these institutions are concentrated in urban areas (see Section 12.3).

The situation of carers should also be considered since large inequalities exist between EU countries with regard to the provision of carers. Thus, paid carers' leave is not generally available throughout the European Union. While caregiving leave schemes for parents of disabled children exist in all European countries (except Slovakia), only some countries provide some form of leave for employees caring for frail elderly people. Even fewer countries provide—paid or non-paid—caregiving leave schemes regardless of the age of the dependent person (AT, DE, DK, IE, IT, NL, SE, UK) (Bouget et al., 2016, 2017).

A carer's allowance exists only in a very few countries. Such an allowance is specifically provided to the family carer, who must apply for it (e.g., in BE; allowance for assistance to the elderly in MT, PL, RO, SK, UK). The schemes may require that the informal carer has no (e.g., PL, UK) or only a limited number of employment hours outside the house (e.g., HU, IE). In Finland, a contract must be drawn up between the carer and the municipality. Cash benefits for carers may be means-tested (e.g., IE, SK) and may be limited to persons giving care to a severely disabled person (e.g., SI, SK). In some countries, the benefit can be shared between two persons (e.g., IE). Cash benefits for the carer are rather symbolic and merely meant as a recognition of the work done by the carer.

12.2.2 Informal Care: The Employment Challenge for Women

As mentioned in the Introduction (Section 12.1), LTC can be considered an 'invisible' welfare scheme: the incidence of informal care in most EU Member States is so high that LTC is considered to be an 'informal economic sector', estimated to range between 50% and 90% of the overall cost of formal LTC provision (Bouget et al., 2017; European Commission, 2016). In countries which underinvest in this area, informal care may be the only, or main, form of care available, particularly for low-income persons and families (Bouget et al., 2017). For instance, in Portugal, the work performed by informal carers is estimated to represent more than 2% of GDP, while formal care is estimated at 0.2% (Spasova et al., 2018).

An *informal carer* is a person who provides care, in principle unpaid, to a care-dependent older person, not on a professional or formal employment basis; the informal carer is, in general, a person with whom the care-dependent has a social relationship. Caring responsibilities for parents are enshrined in law in some countries (e.g., HU, LV, LT). The main reasons for the high incidence of informal LTC are the shortage of accessible formal LTC facilities, their poor quality, the non-affordability of LTC, and, finally, the traditional model of intergenerational and family relations.

It is difficult to estimate the number of informal carers for older people. Data from the Labour Force Survey (LFS) show that looking after children or incapacitated adults was the main reason for inactivity for 5.4% of inactive women aged 50–64 years in 2016 in the European Union. The equivalent percentage for men was 1.4%. With figures of, respectively, 11.7% (compared with 3.9% for men) and 12.3% (compared with 6.7% for men), IE and the UK have the highest shares of female inactivity on the grounds of care (see Figure 12.5).

It should be noted that migrants play a specific role in informal care provision, as families frequently rely on them to assist with care tasks for older people. However, there are frequent issues with regard to their qualifications and working conditions (e.g., irregular contracts and low social protection coverage).

12.2.3 The Financial Sustainability of LTC Provision: The Unknown Equation

Public expenditure on LTC as a percentage of GDP has been increasing over the past 20 years in European countries and is expected to grow by 70%—from 1.6% to 2.7% of GDP—between 2016 and 2070 due to population ageing. However,

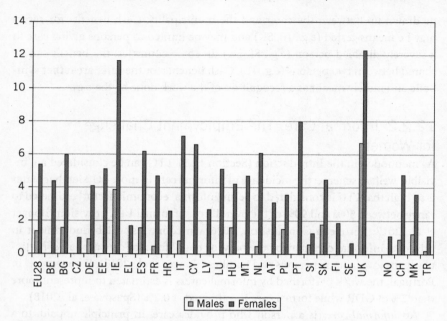

Figure 12.5 Percentage of inactive men and women (50–64) not working on the grounds that they are looking after children or incapacitated adults (2016).
Source: Eurostat, LFS, [lfsa_igar] in Spasova et al. (2018).

projections vary widely between countries. Nordic and Eastern countries are expected to spend generously on LTC. Currently, Nordic and Continental countries are among the leaders in expenditure on LTC (e.g., SE 2.90%, NL 2.62%, BE 2.55%, DK 2.53%) while Eastern European countries score the lowest, at around 0.3% (e.g., BG 0.01%) in 2015 (see Figure 12.6).

Considering the different challenges facing national LTC systems, financial sustainability may be an issue for a number of reasons. It may be affected by fragmentation of care due to a lack of coordination between health and social care entities. An absence of clear financial strategies by the territorial entities responsible for LTC may also lead to unpredictable LTC spending.

Similarly to the LTC health component, for the LTC social component[7] expenditure in terms of GDP is highest in the Netherlands (1.34%), then in Finland (0.96%) and Portugal (0.73%) (see Figure 12.7).

---

7   Assistance care services (IADL) are considered as LTC (social). This indicator may refer to ancillary services (nonspecified by function), healthcare, or LTC-related services nonspecified by function and nonspecified by mode of provision, which the patient consumes directly, in particular during independent contact with the health system and which are not an integral part of a care service package, such as laboratory or imaging services or patient transportation and emergency rescue. For more details,

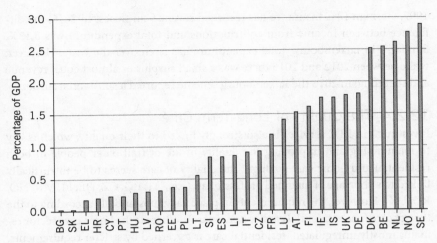

Figure 12.6 Long-term care expenditure (health) in terms of gross domestic product (GDP) (2015).
Source: Eurostat 2015, Spasova et al. (2018).

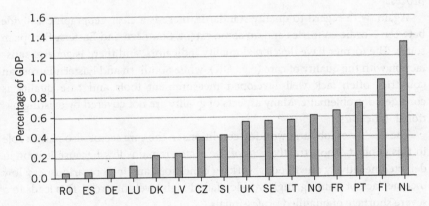

Figure 12.7 Long-term care expenditure (social) in terms of gross domestic product (GDP) (2015).
Source: Spasova et al. (2018).

To ensure the sustainability of its LTC scheme, Germany has been increasing social contribution rates since the scheme began in 1996, up to 2.55% (2.80% for childless insurance members) in 2017. At the same time, LTC expenditure in Germany has steadily increased in recent years, from €14.3 billion in 1997 to €28.3 billion in 2016. In 2016, 24.0% of total expenditure was on care allowances, 13.4% on home care (in kind), and 38.5% on residential care. Importantly, since

see online (Eurostat Healthcare expenditure statistics https://ec.europa.eu/eurostat/statistics-explained/index.php/Healthcare_expenditure_statistics).

1997, German LTC insurance has recorded revenue surpluses. In 2016, the difference between income from contributions and total expenditure was 3.13%. Similarly, in Luxembourg, total expenditure has risen over the years. However, while between 2012 and 2015 there was a small surplus or almost equal revenue and spending, in 2016 the Luxembourg scheme reported a substantial surplus.

12.2.4 The Quality of Long-Term Care

Investment in LTC services is also strongly linked to their quality, which is key to maintaining and improving the quality of life of frail older people in both residential and home care settings. The quality of care seems to be intrinsically linked to a shortage of qualified professionals (e.g., AT, BG, CZ, DE, LI, MK, NO, RO, UK). However, the requirements in place vary substantially according to the type of care (i.e., residential care or home care). Whereas the home care sector remains mostly unregulated, residential care is governed by stricter requirements. Such quality control measures seem to be a first step towards ensuring quality commitment, but some countries have problems in implementation due to limited resources, a lack of qualified inspectors, and/or a lack of transparency in the process.

Again, with regard to quality standards, there is a clear geographical divide between Nordic countries and, to some extent, Southern and Eastern European states. The former have developed quality indicators, and there is general satisfaction with the quality of care (e.g., DK), while Southern and Eastern European countries often lack well-developed measurement tools and care quality is considered problematic. Many aspects of quality are not covered by existing national indicators.

The quality of jobs and working conditions in the care sector also plays a role in this context. The attractiveness of the sector remains low because it is often depicted negatively due to poor working conditions and job precariousness: low income, lack of training, high workload, and high levels of stress. This leads to a severe shortage of qualified professionals.

12.3 AVAILABILITY AND AFFORDABILITY OF LTC PROVISION: WHAT BALANCE BETWEEN HOME CARE AND RESIDENTIAL CARE?

When considering the availability of LTC provision, one of the main challenges is the access to home-based and community-based services. As mentioned already, the main domestic and EU discourses tend to prioritize these types of services. What is more, several countries have implemented policies favouring deinstitutionalization of care for the elderly, thus further increasing inequalities in provision between Member States.

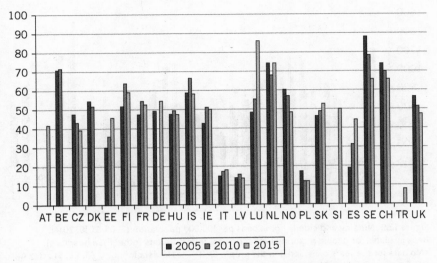

Figure 12.8 Beds in residential long-term care facilities (65+, per 1,000 population, 2005, 2010, 2015)
We have included IS and NO in this figure in order to have a full picture of Nordic countries' LTC provision. TR and CH are included to give a broader European perspective.
* EU countries not included in the dataset: BG, CY, EL, HR, LI, LT, MK, MT, PT, RO. **No data for the years considered in the graph: 2005: AT, SI 2010 AT, DE, SI; 2015: BE, DK.
Source: OECD.

12.3.1 Residential Care for the Elderly: Inequalities in Provision

While deinstitutionalization patterns are fairly strong in Nordic and Continental Europe, the opposite trend can be observed in Southern and Eastern Europe. Nordic countries have considerably reduced their provision of residential places since the mid-1990s (WHO, 2016; see Figure 12.1). But the overall picture is less clear-cut. If we take into account a more recent period (2005–2015), some clear trends emerge for a group of countries (Figures 12.8 and 12.9).

The WHO indicator on the elderly shows that the number of residential beds in the EU28 has been on the rise. However, the Nordic countries have promoted a significant process of deinstitutionalization coupled with a greater emphasis on the development of home care. The number of residential beds for persons aged 65 and older has steadily diminished since 2005 (DK, NO, SE). Yet in some of these countries, new residential places were created between 2005 and 2010 (FI, IS), and deinstitutionalization became a common trend especially after 2010 (FI, IS, NO, SE) (Figures 12.8 and 12.9). The steepest fall can be observed in Sweden, where the number of recipients (65+) in residential facilities dropped from 7.7% to 4.5%, and the number of recipients aged 80 and older decreased from 20.7% to 17.2% during the period 2000–2014, as can also be seen in Figure 12.10.

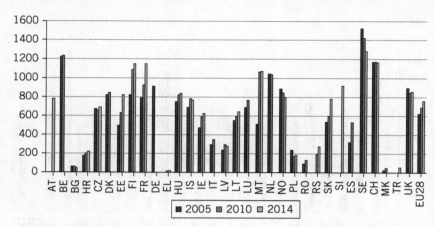

Figure 12.9 Nursing and elderly home beds per 100,000 population (2005, 2010, 2014).
Beds available for people requiring long-term care in institutions (other than hospitals).
*No data for the years considered in the graph: CY, PT. **No data for 2005: AT, EL, SI 2010 AT,
DE, SI; 2014: DE, MK, RO.
Source: World Health Organization (WHO).

In the United Kingdom there has been a steady decrease in the number of residential beds over the period 2003–2014: from 57.7 to 47.7 beds per 100,000 population, a trend which accelerated due to austerity policies after 2009. Moreover,
there has been a strong tendency towards the privatization and marketization
of LTC. For, instance, in England, 89% of domiciliary services and 94% of residential beds for older people are supplied by private providers. The residential

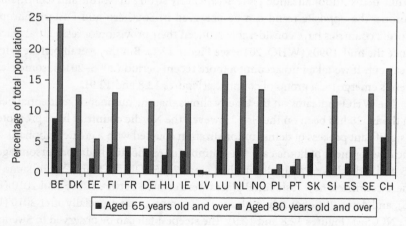

Figure 12.10 Long-term care (LTC) recipients in institutions (other than hospitals) (2014).

OECD data, LTC beds per 1,000 population aged 65+.
* EU countries not included in the dataset: AT, BG, EL, CY, HR, IT, LT, MT, RO. **No data for the
years considered in the graph: CZ, UK. ***No data for 80+ for FR and SK.
Source: OECD.

market in particular is dominated by several large chains backed by private equity capital and reliant on risky financial structures (Glendinning, 2018).

Continental countries have different patterns of provision of care: these are the countries with the highest usage of residential places. The number of residential beds (65+) has increased in France and Germany, fallen only slightly in the Netherlands, and has remained stable in Belgium (2005–2015). The only exception is Luxembourg, where the number of beds per 1,000 inhabitants increased from 41.1 in 2001 to 83.7 per 1,000 inhabitants in 2016.

Similarly, as Figure 12.10 clearly shows, these Continental countries have among the highest numbers of LTC recipients in institutions, with Belgium topping the charts at 8.8% (65+) and 24% (80+). In all these countries, with the exception of the Netherlands, the number of LTC recipients in institutions increased over the period 2000–2014.[8]

The situation in Ireland is similar to that in the Continental countries: there is a bias towards residential care, and the number of residential places has steadily increased since 2005; the number of recipients aged 65+ was 3.6%, and 11.4% for those aged 80+ in 2014. As of 2015, approximately 60% of the budget for supporting older people was spent on long-term residential care, effectively catering for only about 4% of the population older than 65. As in the United Kingdom, however, in 2013, 66.8% of all long-stay beds were provided by the private sector, 10% by the voluntary sector, and only 23.1% by the public sector. Most places are majority-funded by the state, regardless of the sector.

Southern and Eastern European countries face very similar challenges with regard to residential care provision despite very different historical developments. These are countries belonging to the traditional familialistic model: care duties are traditionally provided by family, and there are few publicly provided alternatives to this family care. These countries rely heavily on informal care (see Section 12.2). Other challenges include a steep increase in the old-age dependency ratio (especially in Bulgaria), changes in the family structure, and an increase in the pensionable age (especially for women). Moreover, some young and middle-aged people are emigrating, which challenges the 'familialist' model of caring for the elderly at home.

Figures 12.8 and 12.9 show that in most of Southern Europe there is a clear trend towards increasing the number of LTC beds for those 65 and older (e.g., ES, IT, PT), and this trend is also seen in some Central and Eastern European countries (BG, EE,[9] LT, RO). The country with the steepest increase in residential places for the elderly is Spain, with significant growth in the availability of residential beds, from 8.9% to 44.4%; in Italy, the number of beds increased from 12.2 to 18.5 (2000–2015). Interestingly, in Spain, even with a low number of

8 OECD indicator, LTC recipients in institutions (other than hospitals), 2014 https://stats.oecd.org/index.aspx?queryid=30143
9 OECD data, LTC beds per 1,000 population aged 65+.

residential places at the beginning of the 2000s, there was an oversupply—these places were not occupied mostly due to their cost or because of a cultural preference for care provided by relatives at home. National data from Portugal show that even though there has been a steady increase in the number of residential beds, only 8,400 beds of the 14,640 established as a target had been created by the end of 2016 (Spasova et al., 2018). In general, these countries have increased their numbers of residential places, but demand significantly exceeds supply.

In Eastern Europe also the supply of residential care cannot keep up with demand: considerable inequalities can also be seen, partly due to the development of private residential care. As mentioned earlier, the trend is towards an increase in residential facilities even though this trend is less clear-cut than in Southern European countries. According to OECD data, in some countries there has been a slight but steady decrease in the number of residential beds since the 2000s (e.g., CZ, LV, PL). This is the case for Poland, which cut places from 17.6 to 12.2 (2003–2015). However, these data should be viewed with some caution as it seems that in the social sector the number of beds remains stable (Spasova et al., 2018). In other countries, national data show a certain increase in the number of residential homes (e.g., BG, EE, LT, RO). In Estonia, the number of beds rose from 29 to 49.5 for the period 2000–2015 (see also Figure 12.3).

National data show a spectacular increase of private sector residential institutions in Romania: from 51 in 2009 to 249 in 2016, while the total number of public homes for the elderly increased from 98 to 123 over the same period. The number of users (total public and private) rose from 7,379 to 14,590. Thanks to this increase, the proportion of pending applications out of the total capacity—for both private and public institutions—fell from about 40% in 2009 to about 14% in 2016, reflecting a fairly constant 'active demand' for institutionalization.

In Bulgaria, 11,000 people were placed in 161 homes for adults and elderly people needing institutionalized LTC in 2016. This number has remained virtually unchanged since 2003, leading to waiting lists of people amounting to one-third of the existing capacity in 2017. In the Czech Republic, in 2016, there were 37,247 beds in homes for the elderly and almost 67,000 unsettled applications. In Lithuania, in 2014, 47% of the elderly in need of LTC were on a waiting list for residential care, with an average waiting time of 6 months.

12.3.2 Home Care for the Elderly: The Poor Cousin of LTC Provision

Home care services and community-based care are the biggest challenge for effective access since in many countries these options are underdeveloped. There is a clear split between European countries in this respect. Home and community-based services are most developed in the Nordic countries (DK, IS, FI, NO, SE) and some Continental countries (e.g., BE, DE, FR). On the other hand, Southern (e.g., CY, EL, ES, MT, PT) and especially Eastern European countries (e.g., BG, CZ, EE, LV, LT, MK, PL, RO, RS, SI, SK) have insufficient availability of home

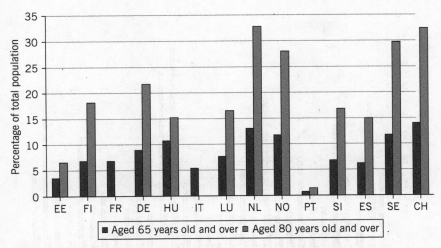

Figure 12.11 Long-term care (LTC) recipients at home (65+ and 80+) (2014).

care provision, which is often targeted at persons with a high degree of dependency. Some of these trends are quite strongly visible from the OECD indicator on LTC recipients at home as a share of the population aged 65 or older (see Figure 12.11). At the same time, these countries also have among the highest percentages of home care: in Germany (8.9%) and the Netherlands (13.1%) for those aged 80 and older, these values are, respectively, 21.9% and 32.8%.

The Eurostat indicator[10] shows similar patterns (see Figure 12.12). The Nordic (e.g., NO, SE) and Continental countries (BE, FR, NL) score among the highest, while Southern and Eastern European countries have among the lowest values. The insufficient supply of institutional care described in Section 2.2 also goes hand in hand with the unavailability of home care in these countries. The percentages of LTC recipients at home are quite low in Eastern and Southern European countries: for instance, 3.5% (65+) and 6.5% (80+) in Estonia, and 0.7% (65+) and 1.4% (80+) in Portugal. The older people grow, the greater use of home services is reported. In all countries except Bulgaria, the percentages of self-reported use of home care services are on average at least double and, in some cases, even four times higher, for persons aged 75 and older.

These geographical inequalities in access and usage of home care are corroborated by the Eurostat results on persons using or not professional homecare services, from the Eurostat ad hoc module on access to services.[11] In

10 *Source:* Eurostat [hlth_ehis_am7u]; * ESPN countries not included in the dataset: CH, LI, MK, RS.

11 Persons using or not professional homecare services by household type, income group, degree of urbanization, and reason for not using professional homecare services [ilc_ats15].

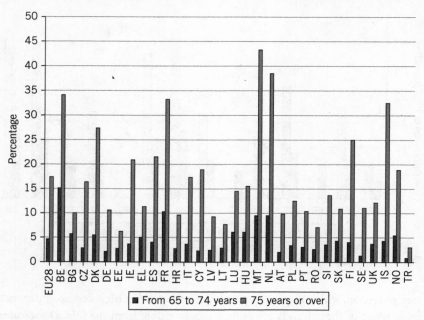

Figure 12.12 Self-reported use of home-care services by age (2014).

the European Union, as many as 8.2% of people aged 65+ do not use professional home care services because they perceive them to be unavailable. Important inequalities in perceptions of unavailability exist between countries: Southern and Eastern European Countries have the highest percentage of people aged 65+ reporting unavailability of home services as a reason for not using them (Italy 27%, Ireland 18.8%, and Estonia 18%). By contrast, in Nordic and Continental countries, these percentages are considerably lower (e.g., FR 2.1%, SE 4.5%).

In Ireland, about three-quarters of formal care services are provided by the for-profit sector. Private commercial providers are increasing their share of the sector in a context where nursing home occupancy rates are as high as 94% and demand outstrips supply.

12.3.3 Affordability of LTC Provision: Measuring Sufficiency

Affordability of LTC provision is a source of serious inequalities between countries and within the same country. Unfortunately, there are no EU indicators to measure affordability of LTC provision. The aforementioned Eurostat ad hoc module on access to services can provide some insightful results, and it shows that serious regional inequalities follow the same geographical pattern as availability of LTC. People in Nordic and Continental countries have fewer problems affording home-based services contrary to people in Southern (with the exception of Malta) and Eastern European countries. People older than 65 years in Romania, Cyprus, Bulgaria, and Greece report the most difficulties in paying

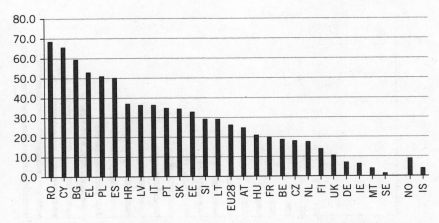

Figure 12.13 Persons, 65+ using or not professional homecare services for financial reasons (2016).
Source: Eurostat 2018, [ilc_ats15].

for home care services: respectively 68.7%, 65.8%, 59.7%, and 53.2%. In Sweden, Malta, and Iceland, these percentages are spectacularly lower: 1.2%, 3.9%, and 4% (Figure 12.13).

Persons on a low income (less than 60% of the median equivalized income, 65+) in Bulgaria, Greece, and Spain often report inability to access services for financial reasons (66.2% 56.3%, and 49.9%, respectively). Remarkably, the values in the same countries for people 65+ above the median equivalized income are no lower: 61.2%, 61.0%, and 50.3%, respectively.[12]

Another way of measuring the affordability of LTC provision is to look at household out-of-pocket (OOP) expenditure on LTC (see Figure 12.14). The United Kingdom (6%), Switzerland (5.9%), Germany (5%), and Ireland (4.8%) top the charts in terms of voluntary private insurance and out-of-pocket spending while France, Greece, and the Czech Republic have among the lowest levels. As mentioned in Section 2.2, the UK and Ireland, for instance, have made large cuts to their public spending on LTC.

OOPs may be an important source of inequalities in access to LTC. In nearly all countries, these may be required both for home care services and for residential care. In some countries, the full price is directly paid by the resident (e.g., AT, EE). In others countries, home care services are free of charge (e.g., DK, TR, and LU) or charges are very low (e.g., MT, BG, SE, Scotland, Wales, and Northern Ireland). OOPs for home care are means-tested in the UK.

---

12 EurostatPersons using or not professional homecare services by household type, income group, degree of urbanization, and reason for not using professional homecare services (2016) [ilc_ats15].

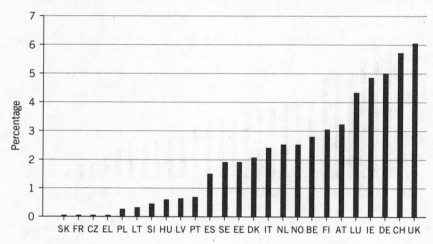

Figure 12.14 Voluntary schemes/household out-of-pocket payments on long-term care (health) (2015).
* EU countries not included in the dataset BG, CY, HR, MT, RO.
Source: OECD, Health expenditure and financing.

Accommodation costs (meals, housing) in residential settings are usually borne by the residents (e.g., AT, BE, CH, DE, DK, FR, LU, NL, SI). In case of insolvency of the cared-for person, the family bears these costs in many countries (e.g., BE, EL, HU, LV, RO). There may be a cap on the price (e.g., HR), on the total amount to be paid by the resident (e.g., DK, SE), or on the amount as a percentage of the income (and assets) due (e.g., AT, HU, IE, IS, LT, LV, MT, NL, RO) in state care homes. In many countries, a certain amount or percentage of the residents' income is safeguarded as pocket money (e.g., AT, IS, LU, LV, MT, UK).

OOPs can also depend on the income of the resident (e.g., HU, IE, IT, LT, LV, MT, NL, NO, PL, SI, UK) or the income of both the resident and his family (e.g., RO). In some countries a cash benefit can be used to (partially) cover the cost of formal services, both for home and residential care (e.g., AT). In most countries, municipalities (e.g., AT, BE, DE, LT, LV, NL, RO, SI), the state/region (e.g., AT, IE, FR, LU), or insurers (for example) cover the costs of those care-dependent persons who themselves, or their relatives, are unable to pay the cost of the care. Accommodation costs for residential care are usually borne by the resident.

In general, residential care is considered expensive mostly in continental Europe. In France, residential care homes are considered to be expensive, with the average remaining cost to be met by residents estimated at between €1,470 and €1,758 per month (excluding social housing benefit for the poorest). In Germany, in 2017, benefit recipients had to pay €1,691 per month (May 2017) for residential care: this is considered expensive in relation to national standards.

In Eastern Europe, the beneficiary is expected to pay OOPs of around 20–30% for publicly run homes. In Romania, there has been a significant decrease in state

Table 12.1 Reform trends in European Union countries

Reforms improving access and affordability	Reforms aimed at improving financial sustainability
AT, CZ, DE, DK, EE, FI, IT, MT, PT, PL, RO, SE	DE, DK, ES, IE, HR, HU, LU, PT, SE, UK

subsidies, which correlates with an increase in beneficiaries' contributions. In the case of public homes under the responsibility of local authorities, beneficiaries' contributions rose from 26% in 2012 to 30% in 2016; for private homes, the beneficiaries' own contributions have even increased from 56% to 74% over the past 4 years.

Inequalities in affording LTC seem to be increased by the tightening of eligibility criteria, thus restricting services to individuals with the most severe care needs (e.g., UK/England). In some countries (SE, UK/England), private for-profit and non-profit institutions have developed as a result of deliberate policies to increase competition and create markets in LTC provision.

12.4 REFORM PATTERNS IN LONG-TERM CARE

LTC provision has been subject to several reforms in most EU Member States over the past 10 years (2008–2018). There have been two main trends with regard to different aspects of LTC care: a) measures addressing financial sustainability and b) better access and affordability of provision, including improvements to the status of informal carers (see Table 12.1).

With regard to financial sustainability, there have been various trends across Europe, such as cuts in funding for residential care, increases in the OOP payments required from beneficiaries, rises in contributory rates for LTC insurance (DE, LU), and tightening of the eligibility conditions for benefits (e.g., PT). Budgetary restrictions were implemented during the crisis and the post-crisis period in several countries (e.g., DK, ES, PT, IE, UK).

For instance, in Spain, a budgetary adjustment made to the long-term programme in 2012 is thought to have resulted in a 37,405 drop in beneficiaries by 2015. Moreover, the government ceased to require social security payments from non-professional home carers in July 2012. Ireland, Croatia, and Sweden have refocused home care towards individuals with the most severe care needs. In Denmark, the total hours of home services provided fell by 18%, and the number of persons receiving home help decreased by 12% between 2010 and 2016. Likewise, in Portugal, there has been a recent drop in the number of places available within the home-based health and social care teams. In Ireland, there has been a significant decline in the home care sector: home help services have decreased from more than 55,000 in 2008 to fewer than 47,000 in 2016; the number of beneficiaries decreased by almost 10,000 between 2008 and 2012.

There were approximately 4,600 people on waiting lists for home care in 2017 in Ireland.

Another major trend in several countries has been a search for ways to improve the access and affordability of LTC provision. These measures range from providing increasing funding for some components of LTC, to tackling the status of informal carers, to improving access to LTC provision. As for the latter, Austria prohibited in 2018 recourse to the assets of persons living in inpatient LTC facilities as well as recourse to the assets of their relatives. Estonia has been tackling the shortage of home care services by allocating additional funds from the EU structural funds.

In addition to these reforms affecting individual parameters of the LTC system, more comprehensive reforms are ongoing in a few countries (e.g., CY, FI). The whole Finnish social and healthcare service system—including LTC—will be overhauled when the social and health care reform (SOTE) comes into force in 2020. This reform is expected to result in an important territorial re-organization of LTC, introducing new personal budgets and more room for private for-profit service providers to operate. It will thus open up even more opportunities for private companies.

Similarly, in several countries there has been a trend towards the privatization and marketization of care (e.g., DE, FI, LT, UK). In the UK (England), there are growing pressures for new policies to ensure funding sustainability, for example through a social insurance approach. Debates are also focusing on the impact of Brexit on the care workforce: 7% of care workers are from other European Economic Area countries and 9% from non-EEA countries. Restricting recruitment from overseas, a possible post-Brexit development, would have a major impact on recruitment in England, where almost 40% of the care workforce are not British-born.

CONCLUSION

In this chapter, we analysed the main issues related to inequalities in access and affordability of LTC provision in the European Union. Although in a comparative perspective Europe, and in particular the EU as a region, leads the field in providing LTC services to its citizens, significant inequalities in expenditure on LTC, services, and benefits provided, and in the situation of informal carers, exist between Member States and even within individual countries.

Although LTC provision is most strongly developed in the European Union and less unequal than elsewhere, two types of superposed inequalities remain in access to LTC. First, access to LTC may be particularly hindered by the institutional split (between healthcare and social care) and geographical fragmentation of LTC provision. Second, often in the countries' mix of LTC provision—home care and residential care—home-based services are the poor cousin of LTC provision in terms of availability and affordability.

The clear trend towards prioritizing home care in national policy-making and EU discourse has not always been matched by sufficient and affordable service supply, especially in Southern and Eastern European countries where home care remains underdeveloped. With regard to access to home-based services, these two EU 'regions' are clearly both lagging far behind the Nordic and Continental countries.

But this is not the only issue for concern: residential care should also be considered. In countries with a long tradition of residential care, especially the Nordic countries, there has been a clear process of deinstitutionalization, matched with the development of home-based services. In contrast to this process of deinstitutionalization in most of the European Union, Southern and Eastern European countries have, however, seen an increase in residential places, although the demand for care considerably—and increasingly—exceeds supply. However, the most common situation in these countries is an inadequate supply of residential care coupled with insufficient and difficult-to-afford home-based services. As the Eurostat data show, in countries such as Bulgaria, Romania, and Greece, single adults aged 65 and older face significant difficulties in affording home care, regardless of whether their income is below or above the poverty threshold.

In some Member States, to some extent due to shortages in supply, there is an increasingly important trend towards the privatization and marketization of LTC and the rapid growth of a commercial sector. The main consequences of these developments are the growing OOP payments for beneficiaries, resulting in greater inequalities and, in some cases, problematic monitoring of the quality of LTC.

Although our chapter does not particularly focus on the role of informal carers, we highlighted the high incidence of informal care in most EU Member States. The abovementioned issues of access and affordability, coupled with the lack or underdevelopment of special provisions for carers in many countries, are closely linked to this situation. This negatively impacts female labour market participation and the quality of work–life balance.

It would be naïve and even undesirable to wish for informal care to disappear or be reduced to very low levels. Intergenerational, family, friendship, and/or neighbourhood solidarity has its place in care. Ideally, however, the carer and the cared-for person should have access to adapted and affordable services. One of the first steps on the road to adequate policies is proper measurement: policymakers and stakeholders should tackle the blatant lack of data and appropriate indicators, especially per age group, to measure the needs and the degree of provision of LTC.

REFERENCES

Becker, U. and. Reinhard, H. J. (2018) (eds.). *Long-term care in Europe*. Cham: Springer.

Bonoli, G. (2005). The politics of the new social policies. Providing coverage against new social risks in mature welfare states. *Policy and Politics*, 33(3). 431–449.

Bouget D., Saraceno C., and Spasova S. (2017). Towards new work-life balance policies for those caring for dependent relatives? In B. Vanhercke, S. Sebastiano, and D. Bouget (eds.). *Social policy in the European Union: State of play 2017* (pp. 155–179). Brussels: European Trade Union Institute and European Social Observatory.

Bouget D., Spasova S., and Vanhercke B. (2016). *Work-life balance measures for persons of working age with dependent relatives in Europe. A study of national policies*. European Social Protection Network (ESPN). Brussels: European Commission.

Esping-Andersen, G. (2009). *The Incomplete Revolution: Adapting to Women's New Roles*. Cambridge: Polity Press.

Eurofound (2015). *Working and caring: Reconciliation measures in times of demographic change*. Publications Office of the European Union, Luxembourg.

European Commission. (2014). *Adequate social protection for long-term care needs in an ageing society*. Report jointly prepared by the Social Protection Committee and the European Commission. Brussels: European Commission.

European Commission. (2016). *Joint report on health care and long-term care systems and fiscal sustainability and its country reports*. Directorate-General for Economic and Financial Affairs and Economic Policy Committee (Ageing Working Group). Brussels: European Commission.

European Commission. (2018). *The 2018 ageing report, economic and budgetary projections for the 28 EU Member States (2016–2070)*. Directorate-General for Economic and Financial Affairs. Brussels: European Commission.

Greve, B. (2017). Long-term care for the elderly in Europe: Development and prospects. Ashgate: Farnham.

International Labour Organisation (ILO). (2018). *Care work and care jobs for the future of decent work*. Geneva: ILO.

Glendinning, C.(2018), ESPN *Thematic Report on Challenges in long-term care, United Kingdom, European Social Policy Network (ESPN)*. Brussels: European Commission.

Saraceno, C. (2004). De-familization or re-familization? Trends in income tested family benefits. In T. Knijn and A. Komter (eds.), *Solidarity between the sexes and the generations: Transformations in Europe* (pp. 68–88). Cheltenham: Edward Elgar.

Spasova, S., Baeten, R., Coster, S., Ghailani, D., Peña-Casas, R. and Vanhercke, B. (2018). *Challenges in long-term care in Europe. A study of national policies. European Social Policy Network (ESPN).* Brussels: European Commission.

Taylor-Gooby, P. (2008). The new welfare state settlement in Europe. *European Societies*, 10(1), 3–24.

Torella, E. Caracciolo di and Masselot A. (2010). *Reconciling Work and Family Life in EU Law and Policy.* New York: Palgrave Macmillan.

World Health Organisation (WHO). (2016). *Integrated care models: An overview.* Working document. Copenhagen: WHO.

13

INDUSTRIAL RELATIONS AND INEQUALITY IN THE EU

Gerhard Bosch

13.1 INTRODUCTION

During the past several decades, income inequality in most countries belonging to the Organisation for Economic Cooperation and Development (OECD) has increased significantly. In some countries the inequality is now as high as it is was before World War I, and the trend shows no sign of reversing. Such high levels of inequality are not only incompatible with widely held norms of social justice and equality of opportunity; they also reduce economic growth substantially because demand and productivity are declining and an increasing number of poor people are no longer able to invest in their skills and the education of their children (Wilkinson, 2005).

Research has shown that the level of inclusiveness of the wage-setting system is the main factor in explaining the inequality of market incomes for dependent employees, under and above the median wage level. By contrast, inclusive systems allow workplace negotiations to be managed collectively by employees with varying degrees of bargaining power. The agreed terms are then made universal for all employees working in that particular company or industry or for the overall economy. If these agreements are to achieve macroeconomic distributional effects, they have to be implemented at an industry-wide or national level.

In exclusive wage-setting systems, employees with strong bargaining power negotiate only the terms of their own wages and social security benefits, which means that the outcomes of their negotiations have no bearing on the wages and benefits of those employees with less bargaining power, thus fuelling the

Gerhard Bosch, *Industrial Relations and Inequality in the EU* In: *Europe's Income, Wealth, Consumption, and Inequality*. Edited by: Georg Fischer and Robert Strauss, Oxford University Press (2021). © Oxford University Press.
DOI: 10.1093/oso/9780197545706.003.0013

social divide between well-paid and poorly paid employees. On the other hand, company bargaining at the company level has only limited aggregate impact. It is therefore unsurprising that the only systems that actually reduce income inequality are coordinated wage-setting systems with a higher coverage by collective agreements (Bosch et al., 2010).

Skills, productivity, gender, ethnicity, national origin, and other factors all play a role in explaining differences in wages paid across industry and occupation, but I concentrate here on institutions of industrial relations that are explicitly designed to determine what workers earn. The most important of these institutions in most European countries is the national system of collective bargaining. The national minimum wage is probably the next most important national pay-setting institution and is particularly important in countries where collective bargaining is limited in its reach. I also stress that a largely unregulated competitive labor market is a key pay-setting institution, with important implications for the prevalence of low-wage work, particularly in the absence of strong collective bargaining or a binding national minimum wage. Two less obvious pay-setting institutions are nonstandard work arrangements (such as part-time, posted, and temporary work) and product-market regulations. The many complex and evolving forms of nonstandard work arrangements grant different rights and responsibilities to firms and workers, frequently shifting the relative bargaining power of employers and employees, with direct effects on low-wage work. Efforts to open product markets to national and international competition often increase competitive pressures on national workers, especially by putting national workers in direct competition with workers from other countries.

The social partners' influence on the distribution process depends on their strategic capacities, their power resources (Korpi, 2006), and their ability to use them strategically and effectively (Lèvesque and Murray, 2010). These power resources result from the social partners' organizational and institutional powers. The term 'organizational power' denotes the specific power resources that can be mobilized during distribution disputes, examples of which include level of membership, financial reserves, and also the narrative resources available to persuade large sections of the companies that the central demands of the negotiation are beneficial. The power resources that are guaranteed by law are also embedded in the employment system's central institutions, which emerged from historical compromises between labour and capital. The German sociologist Theodor Geiger described the development of inclusive wage setting systems in many European welfare states after World War II as early as 1949, as the 'institutionalization of the class struggle'. Its function was to turn those aspects of the struggle that threatened the system into procedures that could be controlled, thereby depoliticizing the process (Geiger, 1949).

In the recent decades, we can observe a process of 'deinstitutionalization' of the former inclusive wage systems in many European countries. Streeck and Thelen (2005) underlined that institutional change can take place in very different forms.

Displacement by removal of existing institutions is clearly the most obvious form of institutional change. But there are other more subtle forms. *Layering* refers to the process of attaching new institutions to existing institutions, which may change their functioning. Cross-border posting of workers is a good example of layering in the European Union (EU). *Drift* describes a situation where institutions lose their impact because they fail to adjust to a changing environment. Examples are outdated collective agreements that are not modernized by the social partners. *Exhaustion* refers to new forms of behaviour or new strategies by main actors which undermine institutions. Noncompliance with collective agreements or using exit options that delocate jobs in non-covered companies are good examples. This typology helps to us understand that a straightforward deregulation of inclusive wage systems is important but is only one form among many that can weaken inclusive wage systems.

Because of differing traditions and system, EU Member States reserved their right from the outset to regulate their industrial relations themselves. Major changes to industrial relation systems like the Hartz laws in Germany and the UK Thatcher reforms in the 1980s were decided upon at a national level.

The European Union had only limited powers to strengthen social rights. Until the 1990s and the early 2000s, however, it used its limited room to manoeuvre effectively. Examples include the EU directive on European works councils, the working time directive, and the directives on the equal treatment of part-time and temporary agency workers. This last directive, when compared with the legally possible unequal treatment of precarious work forms in other parts of the world (e.g., the United States, Canada, or Japan) is a major achievement. This situation began to change, however, with an increasing number of cross-border postings that led to open conflict between freedom of competition in the EU's expanded market and the territorial principle that governs the organization of national labour markets and welfare systems. A number of judgments by the European Court of Justice (ECJ), known as the *Laval Quartet*, restrict the freedom of nation states to organize industrial relations in their territories. It is true that the EU's posted workers directive explicitly enables Member States to lay down minimum terms and conditions of employment for posted foreign workers. However, these had to be 'proportional'; that is to say, not anti-competitive. Moreover, specification of the minimum conditions was made subject to certain formal requirements, such as the extension of collective agreements, which had not been the practice in all Member States for a long time. Monti wrote that this indirect extension of EU competence into the hitherto protected sphere of industrial relations had the potential 'to alienate from the single market and the EU a segment of public opinion, workers' movements and trade unions, which has been over time a key supporter of economic integration' (Monti, 2010: 68).

The direct interventions in the national wage and welfare systems of those countries that were under risk of default on their financial liabilities following the financial crisis and that had to apply for loans also contributed to this alienation.

The so-called *Troika* or *Institutions* coordinated by the Euro-Group, including the European Commission, the International Monetary Fund (IMF), the Euro Rescue Fund, and the European Central Bank, demanded that, in order to restore their creditworthiness, Portugal, Spain, Greece, and Romania should, among other things, cut minimum wages, deregulate collectively agreed wage rates, and radically reduce welfare benefits. Precisely those social policy institutions—modelled on the welfare systems of other EU Member States—that had been introduced in these countries after the end of their various dictatorships were weakened or dismantled. As a consequence, income inequality in these countries has increased significantly.

Many observers believe that 2017 saw an about-face after the Member States agreed on the European Pillar of Social Rights, which is built on 20 key principles. These include the right of employees 'to fair wages that provide a decent standard of living', which is enshrined in Principle 6. It was hoped that these pillars would be followed by legislation at the EU and national levels and that the pillars might be used as reference in the ECJ or in future Memorandi of Understanding (MoU). It is fair to say that the pillars already helped to initiate a number of new legislative actions in the labour field, thus ending the de facto legal stand-still mentioned earlier. The most important is the 2018 Revision of the Posting of Workers Directive (2018) which established the principle of equal pay for posted workers from the first day on.

My purpose in this chapter is to examine in greater detail the pillar of the European social model that has been most seriously damaged in the past two decades, namely industrial relations (Vaughan-Whitehead, 2015, 2019). Industrial relations include negotiations on working and employment conditions between employers and employers' associations, on the one hand, and negotiations among employees and/or their collective representatives, the trade unions, on the other. The object of these negotiations is essentially market incomes (i.e., primary distribution). Market incomes include, in addition to wages, other improvements to employment conditions that incur costs, such as company benefits or reductions in working time with wage compensation. In many countries, the state acting alone or in conjunction with the social partners is a key actor in industrial relations. If the social partners are too weak, the state can become the dominant actor in the regulation of working and employment conditions.

The chapter begins with a summary, based on a number of key indicators, of the evolution of industrial relations in Europe (Section 13.2). The fundamental importance of the primary distribution of income through minimum wages and collective agreements, two of the key wage-setting and industrial relations institutions, is then explained (Section 13.3). In Section 13.4, an example of the interactions between minimum and collectively agreed wages is used to develop a typology of the various wage-setting 'architectures' in the European Union. In a *monetary union* the debate on the appropriate wage policy cannot be conducted on a country-by-country basis because wage moderation or expansive wage increases can have both positive and negative effects on other countries. Finally, the interventions by nation states and the Troika in collective bargaining systems will be investigated using examples from several Member States (Section 13.5).

13.2 THE EVOLUTION OF INDUSTRIAL RELATIONS IN THE EU: AN OVERVIEW

For a long time it was taken for granted in the European Union that working and employment conditions for the majority of employees would be determined by collective agreements negotiated between social partners. This has clearly changed in recent decades. In many EU Member States, trade unions have seen membership numbers dwindle, in some cases dramatically so. As a result, they have also in many cases lost the power to force employers to the negotiating table, if necessary through industrial action. Membership losses were particularly heavy between 2000 and 2016 in Central and Eastern Europe (Figure 13.1). The variability of trade union membership in the European Union has increased significantly. Union density ranges from just 4.5% in Estonia to more than 65% in Sweden, Denmark, and Finland.

The literature agrees that the declining bargaining power of unions in an increasingly globalized world, the increasing number of exit options for employers, and the lack of institutional help by the state or even the proactive displacement of labour market institutions (see Section 13.5) that help unions to organize

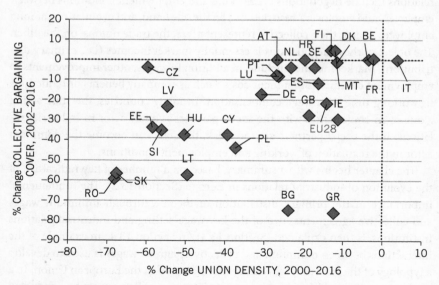

Figure 13.1 Change in trade union density and collective bargaining (2000–2016).
Source: Vaughn-Whitehead/Vazquez-Alvarez 2019: 22.

and mobilize employees are contributing most to the decline of trade unions density. With the threat of delocating production in another country or even within a country in companies which are not covered by a collective agreement, employers are in a strong position to undermine existing wage setting institutions without formally changing the rules (exhaustion). The increasing number of nonstandards forms of work with different regulations (layering) and the fragmentation of formerly vertically integrated companies in many independent legal units create so-called 'fissured workplaces' (Weil, 2014) which facilitate trade union busting or avoidance. Unions often face nearly insurmountable barriers to organize the fragmented workforce in such workplaces especially if the employer is a multinational company with a coordinated and powerful anti-union policy like McDonalds or Amazon. The increasing fragmentation of the workforce is one of the main reasons why unions are weak where they are most needed.

Trade union density currently exceeds 50% only in those countries in which the state sets high incentives to join a union. This is the case in those countries with so-called *Ghent systems* (Denmark, Finland, Sweden, and Belgium), in which trade unions administer the unemployment insurance funds.

In addition to these main reasons, other factors play a role. Political splits may weaken trade unions, and history is full of missed opportunities because unions were caught in their past. The British unions, in an overestimation of their own strength, for example did not sufficiently support the proposals of the Bullock Report to introduce employee representation in company boards (Creighton, 1977) and are today (with the exception of European works councils) without company representation. Also in an overestimation of their own strength, in the 1990s German unions did not demand an extension of their collective agreements in the public services which were opened through EU directives for private providers. The former 100% coverage by collective agreements in most of these industries (waste, postal services, public transport, etc.) has declined substantially, and, in the extremely competitive markets, unions were often not able to organize members in new provider companies. But in spite of these missing opportunities—which, by the way, are also missed opportunities for their respective governments—one cannot blame only the unions for their declining membership (Dromey, 2018). Strong unions and a strong social partnership require institutional help from the state (Bosch and Weinkopf, 2017).

Trade unions' organizational weakness can to some extent be compensated for by institutional power. One important instrument in this regard is the extension of collective agreements to all employees and employers in the sector in question and the protection of collective agreements by the so-called *favourability principle*, which prohibits the undercutting of collective agreements or permits it only with the agreement of the social partners via 'opening' or derogation clauses. It can clearly be seen that those countries with high trade union densities are able through their own efforts to ensure a high level of collective bargaining coverage. In those countries with a trade union density of 40%, the correlation between collective bargaining coverage and trade union density can no longer be observed since institutional power here is highly variable. In most Eastern and Central European countries, the state supports collective bargaining coverage only in individual cases, so that coverage and trade union density are similarly low. In other countries, such as France, Spain, and the Netherlands, the practice of extending collective agreements is the rule or in such widespread use that collective bargaining coverage is considerably higher than union density (Figure 13.2).

Finally, collective bargaining coverage can also be protected by companies' membership in employers' associations. Only in Austria are companies obliged to be members of a chamber of commerce, with the result that collective bargaining coverage is nearly 100%. Voluntary membership of an employers' association is generally high in those countries in which trade unions are also strong or collective agreements are extended. Companies in these countries have an interest in maintaining collective representation and participation in negotiations since they ultimately have to comply with the resultant collective agreements. Furthermore, they rely on assistance from the employers' associations to implement and interpret the agreements. When trade union density and collective agreement coverage are low, on the other hand, employers lose interest in belonging to an employers' association since they are able to determine employment conditions themselves within the legal framework. In cases of dispute, they prefer to have recourse to specialist law firms, as has long been customary in the English-speaking countries. However, when employers' associations not

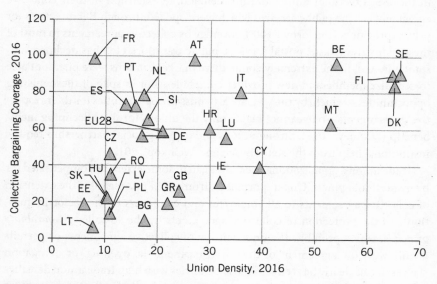

Figure 13.2 Collective bargaining coverage and trade union density in the EU (2016)
Source: Vaughn-Whitehead/Vazquez-Alvarez 2019: 21.

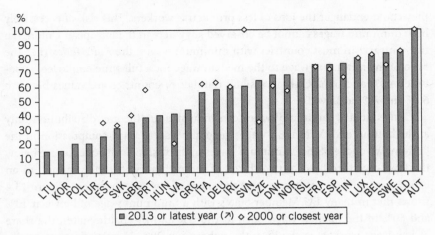

Figure 13.3 Employer organization density.
Source: OECD (2017: figure 4.4).

only take part in collective bargaining but also act as lobbying organizations representing business interests, companies' interest in membership may increase, regardless of the state of industrial relations. It is precisely this interest generated by the dual function of many employers' associations that seems to explain why they are more stable than trade unions (Brandl and Lehr, 2016) (Figure 13.3).

All things considered, it can be stated that trade unions have lost a considerable amount of organizational power in recent decades and that collective agreement coverage has also declined in most countries. Only in countries in which the unions enjoy considerable organizational power or where coverage is strengthened institutionally by the state has collective bargaining coverage remained high. As a result, the labour markets in EU Member States have become more diverse. In a growing number of countries—particularly in Central and Eastern Europe and in the UK and Ireland—wages are largely determined unilaterally by employers. This development is the most important factor in explaining the growing wage inequality prior to state redistribution (Salverda and Mayhew, 2009; Sniekers, 2010). For this reason, the next section investigates the important role of minimum and collectively agreed wages in reducing inequality.

13.3 MINIMUM WAGES, COLLECTIVE AGREEMENTS, AND SOCIAL INEQUALITY

Minimum wages and collective agreements are two of the most effective instruments for influencing market incomes. Minimum wages set lower limits on pay rates, which prevent wages from plunging downwards. Since they generally apply to all or at least most employees, they cannot be set too high, otherwise they could endanger the jobs of less productive workers. This risk of excessively high minimum wages cannot be observed anywhere in the European Union. On the contrary! In most countries with minimum wages, the *Kaitz Index* (i.e., the ratio of the minimum wage to the median wage for a full-time employee) is between 40% and 60%. Only in a small number of countries are values between 60% and 70% achieved.

Consequently, minimum wages can influence the income distribution only at the bottom end. Minimum wages generally lead to wage compression in the bottom two deciles. Since minimum wages in the vast majority of cases are below the low-wage threshold of two-thirds of the median wage, they cannot, as an isolated instrument, usually reduce the share of low-wage workers. Figure 13.4 shows that in many EU Member States with a minimum wage of between 40% and 60% of the median wage, such as the UK and the Baltic States, the share of low-wage workers is significantly higher than 20%. Nevertheless, a correlation, albeit a weak one, between the level of the minimum wage and the share of low-wage workers can be observed, which is a consequence of so-called ripple effects or a high level of collective agreement coverage, which will be investigated shortly.

The correlation between collective agreement coverage and the share of low-wage earners is significantly stronger. This is hardly surprising since differentiated pay grids are negotiated in collective agreements. As a result, skilled employees, employees with particularly heavy workloads, or those with management responsibilities are paid considerably more than the minimum

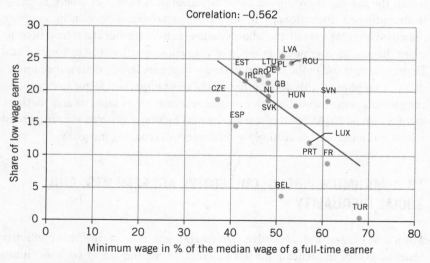

Figure 13.4 Correlation between the level of minimum wages and the share of low wage earners (EU and Turkey, 2014).
Source: Eurostat, Lübker and Schulten (2018), author's calculations.

wage. Unfortunately there is as yet no international comparative research on the relative level of the highest collectively agreed rates of remuneration that would capture the varying degrees of influence that collective agreements exert on the distribution of market incomes. In most countries with high levels of collective agreement coverage, their influence reaches into the middle of the income distribution, and, in a few cases, such as the German public services, even into the upper reaches of the distribution (Figure 13.5). However, this cannot explain the prodigious increases in the salaries of top managers, which are negotiated individually.

It is argued in mainstream economics that both minimum and collectively agreed wages restrict wage flexibility and prevent wages from rapidly adjusting to the equilibrium level in the event of high unemployment or external shocks, such as the financial crisis. In the general equilibrium model, with perfect competition, high unemployment is seen as a consequence of institutional rigidities in the labour market that have to be eliminated.

In so far as economics is understood not as a substitute religion that is immune to facts but as an empirical science, it will soon be agreed that the explanatory power of the theoretical model must be tested empirically. Recent research on minimum wages, the results of which have been summarized in several meta-studies (see, e.g., Belman and Wolfson, 2014; Doucouliagos and Stanley, 2009; Dube et al., 2010), has shown that minimum wages do not have a statistically significant negative effect on employment. These recent research results and comparable results from the evaluation of minimum wages in eight industries dispelled the German government's fear that the introduction of a statutory minimum wage could lead to dramatic job losses, as most established

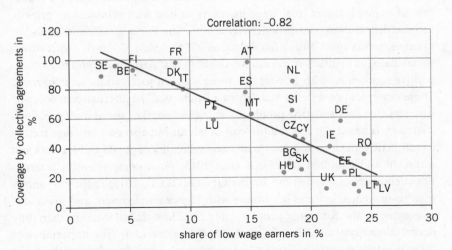

Figure 13.5 Correlation between coverage by collective agreements and the share of low wage earners in the EU (2014).
Source: Visser (2016), Eurostat, author's calculations.

German economists maintained in their horror scenarios. The German minimum wage, which came into force in 2015, and the UK minimum wage, introduced in 1998, are both success stories. They have been able to raise wages significantly at the bottom end without any negative effects on employment levels. In Germany, there can also be seen a positive effect towards improving the structure of employment. 'Only so-called mini-jobs (marginal part-time employment) declined noticeably at the start of 2015. Many of these lost mini-jobs were upgraded to regular, socially insured employment' (European Commission, 2018: 28).

There are considerably fewer research results on the employment effects of collective agreements. Evaluation of those effects is also considerably more difficult since collective bargaining leads to agreements not only on a single wage rate but also on a number of very different wage grids and many other topics besides, including working time, codetermination, vocational training, continuing training, additional social benefits, and dismissal protection. The time frame within which the effects of individual settlements make themselves felt also varies considerably. Wage increases have a more or less immediate effect, whereas agreements on codetermination, vocational training, and continuing training usually bear fruit only in the long term. And since negotiations are often conducted on packages of different topics, the tradeoffs (i.e., the mutual concessions made by both sides) have also to be taken into account.

The most recent studies and reviews of existing empirical studies (ILO, 2016; Hayter and Weinberg, 2011; Braakmann and Brandl, 2016; Eurofound, 2015; Traxler et al., 2001) come to the conclusion that centralized and coordinated wage-setting systems are more effective than fragmented, uncoordinated, and decentralized systems. The main criteria for determining efficacy are the reduction of unemployment, real wage increases in line with productivity growth, income distribution, and productivity effects. The European Commission, for example, writes in its 'Industrial Relations 2014' report: 'Countries with strong social dialogue institutions are among the EU's best performing and most competitive economies, with a better and more resilient social situation than most. These examples point to the viability of a "high road" to international competitiveness that harnesses the problem-solving potential of social dialogue. Such a strategy is based not only on the cost of labour but also on non-wage factors in competitiveness, such as the quality and reliability of goods and services and a trained and educated workforce' (EU, 2015: 7). A comprehensive international comparison carried out by the OECD (OECD, 2018: chapter 3) shows that 'co-ordinated systems are linked with higher employment and lower unemployment, also for young people, women and low-skilled workers, than fully decentralized systems' (Carcillo et al., 2018) (Figure 13.6). The importance of these research results can hardly be exaggerated. They demolish, with all the authority of important international organizations, some of the fundamental articles of faith of neoliberal ideology that the OECD itself, in its 1994 jobs study

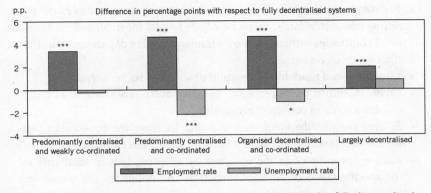

Figure 13.6 Employment and unemployment in coordinated compared to fully decentralized collective bargaining systems.
Note: ***,**,*: statistically significant at the 1,5 and 10% levels, respectively. Results are based on OLS regressions including country and year dummies, collective bargaining coverage, log of average years of education, female employment share and institutional variables: (tax wedge, product market regulation, employment protection legislation (both temporary and permanent), ratio of minimum wage to median wage and gross unemployment benefit replacement rate). p.p.:percentage points. *Source:* OECD estimates. Details on sources and definitions can be found in Chapter 3 of the Employment Outlook 2018.
Source: Carcillo et al. (2018).

(OECD, 1994),[1] and the EU Commission, in the conditions pertaining to deregulation imposed on the debtor countries after the financial crisis, disseminated and which still today form the basis of the conditions that the IMF imposes on borrower countries.

These statistically often highly sophisticated studies on the economic impacts of collective bargaining often do not explain the reasons for the positive outcomes of coordinated wage systems. Country and industry case studies on industrial relations have opened this 'black box' and help us to understand these reasons. Collective agreements with a high coverage

- *Create a level playing field for companies.* They can invest in skills and retain experienced employees by paying decent wages without being undercut by competitors who are not covered by a collective agreement;
- *Direct the competition between companies from wage reductions to improvements of the work organization* and quality of the products or services;

---

1   Thus the OECD recommended, among other things, the following interventions in collective bargaining: 'The practice of administrative extension of agreements which impose inflexible conditions should be phased out. . . . Introducing "opening clauses", which allow higher-level collective agreements to be renegotiated at a lower-level' (OECD, 1994: Part 3b).

- *Reduce transaction costs for companies in creating accepted procedures for setting labour standards.* This is especially helpful for small and medium-sized companies without their own human resource departments and/or tight financial resources;
- *Establish social peace* by the creation of accepted social norms;
- *Create incentives for employers to join employers' organizations* in order to have a voice in collective bargaining;
- *Enlarge the distributional coalitions* and increase the probability that macro-effects on employment and inflation are taken into account;
- *Reduce bureaucracy in the economy* by adapting labour standards to the specific needs of different industries and unburden the state from interventions in wage setting;
- *Extend the scope and the time horizon of collective bargaining.* This supports negotiations on new issues like skill improvement, innovation, or productivity growth;
- *May help to reduce the gender pay gap* if the social partners agree on this issue and proactively undertake joint efforts to reduce this gap.

Whether these potential benefits of collective bargaining are actually realized depends, of course, on the actors' foresight and willingness to innovate. There is a world of difference between the forward-looking agreements on lifelong learning, skill development, modern management methods, working time flexibility, and equal opportunities in the Scandinavian countries and traditional agreements with their rigid protective regulations. A good example of a forward-looking collective agreement is the 'Industry Agreement 2016–2018' (Industry Agreement, 2016) in Norway, which governs a wide range of working and employment conditions and consists predominantly of procedural arrangements that can be concluded only on the basis of a high level of mutual trust.

In some cases, traditional agreements with rigid regulations also survive because of the weakness of the trade unions. They see themselves forced to stick with the successes of the past because they are no longer in a position to achieve a comparable level of protection in new negotiations (drift). A good example here is the highly variable state of collective bargaining in Germany. In those sectors where the unions are strong, such as in the metalworking and chemical industries and the German Federal Railways, they have been able to negotiate new wage grids with equal pay between manual and white-collar workers and modern collective agreements on training and flexible working times that give employees new options in respect of continuing training and working time and which employers also use to their advantage (Bosch, 2018). In other sectors, such as the retail trade, they cling to wage structures rendered obsolete by new technologies since they fear they would be unable to prevent pay cuts if they entered into such negotiations.

However, besides this conservatism born of weakness, there is also political conservatism. It is increasingly widespread among those companies that are less and less willing to reach a compromise with the unions as they did in the immediate postwar period or after the ending of the dictatorships in Southern Europe. Such conservatism is also found in the trade unions, as in Greece, for example. The trade unions there are closely allied with PASOK and see themselves above all as the political opposition to the government and less as the representatives of workers' interests (Vogiatzoglou, 2018).

Finally, it should be noted that the establishment of trust relations, the agreement of framework conditions that will remain in place over the long term in order to foster economic development and a widening of the range of subjects covered by negotiations, require stable structures and a capacity to act on the part of both partners. Declining trade union density threatens the capacity of the trade unions to take action because they lack the members and the funds to do so. If collective bargaining is also decentralized, they will be hopelessly out of their depth in attempting to coordinate the numerous negotiations taking place at company level—which, of course, is the intention. Consequently, it is scarcely conceivable that working and employment conditions can be sustainably determined through collective bargaining in the absence of stable industry-wide agreements. Political interventions, such as the abolition of the practice of extending collective agreements, which in many countries ensures the stability of industry-wide agreements, have far-reaching consequences for the entire institutional fabric of industrial relations. Brandl and Ibsen (2018) show, in a comparison of 34 industrialized countries that draws on data from 1965 to 2014, that the main factors explaining the positive effects of industrial relations on unemployment and inflation are trust, certainty, and stability. Interventions increase transaction costs for companies and consequently have negative effects in the short term. Such interventions are not purely technical corrections of individual variables in an economic model, which can be reversed at any time and have no far-reaching secondary effects. In fact, they alter power relations in the labour market and usually do so for a long time since it takes considerably longer to build up social institutions than it does to dismantle them. In the following section, the various complex industrial relations structures will be clarified by taking as an example the interactions between minimum wages and collectively agreed wages.

13.4 TYPOLOGY OF THE INTERACTIONS BETWEEN MINIMUM WAGES AND COLLECTIVELY AGREED WAGES

To grasp fully the effects of collective agreements and minimum wages, it is necessary to understand the entire architecture of a country's wage-setting institutions (i.e., the interactions between these two labour market institutions).

It is only in recent years that the effects of minimum wages on wages higher up the wage distribution, the so-called *ripple effects*, have become an object of empirical research. Wicks-Lim (2008) discovered that the effects of increases in the US minimum wage reach into the fourth decile of the wage distribution and that those effects are particularly strong in sectors in which wages are concentrated just above the minimum wage. On the other hand, Stewart (2010) was unable to identify any ripple effects produced by the minimum wage in the UK. His quantitative results are supported by case studies in typical low-wage sectors (Grimshaw, 2010). These show that after increases in the statutory minimum wage the wage differentials between the various categories of employees were not re-established. Stewart even identified negative ripple effects in some sectors, in which the gap between the statutory minimum wage and wages further up the distribution actually narrowed. The reasons for this are to be found in the weakening of the British collective bargaining system and the topping-up of low wages by state subsidies (*in-work benefits*), which reduce employees' incentives to negotiate higher wages.

Research in France has produced quite different results. Koubi and Lhommeau (2007) found that an increase in the minimum wage (SMIC) led to wage increases up to the middle of the income distribution. Gautier (2017) investigated the effects not only on the wages actually paid but also on the collectively agreed pay scales. The ripple effects here are strong up to pay levels of one and half times the minimum wages but then tail off up to levels of twice the minimum wage.

The German research on sectoral minimum wages shows that, in sectors with high shares of skilled workers, increases in the minimum wage have shifted the wage curve in Western Germany upwards, with considerable ripple effects being felt up to a level significantly above the median wage for the sector in question. In Eastern Germany, on the other hand, the wage structure has been compressed (Bosch and Weinkopf, 2012).

Reference is made in wage theories to the significance of so-called *key rates*, which serve as reference points for the wages of other workers (Dunlop, 1957). The wages of employees with better qualifications, longer job tenure, or higher positions in the hierarchy rise when these key rates change within so-called *wage contours*, a term used to denote relatively stable wage structures in industries, occupational groups, or regions (Dunlop, 1957: 131). In the case of the United States in 1957, Dunlop was still able to assume that 'collective bargaining must be taken as the normal case' (125), such that, at that time, he was still equating the wage contours with the wage grid agreed by the social partners. However, as trade union power has weakened and wage-setting has become decentralized and individualized, so the wage contours in many countries have become more informal and, above all, more unstable, so that in OECD countries today the ripple effects not only range from positive to negative but can also change over time.

Authors from countries with low levels of collective agreement coverage and considerable freedom in decision-making at company or establishment level attribute positive ripple effects primarily to employers' desire to maintain internal wage differentials. In order to sustain employee morale, motivation, and productivity, wages for the more highly skilled have to rise as well (Wicks-Lim, 2008: 199; Stewart, 2010: 2). However, this obviously did not deter many companies in the United Kingdom from financing the costs of an increase in the minimum wage by a reduction in the wages of employees higher up the earnings distribution. Since they are not bound by collective agreements, they are able unilaterally to alter the wage structure. Since labour was in plentiful supply because of high unemployment and the simultaneous disintegration of wage structures in rival companies, employers could obviously afford to do this without any terribly negative effects on employee morale. The differing results of the US and UK analyses show how much the ripple effects depend on the particular labour market situation.

The situation in France, where collective agreement coverage is greater than 90%, is quite different. Here, increases in the minimum wage cannot be financed by wage cuts for the more highly paid. On the contrary: increases in the minimum wage in France are the trigger for collective bargaining. Thus in 2016, for example, 89% of the lowest pay grades in the so-called *secteur général*, which comprises a total of 174 separate industries and encompasses the entire service sector, were on the level of the SMIC (DARES, 2017: 371). The figures for other sectors (e.g., metal working and construction) were just as high. When the statutory minimum wage is raised at the end of every year, the social partners in most sectors negotiate new wage rates in the first months of the following year. As a result, the wage grid with its fixed proportions between the various pay scales is raised again to the level of the new SMIC. The high ripple effects in France are hardly surprising since they have actually been institutionalized. Above the collectively agreed wage grid, however, they fall off rapidly since the higher wages tend to be determined by bonuses and individual agreements.

All things considered, the findings just outlined suggest that the interactions between minimum wages and collective agreements are not unvarying but depend rather on the architecture of the wage-setting institutions, the strength and actions of the key actors, and the labour market situation (Grimshaw and Bosch, 2013). Thus the explanations advanced by Wicks-Lim (2008), which are based on efficiency wage theories, must be supplemented by an analysis of the wage-setting institutions and the power relations if the ripple effects, and particularly their various dimensions and stability, are to be properly understood. In companies without collective agreements or strong workplace interest representation, ripple effects are a product solely of management decisions from which not all employees necessarily benefit and which can be reversed if the economic situation changes. It is precisely because of this stabilizing effect that collective agreements are also characterized in neoliberal terminology as 'rigidities' (Gautier, 2017).

On the basis of several comparative country studies (Bosch, Weinkopf et al., 2011; Grimshaw, 2013; Bosch/Weinkopf, 2013a), the following types of interactions between minimum wages and collective agreements can be identified (Figure 13.7):

1. *Direct interaction*: In this type, there is no or only a small gap between the minimum wage and the lowest collectively agreed pay scales. The trade unions are too weak to negotiate wages above the minimum wage in free collective bargaining without state assistance. Every increase in the statutory minimum wage leads to a renegotiation of the collectively agreed wage rates, the lowest of which have to be raised to the level of the minimum wage. Since every increase in the minimum wage shifts the entire collectively agreed wage structure upwards, the ripple effects are strong. A good example of this is France. The high share of employees who are paid at or just slightly above the minimum wage despite very high collective agreement coverage points to a close link. As a consequence, the statutory minimum wage has become highly politicized and the collective bargaining system extends each increase to all employees covered by collective agreements. The close link is firmly institutionalized by the practice of extending industry-wide agreements across virtually the entire country.

2. *Coexistence at arm's length*: In this type, a tradition of free collective bargaining between strong social partners has produced a situation in which the vast majority of collectively agreed wage rates are significantly higher than the minimum wage, and wage bargaining is not

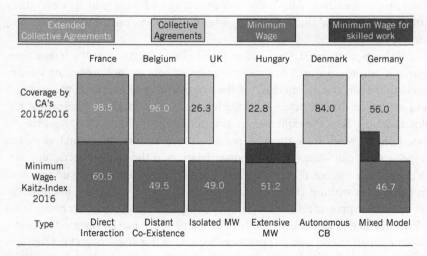

Figure 13.7 Links between minimum wages and collective bargaining: A typology (2015–2016).
Source: Updated and modified version of the typology in Bosch/Weinkopf (2013b).

determined directly by increases in the minimum wage. The lower than average shares of low-wage workers in Belgium are attributable less to the minimum wage than to the high level of collective agreement coverage with collectively negotiated wage rates. In contrast to France, where trade union density is only 7.9% of employees (2015), the Belgian unions, with a density of 54.2% (2015), are strong enough in their own right to negotiate wage rates significantly above the minimum wage even in the lower reaches of the pay scales. High union density is maintained—as in Sweden—by the Ghent system, in which the unemployment insurance funds are managed by the trade unions. And the practice of extending collective agreements means that they apply to virtually all employees.

3. *The isolated minimum wage*: In this type, collective agreement coverage is low since agreements are not extended. Only in the public sector and in a few isolated industries in the private sector (e.g., construction) are industry-level collective agreements with pay grids above the minimum wage still negotiated. Since trade unions in the private sector are very weak, pay is mainly determined unilaterally by employers, who on the whole are concerned solely with efficiency and the labour market situation. When labour is in plentiful supply and workers are largely interchangeable, the ripple effects may even be negative. The most obvious example of this type is in the UK, where the strong industry-level collective agreements that still existed in the private sector in the 1960s have now completely disappeared. After the collapse of industry-level collective bargaining, unions and policymakers have concentrated almost exclusively on raising the statutory minimum wage (Grimshaw, Shepherd et al., 2010). The isolated minimum wage is also the dominant type in Central and Eastern Europe.

4. *Free collective bargaining*: In countries with high collective agreement coverage and trade unions that enjoy considerable power to act independently, statutory minimum wages are rejected as an unwelcome intervention in the collective bargaining system. Since collective agreement coverage is virtually complete, the lowest collectively agreed pay scales function as minimum wages. The Scandinavian countries are examples of this type, even though, following a number of ECJ judgments (Laval, Viking), the comprehensive coverage by collective agreement has now acquired a few cracks around the edges as a result of cross-border postings (Eldring and Alsos, 2012; Bosch/Weinkopf, 2013b). High trade union density (67.2% in Denmark in 2016) and the wide-ranging codetermination rights at establishment and company level, together with the institutionalization of trade union power through the Ghent system, serve to consolidate the unions' bargaining power.

5. *Extensive minimum wage:* When the social partners are weak and collective agreement coverage is low but the government still wishes to put in place wage structures similar to those established through free collective bargaining, then it can differentiate the minimum wage. Hungary is a good example of this type. In 2006, three different minimum wages were introduced; the lowest rate was for semi-skilled and unskilled workers, the intermediate rate for skilled workers, and the highest rate for university graduates. However, the top rate was abolished in 2009 and since then has been merely recommendatory. With the introduction of the two other minimum wages, which remain in force today, Hungary put in place a basic framework for company and collectively agreed wage structures that significantly restrict negative ripple effects for skilled workers (Neumann, 2010). More recently, the minimum wage for skilled workers has been raised even further on several occasions and is now 27% higher than the lower minimum wage[2] (Rödl and Partner, 2016).

6. *Hybrid type:* Germany used to be one of the countries with free collective bargaining and no minimum wage. Until German reunification, collective agreement coverage was 85% (Visser, 2016) and the social partners were able—as they are in Sweden still today—to set effective minimum standards unaided. Collective agreement coverage has now declined to just 55% (WSI Tarifarchiv, 2018). In some sectors, especially in manufacturing, the public services, the energy industry, and banking and insurance, collective agreement coverage remains very high and the old free collective bargaining system continues to function very well. In other sectors, coverage has declined greatly and the social partners are attempting, with government assistance, to set industry-specific standards. The employers' umbrella organization, the Bundesvereinigung der Arbeitgeberverbände/Confederation of German Employers' Associations (BDA), largely rejects the practice of extending collectively agreed wage rates. Consequently, a new solution has been adopted that involves the negotiation of industry-specific minimum wages that can be declared generally binding by the state in accordance with the Posted Workers Act without the agreement of the *Tarifauschuss*, the tripartite committee that negotiates extensions, on which the BDA is represented. As of December 2018, such minimum wages had been agreed in 15 industries at levels higher than the statutory minimum wage. In certain subsectors of the construction industry, a higher minimum wage for skilled workers, like that in Hungary, has been agreed. At €15.79, the highest sectoral minimum

---

2   At the beginning of 2017, the minimum wage for skilled workers was raised by 25%, while the lower minimum wage was increased by only 15%.

wage in 2019, that for teachers with bachelor's degrees and undertaking further training, is €6.60 euros higher than the statutory minimum wage of €9.19 euros. In many service industries in particular, collective agreement coverage has declined sharply. In the large retail and hotel and catering sectors there are still a few segments where workers are covered by collective agreements. In most companies, only the isolated minimum wage still applies.

Using the example of two typical wage curves (Figure 13.8), the distribution effects can be summarized by reference to two of these six types. The wage curve for the United Kingdom in 2014 is characteristic of the *isolated minimum wage* type. The peak of this curve is close to the statutory minimum wage, and high shares of employees are paid a wage close to the minimum wage while the middle income brackets are thinly populated. In the *free collective bargaining* type, which is dominant today in Scandinavia and still prevailed in Germany as recently in 1995, the peak of the income distribution is in the middle and the lower income brackets are thinly populated. Thus the middle income brackets in the primary distribution are constituted not by the market but by collective agreements. Countries in the *coexistence at arm's length* type have similar wage curves to those of countries in the *free collective bargaining* type. In *direct interaction* countries, the middle will be closer to the minimum wage. In Hungary, there will be a second peak above the higher of the two minimum wages before the curve flattens out. In Germany, finally, the middle had flattened out significantly by 2018 because of the erosion of collective agreement coverage.

13.5 POLITICAL INTERVENTIONS IN NATIONAL INDUSTRIAL RELATIONS SYSTEMS

The decline in collective agreement coverage in many European countries that was described in Section 13.2 certainly has many causes. They include the structural shift away from manufacturing towards services and from large, vertically integrated companies to extended value chains with numerous suppliers as well as the growing share of economically active women. As a result, the former bastions of trade union power have lost much of their importance. However, such structural, seemingly politically neutral explanations overlook the possibilities that exist for stabilizing industrial relations by political means, even in times of massive structural change. In countries such as France, Belgium, and the Netherlands, collective agreement coverage is high even in the new service industries because of the practice of extending collective agreements, even though the trade unions' organizational power has declined. In the Scandinavian countries, the trade unions, with institutional support in the shape of the Ghent system and codetermination at establishment and company level, have succeeded

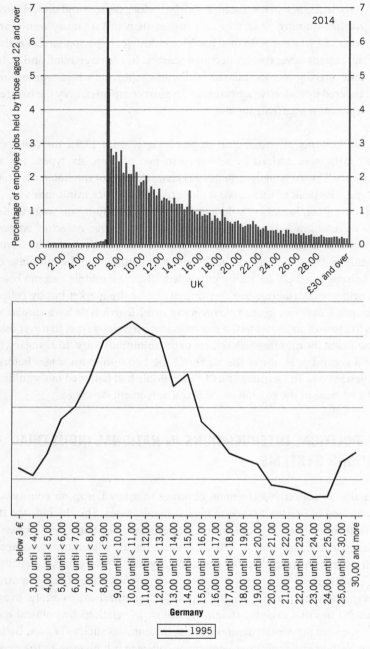

Figure 13.8 Distribution of hourly wages curves in UK (2014) and Germany (1995).
Source: SOEP (2012), author's calculations; Dickens (2015): The Low Pay Commission and the National Minimum Wage. Presentation to NEDLAC, Johannesburg (S.A.).

in organizing workers in the new service industries, including women. In contrast to the rest of Europe, the union membership rate is now actually higher for women than for men since the unions in those countries, with strong support from the state, successfully introduced arrangements to facilitate the reconciliation of paid work and family life considerably earlier than in the other European countries.[3] Most importantly, the majority of economically active women have not remained trapped in precarious part-time work. Rather, as a result of the generous parental and training leave arrangements, part-time work has become a normal episode in a new, more flexible standard employment relationship that enables employees to return to full-time work after parental leave and after further training. The low wage differentials between sectors and between large and small companies resulting from the high level of collective agreement coverage and a solidaristic wages policy,[4] together with the wide-ranging abolition of traditional seniority rules (Anxo et al., 2010), further reduce the risks of a change of employer. Thus high collective agreement coverage is a central pillar of the Scandinavian flexicurity policy (Bekker et al., 2008).

It can certainly with some justification be pointed out that the trade unions in other European countries, as well as employers' associations and governments, clung for too long to the single male breadwinner model and failed to develop a socially just regulatory framework for the new service industries with their high shares of female workers and above-average rates of labour turnover.

However, shifts in political power are the dominant cause of the wholesale collapse of collective agreement coverage. In recent decades, policymakers have seen themselves increasingly less as part of the 'enabling state' that promotes social partnership so that all employees can have a share in productivity gains. In many European countries and also in the European Commission, neoliberal views have become increasingly dominant; influenced by the OECD's Jobs Study (1994), holders of such views have sought to decentralize wage-setting. The EU Directorate-General for Economic and Financial Affairs (DG ECFIN) has unambiguously called for 'employment-friendly reforms' that 'result in an overall reduction of the wage-setting power of trade unions' (European Commission, 2012: 104). Most of the finance ministers in the EURO Group, which together with the IMF coordinated the obligations imposed on the debtor countries, shared this position.

The essence of the new disabling state approach is to deprive trade union bargaining power in collective bargaining systems of its 'institutional anchors'

---

3 Thus, in 2009, 73% of women and 68.5% of men in Denmark were members of a trade union; the figures for Sweden for 2013 were 70.3% and 65.2%, respectively (Visser, 2016).

4 To reduce the gender pay gap and facilitate mobility, the Scandinavian countries have, by adopting a solidaristic wages policy, narrowed the pay gap in recent decades between the manufacturing and service sectors.

(Grimshaw and Lehndorff, 2010). These interventions range from selective adjustments to the complete demolition of the traditional institutional fabric. A number of examples can be cited. Even in the Scandinavian countries, trade union membership is crumbling because governments have in recent years authorized the establishment of private unemployment insurance funds without compulsory trade union membership (e.g., Böckerman and Uusitalo, 2006, Høgedahl and Kongshøj, 2017). In Germany, the European Union's exercises in product market deregulation in the 1990s have drastically reduced the 100% coverage by collective agreement in what were previously purely public services, such as the German Post Office, telecommunications, local transport, German railways, and waste disposal. Private providers not bound by collective agreements quickly won high market shares by paying lower wages, and the previously public providers outsourced many of their activities to sectors not covered by collective agreements or were forced into concession bargaining. The posting of workers on domestic rates of pay to other EU Member States is another element in the deregulation of product markets (Bosch and Weinkopf, 2013b) that can render collective agreements ineffective unless they have been declared generally binding.

The intensification of price competition in deregulated product markets usually leads very quickly to a decline in collective agreement coverage in labour markets without generally binding collective agreements if wages have not been taken out of competition by such agreements or by strong trade unions. This is extremely well known, and the OECD has on several occasions recommended starting with product market deregulation if labour market deregulation is politically unachievable since the two measures are 'complements' (Nicoletti and Scarpetta, 2005). Thus it has stated, for example, that research 'provides evidence that product market deregulation . . . leads to an easing of bargaining institutions, as measured by a decrease in the principal component of union density and union coverage. Thus, from a political economy perspective, product and labour market deregulation can be classified as 'complements'. . . . A related implication is that sequencing reforms to deal first with product markets could make it easier to overcome political opposition to labour market deregulation later on (Fiori et al., 2007: 26–27). The term 'sequencing reforms' describes very well what happened in Germany. The Hartz Acts, which restricted the trade unions' bargaining power by cutting support for the unemployed, deregulating precarious employment forms, and requiring the inclusion of 'opening' or derogation clauses in collective agreements, came into force in 2004, when the service-sector unions in particular had already been hugely weakened by product market deregulation.

In France, Macron initially proposed turning the hierarchy of norms on its head by abolishing the favourability principle. This would have made it possible to conclude company agreements sanctioning departures from any or all of the regulations laid down in industry-wide collective agreements. This would have triggered a stealthy erosion of industry-wide collective agreements, particularly since the French trade unions are much too weak at company level to coordinate these departures from the collective agreements, as IG Metall in Germany has managed to do, at least in medium-sized and larger companies (Haipeter and Lehndorff, 2014). The unions were able, in negotiations held over the summer of 2017, to draw some of the teeth from this draft bill. Nevertheless, temporary departures from the collective agreement have been possible since then in respect of the length of working time and the payment of overtime. Furthermore, divergent agreements can now be negotiated in small and medium-sized companies with employee representatives rather than the trade unions, which gives employers good opportunities to dictate working and employment conditions.[5] It remains to be seen what effects these arrangements will have in practice.

The most radical interventions were initiated by the Troika (aka the 'Institutions'[6]) in the Southern and Eastern European debtor nations (Portugal, Spain, Greece, and Romania) following the financial crisis. In essence, the objective was to reduce wages on the assumption that this would restore these countries' competitiveness and boost exports. Negative effects on domestic demand were not expected. The institutions based their forecasts on very low multiplier effects.

The most obvious interventions were those in Greece. The minimum wage in Greece had previously been freely negotiated by the social partners, and industry-wide collective agreements were extended almost automatically, so that collective agreement coverage was at 83% despite the large number of small and medium-sized enterprises (Karamessini, 2016). The minimum wage was reduced by 22% (and by 32% for young workers) and frozen. Industry-wide collective agreements could no longer be extended. Abolition of the favourability principle enabled employers to withdraw from existing collective agreements and to conclude divergent agreements with so-called 'associations of persons' (i.e., groups of company employees), an arrangement of which employers made extensive use. Furthermore, the after-effect of collective agreements was limited to 3 months in order to force the unions into concessions since they were bound to be afraid of having no agreement at all after 3 months. Collective agreements were to remain in force for 3 years only, which excluded the standard practice across Europe of concluding longer term agreements on the basic framework conditions in an industry, such as the wage grid. In addition, severe limitations were placed on the right to strike, dismissal protection, and other labour laws.

---

5 https://www.journaldunet.fr/management/guide-du-management/ 1165976-loi-travail-2018/

6 The Troika (European Commission, IMF, and European Central Bank) was joined by the euro rescue fund. The Troika thus became a quadriga which, at the request of the Greek government, which did not want the external dictates to be called by Greek names, was named the 'Institutions' instead.

The effects were dramatic. Gross wages fell in a short time by around 24% and collective bargaining collapsed. The Commission for the Review of Greek Labour Market Institutions, nominated by both the Institutions and the Greek government noted: 'The coverage by collective agreements fell sharply from 83% in 2009 to 42% in 2013 with a clear further downward trend. The main drivers for this fall were the abolition of the extension mechanism and the favourability principle which turned around the hierarchy of norms. The number of sectoral agreements dropped from 163 in 2008 to only 12 in 2015' (Expert Group, 2016: 21–22).

It can scarcely be denied that the countries in crisis had, between 2000 and 2008, raised wages considerably more quickly than productivity and that a correction was consequently necessary. However, why an entire well-functioning collective bargaining system is displaced in the process is difficult to understand. A one-off, socially differentiated, and considerably smaller reduction in collectively agreed rates would have sufficed, and, as the Expert Group (2016) suggested, the parties to collective bargaining would have been able to play an important role in reducing social inequality. The result was not, as is usually maintained, the decentralization of collective bargaining but rather its wholesale abolition. The weakened trade unions have no presence in most small and medium-sized enterprises, so employers are able to set wages unilaterally.

How misguided all the basic economic assumptions were can be demonstrated by comparing the forecasts with subsequent developments (Figure 13.9). The drastic cure that was prescribed was unsuccessful since domestic demand collapsed, and, despite the massive reduction in wage costs, exports actually declined slightly, contrary to the assumptions (iAGS, 2018: 18). The IMF's former chief economist has since calculated that the IMF and the European Commission had considerably underestimated the multiplier effects (Blanchard and Leigh, 2013).

It has to added that in spite of much lower wage and unit costs the promised export boom failed to appear. Greek exports have even been declining after the financial crisis, which has partially to do with the high share of shipping exports which suffer from declining freight rates. The OECD explains the sluggish response of Greek exports with its low non-cost-competiveness (OECD, 2016: 13). A successful export strategy seems to require an upgrading of exports through investments in innovation and skills. In a detailed analysis of the export surpluses in the European Union, the European commission came to the conclusion that 'overall there is no evidence that wage developments are at the root of the development' (European Commission, 2012: 91).

Many policy actors now admit that. On 18 February 2018, Jean-Claude Juncker said, for example: 'We have sinned against the dignity of the people of Greece, Portugal, and sometimes Ireland. . . . Everything that's called austerity policy is not necessarily austerity policy. Because often those austerity policies end up being excessive' (see Mody, 2018). The European Commission obviously

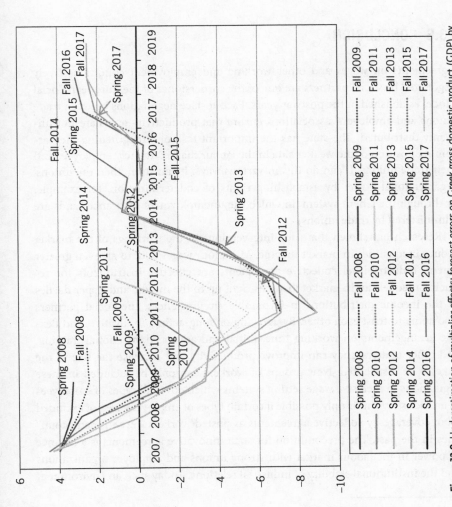

Figure 13.9 Underestimation of multiplier effects: forecast errors on Greek gross domestic product (GDP) by EU Commission.

Source: EU Commission, author's compilation.

no longer objected that the Greek government reintroduced at least a weaker version of the former extension mechanism of collective agreements[7] after the end of direct supervision by the Institutions and until February 2019, 11 collective agreements covering 200,000 employees were extended. The IMF made clear, however, that it would insist on abolishing this regulation again if Greece asks the IMF for credits again.

13.6 CONCLUSION

Agreements on wages and other working and employment conditions freely negotiated by social partners are one of the cornerstones of the European Social Model established in the postwar years. Face-to-face negotiations between trade unions and employers' associations ensure that productivity gains are not unevenly distributed. The state has the important task of strengthening the bargaining position of the weaker side in the labour market, namely employees and their trade unions. It can do this in various ways. It can strengthen the unions' organizational power by establishing rights of codetermination, for example, or through the Ghent system, in which the unemployment insurance funds are administered by trade unions.

Research has shown that such interventions in the workings of the market reduce inequalities in market income. Minimum wages and, to an even greater extent, industry-level collective agreements are effective instruments for reducing inequalities in market incomes right up to the middle and upper deciles of the income distribution. In favourable circumstances, the social partners also come to trust each other. By agreeing on long-acting, innovative, and flexible arrangements on working time, initial and advanced vocational training, and other matters, they can improve productivity and increase the size of the cake to be distributed. New groups of workers can only be included in these regulations in inclusive wage setting systems which cover all types of employees in an industry. This is only possible if certain types of employees are not excluded from coverage by collective agreements as posted workers were in many countries in the past. The precondition for such innovative agreements is a balance of power in the labour market with strong unions and employer organizations and the institutional stability of industrial relations. Today such an environment

---

7   According to this new regulation, collective agreements can only be extended if 50% of the employees of an industry are already covered. If this is the case, it can be checked in real time through a new national database called Ergani. This strict regulation makes extensions extremely difficult, especially in the Greek context with mainly small and medium-sized firms. In these companies, the coverage by collective agreements has been dropped substantially in the past years, and the minimum wage has become the 'going rate'. To establish such a database took the minority vote of two members of the Expert Group. The majority of the members recommended that collective agreements

of institutional stability of industrial relations is only found in a minority of European countries. In many others countries major institutions supporting collective bargaining have been displaced or weakened through incremental forms of institutional change like layering or exhaustion (Streeck and Thelen, 2005).

The OECD has recently provided good evidence that countries in which collective bargaining is coordinated at the industry level have higher employment rates and a lower unemployment rate than do countries in which wage setting is decentralized. Furthermore, it has been demonstrated that minimum wages have no negative employment effects. Also a recent study of the IMF on the impact of different wage-setting procedures found that 'the erosion of labour market institutions in the advanced economies is associated with an increase of income inequality' (Jaumotte and Buitron, 2015: 27). Since fighting inequality is on the agenda of the IMF, the logical conclusions would be supporting higher minimum wages and industry-wide collective agreements.

Contrary to these research findings, many countries and international bodies have tried to reduce trade union influence on wage setting. Labour market institutions that protect wages from direct market influences are still seen as rigidities that have to be eliminated. The British economist Alan Manning (2005: 338) writes that many economists find it difficult even simply to give consideration to the possibility that something such as power imbalances might exist in the labour market and that labour market institutions, such as minimum wages or industry-level collective agreements, do not destroy employment, almost as if they were asked to call into question incontrovertible scientific principles such as the law of gravity.

Only such ideologies, immune as they are to the results of empirical research, can explain the massive interventions in collective bargaining systems in the past two decades at national level and in particular by the Troika at the international level. For the Troika in particular, it was not simply a question of making a few selective corrections for the purpose of internal devaluation but rather of bringing about a total system change: namely, the displacement of the 'institutional anchors' of industry-level collective agreements. Because the trade unions have been weakened, they have been replaced not by decentralized bargaining—as was disarmingly asserted—but rather by unilateral wage-setting by employers. As a result, wages have tended to cluster around the minimum wage, as they have in the United Kingdom (Figure 13.8). The middle income brackets have been

---

should also be extended if there is 'public interest' in extending a collective agreement. A high share of low-wage earners in an industry could be an indicator of a 'public interest'. The Expert Group wrote: 'The extension because of a "public Interest" also follows European best practice to guarantee decent wages in only loosely organized parts of the labor market, in which unions and employers are unable to develop stable industrial relations' (Expert Group, 2016: 41).

thinned out, and the state is unable, via the welfare state (i.e., secondary distribution) to halt the shrinking of the middle class (Vaughn-Whitehead, 2016).

Have the lessons from the Greek drama been learned? Relating to the IMF, Mody is pessimistic, writing: 'The IMF commits the same errors again and again. In the Greek program, the errors were repeated within the course of the long operation even though the evidence was there to behold' (Mody, 2018). At the European level there are some signs of a turn-about, with the declaration of the European Pillar of Social Rights and some legislation ending a long halt in reforms.

The successful campaigns for minimum wages, as that in Germany, are also an important step forward. If there is a genuine desire to combat inequality, however, significantly greater ambition is required. The middle strata of wage earners can be protected only by extending collective agreement coverage. Under present conditions, the trade unions in most countries are too weak to achieve this unaided. The state must therefore extend the practice of declaring collective agreements generally binding to all companies in an industry. In sectors without collective bargaining arrangements, sectoral employment commissions could be set up, as British labour lawyers have proposed; these commissions would negotiate sectoral collective agreements that would be declared generally binding. Trade unions and employers would be represented in equal numbers on these commissions. Additional representatives, of a reinstituted Ministry of Labour in the UK, for example, would be appointed to prevent stalemates (Ewing et al., 2016). After a similar system based on wages councils with seven members, including an official arbitrator, was introduced in Uruguay, collective agreement coverage has been raised in recent years to 96% (Mazzuchi, 2018). As a result, Uruguay has become the South American country with the lowest level of income inequality. If the political will was there, such reforms could also be possible again in Europe.

REFERENCES

Anxo, D., Bosch, G., and Rubery, J. (2010). Shaping the life course: A European perspective. In D. Anxo, G. Bosch, and J. Rubery (eds.), *The welfare state and life transitions: A European perspective* (pp. 1–77). Cheltenham: Elgar.

Belman, D., and Wolfson, P. J. (2014). What does the minimum wage do? Kalamazoo, MI: Upjohn Institute for Employment Research.

Bekker, S., et al. (2008, March/April). Flexicurity: A European approach to labour market policy. *Intereconomics*. doi: 10.1007/s10272-008-0244-0

Blanchard, O., and Leigh, D. (2013). *Growth forecast errors and fiscal multipliers.* Research Department, IMF Working Paper IWP/13/1. Washington, DC: IMF.

Böckerman, P., and Uusitalo, P. (2006). Erosion of the Ghent System and union membership decline: Lessons from Finland. *British Journal of Industrial Relations*, 44(2), 283–303.

Bosch, G. (2018). Social dialogue in Germany. Innovation or erosion? In D. Vaughan-Whitehead (ed.), *Reducing inequalities in Europe. How industrial relations and labour policies can close the gap* (pp. 208–256). Cheltenham: Elgar.

Bosch, G., and Lehndorff, S. (2017). Autonomous bargaining in the shadow of the law: From an enabling towards a disabling state. In D. Grimshaw, C. Fagan, G. Hebson, and I. Tavora (eds.), *Making work more equal. A new labour market segmentation approach*. Manchester: Manchester University Press.

Bosch, G., Mayhew, K., and Gautié, J. (2010). Industrial relations, legal regulations, and wage setting. In J. Gautié and J. Schmitt (eds.), *Low-wage work in the wealthy world* (pp. 147–182). New York: Russell Sage.

Bosch, G., and Weinkopf, C. (2012). *Wirkungen der Mindestlohnregelungen in acht Branchen. Expertise im Auftrag der Abteilung Wirtschafts- und Sozialpolitik der Friedrich-Ebert-Stiftung*. Bonn: FES. WISO Diskurs.

Bosch, G., and Weinkopf, C. (2013a). Wechselwirkungen zwischen Mindest- und Tariflöhnen. *WSI-Mitteilungen*, 66(6), 393–404.

Bosch, G., and Weinkopf, C. (2013b). Transnational labour markets and national wage setting systems in the EU. *Industrial Relations Journal*, 44(1), 2–19.

Bosch, G., and Weinkopf, C. (2017). Reducing wage inequality: The role of the state in improving job quality. Special issue: Making jobs better: Interventions to improve job quality. *Work and Occupations*, 44(1), 68–88.

Braakmann, N., and Brandl, B. (2016). The efficacy of hybrid collective bargaining systems: An analysis of the impact of collective bargaining on company performance in Europe. MPRA Paper 70025. Munich: University Library of Munich.

Brandl, B., and Ibsen, C. L. (2018). Collective wage bargaining and the role of institutional stability: A cross-national comparison of macroeconomic performance. *Cambridge Journal of Economics*. https://doi.org/10.1093/cje/bey041

Brandl, B., and Lehr, A. (2016). The strange non-death of employer and business associations: An analysis of their representativeness and activities in Western European countries. *Economic and Industrial Democracy*, 1–22.

Carcillo, S., Denk, O., and Garnero, A. (2018). OECD Employment Outlook 2018. The role of collective bargaining systems for good labour market performance. LIVE WEBINAR, 4 July 2018. https://www.oecd.org/els/emp/WEBINAR_EMO_CollectiveBargaining.pdf

Creighton, W. B. (1977). The Bullock Report: The coming of the age of democracy. *British Journal of Law and Society*, 4(1), 1–17.

DARES. (2017). *Bilans et rapports: La Négociation Collective en 2016*. Paris: Ministère du Travail, de lEmploi et de la Santé.

Doucouliagos, H., and Stanley, T. D. (2009). Publication selection bias in minimum-wage research: A meta-regression analysis. *British Journal of Industrial Relations, 47*(2), 406–428.

Dromey, J. (2018), Don't blame trade unions for their declining membership. *New Statesman.* https://www.newstatesman.com/politics/staggers/2018/06/don-t-blame-trade-unions-their-declining-membership

Dube, A., Lester, T. W., and Reich, M. (2010). Minimum wage effects across state borders: Estimates using contiguous counties. *Review of Economics and Statistics, 92*(4), 945–964.

Dunlop, J. T. (1957). The task of contemporary wage theory. In G. W. Taylor and F. G. Pierson (eds.), *New concepts in wage determination* (pp. 117–139). New York: McGraw-Hill.

Eldring, L., and Alsos, K. (2012). *European minimum wage: A Nordic outlook.* Fafo-report 2012: 16. Oslo: FAFO.

Ewing, K. D., Hendy, J., and Jones, C. (2016). *A manifesto for labour law: Towards a comprehensive revision of workers rights.* Liverpool: Institute of Employment Rights.

Eurofound. (2015). *Pay in Europe in different wage bargaining regimes.* Luxembourg: Publications Office of the European Union.

European Commission. (2012a). *Labour market developments in Europe 2012, European Economy 5/2012.* Luxembourg: Publications Office of the European Union.

European Commission. (2012b). *Current account surpluses in the EU. European Economy, 9.*

European Commission. (2015). *Industrial Relations 2014.* Luxembourg: European Commission.

European Commission. (2018). *Country report Germany 2018: Including an in-depth review on the prevention and correction of macroeconomic imbalances.* SWD(2018), 204 final. Luxembourg: European Commission.

Expert Group. (2016, 27 September). Recommendations of the Expert Group for the review of Greek labour market. http://www.ieri.es/wp-content/uploads/2016/10/Final-Report-Greece-September-2016.pdf

Fiori, G., Nicoletti, G., Scarpetta, S., and Schiantarelli, F. (2007). *Employment outcomes and the interaction between product and labor market deregulation: Are they substitutes or complements?* IZA DP No. 2770. Bonn: IZA.

Fischer, G. (2018). Social Europe: The Pillar of Social Rights. In: E. Nowotny, D. Ritzberger-Grünwald and Helene Schuberth (eds.), *Structural Reforms for Growth and Cohesion* (pp. 32–45), Cheltenham: Edward Elgar Gautier, E. (2017). *Rigidité des salaires et accords collectifs: Une analyse à partir de données individuelles en France.* DARES Mieux comprendre lévolution des salaires depuis la crise. Comparaisons internationales, Colloque 13.12.2017. Paris:DARES.http://dares.travail-emploi.gouv.fr/dares-etudes-et-statistiques/

colloques-et-appels-a-projets/manifestations-et-colloques/passes/article/
mieux-comprendre-l-evolution-des-salaires-depuis-la-crise-comparaisons

Geiger, T. (1949). *Die Klassengesellschaft in Schmelztiegel.* Cologne: Hagen.

Grimshaw, D. (2010). United Kingdom: Developing a progressive minimum wage in a liberal market economy. In D. Vaughan-Whitehead (ed.), *The minimum wage revisited in the enlarged EU* (pp. 473–508). Cheltenham/Geneva.

Grimshaw, D. (ed.). (2013). *Minimum wages, pay equity, and comparative industrial relations.* New York/London: Routledge.

Grimshaw, D., and Bosch, G. (2013). The intersections between minimum wage and collective bargaining institutions. In D. Grimshaw (ed.), *Minimum wages, pay equity, and comparative industrial relations* (pp. 50–80). New York/London: Routledge.

Grimshaw, D., and Lehndorff, S. (2010). Anchors for job quality: Sectoral systems of employment in the European context. *Work Organisation, Labour and Globalisation*, 4(1), 24–40.

Grimshaw, D., Shepherd, C., and Rubery, J. (2010). *National Report UK. EC project—Minimum wage systems and changing industrial relations in Europe.* http://research.mbs.ac.uk/european-employment/Portals/0/docs/UKReport_000.pdf

Haipeter, T., and Lehndorff, S. (2014). Decentralisation of collective bargaining in Germany: Fragmentation, coordination and revitalization, *Economia & Lavoro*, 48(1), 45–64.

Hayter, S., and Weinberg, B. (2011). Mind the gap: Collective bargaining and wage inequality. In S. Hayter (ed.), *The role of collective bargaining in the global economy: Negotiating for social justice* (pp. 136–186). Cheltenham.

Høgedahl, L., and Kongshøj, K. (2017). New trajectories of unionization in the Nordic Ghent countries: Changing labour market and welfare institutions. *European Journal of Industrial Relations*. https://doi.org/10.1177/0959680116687666

iAGS. (2017). The elusive recovery. Special studies on Greece and Germany. https://www.socialistsanddemocrats.eu/sites/default/files/iAGS%202017%20THE%20ELUSIVE%20RECOVERY%20-%20Special%20studies%20on%20Greece%20and%20Germany%204_1.pdf=

ILO. (2016). *Report evaluating the effects of reforms on collective bargaining in Greece.* Geneva: ILO.

Industry Agreement 2016–2018 (2016). Agreement between the Confederation of Norwegian Enterprise (NHO) and the Federation of Norwegian Industries (Norsk Industri) of the one part and the Norwegian Confederation of Trade Unions (LO) and the Norwegian United Federation of Trade Unions (Fellesforbundet) of the other part. https://www.fellesforbundet.no/globalassets/lonn-og-tariffsaker/overenskomster-2016-2018/industrioverenskomsten-2016-2018-engelsk.pdf

Jaumotte, F., and Buitron, C. O. (2015). *Inequality and labour market institutions.* IMF Staff Discussion Note 15/14. Washington, DC: IMF.

Karamessini, M. (2015). Greece as an international test-case: Economic adjustment through a Troika/state-induced depression and social catastrophe. In S. Lehndorff (ed.), *Divisive integration: The triumph of failed ideas in Europe—revisited* (pp. 95–126). Brussels: European Trade Union Institute.

Korpi, W. (2006). Power resources and employer-centered approaches in explanations of welfare states and varieties of capitalism: Protagonists, consenters, and antagonists. *World Politics, 58*(2), 167–206.

Koubi, M., and Lhommeau, B. (2007). Les effets de diffusion de court terme des hausses du Smic dans les grilles salariales des enterprises de dix salariés ou plus sur la période 2000–2005. Les salaires en France, édition 2007.

Koukiadaki, A., and Kokkinou, C. (2016). Deconstructing the Greek system of industrial relations. *European Journal of Industrial Relations, 19*(4), 295–308.

Lehndorff, S. (ed.). (2012). *A triumph of faled ideas: European models of capitalism in the crisis.* Brussels: ETUI.

Lehndorff, S., Dribbusch, H., and Schulten, T. (eds.). (2018). *Rough waters: European trade unions in a time of crises.* (2nd and updated ed.). Brussels: ETUI.

Lèvesque, C., and Murray, G. (2010). Understanding union power: Resources and capabilities for renewing union capacity. *European Review of Labour and Research, 16*(3), 333–350.

Lübker, M., and Schulten, T. (2018). *WSI-Mindestlohnbericht 2018: Preisentwicklung dämpft reale Lohnzuwächse.* WSI-Mitteilungen 2/2018: 124–131.

Manning, A. (2005). *Monopsony in motion: Imperfect competition in labor markets.* Princeton, NJ: Princeton University Press.

Mazzuchi, G. (2018). *La negociación colectiva en el sector textil vestimenta en Uruguay.* Serie Condiciones de Trabajo y Empleo; no. 96. Geneva: ILO.

Mody, A. (2018, 4 September), The IMF abetted the European Unions subversion of Greek democracy. In Briefings for Brexit. https://briefingsforbrexit.com/the-imf-abetted-the-european-unions-subversion-of-greek-democracy/

Monti, M. (2010). *A new strategy for the single market: At the service of Europe's economy and society.* Report to the President of the European Commission José Manuel Barroso. Brussels: European Commission

Neumann, L. (2010). *National Report Hungary. EC project: Minimum wage systems and changing industrial relations in Europe.* http://research.mbs.ac.uk/european-employment/Portals/0/docs/HungarianReport.pdf

Nicoletti, G., and Scarpetta, S. (2005). *Product market reforms and employment in OECD countries.* OECD Economics Department Working Papers, No. 472. Paris: OECD.

OECD. (1994). *The OECD jobs study: Facts, analysis, strategies.* Paris: OECD.

OECD. (2016). *Economic survey of Greece 2016.* Paris: OECD.

OECD. (2017). *Employment outlook 2017.* Paris: OECD.

OECD. (2018). *Employment outlook 2018*. Paris: OECD.

Rödl and Partner. (2016). Newsletter Ungarn 4/2016. Aktuelles aus den Bereichen Steuern, Recht und Wirtschaft in Ungarn. http://www.roedl.net/fileadmin/user_upload/Documents/Newsletter/Newsletter-Ungarn-4-2016.pdf

Salverda, W., and Mayhew, K. (2009). Capitalist economies and wage inequality. *Oxford Review of Economic Policy, 25*(1), 126–154.

Sniekers, F. (2011). *The changing impact of labour market institutions on earnings inequality: A study of the effects of trade unions and the minimum wage in advanced industrial countries since the 1980s*. Amsterdam: Tinbergen Institute.

Stewart, M. B. (2010). *Individual-level wage changes and spill-over effects of minimum wage increases*. Warwick: University of Warwick/ESRC.

Streeck, W., and Thelen, K. (2005). Introduction: Institutional change in advanced political economies. In W. Streeck and K. Thelen (eds.), *Beyond continuity: Institutional change in advanced political economies* (pp. 1–39). New York: Oxford University Press.

Traxler, F., Blaschke, S., and Kittel, B. (2001). *National labour relations in internationalized markets: A comparative study of institutions, change and performance*. Oxford: Oxford University Press.

Vaughan-Whitehead, D. (ed.). (2015). *The European Social Model in crisis: Is Europe losing its soul?* Cheltenham/Geneva: Edward Elgar and ILO.

Vaughan-Whitehead, D. (ed.). (2016). *Europe's disappearing middle class? Evidence from the world of work*. Cheltenham: Elgar.

Vaughan-Whitehead, D., and Vazquez-Alvarez, R. (2019). Convergence in the EU: What role for industrial relations? In D. Vaughn-Whitehead (ed.), *Industrial relations in Europe*: Fostering equality at work and cross-country convergence (pp 1–34). Cheltenham: Edgar Elgar).

Visser, J. (2016). Institutional characteristics of trade unions, wage setting, state intervention and social pacts (ICTWSS). An international database, Version 5.1. Amsterdam: Amsterdam Institute for Advanced Labour Studies (AIAS).

Vogiatzoglou, M. (2018). Re-paving the path to hell? Greek trade unions amid crisis and austerity. In S. Lehndorff, H. Dribbusch, and T. Schulten (eds.), *Rough waters: European trade unions in a time of crises* (2nd and updated ed.) (pp. 117–134). Brussels: ETUI.

Weil, D. (2014). *The fissured workplace: Why work became so bad for so many and what can be done to improve it*. Cambridge, MA/London.

Wicks-Lim, J. (2008). Mandated wage floors and the wage structure: New estimates of the ripple effects of minimum wage laws. In R. Pollin, M. Brenner, J. Wicks-Lim, and S. Luce. (eds.), *A measure of fairness: The economics of living wages and minimum wages in the United States* (pp. 199–215). Ithaca.

Wilkinson, R. G. (2005). *The impact of inequality*. London: Routledge.

WSI Tarifarchiv. (2018). *Statistik Tarifbindung*. Düsseldorf. https://www.boeckler.de/wsi-tarifarchiv_2257.htm

14

EUROPE'S MIGRATION EXPERIENCE AND ITS EFFECTS ON ECONOMIC INEQUALITY

Martin Guzi, Martin Kahanec, and Magdalena M. Ulceluse

14.1 INTRODUCTION

Economic inequality refers to the disparity of wealth, income, consumption, or other economic variables within or across societies. A certain degree of economic inequality may provide incentives to work and invest in human or social capital and stimulate growth and social progress (Grusky, 2018). However, the literature also shows that high levels of economic inequality within countries hinder productivity and contribute to social problems, including health problems such as obesity, poor educational performance, or violence (Wilkinson and Pickett, 2009; Ravallion, 2014; Chetty et al., 2016). The role of the government has been emphasized in reducing economic inequality and encouraging upward intergenerational social mobility.

Among the various demographic, economic, social, institutional, and political variables affecting economic inequality (Acemoglu et al., 2001; Milanovic, 2011; Piketty, 2014), migration stands out as one that has recently received considerable attention in the political discourse in Europe, but also the United States and other parts of the world. One of the reasons for this attention is that migration changes the composition of the sending and receiving populations, which may affect the competition for jobs and welfare and create winners and losers in the sending and receiving regions, with consequences for economic inequality.

The extent to which economic inequality in the receiving and sending countries is affected by migration depends on a range of factors. One of them is

Martin Guzi, Martin Kahanec, and Magdalena M. Ulceluse, *Europe's Migration Experience and Its Effects on Economic Inequality* In: *Europe's Income, Wealth, Consumption, and Inequality.* Edited by: Georg Fischer and Robert Strauss, Oxford University Press (2021). © Oxford University Press. DOI: 10.1093/oso/9780197545706.003.0014

the selection of migrants: who goes, where to, and when (e.g., whether the migrants are men or women, young or old, skilled or unskilled, or wealthy or poor; whether they go to booming or declining regions, occupations, or industries; and whether they come in good or bad times, and how long they plan to stay). Migration may affect wages or employment in sending and receiving countries because some migrants send remittances to their families left behind. The response of the stayers and natives matters because they may invest in their human capital, change their occupation, and they themselves may move. Migration may also affect governmental policies, such as redistributive policies and access to welfare. Migration may result in technological transfer, trade, or capital flows. The effects of migration also depend on how immigrants integrate in the receiving societies and how the sending and receiving societies adjust to migration.

Understanding the relationships between migration and economic inequality is not only instrumental for the design of migration, economic, and welfare policies, but also for the understanding of the current political and public debates on migration in the European Union (EU). In this effort, it is important to take into account the idiosyncrasies of migration patterns and the changing policy contexts that have characterized the European Union over the past decades.

The COVID-19 pandemic that hit Europe and the world in early 2020, causing many fatalities and a severe health crisis in a number of countries, provides a rare opportunity to study the nexus between migration and inequality because severe restrictions on international migration have been imposed in Europe and elsewhere in response to it. The pandemic provides a natural experiment to enable researchers to identify causal impacts of migration (or the lack of it) on economic inequality. As the data were not yet available when this chapter went to print, however, this opportunity will remain for future research.

This chapter provides the historical context for the past half-century in Europe and the European Union, focusing specifically on the link between migration and economic inequality. It reviews the literature about the migration–inequality nexus from the perspective of both intra- and within-country economic inequality, and it studies the effect of migration on income inequality in receiving societies in a longitudinal analysis of 25 EU countries covering the 2003–2017 period. We document multiple effects of migration on economic inequality within and between countries and suggest that immigration contributes to reducing inequality in receiving countries. Section 14.2 provides the historical context in Europe and the European Union; Section 14.3 presents a conceptual framework of the migration–inequality nexus, recognizing within- and between-country inequality; Section 14.4 empirically analyses this relationship; and Section 14.5 concludes.

14.2 MIGRATION AND INEQUALITY IN THE EU

Human migration has always been an integral part of the European experience. It has affected and responded to the economic, social, and political situations of European societies. The modern era of European migration begins shortly after World War II, when the postwar recovery and strong economic growth resulted in demand for labour that could no longer be satisfied domestically. Countries with a colonial history, such as Belgium, France, the Netherlands, and the United Kingdom, were able to draw on a vast supply of low-skilled labour from their former colonies (Hansen, 2003). The United Kingdom experienced immigration primarily from India, Pakistan, Kenya, and Malaysia; France from Algeria, and later Tunisia and Morocco; Belgium from Congo; and the Netherlands from Indonesia (Van Mol and de Valk, 2016). Several countries, most notably Germany, but also Austria, Belgium, Denmark, Sweden, Switzerland, and to a lesser degree France and the Netherlands, implemented guest worker programmes aimed at providing a supply of much-needed labour. For example, the German government negotiated guest worker programmes with Italy (1955), Greece and Spain (1960), Turkey (1961), Morocco (1963), Portugal (1964), Tunisia (1965), and Yugoslavia (1968) (Hansen, 2003). During this time, migration flows were strongly affected by income inequalities and differences in economic development between the sending and receiving countries. Countries with a flourishing economy, strong labour demand, and high wage levels became attractive for immigrants from countries with high unemployment rates, low wage levels, and stagnating economies (Fassmann and Munz, 1992). Within the source countries, most migrant workers originated from poor agricultural regions with weak labour demand, such as northern Portugal, western Spain, southern Italy, and northern Greece (Bade, 2003). A comparison of gross domestic product (GDP) per capita (in current US dollars) in 1960 documents significant economic inequality between sending and receiving countries. Per capita GDP in the sending countries ranged from US$164 in Morocco; US$360 in Portugal; US$396 in Spain; US$533 in Greece; and US$804 in Italy, compared to US$1,787 in Switzerland; US$1,983 in Sweden; US$1,068 in the Netherlands; US$1,380 in the UK; and US$1,338 in France, representing some of the key receiving countries (World Bank, 2018).

By the early 1970s, 2.0 million foreign workers and 690,000 dependants had entered France, while 2.6 million workers had entered Germany (Castles and Miller, 1998). Migration during this period had mostly positive effects on both sending and receiving countries. For receiving countries, it provided a much-needed labour force to sustain their economic growth, while for sending countries it provided relief from unemployment and strengthened income through remittances (Zimmermann, 2005). In the Mediterranean region, emigration helped to alleviate imbalances and excess supply in the labour market as the region was characterized by low productivity and income and high unemployment (Page Moch, 2003). In Turkey, for example, remittances became a vital source of income (Barou, 2006).

Increasingly large numbers of immigrants and the realization that immigration was becoming permanent, along with the 1973 oil crisis, prompted the receiving countries to stop or severely restrict immigration. Active labour recruitment was effectively stopped in all receiving countries in the early 1970s.[1] Despite this, South–North migration continued through family reunification and later through family formation, particularly among immigrants from non-EU countries such as Turkey or Morocco. Although guest worker programmes were intended to foster temporary migration, return migration was slow (Zaiceva and Zimmermann, 2008). Nevertheless, the abrupt discontinuation of guest worker programmes stymied migration flows in Europe, and the resulting sharp decline in remittances adversely affected or even economically destabilized some of the sending countries (e.g., Turkey) (Barou, 2006).

In the aftermath of the first oil crisis of the early 1970s, Italy, Greece, Spain, and Portugal experienced return migration from former labour-recruiting countries, and, by the 1980s, they had turned into receiving countries for immigration from Africa, Asia, and Latin America (Castles and Miller, 1998). Several factors contributed to this transition from emigration to immigration countries. First, Italy, Spain, and Greece experienced robust economic growth, which, coupled with a population decline, triggered labour shortages. In addition, restrictive immigration policies introduced by Germany and France diverted migrant flows to the emerging southern economies, where migrants found demand for labour and relatively open immigration policies.

Contemporaneously, the level of economic inequality between sending and receiving countries decreased significantly, as evidenced by smaller differences between the levels of GDP per capita in 1988 and those reported earlier for 1960: US\$15,027 in Portugal; US\$18,972 in Greece; US\$20,703 in Spain; and US\$29,294 in Italy, compared to US\$27,925 in the UK; US\$30,658 in France; US\$33,040 in the Netherlands; and US\$36,795 in Sweden. The highest income in 1980 was 2.4 times higher than the lowest income (Sweden vs. Portugal), down from 5.5 times in 1960.

The beginning of the 1990s gave way to new patterns of migration in Europe (Zimmermann, 2005; Van Mol and de Valk, 2016). The fall of the Iron Curtain triggered a wave of East–West migration from Eastern Europe, much of it ethnically driven (e.g., ethnic Germans from Poland and Romania moving to Germany) (OECD, 2001). Ten countries joined the European Union in 2004 (Cyprus, Czechia, Estonia, Hungary, Latvia, Lithuania, Malta, Poland, Slovakia,

---

1 The guest worker programmes were discontinued in 1970 in Switzerland, in 1971 in the UK, in 1972 in France, in 1973 in Germany, and in 1974 in the Benelux countries (Van Mol and Helga de Valk, 2016; Hansen, 2004).

and Slovenia), followed by Bulgaria and Romania in 2007, and Croatia in 2013. These enlargements extended the right of free movement of workers to more than 100 million new EU citizens and led to significant East–West and East–South mobility within the Union (Kahanec and Zimmermann, 2010, 2016; Kahanec, Pytlikova, and Zimmermann, 2016).[2] An additional migration stream of asylum seekers and refugees was driven by conflicts in the former Yugoslavia in the 1990s, Afghanistan and Iraq in the 2000s, and Syria in the 2010s.

As with the previous migration patterns, East–West and East–South European migration after 2000 was motivated by deep economic disparities between the sending and receiving countries. In 2004, Poland's GDP per capita was US$5,632, compared to US$38,813 in the United Kingdom and US$49,678 in Ireland, two of the main destinations for Polish workers. Similarly, in 2007, Romania's GDP per capita of US$8,061 was substantially below the levels in Spain (US$32,460) and Italy (US$38,237), the main migration destinations for Romanians. EU enlargement has triggered large flows of migrants from the Member States that joined the EU in 2004 and 2007 to the incumbent Member States, increasing the total population of citizens from these new members to the old members from about 2.0 million in 2004 to 5.0 million in 2009; these flows gradually declined and stabilized after this period (Kahanec and Zimmermann, 2016).

The economic and financial crisis of the late 2000s, also called the Great Recession, affected some of the peripheral countries more than the rest of the European Union. Figures 14.1 and 14.2 show GDP per capita and unemployment rate trends in the EU countries. Whereas some countries experienced deep recessions followed by sluggish (e.g., Greece and Italy) or more rapid (e.g., Cyprus, Portugal, and Spain) recovery, a number of countries were affected less dramatically and went through just a short period of contraction before returning on the same trend of GDP growth (Germany, Lithuania, Slovakia). Poland was the only EU Member State that did not record a recession during this period. These trends in GDP per capita were, usually with some delay, reflected in the patterns of unemployment in across the Union (Figure 14.2).

A new migration wave emerged from countries such as Greece, Ireland, Italy, Portugal, and Spain (Van Mol and de Valk, 2016). Spain, Ireland, and Greece experienced negative net migration as the size of the emigration flows exceeded that of immigration between 2009/2010–2015 (Eurostat, 2018). During this period, migrants' countries of origin became more varied and intra-EU migration intensified (Eurostat, 2018). A notable development throughout this period is the creation of a dichotomy between EU and non-EU immigration, with each type governed by different sets of policies.

---

2 The so-called *transitional arrangements* enabled the incumbent EU Member States to apply domestic legislation and delay the full implementation of free movement of workers vis-à-vis the new EU citizens for up to 7 years.

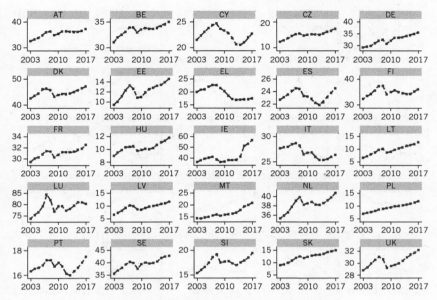

Figure 14.1 Gross domestic product (GDP) per capita trends in the EU.
Constant 2010 prices, EUR in thousands. 2003–2017. AT, Austria; BE, Belgium; CY, Cyprus;
CZ, Czechia; DE, Germany; DK, Denmark; EE, Estonia; EL, Greece; ES, Spain; FI, Finland; FR,
France; HU, Hungary; IE, Ireland; IT, Italy; LT, Lithuania; LU, Luxembourg; LV, Latvia; MT, Malta;
NL, the Netherlands; PL, Poland; PT, Portugal; SE, Sweden; SI, Slovenia; SK, Slovakia; UK, the
United Kingdom.
Source: Eurostat.

The European Union's so-called migration crisis of the mid-2010s
deepened the existing cleavages within and between its Member States with
profound socioeconomic and political consequences. The arrival of an unprecedented number of asylum seekers—more than 1.2 million applications
in Germany, 206,000 in Italy, 200,000 in Hungary, and 191,000 in Sweden in
2015–2016 (Eurostat, 2019b)—led to a polarized political climate, with national interests trumping the efforts for a common EU response. The burden
of receiving and processing asylum requests and caring for refugees was unevenly distributed across Member States, often with the resource-strained
countries like Greece, Italy, or Bulgaria taking a heavier share of the burden.
Immigration became the political and policy issue of the time, not only in
traditional immigration countries, but in new Member States like Hungary,
Poland, Czechia, or Slovakia (Taggart and Szczerbiak, 2018). These states
were reluctant to admit refugees under the EU re-allocation scheme, which
intended to redistribute refugees from Member States of first entrance to
those with comparatively low numbers of refugees. By contrast, Germany
and Sweden pledged to take in a significant number of refugees under relatively generous asylum policies.

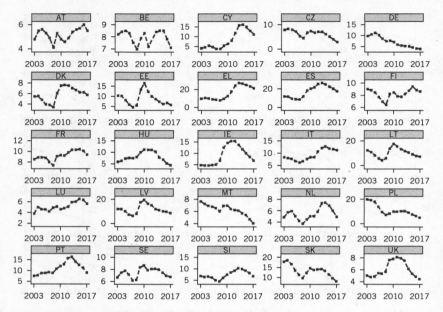

Figure 14.2 Unemployment rates in the European Union.
For 2003–2017. AT, Austria; BE, Belgium; CY, Cyprus; CZ, Czechia; DE, Germany; DK, Denmark; EE, Estonia; EL, Greece; ES, Spain; FI, Finland; FR, France; HU, Hungary; IE, Ireland; IT, Italy; LT, Lithuania; LU, Luxembourg; LV, Latvia; MT, Malta; NL, the Netherlands; PL, Poland; PT, Portugal; SE, Sweden; SI, Slovenia; SK, Slovakia; UK, the United Kingdom.
Source: Eurostat.

The migration crisis came on the heels of the economic and financial crisis of 2008, which had already decreased in the standard of living of many EU citizens, particularly in Southern European countries, and triggered significant intra-EU migration flows even before the European migration crisis (Trenz and Triandafyllidou, 2017; Recchi and Salamońska, 2015). Building upon a growing discontent with policies and the response to the migration crisis in particular, populist parties acceded to political significance in many countries across Europe. In Germany, the Alternative für Deutschland (AfD) gained popularity almost exclusively based on anti-immigration rhetoric. Similar parties include Vlaams Belang in Belgium, the Finns Party in Finland, Front National in France, Fidesz and Jobbik in Hungary, Northern League in Italy, Party for Freedom in the Netherlands, and Law and Justice in Poland. Last, migration became the defining issue in the Leave campaign leading up to the Brexit vote in 2016. Devized as a movement to regain national sovereignty and in which seizing control over migration played a major role, the Leave campaign came on the eve of a migration crisis that created the image of a European Union not capable of handling the situation (Outhwaite, 2019). The recent literature explains that the UK referendum on Brexit was driven by a mix of economic determinants (Arnorsson and Zoega, 2018) including the impact of fiscal austerity (Becker et al., 2017; Alabrese et al.,

2018). Other authors argue that subjective sentimental factors were more important than objective determinants (Eichengreen, Mari, and Thwaites, 2018). In any case, this surge in the popularity and activity of far-right populist parties has signified heated and polarized debates over immigration within and across the EU states and undermined the efforts to respond to the migration crisis and, more generally, to labour mobility.

However, the increasingly anti-immigration political discourse across Europe does not seem to have translated into a seismic shift in citizens' attitudes towards migration. Rather, these attitudes have remained fairly constant over the past decade, even becoming somewhat more positive in some cases. A comparison between the 2002 and 2014 rounds of the European Social Survey (ESS) reveals that in only two countries—Austria and Czechia—have the attitudes towards immigration have become slightly more negative (Heath and Richards, 2016). Overall, the Nordic countries tended to express more positive attitudes towards immigration, while Eastern European countries more negative (Heath and Richards, 2016). The comparison of attitudes towards EU and non-EU immigration between 2014 and 2018 confirm these trends. While the share of very negative attitudes towards non-EU immigrants seems to have decreased over this period, which encompasses the 2015 migration crisis, the share of respondents with a positive attitude has increased. Concerning intra-EU migration, about half of the respondents have a fairly positive attitude, up from about 40% in 2014, with a corresponding decrease in negative attitudes over the same time period. The relative stability of attitudes to migration over time and across countries might just reflect the inertia at the individual and societal levels regarding preferences, social norms, or attitudes. However, it may also be due to the balancing out of opposing forces, cancelling out some of the positive and negative effects on attitudes towards immigrants.

14.3 MIGRATION AND INEQUALITY: WHAT DO WE KNOW?

In its manifold forms and contexts, economic inequality has been a key public policy issue and a central topic in the economic literature (see Milanovic [2011] for a thorough review). The literature points to a complex relationship between economic inequality and migration. Migration changes the composition of the sending and receiving countries' populations in terms of the distribution of social and demographic characteristics, such as skills, gender, and age. Kahanec and Zimmermann (2011, 2014) provide an overview of migration's impacts on economic inequality, modelling the anatomy of the relationship using the Gini coefficient as the measure of inequality. Migrants move with their human capital, sometimes with their welfare benefit entitlements, and usually with a part of their wealth. They make many decisions affecting their social and labour market integration in the receiving countries. Migrants also affect the choices made by other actors, including the natives in the receiving countries (e.g., whether to invest in additional human capital), stayers in the sending countries (e.g., how much labour to supply given the remittances from family members abroad), and firms (e.g., how much, in which location, and in what technology to invest). More broadly, the effects of migration depend on the extent to which immigrants are integrated into the host society's labour market (Kahanec and Zimmermann, 2011). All of this may have consequences for how migration affects both within- and between-country economic inequalities.

14.3.1 Migration and Cross-Country Inequality

The neoclassical economic theory predicts that income differentials trigger migration and that, in the long-run, migration contributes to reducing inequality. Specifically, the theory posits that imbalances in the supply of and demand for labour between countries result in earnings differentials, which drive migration flows from low-wage countries to those with higher wages (Harris and Todaro, 1970). Migration of labour has the potential to improve the efficiency of the allocation of production factors and thus to benefit both the sending and receiving economies (de Haas, 2010; Kahanec and Zimmermann, 2016; Kahanec and Guzi, 2017). The receiving countries gain an additional labour force available to domestic employers while the sending countries benefit from remittances and skills acquired by return migrants. As migration alleviates the initial imbalances and wages converge, the baseline model predicts lower levels of income inequality between countries in the long run.

Going beyond the baseline model, the effects of immigration on wages and employment in the receiving countries have been studied using three main approaches: the *spatial correlations approach*, comparing the impact on natives in regions with high and low immigration; the *skill-based approach*, comparing the impacts of immigration on natives across skill (or occupation) groups using a production function; and a *mixed approach* that exploits immigration both across skill groups and across regions (Dustmann et al., 2016). Under all these approaches, the extent to which migration affects inequality positively or negatively largely depends on the skills of immigrants and, in particular, on whether immigrants and natives are substitutes or complements (Borjas, 2003; Card, 1990; Constant and Massey, 2005; Ottaviano and Peri, 2012; Peri and Sparber, 2009; Peri, 2007; Roy, 1997).[3] These studies, reviewed by Constant (2014) and Peri (2014), mostly find no adverse employment or earnings effects of immigrant inflows on natives at the aggregate level, although some of them find a degree of substitutability and competition among low-skilled workers (typically uneducated, young and inexperienced, or recent immigrants).

---

3   See Figure 14.3 for the skill composition of migration in Europe.

Several studies identify positive income, productivity, and employment effects of immigration in the receiving countries (Constant, 2014; Peri, 2014). A World Bank report (2005) estimates that migration from developing countries increases the labour force of high-income countries by 3%, and the income of natives in high-income countries by 0.4%. This result is supported by Ortega and Peri (2009), who estimate that a 1% increase in immigration raises the total GDP in OECD countries by about 1% without affecting average wages or labour productivity. Felbermayr et al. (2010) use international bilateral migration data for 2000 to provide evidence that an increase in the immigrant population leads to an income gain (per capita) in the receiving economy. D'Amuri and Peri (2014) document a positive effect of immigration on the employment and occupational attainment of natives, especially in countries with more flexible labour market regulation. Cattaneo et al. (2015) find a similar effect on native self-employment. Ottaviano, Peri, and Wright (2013) find evidence that immigration reduces offshoring of jobs. Kahanec and Guzi (2017) and Guzi et al. (2018) show that immigrants in the European Union respond to skill shortages more flexibly than do the natives, putting their skills to use where they are most needed and greasing the receiving countries' labour markets. Kahanec and Pytliková (2017) show positive effects on the employment rate and GDP per capita in the old EU states of immigration from the new EU Member States and mixed effects for immigration from Eastern Partnership countries. These studies suggest that immigration may strengthen the economies of receiving countries and thus cast doubts on the baseline model's implication that migration reduces between-country inequality.

However, there is also evidence of positive effects of out-migration on the per capita income of sending countries. This may occur by means of increased wage growth, the improved employment of stayers, or the positive impact of remittances on economic development. The EU enlargements in 2004 and 2007 led to higher labour mobility within the Union and contributed to increasing wages and decreasing unemployment in the new Member States (Kahanec, 2013; Zaiceva, 2014). Two studies using household survey data by Dustmann, Frattini, and Rosso (2015) and Elsner (2013) show that emigration had a positive effect on the wages of stayers in Poland and Lithuania, respectively. Dustmann et al. (2015) find the largest wage gain for workers with intermediate skills—the group that experienced the largest reduction through emigration in Poland.

The sending countries may benefit from emigration through remittances, technological transfers (Fassio et al., 2019), or trade and capital flows (Kugler and Rapoport, 2005). Remittances, in particular, have been shown to contribute to economic growth (Catrinescu et al., 2009; Glytsos, 2002), thus potentially reducing inequality between countries. Catrinescu et al. (2009) find a positive effect of remittances on economic growth in a dynamic panel data analysis of 162 countries followed over a 34-year period. An important finding is that the extent to which remittances impact economic development depends on the quality of political and economic policies and institutions. Fayissa and Nsiah (2010) show that remittances provide an alternative way to finance investment and help to overcome liquidity constraints in African countries and thus contribute to economic growth. Some studies find a negative correlation between remittances and economic growth. Chami, Fullenkamp, and Jahjah (2005) use data on 113 developing countries over the 1970–1998 period to show the existence of a public moral hazard: the income from remittances reduces the incentives of the receiving household to take up employment, thus reducing overall productivity.

The sending countries are, however, also affected by the loss of population and human capital, referred to as a 'brain drain'. The outflow of skilled workers may leave a developing country in a poverty trap while increasing the productivity of the developed world (Ozden and Schiff, 2006). On the other hand, Mountford (1997) presents a theoretical model of a small open economy with endogenous education decisions to show that the possibility of emigration increases the human capital accumulation which, in the long-run, outweighs the losses incurred by a brain drain. In the same vein, Stark (2004) argues that the behavioural response to the prospect of migration can lead to both a brain drain and a brain gain: as migration rewards those with an education, more individuals are incentivized to get an education, which may stimulate economic development. There are additional effects that may mitigate the negative direct impacts of a brain drain for the sending countries, including higher remittances; positive externalities from the diaspora; return or circular migration channelling experienced, up-skilled professionals back home; and the creation of trans-border investment, business, trade, and knowledge networks fostering economic activity and the transfer of capital, technology, and innovation between sending and receiving countries. Docquier (2006) reviews a large strand of literature focusing on the gains and losses of a brain drain and concludes that the optimal emigration rate of skilled workers that maximizes (both sending and receiving) country gains is between 5% and 10%, whereas emigration of more than 15% of the source population becomes harmful for the country's development. Kahanec (2013) argues that increased migration within the European Union after the 2004 and 2007 enlargements contributed to some gainful 'brain circulation' for the sending countries, although relatively large out-migration from some of the new Member States poses serious risks for their long-run prosperity and public budgets.

Several studies looked at the overall impacts of migration on economic inequality across countries. While international migration is seen as a positive-sum game because it generates income gains at the international level, Sanderson (2013) argues that the gains are highest for wealthier countries. High-income countries boast highly developed technological infrastructures, advanced forms of production, and an educated labour force that enable them to benefit from immigration (Sanderson, 2013). Moreover, in a global labour market, certain countries act as magnets for the highly skilled, which further reinforces their human capital, possibly to the detriment of others (Perrons, 2009). Although the sending countries may benefit as well, their benefits from migration depend on a number of factors such as the nature of migration (temporary, permanent, circular, transnational), the total flow of remittances and their spending, the magnitude and selection of return migration, and the engagement between the diaspora and home region through capital or skill transfers (Perrons, 2009). Kapur and McHale (2009) use a sample of 134 countries to estimate that international migration raises global income per capita by 1% and reduces between-country inequality by 2%. Based on this evidence, whether migration exacerbates or alleviates income inequalities between countries remains an open question.

14.3.2 Migration and Within-Country Inequality

The effects of migration on within-country inequality differ for receiving and sending countries. Empirical studies suggest a U-shaped relationship between migration and inequality in sending countries: migration increases inequality in the short-term and has an equalizing effect once migration networks grow (Mckenzie and Rapoport, 2007). This is because the initial migration is costly and migration networks are not well developed. Thus, migrants tend to be overrepresented from the upper or middle ranges of the wealth distribution of households. In this case, migration increases inequality as households in the upper and middle part of income distribution benefit from the remitted income earned abroad.

Migration networks expand over time, which helps to decrease the cost of migration and improves access to economic resources, thus enabling also poorer individuals to migrate. The benefits of migration are then spread to a broader range of members of society, and the overall impact of migration may reduce inequality. Depending on which part of the income and wealth distributions the migrants originate from, their departure by itself may increase or decrease economic inequality.

There is overwhelming evidence that the country of origin of immigrants matters for their labour and social outcomes in the receiving countries (e.g., Zimmermann, 2005; Chiswick, 1978; Borjas, 1985, 1987). Interestingly, Borjas (1987) finds that immigrants from countries with higher income inequality exhibit less favourable labour market outcomes in the United States. Stark (2006) argues that an important feedback loop works through the selectivity of migrants with different skill levels as a function of inequality in the receiving countries. The basic framework that explains self-selection into immigration is the *Roy model* (see Borjas [1987] for a formalization of the model based on Roy, 1951). The model predicts that high-skilled immigrants are attracted to more unequal countries and low-skilled immigrants are attracted to less unequal countries. Dustmann et al. (2011) present a dynamic Roy model in which skills vary over time, and they show a potential brain gain associated with return migration.

The overall effects of migration on inequality also depend on the effects of immigration on wages. In line with conventional economic thinking, Davies and Wooton (1992) suggest that unskilled immigration is likely to increase income inequality by lowering wages in the low-skill segment of the labour market, while skilled immigration is likely to reduce income inequality by lowering the high-skill wage premium. Kahanec and Zimmermann (2010, 2016) distinguish the effects taking place through the changing skill composition of the labour force and the effects operating through wage adjustment. They argue that the effect of immigration on inequality depends on the skills of the immigrants and the substitutability of labour between immigrants and natives, but also on the distribution of skills in the receiving countries.

To illustrate the changing structure of migration in Europe we calculate the share of skilled immigrants residing in the European Union using the Institute for Employment Research (IAB) brain-drain dataset (Brücker et al., 2013). These data are available for 14 EU countries in 5-year intervals until 2010 and include the number of immigrants residing in each country by educational level. Figure 14.3 documents the increasing share of immigrants with upper secondary and

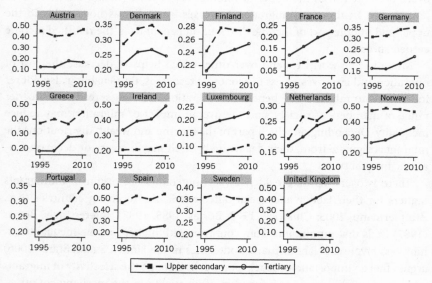

Figure 14.3 The share of immigrants by educational level.
For 1995–2010. The underlying data refer to the total number of foreign-born individuals aged 25 years and older living in a country, distinguished by educational level. The category representing the share of immigrants with lower secondary, primary, and no schooling is omitted from the graph. Data are only available for 14 EU countries in 5-year intervals until 2010.
Source: Authors' calculation based on Brücker et al. (2013).

tertiary education during 1995–2010 in the selected EU countries. Notably, most countries have registered a steep increase in the share of skilled immigrants during the period. One exception is Denmark, where the increasing trend reverted in 2010. Importantly, in 12 of the 14 countries, highly qualified migrants (with upper secondary or tertiary education) comprised the majority of the immigrant population in 2010.

Figure 14.4 reports the varying levels of the Gini coefficient calculated using disposable income. Between 2003 and 2017, inequality has decreased in many countries including Belgium, Czechia, Estonia, Finland, Latvia, Poland, Portugal, Slovakia, and the United Kingdom although inequality increased steeply in Cyprus, Germany, Denmark, France, Luxemburg, Malta, Spain, and Sweden and remained rather flat in Austria, Greece, Hungary, Ireland, Italy, Lithuania, the Netherlands, and Slovenia.

In much of Europe, the Gini is below 30 indicating the relatively low income inequality that is generally attributed to governments' redistribution policies.

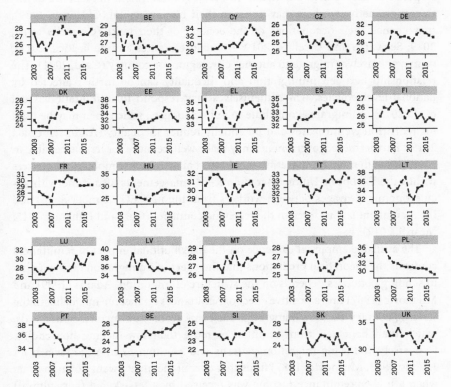

Figure 14.4 Inequality in the EU.
For 2003–2017. The Gini coefficient is calculated based on equalized disposable income.
Source: Authors' calculation based on Eurostat (2019a).

Avram, Levy, and Sutherland (2014) calculate that the redistributive effect of taxes and benefits in the whole EU27 is, on average, around 20 Gini points. The extent of redistribution varies from 11 points in Cyprus to 26.5 points in Belgium, and authors find that the public pensions and income tax schedules are the strongest determinants of redistributive effect.

Comparing migration and inequality in different US cities between 1980 and 2000, Card (2009) proposes that immigration had only a small impact on wage inequality among natives. However, as immigrants are concentrated in the upper and lower tails of skill distribution, Card argues that a larger share of immigrants contributes to higher overall income inequality in the United States. On the other hand, Kahanec and Zimmermann (2014) argue that immigration reduced inequality in the OECD countries. They explain that this effect is caused by the increasing share of skilled workers in the economy (through immigration or the upskilling of natives) that narrows the wage differential between high- and low-skilled workers.

The effect of immigration on inequality is further inflated or deflated by the response of the resident population to the migration influx. In response to immigration, native workers may invest in their human capital (Chiswick, 1989), may change their occupations or the content of their tasks (Giuntella et al., 2019; Sebastian and Ulceluse, 2019; Amuedo-Dorantes and de la Rica, 2011), or may themselves migrate to another city, region, or country (Card, 2001). The relationship between immigration and inequality can be further affected by national-level policies, which themselves may respond to immigration (Guzi et al., 2015). Immigrants contribute to public budgets, which then may be used for redistributive measures and potentially reduce inequality (Andersen et al., 2019). Furthermore, governments may make welfare more (or less) accessible in countries with more immigration (Giulietti et al., 2013). The mobility of workers within the European Union after the recent enlargements also came with socioeconomic cleavages between workers from the new EU Member States and the incumbent labour force in the receiving countries (Guzi and Kahanec, 2015; Meardi, 2012).

The available empirical evidence on the distributional impact of remittances confirms the theoretical predictions that the effect of immigration on inequality in sending countries depends on the structure of migration. Adams (1989) and Milanovic (1987) find a positive effect of remittances on income inequality in the sending country because many migrants came from high-income households, which then benefited from remittances more than low-income households. Conversely, following migration patterns and remittances in Yugoslavia from 1973 to 1983, Milanovic (1987) finds that overall inequality went down in years when a higher remittance income was received by a less-skilled (agricultural) household.

14.4 IMMIGRATION AND ECONOMIC INEQUALITY IN EU MEMBER STATES

14.4.1 Data and Descriptive Statistics

To empirically assess the effects of migration on inequality in the European Union, we construct an unbalanced panel of 25 countries over the 2003–2017 period.[4] The estimation sample includes 311 country-year observations. Our measure of income inequality is the Gini index based on equalized disposable income (Eurostat, 2019a). This measure is calculated based on household income from the EU Statistics on Income and Living Conditions (EU-SILC) that is harmonized and standardized both over time and between countries. To analyse the connection between migration and inequality, we use the migration inflow and stock variables from Eurostat (Eurostat, 2019b). The definition of a migrant is based on foreign citizenship. Unfortunately, statistics on migration are not available for all years and all EU countries, and the data do not permit us to distinguish migration statistics by different origins. To control for a range of possible confounding factors, we further compile data on the GDP per capita, unemployment rate, trade openness (measured as exports plus imports as a share of GDP), inflation, the share of population with tertiary education, and industry structure (employment in the agricultural sector). Table 14.A1 in the Appendix provides the definitions and sources of all the variables.

The basic descriptive statistics of the main variables used in the analysis are reported in Table 14.1 separately for periods before and after the beginning of the Great Recession. Additionally, we split countries by the size of immigrant stock into high (above-median) and low (below-median) groups. The migration variables are expressed per 1,000 population and exhibit large variation in the studied sample. The average annual migration inflow is 0.8% (7.5 per 1,000), and the average share of immigrants in the total population is 6.6%. The countries with high immigrant stocks exhibit larger immigrant inflows, but the rate of growth of the immigrant stocks is relatively faster in low immigrant countries. Countries with higher immigrant stocks have on average a higher GDP per capita and unemployment, lower government expenditures, more educated workforce, higher trade openness, and lower employment in agriculture. Many of the differences between high and low immigrant countries have become narrower in the period

---

4   The sample includes Austria (AT), Belgium (BE), Cyprus (CY), Czech Republic (CZ), Denmark (DK), Estonia (EE), Finland (FI), France (FR), Germany (DE), Greece (EL), Hungary (HU), Ireland (IE), Italy (IT), Latvia (LV), Lithuania (LT), Luxemburg (LU), Malta (MT), Netherlands (NL), Poland (PL), Portugal (PT), Slovakia (SK), Slovenia (SI), Spain (ES), Sweden (SE), and the United Kingdom (GB). We could not include Bulgaria, Croatia, and Romania in the sample due to missing migration data in the Eurostat database.

Table 14.1 Summary statistics for the main variables

Period	2003–2009		2010–2017	
Immigrant stock	High	Low	High	Low
Gini	29.84	30.48	30.88	30.27
Inflow per 1,000	10.6	5.7	9.7	6.5
Stock per 1,000	91.3	40.7	100.3	55.9
Government expenditure	44.4	46.9	45.8	48.6
GDP per capita	10.23	10.04	10.27	10.10
Unemployment rate	9.4	8.0	11.5	8.8
Trade openness	75.4	70.0	87.9	80.8
Tertiary education	25.8	22.6	30.6	29.2
Employment in agriculture	3.8	4.9	3.2	3.8
Inflation	2.2	2.3	1.3	1.5

Countries are split by the size of immigrant stock into high (above-median) and low (below-media) group. Figures are weighted by population size.
Source: Eurostat

after the beginning of the Great Recession. Interestingly income inequality remains very similar in these two groups of countries over time.

14.4.2 The Empirical Framework

The empirical framework is based on a standard dynamic linear panel model that exploits variation within countries over time:

$$gini_{ct} = \beta_1 inflow_{ct-1} + \beta_2 stock_{ct-1} + X_{ct-1}\gamma + \eta_t + \eta_c + \varepsilon_{ct} \text{ (1)}$$

where $gini_{ct}$ measures net income inequality for country c in period t; $inflow_{ct-1}$ and $stock_{ct-1}$ are lagged measures of the annual immigrant inflow and the size of migrant population relative to population size in a country; $X_{ct-1}\gamma$ is a vector of lagged control variables and their corresponding coefficients; η_t and η_c denote a time effect and a time-invariant country-specific fixed effect; and ε_{ct} is an idiosyncratic error term. Including country-fixed effects helps to remove the effect of time-invariant institutional differences that may affect income inequality but do not vary over time during the studied period. All of the explanatory variables are lagged by 1 year to partly alleviate the possible problem of simultaneity. A simultaneity bias could affect our results if a reverse channel of causation was present and inequality was affecting, rather than being driven by, those explanatory variables. Observations are weighted by countries' population size, and standard errors are corrected by applying the Huber and White robust variance estimator.

A particular problem of simultaneity arises with respect to the key explanatory variable, migration flows and stocks. Based on the literature reviewed earlier, it is possible that immigration flows and stocks are endogenous, responding to inequality in receiving countries. We address this endogeneity problem with the instrumental variable, or two-stage least squares (2SLS) approach. A suitable instrumental variable is required to be independent of ε_{ct} in Equation 1, but correlated with the migration variables. We construct instrumental variables based on historical immigration. There is a consensus in the literature that migrant networks facilitate immigration as immigrants are attracted to settle where there are existing networks with the same cultural or linguistic background as themselves (Borjas, 1994; Card, 2001). Therefore, past immigrant inflows are a good predictor of contemporary inflows. We assume that past inflows are not directly correlated with current income inequalities if measured with a sufficient time lag. We use past migration variables with a 4-year lag as instruments.[5] The identification thus rests on the assumption that current inequalities are not affecting past immigration through expectations or serial correlation of the migration variables.

Columns 1 and 2 in Table 14.2 report the ordinary least squares (OLS) estimates from fixed and random effects models. The random effects model emphasizes the importance of modelling heterogeneity using random coefficients and is more efficient than the fixed effects model.[6] Column 3 presents the results from the second stage of the 2SLS regression.[7] The key result of this analysis is that the estimated coefficients consistently show across all three models that migration inflows and immigrants stocks decrease income inequality in the receiving countries. In the 2SLS model, the effect of immigrant stocks remains negative but loses significance. The calculated elasticities based on 2SLS estimates are 0.035 and 0.031 for inflow and stock variables, respectively. This implies, approximately, that a 10% increase in migration inflow decreases the Gini index by 0.3%. As for the other variables, the results are generally consistent with the literature. We find that government spending, openness to trade, and the share of the educated labour force decrease economic inequality, while unemployment and employment in agriculture increase economic inequality. These results are consistent with the previous literature (see, e.g., Kahanec and Zimmermann, 2014; Guzi and Kahanec, 2019).

---

5 The results are practically identical when the inflows lagged by 3 years are used.

6 We run a Hausman test, which confirms that the results of both models are consistent (i.e., the test cannot reject the random effects model).

7 The first-stage regressions (presented in Table 14.A2 in the Appendix) are estimated for each migration variable separately and with the same controls as well as country and year fixed effects as the second stage. The estimated coefficient on the lagged migration variables from the first-stage are significant. The first-stage Cragg–Wald F statistics are equal to 27 and 87, which surpass the value 10 for the test of weak instrument (Stock et al., 2002). We can also reject at the 1% level the null hypotheses of underidentification and weak instruments as proposed by Sanderson and Windmeijer (2016).

Table 14.2 Determinants of income inequality

	RE	FE	2SLS
	(1)	(2)	(3)
Inflow per 1,000	−0.063**	−0.072**	−0.123**
	(0.025)	(0.032)	(0.056)
Stock per 1,000	−0.013*	−0.023**	−0.016
	(0.007)	(0.010)	(0.012)
Government expenditure	−0.175***	−0.138*	−0.148***
	(0.035)	(0.067)	(0.048)
GDP per capita	−38.933**	−27.63	−27.319
	(18.486)	(22.626)	(28.766)
GDP per capita square	2.168**	1.67	1.671
	(0.916)	(1.149)	(1.451)
Unemployment rate	0.146***	0.142***	0.121**
	(0.029)	(0.047)	(0.050)
Trade openness	−5.123***	−5.556**	−5.083**
	(1.021)	(2.193)	(2.313)
Tertiary education	−0.205***	−0.273***	−0.281***
	(0.038)	(0.073)	(0.059)
Employment in agriculture	0.396***	0.525**	0.523**
	(0.144)	(0.205)	(0.214)
Inflation	0.088	0.092	0.11
	(0.074)	(0.124)	(0.079)
Constant	233.6**	176.8	169
	(94.258)	(114.143)	(144.690)
Sample size	311	311	311
R2/Within R2	0.42	0.43	
First stage F–stat (inflow)			27.4
First stage F–stat (stock)			87.3

Estimates from fixed effects (FE), random effects (RE) and two-stage least squares (2SLS) regression analysis. Dependent variable is the Gini index based on equivalized disposable income. Explanatory variables are lagged 1 year and all models include year fixed effects. Observations weighted by population size.
* < 0.10, ** <0.05, *** < 0.01.

Source: Authors' calculations based on data from Eurostat.

We note several limitations to our analysis. First, we employ data on immigration flows from the Eurostat that provides data for only a limited number of countries and for a relatively short period, possibly insufficient to detect long-run effects of immigration on inequality. Additionally, the available data do not allow us to distinguish between different types of flows (e.g., high- vs. low-skilled) or between different countries of origin. Third, our results reflect an aggregate effect across countries and over time. It is possible that the magnitude (and perhaps the direction) of the effect would be different for different (groups of) countries. Nevertheless, this analysis provides an insight into the relationship between immigration and within-country inequality in the context of the European Union, a significant immigrant destination.[8] Future research aimed at distinguishing between, for example, the effects of high- and low-skilled immigration, immigration from different origins, or immigration under different institutional and policy regimes would be needed to shed more light on this complex relationship.

14.5 DISCUSSION AND CONCLUSION

Human migration affects the size and composition of populations in the sending and receiving countries. In consequence, it has an impact on the supply and demand and the nature of competition in their labour markets. Additional effects arise in the markets for goods, services, capital, and technologies. Migration may have further economic impacts through its effects on preferences, social norms, or behaviours and on choices of receiving and sending populations and migrants themselves.

This chapter reviews what we know about the effect of migration on income inequality within and across countries of the European Union. The review of the existing literature suggests that the baseline economic model of migration, which predicts that the international mobility of workers should decrease international wage differentials, does not capture important effects that may in fact work against this prediction. This is not least because labour is heterogeneous, and immigrant workers bring along skills to countries, sectors, and occupations where they are most needed and where they complement the skills possessed by the natives. The receiving countries may also benefit from brain gain and the creation of new trade, investment, and knowledge networks facilitated by immigrants. Hence, immigration provides new economic resources and helps to fill in the bottlenecks and grease the wheels of economic growth and wealth creation in the receiving countries. On the other hand, while the sending countries may lose due to brain drain, they also may benefit from remittances, brain circulation, or the positive effects of out-migration on wages and employment

---

8 As a robustness check, we split the sample into two subperiods. We confirm that estimates from 2SLS regression remain significant in the period after the crisis (2010–2017) while estimates in the pre-crisis period are not significant. Furthermore, we find that the estimates are significant in countries hit less by the financial crisis (when measured by the increase in unemployment after 2009). In our estimations, observations are weighted by countries' population size, so that results are not driven by small countries (e.g., omitting Luxembourg from estimation sample has no impact on our results).

opportunities. The overall net effect of migration on economic inequalities across countries thus remains an open empirical question.

Looking at the effects of migration on within-country economic inequality, the literature establishes that they largely depend on the skill mix of migrants or, more precisely, on migration's impacts on the composition of the labour force in the respective labour market. While high-skilled immigration presents the potential to reduce inequality by lowering the gap between the wages of low- and high-skilled workers in the receiving countries, low-skilled immigration can increase inequality by expanding the supply of low-skilled workers in receiving countries and decreasing their wages or increasing their unemployment. The corresponding opposite effects can be expected for out-migration. Additional effects on the skill composition of workers may arise through the reaction of the incumbent labour force in the receiving labour markets or the stayers in the sending countries, as well as through the effects of remittances and public budgets and redistribution. Several channels of interaction between migration and inequality may be at play simultaneously, and their salience is likely to vary across migration sources, types, and selectivity; economic, demographic, and institutional and policy contexts; and the responses of the receiving society and migrants themselves. The overall net effect of migration on within-country inequality is the composite of these effects and is context-dependent. At the very general level, labour mobility empowers workers and provides them with additional alternatives, which can be expected to increase labour's share in income and, because capital income is more concentrated than labour income, decrease income inequality.

Our own empirical results show that immigration has contributed to reducing inequality within the 25 EU countries over the period analysed. Importantly, as we show that EU Member States have attracted relatively highly qualified immigrants throughout this period, our results are consistent with the ameliorating effect of skilled immigration on within-country inequality, as predicted by theory. This finding has important policy implications for receiving countries that experience an acute need for skilled labour and are increasingly aware of the detrimental effects of inequality for their societies. Specifically, our findings suggest that immigration may be a mechanism that reduces income inequality. By attracting qualified immigrants, receiving societies may satisfy two needs with one deed: respond to the existing demand for skilled labour and reduce economic inequality.

To conclude, migration and inequality interact through a variety of channels, some of which work through the composition of the sending and receiving populations, others through the effects on the nature of competition in the sending and receiving labour markets, and yet others through the effects of migration on business, trade, investment, and innovation patterns. Institutions and policies may affect or intermediate the relationship between migration and inequality. In fact, they may respond to migration; Giulietti et al. (2013) provide some evidence that redistribution policies become more generous in countries that have experienced more immigration. The literature and our own results suggest that immigration may decrease inequality in the receiving EU countries. However, the relationship between migration and economic inequality requires further research to map its complex interactions with various institutional and policy contexts, its dependence on different types of migration, and its origins and destinations. That attitudes towards immigration did not deteriorate and, in fact, might have improved in spite of what is called the European migration crisis, gives hopes that the European Union will be able to reach a compromise over its migration framework that will nurture the benefits from migration and immigration and at the same time win acceptance by its citizens.

The 2020 COVID-19 pandemics and its dire consequences will make reaching these objectives increasingly more complex, but they may also catalyse new innovative approaches to the governance of (global) public goods, including migration and labour mobility. Certainly, it will provide a rare opportunity to study the impacts of migration on economic inequality in a natural experiment setting.

ACKNOWLEDGEMENTS

The authors gratefully acknowledge the support from Slovak Research and Development Agency (grant APVV-15-0765: Inequality and economic growth). Martin Guzi acknowledges the support from the Czech Science Foundation (grant no. 20-31615S). Martin Kahanec very much appreciates the support by his Mercator Fellowship at Bruegel during the final stages of writing this chapter.

REFERENCES

Acemoglu, D., Johnson, S., and Robinson, J. A. (2001). The colonial origins of comparative development: An empirical investigation. *American Economic Review, 91*(5), 1369–1401. https://doi.org/10.1257/aer.91.5.1369

Adams, R. H. (1989). Worker remittances and inequality in rural Egypt. *Economic Development and Cultural Change, 38*(1), 45–71. https://doi.org/10.1086/451775

Alabrese, E., Becker, S. O., Fetzer, T., and Novy, D. (2019). Who voted for Brexit? Individual and regional data combined. *European Journal of Political Economy, 56*, 132–150.

Amuedo-Dorantes, C., and de la Rica, S. (2011). Complements or substitutes? Task specialization by gender and nativity in Spain. *Labour Economics, 18*, 697–707.

Andersen, L. H., Dustmann, C., and Landersø, R. (2019). *Lowering welfare benefits: Intended and unintended consequences for migrants and their families.* The Rockwool Foundation Research Unit. Study Paper No. 138. Copenhagen: Rockwood Foundation.

Arnorsson, A., and Zoega, G. (2018). On the causes of Brexit. *European Journal of Political Economy, 55*, 301–323.

Avram, S., Levy, H., and Sutherland, H. (2014). Income redistribution in the European Union. *IZA Journal of European Labor Studies, 3*(1), 22.

Bade, K. (2003). *Migration in European history.* London: Blackwell Publishing.

Barou, J. (2006). *Europe, Terre d'immigration: Flux Migratoires et Intégration.* Grenoble: Presses Universitaires de Grénoble.

Becker, S. O., Fetzer, T., and Novy, D. (2017). Who voted for Brexit? A comprehensive district-level analysis. *Economic Policy, 32*(92), 601–650.

Borjas, G. J. (1985). Assimilation, changes in cohort quality, and the earnings of immigrants. *Journal of Labor Economics, 3*(4), 463–489. https://doi.org/10.1086/298065

Borjas, G. (1987). Self-selection and the earnings of immigrants. *American Economic Review, 77*, 31–553.

Borjas, G. (1994). Economics of migration. *Journal of Economic Literature, 32*(4), 1667–1717.

Borjas, G. J. (2003). The labor demand curve is downward sloping: Reexamining the impact of immigration on the labor market. *Quarterly Journal of Economics, 118*(4), 1335–1374. https://doi.org/10.1162/003355303322552810

Brücker, H., Capuano, S., and Marfouk, A. (2013). Education, gender and international migration: insights from a panel-dataset 1980–2010. *Methodology Report.* http://doku.iab.de/daten/brain-drain/iabbd_8010_v1_methodology.pdf

Card, D. (1990). The impact of the Mariel Boatlift on the Miami labor market. *ILR Review, 43*(2), 245–257. https://doi.org/10.1177/001979399004300205

Card, D. (2001). Immigrant inflows, native outflows and the local labor market impacts of higher immigration. *Journal of Labor Economics, 90*(2), 360–367.

Card, D. (2009). Immigration and inequality. *American Economic Review, 99*(2), 1–21. https://doi.org/10.1257/aer.99.2.1

Castles, S., and Miller, M. J. (1998). *The age of migration* (2nd ed.). Houndmills, UK: Macmillan.

Catrinescu, N., Leon-Ledesma, M. Matloob Piracha, M., and Quillin, B. (2009). Remittances, institutions, and economic growth. *World Development, 37*(1), 81–92. https://doi.org/10.1016/j.worlddev.2008.02.004

Cattaneo, C., Fiorio, C. V., and Peri, G. (2015). What happens to the careers of European workers when immigrants 'take their jobs'? *Journal of Human Resources, 50*(3), 655–693. https://doi.org/10.3368/jhr.50.3.655

Chami, R., Fullenkamp, C., and Jahjah, S. (2005). Are immigrant remittance flows a source of capital for development? *IMF Staff Papers, 52*(1), 55–81.

Chetty, R., et al. (2016) The association between income and life expectancy in the United States, 2001-2014. *Journal of the Americal Medical Association,* 315(16), 1750–1766.

Chiswick, B. R. (1978). The effect of Americanization on the earnings of foreign-born men. *Journal of Political Economy, 86*(5), 897–921. https://doi.org/10.1086/260717

Chiswick, C. U. (1989). The impact of immigration on the human capital of natives. *Journal of Labor Economics, 7*(4), 464–486. https://doi.org/10.1086/298217

Constant, A. (2014). Do migrants take the jobs of native workers? *IZA World of Labor.* https://doi.org/10.15185/izawol.10

Constant, A., and Massey, D. S. (2005). Labor market segmentation and the earnings of German guestworkers. *Population Research and Policy Review, 24*(5), 489–512. https://doi.org/10.1007/s11113-005-4675-z

D'Amuri, F., and Peri, G. (2014). Immigration, jobs, and employment protection: Evidence from Europe before and during the great recession: Immigration, jobs, and employment protection. *Journal of the European Economic Association, 12*(2), 432–464. https://doi.org/10.1111/jeea.12040

Davies, J. B., and Wooton, I. (1992). Income inequality and international migration. *Economic Journal, 102*(413), 789. https://doi.org/10.2307/2234577

de Haas, H. (2010). Migration and development: A theoretical perspective. *International Migration Review, 44*(1), 227–264.

Docquier, F. (2006). *Brain drain and inequality across nations.* IZA Discussion Paper No. (2440). Bonn: IZA.

Dustmann, C., Fadlon, I., and Weiss, Y. (2011). Return migration, human capital accumulation and the brain drain. *Journal of Development Economics, 95*(1), 58–67. https://doi.org/10.1016/j.jdeveco.2010.04.006

Dustmann, C., Frattini, T., and Rosso, A. (2015). The effect of emigration from Poland on Polish wages. *Scandinavian Journal of Economics, 117*(2), 522–564. https://doi.org/10.1111/sjoe.12102

Dustmann, C., Schönberg, U., and Stuhler, J. (2016). The impact of immigration: Why do studies reach such different results? *Journal of Economic Perspectives, 30*(4), 31–56. https://doi.org/10.1257/jep.30.4.31

Elsner, B. (2013). Does emigration benefit the stayers? Evidence from EU enlargement. *Journal of Population Economics, 26*(2), 531–553. https://doi.org/10.1007/s00148-012-0452-6

Eurostat. (2018). *Demography and migration database.* Luxembourg: Eurostat.

Eurostat. (2019a). *Gini coefficient of equivalised disposable income.* Luxembourg: Eurostat.

Eurostat. (2019b). *International migration statistics.* Luxembourg: Eurostat.

Fassio, C., Montobbio, F., and Venturini, A. (2019). Skilled migration and innovation in European industries. *Research Policy, 48*(3), 706–718. https://doi.
org/10.1016/j.respol.2018.11.002

Fassmann, H., and Munz, R. (1992). Patterns and trends of international migration in Western Europe. *Population and Development Review, 18*(3), 457.
https://doi.org/10.2307/1973654

Fayissa, B., and Nsiah, C. (2010). The impact of remittances on economic growth
and development in Africa. *American Economist, 55*(2), 92–103. https://doi.
org/10.1177/056943451005500210

Felbermayr, G. J., Hiller, S., and Sala, D. (2010). Does immigration boost per
capita income? *Economics Letters, 107*(2), 177–179. https://doi.org/10.1016/
j.econlet.2010.01.017

Giulietti, C., Guzi, M., Kahanec, M., and Zimmermann, K. F. (2013).
Unemployment benefits and immigration: Evidence from the EU. Edited by
Alan Barrett. *International Journal of Manpower, 34*(1), 24–38. https://doi.
org/10.1108/01437721311319638

Giuntella, O., Mazzonna, F., Nicodemo, C., and Vargas-Silva, C. (2019).
Immigration and the reallocation of work health risks. *Journal of Population
Economics, 32*(3), 1009–1042. https://doi.org/10.1007/s00148-018-0710-3

Glytsos, N. P. (2002). The role of migrant remittances in development: Evidence
from Mediterranean countries. *International Migration, 40*(1), 5–26. https://
doi.org/10.1111/1468-2435.00183

Grusky, D. (2018). *The inequality reader: Contemporary and foundational readings
in race, class, and gender* (2nd ed.). Edited by D. B. Grusky and S. Szelényi.
Abingdon, UK: Routledge. https://doi.org/10.4324/9780429494468 Bo

Guzi, M., and Kahanec, M. (2015). Socioeconomic cleavages between workers
from new member states and host-country labour forces in the EU during the
Great Recession. In M. Bernaciak (ed.), *Market expansion and social dumping
in Europe* (pp. 97–121). London: Routledge.

Guzi, M., and Kahanec, M. (2019). *Income inequality and the size of government: A causal analysis.* IZA Discussion Paper No. 12015. Bonn: IZA.

Guzi, M., Kahanec, M., and Kurekova, L. M. (2015). *What explains immigrant-
native gaps in European labor markets: The role of institutions.* IZA DP No.
(8847). Bonn: IZA.

Guzi, M., Kahanec, M., and Kurekova, L. M. (2018). How immigration grease is
affected by economic, institutional, and policy contexts: Evidence from EU
labor markets. *Kyklos, 71*, 213– 243. doi: 10.1111/kykl.12168.

Hansen, R. (2003). Migration to Europe since 1945: Its history and its
lessons. *Political Quarterly, 74*(s1), 25–38. https://doi.org/10.1111/
j.1467-923X.2003.00579.x

Harris, J., and Todaro, M. (1970). Migration, unemployment and development: A
two-sector analysis. *American Economic Review, 60*(1), 126–142.

Heath, A., and Richards, L. (2016). Attitudes towards Immigration and Their Antecedents: Topline Results from Round 7 of the European Social Survey. European Social Survey, http://www.europeansocialsurvey.org/docs/findings/ESS7_toplines_issue_7_immigration.pdf.

Kahanec, M. (2013). Labor mobility in an enlarged European Union. In A. F. Constant and K. F. Zimmerman (eds.), *International handbook on the economics of migration* (pp. 137–152). London: Edward Elgar Publishing.

Kahanec, M., and Guzi, M. (2017). How immigrants helped EU labor markets to adjust during the great recession. *International Journal of Manpower, 38*(7), 996–1015. https://doi.org/10.1108/IJM-08-2017-0205

Kahanec, M., and Pytliková, M. (2017). The economic impact of east–west migration on the European Union. *Empirica, 44*(3), 407–434. https://doi.org/10.1007/s10663-017-9370-x

Kahanec, M., and Zimmermann, K. (2009). International migration, ethnicity and economic inequality. In W. Salverda, B. Nolan, and T. M. Smeeding (eds.), *Oxford handbook on economic inequality* (pp. 455–490). Oxford: Oxford University Press.

Kahanec, M., and Zimmermann, K. (2010). *EU labor markets after post-enlargement migration*. Berlin: Springer.

Kahanec, M., and Zimmermann, K. (2011). *International migration, ethnicity, and economic inequality*. Oxford: Oxford University Press. https://doi.org/10.1093/oxfordhb/9780199606061.013.0019

Kahanec, M., and Zimmermann, K. (2014). How skilled immigration may improve economic equality. *IZA Journal of Migration, 3*(1), 2. https://doi.org/10.1186/2193-9039-3-2

Kahanec, M., Pytlikova, M., and Zimmermann, K. (2016). The free movement of workers in an enlarged European Union: Institutional underpinnings of economic adjustment. In Kahanec, M., and Zimmermann, K. (eds.), *Labor migration, EU enlargement, and the Great Recession*. Berlin: Springer, 1–34.

Kahanec, M., and Zimmermann, K. (2016). *Labor migration, EU Enlargement, and the Great Recession*. Berlin: Springer Berlin Heidelberg.

Kapur, D., and McHale, J. (2009). International migration and the world income distribution. *Journal of International Development, 21*(8), 1102–1110. https://doi.org/10.1002/jid.1649

Kugler, M., and Rapoport, H. (2005). *Skilled migration, business networks and foreign direct investment*. CESifo Working Paper No. (1455). Munich: CESifo.

Mckenzie, D., and Rapoport, H. (2007). Network effects and the dynamics of migration and inequality: Theory and evidence from Mexico. *Journal of Development Economics, 84*(1), 1–24. https://doi.org/10.1016/j.jdeveco.2006.11.003

Meardi, G. (2012). *Social failures of EU enlargement: A case of workers voting with their feet*. New York: Routledge.

Milanovic, B. (1987). Remittances and income distribution. *Journal of Economic Studies, 14*(5), 24–37. https://doi.org/10.1108/eb002657

Milanovic, B. (2011). *Worlds apart: Measuring international and global inequality*. Princeton, NJ: Princeton University Press.

Mountford, A. (1997). Can a brain drain be good for growth in the source economy? *Journal of Development Economics, 53*(2), 287–303. https://doi.org/10.1016/S0304-3878(97)00021-7

OECD. (2001). *Migration policies and EU enlargement: The case of Central and Eastern Europe*. Paris: OECD. https://doi.org/10.1787/9789264189324-en

Ortega, F., and Peri, G. (2009). The causes and effects of international labor mobility. Evidence from OECD Countries 1980–2005. Human Development Research Paper 2009/06. Paris: OECD.

Ottaviano, G. I. P., and Peri, G. (2012). Rethinking the effect of immigration on wages. *Journal of the European Economic Association, 10*(1), 152–197. https://doi.org/10.1111/j.1542-4774.2011.01052.x

Ottaviano, G. I. P, Peri, G., and Wright, G. C. (2013). Immigration, offshoring, and American jobs. *American Economic Review, 103*(5), 1925–1959. https://doi.org/10.1257/aer.103.5.1925

Outhwaite, W. and Menjívar, C. (2019). Migration Crisis and "Brexit". In Menjívar, C., Ruiz, M., and Ness, I. (eds.). *The Oxford Handbook of Migration Crises*.

Ozden, Ç., and Schiff, M. (2006). *International migration, remittances, and the brain drain*. Washington, DC: International Bank for Reconstruction and Development/World Bank.

Page Moch, L. (2003). *Moving Europeans: Migration in Western Europe since 1650*. Bloomington: Indiana University Press.

Peri, G. (2007). *Immigrant's complementarities and native wages: Evidence from California*. National Bureau of Economic Research Working Paper 12956. Cambridge, MA: NBER.

Peri, G. (2014). Do immigrant workers depress the wages of native workers? *IZA World of Labor*. https://doi.org/10.15185/izawol.42

Peri, G., and Sparber, C. (2009). Task specialization, immigration, and wages. *American Economic Journal: Applied Economics, 1*(3), 135–169. https://doi.org/10.1257/app.1.3.135

Perrons, D. (2009). Migration: Cities, regions and uneven development. *European Urban and Regional Studies, 16*(3), 219–223. https://doi.org/10.1177/0969776409104689

Piketty, T. (2014). *Capital in the twenty-first century*. Cambridge, MA: Harvard University Press.

Ravallion, M. (2014). Income inequality in the developing world. *Science, 344*(6186), 851–855. https://doi.org/10.1126/science.1251875

Recchi, E., & Salamońska, J. (2015). Bad Times at Home, Good Times to Move? The (Not So) Changing Landscape of Intra-EU Migration. In *Europe's Prolonged Crisis* (pp. 124–145). Palgrave Macmillan, London.

Roy, A. S. (1997). Job displacement effects of Canadian *Immigrants by Country of Origin and Occupation. International Migration Review, 31*(1), 150–161. https://doi.org/10.1177/019791839703100109

Sanderson, M. R. (2013). Does immigration have a Matthew Effect? A cross-national analysis of international migration and international income inequality, 1960–2005. *Social Science Research, 42*(3), 683–697. https://doi.org/10.1016/j.ssresearch.2012.12.004

Sanderson, E., and Windmeijer, F. (2016). A weak instrument F-test in linear IV models with multiple endogenous variables. *Journal of Econometrics, 190*(2), 212–221.

Sebastian, R., and Ulceluse, M. (2019). The effect of immigration on natives' task specialization: The case of Germany. *International Journal of Manpower, 40*(5), 939–957.

Stark, O. (2004). Rethinking the brain drain. *World Development, 32*(1), 15–22. https://doi.org/10.1016/j.worlddev.2003.06.013

Stock, J. H., Wright, J. H., and Yogo, M. (2002). A survey of weak instruments and weak identification in generalized method of moments. *Journal of Business & Economic Statistics, 20*(4), 518–529.

Taggart, P. and Szczerbiak, A. (2018). Putting Brexit into perspective: the effect of the Eurozone and migration crises and Brexit on Euroscepticism in European states. *Journal of European Public Policy, 25*(8), 1194–1214.

Trenz, H. J., and Triandafyllidou, A. (2017). Complex and dynamic integration processes in Europe: intra EU mobility and international migration in times of recession. *Journal of Ethnic and Migration Studies, 43*(4), 546–559.

Van Mol, C., and de Valk, H. (2016). Migration and immigrants in Europe: A historical and demographic perspective. In B. Garcés-Mascareñas and R Penninx (eds.), *Integration processes and policies in Europe* (pp. 31–55). Cham: Springer. https://doi.org/10.1007/978-3-319-21674-4_3

Wilkinson, R. G., and Pickett, K. (2009). *The spirit level: Why more equal societies almost always do better.* Harmondsworth: Penguin.

World Bank. (2005). *Global economic prospects 2006: Economic implications of remittances and migration.* Washington, DC: World Bank. http://documents.worldbank.org/curated/en/507301468142196936/Global-economic-prospects-2006-economic-implications-of-remittances-and-migration

World Bank. (2018). *World development indicators.* Washington, DC: World Bank.

Zaiceva, A. (2014). Post-enlargement emigration and new EU members' labor markets. *IZA World of Labor.* https://doi.org/10.15185/izawol.40

Zaiceva, A., and Zimmermann, K. F. (2008). Scale, diversity, and determinants of labour migration in Europe. *Oxford Review, of Economic Policy, 24*(3), 427–451. https://doi.org/10.1093/oxrep/grn028

Zimmermann, K. (2005). *European migration: What do we know?* Oxford: Oxford University Press. https://global.oup.com/academic/product/european-migration-9780199257355?cc=us&lang=en&.

APPENDIX

Table 14.A1 Variable definitions

Variable	Source	Variable definition
Gini index	Eurostat (ilc_di12)	Gini coefficient for equivalized disposable income (based on EU-SILC)
Inflow	Eurostat (migr_imm1ctz)	Immigration of citizens with foreign citizenship and stateless
Stock	Eurostat (migr_pop1ctz)	Population with foreign citizenship and stateless
Government expenditure	Eurostat (gov_10a_main)	Total general government expenditure (% of GDP)
GDP per capita	Eurostat (nama_10_pc)	Gross domestic product at market prices, euro per capita, in log
Unemployment rate	Eurostat (tsdec450)	Total unemployment rate
Trade openness	Eurostat (nama_gdp_c)	Sum of exports and imports (% of GDP), in log
Tertiary education	Eurostat (edat_lfse_03)	Population by educational attainment level
Inflation	Eurostat (prc_hicp_manr)	Harmonized index of consumer prices (HICP), yearly averages of monthly data
Employment in agriculture	Eurostat (lfsa_egana, lfsa_egan2)	Employment share in agriculture (including fishing, hunting, and forestry)

Table 14.A2 First-stage results

Dependent variable	Inflow	Stock
	(1)	(2)
Inflow per 1,000 lag	0.20**	1.57***
	(0.09)	(0.21)
Stock per 1,000 lag	−0.12***	0.49***
	(0.02)	(0.04)
Government expenditure	−0.16*	0.26
	(0.09)	(0.19)
GDP per capita	23.92	−192.58
	(52.49)	(129.46)
GDP per capita square	−1.36	7.94
	(2.74)	(6.54)
Unemployment rate	−0.16	−0.77***
	(0.13)	(0.20)
Trade openness	−4.23	−31.81***
	(4.36)	(7.82)
Tertiary education	0.07	−0.63*
	(0.19)	(0.35)
Employment in agriculture	−0.01	−0.33
	(0.29)	(0.81)
Inflation	0.68***	1.23***
	(0.19)	(0.37)
Constant	−49.98	1353.94**
	(247.15)	(640.50)
Sample size	311	311
R2/Within R2	0.42	0.43
F statistics	17.97	98.94
SW F–stat	27.37	87.3

We use past migration variables with a four-year lag as instruments. Reported are F-statistic and Sanderson-Windmeijer (SW) first-stage F statistic. Models include year and country fixed effects. Observations are weighted by population size. * < 0.10, ** <0.05, *** < 0.01.

Source: Authors' calculations based on data from Eurostat.

15

CAN THE EUROPEAN UNION CONTAIN AND IMPROVE INCOME INEQUALITY?

Wiemer Salverda

15.1 INTRODUCTION

The European Union (EU), its monetary union (the Euro Area [EA]), and its social model are unique features of this continent, and the question must be asked what the results are of action at the EU level and its coordination with the national level of the member countries in the field of inequalities. The single currency (Euro) has been introduced while the European Monetary Union was and still is under construction and has gone through a life-threatening experience as a result of the double crisis: the financial crisis and the Euro crisis in its wake. This has not exactly promoted the European Social Model, which came under pressure from economic unification itself as well as the dominance of financial and economic policymaking at the EU level in the face of both that unification and the pressing crises. Notably, only the European Union can provide the agency capable of policymaking at the European level.

To discuss this I briefly revisit first, in the rest of this introduction, the most relevant arguments concerning the European Union made in earlier chapters that cover EU countries.[1] Next, in Section 15.2, I complement that discussion with a comprehensive picture of EU income inequality and poverty, discuss its links to labour earnings, and explore the perspective of the EU-wide distribution. Note

---

1 I leave out Chapters 7 and 8 on the Western Balkans and Turkey, respectively, as they are not EU members and not involved in relevant EU policymaking nor included in relevant EU data.

Wiemer Salverda, *Can the European Union Contain and Improve Income Inequality?* In: *Europe's Income, Wealth, Consumption, and Inequality.* Edited by: Georg Fischer and Robert Strauss, Oxford University Press (2021). © Oxford University Press. DOI: 10.1093/oso/9780197545706.003.0015

that the focus is policies and instruments and not explanations and drivers of inequality. In Section 15.3, I examine the EU's policymaking on poverty, the main action in the field of inequality, and the lessons that can be drawn more broadly for relevant aspects of the current debate on the content and organization of future policies concerning inequality. Section 15.4 concludes.

The preceding chapters contribute many important observations. In Chapter 2 Andrea Brandolini and Alfonso Rosolia lay the broad foundation for the volume. They draw the aggregate picture of postwar developments for the European Union as a whole (EU28) and its 'old' part (EU15).[2] This shows favourable and converging trends in employment, productivity, and incomes which, unfortunately, began to deteriorate and diverge under the influence of the combined financial and Euro crises. From existing 'fragile' evidence they observe a narrowing of the income distribution until the 1980s/1990s.[3] From 2005 onwards, they construct the aggregate distribution for EU28, which ranks all 500 million persons in the European Union by their equivalent incomes, benchmarked against the single-person household. Income inequality is lower but increasing for EU15 and higher (but still below the United States) but decreasing for EU28 and, by implication, for the new Member States (NMS).[4] In a comparison of Member States on the same footing of purchasing power parities, they find strong movements in real incomes that uplift the European bottom 30% while the upper 70% stagnate (Figure 2.9). Behind this is formidable growth across the board in the NMS, which more than compensates for strong declines at the bottom of 'peripheral' countries[5] that suffered most from the crisis and corresponding policies of austerity. In the seven countries at the core of the EU,[6] higher incomes grow more strongly while the highest incomes in Sweden, Denmark, and the United Kingdom register some decline.

Four chapters elaborate on regional groupings of EU countries: France and Germany at the centre of EU15, the Southern countries, Central and Eastern countries (CEE), and Northern countries, respectively. The chapters discuss national differences and commonalities with a broad coverage of subjects, such as (mostly) the level and inequality of incomes, social exclusion, employment, consumption, satisfaction, and redistribution policy. I touch briefly on the most salient intraregional commonalities and differences in recent years. Balazs Palvolgyi, Johannes Ziemendorff, and Lucia Granelli (Chapter 3) draw a detailed

---

2 Austria, Belgium, Denmark, Finland, France, Germany, Greece, Ireland, Italy, Luxembourg, Netherlands, Portugal, Spain, Sweden, and UK.

3 Various sketches (Darvas, 2016, figure 10; Blanchet et al., 2019, figure A.3) suggest an increase in inequality from the 1980s up to the mid-1990s followed by a long trajectory of gradual decrease until 2007.

4 Bulgaria, Cyprus, Czech Republic, Estonia, Hungary, Latvia, Lithuania, Malta, Poland, Romania, Slovenia, and Slovakia.

5 Greece, Ireland, Italy, Portugal, and Spain.

6 Austria, Belgium, Finland, France, Germany, Luxembourg, and Netherlands.

comparison of Germany and France. They argue that Germany has done better over the double crisis than France because of a greater degree of flexibility in the labour market that spills over into a flexibility of wages and working hours. However, the long run is an alternation of episodes that one country leads the other and vice-versa. This occurs in spite of major differences in the two models of economic growth and their sets of labour-market institutions. As a result, the German distribution of market incomes is more unequal and poverty is higher than in France. However, due to differences in the redistribution of incomes, the distribution of disposable incomes is similar—in the aggregate, though not for separate (age) groups. For the four Southern countries,[7] Manos Matsaganis (Chapter 4) depicts strong declines in gross domestic product (GDP), incomes, and consumption. Their income inequalities had converged on the eve of the crisis, albeit at a level near the top of EU countries' income inequalities, and they show remarkably little increase over the double crisis. Incomes suffer also higher up the distribution. The redistribution of incomes in these countries is below EU average. Monetary poverty increases modestly (+1 to 2 percentage points) if measured relative to the current median income, but hugely (+5 to 30 percentage points) if measured against the poverty threshold anchored at its purchasing level of 2008. Apparently, many of the non-poor are less able to afford durables or make ends meet than they could in 2008. In Matsaganis's view, renewed convergence hinges on the rebalancing policy of the European Union and the national control of internal political (in)stability. Márton Medgyesi and István Tóth (Chapter 5) consider 10 CEE countries.[8] In spite of the recessions due to transition in the 1990s and the financial and Euro crises, these have managed to reduce their disadvantage compared to EU15 countries in many respects. The European Union provides important help to their institutional development and was, until the double crisis, a major source of private foreign direct investment (FDI) inflows and of public investment via the Cohesion funds. However, this did not benefit regions and social groups equally, creating tensions which the crisis has exacerbated. Income inequalities have significantly increased, albeit heavily depending on specific factors in the countries. The authors advocate making future growth more inclusive and targeting lagging regions and sectors. The broad lines of these two chapters confirm the findings of Chapter 2: rising incomes in the East and falling in the South. Chapter 6 adds the fourth EU grouping: the Nordic countries.[9] Erling Barth, Karl Ove Moene, and Axel West Pedersen find increasing income inequality and increasing relative income poverty but in a context of economic growth so that those falling behind do not often suffer absolute declines in material well-being. Coming from a low level of

---

7 The five 'peripheral' countries except Ireland. All four are comprised in EU15.
8 The 12 NMS countries except Cyprus and Malta.
9 Denmark, Finland, Sweden, and also Norway (not a EU member but a de facto rule-taker in many fields; I leave it out in the rest of this chapter).

inequality, Nordic inequalities are still smaller than elsewhere. Labour earnings compression and generous welfare states appear to reinforce each other ('equality multiplier'), but, in the authors' view, this can also work the other way: growing earnings inequality might put pressure on the generosity of the welfare states. A majority of voters and politicians may feel that they can no longer afford generous welfare states, especially in Sweden and Finland, which suffered major recessions in the 1990s. The same pattern can be found in many other European countries. However, the authors hope that sustained high Nordic levels of trust and social cohesion will produce the potential for collective action that stabilizes the economic and political system and may also act as a countervailing power against rising inequality. Taken together, these four chapters provide substantial coverage of the European Union, but also leave out a significant set of countries,[10] which I discuss next.

15.2 DYNAMICS OF EUROPEAN INCOME INEQUALITY

This section provides a comprehensive and stylized picture of EU income inequality and poverty covering all member countries.[11] First (Section 15.2.1.), I compare the inequalities of both market incomes and disposable incomes and the redistributive actions underlying the differences for all incomes and for poverty. Second (Section 15.2.2), I consider their linkages to the most important source of incomes: individual wage earnings. Third, I explore the insights offered by the perspective of the EU-wide distribution advocated by Brandolini and Rosolio. I consider EU27[12] as a whole, together with a split into three main EU regions, which aims to avoid the flurry of 27 individual country situations and is inspired by the preceding chapters. These regions are

NMS12: The 12 new Members States that joined in 2004 and later: Bulgaria, Czech Republic, Cyprus, Estonia, Hungary, Latvia, Lithuania, Malta, Poland, Romania, Slovakia, and Slovenia

10 Austria, Belgium, Ireland, Luxembourg, Netherlands, and the UK, with Cyprus and Malta—covering 22% of EU27 population.
11 Unfortunately, it is beyond the scope of this chapter to analyse inequality at the level of within-country regions however important the distinction (especially between urban environments and the countryside) may seem to be for recent political developments (e.g., Trump, Brexit, *gilets jaunes*). Filauro (2018) finds a somewhat more important role for between-region inequality compared to between-country inequality but largely the same downward trend between 2006 and 2014.
12 Croatia, a member country since 2013, is left out throughout the chapter for lack of data over longer years. It makes up 0.8% of the EU28 population. The UK is included as still being a EU member over the period up to the time of writing.

PERI5: The 5 'peripheral' countries which stood out during the financial and Euro crisis: Greece, Ireland, Italy, Portugal, and Spain

CORE10: The 10 remaining countries: Austria, Belgium, Denmark, Finland, France, Germany, Luxembourg, Netherlands, Sweden, and the UK (taken together with PERI5 they make up 'old' EU15)

The result is necessarily stylized, but further country details can be found in Chapters 3 to 6. I focus on the period since 2006 because, first, available data are better comparable and comprehensive, and, second, it enables us to consider the effects of the double crises and concomitant policymaking.

15.2.1 Market Income, Disposable Income, and Poverty: Strong Divergences

15.2.1.1 Market Income, Disposable Income, and Redistribution

Figure 15.1 compares the trajectories of inequalities of market incomes and disposable incomes and the effects of social transfers and pensions, respectively, which explain the reduction from market income inequality to disposable income inequality. Unweighted country averages are used to indicate what countries generally do irrespective of their demographic or economic size.[13]

Panel A shows high levels of market income inequality, with Gini coefficients ranging between 0.456 and 0.550. The average inequality in EU27 countries decreases from 0.479 in 2006 to 0.470 in 2007 but subsequently increases continuously to 0.506 in 2014, followed by a gradual decline to 0.493 in 2018. Levels for the regions differ very modestly (1.2 points) in 2006 but fan out strongly until in 2014 a gap is reached of 6.6 points, which subsequently declines to 4.9 points in 2018. An early and brisk but short-lived increase brings CORE10 inequality up by +0.28 points between 2007 and 2009, likely under the shock of the financial crisis; it remains slightly higher at around 0.509 from 2014 onward. This is accompanied by a long and ultimately much larger increase of PERI5: +0.75 points from 0.485 to 0.550 in 2014, likely reflecting lesser sensitivity to the financial crisis and strong exposure to the Euro crisis and concomitant austerity policies. A subsequent fall, however, to 0.517 in 2018 takes away half the increase. NMS12 start with a significant decrease (−0.24 points) until 2009, subsequently neutralized by a +0.28 point increase until 2014. This is followed by a decline to 0.468 in 2018. All three regions, and EU27 with them, reach maximum inequality in 2014, after which PERI5 and NMS12 decrease while CORE10 remains unchanged. Throughout, the level for NMS12 is the lowest, well below the EU27 average and CORE10, while the PERI5 level is always the highest.

---

13 This treats countries' (and regions') experiences equally irrespective of size for a better comparison (cf. European Foundation, 2018: 22). For weighted outcomes, see European Commission, Social Situation Monitor, Distribution of market income tables. https://ec.europa.eu/social/main.jsp?catId=1050&langId=en.

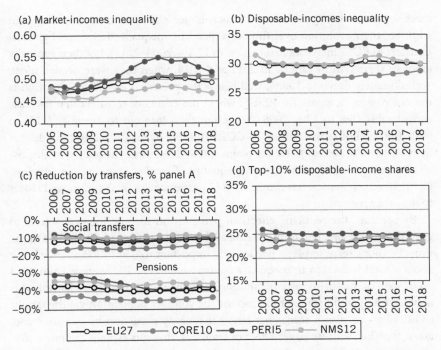

(a) Market-incomes inequality

(b) Disposable-incomes inequality

(c) Reduction by transfers, % panel A

(d) Top-10% disposable-income shares

—o— EU27   —•— CORE10   —•— PERI5   —•— NMS12

Figure 15.1 Gini coefficients of market and disposable incomes and the percentage reductions of market income inequality by social transfers and pensions, by EU regions (2006–2018). The average Gini coefficient of market incomes for PERI5 countries attains 0.55 in 2014 (panel A). The more negative the values in panel C the larger the redistribution.
All incomes are equivalized for household size and composition and shown for all persons in the household. Country averages are unweighted. Market incomes are before social transfers and pensions. Effects of social transfers and pensions are both percentages of market incomes. The NMS12 level for 2006 includes Romania, whose value (56.5) is extrapolated backwards from 2007 and 2008. EU27 excludes Croatia. Top incomes are for disposable income, whereas they are for gross incomes in the literature (Atkinson and Piketty, 2007).
Source: Author's calculations from Eurostat, EU Statistics on Income and Living Conditions (EU-SILC): ilc_di12, ilc_di12b, ilc_di12c and ilc_di01 (update 17 December 2019).

The evolution of disposable income inequalities (panel B) shows a significant contrast. Levels are substantially lower (−15 to 23 points, or 31% to 45%). Time trends are much flatter by comparison but still show the initial declines for PERI5 and NMS12 and the increase for CORE10. In particular, PERI5 does not show the strong growth to 2014, but also not the slight decline afterwards. The highest level is again for PERI5, but here CORE10 is well below NMS12 which now exceeds the EU27 average.

The gap between the two distributions embodies the redistribution of income as practised in the countries. This has two different components (see, e.g., Inchauste and Karver, 2017): social transfers, mainly for persons in the working-age bracket, and pensions, mainly for old age. Panel C indicates their importance: social transfers reduce market inequality by 11% on average across the three regions, while pensions sort much larger effects of 27% on average. In addition, their evolution over time diverges. The inequality reduction by social transfers in EU27 increases first (11.7% to 12.4%, 2006–2011), but then generally tends to shrink, most rapidly in 2012 and 2014, when they were needed most, and ultimately down to 10.5%, well below the pre-crisis level. The evolution is much stronger, however, for PERI5, where the effects of transfers first increase considerably (8% to 12%, 2006–2011), but then lose out to austerity (12% to 9%). The level of redistribution in CORE10 (15% average) clearly exceeds that in NMS12 (9% average). This explains CORE10's lower inequality of disposable incomes in spite of its higher inequality of market incomes. Nonetheless, CORE10 redistribution has diminished (3 percentage points) and moved closer to the other regions.

By contrast, the reducing effects of pensions on income inequality tend to grow during the first half of the period and remain unchanged for the rest of the time. Pensions seem to play a particularly important role in PERI5 as they bring about a total reduction in inequality comparable to the EU average from 2014 on in spite of the shrinking contribution made by social transfers. Plausibly this may have helped fill some of the gap for the younger population via the family. CORE10 shows also a somewhat larger inequality reduction by pensions and, taken together with its larger effect of transfers, this can explain the more substantial reduction from market to disposable incomes; however, both effects have been shrinking slightly since 2014.

Finally, panel D shows the evolution of the shares in equivalized incomes of the top decile of households. Declines and increases in the earlier years change to rather steady levels since 2008. Also here PERI5 attains the highest level of the three regions, but mutual differences seem rather modest.[14]

15.2.1.2 Poverty

Generally, anti-poverty policy is as close as explicit policymaking often comes to addressing income inequality. Figure 15.2 spells out the evolution of what in the European Union is officially called the incidence of 'at-risk-of-poverty' (AROP), though it is unclear what exactly is meant by 'at risk of' (Darvas, 2019b). The figure enables comparison to Figure 15.1. Panel A indicates what the incidence of poverty looks like in the space of market incomes, which is before the effects of social transfers and pensions kick in. Again, there is a considerable increase and decrease for PERI5, and the lowest level is for NMS12. Panel B indicates the rate of monetary poverty AROP, applied as usual to equivalized disposable incomes. It varies between 14% and 21%. Only in NMS12 did the level actually decrease (19% to 17%) but it is remarkably similar to the other regions, and all are relatively stable. Interestingly, the AROP rate of PERI5 exceeds that of NMS12 from

---

14 Note that the Statistics on Income and Living Conditions (SILC) survey does not oversample top incomes and may err downwards on their level and evolution.

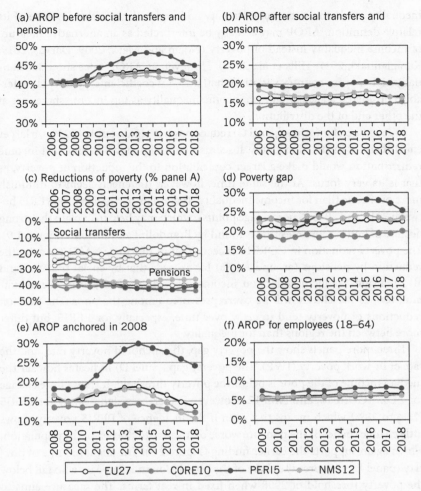

Figure 15.2 At-risk-of-poverty (AROP) levels before and after social transfers and pensions, by EU regions (2006/2009–2018).

In 2014, the level of poverty before transfers and pensions reaches 48.3% for PERI5 (panel A). Poverty is for all incomes equivalized for household size and composition below 60% of median household income and shown for all persons. Country averages are unweighted.

Effects of social transfers and pensions are both percentages of poverty before social transfers and pensions. Panels D, E, and F are after transfers and pensions. The NMS12 level for 2006 includes Romania whose value (46.1) is extrapolated backwards from 2007 and 2008. EU27 excludes Croatia.

Source: Author's calculations on Eurostat: ilc_li02, ilc_li09b, ilc_li10, ilc_li11, ilc_li22b, ilc_iw01 (update 17 December 2019).

the start and shows equally little change, while the rate for CORE10 is consistently lower, as was the case before for disposable income inequality. The developments look very similar to Figure 15.1 panels A and B: market income inequality shows the same divergence from a similar level at the start, and disposable income inequality levels show the same stability and regional hierarchy. Because of its relative definition, AROP may actually be interpreted as an alternative measure of income inequality instead of poverty (Nolan and Marx, 2009; Darvas, 2019; Karagiannaki, 2017; Hills et al., 2019). However, as AROP rates show substantially higher cross-country variation than the Gini coefficients, poverty is preferably considered a special take on income inequality as top income shares are at the other end of the distribution.

Indeed, social transfers (panel C) reduce poverty significantly (−25%), a larger effect than for income inequality. It seems a natural policy outcome that income redistribution would make a larger contribution to the reduction of poverty, as that is its very focus. At the same time, however, the effects seem to diminish more over time than for income inequality. That holds particularly for PERI5 between 2010 and 2016 (5 percentage points), which may help to explain the strong decline of bottom incomes that is found by Brandolini and Rosolio (Figure 1.9). The poverty reduction in CORE10 exceeds that in PERI5 or NMS12. Again, the reduction by pensions (around −40%) far exceeds that by social transfers and also pensions' reducing effect on income inequality (−25%). This seems natural, too, as the elderly will be overrepresented among the poor. The pension reductions of poverty tend to grow over time, especially for PERI5, but differ more between the regions than for inequality.

Three more panels show the poverty gap, the anchored poverty rate, and the rate of in-work poverty (IWP). The poverty gap (panel D) indicates how far the median income of the poor is below the poverty threshold. It shows little change for EU27, CORE10, and NMS12. However, it increases significantly for PERI5 (23% to 28%) which means that even if the incidence of PERI5 poverty shows little change (panel B) the poor are worse off relative to the rest of the population, which again supports the earlier finding (Figure 2.9). The anchored rate of poverty (panel E) measures the share of the population in later years who fall below the poverty threshold of 2008 when fixed in real terms. The measure aims to repair an important weakness of the relative poverty measure (Nolan and Marx, 2009). If a country's real incomes rise or fall across the board this does not necessarily show up in AROP in spite of the fact that life might become easier or more difficult for the poor. It is telling that in Greece, where both median and mean income fall by one-third, the AROP rate increases only little from 2008 (20.1%) to 2012 (23.1%) and then falls again to 18.5% in 2018, ducking below the initial level for the first time. The anchored rate points more strongly in the same direction. The rate of PERI5 shows explosive growth, from 19% to 30%, followed by a fall only half as large—to 24.4% in 2018. This contrasts strongly with the 1 percentage point increase of the AROP rate of panel A. It also far exceeds the 3 percentage points growth in NMS12 while CORE10 shows virtually no change. It implies that by 2014, 11 percentage points more of the PERI5 population share the experience of the poor of 2008. Unfortunately, an anchored poverty gap is not available. Finally, IWP levels among employees (panel F, available since 2009 only) are between two and three times lower than for the population in general (panel B), depending on the region.[15] Indeed, taken as a rate among the total population, IWP is between 3% and 5%, or about one-third of the total AROP rate, implying that policies aimed at diminishing IWP make at best only a small contribution to reducing total poverty. IWP levels show a slight increase, and regional differences are rather small although PERI5 levels still exceed the other regions and grow more.

15.2.2 Wage Earnings and Incomes: An Essential Mechanism Shared Across Europe

The redistribution from market incomes to disposable incomes raises the question how the inequality of market incomes comes about and whether that may affect the redistribution. For this I examine how wage earnings, by far the most important source of market income (and also of taxes and social contributions), get distributed over households and how the latter distribution relates to that of hourly wages. Of crucial importance is households' joint labour supply, which reflects the demise of the traditional single breadwinner and implies a combination of different levels of pay within the household (Figure 15.3).

This has important implications for the distribution and redistribution of incomes and concerns potentially one 'underlying force that has raised inequality' (Chapter 6). The focus is on 'labour households', defined as those deriving the greater part of their gross incomes from gross annual earnings,[16] and their position in the distribution of household incomes, regardless of the number of persons in the household. I examine this in cross-section for the year 2014, using the latest Statistics on Income and Living Conditions (SILC) data available at the time of starting this research,[17] with the continued use of unweighted country averages (but see the EU-wide perspective later).

15.2.2.1 Wage Earnings Are the Primary and Skewed Source of Incomes

The earnings are strongly skewed towards the top of the distribution of household gross incomes.[18] Panel A indicates the importance of households' annual

---

15 Poverty rates among the self-employed are much higher and vary between 16% and 24%, often exceeding total AROP levels. Income data for the self-employed may be less reliable (Guio, 2009).

16 The EU counts 113 million such households, comprising 186 million individual employees. Other households comprise 24 million employees, or 12% of all employees, who receive only 5% of all earnings.

17 However, see Salverda and Haas (2014) for an earlier version that largely resembles the current situation, and Salverda (2015a, 2016, 2018) for further discussion.

18 In this section gross incomes are not equivalized, contrary to their frequent equivalization also for market incomes for that matter (e.g., OECD Income Inequality

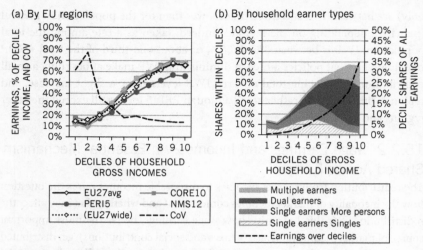

(a) By EU regions

(b) By household earner types

(c) Earnings as % of total income of all households

	EU27	CORE10	PERI5	NMS12
Total	56%	59%	47%	58%
Single earners Singles	7%	10%	5%	6%
Single earners More persons	10%	8%	12%	9%
Dual earners	30%	32%	25%	30%
Multiple earners	10%	8%	5%	13%

Figure 15.3 Shares of household earnings in deciles of the overall distribution of household gross incomes, earnings as percentage of all income within deciles, EU27 (2014).
Labour households in CORE10 comprise 70% of the income of all households in the 9th decile (panel A); earnings in the top decile amount to 35% of all earnings of labour households (panel B).
CoV is coefficient of variation across all countries.
Source: Author's calculations on EU Statistics on Income and Living Conditions (EU-SILC) 2015 for annual outcomes of 2014.

earnings within the 10 deciles of the overall income distribution. In total, 56% of total income depends on earnings, varying from 15% in the bottom decile to 67% in the top 10%.[19] Unsurprisingly, PERI5 is the laggard, with earnings comprising 47% of total income, more than 10 percentage points below CORE10 and NMS12. The higher the decile, the more the countries resemble each other: witness the

---

Database). Such equivalization tends to inflate the role of redistribution and ignores that of equivalization itself. For example, the average EU27 difference between the Gini coefficients of gross and net incomes amounts to 0.056 non-equivalized and 0.066 equivalized (author's calculation for 2014).

19 The overall income of labour households substantially (30%) exceeds their earnings and equals 73% of total income: varying from 17% in decile 1 to 85% in decile 10. Their average gross income is almost 2.5 times higher than the average of all other households.

declining value of the within-decile coefficient of variation for all 27 countries. Nonetheless, the increase in PERI5 is less than in the other two regions, particularly because of its lower employee-to-population ratio.[20]

The role of joint household earnings behind this pattern is shown in panel B, for the average of the 27 countries and detailed for the three regions in panel C, the appended table.[21] It distinguishes four types of labour households depending on the number of earners that they field and whether the household comprises one person or more. Single-earner singles concentrate in the middle and the left of the distribution, and their earnings match only 7% of total income; single earners in more-person households stretch only slightly more to the right and obtain 10% of total income. Dual-earner households and multiple-earner households (with three or more earners) accumulate in the upper half, with earnings equal to 40% of total income, the remnant of the total percentage of 56%.

The dashed line shows the distribution of earnings alone (on the right axis). More than half of all earnings are received by the households in the ninth (21%) and tenth (35%) deciles taken together; this contrasts with less than 8% in each of the lowest six deciles. Household joint labour supply has put dual-earner and multiple-earner households at the heart of the labour market and the income distribution (Salverda and Checchi, 2015). The relative contribution of dual earners, 30% out of 56% for EU27, is more than half in all regions including PERI5.[22] Pattern differences concentrate among the other three earner types: multiple earning is more important in NMS12 (13%), traditional single earning in more-person households in PERI5 (12%), and singles' single earning in CORE10 (10%). Table 15.1 provides more detail for household earner types as well as the top income decile by gender, age, and educational attainment. Female earners make up 40% of all earners in EU27 but account for two-thirds of second dual earners—with little regional difference. Youths comprise 4% of all earners, but 29% of them are members of top-decile households. The highly educated receive almost half (47%) of all earnings, and half of them are members of top-decile households. Notably, their role is more important in PERI5.

The flip side of all this is that currently almost three-quarters of all employees share a household with another employee while little more than 25% are still single earners, in either one-person or more-person households. This reflects the universal demise of the single breadwinner and suggests that globalization and the doubling of the global labour force, made famous by Richard Freeman

---

20 Average employee-population ratios (15–64 years) are for EU27, 55%; CORE10, 62%; PERI5, 45%; and NMS12, 54% in 2014 (Eurostat, lfsa_ergan). The PERI5 ratio fell from 50% in 2008. This seems a phenomenon with potentially significant policy implications that extend to, for example, the generation of tax receipts or of job vacancies.

21 The somewhat less skewed distribution of employee numbers (not shown) combines with rising average earnings to the right.

22 Dual-earner shares across the 27 countries show a 9% coefficient of variation only.

Table 15.1 Earnings distribution by earner characteristics and top 10% by European Union regions (2014)

	All (%)	Single earners, single person (%)	Single earners more-person (%)	Dual earners First (%)	Dual earners Second (%)	Multiple earners First (%)	Multiple earners Second (%)	Multiple earners Third+ (%)	D10 horizontal (%)	D10 vertical (%)
All										
EU27	100	12	17	35	18	9	5	3	35	100
CORE10	100	17	14	37	18	8	4	2	34	100
PERI5	100	10	25	36	18	6	3	2	37	100
NMS12	100	10	16	34	17	11	7	4	35	100
Women										
EU27	40	6	5	10	12	3	2	2	32	13
CORE10	39	7	5	9	13	2	1	2	30	12
PERI5	40	6	7	11	12	2	1	2	34	13
NMS12	41	6	4	10	12	4	3	2	33	14
Youths										
EU27	4	0	0	0	1	0	0	0	29	1
CORE10	5	1	0	1	1	0	0	0	24	1
PERI5	3	0	0	0	0	0	0	0	27	1
NMS12	4	0	0	1	1	1	1	1	34	1
Low-educated										
EU27	11	1	2	3	2	3	1	2	15	11
CORE10	10	2	2	2	2	1	1	1	16	10
PERI5	20	2	6	6	3	6	2	0	13	20
NMS12	9	1	2	2	1	2	1	1	15	8

Middle-educated

EU27	41	5	7	13	3	2	23	41
CORE10	39	7	5	14	2	2	22	40
PERI5	28	3	7	9	1	2	26	30
NMS12	46	4	7	14	3	3	24	47

High-educated

EU27	47	6	8	18	4	4	50	48
CORE10	49	8	7	19	3	0	46	50
PERI5	52	6	12	20	3	3	53	50
NMS12	44	5	7	17	5	1	51	45

In EU27 12% of all earnings of labour households were received by single-earner singles, while all earnings 35% was found in top 10% households.

Source: Author's calculations on SILC 2015 for annual outcomes of 2014.

(2007), are not the only forces that have drastically altered the shape of European (and American) labour markets. There has been also a more gradual and less noticed 'second doubling': the within-country rise of female employment participation, in conjunction with the rapid increase in female educational attainment and often also of part-time employment.[23] Most of this increase has landed in households already having an employee, thus leading to an EU average of 1.7 employees per labour household. The phenomenon is broadly shared across countries. It is an ongoing process that is especially relevant to consider for future inequality.

The relationship of hourly pay and household incomes has changed fundamentally as a consequence of this joint earning. So far, the argument was fully based on annual earnings as found in SILC, which depend on the hours worked and hourly pay. In the bygone days of the full-time working single earner, the hours worked were roughly uniform (i.e., full-time) and the annual earnings directly mirrored the distribution of hourly pay; and, as there was only one worker in the household, his or her annual earnings in turn were directly mirrored in the annual household income. Low hourly pay thus meant low income. This is no longer so, as the large role of dual-earner and multiple-earner households spreads low pay over the entire income distribution, far beyond the segment of lower incomes.

The two panels of Figure 15.4 present an approximate sketch of the current relationship viewed from two angles,[24] which both horizontally allocate employees over the distribution of hourly pay. Panel A ranks them vertically by their households' positions in the 10 deciles of the overall distribution of income, while panel B sorts them by their earner positions in the household. The former panel shows a clear correlation between household income and the level of pay. Employees from top 10% households make up two-thirds of employees earning top 10% pay. However, the correlation is far from perfect, and employees from such high-income households are effectively spread over the entire wage distribution; among them only roughly one-third is paid a top 10% wage. The box inserted at the left-hand side of the panel delineates the low-wage segment of the labour market, defined commonly as lying below two-thirds of median hourly pay. It covers more than 17% of all employees. They are spread over all 10 income

---

23 This holds for CORE10 and PERI, while under communism CEE countries had dual and multiple earning almost by definition.

24 SILC allows an approximation only for reasons of principle: income data from the preceding year need to be combined with current labour market positions, which may have changed, and for practical reasons: substantial missing values for hours of work in the survey (17%). This likely leads to an underrepresentation of low pay, plausibly also for the top of the income distribution, as it coincides with a known underrepresentation of youths (−41%), who have an important presence as 3+ earners at the top, of whom also 42% are missing—particularly in Denmark, Finland, the Netherlands, and Sweden.

(a) Employees by household gross-income level

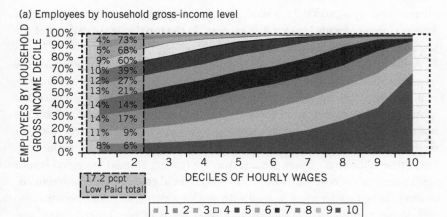

(b) Employees by household earner type

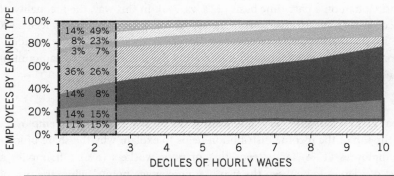

Figure 15.4 Labour household earners over the distribution of hourly wages, EU27 average (2014).
The share of employees from 1st decile households in the hourly wage distribution is very small, and though 73% are low-paid their share among all low-paid is 4% only. Percentages in the low-pay boxes concern the vertical distribution left, the horizontal incidence right.
Source: Author's calculations on EU Statistics on Income and Living Conditions (EU-SILC) 2015.

deciles, and 8% are in the top decile alone (twice as much as actually are in the bottom decile), varying from 6% in PERI5 to 9% in CORE10. Conversely, 6% of all employees in top 10% households are low paid, with little regional variation. This can be understood from the second panel, which shows a rather even distribution of the four main household earner types over the hourly wage distribution. Within dual-earner and multiple-earner households, however, there is a clear difference between first earners—defined as having the largest earnings in the household—and additional earners. The former reach higher up the wage distribution while the latter remain lower down. Consequently, additional earners make up 61% of the low paid, and they face a higher incidence of low pay, 28% as compared with 11% for first earners. At the top decile virtually all of the low paid are additional earners.

Apparently, the current income distribution is far from simply reflecting the wage distribution, as low-paid jobs (and low-skill jobs for that matter) are present up to the very top of the income distribution.[25] Conversely, this implies that most employees operating in the low-wage segment of the labour market are not members of low-income households. Subsequently, as there will often already be a better-paid first earner in the household, the household situation may lend those additional earners some leeway for trading off paid work and labour conditions against other activities such as household care or participation in education. They may be more at ease with working part-time[26] and perhaps also with looser contractual conditions and lower levels of pay. Indeed, additional earners more often work on temporary contracts than first earners (17% vs. 9%) and more often on a part-time basis (22% vs. 7%). In this way, the inequality of the income distribution arising from the labour market can potentially feed back to the labour market and increase wage inequality by enhancing the competition for simple low-wage jobs and moderating the demands for the amount of working time and the level of wage compensation.[27]

15.2.2.2 Earnings and Poverty

Low pay and IWP diverge very significantly. The presence of low-paid employees up to the top of the income distribution helps to explain why the share of low-paid employees (17%) far exceeds that of poor workers (8%).[28] It implies a modest overlap only between the two (3.6 percentage points) while the rest of the in-work poor (2.5 percentage points) are actually better paid by the hour but also poor because of their household composition (Figure 15.5).[29] Across the EU regions the picture is largely the same, with only modest variation (16–18%). Again, the highest incidence of low pay (18.3%) is found in PERI5, where the overlap of the low-paid and poverty (4.4%) is also the highest.

Combining earnings helps labour households to stay out of poverty. A total of 15 million poor earners in these households make up 18% of all poor persons. Poverty rates differ very significantly between the four household types, as Figure 15.6 panel A illustrates. The aggregate risk among employees in labour households is less than 8%, well below the 17% risk of the total population

---

25 See also Matsaganis et al. (2015)

26 Nineteen per cent of all low-paid workers work part-time, 70% of them as additional earners and almost 80% of them coming from households in the upper half of the income distribution.

27 Salverda and Rook (forthcoming) elaborate on this vicious circle.

28 See Figure 15.6 panel A. This concerns the working poor who are members of labour households only, while Figure 15.2 .F covers all employees.

29 Compare Salverda (2018a) for a further discussion.

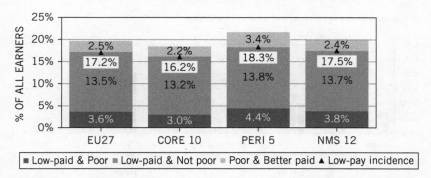

Figure 15.5 Poor employees and low-paid employees, % of all employees, by EU regions (2014). In the average EU27 country 13.5% of employees are low paid but not in a poor household. The working poor equal the low-paid poor and the better-paid poor taken together, while the low-paid equal the poor and non-poor low-paid taken together. Better pay is above the low-pay threshold of 66% of the median hourly wage.
Source: Author's calculations on EU Statistics on Income and Living Conditions (EU-SILC) 2015.

(Figure 15.2, panel B). However, among them, the traditional single earners in more-person households run a risk of poverty (20%) that exceeds the general average. This is five times higher than for dual earners and eight times higher than for multiple earners. Apparently, the pooling of earnings, including from low-paid jobs, helps keep their two rates low, though often the first earnings in those households are already sufficient for that purpose. Unsurprisingly, more-person single earners make up a large fraction of the working poor (41%), more than half (53%) in PERI5.

The reducing effect of income redistribution is limited. Poverty is defined on equivalized disposable household incomes, which result from gross earnings after, first, redistribution (payment of taxes and transfers and receipt of social transfers) and, second, equivalization for household size and composition. The working poor are all found down in the bottom two deciles of the net-equivalized income distribution. However, when we follow them back to the gross-income distribution, only a minority of 39% of them are found in the two bottom deciles, while the annual earnings of the rest spread up to the 7th decile. Depending on household size and number of earners, employees may actually be rather well paid while their household is still poor.[30] Tracing them back again in two steps, the transition from gross to net incomes shows the effects of income redistribution while the transition from net to equivalized disposable incomes indicates the effect of equivalization (Figure 15.6, panel B).

---

30 Likewise, in the United States, poor households receiving the Earned Income Tax Credit are found up to the 7th and 8th of the individual distribution of broad pre-tax income; see https://www.taxpolicycenter.org/model-estimates/individual-income-tax-expenditures-october-2018/t18-0203-tax-benefit-earned-income

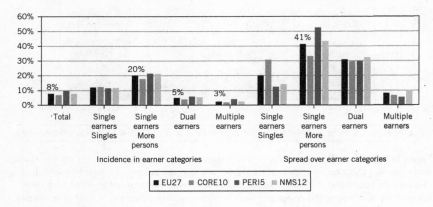

(a) Poor employees' incidence among and spread over earner types

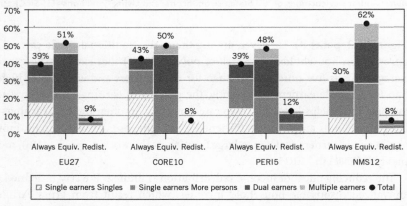

(b) Distributive shifts of poor employees due to redistribution and equivalisation

Figure 15.6 Poor employees: Incidence, spread, and effects of redistribution and equivalization, by EU regions (2014).
Of all employees in labour households in EU27, 8% are in a poor household (left half of panel A); they make up 20% of all poor employees (right half).
The three columns for each area in panel B add up to 100%.
Source: Author's calculations on EU Statistics on Income and Living Conditions (EU-SILC) 2015.

The redistribution of income appears to shift them only marginally down the distribution (9% for EU27), while the subsequent transition to equivalized incomes has a highly significant impact (51%). Apparently, income redistribution has little effect and sometimes even worsens their position; it certainly does not neutralize the effects of household size and composition on poverty. This seems logical as far as taxes and contributions do not take households characteristics into account.[31] Notably, the large contribution made by equivalization is

---

31 The redistributive effect differs between countries (3–21%) but is always much smaller than for equivalization (38–71%).

not perceived by the AROP approach (Figure 15.2) as gross incomes are already equivalized.

These basics are shared by the three regions with modest variation. The downwards effect of redistribution is larger in PERI5 (12%), especially for traditional single earners and dual earners. For CORE10, redistributive effects are confined to single-earner singles, who also have a substantial share in poverty from the start (22%). The effect of equivalization is larger in NMS12 (62%), especially due to traditional single earners but also to the larger mass of multiple earners in this region. As a result, NMS12 witnesses the largest combined downwards shift of redistribution and equivalization (70%). Equivalization effects for dual earners, however, are the same across the regions (23%). Equivalization effects for singles are zero by definition of equivalization.

15.2.3 Europe-wide Perspective on Income Inequality Selectively Widens the Differences

I now turn to income inequality in the European Union viewed as a single aggregate, with all countries brought to the same monetary denominator for incomes and earnings, on which there is now a rapidly developing literature. Brandolini and Rosolia (Chapter 2) argue the importance of this perspective on inequality. It provides an important complementary perspective to the national inequalities as it can tell how the income distribution of the European Union viewed as a single entity behaves and how individual member countries fit into that picture. It serves in studying the cohesion and the (in principle, upward) convergence of incomes and examining possible effects on inequality of economic unification itself. Through decomposition, it can indicate also where most of the action regarding inequality is located: at the EU level or at the individual country level, or, in other words, between or within countries? Finally, it enables comparing European income inequality to that of the United States more appropriately than by comparing it to individual EU countries. This can help focus the mind on where the European Union currently stands, where it may be moving in future, or what it might need to undertake.

For this, the EU countries need to be added together. This can be done directly for physical entities such as employed or unemployed persons. Incomes, by contrast, need to be measured comparably first with the help of national purchasing power parities of the euro, which, as discussed by Brandolini and Rosolio, correct for the fact that similar nominal amounts buy more (in poorer countries) or less (in richer countries) depending on the general price level. A single EU distribution of incomes can then be produced with a corresponding level of inequality that likely differs from the weighted (Eurostat) or unweighted (previous sections) average of the national inequalities of the 27 EU countries. Note that the use of purchasing power parities amounts to a linear transformation of all incomes in a country, one that leaves the national inequalities unchanged.

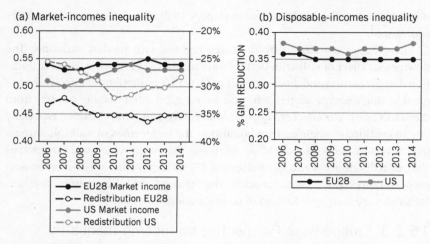

Figure 15.7 Gini coefficients of market and disposable incomes, EU-wide and United States (2006–2017).
In 2006, the Gini coefficient of EU market income attains 0.54 (left axis), and redistribution lowers the US coefficient by 25% (right axis).
Incomes are equivalized for household size and composition and purchasing power parity (PPP)-based, also across American states. They are shown for households. Market incomes exclude pensions and inequality may be underestimated. EU-wide includes Croatia.
Source: Filauro and Parolin (2019), figures 1 and 2, reconstructed on the basis of their online dataset (which is two-digit only). They use data from EU Statistics on Income and Living Conditions (EU-SILC) for EU and from Current Population Survey, Annual Social and Economic Supplement, for the United States. Author's calculations for redistributive efforts.

Recent research by Francesco Filauro and Zachary Parolin (2019) finds an EU-wide level of market income inequality around 0.54 (Figure 15.7, panel A).[32] This is consistently higher that the unweighted average of between 0.470 and 0.506 (Figure 15.1) or the weighted average between 0.496 and 0.520 (Eurostat, ilc_di12b). Strikingly, it is consistently a tad higher than for the United States.[33] At the same time, the European redistribution of incomes (−35%) exceeds the American (around −30%) sufficiently to generate a lower level of disposable income inequality in Europe (0.35, panel B). So, EU market income inequality is

32 Filauro and Parolin carefully define income in a comparable way for the two blocks, they optimize the data for comparison by adjusting the American data for the underreporting of means-tested benefits, and they correct for price-level differences between US states as is done for the European countries with purchasing power parity adjustment.

33 Capital gains and imputed rent are excluded from the income concept. For the working age population, the two Gini's are not significantly different (Filauro and Portalin, 2018: fn 8). The Gini coefficient may not adequately capture inequality at the top of the distribution. Blanchet et al. (2019) find substantially higher top-income shares for the United States compared to Europe, largely due to their much stronger growth since 1980.

high but so is EU redistribution. The EU–US difference in disposable income inequality is minor but significant nonetheless (Filauro and Parolin, 2019: 550). That EU level, however, is clearly higher than the unweighted (0.30) or weighted (0.303–0.310) EU average (in 2014).

The evolution of EU market income inequality is more muted compared to the small increase of Figure 15.1, and the inequality of disposable incomes remains equally flat after an initial decline. In Europe, the effect of redistribution increases from 32% in 2007 to 35% in 2009, at the onset of the crisis, and thus makes a partial contribution to the initial decline in disposable income inequality. Though the American effort is consistently smaller, the difference is surprisingly modest. It increases substantially in the United States up to 2010, from 25% to 32%. The change is larger and continues for longer than in the European Union, and, as a result, the mutual gap is more than halved, from 8 to 3 percentage points. However, after 2010, it widens again, to 7 percentage points in 2014.

It is surprising that the long years of financial crisis and its sequel, the euro crisis, which hit the European economy strongly between 2008 and 2014, have not prompted an increase in inequality. The picture is much the same for other measures of inequality, such as the top 10% income share (Filauro, 2018, figure 4.a; Darvas, 2018, figure 1; Blanchet et al., 2019, figure 16), the Theil index (Bönke and Schröder, 2015, figure 6), the mean log deviation (Heidenreich, 2016, table 2.2), or the percentile ratios, especially in the upper half of the distribution: P90:P50 (Benczúr et al., 2017, figure 3). The EU-wide percentage real income growth curve (Brandolini and Rosolia, this volume Chapter 2, figure 2.9) shows a sharp increase at the bottom of the distribution, implying a decline in inequality. This is consistent with the pattern of initial inequality decline followed by stagnation, as that bottom growth is concentrated almost entirely in the first few years before 2008 and no longer found for the remaining years (personal communication with the authors). Similarly, Darvas (2019, figure 1) shows an increase in the income share of the bottom 40% between 2007 and 2016 (16.7% to 18.2%), which is largely concentrated before 2010 (17.8%). He also finds a decrease for the top 10% income share: 26.1% to 25.4% from 2007 to 2012, followed by stagnation.

Country shifts oppose between east, south, and north/west. The EU-wide inequality can be decomposed into the contributions made by inequalities between the member countries, on the one hand, and those within each of the countries, on the other hand. Note, however, that there is no simple general rule that the between-country component relates to the Union while the within-country component relates to the countries. Within-country inequalities may be affected by the effects of unification on the economy (Bertola, 2010, 2018; Beckfield, 2006, 2009), and within-country transfers can be fed by EU contributions to the country.[34]

---

34 For example, for the United States, Filauro and Parolin (2019, 553) find a between-component for the US of less than 1 per cent only but they relate transfers to the state

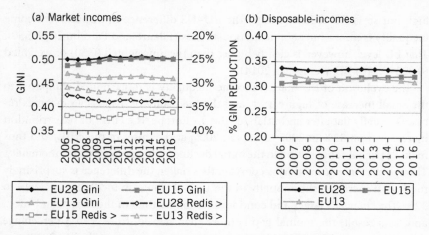

Figure 15.8 Gini coefficients of region-wide incomes for EU15 and EU13 (2006–2016). EU28 Gini of market incomes is 0.500 in 2006 and 0.502 in 2016. Purchasing power parity (PPP)-based. EU13 is NMS12 plus Croatia.
Source: Author's calculations on dataset underlying Darvas (2016), LD version of Gini, data update of 2 July 2019: http://www.bruegel.org/publications/datasets/global-and-regional-gini-coefficients/

A Theil decomposition performed by Filauro (2018, figure 5.A) indicates that by far the largest contribution, up to almost 80% of total inequality, is made by within-country inequalities. Between-country inequality plays a much smaller role, just above 20%, but interestingly its importance evolves in parallel to the overall inequality, declining during the first few years and remaining stable after that. By the looks of it, this decomposition exudes the same calm as the EU-wide inequality. However, significant country shifts remain hidden in each of the two components. Similar decompositions based on the same data applied to the disaggregate level of EU regions show different levels of inequality and opposing trends. The most important distinction among EU countries concerns the split between the countries of the EA[35] who share the same currency and the remaining nine countries who maintain their own currency.[36] First, EA inequality is well below the EU-wide level but has been rising from 2009 to 2013 (Filauro, 2018, figure 1). Second, decomposition for the EA shows a contribution of between-country inequalities less than half as large as for EU28 as a whole,

---

level in spite of the fact that significant shares (UI benefits, Medicaid etc.) are financed by the federal government, as is the EITC.

35 *Austria, Belgium,* Cyprus, Estonia, *Germany, Finland, France, Greece, Ireland, Italy,* Lithuania, Latvia, *Luxembourg,* Malta, *Netherlands, Portugal,* Slovakia, Slovenia, and *Spain.* The 12 countries in italics started in 2002, the other seven joined between 2007 and 2015.

36 Bulgaria, Croatia, Czech Republic, Denmark, Hungary, Poland, Romania, Sweden, and the UK.

which also gradually increases after 2008, implying a higher but also decreasing between-country contribution for the other nine countries.

Similarly, inequality in the 'old' EU15 country group has been rising for market incomes throughout the period up to 2013 (0.487 to 0.504), followed by a slight decline. It became markedly higher than for EU13, where inequality fell until 2008 and remained unchanged for the rest of the period (Figure 15.8, panel A). Interestingly, redistribution is at the same time also more substantial in EU15, slightly decreasing from 37% to 36%, when compared to EU13, but there it increased (31% to 33%). Due to these opposing trends, EU13's inequality of disposable incomes fell from 0.325 to 0.310 and is now below EU15's level, which grew from 0.307 to 0.321 (panel B). A Gini-based decomposition of EU15 versus EU13 points in a similar direction (Darvas, 2016, figure 12, panels c and d).[37] Between-country inequalities in EU15 have grown since 2008, while they declined in EU13, primarily reflecting divergence and convergence, respectively, of countries' mean incomes in the two groups.

Confirmation with more country detail is provided by the four country groupings of Chapter 2. After 2007, the sharp real income growth at the bottom of NMS (NEU15) incomes of Figure 2.9 flattens out but remains high (some 30%), while EU-wide growth disappears entirely (personal communication from the authors). In contrast, the shocking decline of the bottom incomes of the PERI5 countries[38] seems entirely concentrated in the later period 2007–2015. Péter Benczúr et al. (2017) find steep inequality growth also for the region of Mediterranean countries.[39] As observed by Zsolt Darvas (2019), southern Europeans have been pushed down substantially along the EU-wide distribution of incomes. In particular, the Italian presence in the EU-wide bottom 20% has doubled, while it has hardly changed in the top 10%. The observations of Manos Matsaganis (Chapter 4) confirm the dire straits of Southern European countries. Interestingly, Timm Bönke and Carsten Schröder (2014) break down Eurozone between-country inequality by means of pairwise decompositions of the (10) countries involved. They point to the important contribution made by declining living standards in Greece and Spain to the EA's growing between-component. István Tóth and Márton Medgyesi (Chapter 5) confirm that, in spite of the two recessions, during the period, CEE disadvantages to EU15 have actually diminished.[40] Benczúr et al. (2017) confirm the decline of the Gini coefficient for the collective of Eastern and Central European countries.

---

37 Note that Darvas in the decomposition keeps a mean income component apart from a relative population size component and also addresses interactions between the three components.

38 Greece, Ireland, Italy, Portugal, and Spain.

39 Cyprus, Greece, Spain, Italy, Malta, and Portugal.

40 Note, however, that Alcidi et al. (2018) find important diverging patterns within these countries, with growth being strongly concentrated in capital cities while other regions are left behind. See also Heidenreich (2016) who integrates the regional dimension with the country dimension. Compare Sandbu (2018).

The middle of the income distribution goes missing. The EU-wide approach to income inequality informs about the relative position of the member countries vis-à-vis each other, as it nests the national distributions higher or lower within the EU-wide distribution (Vacas-Soriano and Fernández-Macías, 2018, figure 1) and shows their shifting over time (Brandolini and Rosolia, this volume, figure 2.10). The higher or lower insertion sheds a different light on parts of the national distributions. This is especially visible at both ends of the distribution: the rate of income poverty and the top incomes shares. Poverty in a country, defined in accordance with EU usage as below 60% of median household income, looks radically different if the national median or the EU-wide median is used, as is also pointed out by Brandolini and Rosolia (Chapter 2, this volume), Salverda (2015), Goedemé and Collado (2016), and Goedemé et al. (2017).

Figure 15.9 panel A indicates how EU-wide measurement of poverty (22%) significantly exceeds the national measurement (16%). The number of poor households is enhanced accordingly from 37 million to 48 million. The point is not that the EU-wide approach provides a superior measure of poverty compared to the national one, but that it complements this and offers a pertinent indication of the distance the European Union has to travel to eradicate poverty in the Union as a whole. It also tells that, in itself, the lowering of the national poverty rates, which is an important policy aim of the Europe 2020 Strategy, may do little or nothing to improve the situation from the perspective of European cohesion.

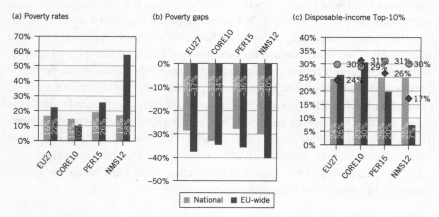

Figure 15.9 National versus EU-wide household poverty rates and top-income shares (2014). The EU27 average poverty rate is 16%, the EU-wide one is 22%. The dots in panel C concern shares in gross income, as in the literature.

For consistency with poverty rates, the top shares are given for equivalized disposable incomes, which contrasts with the gross-income shares common to the top-incomes literature (see Atkinson and Piketty, 2007). Purchasing power parity (PPP)-based and regional totals for EU-wide; country averages for National.

Sources: Author's calculations for annual incomes 2014 on EU Statistics on Income and Living Conditions (EU-SILC) 2015 including exchange rates, PPP's from Eurostat [prc_ppp_ind], accessed 13 October 2017.

The EU-wide CORE10 poverty rate (10%) falls below its national rate (14%) and substantially below the 22% rate for EU27. This contrasts with PERI5, where the poverty rate increases from 19% nationally to 26% EU-wide, and particularly with NMS12, where the rate jumps very strongly from 17% nationally to 58% EU-wide. The EU-wide perspective on the poverty gap (panel B), which is defined as the percentage of the poverty threshold level that the average income of the poor households lies below that threshold, shows a rather different picture. The gap increases for EU27 from 29% nationally to 37% EU-wide. Surprisingly, the gap is not much different for CORE10 and rises from 29% to 34%. Apparently, there are deep pockets of poverty hidden in the national rates of the richer countries. Nonetheless, the gap grows most in NMS12, from 28% to 40%.

A similar comparison for the income shares of households belonging to the top decile (panel C) shows a small difference for the European Union, as the EU-wide level exceeds the country-based level by 2% only. At the regional level, however, the effects are substantial. NMS12, in particular, sees the average share decline from 25% to 7%, and PERI5 from 25% to 20%. This contrasts with a rise from 23% to 30% for CORE10. For gross incomes—common currency of the top incomes literature—the difference is 6% for EU27. For NMS12, they are almost halved (30% to 17%), for PERI5 the difference is 4%, and for CORE10 it is surprisingly small (29% to 31%). Strikingly, the CORE10 top 10% retains about the same share for both gross and disposable EU-wide incomes. Taking poverty and equivalized top incomes together, the EU-wide distribution appears to be more compressed as the middle between those two ends is squeezed from 59% to 52%. The effects are tiny for CORE10, where its size stays around 60%, and for PERI5 (around 55%) and are almost entirely concentrated in NMS12, where the middle share dwindles from 58% nationally to 35% on a EU-wide basis. It implies that there is a long way to go to build a broad European middle class.

15.2.4 Summary

Behind the steady inequality of equivalized disposable income for EU27 since the mid-2000s lies growing market income inequality, irrespective of whether we average national inequalities or aggregate EU-wide incomes, which now is high enough to exceed the American one. Growing income redistribution via pensions and roughly stable redistribution via social transfers explain the calm of disposable income inequality and its level below corresponding American inequality. Underneath the calm surface, however, lurks significant regional divergence from similar levels in 2006 that affects particularly strongly the level and evolution of inequality in the peripheral countries of Greece, Ireland, Italy, Portugal, and Spain (PERI5) in comparison with the NMS (NMS12) and the remaining 10 countries (CORE10). PERI5's rapid rise in market incomes is kept in check by rising pensions but goes together with the lowest level of social transfers and generates the highest of level of disposable income inequality. The lowest incomes in PERI5 have declined existentially in the EU-wide perspective.

Compared to CORE10, NMS12 combines low market inequality with less redistribution into relatively higher disposable income inequality.

The relative rate of income poverty draws essentially the same picture, albeit with a stronger and universal decline in social transfers at the time they were most needed and a larger increase in pensions. It shows very similar changes and relative levels for PERI5, including a high and growing poverty gap. Its anchored poverty rate (2008) increases substantially, confirming doubts surrounding the significance of the running rate's stability. The national averages of poverty differ rather little (16–19%) between regions, but the EU-wide poverty rate of NMS12 pulls up very high (58%) above EU27 (22%), reflecting much lower incomes overall in NMS12. Rather similar, IWP points to the varying incidence of other poverty. Top 10% income shares change little over the years but differ again strongly for NMS12 between average national distributions (25%) and the EU-wide approach (7%).

For NMS12, cohesion with the rest of EU has improved but the gap remains very substantial; cohesion within PERI5 and between them and other countries has suffered since the onset of the Euro crisis and concomitant policymaking. Cohesion within CORE10 diminishes but exceeds other regions.

In all countries, wage earnings and their combination in households make an essential contribution to income and income inequality and to poverty. Dual and multiple earners are a large majority and concentrate in the highest deciles. High-educated homogamous dual earners play a particularly important role in the top decile. This contrasts with the dwindled importance of traditional single earners with a family, though they retain a significant role in PERI5. CORE10, by contrast, experience the largest role for single-person single earners. These two categories concentrate in the lower deciles and experience much higher rates of poverty. The high frequency of more than one earner in a household implies a breakdown of the simple relationship between the distributions of hourly wages and household incomes. The low-paid are found across the entire income distribution. Consequently, only a small minority of them are also poor, while the others are not; conversely, a substantial chunk of the in-work poor are actually better paid (by the hour). Incomes of the poor stretch up to the 7th decile of gross incomes. They shift down only a little in the distribution of disposable incomes after tax and social contributions. The major factor that can explain their poverty is their household characteristics.

15.3 EUROPEAN POLICIES FOR INCOME INEQUALITY

The principal aims of the European Union include the promotion of the well-being of the peoples; economic, social, and territorial cohesion; and solidarity between the member countries (Article 3 of the Treaty on European Union). The European Union has the competence to attain objectives which the participating countries have in common, but only if defined in the Treaty and in accordance with principles of subsidiarity and proportionality. As a consequence, and in strong contrast with the United States, the European Union is responsible for no more than 0.3% of total public social expenditure in the EU countries while the remainder is in the hands of the countries (European Commission, 2017, 24). This underlines the great importance of national policymaking in this field, for better or for worse, and indicates the legal restrictions on EU-level social policymaking and the tensions with Member States that this may generate. Essentially, EU policy in this area amounts to herding ('guiding') the countries by enticing them to subscribe to common social goals and assisting their implementation. This makes the organizational side of European social policy as important for the results as the conceptual side. That organizational side involves both the way social policy is embedded in the structure of EU governance and the instruments it is given for realizing its aims. The conceptual side concerns the content or nature of the policy: its specific purpose and targets. Without proper instruments, the content risks becoming a pious wish; without proper embedding, the content and the instruments run the risk of standing apart from mainstream policymaking and remaining temporary and vulnerable to changes in the political climate. Naturally, the three—content, instruments, and embedding—are intricately related aspects. The natural questions to pose are, what policy does the EU currently have regarding inequality, and how has that worked out? And, what new policy initiatives are or can be developed to conceptually improve inequality policy and organizationally strengthen it? Thus, we can see what may be learned for future policies and bring this to bear on future developments.

The European Union has no policy addressing income inequality as such but concentrates extensively on poverty—as do most individual member countries and the United States as well. Anti-poverty policies do have relevance for income inequality as they concern the lower end of the income distribution, but, at the same time, they miss out on the higher end—often consciously so in recent decades, on the presumption that income from the top will come trickling down the distribution. Plausibly, this has permitted inequality to rise as top incomes have run away from the rest in many places while the claim of trickling down is contested (e.g., Nolan, 2018). The resulting inequality has become the subject of intense public debate worldwide—witness the current volume. First, I evaluate the conceptual and organizational experiences of the Europe 2020 policy on poverty and social exclusion, and, second, I consider how the new initiative of the European Pillar of Social Rights (EPSR), proclaimed in November 2017, may strengthen European policymaking for inequality.[41] The governance structure of

---

41 It is beyond the possibilities of this chapter to deal with EU regional policy where the Union maintains a long tradition. A whole array of funds invests in economic and social restructuring of less-developed regions to promote employment growth (European Commission, 2014) involving monetary transfers between countries

the European Union is an ongoing debate and a project of construction aimed at reconciling the union level with the national level and the economic aspect with the social aspect, all under the particular pressure of building the monetary union. I discuss the experiences of the past decade, which notably comprise the years of the financial and Euro crises. The focus is European policy effects and not the analysis of the drivers of inequality or the incidence of poverty.

15.3.1 Europe 2020 Anti-Poverty Policy: Weakness of Content, Instruments, and Organization

In 2000, the 'old' EU15 established the *Lisbon Strategy* for the period until 2010, aimed at furthering job growth and social cohesion.[42] As a means for improving the coordination of country-level social policies, it established a long list of indicators (Laeken indicators), with the poverty rate (AROP) as *primus inter pares*. This rate was and still is defined as a measure of monetary poverty of households relative to the country's distribution of net equivalized incomes. Households and their individual members are considered to be poor if the income of the household remains below the poverty threshold of 60% of (national) median household income. This relative approach can be understood on the grounds of intercountry comparability, but it also avoids the problem of the absolute approach to poverty: How to specify a basket of goods and services and, in particular, how to adjust this over time to maintain its significance in view of rising prices and structural change in products, population, and incomes?[43] However, the relative approach creates a critical problem of comparability over time as the rate may decline or rise if a country's incomes in general decline or rise. The poor of one year may be able to buy much more/less than those of another year. The national approach creates the equally critical problem of a wide

---

running via the EU level. Though it is not the aim to influence income inequality, the results may actually do so, both within and between countries. Unfortunately, regional income differences have been growing, which has stimulated worries about urban/rural and star-cities/other-cities inequalities similar to those in the United States (Roses and Wolf, 2018; Iammarino et al., 2018; European Commission, 2017; Hendrickson et al., 2018).

42 Formally the policy indicators of poverty and social exclusion make mention of 'at risk of'. However, as Darvas (2019, 1088) observes, the level of risk is left unspecified while it should be significant if it is to have substantive meaning. In contrast, for example, low work intensity (LWI) is actually observed. Therefore, I drop the 'at risk of' part in the text but stick to the acronyms of AROP for poverty and AROPE for poverty and social exclusion.

43 The United States is a case in point because it still adheres to a basket of goods defined in the 1960s (https://www.census.gov/library/working-papers/1997/demo/fisher-02.html). It maintains a plethora of precise poverty lines depending on household size and composition. The EU measure does the same but leaves such differences implicit in the equivalization of income, which depends equally on household size and composition.

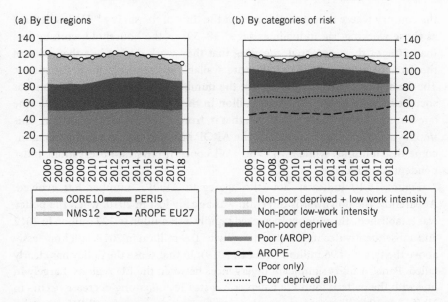

(a) By EU regions

(b) By categories of risk

Figure 15.10 Persons at risk of poverty and social exclusion, × million, EU27 (2006–2018). The 'Poor deprived all' include also the deprived facing low work intensity.
Source: Author's calculations on Eurostat, Intersections of Europe 2020 poverty target indicators by age and sex [ilc_peeso1] (update 17 December 2019).

variation in the purchasing power of the poverty thresholds across EU countries, stretching from a minimum of €2,600 in Romania to a maximum of €17,600 in Luxembourg in (Darvas, 2019, 1097). It gives the concept of poverty very different meanings: the poor in Luxembourg may buy almost seven times as much as those in Romania.

When the Lisbon Strategy expired in 2010, the EU27 agreed to the Europe 2020 Strategy. This explicitly introduced poverty and social exclusion as a field of action, with a 'flagship' policy initiative concerning poverty/inequality.[44] The new Strategy extended beyond monetary poverty to social exclusion. Copeland and Daly (2012) describe the process of political comprise underpinning this, as part of which the composite indicator AROPE was developed. It tops up the monetary poor (AROP) with persons in households that suffer from severe material deprivation (SMD)—an absolute, basket-type element—and/or have very little attachment to the labour market—'low work-intensity' (LWI)—even if they are not poor monetarily.[45]

SMD is observed when the household cannot afford four out of nine items necessary or desirable for people to have an 'acceptable' standard of living in

---

44 Four other fields concern the employment/population rate, spending on research and development, climate change, and the population's educational attainment.
45 Evidently, LWI is left out for pensioners (Verbunt and Guio, 2019).

the country where they live, observed at the time of the survey.[46] LWI is defined as those working-age individuals (aged 18–59) in the household working less than 20% of their potential, meaning that they work during less than 20% of the seven or more months that they are available in the year prior to the survey. The Strategy set the target to reduce the number of persons in poverty and/or social exclusion in the EU by 20 million in the year 2020 relative to 2008 (the latest available year of data in 2010); that is, from 116 million to 96 million. This implies a 17% decrease. As before, the AROP part derives from the national income distributions, while SMD and LWI concern physical observations independent from income.

Figure 15.10 indicates how the aggregate AROPE number has evolved. Apparently, the downwards direction was already lost in 2010, when the policy was established. The number increased rapidly by 8 million to 122 million in 2012 and subsequently declined only gradually to 109 million in 2018, still hopelessly above the target of 96 million (Darvas, 2019). In that sense the policy has clearly failed. Panel A finds significant divergences between the EU regions. Largely in line with the pattern found in Chapter 2, a steady and strong decrease occurs in NMS12 (−10 million) together with a significant increase in the PERI5 countries (+6 million up to 2014) followed by a decrease (−3 million). CORE10 occupies the middle position with a basically stable number: a 3 million growth up to 2014 followed by a 3 million fall to 2017, but then deceptively again increasing by 1 million in 2018.

Apparently, NMS12 have realized a 30% decline (corrected for their 2% population decline), and, had the other two regions followed suit, the 2020 target would have been within easy reach. So, why didn't or couldn't they? Panel B dissects the AROPE numbers in their three component parts: monetary poverty (AROP) and the non-poor top-up split between SMD and LWI and their small overlap. Their dynamics clearly differ. Monetary poverty increases, by 6 million up to 2016, falls slightly in 2017, and increases again in 2018, remaining well above the level of 2008 (+5%). This contrasts with the non-poor SMD who share the initial rise between 2009 and 2012 (+3 million) but then fall quickly to 12 million, well below 2008 (22 million). This fall largely equals the decrease in total AROPE for NMS12. The third category, non-poor with LWI, increases very little and then falls to a level in 2018 (10 million), 18% below 2008 (13 million).

---

46 The nine desirable items are (1) paying rent, mortgage, or utility bills; (2) keeping home adequately warm; (3) facing unexpected expenses; (4) eating meat or proteins regularly; (5) going on holiday; and (6) owning a television set, (7) a washing machine, (8) a car, or (9) a telephone. Numbers are corrected for respondents not wanting or needing certain items. Items 1 to 5 concern 'economic strain' of the households, 6 to 9 'durables'; see https://ec.europa.eu/eurostat/statistics-explained/index.php?title=Glossary:Material_deprivation. Since 2010, more indicators have been developed (Guio et al., 2012) which are left aside here.

The area below the dashed line in the graph indicates the occurrence among the monetary poor of 'sole poverty'; that is, non-overlapping with SMD or LWI. The subsequent area up to the dotted line indicates the poor who are simultaneously poor and deprived while the remaining area of the poor above this line concerns their overlap with LWI. Sole poverty falls between 2008 and 2013 and then rises up to 2018 (+10 million), during the same years that the overall indicator shows a decline. SMD among the poor (including the overlap with LWI) evolves largely similar to the non-poor, diminishes strongly (−7 million, 2012–2018) after a significant increase (+4 million 2009–2012). In contrast, poor LWI retains its role among the increasing and decreasing numbers of the poor, as it grows from 19 million in 2008 to 24 million in 2014 and shrinks to 20 million in 2018. However, the share of the poor among LWI increases, especially after 2014, and as a result LWI now associates more closely with poverty than before.

The diverging territorial dynamics of panel A are consistent with a key organizational weakness of the policy. Though the EU2020 Strategy sets the target at the EU level, it is actually no more than an international agreement that all countries aim at a reduction in poverty. While it asks countries to declare their intentions concerning the targets, it does not specify the country contributions, pro rata or otherwise,[47] to be made to the overall AROPE outcome, nor does it stipulate that the countries' broader policies shall indeed focus on poverty and social exclusion.[48] Thus there is a European policy in the sense of a common desire, but not in the sense of the measures to be taken. Here is a major difference with the United States, where the measurement of poverty[49] is directly linked to a federal policy instrument aimed at reducing that incidence, the Earned Income Tax Credit (EITC), which is wielded by the federal government across all states.[50]

---

47 Countries' known quantitative intentions in the policy area add up to a good 10 million decline in EU's AROPE level, only half of the 20 million needed (SPC, 2018, table 1).

48 Nine countries adopted an indicator different from AROPE (but often covering a part of it): Bulgaria, at risk of poverty; Germany, long-term unemployed; Denmark, persons living in households with LWI; Estonia, at risk of poverty; Ireland, combined poverty, defined as those severe materially deprived who are also at risk of poverty; Latvia, at risk of poverty and/or living in households with very low work intensity; the Netherlands, people aged 0–64 living in a jobless household; Sweden, per cent of women and men aged 20–64 who are not in the labour force (except full-time students), the long-term unemployed, or those on long-term sick leave; United Kingdom, numerical targets from the 2010 Child Poverty Act and Child Poverty Strategy 2011–2014, which are in turn different versions of the 'at risk of poverty' rate (Darvas, 2019: fn 5; see also Salverda, 2015: 40).

49 The United States specifies 48 poverty thresholds, depending on household size and composition, ranging from $12,043 to $ 55,613 in 2018 and applicable to all states; https://www.census.gov/data/tables/time-series/demo/income-poverty/historical-poverty-thresholds.html

50 In the United States in 2018, EITC and child tax credit reached 28.1 million persons, of whom 10.6 million were lifted out of poverty while income was improved for

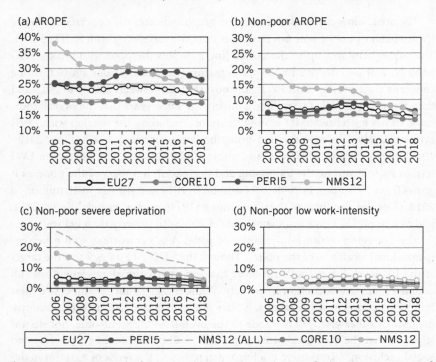

Figure 15.11 Persons at risk of poverty and social exclusion, by type of risk and EU regions, % of respective populations (2006–2018).
The AROPE rate for NMS12 in 2006 is 38%.
Percentages are taken on the groupings' full populations and can be compared per grouping across the panels. The dashed line in panel C indicates severe deprivation including its overlap with the poor; panel D is the same for low work intensity.
Source: Author's calculations on Eurostat, Intersections of Europe 2020 poverty target indicators by age and sex [ilc_peeso1] and In-work at-risk-of-poverty rate by age and sex—
EU Statistics on Income and Living Conditions (EU-SILC) survey [ilc_iwo1] (updates 17 December 2019).

The AROPE rate in NMS12 stagnates around 31% from 2008 to 2013 and then falls to 22% in 2018. In PERI5, it rises from 25% to a plateau of 29% between 2012 and 2016 and then falls to 26% in 2018, still somewhat above the initial level 10 years later and considerably above NMS12. The level fluctuates very little in CORE10, between 19% and 20% only (Figure 15.11 panel A).[51] Have the NMS12 simply been more disciplined in putting effort into their policymaking, compared to the PERI5 and CORE10 whose lack of effort has then supposedly

---

the remaining 17.5 million; https://www.cbpp.org/blog/child-tax-credit-and-earned-income-tax-credit-lifted-106-million-people-out-of-poverty-in-2018

51 Note that the NMS12 population fell by 2%, possibly mainly because of emigration to Western Europe (the Netherlands alone registered an inflow of 0.2% of the total NMS12 population), where they may have augmented AROPE, directly or indirectly.

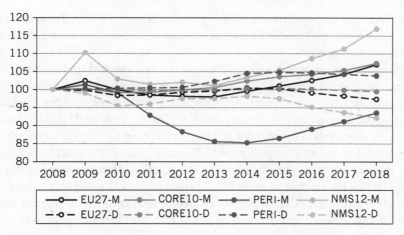

Figure 15.12 Mean equivalized income (national prices of 2018), 2008 = 100, versus the rate of severe material deprivation (poor plus non-poor), cumulative percentage-point change since 2008 set at 100 (2008–2018).
Mean real equivalized household income in NMS12 in 2018 is 17% higher than in 2008.
Extensions M for means, and D for deprivation.
Source: Author's calculation on Eurostat, Mean and median income by household type— EU Statistics on Income and Living Conditions (EU-SILC) survey [ilc_dio4] and see Figure 15.11 for severe deprivation (updates 17 December 2019).

thwarted attaining the common goal? This is no foregone conclusion in the light of panel B, which shows that the NMS12 decline concentrates entirely in the non-poor part of AROPE (8% out of 9% between 2008 and 2018), which in turn rests almost entirely on a decline in the non-poor SMD (8% out of 8%, panel C) while LWI accounts for the rest (1%, panel D). Including the poor, the rate of SMD in NMS12 falls from 28% to 11% (dashed line). The decline is unique and brings NMS12 down from an order of magnitude above the other EU countries to a very similar level. So, even if they would, the other countries could not possibly have matched the great advance of NMS12 as non-poor SMD was much smaller from the start. CORE10's rate is steady, and even in PERI5 the rise is limited to 2 percentage points. It suggests also that a further decline in AROPE for NMS12 may now be as difficult as for the other countries. The same holds *a fortiori* for LWI, where NMS12 is already doing better than the rest.

It seems unlikely that special efforts of poverty policy can be held responsible for the SMD decline, given NMS12's small and shrinking income redistribution wrought by social transfers, the growing poverty gap, and the rise of anchored poverty.[52] The rise (17%) in average real incomes in NMS12, their decrease (6%) in PERI5, and slow growth (7%) in CORE10 seem better candidates

---

52   Also Darvas and Wolff (2014).

for explaining the regional trends in deprivation (Figure 15.12).[53] These relate to the economy more broadly, as the contribution of deprivation among the non-poor would suggest.[54]

One conceptual unease with SMD regards its international application, as the significance of the nine desirable items on which it is based is effectively reduced to five in the richer member countries, because TV, telephone, washing machine, and car are deemed universally available, thus driving down SMD in those countries. To mend this, a broader list of 13 items has been developed, out of which five should be missing to qualify for SMD (Guio et al., 2012, 2017; SPC, 2015), but this has not been officially adopted yet.[55] Another, deeper concern relates to the fact that the amount of money that people need (and miss) for the items is not observed in EU-SILC. It throws a different light on SMD among the non-poor.[56] This makes it less desirable to follow Darvas's (2019) suggestion to consider SMD as a useful indicator of poverty EU-wide.[57]

The Holy Grail of poverty measurement remains out of reach. The income-based indicator is conceptually seen as a snapshot and as focusing on the inputs of the household while ignoring the outcomes that households manage to realize (Nolan and Marx, 2009; Guio, 2009). SMD and LWI add absolute components aimed at compensating for the shortcomings of the monetary approach (AROP) and accounting for the multidimensional nature of poverty (Nolan and Whelan, 2018: 101) and the exclusion from the labour market (SPC, 2015: 5, 10). Anchoring the poverty threshold in real terms in a certain year has been tried as a solution. It does add useful information, indeed, as shown earlier, but also generates new problems.[58] However, instead of anchoring to a single year for a longer period, the annual change in poverty anchored just to the preceding year could perhaps help interpret the parallel changes in AROP.

---

53 In 2017, median incomes in purchasing power parities are 8,200 for NMS12 compared to 12,900 for PERI5 and 17,100 for CORE10. Given poverty gaps, mean incomes of the poor were 3,700, 5,500, and 8,300, respectively.

54 Next to changing incomes, cheap imports may have eased the ownership of durables by lowering prices and have improved infrastructure.

55 Eurostat publishes the statistic (ilc_mdsd01) from 2014 on. It increases the CORE10 and PERI5 levels and lowers the NMS12 level. The trend for NMS12 is virtually identical to SMD.

56 SILC asks whether the lack of an item is 'enforced' (Guio, 2009). SMD still concerns 4% of persons in the highest income quintile of NMS (Eurostat, ilc_mdsd02). For example, higher income households' incomes may contract correspondingly higher mortgages and encounter similar problems of payment as those with lower incomes as a consequence. See also Darvas (2019).

57 Notably, SMD rates show an international coefficient of variation (21–27%) twice that for the Gini coefficients.

58 The choice of anchor year seems arbitrary. Eurostat, ilc_li22, anchors in 2005, the European Commission once did in 2004; see https://ec.europa.eu/social/main.jsp?ca tId=1050&intPageId=1889&langId=en

To conclude this discussion of anti-poverty policy, I look briefly at the Europe 2020 Strategy to consider what significance the measures that were implemented in two other relevant policy areas than poverty may have for income inequality. The areas concern employment, where the aim is to increase the rate of persons in employment to 75% of the working-age population in 2020,[59] and education, with the objective of increasing the rate of persons holding a tertiary degree to 40% among the 30- to 34-year-old age cohort. Both targets seem well within reach, given levels of 73% and 41%, respectively, in 2018. Without doubt the two measures are worthwhile in their own right: the question here is, however, whether they might also pose a risk of growing inequality that needs to be addressed in conjunction with the policy. Section 15.2.2 made it clear that increasing the employment rate is not a self-evident route to shifting people into employment aimed at lifting their households out of poverty (Marx, 2018). The massive role of dual- and multiple-earning mirrors has increased the odds that new jobs—including low-paid ones—are taken up in households already having a job and potentially contribute to increasing inequality.[60] The risk of growing inequality is even stronger for boosting the rate of tertiary educational attainment: witness the significant role of high-educated dual earners at the top of the income distribution. In addition, there is a greater attraction for the highly educated of migrating from lower to higher income countries because of greater potential income gains.[61] Their migration can negatively affect the growth potential of the country that they leave.

To this can be added a few issues that seem to be missing from the policy debate. Organizationally, all cards are put on Member State actions which the EU level aims to inspire but hardly even coordinates. Thus, the EU level itself can take no action on poverty and social exclusion. It cannot counteract the inequality effects of unification itself, which are outside the scope of the national governments, nor can it weigh to compensate for the effects on inequality of actions in other areas at the EU level, as Troika policymaking for Greece has demonstrated.

Finally, the poverty measures pay no attention to persons' access to public services such as good education (Sutherland and Tsakloglou, 2012) nor to people's profit from tax expenditures (Avram, 2018). For the former, new deprivation measures are conceivable; for the latter, the concept of transfers could be broadened.

---

59 This is on a head-count basis including growing part-time employment; the full-time employed (FTE)-based employment rate is at 66% (European Commission, *Employment and Social Developments in Europe Annual Review*).

60 Salverda (2016) examines the link with part-time employment for 10 EU countries.

61 They may double their annual earnings when moving from the top decile of NMS12 to that of CORE10 (author's calculation on SILC 2015).

In summary, the anti-poverty policy has been unsuccessful. The overall target is not at all within reach and actually combines an increase in monetary poverty with a decline in SMD that has been so rapid and geographically concentrated that it puts doubt on the validity of that very indicator. The NMS12 have profited from the decline, but plausibly not as a result of any special policy efforts. This decline has brought these countries roughly in line with the other Member States, which suggests that future progress may become equally challenging to them. By contrast, the Southern European countries and Ireland have combined higher monetary poverty and smaller redistributive efforts with a significant increase in SMD. They have been the clearest victims of the Euro crisis. All in all, the developments of the EU's anti-poverty policy bear out the risks feared by Copeland and Daly (2012) of incoherence as a policy approach to social policy and ineffectiveness in advancing policy actions undertaken by the countries. All policy efforts have been relegated to the national governments, without strictly uniform criteria and with no clear instruments attached.

Anyway, the Europe 2020 policies is now coming to an end. For sustainable European capacity, we need to look beyond this and ask whether new initiatives will be able to offer, conceptually and organizationally, what those anti-poverty policies have been unable to accomplish.

15.3.2 Future Inequality Policy: Uncertain Improvements Under Construction

The launch in 2010 of the Europe 2020 policy on poverty and social exclusion was ill-starred, being set on the brink of the Euro crisis. The crisis exposed the massive capital movements between Member States which the Economic and Monetary Union (EMU) had stimulated but also left unchecked. This provoked a threatening split between debtor countries, also called 'peripheral countries' (PERI5), and creditor countries. They were two sides of the same coin as big banks—deeply weakened by the financial crisis—in large creditor countries bore joint responsibility for these capital flows together with the debtor country lenders. The large creditor countries effectively forced all Eurozone countries to contribute to recouping the lost capital flows (Minenna, 2018), as a result of which government debt rose significantly in Greece, Ireland, Spain, and Portugal. This crisis of its own making led the EA to the adoption of austerity policies for all member countries, very strong ones for the four countries just mentioned, and to an anxious institution building at the Eurozone level. This generated new rules and a new institutional forum, the *European Semester*, which jointly moved crucial elements of economic and financial policymaking away from the national level and gave those leverage over social policymaking.[62] The Eurozone counted 16 members at the time, but the institution building regarded all (except Denmark and the

---

62 Six Pack: EU directive 2011/85 stipulating requirement for Euro Area countries' budgets, Two Pack: Regulation 473/2013 for assessing countries' budgetary plans and

UK) who are obliged to join the EA in due course. Consequently, the two—the European Union and the Eurozone—overlapped strongly in the intertwined response of policymaking and institution building, and the European Commission became deeply involved. Hence the new Europe 2020 policy on poverty and social exclusion has faced a prolonged and deepening economic recession due to overacting policies of austerity and their dominance. This was based on the purpose-built support of the new institution, the European Semester, which aimed to decide also about social reform but ignored concerns of poverty and inequality. The adverse developments in PERI5 merit as much consideration as an effect of European unification as the favourable trends in NMS12. The whole approach has clearly contributed to the failure of Europe 2020 to reduce poverty (Darvas and Tschekassin, 2015; Maquet et al., 2015; De Agostini et al., 2016). The actual efforts of soft-law anti-poverty policy were too weak to overcome the negative economic effects of the crisis and counteract the effects of the hard-law economic and financial policies. Note, however, that the European Commission is not a singular monolith and, though financial and economic policymaking have certainly had the upper hand, certain social improvements have been made, too. This concerns in particular the European Structural and Investment Funds, which are the Commission's responsibility, which were required to spend more on social inclusion during the 2014–2020 period. In 2014, a new small-scale programme was added, the Fund for European Aid to the Most Deprived (FEAD), that subsidizes the provision of food, basic consumer items, and school supplies to those most in need in member countries. It has more than proportionally benefited PERI5 and NMS12.[63]

Can the European Union get its act together to address inequality and improve the content of its policymaking, by making it more adequate in relation to poverty and also widening beyond that; its organization, by adjusting governance at the EU level and coordination with the national level; and also the instruments for implementation, by accounting more effectively for underlying and evolving mechanisms of inequality? I briefly explore the response the European Union is currently developing to these challenges: the introduction of the ESPR and the integration of social policy into the governance structure of the European Semester. There is growing debate whether the EPSR can become

---

correcting excessive deficits, and Treaty on Stability, Coordination and Governance in the Economic and Monetary Union in 2011.

63 Up to 2016, FEAD spent €500 million (in purchasing power parities, 400 million in plain euros). Half of this was spent in PERI5, and 40% in NMS12 (EC-FEAD, 2018). See also Greiss et al. (2019). In a similar vein, see Varoufakis's Modest Proposal of an Emergency Social Solidarity Programme to guarantee access to nutrition and to basic energy needs for all Europeans; https://www.yanisvaroufakis.eu/modest-proposal/4-the-modest-proposal-four-crises-four-policies/policy-4-emergency-social-solidarity-programme-essp/#top)

a game changer towards reinforcing the social dimension of the European Union, not only conceptually but also organizationally, as it is being built into the Semester. In that sense, the Pillar provides not an updated version of the standalone Europe 2020 Strategy but an agenda for action within the mainstream of EU governance. Will the Pillar's agenda be adequate to address inequality, and will the governance structure, hastily built with an overarching economic and financial remit in response to the Euro crisis, adjust and reinforce that agenda? Will it manage to mainstream social policy, which means not just admitting it to the mainstream policymaking but also allowing it to influence this on an equal footing?

15.3.2.1 Pillar of Social Rights

The EPSR is an official Proclamation signed by the EU's three top organisms: Parliament, Council (of governments), and Commission, in November 2017.[64] It aims at fostering a high level of social protection, combatting social exclusion, and making the associated rights more understandable and explicit for citizens (European Commission, 2018a). The EPSR by itself, however, lends no individual, enforceable entitlements because that would conflict fundamentally with EU legalities (Vandenbroucke, 2018). Such rights depend instead on their implementation by national governments in national laws.

First, as to content, the Pillar identifies 20 'principles' which specify 30-odd rights, including some rights within rights, some already existing in binding provisions of EU law, and some new additions to the *acquis social* (e.g., on adequate minimum wages).[65] These principles divide over three social dimensions: equal opportunities and access to the labour market, fair working conditions, and social protection and inclusion. Most relevant are five principles. Principle 6 stipulates that IWP shall be prevented by adequate minimum pay; Principle 11 entitles children to protection from poverty; Principle 14 entitles persons without sufficient resources to minimum benefits that allow a 'life in dignity'; Principles 15 and 17 promise the same to persons in old age or the disabled. Word for word, the Pillar overlaps modestly with the existing poverty policy but it offers also a much broader coverage of the social domain and addresses several mechanisms that contribute to income inequality. It falls short, however, of a broad grasp of inequality including top incomes, and it does not

---

64 European Union (2017) and https://ec.europa.eu/commission/priorities/deeper-and-fairer-economic-and-monetary-union/european-pillar-social-rights/european-pillar-social-rights-20-principles_en

65 The 1989 Community Charter of the Fundamental Social Rights of Workers (Deakin, 2017), the 2000 Charter of Fundamental Rights of the European Union, and the 1961 European Social Charter of the Council of Europe and its 1996 revision (De Schutter, 2018).

consider the potential inequality effects individual principles may have.[66] On this basis, the Pillar has put on the agenda of the EU institutions a broad set of regulations, directives, and recommendations to initiate. These aim at giving body to the rights (e.g., employment guidelines, parental leave, posting workers, written labour contracts, labour authority, etc.; Commission, 19/2/2019; 17/11/2018). EPSR might risk squandering its energy if it does not prioritize a few principles in the first stage. Minimum income protection and child poverty provide the strongest moral stepping stones conceptually, while unemployment benefit reinsurance may provide an organizational example to follow.[67]

Second, with regard to organization, like Europe 2020 before it, the Pillar's progress hinges on the actions to be taken—or not—by the national governments. While the rights expressed in the Pillar are per se not enforceable, the Commission suggests, for certain principles, legal acts to make them binding across the Member States. As there may be more legal leverage over Member States in the field of labour, they concern mainly labour rights, with substantial relevance for so-called non-standard employment, and include also paid family and care leave. The EPSR is said not to affect the rights of Member States to define the fundamental principles of their social security systems or the financial equilibrium of those systems (European Commission, 2018a, 5). The European Commission has to work together with the countries with the help of the Open Method of Coordination (OMC), which is a voluntary process of political co-operation, reviewing and providing best-practice advice on commonly agreed objectives and indicators. To support this herding of the Member States, the Council has adopted a Recommendation on access to social protection for all workers and the self-employed, adopted in December 2018—the countries will need to explain what they have done on the subject. The herding may be helped also by the fact that, more than before, the EPSR may receive (some) financial leverage from the Social Investment Package 2013 and the European Social Fund Plus (Andor, 2018). All in all, the EPSR may serve to increase political pressures to work towards the common objectives, even though the Proclamation is not legally binding to the Members States (Costamagna, 2019). Maurizio Ferrera (2018) interprets the rights beyond legal entitlements as sources of power, of normative, enforcement, and instrumental resources, where the European Union can actually play a role to support its citizens. Nonetheless, the organizational setup continues to ignore the actions at the EU-level and interaction effects between countries due to unification itself, which need addressing at the EU level.

---

66 As discussed earlier for the employment and tertiary education policies of Europe 2020, parental leave is very worthwhile in its own right. However, it may more than proportionally benefit higher incomes given the income position of dual earners.

67 Cantillon (2019) strongly advocates granting Principle 14 (minimum income protection) first priority among the 20 principles.

Next to national governments, the Pillar attributes a key role for the delivery of social rights to the social dialogue of trade union and employer associations at EU and national levels. The Commission's relaunching of the 'social dialogue' promotes social partner involvement in national consultation processes (ESDE, 2018: 171; European Commission, 2018a: 40).[68] The realization, however, depends on national governments.[69] Clearly, the commitment of the social partners is of utmost importance for the much needed support for the EPSR to flourish. Also, the social dialogue is of great value in itself and can help to reduce inequalities (Bosch, Chapter 13 this volume; Vaughan-Whitehead, 2018). Nonetheless, its role for the EPSR, poverty, and income inequality is not straightforward. First, the importance and nature of the social dialogue differs significantly between countries (Eurofound, 2016), yet the Pillar has no indicators for the presence and quality of the dialogue (Salverda, 2019). Using the rate of collective bargaining coverage as a headline indicator is proposed (European Economic and Social Committee [EESC], 2018: 18), but that may not be sufficient. However broad the spread of collective bargaining, the outcomes depend on the relative power of the parties. Unions, when they are weak, may cave in to employer demands, and employer associations may be too weak to discipline the behaviour of their members in accordance with agreements reached in the dialogue.[70] Second, fair working conditions, the social dimension nearest to the social partners' hearts, risk overshadowing the other two, particularly social protection and inclusion. For example, the Commission invites Member States to take complementary measures to avoid IWP (European Commission, 2018a: 34). Needless to say that IWP is an utterly distressing phenomenon. Nonetheless, for political priorities, it needs to be set against poverty in general, which is 3 to 10 times more frequent.[71] Third, it is not straightforward that social partners, through their wage bargaining, can diminish the problem as employers will normally (and correctly) not be familiar with the poverty status of their employees (Bennett, 2018), for the two reasons discussed earlier: low-paid jobs are present up to the top of the income distribution and differ from IWP, and, earners' families can be poor in spite of higher

---

68 This revives a common objective of the European Union and its Member States (Articles 151–155 TFEU).

69 Trade unions harbour severe doubts whether the governments will involve them and, if so, how (EESC, 2018: ii).

70 For example, Salverda (2019) shows the drastic increase in temporary employment in the Netherlands, to about the highest rate in the European Union and plausibly way beyond what the Pillar's Principle 5 (on secure and adaptable employment) aims at, and he discusses in detail how this could occur in spite of the two EU Directives: 1999/70 on temporary work and 2008/104 on temp work agencies.

71 IWP varies across countries between 10% and 32% of AROP (IWP rate × employed persons]/AROP persons).

earnings.[72] Note that the suggestion of introducing a EU reinsurance scheme for national systems of unemployment benefits (e.g., Beblavý and Lenaerts, 2017; Vandenbroucke, 2018) tends in the same labour-focused direction. Involving the social partners is viewed in an instrumental perspective as 'crucial to increase the ownership of reforms' (Joint Employment Report, 2017: 4).

Third, on the instrumentation, the Commission closely monitors developments at EU and country levels as a means of herding governments towards the realization of the Pillar's aims and rights. This is done with the help of the *Social Scoreboard*, with close to 100 indicators,[73] many of them retained from the earlier monitoring of various Europe 2020 policies and some new additions for income growth and income inequality. Fourteen are integrated as headline indicators concerning the EPSR in the European Semester's policymaking. These include AROPE and the impact of social transfers on poverty, which are joined by the income quintile shares ratio (S80/S20) for income inequality, the cumulative change in real average disposable household income, and the net earnings of a full-time single worker without children earning the average wage for income growth (European Commission, 2018b: 3).[74] Secondary indicators of the Scoreboard include AROP, SMD, LWI, and IWP. It implies retaining the weaknesses of Europe 2020 discussed earlier. The Pillar improves, though, by going beyond the preoccupation with financial efforts to reduce poverty. Importantly, some rights (e.g., minimum pay) may be considered as instruments for realizing other rights. Although quantitative indicators have been retained, the Pillar does not specify target levels or time paths for its implementation but gives mainly a sense of direction. However, some of the principles and ensuing rights could easily be attributed precise target levels. What else can 'Children have the right to protection from poverty' (Principle 11) sensibly mean than a zero-poverty rate among them? Similarly, minimum income protection (Principle 14) can be linked to the poverty threshold (Crepaldi et al., 2017: 87), filling a lacuna of Europe 2020 policies. Unfortunately, the Child poverty rate and the Poverty gap are not part of the Social Scoreboard or the Semester headline indicators.

15.3.2.2 European Semester
EPSR headline indicators have made their way to the heart of EU decision-making since the Employment Guidelines, on which European Semester policymaking is traditionally based; they have been updated in July 2018 to incorporate various

---

72 A sensible indicator could be the IWP rate of single workers alone as it avoids complex calculations (EESC, 2018: 17) and may also bring out more clearly the effects of wage bargaining and a minimum wage.

73 https://composite-indicators.jrc.ec.europa.eu/social-scoreboard/

74 The latter replaced the average compensation of employees per hour worked (European Commission, 2018, Joint employment report 2019: 23), in response to demands made by member states (Joint employment report 2018: fn 16).

criteria based on the EPSR. The European Semester is the most relevant channel for policymaking in an interaction between the national and EU levels. It allows the Commission to evaluate the performance of individual countries regarding the common criteria and to propose to the Council (of governments) specific country recommendations for further development, which the countries supposedly put in practice in their reform plans and national budgets for the following year. But will the EPSR's impact in the Semester go beyond or stop at the addition of indicators, as suggested by Costamagna (2019)? The insertion of the EPSR was extensively discussed in the Joint Employment Reports of 2018 and 2019, which are important preparatory documents that each year kick off the trajectory of the Semester. The reports now examine the progress of EPSR in one chapter with that of the Employment Guidelines in another. The latest version, the draft Report for 2020 of 17 December 2019, however, illustrates how weak the role of the social still is in EU policymaking. In a detailed discussion of the EPSR headline indicators, the Report shows that as the impact of social transfers on poverty shrinks, the inequality of incomes (i.e., the quintile shares ratio) grows, and IWP remains high.[75] Surprisingly, these red lights flashing for inequality solicit no stronger response than that they require 'action by Member States in different areas' (5). This contrasts sharply with the significant policy discussions that follow the examination of each of the Employment Guidelines.

Therefore, one may doubt the impact that the EPSR in and of itself will really have on the EU process of political decision-making. The Semester has a broad remit, and social protection and cohesion are but one element that has now been added, but it remains at risk of being overwhelmed by other policy concerns. Even now, in 2020, everything in the explanation of the Semester continues to read exactly as before: the priorities are economic, with the explicit goals being sound public finance, macroeconomic balance, structural reform, and investment growth.[76] It tends also to put social policy in a straitjacket of structural reform and international uniformity and to ignore the contribution that increasing the financial means might make to improving social protection. There is no a priori need for such a uniform approach (Bertola, 2018).[77] The United States is

---

75 It actually increased for EU28 (Eurostat: TESPM070).

76 Witness   https://ec.europa.eu/info/business-economy-euro/economic-and-fiscal-policy-coordination/eu-economic-governance-monitoring-prevention-correction/european-semester/framework/european-semester-why-and-how_en (accessed 19 January 2020). Neither has there been much change in the broader environment of the Semester: no mention of poverty or inequality in the Commission's annual State of the Union of 2017 or 2018, no mention of the social side in the Commission's Roadmap of December 2017 for deepening Europe's economic and monetary union in 2018.

77 The concept of a European Social Union (Vandenbroucke et al., 2017; Vandenbroucke, 2018) as a union of welfare states—not a unified welfare state—takes national decision-making on welfare as leading and adds the protection of a union.

the monetary union par excellence, with substantial interstate transfers and a far larger role for the federal government compared with the EU institutions. Yet it is characterized by substantial and enduring differences in economic outcomes across the states, such as income inequality (Salverda, 2015b), employment- and unemployment-to-population ratios, and social institutions such as the minimum wage and union membership. For the Pillar and its rights to become a permanent success, the suitability of the hastily built EU governance structure and its overarching policy preferences need evaluation and re-equilibration between hard and soft law to prevent a weakening of social policy at the moment it is most needed. Will EPSR rights survive better materially than Europe 2020 policies if a new bout of austerity policies were initiated and implemented at EU level, particularly in countries subject to similar far-reaching Troika-type treatments with strong distributive effects (Kornezov, 2017)? It seems worthwhile to explore how retaining social responsibility at the national level can actually assist countries in obtaining the comparable economic outcomes they apparently seek as an outcome of monetary union (witness, e.g., the identical 75% employment rates and 40% educational attainment rates they have all wanted to subscribe to for Europe 2020) and avoid a future of Europe where economic and employment growth are predominantly concentrated in the geographical area around London, Amsterdam, Munich, Milano, and Paris while large regions if not entire countries have to live with the choice between becoming a rustbelt or a holiday dependency. Clearly, with long histories of self-determination, neither the peoples of Germany, France, Belgium, the Netherlands, and the UK nor those of other countries at the losing end will expect such outcomes from European unification for themselves.

15.3.2.3 Consequences of Unification

I conclude with a word about the missing capstone of both the Pillar's content and the Semester's organizational setup, which I relate to the high end of income inequality. Economic unification can offer leverage beyond what individual countries can accomplish and where they would do well to cede to the EU level—compare Commission proposals for fair taxation of the digital economy.[78] However, unification also enhances interrelated risks between the participating countries. Increased competition and growing economies of scale may pull firms from one country to another while workers are left behind, unemployed and dependent on the first country's protection system. Or people may migrate more easily, taking their human capital with them at a cost to their own country's educational investment and its productive potential, but to the advantage of another country.

---

78 https://ec.europa.eu/taxation_customs/business/company-tax/fair-taxation-digital-economy_en

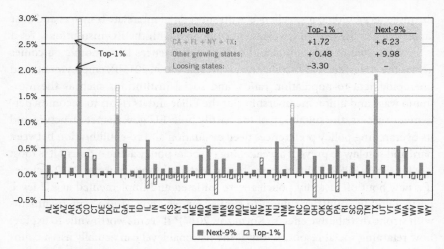

Figure 15.13 Shifting top 1% and next 9% income shares across American states: Percentage point of aggregate income in 2012 minus 1980.
Alaska's share of next 9% incomes in total income 2012 exceeds that of 1980 by 0.17%, that of top 1% incomes decreases by 0.11%.
Source: Author's calculations on Frank et al. (2015).

Similarly, the greater ease of financial transactions across countries, especially if monetary union takes away the exchange risk, may help to geographically concentrate incomes and wealth. Figure 15.13 serves to illustrate such growing concentration in the United States. It shows how the top 1% and next 9% (top 10% excluding top 1%) shares in total income have changed nationally and across the 50 states. The four states California, Florida, New York, and Texas have witnessed substantial increases for both shares; several other states have booked small increases for one or both; whereas a substantial number, with negative values, witnessed declining participation in the top 1%. It cannot be left to single countries to deal with such a phenomenon but warrants attention in an integrated setup of national and EU-level policymaking that allows for effects of the unified aggregate. This underlines also the need to broaden the focus of inequality policy beyond poverty and redistribution to top incomes and their formation as market incomes also at the EU level. The 'Manifesto to Save Europe from Itself' of Thomas Piketty and others suggests a possible solution of a European tax on, inter alia, incomes exceeding €200,000; Piketty et al., 2018). This would evidently help to reduce the incentives for persons to move within the European Union due to tax arbitrage.

15.4 CONCLUSION

I have taken four steps to get here: examining inequality trends and regional differences, exploring the main transmission mechanism from wage earnings to household incomes, assessing existing EU policy experiences, and reviewing options for future improvement of Europe's social policymaking. The upshot is that inequality for the European Union has been largely stable but only as a balance of opposing trends: a sharp increase in PERI5 countries, characterized by a disastrous falling away of the lowest incomes and also at least partly due to EU-level policymaking; a modest increase in CORE10, plausibly due to unsatisfactory redistribution in view of rising market income inequality; and a relatively strong decrease in NMS12 which cannot be attributed to increased redistributive effort but seems to relate to general improvements in income. By and large, the European Union has been unable to make noticeable progress on poverty reduction and diminution of inequality. What adds to the worry, even more on the future of European unification than of income inequality, is the potential responsibility of European policy for the outcomes in 'peripheral' countries. These disappointing experiences are not a loss, but instead can offer lessons for building a sustainable capacity for dealing with income inequality as long as the lessons shed a fresh light on the problems of constructing adequate policies and of relating the national and the EU levels.

Though Europe does not improve on the United States for market incomes, it does provide stronger redistribution in virtually all Member States that leads to lower inequality of disposable household incomes. Here the new EPSR can offer the perspective of improvement by its breadth and the instruments it brings in as a result, certainly when circumstances remain relatively favourable and help to build political momentum. The first priority remains the reduction of poverty, for which improvement of minimum income protection, child benefits, and minimum wages can be pursued on the basis of the Pillar.

To endure and play its protective role also under adverse circumstances the Pillar needs a solid embedding in EU governance, the European Semester, which then needs adjustment to allow the Pillar to influence policy priorities and policy integration more general. The European perspective cannot be missed because it will become only more important and perhaps threatening. The point is not that country trends diverge but that divergences may hang together. Here the countries and the EU level should nurture what can better be addressed together. In addition, national successes in the fight against poverty will do little to change EU-wide inequality, and an exclusive focus on poverty will have little effect on the growing inequality of market incomes, which implies a growing need for income redistribution. This inequality growth will persist due to further economic integration as well as changing household labour market behaviour. These developments are widely shared and progressively invalidate traditional remedies to inequality. Looking for the right answers is a challenge shared by all countries.

Households living mainly on wage earnings provide the backbone to income inequality, not only because earnings are by far the most important source of income but also because they massively rank in the highest deciles of the income distribution. That is due primarily to the combined earnings of employees in dual- and multiple-earner households, a situation that reflects—on the positive side—the secular increase in opportunities for many to find employment and generate an own income. As this has gone hand in hand with the improved educational attainment of many—women in particular—that upward skewing of household earnings goes together with a strong gradient of educational attainment. In other words (and another worry), highly educated homogamy has become a core feature of dual-earner households at the top of the income distribution in various countries and will inevitably spread to other countries. Nowadays, 75% of employees share a household with another employee, while among the remaining single breadwinners very few manage to reach the top of the income distribution and many are found among the working poor. The distributions of hourly wages and household incomes are no longer Siamese twins. Via additional earners in dual- and multiple-earner households low pay is found up to the top of the income distribution. As educational attainment will only increase over the coming years, these are worrying trends that may be expected to continue to reinforce market income inequality and perhaps also to simultaneously diminish the political demand for redistribution.

In response to these findings I advocate paying separate attention to the negative and positive effects of unification and providing room for policymaking at the EU level based on indicators (e.g., geographical measures of concentration of employment by firms, industries, and personal characteristics such as educational attainment) that look more directly and precisely at such effects than at macroeconomic imbalances. To improve on policymaking regarding poverty, I suggest focusing on the poverty gap—ultimately, reducing this to zero will amount to eradicating poverty and providing adequate minimum income protection. The gap offers the advantage of relatively small country differences in both the national and the EU-wide perspective (Figure 15.9, panel B), which implies two things: all countries can profit, and a change in due course from the national to the EU-wide perspective has no major effects. An adequate reduction policy could be designed for the individual countries to implement while their costs will be subsidized by the European Funds on the basis of the success they achieve in reducing the gap. Such a policy could comprise at least, first, a European child benefit (Atkinson, 2015: proposal 12) because of its great effectiveness (Levy et al., 2013, Leventi et al., 2019) together with, second, a combination of a kind of broad EITC because this can remedy the skewed distribution of dual and multiple earners and, at the same time, preserve individual taxation when combined with a minimum wage that serves to ensure that the benefits of the EITC accrue to households instead of firms. More elements can be added and also address the top incomes.

ACKNOWLEDGEMENTS

I am very grateful to Veerle Rook for her treatment of the SILC 2015 data.

REFERENCES

Alcidi, C., Núñez Ferrer, J. Di Salvo, M., Musmeci, R., and Pilati, M. (2018, 9 January). *Income Convergence in the EU: A tale of two speeds.* Commentary. Brussels: CEPS.

Andor, L. (2018). *A timely call for a social union.* http://www.euvisions.eu/issues/europea-social-union-public-forum-debate/

Atkinson, A. (2015). *Inequality. What can be done?* Cambridge, MA: Harvard University Press.

Avram, S. (2018). Who benefits from the 'hidden welfare state'? The distributional effects of personal income tax expenditure in six countries. *Journal of European Social Policy, 28*(3), 271–293.

Beblavý, M., and Lenaerts, K. (2017). *Feasibility and added value of a European unemployment benefits scheme.* Brussels: CEPS. https://www.ceps.eu/system/files/EUBS%20final.pdf

Beckfield, J. (2006). European integration and income inequality. *American Sociological Review, 71*(6), 964–985.

Beckfield, J. (2009). Remapping inequality in Europe. *International Journal of Comparative Sociology, 50*(5–6), 486–509.

Benczur, P., Cseres-Gergely, Z., and Harasztosi, P. (2017). *EU-wide income inequality in the era of the Great Recession.* JRC Working Papers in Economics and Finance. Ispra, IT: Joint Research Centre. doi:10.2760/244655

Bennett, F. (2018). Rethinking low pay and in-work poverty. *IPPR Progressive Review, 24*(4), 354–360.

Bertola, G. (2010). Inequality, integration and policy: issues and evidence from EMU. *Journal of Economic Inequality, 8,* 345–365.

Bertola, G. (2018). It's OK to be different: Policy coordination and economic convergence. European Economic Advisory Group (*EEAG) report on the European economy* (pp. 64–82). Munich: CESifo.

Blanchet, T., Chancel, L., and Gethin, A. (2019). *How unequal is Europe? Evidence from distributional national accounts, 1980–2017.* Working paper 2019/06. World Inequality Database WID.world. https://wid.world/document/bcg2019-full-paper/

Bönke, T., and Schröder, C. (2015). *European-wide inequality in times of the financial crisis.* Discussion Paper 1482. Berlin: DIW.

Brandolini, A., and Viviano, E. (2017). Extensive versus intensive margin: changing perspectives on the employment rate. In Atkinson, A.B.,

Guio, A-C., and Matlier, E. (eds.), *Monitoring social inclusion in Europe 2017 Edition* (chapter 14). Luxembourg: Eurostat.

Cantillon, B. (2019). *The European Pillar of Social Rights: Ten arguments for prioritising principle 14 on minimum incomes.* http://www.euvisions.eu/issues/europea-social-union-public-forum-debate/

Copeland, P., and Daly, M. (2012). Varieties of poverty reduction: Inserting the poverty and social exclusion target into Europe 2020. *Journal of European Social Policy,* 22(3), 273–287.

Costamagna, F. (2019). *The European Social Union as a 'union of national welfare states: a legal perspective.* http://www.euvisions.eu/issues/europea-social-union-public-forum-debate/

Crepaldi, C. et al. (2017). *Study: Minimum income policies in EU Member States.* European Parliament EMPL Committee. Brussels: European Parliament.

Darvas, Z. (2016). *Some are more equal than others: New estimates of global and regional inequality.* Working Paper 8. Brussels: Bruegel.

Darvas, Z. (2018). *EU income inequality decline: Views from an income shares perspective.* Brussels: Bruegel. http://bruegel.org/2018/07/eu-income-inequality-decline-views-from-an-income-shares-perspective/

Darvas, Z. (2019). Why is it so hard to reach the EU's poverty target? Social Indicator Research, 141 (3), 1018-1105. https://doi.org/10.1007/s11205-018-1872-9

Darvas, Z., and Tschekassin, O. (2015). *Poor and under pressure: the social impact of Europe's fiscal consolidation.* Bruegel Policy Contribution Issue 2015/04. Brussels: Bruegel. www.bruegel.org March 2015

Darvas, Z., and Wolff, G.B. (2014). *Europe's social problem and its implications for economic growth.* Bruegel Policy Brief 2014/03. Brussels: Bruegel. https://www.bruegel.org/2014/03/europes-social-problem-and-its-implications-for-economic-growth/

De Agostini, P., Paulus, P. A., and Tasseva, I. (2016). *The effect of changes in tax-benefit policies on the income distribution in 2008-2015.* Euromod Working Paper EM 6/16. https://www.euromod.ac.uk/sites/default/files/working-papers/em6-16.pdf

Deakin, S. (2017). What follows austerity? From Social Pillar to New Deal. In Vandenbroucke, F. et al. (eds.). *A European Union after the crisis,* chapter 8. Cambridge: Cambridge University Press.

De Schutter, O. (2018). T*he European pillar of social rights and the role of the European social charter in the EU legal order.* Study for European Social Charter and of the CoE-FRA-ENNHRI-Equinet Platform on Economic and Social Rights. Strasbourg: Council of Europe.

EC-FEAD: *Report from the Commission to the Council and the European Parliament Summary of the annual implementation reports for the operational programmes co-financed by the Fund for European Aid to the Most Deprived in 2016, Annex*. Brussels: European Commission, 14 November 2018 COM(2018) 742 final

ESDE: Employment and Social Developments (2018). *Employment and Social Developments in Europe Annual Review 2018*. Brussels: European Commission.

Eurofound: European Foundation for Living and Working Conditions. (2016). *New topics, new tools and innovative practices adopted by the social partners*. Dublin: Eurofound.

Eurofound: European Foundation for Living and Working Conditions. (2018). *Upward convergence in the EU: Concepts, measurements and indicators*. Dublin: Eurofound.

European Commission. (2014). *The European Unions explained: Regional policy*. Brussels: European Commission. doi:10.2775/74781

European Commission. (2017). *Reflection paper on the social dimension of Europe*. COM(2017) 206. Brussels: European Commission.

European Commission. (2018a). *Monitoring the implementation of the European Pillar of Social Rights*. SWD67. Brussels: European Commission.

European Commission. (2018b). *Summary of the annual implementation reports for the operational programmes co-financed by the Fund for European Aid to the Most Deprived in 2016*. COM(2018) 742 final. Brussels: European Commission.

European Economic and Social Committee (EESC). (2018). *Study: Implementing the European Pillar of Social Rights: What is needed to guarantee a positive social impact*. Brussels: European Commission.

European Union. (2017). *European Pillar of Social Rights*. Booklet. https://ec.europa.eu/commission/sites/beta-political/files/social-summit-european-pillar-social-rights-booklet_en.pdf

Ferrera, M. (2018). *Crafting the ESU: Towards a roadmap for delivery*. http://www.euvisions.eu/issues/europea-social-union-public-forum-debate/

Filauro, F. (2017). *European incomes, national advantages: EU-wide inequality and its decomposition by country and region*. Research Paper Series No. 05/2017. Brussels: EERI.

Filauro, F. (2018). *The EU-wide income distribution: inequality levels and decompositions*. European Commission. Luxembourg: Publications Office of the European Union .Filauro, F., and Parolin, Z. (2019). Unequal unions? A comparative decomposition of income inequality in the European Union and United States. *Journal of European Social Policy, 29* (4), 545–563.

Frank, M., Sommeiller, E., Price, M., and Saez, E. (2015, July.). Frank-Sommeiller-price series for top income shares by US states since 1917. WTID Methodological Notes. https://wid.world/document/wid_methodology_notes_2015_7_us/

Freeman, R. (2007). The great doubling: The challenge of the new global labor market. In J. Edwards., M. Crain, and A. Kalleberg (eds.), *Ending poverty in America: How to restore the American dream* (chapter 4). New York: New Press.

Goedemé, T., and Collado, D. (2016). The EU convergence machine at work: To the benefit of the EU's poorest citizens? *Journal of Common Market Studies,* 54(5), 1142–1158.

Goedemé, T., Trindade, L., and Vandenbroucke, F. (2017). *A pan-European perspective on low-income dynamics in the EU.* Working paper 17/03. CSB: Center for Social Policy Herman Deleeck. Antwerp: University of Antwerp.

Greiss, J., Cantillon, B., Marchal, S., and Penne, T. (2019). *Europe as agent that fills the gaps? The case of FEAD.* Working Paper 1903. CSB: Center for Social Policy Herman Deleeck. Antwerp: University of Antwerp.

Guio, A.-C. (2009). *What can be learned from deprivation indicators in Europe.* Eurostat Methodologies and working papers. Luxembourg: Eurostat.

Guio, A.-C., Gordon, D., and Marlier, E. (2012). *Measuring material deprivation in the EU. Indicators for the whole population and child-specific indicators.* Eurostat Methodologies and working papers. Luxembourg: Eurostat.

Guio, A.-C., Gordon, D., Najera, H., and Pomati, M. (2017). *Revising the EU material deprivation variables. 2017 Edition.* Eurostat, Statistical Working Papers. Luxembourg: Eurostat.

Hendrickson, C., Muro, M., and Galston, W. (2018). *Countering the geography of discontent: Strategies for left-behind places.* Washington, DC: Brookings.

Heidenreich, M. (2016). The Europeanisation of income inequality before and during the eurozone crisis: Inter-, supra- and transnational perspectives. In M. Heidenreich (ed.), *Exploring inequality in Europe: Diverging income and employment opportunities in the crisis* (pp. 22–45). London: Edward Elgar.

Hills, J., McKnight, A., Bucelli, I., Karagiannaki, E., Vizard, P., and Yang, L., with Duque, M., and Rucci, M. (2019). *Understanding the relationship between poverty and inequality. Overview report.* CASE report No. 119 LIPpaper 10. London: Centre for Analysis of Social Exclusion CASE, London School of Economics and Political Science.

Iammarino, S., Rodriguez-Pose, A., and Storper, M. (2018). Regional inequality in Europe: Evidence, theory and policy implications. *Journal of Economic Geography,* 1–26. doi:10.1093/jeg/lby021

Inchauste, G., and Karver, J. (2017). Fiscal redistribution in the European Union. World Bank. http://pubdocs.worldbank.org/en/632981520461235859/EU-IG-Report-Fiscal-Redistribution.pdf

Joint Employment Report (2017). *Joint employment report from the Commission and the Council as adopted by the EPSCO Council 3 March 2017.* Brussels: European Commission.

Joint Employment Report (2018). *Joint employment report from the Commission and the Council as adopted by the EPSCO Council 15 March 2018.* Brussels: European Commission.

Joint Employment Report (2019). *Joint employment report from the Commission and the Council as adopted by the EPSCO Council 15 March 2019.* Brussels: European Commission.

Karaganniaki, E. (2017). *The empirical relationship between income poverty and income inequality in rich and middle income countries.* CASE paper No. 206 LIPpaper 3. London: Centre for Analysis of Social Exclusion CASE, London School of Economics and Political Science.

Kornezov, A. (2017). Social rights, the Charter, and the ECHR: Caveats, austerity and other disasters. In Vandenbroucke, F. et al. (eds.). *A European Union after the crisis*, chapter 16. Cambridge: Cambridge University Press.

Leventi, C., Sutherland, H., and Tasseva, I.V. (2019). Improving poverty reduction in Europe: What works best where? *Journal of European Social Policy*, 29(1), 29–43.

Levy, H., Matsaganis, M., and Sutherland, H. (2013). Towards a European Union Child Basic Income? Within and between country effects. *International Journal of Microsimulation*, 6(1), 63–85.

Maquet. I., et al. (2015) for European Commission, DG Employment. *High and rising inequalities: What can be done about it (at EU level)?* Analytical Web Note 6/2015. Brussels: European Commission.

Marx, I. (2018). Europe's poor need more than jobs. *Social Europe*. https://www.socialeurope.eu/europes-poor-need-jobs

Matsaganis, M., Medgyesi, M., and Karakitsios, A. (2015). *The interaction between minimum wages, income support, and poverty.* Research note 10/2015. European Commission, DG Employment and Social Affairs. Brussels: European Commission.

Minenna, M. (2018). A look back: What Eurozone 'risk sharing' actually meant. *Financial Times/Alphaville*, 10 October. https://ftalphaville.ft.com/2018/10/10/1539147600000/A-look-back--what-Eurozone--risk-sharing--actually-meant/

Nolan, B. (2018). *Inequality and inclusive growth in rich countries: Shared challenges, and contracting fortunes.* Oxford: Oxford University Press.

Nolan, B., and Marx, I. (2009). Poverty and social exclusion. In: Salverda, W., Nolan, B., Checchi, D., Marx, I., McKnight, A., Tóth, I.G., and Van de Werfhorst, H. (eds). *Changing Inequalities in Rich Countries: Analytical and Comparative Perspectives*, Chapter 13. Oxford: Oxford University Press.

Nolan, B., and Whelan, C. (2018). Poverty and social exclusion indicators in the European Union: The role of non-monetary deprivation indicators. In R. M. Carmo, C. Rio, and M. Nedgyesi (eds.), *Reducing inequalities. A challenge for the European Union?* (pp. 97–114). London: Palgrave Macmillan.

Piketty, T., et al. (2018, 10 December). *Our manifesto to save Europe from itself.* *The Guardian.* https://www.theguardian.com/commentisfree/2018/dec/09/manifesto-divided-europe-inequality-europeans

Roses, J., and Wolf, N. (2018). *Regional economic development in Europe, 1900–2010: A description of the patterns.* CEPR Discussion Paper 12749. Washington, DC: CEPR.

Salverda, W. (2015a). Individual earnings and household incomes: mutually reinforcing inequalities? *European Journal of Economics and Economic Policies: Intervention*, 12(2), 190–203.

Salverda, W. (2015b). EU policy making and growing inequalities. European economy. Discussion Paper 008. European Commission, Directorate-General for Economic and Financial Affairs. http://ec.europa.eu/economy_finance/publications/eedp/dp008_en.htm

Salverda, W. (2016). *The tsunamis of educational attainment and part-time employment, and the change of the labour force 1960–2010: What can be learned about self-reinforcing labour-market inequality from the case of the Netherlands in international comparison?* ImPRovE Working Paper No. 16/04, Antwerp: Herman Deleeck Centre for Social Policy—University of Antwerp.

Salverda, W. (2018, June). Household income inequalities and labour market position in the European Union. *CES Ifo Forum*, 19(2), 35–43. https://www.cesifo-group.de/DocDL/CESifo-Forum-2018-2-salverda-income%20inequality-june.pdf

Salverda, W. (2018a). Low earnings and their drivers in relation to in-work poverty. In H. Lohmann and I. Marx (eds.), *Handbook of research on in-work poverty* (pp. 26–49). London: Edward Elgar.

Salverda, W. (2019). The Netherlands: From convergence to divergence in Europe? Social dialogue and industrial relations in the face of household labour supply. In D. Vaughan-Whitehead (ed.), *Industrial relations in Europe: Fostering equality at work and cross-country convergence?* Geneva/London: ILO/ Edward Elgar.

Salverda, W., and Chechhi, D. (2015). Labour-market institutions and the dispersion of wage earnings. In A. B. Atkinson and F. Bourguignon (eds.), *Handbook of income distribution (Vol. 2B)* (pp. 1535–1727). Handbooks in Economics. Amsterdam: Elsevier/North Holland.,

Salverda, W. and Haas, C. (2014). Earnings, Employment and Income Inequality. In: Salverda, W., Nolan, B., Checchi, D., Marx, I., McKnight, A., Tóth, I.G., and Van de Werfhorst, H. (eds) *Changing Inequalities in Rich Countries: Analytical and Comparative Perspectives*, Chapter 3. Oxford: Oxford University Press.

Salverda, W., and Rook, V. (Forthcoming). *Does income inequality reinforce labour market inequality in Europe?* Paper in preparation.

Sandbu, M. (2018, 30 November). The economic problem tearing countries apart. *Financial Times blog. https://www.ft.com/content/ab2f8a30-f47c-11e8-ae55-df4bf40f9d0d*

SPC: Social Protection Committee (2015). *Portfolio of EU Social Indicators for the Monitoring of Progress Towards the EU Objectives for Social Protection and Social Inclusion*. Brussels: European Commission.

SPC: Social Protection Committee (2018). *Annual Report 2018*. Brussels: European Commission.

Sutherland, H., and Tsakloglou, P. (2012). Accounting for the distributional effects of noncash public benefits. In D. Besharov and K. Couch (eds.), *Counting the poor: New thinking about European poverty measures and lessons for the United States*, Chapter 5. Oxford: Oxford University Press.

Vacas-Soriano, C., and Fernández-Macías, E. (2018, June). Income inequality in the great recession from an EU-wide perspective. *CES Ifo Forum, 19*(2), 9–18.

Vandenbroucke, F. (2018). *The European Pillar of Social Rights: From promise to delivery*.http://www.euvisions.eu/issues/europea-social-union-public-forum-debate/

Vandenbroucke, F., Barnard C., and De Baere, G. (eds.). (2017). *A European Social Union after the crisis*. Cambridge: Cambridge University Press.

Vaughan-Whitehead, D. (ed.) (2018). *Industrial relations in Europe: Fostering equality at work and cross-country convergence?* Geneva/London: ILO/Edward Elgar.

Verbunt, P., and Guio, A-C. (2019). Explaining Differences Within and Between Countries in the Risk of Income Poverty and Severe Material Deprivation: Comparing Single and Multilevel Analyses. *Social Indicators Research*, 144, 827–868.

INDEX

For the benefit of digital users, indexed terms that span two pages (e.g., 52–53) may, on occasion, appear on only one of those pages.

Tables and figures are indicated by an italic *t* and *f* following the page/paragraph number.